The Global Cold War

Suez Canal, 1906
Hungarian rebellion

The Cold War shaped the world we live in today – its politics, economics, and military affairs. This book shows how the globalization of the Cold War during the last century created the foundations for most of the key conflicts we see today, including the War on Terror. It focuses on how the Third World policies of the two twentieth-century superpowers – the United States and the Soviet Union – gave rise to resentments and resistance that in the end helped topple one superpower and still seriously challenge the other. Ranging from China to Indonesia, Iran, Ethiopia, Angola, Cuba, and Nicaragua, it provides a truly global perspective on the Cold War. And by exploring both the development of interventionist ideologies and the revolutionary movements that confronted interventions, this book links the past with the present in ways that no other major work on the Cold War era has succeeded in doing.

ODD ARNE WESTAD is Director of the Cold War Studies Centre at the London School of Economics and Political Science, where he teaches Cold War history and the history of East Asia. He has written or edited ten books on contemporary international history, the most recent of which are *Decisive Encounters: The Chinese Civil War, 1946–1950* (2003) and, with Jussi Hanhimäki, *The Cold War: A History in Documents and Eyewitness Accounts* (2003).

P9-DIE-014

Sandy ZHU

The Global Cold War

Third World Interventions and the Making of Our Times

Odd Arne Westad

CAMBRIDGE
UNIVERSITY PRESS

CAMBRIDGE UNIVERSITY PRESS
Cambridge, New York, Melbourne, Madrid, Cape Town, Singapore,
São Paulo

Cambridge University Press
The Edinburgh Building, Cambridge CB2 2RU, UK

Published in the United States of America by Cambridge University Press,
New York

www.cambridge.org
Information on this title: www.cambridge.org/9780521703147

© Odd Arne Westad 2007

First published 2005
First paperback edition 2007

Printed in the United Kingdom at the University Press, Cambridge

A catalogue record for this publication is available from the British Library

ISBN 978-0-521-85364-4 hardback
ISBN 978-0-521-70314-7 paperback

For
Ruth First
and
Sayed Ali Majrooh

Contents

Illustrations

Maps

Acknowledgments

A book that aims to integrate more than fifty years of the international history of five continents obviously works up a fair amount of debts, intellectual or otherwise. My primary debt is to those many scholars who have written accounts of various aspects of the Cold War in Africa, Asia, and Latin America that I have drawn on for this volume. They have created a big literature, spread over many different fields of investigation, from history to sociology and social anthropology. Each of these fields are fascinating in their own right, and I have written this book in the spirit of helping to connect them further.

Another debt is to the members of my graduate seminar at the LSE over the past four years, especially Alita Byrd, Jeffrey Byrne, Jan Cornelius, Tanya Harmer, Julia Huber, Alex Martinos, Alessandra Migliaccio, David Milne, Claudia Schleipen, Sim Chi-yin, Candace Sobers, Amal Tarhuni, David Walsh, Valdis Wish, Louise Woodroofe, and Cynthia Wu. They and their cohorts made for many good discussions and much good cheer while helping to shape this book.

I am also deeply indebted to those scholars who agreed to read the whole or part of the manuscript as it was being prepared. My coeditor of the Cambridge History of the Cold War, Melvyn Leffler, is a wonderful critic and a great friend, whose reading influenced the manuscript in many different ways (although I think we still disagree on its basic argument). At LSE my colleagues McGregor Knox, Piers Ludlow, Nigel Ashton, and Steven Casey provided important input. During my stay at New York University in the spring of 2002, Marilyn Young read and commented on the first chapter. At the University of California, Santa Barbara, Tsuyoshi Hasegawa and Fred Logevall (now of Cornell University) helped organize a seminar to discuss my main findings in the spring of 2003, and Campbell Craig did the same at the University of Canterbury, New Zealand. At Peking University in the spring of 2004 Niu Jun and his colleagues helped make this a better book, and in Moscow Aleksandr Chubarian and his staff at the Institute of General

History of the Russian Academy of Sciences helped during my many research trips in more ways than I can mention. Closer to home, at Cambridge David Reynolds, Jonathan Haslam, and Christopher Andrew gave advice during many discussions and seminars. At Oxford I learnt much from presenting to a seminar at All Souls during John Lewis Gaddis' tenure as Eastman Professor at Balliol in 2001.

While some of this work is based on published sources or easily available document collections, I had to do primary research in archives in many corners of the globe in order to complete the picture. In Moscow I am grateful to the director of the Archive of Foreign Policy of the Russian Federation, Aleksandr Churilin, and his predessors; to the director of the Russian State Archive of Socio-Political History, Kirill Anderson; to the director of the Russian State Archive of Contemporary History, Natalia Tomilina; and to the Archive of the President of the Russian Federation. In Beijing Zhang Sulin of the Chinese Foreign Ministry Archives was helpful beyond the call of duty. In Belgrade the staff of the Federal Archives of Serbia and Montenegro – and especially Deputy Director Miladin Milosevic – provided access to hitherto untapped sources. In Pretoria Niels Mueller of the Department of Foreign Affairs archives arranged for easy access and for much help in finding my way in the South African documents. In Berlin the staff of the Federal Archives' Department for Parties and Mass Organizations of the GDR was wonderfully helpful, and in Rome the Gramsci Institute Archives proved – in large part through the efforts of their archivists – to be a gold mine for an international historian.

It would have been impossible to complete this study without the help of the Cold War International History Project (CWIHP) and the National Security Archive – those two outstanding Washington institutions at which the quests for global archival openness and global scholarly collaboration go hand in hand. I am much indebted to the former directors of CWIHP, James Hershberg and David Wolff, and to its present director, Christian Ostermann. At the National Security Archive I have been much helped by its director, Thomas Blanton, and by Malcolm Byrne, William Burr, Svetlana Savranskaya, and Vladislav Zubok (now of Temple University).

As always, it is Ingunn, Anders, and Jenny who make it all worthwhile. They will forgive me for dedicating this book not to them, but to two friends of mine who died during the Cold War: Ruth First, a South African Communist who was assassinated by agents of the apartheid regime in Maputo in 1982, and Sayed Ali Majrooh, an Afghan Muslim and democrat who was killed by Islamist extremists in Peshawar in 1988. *Bis vivit qui bene vivit.*

Abbreviations

AIOC	Anglo-Iranian Oil Company
ANC	African National Congress (South Africa)
ARAMCO	Arabian-American Oil Company
ASEAN	Association of South East Asian Nations
BOSS	Bureau of State Security (South Africa)
CC	Central Committee
CCP	Chinese Communist Party
CIA	Central Intelligence Agency (US)
Comintern	Communist International
CPP (m-1)	Communist Party of Philippines (Marxist-Leninist)
CPSU	Communist Party of the Soviet Union
CWIHP	Cold War International History Project
DCI	Director of Central Intelligence (US)
DPK	Democratic Party of Kurdistan
DPRK	Democratic People's Republic of Korea
ELF	Eritrean Liberation Front
EPLF	Eritrean People's Liberation Front
EPRP	Ethiopian People's Revolutionary Party
FAPLA	Forças Armadas Popular para Libertação de Angola (People's Armed Forces for the Liberation of Angola)
FLN	Front de Libération Nationale (Algeria)
FMLN	Frente Farabundo Martí para la Liberación Nacional (Farabundo Martí Front for National Liberation, El Salvador)
FNLA	Frente Nacional de Libertação de Angola (National Front for the Liberation of Angola)
FRELIMO	Frente de Libertação de Moçambique (Mozambiquan Liberation Front)
FRETILIN	Frente Revolucionária de Timor Leste Independente (Revolutionary Front of Independent East Timor)

FSLN	Frente Sandinista de Liberación Nacional (Sandinista National Liberation Front, Nicaragua)
GDR	German Democratic Republic
GRU	Glavnoie razvedivatelnoie upravleniie (Chief Intelligence Directorate of the General Staff; USSR)
IBRD	International Bank for Reconstruction and Development
ICP	Iraqi Communist Party
IMF	International Monetary Fund
ISI	Inter-Services Intelligence (Pakistan)
KGB	Komitet gosudarstvennoi bezopasnosti (Committee for State Security; USSR)
KhAD	Khadimat-e atal'at-e dowlati (State Information Service [Security]; Afghanistan)
MCP	Malayan Communist Party
MFA	Movimento das Forças Armadas (Armed Forces Movement; Portugal)
MIT	Massachusetts Institute of Technology
MNC	Mouvement National Congolais (Congolese National Movement)
MO	Mezhdunarodnyi otdel (International Department of the Central Committee of the CPSU; USSR)
MPLA	Movimento Popular de Libertação de Angola (People's Movement for the Liberation of Angola)
NAM	Non-Aligned Movement
NIEO	New International Economic Order
NLF	National Liberation Front (Vietnam)
NPA	New People's Army (Philippines)
NSC	National Security Council (US)
OAS	Organization of American States
OAU	Organization of African Unity
OPEC	Organization of the Petroleum Exporting Countries
PAIGC	Partido Africano da Independência da Guiné e Cabo Verde (African Party for the Independence of Guinea and Cape Verde)
PDPA	People's Democratic Party of Afghanistan
PDRE	People's Democratic Republic of Ethiopia
PDRY	People's Democratic Republic of Yemen
PGT	Partido Guatemalteco del Trabajo (Guatemalan Workers' Party)
PKI	Partai Komunis Indonesia (Indonesian Communist Party)

PLO	Palestinian Liberation Organization
PMAC	Provisional Military Administrative Council (Ethiopia)
POMOA	Provisional Office for Mass Organizational Affairs (Ethiopia)
PRC	People's Republic of China
PRI	Partido Revolucionario Institucional (Institutional Revolutionary Party; Mexico)
SACP	South African Communist Party
SALT	Strategic Arms Limitation Talks
SED	Sozialistische Einheitspartei Deutschlands (Socialist Unity Party; GDR)
SpetsNaz	Voiska spetsialnogo naznacheniia (special purpose forces; USSR)
TANU	Tanganyika African National Union
TPLF	Tigray People's Liberation Front
UAR	United Arab Republic
UNITA	União Nacional para a Independência Total de Angola (National Union for the Total Liberation of Angola)
USSR	Union of Socialist Soviet Republics
VWP	Vietnam Workers' Party
WSLF	Western Somalia Liberation Front

Introduction

"We look into history from motives of two kinds," says the Oxford classicist Jasper Griffin. "There is curiosity about the past, what happened, who did what, and why; and there is the hope to understand the present, how to place and interpret our own times, experiences, and hopes for the future."[1] As with the history of antiquity, the best contemporary history is usually driven by both kinds of motives; those that see the past as past and those that see the past as present. In the spirit of Professor Griffin's injunction, this is a book about the creation of today's world, about how the mightiest powers of the late twentieth century – the United States and the Soviet Union – repeatedly intervened in processes of change in Africa, Asia, and Latin America, and through these interventions fuelled many of the states, movements, and ideologies that increasingly dominate international affairs. In its choice of topic it is, in other words, an unabashedly presentist book, even though it is also an historical account, written by a historian.

The volume grew out of my interest in the motives and decisions of the Cold War superpowers in their Third World policies, which I felt needed to be reinvestigated now that archival materials from both sides are available for the first time. During the research, however, the subject of the book turned into something broader: I found it impossible to understand Moscow's and Washington's decisions without exploring both the ideological origins of their Cold War interventionisms and the transformation of Third World politics that precipitated the superpower involvement. What had started out as a book about interventions increasingly became one about Third World processes of change. Its perspective shifted south.

Such a shift may not have been presaged exclusively by the historian's curiosity. It was also, undoubtedly, a residue of having spent much time in Africa and Asia in the late 1970s and early 1980s, where – as a very young man – I was an excited witness to the social and political changes taking place. I sympathized profoundly with those who attempted to achieve a more just and equitable society, and with those who defended their communities against foreign interventions. (As I am writing this, I still recall walking home from a political rally in Maputo on a night some

1

twenty-five years ago, astonished at the courage and determination shown by ordinary Mozambicans in the face of poverty and war.) This sympathy and fascination still remains with me, even though I hope by now to have been weaned off easy political solutions to complex social problems. It certainly made it impossible for me to write a book about the Cold War in the Third World from a superpower perspective only.

A friend of mine, who studies language, noted with more than a touch of friendly irony how chronologically well attuned my choice of conceptual terms for this book is to the topic covered: Both "Cold War" and "Third World" are late twentieth-century neologisms, employed for various purposes and in various cultural settings to create some of the most fundamental hegemonic discourses of the era. My linguist friend is of course right. Neither of these terms existed prior to World War II, and the ways in which they have been used are signals for which side you were on in the last great conflicts of the century. "Cold War" was first used by George Orwell in 1945 to deplore the worldview, beliefs, and social structure of both the Soviet Union and the United States, and also the undeclared state of war that would come to exist between them. "The atomic bomb," Orwell found, may be "robbing the exploited classes and peoples of all power to revolt, and at the same time putting the possessors of the bomb on a basis of equality. Unable to conquer one another they are likely to continue ruling the world between them."[2] Although a critical term at first, the term "Cold War" in the 1950s came to signal an American concept of warfare against the Soviet Union: aggressive containment without a state of war. The Soviets, on their side, never used the term officially before the Gorbachev era, since they clung to the fiction that their country was "peaceful" and only "imperialism" was aggressive, in a way similar to how US (and Western European) leaders used the "Cold War" to imply a Soviet threat.

The concept "Third World" came into being in the early 1950s, first in French and then in English, and gained prominence after the Bandung conference of 1955, when leaders from Asia and Africa met for the first large postcolonial summit. With its French connotations of *tiers état* – the "third estate," the most populous but least represented of the French prerevolutionary social groups – the term "Third World" implied "the people" on a world scale, the global majority who had been downtrodden and enslaved through colonialism, but who were now on their way to the top of the ladder of influence. The concept also implied a distinct position in Cold War terms, the refusal to be ruled by the superpowers and their ideologies, the search for alternatives both to capitalism and Communism, a "third way" (if that expression can be decoupled from present-day Blairite hypocrisy) for the newly liberated states.

My use of these terms may therefore be seen to point in two opposing directions: the term "Cold War" signals Western elite projects on the grandest of possible scales, while the term "Third World" indicates colonial and postcolonial processes of marginalization (and the struggle against these processes). Some critics have claimed that by positioning one "in" the other I do violence to their separateness – I implicitly subsume one discourse under the other. Having reread the literature that was written on the Cold War in the Third World towards the end of the Cold War era, I can sympathize somewhat with this position: the greater amount of these mostly American writings attempted to delegitimize domestic Third World revolutions or radical movements on the grounds that they were Soviet-inspired or Soviet-sponsored.

Still, the argument that the Cold War conceptually and analytically does not belong in the south is wrong, mainly for two reasons. First, US and Soviet interventionisms to a very large extent shaped both the international and the domestic framework within which political, social, and cultural changes in Third World countries took place. Without the Cold War, Africa, Asia, and possibly also Latin America would have been very different regions today. Second, Third World elites often framed their own political agendas in conscious response to the models of development presented by the two main contenders of the Cold War, the United States and the Soviet Union. In many cases the Third World leaders' choices of ideological allegiance brought them into close collaboration with one or the other of the superpowers, and led them to subscribe to models of development that proved disastrous for their own peoples. The latter aspect of the Cold War in the Third World is the least explored, perhaps because it is the most difficult for both former Cold Warriors and their opponents to accept.[3]

For the purpose of this volume my definitions of the key terms are rather straightforward. "Cold War" means the period in which the global conflict between the United States and the Soviet Union dominated international affairs, roughly between 1945 and 1991. "Third World" means the former colonial or semicolonial countries in Africa, Asia, and Latin America that were subject to European (or rather pan-European, including American and Russian) economic or political domination.[4] "Global" means processes that took place on or toward different continents at roughly the same time. "Intervention" means any concerted and state-led effort by one country to determine the political direction of another country. These are brief, operational definitions that make sense in the particular context in which they are used here (but that are obviously open to challenge in any broader context).

In a study that aims both at discussing the origins and the course of Third World revolutions and the superpower interventions that accompanied them some hard choices obviously had to be made in order to avoid the text spilling over into two or three volumes. The focus of the book is on the 1970s and the early 1980s, when superpower conflict in the Third World was at its peak and when developments in the Third World had most significance for the wider conduct of the Cold War. As will be shown later, this is, of course, not to say that the Third World was unimportant for the Cold War conflict in earlier periods, but only that by the 1970s the conditions in the Third World and the capabilities of both superpowers had reached a stage that made events in Africa, Asia, and Latin America central to international affairs. Likewise, not all Third World conflicts in which the superpowers were involved are given equal weight in the chapters. Instead, conflicts in which foreign interventions set both the framework and the course of events are given priority, meaning, for instance, that the Arab–Israeli or the Indo-Pakistani wars (which were governed more by their very specific regional rationale than by their Cold War context) are treated in less depth than they would have been if the purpose was to provide a general survey. Such limitations have made it possible to opt toward inclusivity on other issues, such as the tracing of the historical development of superpower interventionist ideologies and postcolonial Third World politics in the first three chapters.

While serving as comfort for nervous editors concerned with length, the geographical exclusions also serve as useful reminders to the reader that while the Cold War is a central discourse in the international history of the late twentieth century, it is by no means the full story. Other major discourses with geneses that are in part separate from the Cold War – such as the economic rise of East Asia or the upsurge of political Islam – have histories of their own, which for some time existed in parallel to the superpower conflict (and which in the end, as I have argued elsewhere, came to overtake it as the fulcrum of international affairs). The Cold War is a separate, identifiable part of a much richer spectrum of late twentieth-century history, but one that gave shape to a recognizable international system based on two opposing versions of European modernist thought.

This book argues that the United States and the Soviet Union were driven to intervene in the Third World by the ideologies inherent in their politics. Locked in conflict over the very concept of European modernity – to which both states regarded themselves as successors – Washington and Moscow needed to change the world in order to prove the universal applicability of their ideologies, and the elites of the newly independent states proved fertile ground for their competition. By helping to expand the domains of freedom or of social justice, both powers saw themselves as assisting natural trends in world history and as defending their own security at the same time. Both saw a specific mission in and for the Third World that only their own state could carry out and which without their involvement would flounder in local hands.

It is easy, therefore, to see the Cold War in the South as a continuation of European colonial interventions and of European attempts at controlling Third World peoples. I have little doubt that this is how historians of the future will regard the epoch – as one of the final stages of European global control. The means and the immediate motivations of Cold War interventions were remarkably similar to those of the "new imperialism" of the late colonial era, when European administrators set out to save the natives from ignorance, filth, and the consequences of their own actions. In both the early and the late twentieth century the European ideological rationale was that the path toward the future had been discovered by them and that they had a duty to help Third World peoples along that road. Throughout my research I have been astonished at the sense of duty and sacrifice that advisers on both sides showed in aiding friends or opposing foes in, for them, faraway places. The Cold War ethos – for those who accepted it – was at least as alluring and evocative as the imperialist ethos that it replaced, both for Europeans and for their collaborators. (While interviewing leaders of long-forgotten Third World people's republics, I have often been reminded of the Indian writer Nirad Chaudhury's dedication of his autobiography to the memory of the British empire, by which "all that was good and living within us was made, shaped, and quickened."[5])

One crucial comparative distinction needs to be made, however. It is to me less meaningful to talk about patterns of US or Soviet domination as "empires" than to describe them in a specific temporal sense. Different from the European expansion that started in the early modern period, Moscow's and Washington's objectives were not exploitation or subjection, but control and improvement. While this distinction may be rather ethereal seen from the receiving end, it is crucial for understanding the Cold War discourse itself: while imperialism got its social consciousness almost as an afterthought, in the Cold War it was inherent from the very beginning. Both US and Soviet criticisms of early twentieth-century European imperialist practices were genuine and deeply held ideological views. Indeed, some of the extraordinary brutality of Cold War interventions – such as those in Vietnam or Afghanistan – can only be explained by Soviet and American identification with the people they sought to defend. Cold War interventions were most often extensions of ideological civil wars, fought with the ferocity that only civil wars can bring forth.

The need to understand the Cold War in light of the colonial experience has influenced the way this book has been structured. The first three chapters deal with the ideological and political origins of the Cold War in the Third World by exploring the motives of American, Soviet, and postcolonial leaders in an historical perspective. Chapter 1 discusses the development of US thinking on non-European peoples and their relationship to American identity and foreign policy. It argues that discourses on liberty, progress, and citizenship already in the early years of the republic's existence set an ideological pattern of involvement with the Third World that has persisted up to this day. Chapter 2 deals with the origins of Russian discourses on the Third World, from the creation of the empire up to the post-Stalin era. It shows how the Bolsheviks took over many of the problems of the past, and how they tried to transform them through their emphasis on a collective form of modernity, which via the Comintern and Soviet foreign policy they tried to spread to other parts of the world. Chapter 3 concludes this overview of the historical origins of mindsets and ideologies by focusing on Third World resistance against European colonialism and on the development of different forms of anticolonial revolutionary movements. It explains how anticolonial movements interacted with the early Cold War conflict and how some Third World leaders chose to align themselves with one or the other of its competing ideologies, while others defined themselves in opposition to both.

Chapters 4 and 5 discuss the interrelationship between the growing success of the anticolonial resistance and the creation of US Cold War interventionism. Chapter 4 argues that in the period between 1945 and 1960 the United States, through its policies toward Africa, Asia, and Latin America, helped to create the Third World as a meaningful concept in international politics, symbolizing resistance against Western domination. Chapter 5 looks at the foreign policy of Cuba and Vietnam in opposing US control, and at how they provided foci of inspiration for revolutionary movements elsewhere (although mostly in the form of creative misunderstandings, rather than straightforward lessons).

Chapters 6 to 8 deal with key cases of intervention and revolutionary transformation in the Third World during the late Cold War. Chapter 6 provides an overview of the international aspects of the struggle against apartheid and colonialism in Southern Africa, while focusing on the Angolan civil war and the Cold War interventions that accompanied it. Chapter 7 discusses the Ethiopian revolution and its links both with the United States and, especially, with the Soviet Union, and looks at how the Ethiopian-Somalian war helped to undo both the prospects for socialism in the Horn of Africa and also the brief period of *détente* between the superpowers. Chapter 8 shows how the growth of Islamism in both Iran and Afghanistan helped to destroy the modernization enterprises of the regimes, and how the Soviet Union decided to intervene in order to recreate a modernizing, socialist regime in Kabul.

The final two chapters and the conclusion provide a discussion of the Cold War in the Third World in the 1980s and its effects up to our own time. Chapter 9 outlines the Reagan offensive against left-wing revolutionary regimes and against the Soviet Union in Afghanistan, Angola, and Central America. It also discusses the global economic and ideological changes that made the offensive succeed. Chapter 10 shows how Mikhail Gorbachev, after a brief period of euphoric engagement, decided to withdraw the Soviet Union from intervening in Third World conflicts and how he attempted, unsuccessfully, to build an international order around principles of the self-determination of states. The conclusion evaluates the impact the Cold War had in the Third World and how it fuelled continued resistance against foreign domination. It also discusses how interventionism weakened both the Soviet Union and the United States and how it continues to bedevil US foreign policy ideology today.

The literatures on superpower interventions and on Third World revolutions are enormous, and I am indebted to a multitude of scholars for their insights, many more than can be mentioned in the acknowledgments or even in the notes. Strangely enough – and to the detriment of students – these two literatures have so far been mostly unconnected in an intellectual sense; they seem to speak past each other rather than engage across intellectual boundaries in addressing issues that are of consequence to both. An important reason for this deficiency is that the most important research into each field have been divided by disciplines: while historians and international relations experts have been concentrating on aspects of interventions, sociologists and social anthropologists have been studying Third World revolutions and their consequences. It has been my aim to draw insights from all these disciplines on their objects of study (even though the limitations of my own discipline are bound to shine through from time to time).

For me, as an historian, the core reason why this book could be written at all is the extraordinary extension of access to archives in the (former) First, Second, and Third World. While historians of the Cold War up to the last decade had only meager access to archives outside the United States and Western Europe, we can now make use of Soviet and East European archives, as well as an increasing range of collections from countries in Africa, Asia, and Latin America. This increased access to source material carries the promise of changing the field profoundly – both, I hope, in terms of its overall approach and interpretations and also in terms of making it more relevant to a larger number of people as a field of study. The present volume is an attempt at furthering both of these processes.

1 The empire of liberty: American ideology and foreign interventions

In the 1890s, as the United States for the first time prepared to colonize peoples outside the North American continent, the debate over whether a republic could also be an empire raged intensely. When accepting the Democratic nomination for president in 1900, William Jennings Bryan castigated the American colonization of the Philippines, claiming that such policies undermined the essence of republicanism: "Our whole history," Bryan said, "has been an encouragement not only to the Filipinos, but to all who are denied a voice in their own government ...

While our sphere of activity has been limited to the Western hemisphere, our sympathies have not been bounded by the seas. We have felt it due to ourselves and to the world, as well as those who were struggling for the right to govern themselves, to proclaim the interest which our people have, from the date of their own independence, felt in every contest between human rights and arbitrary power.[1]

In the century that followed Bryan's doomed battles for the presidency the complexity of his sentiments was to be often repeated at key moments of making decisions in US foreign policy: could Americans, jealous of their own freedoms, govern others? And, if not, what form should that "interest" in the world that Bryan proclaimed take? Was liberty for Americans enough to satisfy the promise of America, or was the agenda of American liberty the world? If America's mission stopped at its shores, how could the United States in the long run defend its own liberties? And if that mission extended *ad infinitum*, how could American power protect the United States *and* build global freedoms at the same time?

Historians, with their sense of dichotomies, have often seen the 1890s and Bryan's defeats as a struggle between the republican preoccupation with liberty and the Republicans' preoccupation with money and interests – a contest that the latter decisively won. But, at least in terms of foreign policy, the turn of the nineteenth century could as well be seen as a particularly intense moment in a continuous creation of a distinct American ideology, a process that extends back to the eighteenth century and forward to the twenty-first. When Thomas Jefferson in 1785 praised the *principle* of an America concentrated on perfecting freedoms at home, he himself added that avoiding war may be "a theory which the servants of America are not at liberty to follow." The problem, Jefferson found, was in the very foundations of the nation – "our people have a decided taste for navigation and commerce."[2] In the creation of the American state in the nineteenth and early twentieth centuries, "theory" and "tastes" competed for primacy, while becoming increasingly entwined and mutually adjusted.

By the mid-twentieth century both liberty and interests – "theory" and "tastes" – had natural and integrated places in US foreign policy ideology, welded together as symbols and key perceptions in a universalist understanding of America's mission. During the Cold War what set the function of these ideas apart from those of "normal" states within the Western state system was how American symbols and images – the free market, anti-Communism, fear of state power, faith in technology – had *teleological* functions: what is America today will be the world tomorrow. While American universalism and teleology go back to the revolutionary origins of the state, their ideological manifestations developed more slowly, often as much needed compromises between divergent ideas. As historian Michael Hunt has observed, the outer form of these symbols all go back to the revolutionary era, while their content can be strikingly contemporary.[3] It therefore makes sense to speak of an American ideology that goes back two hundred years, but it is an evolving ideology into which generational experiences are interpreted and perceptual conflicts solved.

The history of America's interventions in the Third World is very much the history of how this ideology developed over time and how it framed the policies of the US foreign policy elite. Although there were periods of strong domestic opposition to the policies pursued, the Cold War era stands out as a time when there also was, by American standards, a remarkable consensus as to the immediate aims and means of US policy abroad. This relative lack of political controversy has sometimes made scholars oversimplify the relationship between ideology and practice in how Washington has conducted its international policies. But as the genesis of America's relations with the world shows, the Cold War consensus developed out of profound conflicts in the past over the role and the means a democratic republic could take up when influencing others.

"In every contest"

From its inception the United States was an interventionist power that based its foreign policy on territorial expansion. Its revolutionary message – free men and free enterprise – was a challenge to the European powers on a continental scale. Even for those few who in the early nineteenth century did not believe in divine providence, the core ideas that had led Americans to nationhood were the same ones that commanded them to seize the vastness of America and transform it in their image. Together these ideas formed an ideology that motivated US elites in their relations with the outside world from the federal era to the Cold War.

First among these core ideas was the American concept of *liberty*, with its particular delineations and extensions. Liberty for its citizens was what separated the United States from other countries; it was what gave meaning to the existence of a separate American state. American freedom was, however, sustained by a human condition that was different from that of others. The American, Jefferson argued in the wake of the French Revolution,

by his property, or by his satisfactory situation, is interested in the support of law and order. And such men may safely and advantageously reserve to themselves a wholesome control over their public affairs, and a degree of freedom, which, in the hands of the *canaille* of the cities of Europe, would be instantly perverted to the demolition and destruction of everything public and private ... But even in Europe a change has sensibly taken place in the mind of man. Science has liberated the ideas of those who read and reflect, and the American example has kindled feelings of right in the people. An insurrection has consequently begun ... It has failed in its first effort, because the mobs of the cities, the instrument used for its accomplishment, debased by ignorance, poverty and vice, could not be restrained to rational action. But the world will recover from the panic of this first catastrophe.[4]

To the third president, and his successors, liberty could not exist without private property and the dedication to an ordered society that followed from that particular right. Liberty, therefore, was not for everyone, but for those who, through property and education, possessed the necessary independence to be citizens of a republic. Already during the federal period it was widely accepted that most Europeans could achieve such status if they were enlightened by the American example, and, in ethnic terms, the circle of possible enlightenment widened in the twentieth century. Up to the Cold War, however, most of the world's population – including the internal African colony the Europeans had brought to America – was *outside* that circle. Native and Latin Americans were also excluded. "I join you sincerely, my friend," Jefferson wrote to de Lafayette in 1813, "in wishes for the emancipation of South America.

That they will be liberated from foreign subjection I have little doubt. But the result of my enquiries does not authorize me to hope they are capable of maintaining a free government. Their people are immersed in the darkest ignorance, and brutalised by bigotry & superstition.

Jefferson still held out hope for the Latin Americans, though: "Light will at length beam in on their minds and the standing example we shall hold up, serving as an excitement as well as a model for their direction may in the long run qualify them for self-government."[5]

Central to the American ideology was its *anticollectivism* – the independent individual can be a republican, the *canaille* cannot. The collective symbolized all the fears American eighteenth-century revolutionaries had for the corruption of their republic. Outside the United States the essence of non-liberty consisted in being controlled by others, through feudal bondage or, as in the case of the French revolution, through seduction by a party or a movement. In America – and gradually elsewhere – the countermeasure to this enslavement was in education and "rationality" through science. But there remained, echoing through generations, a risk that if America did not tend and defend its own liberty, then history could move in the opposite direction; that American freedom could be undermined by imported collectivist ideas or by uneducated immigrants who clung to cultural identities US elites did not recognize.

Most Americans of the late eighteenth and early nineteenth century shared a reluctance to accept *centralized political power*. Indeed, much of the ideological discourse in first two hundred years of the American republic centered on ways of *avoiding* a strong state. In order to have the nation's constitution commonly agreed upon in the late eighteenth century, for instance, a number of powers – including the power to declare war – had to be taken away from the executive. One hundred years later this anticentralism prevented America from using the state as an instrument of social reform along European lines, and cast suspicion, in ideological terms, on those countries that followed such a path. During the twentieth century, in spite of occasional attempts at state-led reform and also in spite of the immense growth, in absolute terms, of the federal state, these attitudes were still important in how American elites saw the world and their role in it.

Science as the progenitor of "rational action" underpinned American faith in the new state's universal significance from the very beginning. The United States was the first country created on the "scientific principles" of the Enlightenment. This meant the new state was a pioneer of other states to come – "the light that will bear in on their minds," in Jefferson's terms. But it also meant that an American identity, during the nineteenth century, became connected with the very concept of modernity, closely linking technology with the existing social order in the United States. The only way of becoming modern would be to emulate the American example, to "liberate" productivity and innovation from "ancient" (later "traditional") cultures and ideologies. By the twentieth century the only framework of reference for Americans was America – the completion, one may say, of the self-fulfilling prophesy made at the beginning of the American republic's existence.

Part of the "rational action" of early America was *the market* – the exchange of products and services based on their value in money alone, unfettered by patronage or by need. As we have seen, even Thomas Jefferson – who along with large numbers of nineteenth-century Americans cherished the self-sufficient farmer as the ideal citizen – recognized his countrymen's "taste for navigation and commerce" enough to, as president, send naval forces to North Africa to protect American shipping. As the United States industrialized in the late nineteenth century, the capitalist market became a reality for all Americans, and the participation in that exchange, in one form or another, became a symbol of belonging to America. And as American exports grew at around the turn of the century, so faith in the market transformed itself into a self-serving belief in open international markets, where American companies – more often than not the strongest competitors – could bring their money-making skills and their business organization. Even though this conviction was not always brought to bear on *foreign* access to *American* markets, the free market had become a part of American foreign policy ideology – as an idea, a logical extension of the virtues of capitalism and universal liberty.

Having successfully defended their access to international trade in the war of 1812, American elites of the early nineteenth century turned their attention to the expansion promised at the inception of their state. Up to the end of the century the aims of that expansion were primarily continental – the existence of European colonial empires on American soil was intolerable to liberty as constituted in the United States. During Jefferson's presidency the United States consisted of roughly 800,000 square miles – by 1848 the figure was 3 million square miles, and in 1867, after the acquisition of Alaska from Russia, it was more than 3.5 million. Only the latter can be said to have happened, in historian Bradford Perkins's phrase, as a "freely negotiated transfer." The others – Louisiana, Florida, Texas, the Northwest, the 1848 conquests from Mexico – all resulted either from war or the threat of war. The image that made possession of the continent America's "manifest destiny," a term first used in 1845, expressed as myth what in reality was a rather concrete imperialist program.[6]

But by far the most important US interventions of the nineteenth century took place against Native American nations. In the name of rationality and progress, the American government attempted to control

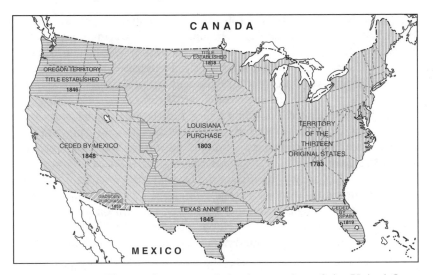

Map 1   The contiguous continental expansion of the United States up to 1914.

and in some cases exterminate all the nations who had settled in what became the United States before the seventeenth century. These interventions – against those who, in spite of competing imperialist claims, in the early part of the nineteenth century were in still in command of most of the continent – set the framework for dealing with countries that for reasons of low levels of "rational action" could not receive liberty as a gift from America. "Control" became the favored method for extending American's aims beyond the seas, to where liberty as yet was not an option.[7]

The issue of control of those not yet worthy of the levels of liberty accorded to white Americans was also crucial for the treatment of the internal African colony that had come with the Europeans. While at least in the nineteenth century slavery was increasingly abhorrent to most Americans, blacks still had to be controlled for fear that their lack of "rational action" could disturb the progress of America. After the reconstruction era, Southern racism and Northern plans for "betterment" effectively disenfranchised the black population up to the late twentieth century, delivering, as we shall see, both techniques of control to be employed abroad and, eventually, an ideological challenge to American concepts of liberty.

In the late nineteenth century, at the same time as the issue of the United States as a transoceanic imperialist power first emerged, the dual face of foreign immigration also became increasingly apparent to many Americans. On the one hand, Americans then – as during the Cold War and today – recognized that increasing immigration was the confirmation of America's success. On the other hand, Northern whites grew increasingly concerned over the threat to "American values" that could come out of the entry of "unassimilable strangers." From 1870 to 1920, as the United States received 26 million new immigrants, racial and ethnic stereotyping came to determine their initial "placing" in American society, and, in some cases, who should rather be kept out. The Chinese Exclusion Act of 1882 was the first of a series of laws, campaigned for by organizations such as the Immigration Restriction League, which attempted to keep out "racially inferior" peoples. Such exclusion was important, it was claimed, because free immigration would prevent America from living up to its global promise. "We believe," said a Wyoming delegate to the United Mine Workers of America in 1904,

that Americans today, as in 1776, stand for independence and the noblest manhood; the Japanese laborer, as we find him in our mines and other industries, stands for neither. The Jap, like the Chinaman, works for whatever the company is pleased to pay him, and returns a portion of his earnings regularly to a Japanese agent, who is called a "boss," doubtless to evade technically the law prohibiting contract labor.[8]

As the concept of manifest destiny fastened its grip on Americans' perceptions of their country's role, the question of where this destiny ended was becoming increasingly controversial. Could an ideology that was in its essence universal and teleological end its applicability at the shores of North America? In the early part of the nineteenth century interventions further afield limited themselves to political support and, in a few South American cases, supplies for favored groups or movements. The United States, John Quincy Adams argued in 1821, had to distinguish between extending sympathies and using military power:

Wherever the standard of freedom and independence has been or shall be unfurled, there will her heart, her benediction, and her prayers be. But she goes not abroad in search of monsters to destroy. She is the well-wisher to the freedom and independence of all. She is the champion and vindicator only of her own.[9]

By the final decades of the century, however, an increasingly strong argument was being put forward that the United States had a duty to assist in the "freedom and independence" of others outside its new borders. There were several reasons for this shift. The successes of American industrialization and the reordering of society along capitalist lines after the civil war increased the confidence of the elites in the international relevance of their message. The takeover of North America had been carried through as far as possible without incorporating inferior Latinos in Mexico or risking conflict with the British empire over Canada. The European imperialist land grabs in Africa and Asia posed the challenge of how "advanced" countries should interact with lesser developed nations. American missionaries had begun carrying the nineteenth-century campaigns for social control and social betterment abroad. And, finally, American commercial expansion led to hopes of new foreign markets, or at least to a fear that such markets, were they to exist, could become the domain of others.

It would still be wrong to see the American occupation of Hawaii (1897) and the occupation of the Philippines and Cuba in the wake of the Spanish–American War (1898) as too radical a departure in US foreign relations. The American involvement with East Asia, both in commercial and political terms, goes back to the 1840s – it was US naval vessels, after all, that forced Western trade on Japan in 1854. The Mexican War of 1846–48 – in which Matthew Perry of later Japanese fame had served with distinction – also brought the United States into closer contact with the Caribbean and Central America. In 1855 the American William Walker set himself up as the ruler of Nicaragua, and numerous other adventurers in the late nineteenth century attempted to follow his example.[10] And, as we know, American interventionism in the Caribbean did not end with Cuba: between 1898 and 1920 US Marines were used on at least twenty separate occasions in the region.

What does set the late 1890s apart, though, was the willingness of the American federal state under McKinley and Roosevelt to take political responsibility for the overseas peoples under its control. In a way historians have been right in seeing the establishment of an American trans-oceanic empire as an aberration – a short-term reaction to the culmination of European imperialism and an attempt at conforming to the global system it created. By taking up "the white man's burden" – as Kipling had implored it to do in his poem – the United States found a place as one among the Western great powers. The problem for the American imperialists was, however, that America was already fast becoming something more than one among many: in terms of its economic and military power, it did not need to conform or to take on a role that, in ideological terms, was foreign to it. Rather than being *one* imperial power, the United States was fast becoming the protector and balancer of a capitalist world system.

It was that role that America formally assumed – even with regard to Europe itself – during World War I. To Woodrow Wilson and many of his contemporaries, the decision for war meant that America could begin to reshape a world in which there were so many wrongs that needed to be put right and where the American experience could serve as a pattern.

Intervention, Wilson had concluded by 1917, was the only way of achieving "a reasonable peace settlement and the reconstruction of the world order."[11] What Wilson felt to be good for the world – as in his Fourteen Points – would also, necessarily, be good for America.

"Foreigners" and anti-Communism

In the overall American approach to global affairs, World War I symbolized first and foremost a reduction of Europe and its main powers almost to the level of nonrational charges. Europe, wherefrom the light that Jefferson spoke of had originally gone forth, had debased itself through an orgy of blood and hatred. It was up to America – a victor in the war and, when it ended, undoubtedly the strongest power in the world – to set things right. President Woodrow Wilson, an interventionist reformer at home and abroad and a (political) scientist who saw America's mission as creating an international order that prevented war between the great powers in the future, focused on two main problems: nationalism and revolution. Understanding his approaches to this twin challenge is crucial for understanding American foreign policy discourse right up to the end of the twentieth century.

Wilson saw nationalism (self-determination, in his terms) as the only mechanism by which stable states could be created, which then, with American aid, could be set on the way to democracy. But, as the war had shown, nationalism also had another face, filled with those wild and vulgar features that had characterized Germany's fate on the road to disaster. As the president had noted already during the war, a very thin line divided "positive longings" from "anarchy" (perhaps Wilson's favorite term of opprobrium), and the postwar situation in Europe gave him plenty of examples of the latter. While Wilson's support for national self-determination helped numerous nationalist projects to become reality on the ruins of war in Central and Eastern Europe, he withheld American support from many others, especially where he feared that radicalism or socialism were the driving engines. Wilson's fear of disorder – inherited from his early years in Reconstruction Virginia – led to an acceptance of the French and British governments' emphasis on stability, rather than on popular will, in the European peace settlements.

For the world outside Europe it was the negative results of European colonialism that presented a challenge after World War I. Instead of uplifting their charges to higher levels of civilization, European colonialists had exploited and mistreated them, thereby creating potential hotbeds of chaos and anarchy. Even for the British colonies such as India – often seen in the nineteenth century as a star example of benevolent colonial rule – American opinion in the interwar period turned increasingly critical. But, from its the very beginning this renewed anticolonial critique ran into problems in terms of alternatives. Since the Europeans had so often failed in their civilizing mission, real independence for the colonies would only lead to more instability and suffering. The Mexican revolution, unfolding on America's very doorstep, was to Wilson a terrible example of what such instability would produce.

By the early 1920s the fear of what instability and ignorance could result in was made worse by the Russian revolution and its effects. At first, in 1917, the collapse of the tsar's government was welcomed by many Americans, who saw tsarism as the most reactionary form of rule in Europe and hoped that the new regime's policies would follow a trajectory not unlike that of the American revolution. But the authoritarian collectivism of the Bolsheviks, and their emphasis on the permanence and internationalism of their revolution, soon drove away any goodwill that may have existed among American elites. On the contrary, over the years that followed Soviet Communism came to be seen as a deadly rival of Americanism, because it put itself forward as an alternative modernity; a way poor and downtrodden peoples could challenge their conditions *without* replicating the American model. Already by 1918 the US government had joined the other imperial great powers in a military intervention against the Bolsheviks.

America's postwar unwillingness to take the lead in the international organizations Wilson had constructed is often written down to a US sense of political betrayal after Europe spurned US positions at the peace conferences. But the so-called "isolationism" of the 1920s and 1930s had deeper roots than concern over diplomatic negotiations. As the United States became the world's primary industrial power, immigration had increased manifoldly, reaching its peak in the years immediately preceding World War I. While in principle accepting the need to import labor in order to keep up with the productivity (and the export potential) of American industry, many Americans were concerned about what "new" groups of immigrants could signify in ideological terms – could the principles of liberty withstand the influx of Latin, Slavic, or Asian immigrants; peoples who in racial terms were not seen as possessing the virtues needed for rational behavior? Could America's involvement with the world quite literally be polluting the idea of liberty at home?

In post-World War I America – the period in which most US Cold War leaders grew up – the idea that Europe and the world had shown themselves not ready for American order, organization, and concepts of rights merged with concern over the effects of immigration. In ideological terms it could be argued that the two perceptions were mutually reinforcing; if foreign countries had not yet reached the necessary levels of civilization needed to receive the American message, what then about the masses from these very same countries who were coming to the United States? Immigration could overwhelm American democracy and defeat it in ways foreign powers were no longer capable of doing. And the way to refute that internal challenge was through limiting immigration by "less civilized" peoples and Americanizing the foreigners who were already inside.

The main obstacle to the process of Americanizing foreigners at home were the ideas with which they were contaminated before arriving on American shores. By the 1920s the most threatening of these were Communism, both because of its revolutionary collectivism and because it purported to represent a version of modernity more advanced than that presented by America. As seen by elites in the United States, the latter claim was not only wrong in essence, but was also a declared challenge to the universalism and teleology embedded in their ideology. There was simply no room, within or without the United States, for a universalist ideology that constructed a world operating according to different principles and with a different endpoint from that of their own images. Communism – and, by implication, collectivism in all of its forms – in this view had to be grouped with the traditionalist and antimodern traits of Europe that had so disastrously manifested themselves in World War I.

The existence of an American Communist Party, from 1921, therefore became an ideological manifestation out of proportion with the very limited following that party came to command. To many Americans, the very existence of such a party (alongside other ills, such as organized crime) proved the need for Americanization and vigilance at home. At the same time, the existence of an American Communist Party did become, for a brief moment during the Depression, a signal to some of those whom Americanism had disenfranchised that other methods for organizing society could be envisaged, even in America. The author Richard Wright, who briefly joined the party after his escape from institutionalized racial oppression in the South, wrote depreciatingly of

our too-young and too-new America, lusty because it is lonely, aggressive because it is afraid, insists upon seeing the world in terms of good and bad, the holy and the evil, the high and the low, the white and the black; our America is frightened of fact, of history, of processes, of necessity. It hugs the easy way of damning those it cannot understand, of excluding those who look different, and it salves its conscience with a self-draped cloak of righteousness.[12]

The great majority of Americans, however, viewed the growth of authoritarian collectivist ideologies in Europe during the Great Depression with suspicion and fear. Although Communism had in many ways been the original challenge, it was not difficult to see similarities between the Communist faith – especially in its Stalinist form – and other contemporary political directions, such as fascism or national socialism. They all represented a challenge to America. "In a world of high tension and disorder, in a world where stable civilization is actually threatened," Franklin Roosevelt said in his 1938 State of the Union address, "it becomes the responsibility of each nation which strives for peace at home and peace with and among others to be strong enough to assure the observance of those fundamentals of peaceful solution of conflicts which are the only ultimate basis for orderly existence."[13]

Although the perceived lessons of World War I led the American administrations of the 1920s and 1930s to question the value of direct military intervention, as such the interwar period in US foreign relations can barely deserve the label "isolationist." On the contrary, these two decades were the breakthrough for America as the center of the global economy, especially with regard to the Third World. In Latin America, the United States replaced Britain as the key economic power, and the American share of exports to East Asia almost tripled between 1920 and 1940. In a world where the Great Depression forced many minds to begin to consider new models for their nations, American ideas followed American products to an extent that few Americans – in their fear of outside challenges – realized. This influence was far more profound than just American models for production or management. In urban popular culture, in Europe and in the Third World, America established itself as the epitome of modernity, conveying ideas that undermined existing concepts of status, class, and identity.

The dichotomy that existed between the domestic elite view of the United States as being under pressure from within and without, and the international view of America as superabundant and expanding, was replicated from the 1930s onwards in the fissures that the Great Depression created in American politics. Roosevelt's New Deal and the state-led reforms that followed were greeted by some as a necessary concession to collectivism, while others feared the administration's initiatives and saw them as confirming the political, cultural, and moral decline that had been forced on America by "foreign" influences. Both directions – "liberal" and "conservative" – were anti-Communist, but the latter was considerably more skeptical to direct military intervention in the 1930s and through most of the Cold War. Both saw international affairs as an extension of their interpretation of America's domestic role, with the conservatives accusing their opponents of being "soft on Communism" and the liberals claiming that the conservatives were unwilling to pay the price of "making the world safe for democracy."

While the responses to the Great Depression were the main progenitors of America's Cold War visions of the world, it was the Second World War that formed its strategies. The Japanese attack in 1941 confirmed that interventionism and global reform were key to America's survival – the "monsters" would have to be destroyed if the United States was ever again to feel secure. It was the liberal interpretation of American foreign policy ideology that made World War II and its aftermath a laboratory for global reform. Like Wilson during World War I, Franklin Roosevelt believed in "positive nationalisms" as the best guard against authoritarian ideologies, but with the crucial difference that America this time could and should assist in finessing the *content* of these nationalisms and the reforms they envisaged for their countries when liberated from the enemy menace. As in America, educated reform could guide the energies of those who had dreamt of revolution in a "modern" direction. Referring to the aftermath of World War I, Franklin Roosevelt in October 1944 promised that "we shall not again be thwarted in our will to live as a mature nation, confronting limitless horizons. We shall bear our full responsibility, exercise our full influence, and bring our help and encouragement to all who aspire to peace and freedom."[14]

The American wartime involvement in China is the best example of how Washington attempted to guide allied regimes deemed deficient in talent, education, and moral strength toward reform. While the Chinese leader Jiang Jieshi (Chiang Kai-shek) saw his alliance with the United States as a marriage of convenience directed, first, against Japan and then, after Tokyo's defeat, against the Chinese Communists, many in Washington viewed Sino-American cooperation as a blank check to reform Chinese society and the state. When Jiang proved himself unwilling to be educated by the Americans, rather than withdrawing, the United States attempted to have the Chinese leader replaced by other anti-Communists who would be more willing to listen to American advice. Although ultimately unsuccessful in China, this was a pattern of intervention that would be repeated elsewhere in Asia later in the century.

The way World War II ended, with the unconditional surrender of its enemies, proved that America could defeat evil on a global scale. But it also proved to most Americans that the world wanted Americanism – through its products and through its ideas. What Americans abroad had seen in Europe, not to mention in China, Korea, or Iran, were peoples who needed to be set free from age-old forms of social and ideological oppression, people whose lives were so different from those experienced in the United States that their very existence formed a challenge to America's global mission. And the two world wars had shown what could happen in such societies if they were *not* exposed to the American form of progress, but rather were hijacked by false forms of modernity – German imperialism or Nazism, Japanese militarism. Other countries, in Harry Truman's phrase concerning Greece and Turkey in March 1947, must be aided before "confusion and disorder" spread.

The wartime alliances with the Soviet Union and Great Britain had remarkably little influence on how US leaders saw the world. Conservatives did criticize the Roosevelt administration for being "naïve" in its relations with the Soviet Union – in part a way to attack reform at home – but with limited success. Roosevelt and his main advisers seem to have been convinced that their very participation on the side of the United States in the war would pull both of its main allies in a more "democratic" and "progressive" direction, since the United States was, by far, the most powerful of the three. Victory in World War II was therefore a victory not just for an alliance, but also for the American way of life itself. It had outproduced and outgunned its enemies; now the time had come to transform both enemies and friends in one's own image.

Beyond Europe

The origins of America's interventions in the Third World form part of the origins of the American state. When Thomas Jefferson intervened against pirates on the North African coast – in the American image, the precursors of twenty-first-century terrorists – the aim was both to secure American commerce and to impose American standards of behavior. It was also to declare to the outside world that the United States was prepared to impose its will abroad. The need for such a declaration – later to be repeated as dogma for Latin America in the Monroe Doctrine – grew out of the visible contrast between building empires overseas, such as the West European powers were doing, and constructing a continental or even "inner" empire, such as Americans did through the twin processes of westward expansion and slavery.

Though much of the American discourse on non-Europeans originated with the colonial encounters with Native Americans, it is through the institution of slavery that the new republic formed its main images of the world beyond Europe. It is therefore doubly wrong to see American Third World policies as a kind of afterthought to US foreign affairs, as some historians have done. Africa was at the heart of the new republic's policies both at home and abroad during the first hundred years of its existence, and Africans for much longer than that. It was through battles over the institution of slavery that much of American foreign policy ideology took shape and the form of liberty that the United States was to stand for in the twentieth century was defined.

Out of the nineteenth-century conflicts over slavery and Reconstruction in the South came two key images for the development of twentieth-century American Third World policies: those of *emancipation* and *guidance*. The first relates to the need to remove the stigma of slavery from American ideals of liberty. Emancipation came to symbolize the removal of the *causes* of slavery, which were taken to be not primarily American economic need but rather the "ignorance, poverty, and vice" of those societies from which the slaves had originated. As such, it was an indictment of most non-European peasant societies and a stipulation that only the removal of the present form of these societies could prevent the conditions of slavery from reemerging. In such a sense, emancipation had a global agenda that was particularly urgent because slavery had existed in America itself and had come to be seen as a direct threat to its liberties, particularly as antislavery Northerners felt the double transformation of wage labor – often referred to as "wage-slavery" – and mass immigration threaten their own personal independence.

The concept of *guidance* and its object, *the ward*, were prominent in American images of African Americans before and during the Civil War, but became issues of key concern during the era of Reconstruction. Because of their wants, former slaves were seen as being incapable of controlling themselves. Even more than recent immigrants, they therefore fell easy victim to a return to the ways of their "underdeveloped" peasant societies of old, or, even worse, to the lures of new collectivist ideologies – such as socialism – competing for influence. The Reconstruction project, and African Americans' intense struggles for equality and justice, proved to many Americans that they were in need of guidance. In the South white elites disenfranchised blacks through political violence and terror. In the North it was often reformers – those who sought to eradicate poverty and vice in the cities – who crushed black aspirations through their insistence on making African Americans conform to white society a condition for their eventual "assimilation."

But the late nineteenth and early twentieth centuries zeal for reform was not only a key to American politics, it also put its stamp on the activities of Americans abroad, especially through the expansion of religious missions. After the United States had forced access to China and Japan at midcentury, American missionaries had spread there and gradually elsewhere, including Africa. While they were hugely important in bringing the "gospel of modernity" – health, education, and consumerism – the missionaries' relative lack of success in spreading the gospel of Christ troubled their audience at home, even though exaggerated figures of souls saved were reported. In the 1910s and 1920s many Americans began to see the "heathen natives," especially in East Asia, as being "ungrateful" for what was offered them through American missions.

The themes of "ungratefulness" and "wasted opportunities" also marked early twentieth-century US views of Latin America, and especially of Cuba, which the United States had taken from Spain in the war of 1898 and later given a ward-like status of semi-independence. In the 1920s and 1930s American commentators repeated much of the nineteenth-century discourse of Latin peoples' unsuitability for true republicanism, but with the added twist that "democracy" in the Cuban case had been subverted from within, after the best American efforts at implanting the seeds of freedom on the island. Instead of taking their cue from the United States' example, Cuban and other Latin American leaders had adopted the worst practices of their former colonial masters. In doing so, they had scuppered the offer of liberty and progress that Washington had presented to them. "If the United States has received but little gratitude," a State Department instructor told new envoys in the mid-1920s,

this is only to be expected in a world where gratitude is rarely accorded to the teacher, the doctor, or the policeman, and we have been all three. But it may be that in time they will come to see the United States with different eyes, and to have for her something of the respect and affection with which a man regards the instructor of his youth and a child looks upon the parent who has molded his character.[15]

The only country in the early twentieth century where the United States could impose its model of development through colonization was the Philippines. Like Cuba, the Philippines had been taken over after the Spanish–American War, but unlike the island in the Caribbean, the Southeast Asian islands were kept under direct American control as a dependency. The possession of the Philippines gave the United States an opportunity to experiment with the transposition of American ideals to a culture regarded as alien. In spite of the initially fierce resistance by the Philippinos to the American colonial project, by the mid-1930s many Americans were convinced that enough progress had been made for the colony to gain its independence within a decade. An alliance in Washington between trade protectionists, New Deal reformers, and fiscal conservatives secured a timetable for decolonization, on the clear understanding that the United States would keep its military bases and most of its political influence intact. The Philippines was seen as a triumph for American reform: it had brought a "new day of freedom" to an Asian people who earlier could have entertained no hopes for such a future.[16]

Much of the postwar agenda for US intervention in the Third World was therefore set from well before 1945 (or 1941, for that matter). What the results of the Second World War offered were new opportunities and requirements: as the main victor, the United States had the possibility, many in Washington believed, to remake the world. But in doing so it faced a challenge from the Soviet Union, the other main power left after the war, over the very content of the American mission. Within Europe, American aims centered on economic rebuilding through the Marshall Plan and security through the North Atlantic Treaty Organization (NATO). Both of these approaches aimed at combating Communism, and – in different forms – later came to form key elements of American policy toward the Third World.

Still, it was the restructuring of Japan that formed the main model for future American initiatives outside Europe. Although there were disagreements among US advisers as to how radical the restructuring of Japan should be, the basic direction was not in dispute: it was only through becoming more like the United States that Japan – the only non-European economic and military power – could be redeemed. The key to success was not only the rebuilding of Japanese institutions, but also the remolding of "the Japanese brain." "Our problem," according to an 1945 instructional film for the occupation forces, "is in the brain inside of the Japanese head. There are seventy million of these in Japan, physically no different than any other brains in the world, actually all made from exactly the same stuff as ours. These brains, like our brains, can do good things or bad things, all depending on the kind of ideas that are put inside."[17]

The mix of coercion, enticement, and appeal to the popular will that the occupation authorities used to put ideas into Japanese brains emphasized the new role that the state had come to occupy in American policy at home and abroad. In the beginning phase of the restructuring of Japan – just as in the implementation of the Marshall Plan in Europe – it was veterans of Franklin Roosevelt's New Deal programs who set the aims, and in doing so they reflected a much more positive view of what the state would be able to do than had been usual in American policy abroad. Even though the Cold War soon saw New Dealers lose influence within the occupation regime and in US foreign policy in general, all postwar American administrations up to Ronald Reagan were much more willing to use state power for social development purposes than any of their predecessors had been.

State power meant, usually, a set of programs carried out by the local government under US guidance. While the experience in Japan set many of the aims of US Third World policies, the European Recovery Program defined the means. As Paul Hoffman – a key Marshall Plan administ put it in 1951: "We have learned in Europe what to do in Asia, for the Marshall Plan we have developed the essential instrument.. .. . successful policy in the arena of world politics."[18] Those instruments were the political and cultural seduction of local elites, access to local markets, and military aid and training. Together, these measures were aimed at creating states that could both be successful in their own development *and* be part of American containment policies against the Soviet Union and its allies.

Although many historians have exaggerated the domestic pressures President Truman faced after World War II for an American withdrawal from an evil world, it is clear that the support many Americans gave to permanent military engagements abroad and to a policy of intervention in the Third World could only come as a result of the rivalry with Soviet Communism. The immense rise in Soviet power as a result of World War II – in which it was the other major victorious state – would have posed a challenge to any great power engaged in Europe or Asia. But it was the American ideological insistence that a global spread of Communism would, if not checked, result from the postwar extension of Soviet might that made the rivalry between the two powers into a Cold War. To elites in the United States, the rise of the Soviet Union as a world power also meant the rise of an alternative form of modernity that America had been combating since 1917. Any compromise with the great power that embodied Communist ideals would have been unlikely in the late 1940s. But the Soviet form of messianic modernism was particularly unfortunate in reaching the peak of its influence just as the United States removed the last limits to its global mission. "What indeed," asked the State Department official Joseph Jones in 1955, "are the limits of United States foreign policy?

The answer is that the limits of our foreign policy are on a distant and receding horizon; for many practical purposes they are what we think we can accomplish and what we think are necessary to accomplish at any given time ... [The Marshall Plan experience shows] not the limits but the infinite possibilities of influencing the policies, attitudes, and actions of other countries by statesmanship in Washington.[19]

But the US move to global interventionism did not happen without intense political debate at home as to the methods that America could use. Especially after the success of the Chinese Communist revolution and the attempt by Korean Communists to reunify their country by force, New Deal liberals came under attack from the Right for their failure to extend interventionism early and decisively enough. To Senator Joseph

McCarthy and his political allies, the determined resistance Jiang Jieshi had shown to American pressures for reform was not reason enough to limit assistance to his regime when faced with a Communist onslaught. In an extreme form of wishing a world of ideological allies, McCarthy attacked the New Dealers for not *exclusively* focusing on the defeat of Communism in the postwar period:

In one area of the world the plan was fight international communism with economic aid: in another area it was to fight international communism with military aid; and in the third area [Asia] it was to turn everything over to the Communists ... We know that at Yalta we were betrayed. We know that since Yalta the leaders of this Government by design or ignorance have continued to betray us ... We are more free than they wish us to be, and we are ready to fight for what we know is right, but we must not fight under the leadership of perfumed, dilettante diplomats.[20]

Although his confrontational rhetoric in the end defeated him, McCarthy would have recognized many of his aims in the policies that the Eisenhower administration implemented toward the Third World in the 1950s. By the end of the Korean War it was abundantly clear to General Eisenhower that there were limits to the sacrifices most Americans were willing to make in order to extend Americanism abroad. His policies of using covert interventions combined with alliances with local elites – rather than US military forces – proved successful in toppling moderate left-wing governments in Iran and Guatemala. The foreign aid that the United States provided to the Third World was primarily military – 95 percent of all aid in 1954 and more than 50 percent in 1960 – and the intention was both to prevent left-wing governments from coming to power and to help local elites resist Soviet pressure (more than half of all aid went to "frontline states" up to 1961).

In terms of American ideology, the wave of decolonization that began in the late 1940s and was mostly completed by the mid-1970s led in two different directions. On the one hand, American elites welcomed the breakup of the European colonial empires because it meant opportunities for extending US ideas of political and economic liberties. It also meant that the European elites – much reduced in stature after the two world wars – could concentrate on defense against Communism and reform at home. As Secretary of State Marshall had commented after discussions on NATO in 1949, "when we reached the problem of increasing the security of Europe, I found all the French troops of any quality were all out in Indochina, and I found the Dutch troops of any quality were out in Indonesia, and the only place they were not was in Western Europe."[21]

Decolonization meant that the future direction of the Third World was becoming an American responsibility, not a European one.

On the other hand, however, decolonization increased the threat of collectivist ideologies getting the upper hand in the Third World. The Chinese Communist revolution, the US-supported wars against Communist guerrillas in Vietnam, Malaya, and the Philippines, the radical orientation of the postindependence regimes in Indonesia, India, and Egypt, and even the successful interventions in Guatemala and Iran convinced the Eisenhower administration that the Third World may not be ready for democracy – the ingratitude shown by Chinese and Indonesians to US efforts to secure their freedom during and after World War II signified a lack of appreciation for the principles America was attempting to further. If that was the case, then a covert strategy for influence would make more sense than open attempts at gaining friends through aid and trade.

If the United States had been a less dynamic society – and had its ideological foundations been different – then the Eisenhower approach to the Third World challenge may have continued for another decade or more. But the same reform impulses that extended American democracy at home in the late 1950s and early 1960s led to an increasing emphasis on reform abroad. To an impatient postwar generation, the containment of Communism in the Third World was not enough. While arguing for the extension of democracy to African Americans and other previously disenfranchised groups, it was increasingly difficult to maintain that peoples of the Third World were not ready for democracy. And if they were, then America had to help them reach that goal. Both Left and Right in American politics emphasized the need for increased American involvement – while the Left deemphasized the Soviet threat and stressed the need for aid, the Right pressed for a more aggressive form of containment and the need to win allies. Both strains came together in the "battle for hearts and minds" in the Third World constructed by the Kennedy and Johnson administrations. Ironically, it was the failure of that joint approach in Vietnam that created much of the critique of American interventionism. But at a time when US foreign policy ideology had turned radically interventionist, that critique centered not on motivations and world views, but on themes of economic exploitation abroad and business dominance at home.

"The world as a market"

To some, American capitalism has always been the centerpiece of US foreign policy. In their view, only through a more profound understanding of its expanding economic role can the political aspects of US foreign affairs be grasped. In the twentieth century there were basically two directions within this school of thought. One was a radical populist and sometimes isolationist direction, which saw the influence of particular business interests as hijacking US foreign policy from the late nineteenth century onward, determining how America's relations with the world should develop. The other was a Marxist critique, which viewed the US state itself as an expression of the interests of the bourgeois class, representing that class in the international arena of competition for market shares. Given the increasing preponderance in international markets of US trade and investments, and the overall growth of its economy, it is not surprising that economic factors – be they seen as conspiratorial or structural – have been placed at the center of critical interpretations of America's global role.

Around 1900, in the 1920s, and in the 1960s – periods when US interventionism faced sustained criticism at home – the key to much of that critique was the undermining of American ideals through the influence of markets. Instead of seeing the role of the market in US foreign policy as part of a comprehensive ideology, many of those who opposed the occupation of the Philippines, Wilson's interventions, and the war in Vietnam saw the pernicious influence of businessmen as steering the direction of foreign policy. Bryan, in 1900, castigated "the commercial argument. It is based upon the theory that war can be rightly waged for pecuniary advantage and that it is profitable to purchase trade by force and violence ... Imperialism would be profitable to the Army contractors; it would be profitable to the shipowners, who would carry live soldiers to the Philippines and bring dead soldiers back; it would be profitable to those who would seize upon the franchises."[22] In the 1962 Port Huron statement, Students for a Democratic Society regretted – in a very Bryanesque way – the fact that "foreign investments influence political policies in under-developed areas – and our efforts to build a 'profitable' capitalist world blind our foreign policy to mankind's needs and destiny."[23]

Both before and during the Cold War there have been occasions when concrete business interests have had a direct and decisive role in American interventions, but the historical record shows that these were few and far between. Normally, presidents – from Jefferson to Reagan – have had little patience with businessmen promoting their self-interests, at least *after* they themselves have been elected to the White House. Those bankers, investors, and exporters who have come to the Oval Office pleading the case of their companies have more often than not received short shrift, somewhat similar to the way Soviet political theorists, scientists, or heads of friendship associations were treated in the Kremlin when they made suggestions on foreign policy.

But this is in no way to say that the capitalist market has played a negligible part in the formation of American foreign affairs. In a way, the Marxists seem to be right in arguing for a *systemic* role for business interests: throughout its existence, the American elite has argued – though in very diverse ways – for the promotion of free market exchanges as being at the core of US "national interest" abroad. While denying individual capitalists, no president has moved away from seeing the protection of such exchanges as a core duty. As Woodrow Wilson put it when he was still a political scientist rather than a practitioner: "Since ... the manufacturer insists on having the world as a market, the flag of his nation must follow him, and the doors of nations which are closed against him must be battered down. Concessions obtained by financiers must be safeguarded by ministers of state even if the sovereignty of unwilling nations be outraged in the process."[24]

The astonishing growth rates of the US economy in the nineteenth century – so far unparalleled in history – made America an economic superpower well before it took on that role militarily and politically. With growth averaging 3.9 percent per year between 1774 and 1909, by the beginning of World War I the United States was by far the largest producer of goods and services in the world. Its aggregate annual output was greater than that of the three main European powers – UK, Germany, and France – combined. While only a small percentage of the American economy then (and today) was engaged in foreign trade and investments, US exports have long been a significant part of world trade, constituting 13 percent of world total exports in 1913 and growing to 20 percent in 1950. A net importer of capital in the nineteenth century, by 1918 the United States was the world's largest capital exporter, a position it would keep until 1981.[25]

The influence of the American economic behemoth on the rest of the world has, of course, been substantial, and not just in terms of trade. In the 1890s and early 1900s the New York–London link created the first real international capital market, engaging American capital worldwide through British and other foreign companies. Between 1897 and 1914 total US investment abroad rose fivefold, and a significant part of these investments were connected to the Third World through European companies engaged in colonial exploitation and through direct investments in Mexico, Cuba, Central America, and to a smaller extent elsewhere in Latin America.[26] Although the relative size of US Third World investments never again reached their pre-World War I levels, after World War II the pattern broadened significantly to include a larger number of countries, industries, and products. By the late 1940s, when the United States produced a full half of the world's manufactured goods, it makes good sense to speak of an American capitalist world system, in which all major economic decisions influenced and were influenced by the US market.

But in spite of its economic and financial preponderance during the Cold War era, the United States has proven itself a reluctant economic imperialist. During every decade – except, perhaps, the 1970s – the huge domestic market always had the upper hand in attracting capital: it was all the outside world (and especially the Third World) was not – rich, socially and geographically mobile, and politically stable. And even though the hope of greater returns always kept American capital coming to the Third World, very few of those investments and trade links turned out to be highly profitable. During the Cold War the government always wanted private companies to increase their investments abroad – and especially in the Third World – in order to create influence and "development" – but with limited success. One of the main reasons why Washington had to turn to direct and indirect aid to Third World countries in the 1950s and 1960s was the lack of a willingness to invest on the side of US business.[27]

Equally problematic for those who wanted to enlist capitalism for America in the Cold War was the question of tariffs. As we have seen, a key component of US ideology is the concept of a unrestricted exchange of goods. But in American history the slightly broader concept of *free trade* has been a domesticated term: it was good for trade within the United States and for American access to foreign markets. But it was *not*, overall, admissible for foreign exports *to* the United States. Arguing that foreign imports threatened American freedoms, because products made by "unfree" workers abroad did away with jobs and profits for its citizens, the United States used massive import substitution and prohibitive tariffs – first on textiles, then on steel and related products – to stimulate its economy in the nineteenth century (the very same measures which the International Monetary Fund has tried to deny Third World countries today).[28] During the Cold War such measures were supported by a majority in Congress up to around 1980, in spite of attempts by successive administrations to gain access for Third World countries to US markets.

During the Cold War it was not the importance of the Third World to the US economy, but the importance of the United States to most Third World economies that counted; and even then, not as much as mutual trade and foreign investments than as products and patterns of production. For people in the Third World, the United States was where advanced goods came from, where machines had done away with much of the drudgery of production, and where productive companies were headquartered. For Americans who traveled or worked abroad, the persistence of US products and the admiration that US living standards and technology met among others were powerful confirmations of the superiority of Americanism, and raised genuine hopes that the American experience could be replicated locally. For those "locals" of some stature who did not believe in the replication of the American dream in the place they knew, there was increasingly another way out. In the mid-1960s Congress abolished the racist national origins quota system for immigration to the United States, replacing job skills for race as the main criterion for admission, and thereby opening up for a flood of new immigrants from Latin America and Asia. In a pattern that had been established in agriculture in the nineteenth century, unemployment was part of the reason why these immigrants came to the United States, since local production had been outcompeted by imports.[29]

The wish to make the world safe for capitalism – and the disappointingly low interest among US capitalists to personally contribute to that process – led US Cold War administrations to embark on extensive aid programs for the Third World from the mid-1950s. It was still the experience in postwar Japan and Western Europe that formed these initiatives: aid was linked to the recipient's acceptance of market access and export of profits, as well as to administrative restructuring and the exclusion of Communists and left-wing socialists from government. The purpose of the aid – often put with remarkable frankness to the recipients – was to reform the states and societies of the countries that received it. As the US Agency for International Development put it, "successful efforts to influence macro-economic and sectoral policies are likely to have greater impact on growth than the added capital and skills financed by aid."[30] In other words, it was the *structure* of society that mattered, rather than capital or training.

The deification of the market in the 1950s was a rather extreme version of the capitalist element in American foreign policy ideology. It came about for two reasons. One was the right-wing's political campaigns against the New Deal's extension of the US federal state. The other was the international collectivist challenge, which by the mid-1950s was more pronounced than ever in the Third World and from the Soviet Union. "I have become personally convinced," Secretary of State John Foster Dulles wrote in 1954, "that it is going to be very difficult to stop Communism in much of the world if we cannot in some way duplicate the intensive Communist effort to raise productive standards."[31] Both the domestic campaign and the international challenges led to a reaffirmation of the market in US foreign policy, but more as ideology than as exploitative practice.

Gradually, during the first part of the Cold War, the United States took on a *systemic* responsibility for the world economy, attempting to define its shape both with regard to Europe and the Third World. Ideology blended well with strategy in this mission: the Third World had to choose the market, in part because the periphery had to sustain the former imperial centers – Western Europe and Japan – through trade, and thereby both contain Communism *and* reduce the need for increased access to US markets. Aid to the Third World was one answer to all of these challenges. In the period 1956–60 – in spite of the fear of Soviet advances – only slightly less than 90 percent of all official aid to the Third World came from advanced capitalist countries, and between 60 and 70 percent of that percentage came from the United States.[32] As an increasing number of Third World countries gained their independence in the 1950s and early 1960s, the availability of such aid set rather crude questions of principles and priorities before their leaders.

On the American side – behind issues of strategy and alliances – lay a conviction that what had worked for the United States would also work for the world. Without the slightest hint of irony given their own practices of tariffs and embargos, "global development education" meant teaching the world to open its markets and encourage the growth of local private capital. Development was a matter of choice, and the model was the United States and its free enterprise. In its exhibitions abroad, its products were proof of America's success, showing, in the words of one reporter, "the freedom offered by washing machines and dishwashers, vacuum cleaners, automobiles, and refrigerators."[33] It was clear to American observers that just as trade carries products, products carry ideas.

Modernization, technology, and American globalism

With the postwar extension of American higher education and a rapid increase in the number of foreigners who came to study in the United States, it was not surprising that much work was set in to provide a theoretical model of Americanism to rival that of Communism. Both academic and government authorities stressed the need for such a model in education at home and in work abroad. Third World elites, underlined the Social Science Research Council in 1957, were looking for a new concrete form for their states and societies, and it was the duty of American social scientists to produce one.[34] The need was felt to be urgent: instead of the clear-cut Marxist theory of social change, the Western experience was a messy, drawn-out series of unheroic social processes, with few concrete points of reference that could enflame young Third World intellectuals. In order to learn, one had to observe the political systems of the "developing areas" and compare them with development in the West. The result, said Princeton professor Gabriel Almond, would not only be a prescriptive tool, but "a major step forward in the nature of political science as science."[35]

As an intellectual enterprise, what came to be called "modernization theory" has many of the same positivist traits as Marxism, with which it self-consciously draws a comparison. Indeed, it could be argued that both constitute a form of "high modernism" that emphasize, in a deterministic form, the unity of all modern development, centered on industry and technology. The Harvard sociologist Talcott Parsons, whose 1937 book *The Structure of Social Action* inspired most of the postwar modernization theorists, had claimed that an integrated and stable transition to industrial society could only be achieved through changes in political and cultural values. But, unlike Marx, Parsons believed that it was the opportunities for the individual to fit into the structures of society that determined the course of history, not economic developments alone. For Parsons, for MIT's Daniel Lerner, and for Walt Whitman Rostow – the Harvard professor whose 1960 *The Stages of Economic Growth: A Non-Communist Manifesto* later became a key text for modernization theory – the form of transition that they described had already taken place, in America. But there were enough "unsuccessful modernizations" – Germany, the Soviet Union, China – to necessitate the search for a grand theory of the road from "tradition" to "modernity."

Rostow's first major attempt at influencing policy-making came with a 1957 book he wrote with his MIT colleague Max Millikan, *A Proposal: Key to an Effective Foreign Policy*. In it, Millikan and Rostow argued that global challenges to the United States were momentous and immediate. "We are in the midst of a great world revolution," they wrote. "For centuries the bulk of the world's population has been politically inert. Outside America and Western Europe, and even in parts of the latter, until recently the pattern of society remained essentially fixed in the mold of low-productivity rural life centered on isolated villages. The possibility of change for most people seemed remote." But two world wars, decolonization, and improvements in communication had given "previously apathetic peoples" a chance to improve their lot. Unfortunately,

the danger is that increasing numbers of people will become convinced that their new aspirations can be realized only through violent change and the renunciation of democratic institutions. The danger ... is greatly increased by the existence of Communism – not because of any authentic attractions in its ideology but because the Communists have recognized their opportunities to exploit the revolution of rising expectations by picturing communism as the road to social opportunity or economic improvement or individual dignity and achievement of national self-respect.

But, according to Rostow and Millikan, the United States could offset the threat of Communism in the Third World through positive intervention. "American society," they wrote, "is at its best when we are wrestling with the positive problems of building a better world. Our own continent provided such a challenge throughout the nineteenth century ... Our great opportunity lies in the fact that we have developed more successfully than any other nation the social, political, and economic techniques for realizing widespread popular desires for change without either compulsion or social disorganization." The two social scientists wanted "to give fresh meaning and vitality to the historic American sense of mission – a mission to see the principles of national independence and human liberty extended on the world scene."[36]

In spite of being obsequiously self-referential, the US-led attempt at understanding the causes of Third World social and political change went far beyond simple apologia and the construction of global hierarchies. At its best, "developmentalism" was plainly intended as a wake-up call for America to take the global problems of hunger and social dislocation seriously and employ its enormous resources to improve the world condition. Designed to accompany the campaigns for social reform and the extensions of American democracy of the 1960s, the great majority of the US Third World programs aimed at improving education and health care, and to show that development intervention was an *alternative* to military intervention. As Millikan and Rostow had concluded, "we need the challenge of world development to keep us from the stagnation of smug prosperity."[37]

In the 1960s the United States saw administrations that eagerly responded to that challenge. John F. Kennedy – and his successor, Lyndon B. Johnson – both firmly believed that international development was an integral part of an American national security strategy. Kennedy, who made Walt Rostow head of the State Department's Policy Planning Council (he later served as Johnson's National Security Adviser), fervently believed that Americans could not escape, as he told Congress in 1961, "our moral obligations as a wise leader ... our economic obligations as the wealthiest people in a world of largely poor people ... and our political obligations as the single largest counter to the adversaries of freedom.

To fail to meet those obligations now would be disastrous; and, in the long run, more expensive. For widespread poverty and chaos lead to a collapse of existing political and social structures which would inevitably invite the advance of totalitarianism into every weak and unstable area ... We live at a very special moment in history. The whole southern half of the world – Latin America, Africa, the Middle East, and Asia – are caught up in the adventures of asserting their independence and modernizing their old ways of life.[38]

For Kennedy and his advisers the key to what America could do to help avoid breakdown in the Third World was held by its technological success. Money in itself could not do the job – only the diffusion of technology and the accompanying know-how could bring Third World countries swiftly across the period of uncertainty in which Communism threatened. Likewise, the receptivity of Third World countries to US technology implied an acceptance of the American leading role in the global drive toward modernity. In an age when even some Americans had begun to doubt that US technological superiority would last, such acceptance was refreshing. "Starting from a position of substantial inferiority in almost all areas, the Soviet Union has caught up with and surpassed us in more categories than are comforting," noted Henry Kissinger, a Harvard professor whose early views of development very much overlapped with those of Rostow and Millikan. Kissinger's 1960 recipe for success was to combine massive increases in US foreign aid with assistance in constructing "enlightened political institutions" in the recipient countries. Noting that "economic assistance is a form of intervention," Kissinger believed that "to offer nothing but bread is to leave the arena to those who are sufficiently dynamic to define their purpose."[39]

Kennedy and Johnson had more to offer than bread alone. Initiatives such as the Peace Corps and the Alliance for Progress were intended to stimulate political as well as economic development. In announcing the Peace Corps – an organization that, by 1965, had sent more than 13,000 Americans to work as volunteers in Third World development programs – Kennedy had promised that "our young men and women, dedicated to freedom, are fully capable of overcoming the efforts of Mr Khrushchev's missionaries who are dedicated to undermining that freedom."[40] The Alliance for Progress, set up to provide economic, technical, and educational assistance to Latin America, had a similar aim. Kennedy's adviser, the Harvard historian Arthur Schlesinger, reported after a tour of the continent that coincided with the launch of the Alliance in the spring of 1961, that the administration had to engineer "a middle class revolution where the processes of economic modernization carry the new urban middle class into power and produce, along with it, such necessities of modern technical society as constitutional government, honest public administration, a responsible party system, a rational land system, an efficient system of taxation."[41] In other words, only by becoming more like the United States could Latin America develop.

In some Third World areas, where Communists or left-wingers had already staged attempts at gaining political power, civilian development had to be accompanied by military development, thorough US assistance programs aiming at establishing a "modern" army capable of fighting the counterinsurgence wars that would keep their opponents at bay. The combination of training and technology would enable the soldiers to hold the ground while the political and economic forces of modernization took hold of society, removing it from the danger of a Communist take-over. Meanwhile, through US education local officers themselves would become an important part of the modernizing middle class that Schlesinger saw emerging. For many of the young military commanders in Third World states it was therefore not only US support for their armies that mattered. Their own fascination with American technology also played a key role in defining the relationship. After Kennedy told General Joseph Désiré Mobutu, the de facto ruler of the Congo, that "there was nobody in the world that had done more than the General to maintain freedom against the Communists," Mobutu's reward, at his own request, was six weeks of parachute training at Fort Benning and at the Special Warfare School at Fort Bragg, and the delivery of a US military command aircraft for his use in the Congo.[42]

The problem for the theory of limited intervention that accompanied the ideas of modernization was that the international enemy, Communism, was seen as increasingly aggressive and dynamic, while one's own side had doubts about direct military engagements, even of limited nature. In the war in Vietnam this problem was visible to US policy makers from the beginning of the 1960s. Rostow, who thought Vietnam a particularly suitable country for showing the relevance of modernization to foreign policy, argued to Kennedy already in November 1961 that

without the troop commitment, the Communists (who have been reading of our fears of white men in Asia ...) will believe that they have plenty of room for maneuver and continue infiltration ... If we move without ambiguity – without the sickly pallor of our positions on Cuba and Laos – I believe we can unite the country and the Free World; and there is a better than even chance that the Communists will back down and bide their time. This we should cheerfully accept; because the underlying forces in Asia are with us, if we do not surrender and vigorously exploit them.[43]

The emphasis on technology as a means of successful intervention abroad is embodied in Kennedy's and Johnson's Secretary of Defense, Robert S. McNamara. Having come to the Pentagon from the Ford Motor Company, at which he had become a director at the age of 30, McNamara firmly believed that the advantage that the United States had over Communism was primarily related to knowledge and the means of processing that knowledge into instruments of policy. That meant, for instance, ordering the right kind of weapons and tactics for the circumstances. But it also meant joining social science with military science: the Strategic Hamlet Program in Vietnam was an attempt at removing the civilian population from an area so that they would be less exposed to Communist propaganda and give anti-Communist forces a chance to wipe out their opponents militarily without risking high civilian casualties. But McNamara also saw the program as having wider aims. "Hard analysis," he explained to Kennedy, showed that hamlet construction gave "individuals an identity as citizens of a community" and promoted general trends of development through centralization and standardization.[44]

Throughout the 1960s and 1970s the numbers of Third World students who came to the United States for part of their education continued to increase. Successive administrations were very aware that these students, on going home, constituted a massive resource for the United States to draw on in its quest to influence and reform Third World countries. Having been confronted with the wealth and the products of America, its educational and jobs opportunities, its communications, ease of travel, and its youth culture, many returning students wanted to achieve modernity for their own countries, although not always, as it turned out, in a form recognizable to their American mentors. For most, the aim became to construct a modernity that in material terms offered the same potential they had witnessed in New York, California, or Ohio, but in a form that could be reconciled with social and ideological trends in their own countries or cultures. In some cases, the visitors turned against the dominant American ideological message and began identifying themselves with different forms of critique of US modernity and especially the US role abroad.

A significant part of the critique of US foreign policy that inspired these students (and many who had never visited) came from within the United States itself. During the 1960s, as a result of the failing war in Vietnam and the civil rights revolution at home, some of the chief ideological tenets of American thinking about the Third World came under attack. Although the criticism was diverse in background and in intention, some of the most sustained critiques came from civil rights leaders who identified their own struggle with that of Third World leaders opposed to US foreign policy. Martin Luther King, Jr., in 1967 spoke of telling the angry young men of the African-American ghettos

that Molotov cocktails and rifles would not solve their problems ... But they asked – and rightly so – what about Vietnam? They asked if our own nation wasn't using massive doses of violence to solve its problems, to bring about the changes it wanted ... I knew that I could never again raise my voice against the violence of the oppressed in the ghettos without having first spoken clearly to the greatest purveyor of violence in the world today – my own government.[45]

Three years earlier, Malcolm X had castigated the United States as a colonial power, internationally and domestically. "There is no system," Malcolm said, "more corrupt than a system that represents itself as the example of freedom, the example of democracy, and can go all over this earth telling other people how to straighten out their house, and you have citizens of this country who have to use bullets if they want to cast a ballot."[46]

The extension of democracy in America that began in the mid-twentieth century led the debate over US Third World policies in two different directions. Within the foreign policy elites the answer was to intensify engagements abroad through the Cold War, vowing to extend America's freedoms there as well as at home. But for many minorities the beginning successes in the battle for status and equality at home meant sympathy for those abroad who fought US power for the same purposes. Though always a minority voice and never politically influential, this persistent critique opened up visions of an America that concentrated on solving its own domestic problems, while engaging in a dialogue with the new countries of the Third World.

For official foreign policy, though, the universal Cold War became the proper symbol of America's aims. It was a globalist vision that fitted the ideology and the power of the United States in the late twentieth Century, while being symmetrical with the character of its Communist enemy, an enemy that also portrayed itself as popular, modern, and international. The Cold War provided an extreme answer to a question that had been at the center of US foreign policy since the late eighteenth century: in what situations should ideological sympathies be followed by intervention? The extension of the Cold War into the Third World was defined by the answer: *everywhere* where Communism could be construed as a threat.

2 The empire of justice: Soviet ideology and foreign interventions

Like the United States, the Soviet state was founded on ideas and plans for the betterment of humanity, rather than on concepts of identity and nation. Both were envisaged by their founders to be grand experiments, on the success of which the future of humankind depended. As states, both were universalist in their approaches to the world and the majority of their leaders believed that friends or enemies on the international stage were defined by proximity or nonproximity to the specific ideological premises on which each of these Powers had been founded. During the Cold War both Soviet and American leaders came to define the potential for such proximity by any country's distance from the other superpower in its foreign policy and domestic political agenda.

In historical terms, much of the twentieth century can be seen as a continuous attempt by other states to socialize Russia and America into forms of international interaction based on principles of sovereignty. In these efforts there were some successes, but many failures. The successes have mainly been connected to crises within the international system that could directly threaten Moscow or Washington themselves. For the United States, as we have seen, the Great Depression, the Second World War, and the end of the Vietnam War all led to a greater degree of accommodation to the interests of other states. For Russia, the period between the 1905 and 1917 revolutions, the aftermath of the German attack in 1941, and the Gorbachev–Yeltsin era signaled such accommodation. But the periods in which both powers have been poised to intervene unilaterally *against* the gradually developing norms of international interaction have been much more prevalent. Given the form that American and – at least during its Soviet period – Russian policy took during the twentieth century, it is reasonable to assume that the two projects – one of state sovereignty and another of global ideological predominance – cannot be reconciled, even though both Cold War superpowers at least in form came to accept alliances and international organizations.

While this chapter will argue that most of the interventionist impulses in Soviet foreign policy were unique to that specific form of a Russian state, the Communists when taking power in Russia of course became successors to an old expansionist empire, in much the same way as the American revolutionaries developed out of the British empire. In both cases the ideologies that justified intervention had developed from concerns that were formed in earlier centuries, under different regimes. For the Russian Communists, this meant that not only did they inherit a multicultural space in which Russian was spoken by less than half the population, but they also took over a state in which the tsars for at least two generations had attempted a policy of Russification and modernization of their non-Russian subjects. Many Russians in the late nineteenth and early twentieth centuries, including some who became Communists, believed that their country had been endowed with a special destiny to clear the Asian wilderness and civilize the tribes of the East.

In the first decade of the twentieth century Vladimir Illich Ulianov – also known as Lenin – created a party that believed in a form of Marxist modernity that would drive away backwardness from European Russia and set the Asian peoples of the empire on the path to modern development. The Bolsheviks – later known as the All-Russia Communist Party and the Communist Party of the Soviet Union – placed the liberation of the productive potential of the people at the core of the political process. To Lenin, as a Marxist, that liberation meant their transformation from peasants to modern workers, but without the oppression that capitalist systems had inflicted on the industrial proletariat in other European countries. The small Russian proletariat could, the Bolsheviks believed, free itself from the capitalist stage of development if led by a revolutionary vanguard – the Communist Party. The party represented the proletariat and would direct Russia's historical development from a peasant society to a society of industrial workers.

While US and Soviet ideologies had much in common in terms of background and project, what separated them were their distinctive definitions of what modernity meant. While most Americans celebrated the market, the Soviet elites denied it. Even while realizing that the market was the mechanism on which most of the expansion of Europe had been based, Lenin's followers believed that it was in the process of being superseded by class-based collective action in favor of equality and justice. Modernity came in two stages: a capitalist form and a communal form, reflecting two revolutions – that of capital and productivity, and that of democratization and the social advancement of the underprivileged. Communism was the higher stage of modernity, and it had been given to Russian workers to lead the way toward it.

The Russian empire and its revolutions

After the fall of the Soviet Union there was – for a time – a commonly held view that Russia had been a normal European state before the Communist experiment (and that it would return to being one after the end of Communism). The first part of that judgment is certainly untrue. The Russian empire, until the very end of its development, had very little in common with the other main European powers in terms of ideology or state structure. The prerevolutionary Russian elite of the nineteenth century was intent on overcoming what they saw as an age-old exclusion of Russia from the continent through recreating European culture under new and better circumstances. What the Europeans saw as backwardness was in reality, it was argued by many, a virgin opportunity to create a more genuine and unpolluted Christian civilization in the east, which, in time, would become the redeemer of a decadent and declining continent. Meanwhile, Russia remained an autocratic state, in which much of the elite's legitimacy was built on continuous continental territorial expansion, especially, in the nineteenth century, towards the east and the south.

Russian territorial expansion had begun in the sixteenth century and had gone into high gear in the early eighteenth century during the reign of Peter the Great. After the Napoleonic Wars Russia's incorporation of its Western neighbors was at an end, and its imperialist designs were turned increasingly toward the Caucasus, Siberia, and Central Asia. By the end of the nineteenth century less than half the empire's subjects were Russians and only around two-thirds were Slavs. The rest, inhabiting around three-quarters of what had been declared Russian territory, consisted of around seventy major ethnic groups, stretching from the Norwegian to the Korean borders. The largest and best organized of these groups outside European Russia were the Muslims of the Central Asian and the Caucasus regions. Although most of the early conquest in Asia had taken place by force, the enormous distances between center and periphery and the lack of qualified imperial administrators had meant that in most places the empire at first had been content with using local elites to administer on behalf of St. Petersburg. In some regions the Crown had even subsidized Islamic proselytizing as a means of "civilizing" heathen parts of the empire.

Toward the middle of the nineteenth century, however, as concepts of Russian uniqueness came together with improved communications to create a much more self-confident imperial elite, the cultural autonomy of distant regions began coming under pressure. In the 1830s, as the final push to conquer all of the Caucasus got under way, the Imperial Council declared that the region would "be connected to Russia as one limb on the same body, and the peoples who live there will be made to speak, think and feel Russian."[1] Such a mission meant that expansion became a necessary part of the imperial state, even for those who wanted reform at home. As the liberal foreign minister Aleksandr Gorchakov framed the dilemma in 1864: "The Russian situation in Central Asia is similar to that of all civilized states that come into contact with half-wild, unsettled peoples who lack a stable social organization. In such cases, both security and trade interests always demand that the civilized state exercise a certain authority over those of its neighbors that create disturbances because of their wild and impetuous habits." But the duties of civilized government were then extended, according to Gorchakov, because the effects of that "authority" meant that the half-wilds would change their behavior and gradually become more civilized, a process which in turn exposed *them* to raids by their neighbors. "And so a state must decide: either to give up this constant task and give its outer borders over to chaos ... or to penetrate ever further into the wild countries." When the latter road is chosen, Gorchakov notes, "it is very difficult to stop ever again."[2]

Faced with resistance to the project of extending civilization, Russia's wars in Asia in the mid-nineteenth century turned genocidal. In the Caucasus large numbers of Muslim noncombatants were killed or driven into exile, their villages and fields taken over by Slav migrants. By the 1860s the empire faced a question that the United States had to deal with in the very same generation: which peoples could be integrated into the state and which could only be controlled or, at worst, exterminated? Because of the way it saw its own mission, the Russian elite's main answer was a massive Russification campaign, which sought to give as many as possible of the empire's inhabitants the opportunity to become Russian and thereby assist in the spreading of civilization. The best way of convincing others of Russian superiority was through letting them take part in the spiritual and material project of extending the empire. "The Russian conquest of Turkestan brought about an immense alleviation in the lot of the common man," Count Konstantin von der Pahlen argued in the early twentieth century, when on an inspection tour of the immense areas over which the empire had taken control.[3] The count believed that seeing the advantages of Russian rule would help Muslims become a part of the imperial project and thereby save themselves from the extermination that noncompliance would lead to.

Increasingly, in the nineteenth century, the project of building the world's largest contiguous state became linked with the debate over reform at home. This debate often centered on the fate of the Russian peasants, most of whom up to Alexander II's Edict of Emancipation in 1861 were held as serfs. Russian serfs had more in common with nineteenth-century American slaves than with European peasants; indeed, it makes sense to speak of them, as the historian Dominic Lieven does, as a form of inner colony within the empire.[4] Without property rights and bound to provide service for the *barin*, or master, the serfs by the mid-nineteenth century stood in the way of developing the workforce a modern capitalist economy needed. But even after emancipation, reformers saw the traditions of the "backward" Russian countryside as a barrier against creating a modern state. Some hailed the capitalist market as one means of redemption. The market, Lenin wrote while exiled to Siberia for revolutionary activities in 1897,

is in all respects progressive, that it is breaking down routine, disunited, small-scale hand production which has been immobile and stagnant for ages; that it is increasing the productivity of social labour, and thereby creating the possibility of higher living standards for the working man; that it is also creating the conditions which convert this possibility into a necessity – namely, by converting the "settled proletarian" lost in the "backwoods," settled physically and morally, into a mobile proletarian, and by converting Asiatic forms of labour, with their infinitely developed bondage and diverse forms of personal dependence, into European forms of labour.

"The European manner of thought and feeling is no less necessary ... for the effective utilisation of machines than steam, coal, techniques," the young Lenin added.[5]

By the late nineteenth century members of the Russian intellectual and economic elite were charging that political and military leaders did not take the project of reforming the state seriously enough, and that they thereby let down all the "new" peoples in the empire, be they Asians or emancipated serfs. While the revolutionaries, such as Lenin, were a distinct and rather isolated minority, the debate between "Westernizers" and "Slavophiles" showed a widespread sense that the empire had lost its direction. Both groups believed that part of Russia's purpose was to fulfill its duty toward non-European peoples, but the first saw salvation in selective learning from the West, while the latter saw Russia's future in an idealized image of its past. While some accepted capitalism as a necessary evil, most increasingly saw a contradiction between the strengthening of the state, which they sought, and the development of free markets. As Russia began to industrialize this contradiction became more acute and created a widespread sense that the empire was being let down by its traditional elites.[6]

The response to the perceived crisis – which was underway well before the empire lost its wars of 1904–05 and 1914–17 – united many Westernizers and Slavophiles in a reconstructed faith in Russia's special mission. While believing in the need to create a new Russia that was

Map 2   The Russian empire in 1914.

representative of its real elite – the intelligentsia – many politicians and writers underlined the fact that their country had to put technology and progress into the service of the people and thereby help create a more just social system. A significant group of reformers turned toward anticapitalism, claiming, as did the philosopher Nikolai Berdiaev, that "to be a bourgeois is ... to be a slave of matter and an enemy of eternity. The perfected European and American civilizations gave rise to the industrial-capitalist system, which represents not only a mighty economic development but the spiritual phenomenon of the annihilation of spirituality."[7] No wonder that Sergei Bulgakov, a Russian Marxist later turned Orthodox priest, saw the Russian intellectual as defined by his "other-worldliness, his eschatological dream about ... a coming empire of justice."[8]

O C E A N

Bering Straits

R. Anadyr

R. Indigirka

R. Kolyma

KAMCHATKA

Siberian Plains

R. Lena

E M P I R E   Yakutsk •   Okhotsk •

Sea of Okhotsk

Lower Tunguska

R. Aldan

SAKHALIN

• Yeniseysk

R. Angara

• Krasnoyarsk

R. Yenisey

•Lake Baikal

• Irkutsk

Nerchinsk

R. Lena

AMUR REGION

MANCHURIA
(occupied 1900–5)

• Vladivostok

MONGOLIA

J A P A N

Russian empire 1796

Acquisitions 1796–1855

Acquisitions 1856–1914

CHINA

K O R E A

What gave the reformist vision of the empire's role its chance in Russian politics – and eventually drove its more extreme elements to the forefront – were the wars of expansion that the traditional elites had begun losing by the beginning of the twentieth century. Already in the late 1850s the wars in the Caucasus had taken up one-sixth of the state income. When confronted with Japanese and German expansionism, the Russian imperial project simply did not have enough readily available resources to compete. Between 1905 and 1917 legitimacy in the political debates began shifting to those who had a more representative and a more inclusive version of the Russian mission to offer. Among these stood the Bolsheviks – a revolutionary party that mixed visions of radical democracy with elitist achievement, and that promised Russians a key role in the future reordering of the world.

It would be unfair on Lenin's party to see its policies – as many Western observers have – as being a direct continuation of Russian expansionist ideology: eternal Russia disguised as proletarian internationalism. Much of the party's nationalist rhetoric – before the revolution and after – was indeed merely propaganda, and was misleading in terms of the party's real internationalist aims. Lenin had no time for Berdiaev's spiritualist Russian exceptionalism; "Marxism," Lenin said, "is materialism. As such, it is relentlessly hostile to religion."[9] The leader of the Bolsheviks – constituted as a separate party from 1912 – also stressed their enmity toward Russification and the oppression of minorities: "Complete equality of rights for all nations; the right of nations to self-determination; the unity of the workers of all nations" were among the slogans Lenin put forward on the eve of the outbreak of World War I, the war that would break the back of the Russian empire and give the well-organized Bolsheviks their chance to take power through a coup in November 1917. But Lenin also warned:

In this situation, the proletariat of Russia is faced with a twofold or, rather, a two-sided task: to combat nationalism of every kind, above all, Great-Russian nationalism; to recognise, not only fully equal rights for all nations in general, but also equality of rights as regards polity, i.e., the right of nations to self-determination, to secession. And at the same time, it is their task, in the interests of a successful struggle against all and every kind of nationalism among all nations, to preserve the unity of the proletarian struggle and the proletarian organisations, amalgamating these organisations into a close-knit international association, despite bourgeois strivings for national exclusiveness.[10]

The Bolsheviks shared with the elites within the Russian empire a conviction that their country would eventually become the center of a new world civilization that would be both modern and just. Lenin believed that having been the first country that experienced a socialist revolution, Russia could do much to help revolutionaries in other countries – it could function as a base area and rear guard for the revolutions in the more advanced countries of Europe, which, Lenin believed, would follow soon. But in spite of the country's social and technological backwardness, Lenin believed that the organization of its proletariat through the Communist Party had given Russia the edge – and that it could teach the lessons of the October Revolution to other proletarian parties. "To wait until the working classes carry out a revolution on an international scale means that everyone will remain suspended in mid-air," Lenin said in May 1918.[11] The very fact that the main imperialist powers had intervened against the new Soviet state in the civil war that followed the October Revolution proved to the Bolsheviks how crucial their section of the front against imperialism was.

Having taken power in the main cities and begun – however slowly – to extend their territory through civil war and to construct their own state,

Fig. 1   Bolshevik soldiers in 1917: the Russian revolution
inspired many Third World leaders.

the Bolsheviks soon found themselves the inheritors not only of Russia,
but also of its empire. In the immediate wake of the 1917 revolution all of
the major nationalities within the empire had broken away to set up their
own administrations. But whenever the principles of national sovereignty
came into conflict with those of the strategic needs of the new Soviet state –
the latter representing the needs not only of proletarians within Russia
but also worldwide – the Communist Party opted for the latter. In the case
of the Ukraine, Lenin told its parliament (Rada) in an ultimatum as early
as December 1917, that "even if the Rada had received full formal
recognition as the uncontested organ of supreme state power of an
independent bourgeois Ukrainian republic, we would have been forced
to declare war on it without any hesitation, because of its attitude of
unexampled betrayal of the revolution and support of ... the bitterest
enemies of the national independence of the peoples of Russia, the
enemies of Soviet power and of the working and exploited masses."[12] In
1921 – having for all practical purposes won the civil war – the
Communists even invaded and occupied Georgia, a former Russian
colony where a socialist regime had come to power through its own
revolution a few years earlier. Josif Vissarionovich Dzhugashvili – a
veteran Georgian Bolshevik calling himself "Stalin" after the pattern of
the great leader – declared that the former socialist regime in Tblisi had
been "a vehicle of bourgeois influence on the proletariat" and that

"in view of the utter hostility of the capitalist states toward the Soviet countries, the totally isolated existence of Soviet Georgia, or of any other Soviet country, is inconceivable both from the military and from the economic point of view. The mutual economic and military support of the Soviet states is a condition without which the development of these states is inconceivable."[13]

As the new Soviet Commissar for Nationalities, Stalin exerted a key influence on Communist policy toward the non-Russian peoples within the "Red Empire." Himself a Russified Georgian, he strongly believed that modernity could only come to the more backward peoples within the union through the extension of the influence of the Russian working class. A crude but dedicated Marxist, Stalin saw development as a set of hierarchies, fashioned throughout by the greater or shorter distance from the existence of a class-conscious proletariat directed by a Communist Party. Similar to some of the Russian imperialists of the nineteenth century, he felt that Russia, being on the periphery of Europe, was in a better position to work with non-European peoples than were other advanced nations. As Lenin lay dying in 1922, even he – who had sanctioned the forced integration into the Soviet Union of the former colonies and the brutal crushing of their nationalist leaderships – sensed that Stalin's centralism might conflict with the party's Marxist creed. "Stalin's haste and his infatuation with pure administration," Lenin wrote in a comment on the Sovietization of Georgia, could hinder the processes of natural social development toward socialism not only in the colonies, but also within Russia itself. "The infinitesimal percentage of Soviet and Sovietized workers will drown in that tide of chauvinistic Great-Russian riffraff like a fly in milk," the leader predicted with characteristic hyperbole.[14]

In the short term, however, the many young Russian Bolsheviks who set out to remake the Asian parts of the new Soviet Union proved their founding father wrong. They were driven not so much by chauvinism as by complete dedication to the Communist ideals of social justice and technological development. Their message was different from that of the former colonial administrators in stressing that colonized peoples had rights, and that the most downtrodden of them – those who had been exploited both by the colonial authorities and by the local elites – were the natural allies of the new regime. Only through profound social change – stimulated by Russia but carried out by the minorities themselves – could their peoples become little wheels in the great machine that would produce Soviet socialism. As would happen later elsewhere in the Third World, the Communist recipe for change was certain to split whole societies apart – on the one hand, a small group of committed local followers wanted to move their countries rapidly toward the common goal, and, on the other, large groups of waverers or resisters whose loyalties lay with their communities or with other ideals. In the Soviet Union none of these could be tolerated. By the mid-1920s all of those who opposed the Communists – anarchists, left-socialists, liberals, tsarists – were driven into exile, imprisoned, or executed, while the waverers had learnt to keep their doubts to themselves. Only among the Muslims of Central Asia did armed resistance continue into the 1930s, in groups that the Bolsheviks called *Basmachi* (bandits), and whose name and ferocious reputation anti-Soviet fighters in Afghanistan would take up as badges of honor two generations later.[15]

The Comintern and the Third World

It was not only inside the Soviet Union that Communism had to expand in order to fulfill its promise of social justice for all. Very few of Lenin's followers saw a sharp distinction in terms of political activity between what had been the Russian empire and countries outside it – indeed, to Lenin the main purpose of his revolution had been to prepare the ground for other revolutions to come; first, in the developed capitalist countries of Europe and then, as their social conditions allowed for it, in the colonial territories. In order to assist and promote such revolutions the Bolsheviks in 1919 set up the Communist International, or Comintern, a world-wide organization headquartered in Moscow, to which all workers' parties were invited as members. Lenin's aim for the Comintern was also to help "Bolshevize" the main socialist parties, but in most cases the opposite result followed – in their eagerness to join the new International, Lenin's supporters abroad found themselves marginalized and often excluded from the mainstream organizations and forced to set up new Communist parties, or, as the Soviets liked to think of them, new local chapters of the Comintern.

From its nineteenth-century origins Marxism had concentrated its analysis and predictions on Europe and America, and had had little time for or interest in those countries in which capitalism had not yet been established as the main vehicle of exploitation. Like his later adherents in Russia, Karl Marx had seen the world as organized in a hierarchy of development, in which the existence of an industrial working class was the key distinguishing factor – those countries that had a proletariat would also be the first to advance toward socialism, through a process that grew directly out of the specific forms of capitalist exploitation that European and American workers lived within and, ultimately, rebelled against. Asia and Africa, Marx conceded, had in the past gone through a different development from Europe – from an historical perspective, the journey of these continents toward capitalism had only just begun. What Marx called the Asiatic mode of production was distinguished by isolated peasant communities vaguely connected to a despotic and inefficient state – a social system that forced people into an "undignified, stagnatory, and vegetative life." Under these circumstances imperialism was an agent for progress, in spite of Marx's sympathy with its victims. "England," he concluded as Britain was crushing the Indian Mutiny in 1853, "has a double mission in India: one destructive, the other regenerating – the annihilation of old Asiatic society, and the laying of the material foundations of Western society in Asia."[16]

As a profoundly unorthodox Marxist, Lenin's thinking – especially toward the end of his life – had begun awarding a much broader tactical role to Marx's "semibarbarian societies." In his key work *Imperialism: The Highest Stage of Capitalism*, written directly before the 1917 revolution, Lenin argued that the intense conflict between European states over colonial possessions in the late nineteenth century had changed capitalism as a system and advanced its decay.

To the numerous "old" motives of colonial policy, finance capital has added the struggle for the sources of raw materials, for the export of capital, for spheres of influence, i.e., for spheres for profitable deals, concessions, monopoly profits and so on, economic territory in general. When the colonies of the European powers, for instance, comprised only one-tenth of the territory of Africa (as was the case in 1876), colonial policy was able to develop – by methods other than those of monopoly – by the "free grabbing" of territories, so to speak. But when nine-tenths of Africa had been seized (by 1900), when the whole world had been divided up, there was inevitably ushered in the era of monopoly possession of colonies and, consequently, of particularly intense struggle for the division and the redivision of the world.[17]

The intensity of capitalist imperial rivalries gave new possibilities and new significance to the anti-imperialist struggle of people in the Third World, according to Lenin, especially after the European revolutions that he had predicted after World War I had failed to materialize. While never openly contradicting Marx's belief in stages of development, Lenin thought that the Russian revolution had shown that some of these stages could be very brief indeed, and began bringing Third World socialists to Moscow already in the immediate aftermath of the 1917 Communist coup. In November 1919, in a speech filled with missionary exhortations, Lenin told one such gathering that their "task is to arouse the working masses to revolutionary activity, to independent action and to organization, regardless of the level they have reached; to translate the true Communist doctrine, which was intended for the Communists of the more advanced countries, into the language of every people."[18] Two years later Lenin had concluded, in desperation, that "the destiny of all Western civilization now largely depends on drawing the masses of the East into political activities."[19]

The first opportunity the Bolsheviks got to implement their credo outside their own borders was in Mongolia, where China had lost control of the government after 1911. A small group of Mongolian revolutionaries, having come into contact with Bolsheviks who had fled there during the Russian civil war, began seeing Communism as incorporating both independence and modernity, and therefore as an ideal vehicle for escaping Mongolia's nomadic and Buddhist past. In 1921 Russian and Mongol Bolshevik soldiers occupied Urga, the winter quarters of the last living Buddha, and made it the capital of a Mongolian People's Republic under the name of Ulaanbaatar (Red Hero). As the first People's Republic, Mongolia became a testing ground for much of Communist policy in the Third World: methods of education, cultural work, collectivization, and antireligious propaganda that would appear later in other countries on other continents were first introduced by Soviet advisers in Mongolia, who ran the country on behalf of its Communist rulers. The young Soviet advisers were in a hurry, not least because support for Mongolia was a drain on scarce resources at home. The Comintern representative instructed the leaders in Ulaanbaatar:

Within ten years we must have built up socialism in Mongolia. In order to fulfill the instructions ... to completely end the importation of flour from the USSR, it is urgently required to develop agriculture. It is required to overfulfill the meat procurement plan. As the external situation of Mongolia is unstable, it is necessary to kill, arrest, and imprison feudal lamas and noblemen.[20]

The Comintern was to be the vehicle through which the Communists should set off rebellions against colonialism. For many of those in the Third World who opposed foreign domination, the Russian revolution had been a signal event: not only did the Bolsheviks want to set up a new state of their own that did away with colonial oppression and ethnic domination, but they also promised to support all movements worldwide that had the same aim. And most important of all – as we will see in the next chapter – the Communists had both a model for how to overthrow the former regime and a pattern for a new state that was just and modern at the same time. The image of the October Revolution that Comintern propagandists spread worldwide was one that many young organizers and intellectuals found immensely attractive as a future for their own countries. No wonder, then, that by the early 1920s Communist parties had been set up in most of the key states in the Third World – China,

India, Indonesia, Turkey, and Iran all saw Communist parties established in 1920 or 1921. The leaders of these parties – those who had not already been arrested or shot by the regimes in power – congregated in Moscow for the Comintern congresses, as did European Communist leaders. The records of the meetings show not only how diverse the early Communist movement was, but also how difficult the encounters between the Russians and Marxists from other backgrounds turned out to be.

The Soviets had expected opposition (and not a little condescension) from Western European Marxists who attended the first Comintern congresses. What surprised them more was the ability and willingness of Third World Marxists to stake out independent positions on the understanding of social developments and the political course of Communism. While in no way presenting a uniform critique of Soviet socialism, the voices of these leaders described some of the difficulties that would prove impossible to overcome in their Third World policy for later generations in the Kremlin. The young Indian Communist Mahabhendra Nath Roy, for instance, criticized Lenin at the Second Comintern Congress for being too reluctant to give Third World Communist parties a leading role in the anticolonial revolutions in their countries. While agreeing with the Soviet leader that the Communists had to ally with the local (or "national") bourgeoisie against the colonial power, Roy believed that the Communists had to propagandize independently among and recruit from all social layers for their own party, which would form a "vanguard of the working class," even in areas where that class was very small relative to the peasant masses. Claiming that an alliance with the Soviet Union could help Third World countries avoid capitalist development altogether, Roy saw the possibility, at least in some areas, of Communist parties coming to power before the working class was fully developed, and therefore having to carry out both "petty bourgeois reforms, such as the division of land" and the construction of proletarian power simultaneously.[21]

Even worse from a Soviet perspective was the critique voiced by the Bashkir Communist Mirsaid Sultan Galiev. Born in 1892 into an ethnic group that had been colonized by Russia, Galiev argued for the revolution as first and foremost meaning the liberation of enslaved peoples. As founder of the "Militant Tatar Organization of Socialists-Internationalists," Galiev had already in 1914 called on Tatar and Bashkir soldiers in the tsar's army to rebel, since the cause of the war was that "Russians, not content to have conquered the Tatars, Bashkirs, Turkestanis, the [peoples of the] Caucausus, etc., wanted to conquer the Turks and Persians as well."[22] Galiev joined the Bolsheviks in Baku in 1917, and soon became the most prominent party leader with a Muslim background. As Stalin's deputy as Comissioner for Nationalities, the Bashkir Communist argued that "all colonized Muslim peoples are pro-letarian peoples" without strong class contradictions, and that the libera-tion of the colonies was an essential precondition for revolutions in the West. "So long as international imperialism ... retains the East as a colony where it is the absolute master of the entire natural wealth," Galiev stressed, "it is assured of a favorable outcome of all isolated economic clashes with the metropolitan working masses, for it is perfectly able to shut their mouths by agreeing to meet their economic demands."[23] Understandably, as Stalin's star rose within the govern-ment, Galiev's fell. He was expelled from the party in 1923, accused of wanting to organize a separate anticolonial International and for claiming a progressive role for Islam in the liberation of Asian peoples.[24]

As Stalin's hold on the Soviet party increased in the 1920s, dissident voices from the Third World were stifled both within the Soviet Union and within the Comintern. Roy was sacked from his leading position in the international Communist organization in 1928 because of his support for a more independent role for the Chinese Communist Party (CCP) within the nationalist alliances that Stalin had ordered it to join. In his last and final battle with Trotsky, Stalin in 1926–27 had made an issue of the need for the CCP to join with the Chinese nationalist party – the Guomindang – in opposing foreign imperialism and in constructing a new Chinese state. Against Trotsky's concept of a permanent revolution, in which the capit-alist stage of development could be a very brief period between the bourgeois and socialist revolutions, Stalin saw these transitions in all cases to be processes in which a fully-fledged capitalist social system came into being before the working class could successfully challenge the bourgeoisie for power. Confronted with Chinese requests to establish its own Communist armed forces, the Soviet leader declared that "we need the [Guomindang] Right. It has capable people who still direct the army and lead it against the imperialists."[25] While Stalin won the political battle in Russia, his advice to the Chinese Communists proved disastrous for the recipients. In April 1927 the Guomindang army under Chiang Kai-shek crushed the Chinese party and arrested or murdered its main leaders. Communism was finished as a main political force in China for almost a decade. But people such as Roy – who claimed that what they had requested for the Chinese was nothing more than what Lenin had done in Russia in 1917 – drew no benefit from having been right.

In the 1930s, as Stalin's real and imagined opponents disappeared into labor camps or killing fields, Soviet Communism created a set of key myths about the October Revolution, all designed to help Stalin's claim to power and his dogmatic views about the Marxist laws of historical development. According to these myths, 1917 was a workers' revolution carried out by the most advanced groups of the industrial proletariat under the direction of the Communist Party. Since the emphasis was on *advanced*, numbers almost did not matter – it was the "objective" role of the Petersburg coup-makers to represent the working class as a whole. What they carried out a revolution against was a bourgeois state that had gradually come into being since 1905, and which had manifestly been in power since February 1917. That way Stalin could emphasize that the Bolsheviks had "in a natural manner" followed the laws of development by replacing a bourgeois regime with a proletarian one (even if the bourgeoisie had only had the blessing of their own state for about eight months). The reason why there could be such a brief period of transition in Russia was *not* a permanent revolution, but the organizing abilities of the Russian Communists, led by Lenin and Stalin. By instituting these myths as an integral part of what now became known as Marxism–Leninism, Stalin emphasized his own role and that of the party, but he also effectively kicked away the ladder that could help impatient Third World Communists climb rapidly toward socialism. "One cannot trifle with the laws of historical development," Stalin said accusingly after the Chinese debacle.[26]

The major internal transformation in Stalin's Soviet Union – and the foundation for the Communists' claim to have modernized Russia – was the collectivization of agriculture. For seven years, between 1929 and 1936, a war was raging in the Soviet republics between Communist officials and peasant resistance, leading to famine and devastation. The battlefront moved back and forth – in March 1930 58 percent had been forced into collectives, by June 1930 more than half of them had escaped. Gradually, by using terror – confiscation of land and supplies, mass arrests, deportations to labor camps, executions – the Bolsheviks turned the tide of opposition. Stalin's purpose was simple: he wanted to create a modern state by liquidating the internal colony that serfs had been in imperial Russia. The only way to achieve this aim, Stalin and his supporters thought, was to do away with the individualistic and localistic "peasant mentality" and to streamline agriculture, like the rest of the economy, under central state control. To the Stalinists, this was the greatest revolution ever and an example of how socialist transformation could happen elsewhere. Making the peasants create the state-controlled surplus that was necessary for jump-starting an industrial economy was a way in which even backward countries and societies could aspire to modernity.[27]

While the Comintern went through several hair-curling twists in its general policies between 1928 and 1941 – from the intensely anti-Social

Democratic "third period" between 1928 and 1933, to "popular front" alliances between 1934 and 1939, to the moribund defense for Stalin's alliance with Hitler – its policies toward the Third World stayed relatively stable. Throughout the prewar period Stalin refused to believe that Africa, Asia, or Latin America had any short-term potential for socialism, because the historical conditions for the creation of proletarian Communist parties did not yet exist there. Although the Soviet leader never quite gave up on Lenin's faith in "backward countries" moving rapidly toward socialism, Stalin was always very willing to use the "non-skipping of stages" to explain Communist setbacks in the Third World, setbacks that often came out of policies he himself had devised. Overall, the Comintern's influence in the Third World declined between 1928 and 1943, with several of the key parties decimated politically or physically by their opponents. In India in the early 1930s, for instance – after the Sixth Comintern Congress had declared war on "Gandhi'ism" because of its "religious conceptions" and "most backward and economically reactionary ways of living" – the Communist Party was reduced to some twenty members (0.000006 percent of the population, as historian Ken Post points out).[28]

The Comintern's importance, and that of the organizations it controlled, was through the many future leaders of the anti-Western resistance who passed through their ranks. For Communists such as Vietnam's Ho Chi Minh or Brazil's Luis Carlos Prestes, their work for the Comintern confirmed a lifetime's dedication to seeing socialism as unified and international. For anticolonialists such as Indonesia's Tan Malaka, who went from the Communist Party to set up an Indonesian nationalist regime with Japanese support, or India's Jawaharlal Nehru, who had been a delegate to the February 1927 Brussels Congress of Oppressed Nationalities organized on Comintern orders, the encounters with Communism and the Soviet Union provided succinct ideas about how to construct their movements and their states. The thousands of activists who studied at schools and universities in the Soviet Union – such as Moscow's Sun Yat-sen University, set up primarily for Asian students – were impressed with their Soviet comrades' dedication to and absolute faith in their cause. Even non-Communists or those who later broke with Communism often continued to believe in the Soviet Union as a progressive country and a model for emulation as a state. The Afro-American leader W. E. B. Du Bois, who first visited in 1928, found "that Russia is a victim of a determined propaganda of lies. And that whether the present Russian Government succeeds or not, the thing that it is trying to do must and will be done sometime if the world continues to progress."[29]

Within the Soviet Union itself, all attempts at devising policies that reflected its own multinational form as a state drowned – quite literally in blood – during Stalin's purges. Most of the early leaders of the minority peoples within the Soviet state perished between 1935 and 1941, to be replaced by a mixture of Russian and local Stalinists. Stalin – the man these new leaders called their *vozhd* (boss) – in November 1937 gave his inner circle a lesson in his views on the role of ethnicity:

The Russian tsars did a great deal that was bad. They robbed and enslaved the people. They waged wars and seized territories in the interests of the landowners. But they did one thing that was good – they amassed an enormous state, all the way to Kamchatka. We have inherited that state ... We have united the state in such a way that if any part were isolated from the common socialist state, it would not only inflict harm on the latter but would be unable to exist independently and would invariably fall under foreign subjugation. Therefore, whoever attempts to destroy that unity of the socialist state, whoever seeks the separation of any of its parts or nationalities – that man is an enemy, a sworn enemy of the state and of the peoples of the USSR. And we will destroy each and every such enemy, even if he was an old Bolshevik; we will destroy all his kin, his family. We will mercilessly destroy anyone who, by his deeds or his thoughts – yes, his thoughts – threatens the unity of the socialist state.[30]

The ruthlessness of Soviet Stalinism and its inability to work with other parties of the Left was shown most clearly in the Spanish Civil War, the main Soviet foreign intervention between the 1920–21 war against Poland and the Hitler–Stalin Pact. The Spanish events are highly important in order to understand later Soviet interventions in the Third World: not only was it the first long-distance intervention directed by Moscow, but it also provided the personal experience that many leaders of the Cold War period fell back on to plan or execute involvements abroad. While most Spanish Republicans saw their state as having been defeated by Franco's armies in part because of Communist sectarianism and Soviet perfidy, Moscow's lessons were quite different. Stalin and his colleagues saw the failure in Spain as resulting from the "carelessness" and "undue haste" of the Spanish Republicans themselves, including many members of the Communist Party. If an "isolated" struggle like the one in Spain was to succeed in the future, it would have to be directed by Soviet officers, even if the aim was defensive rather than offensive. Only if the Soviet experience was brought directly to bear on the local situation, Stalin decreed, could such struggles have any chance of succeeding.

By 1941 the Stalinist regime in Moscow had removed much of the early Communist emphasis on revolution in the Third World. While crushing the aspirations of Soviet minorities for their own autonomous developments, Stalin had focused on building an authoritarian noncapitalist state with his own role and that of the party at the center. While many anti-colonial leaders on other continents continued to see the Soviet party and state as an inspiration – as we shall see in the next chapter – Moscow's direct involvement in Third World affairs had declined precipitously already by the mid-1930s, when Stalin began concentrating on a coming war in Europe. Until Hitler disabused him of the notion in June 1941, Stalin believed that World War II was "between two groups of capitalist countries – (poor and rich as regards colonies, raw materials, and so forth) – for the redivision of the world ... We see nothing wrong in their having a good hard fight and weakening each other ... Next time, we'll urge on the other side."[31] The Soviet leader did expect that the colonies would attempt to rebel during a war between the imperialists, but did not think that any country outside Europe was developed enough to successfully defend such a revolution unless given direction and aid by the Soviet Union.

Defining intervention: Iran, China, Korea

The German attack in 1941 meant a complete redirection of Soviet foreign policy and of Stalin's instructions to international Communism. The Stalinist regime was fighting for its survival against both foreign and domestic enemies, and it now needed to spend all its resources on the war against Hitler and those within the Soviet Union who saw the German attack as a welcome opportunity to rid themselves of Stalin's terror. It also desperately needed allies, and much effort was spent on developing the relationship with Britain and the United States into a firm wartime alliance. While never imagining that such an alliance would much outlast the war, Stalin believed that the two capitalist powers needed an understanding with the Soviet Union as long as the war was still on and, probably, through the initial phase of postwar reconstruction.

Soviet planning for the postwar world began as soon as the German offensive ground to a halt in 1942. Stalin wanted to extend Soviet influence in Europe – crucially, along its western borders, but also, if possible, into Central Europe and Germany itself. But the Soviet leaders had to be very careful with predicting the precise outcome of the war. While convinced from 1942 on that Germany could not win, Stalin expected the capitalist powers to seek peace with Germany after the collapse of Hitler's regime. Fearful that such a separate peace would leave Germany free to continue its war against the Soviet Union, Stalin needed, on the one hand, to minimize friction with his allies and thereby reduce their temptation to throw him to the wolves, while, on the other hand, also to minimize the chances for a Japanese attack on the Soviet Union in the east, an attack that Stalin knew would mean the end of the Soviet state. Moscow therefore had to downplay any revolutionary aims to come out of the war. Communist parties in the Third World were ordered not to engage in anti-imperialist propaganda, but to support the allied war effort. In 1943 the Comintern was formally dissolved, in part as a gesture toward London and Washington, though its *apparat* was kept intact and later, as the core of the international departments of the Soviet Communist Party, came to play a key role in developing its Third World policies.[32]

Toward the end of the war – and finally convinced that his allies were not aiming for a separate peace – Stalin began choosing between the different Marxist perspectives that had been offered to him through Soviet wartime planning. His appetite increased by the Soviet victories on the Eastern Front, the Soviet leader now foresaw a security belt along its western border consisting of states whose foreign policies depended on the Soviet Union. But he also expected postwar Germany – the big prize in terms of Europe's future development – to move toward socialism and an alliance with Moscow. Through attacking a weakened Japan, the Soviet Union would secure its influence on the postwar settlements in China and Korea. Elsewhere in the colonies, the Soviet Union would also stake its claims in the redivision that would follow the war. Stalin based these optimistic perspectives on the continued competition among the main imperialist powers – Britain and the United States – in the coming battle for spoils. While the imperialists continued their rivalry, the Soviets could – through a mix of diplomacy and force – become a socialist world power.

Only gradually, between 1944 and 1947, did it become clear to Stalin that the prediction of intense imperialist rivalries for the redivision of the postwar world was wrong. Instead of powers competing, the weak European states, including Britain, sought protection of their security and the interests of world capitalism as such from the United States. To see this new, unipolar capitalist world was a hard-won realization for the Soviet leaders. It did not fit any of the Marxist maps that had been offered during the war, and it had to be explained as a temporary phenomenon, brought about by the West European capitalists' need to import American capital and technology. What was clear to Stalin was that a world dominated by the United States was much more dangerous for the Soviet Union than a system in which one could play imperialist powers off against each other. The advent of a capitalist hegemony meant that a concerted strategy for strangling the socialist state was in the making, Stalin thought.

The imposition of Communist regimes in the Eastern European countries under Soviet military control, carried out between 1945 and 1948, was to a great extent a response to these new and more pessimistic perspectives on what the postwar world would look like. In processes that later would form important lessons for Soviet thinking about the Third World, Moscow helped plot strategies for Communist control in Poland, Czechoslovakia, Hungary, Romania, and Bulgaria, while helping to set up a separate socialist state in the part of Germany that had been occupied by Soviet troops. Stalin made it clear to the East European Communists that their political strategies could only succeed if supported by the Soviet Union and by its Red Army. Doubtful about the political qualities of the local Communist leaders, the *vozhd* argued to his inner circle that the Soviet steps had been taken more for security than for the sake of immediate social revolution – just like in Russia's outlying provinces after 1917, the Communists and the Soviet Army were needed to hold the line *until* the local society and party were ready to embark on a true revolutionary path – patterned, of course, on that of Russia. Meanwhile, the local Communists set about constructing new states in the only way they and their Soviet advisers knew: through terror and the destruction of all independent opposition.

The change of perspectives that muddled Soviet foreign policy in Europe in the immediate postwar period also hurt its aims in the Third World. Toward a state like Turkey – where Stalin, ironically, saw no hopes for a revolution because of the dominance of Turkish bourgeois nationalism in a multiethnic state – Soviet aims were dominated by security concerns, first and foremost for control of the entrance to the Black Sea. Promising to "drive the Turks into Asia," Stalin had asked rhetorically already in 1940: "What is Turkey? There are two million Georgians there, one and a half million Armenians, a million Kurds."[33] In 1945 the Soviets demanded naval bases at the Straits of Hormuz and border "readjustments" in eastern Turkey, but encountering Turkish determination to defend its possessions – supported by the United States – Stalin already in the fall of 1946 decided that continued pressure on Ankara was not worth the price. The lesson, the Soviets thought, was that the Turkish nationalists were planning to create "an anti-Soviet Eastern bloc" in response to Turkey's own "political and economic crisis and its high level of dependence on American political and military backing."[34] That the Turkish crisis had been provoked by Soviet policies found no place in Moscow's analysis.[35]

Stalin's postwar appetite for Soviet influence in the Third World also extended to the colonies of the defeated Axis powers, both in Africa and in Asia. The Soviet leaders thought that Tripolitania, the western half of the former Italian colony of Libya, was a particularly appropriate spot for Soviet expansion – there "we could establish a firm foothold in the

Mediterranean basin," Maksim Litvinov told the Politburo in June 1945.[36] According to the perspective of a world dominated by post-war imperialist rivalry, the former Commissar for Foreign Affairs told the leadership that a Soviet "presence in North or East Africa will not be opposed by the United States; on the contrary, it will rather be encouraged as an way of weakening English influence."[37] As the United States sided with Britain in blocking the Soviet claim, Stalin made sure that Molotov held to the rather ridiculous line at the Allied Foreign Ministers' meetings that "the Soviet government considered the future of Tripolitania as of primary importance to the Soviet people, and they must press their request to assume trusteeship of that territory."[38] But, again, by the end of 1946 Stalin had concluded that a direct role in North Africa was eluding his grasp because of hardening US policies. While instructing his diplomats to give up on the Soviet demand, he expected them to let the British and the Americans know that "those days when the USSR could consider itself as an insignificant state regarding all kinds of mandate territories, have passed." Justifying his retreat, he added that

we should not be more leftist than the leaders of these territories. These leaders ... in their majority are corrupt and care not so much about the independence of their territories, as about the preservation of their privileges regarding the population of these territories. The time is not yet ripe for us to clash over the fate of these territories and to quarrel over their future with the rest of the world, including their corrupt leaders themselves.[39]

In Iran, the Soviets' biggest neighbor to the south, the problems in Stalin's postwar Third World policy were connected to much higher stakes than in his Libyan adventure. In 1941 the Soviet Union had – in agreement with its Western allies – occupied the northern part of the country to keep it from German control, while Britain had taken over the south. Meanwhile, the British had engineered the ousting of the Iranian emperor – the shah – and replaced him with the young Crown Prince, Mohammad Reza Pahlavi. Within Iran, the shattering experience of foreign occupation had thrown the door open for new political groups and ideas, which challenged not only the traditional authoritarian monarchy, but also the social and religious fundaments for the shah's power. The Communist-led People's Party, or Tudeh, had become the country's largest and best-organized political group, and the voice of a growing movement of industrial and agricultural trade unions. Leaders of the ethnic minorities – Azeris, Kurds, and Arabs – had started agitating for autonomy or outright independence. And in Qum – Iran's leading religious center – young clergymen, among them Ruhollah Khomeini, had begun calling for resistance to the foreign powers and to their agent, the shah.[40]

The sense of national humiliation brought on by the great power occupation intensified political competition in Teheran. The 1943 elections to the national assembly showed strong support for liberal and leftist candidates, although the majority of representatives were still unaffiliated with any party. And although the young shah, helped by the British, managed to appoint a succession of conservative premiers over the next two years, the political initiative in the national assembly, the Majlis, gradually passed to liberal nationalists such as Ahmed Qavam and Mohammad Mossadeq.

While the Tudeh in its messages to Moscow stressed the immediate potential for a revolutionary uprising in Iran, Stalin strongly disagreed with that perspective. His main preoccupations were defensive – denying the imperialists access to the oil resources in northern Iran and securing a treaty with the leftist bourgeois nationalists in Teheran. In 1944, as the Soviet demand for an area of 216,000 sq km in the north to be set aside for joint Soviet–Iranian oil exploration enraged nationalists of all kinds in Iran, Stalin's thinking turned to using northern ethnic separatists rather than the Iranian Communists to reach his aims.[41] The *vozhd* took up a proposal made by the party leader in Soviet Azerbaijan, Mir Bagirov, instructing him to "organize a separatist movement in southern Azerbaijan and other provinces of northern Iran" and to "create a democratic party in southern Azerbaijan under the name 'Azerbaijani Democratic Party,' founded by reforming the Azerbaijani branch of the People's Party of Iran and attracting all supporters of the separatist movement from all layers of society."[42] The Azeri nationalist Bagirov may have hoped for the unification of Soviet and Iranian Azerbaijan, but Stalin obviously intended to use the threat of Soviet support for the disintegration of Iran to pressure the Iranian bourgeoisie into striking a deal with Moscow for oil and influence.[43] The Teheran Communists were understandably furious. "If the enemies of the USSR had created a plan against it, they could not possibly invent anything better than what is taking place at the present time," they wrote to Stalin in September 1945.[44]

But Stalin and Bagirov were not discouraged. All through 1945 and early 1946 the Soviets continued to direct and build an autonomous regime in Iranian Azerbaijan, based in Tabriz, while warning the Tudeh against any attempts at carrying out a revolution.[45] Even in Azerbaijan and the Kurdish areas – where the Soviets supported the Democratic Party of Kurdistan (DPK) – the reforms had to be moderate: "You have been told many times that we do not want to spark a civil war or class struggle among the Azerbaijanis. All forces … must be used against those who disturb us in our battle for the autonomy of Azerbaijan and

northern Kurdistan," Bagirov warned his comrades south of the border.[46]
To some extent the Kurdish nationalist regime in Mahabad was more to
the Soviets' liking than that of Pishevari's socialists, especially since the
DPK president Qazi Mohammad – a well-read and broad-minded Islamic
judge – understood that the occasional use of radical slogans would help in
enlisting Soviet support and got the help of Kurds who had studied in
Teheran to make up a list for official use.[47]

The Iranian elite in early 1946 started realizing that there was a real
danger that their country could split apart and that a military conflict with
the Soviet Union may be approaching. The Majlis turned to Ahmad
Qavam, a wealthy 76-year-old landowner from northern Iran with a
record of political radicalism, as the new prime minister. Qavam wanted
to reform politics and social affairs in Iran and defeat the challenges from
the northern separatists, the Tudeh, and the royalist right wing. The new
prime minister was hated by the British, with whom he had clashed on
several occasions during his long political career, and was distrusted by
the Americans, who viewed him as a shifty and intriguing old-style
politician.[48] The Russians regarded him as a "bourgeois democrat and
nationalist," who realized that he would have to seek support for his
reform plans either from the United States or the Soviet Union. Qavam
wanted a compromise on Soviet oil concessions, and might support
"reforms" in Azerbaijian, but could not grant autonomy to the Azeris
and survive in power, Moscow noted.[49]

The Soviet–Iranian negotiations in Moscow in February–March 1946
showed the limitations of Stalin's approach to the Third World. Stalin
and his foreign minister Molotov wanted Qavam to agree to oil concessions – together with a series of connected "rights" – and some form of
self-rule for Azerbaijian. Any of these two measures would give Moscow
control of northern Iran, a fact which left Molotov free to be "flexible" on
the Azeri question. Some form of compromise could be found, according
to Molotov, whereby real military and political power in the north would
remain with the Teheran government. Pishevari "could die or become
ill."[50] But a solution to the Azeri question, and a timetable for the withdrawal of Soviet forces, both depended on Qavam granting Moscow the
economic concessions Stalin wanted.[51]

Qavam would not accept Stalin's and Molotov's Cold War logic. He
suggested a compromise in which he, in return for a Soviet commitment to
withdraw, would propose to the Majlis limited self-rule for the Azeris and
comprehensive talks with Moscow on political and economic relations. But
Molotov was not impressed. "The Soviet government wants to expedite
the oil issue," the foreign minister said, and if Qavam was in no position to
grant oil concessions, the Soviets would discuss the issue with the

government in Tabriz.[52] Then Molotov presented his own proposals: a limited self-rule scheme for Azerbaijan – which clearly signaled Moscow's disinterest in the overall fate of Pishevari's regime – and the immediate start of negotiations between Iran and the Soviet Union on a concession in northern Iran for a joint oil exploration and production company, 51 percent of which was to be owned by Moscow. "Soviet troops," Molotov wrote, "will be completely withdrawn from Iran as soon as the Iranian government liquidates all enemy and discriminating measures in its relations with the Soviet Union, establishes peaceful conditions in northern Iran, and introduces a friendly policy toward the Soviet Union."[53]

Encountering such demands, and such a negotiating strategy, there is little wonder why Qavam turned to the Americans for support and to crafty diplomacy for time. As US pressure increased for the Soviets to withdraw the Red Army from northern Iran, the Iranian prime minister promised Stalin a treaty on oil concessions to ease the Soviet departure. He also took three members of the Tudeh into his new government after the last of the Soviet soldiers had left at the end of May 1946. Himself confronted by the West and still believing that Qavam and the bourgeois nationalists would have to come to an agreement with Moscow to stave off Western pressure, Stalin decided to drop the Azerbaijani separatist regime. The Tabriz leadership was understandably dejected. As Pishevari told Bagirov during a secret meeting in April 1946:

Having turned the Shah's government against ourselves, we cannot go on our knees before them ... No matter how much I might want to, I just cannot do it. I am prepared to die on the fields of battle in the interest of the people, but I can't sell them out ... With your help, we democrats and leaders followed a path in violation of Iran's constitution, breaking it, discrediting it ... After all that, how can Qavam ever forgive us? Even in the middle of our work ... there were moments when I had my doubts about you, and whether you would help us to the end ... and now, all the more, I don't believe you at all. Comrades, I repeat, I don't believe you anymore.[54]

Stalin, however, would not let the Azerbaijani leaders fall without giving them a final lecture on Marxism. In May 1946 he wrote to Pishevari:

You here want to emulate Lenin [by calling for revolution]. This is very good and laudable ... However, the situation in Iran today is totally different. There is no profound revolutionary crisis in Iran. There are few workers in Iran and they are poorly organized ... We decided to withdraw troops from Iran and China, in order to seize this tool from the hands of the British and Americans, to unleash the liberation movement in the colonies and thereby render our liberationist policy more justified and efficient.

Qavam, Stalin stressed, remained a progressive bourgeois. The Communist aim, in Tabriz, Teheran, and Moscow, should be to "wrench concessions from Qavam, give him support, isolate the Anglophiles."[55] But by the end of 1946 the shah's armies had retaken all the northern areas, where they wreaked a terrible revenge on the Azeri and Kurdish separatists. Conveniently for Stalin, Jafar Pishevari died in a car crash after having fled to the Soviet Union in 1947. With both the Azeri regime and the Red Army gone, the Majlis saw no reason to ratify the Soviet oil treaty. The Communists were soon forced out of the Teheran government, and Ahmad Qavam was dismissed by the shah in December 1947. Two years later, the Tudeh was banned and its leaders driven underground or into exile, as the shah drew increasingly close to the United States.

Stalin's actions in Iran and the dogmatic view of social and political development on which they were based helped defeat the Iranian Left. Although it would have been suicidal to openly question the *vozhd*'s views within the Soviet party, we know that some leaders in Moscow and in Baku were skeptical at least as to the outcome of Stalin's policies and wondered if the Soviet Union could not do better in its competition with the imperialist powers. But for the vast majority of Soviet officials the Iranian debacle was a result of the West's increasingly aggressive policies against the Soviet Union and against socialism. "In all of the Near and Middle East one can observe an intensification of American activity," one intelligence summary noted, "from which rises the smell of oil, military sea- and air-bases, the preparation of an aggressive war. Behind the talks on dollar loans, 'emergency help,' 'control activities' of military and civilian personnel is hidden the ... increased penetration of American imperialism into these countries with the goal of turning them into its military-strategic launching pads."[56]

China – Stalin's old nemesis – was the only major Third World state contiguous to the Soviet Union in which the *vozhd* did not manage to wreck the perspectives of the local Communists on behalf of Soviet security. The main reason why the Chinese Communists succeeded where the Iranians failed was Mao Zedong's determination not to risk his own party's future by following each and every instruction he might be getting from Moscow. While believing in Stalin's strategic genius and in the need to emulate the Soviet experience in China in a concrete form, Mao chose to ignore the Boss's orders to make peace with the Chinese Nationalists, Chiang Kai-shek's Guomindang (GMD), after Chiang had attacked the Communist troops in 1946. As in Iran, Stalin had tried to negotiate a treaty with the Nationalist government in China after the end of World War II, intending to exclude imperialist influence and secure Soviet control of the border areas, but – as in Iran – the government had turned to the United States to successfully resist Soviet pressure. However, unlike the governments of Turkey or Iran, Chiang's regime in China had been significantly weakened by the war and – to make matters worse for itself – began taking on all of its domestic enemies at once in the postwar period. As a result, the Communists not only survived the initial military onslaught, but were gradually able to turn the situation on the battlefield to their advantage. By 1948, as it became clear that the GMD could not defeat Mao's forces and that the Americans were unwilling to bail Chiang's government out of its economic and military predicament, Stalin began a significant program of support for the Chinese Communists. As the GMD armies broke down, Communism finally seemed set to make a major advance in the Third World.

But even in victory Stalin's dogmatic adherence to the Marxist patterns of development shone through. In 1948–49, as Mao's forces were preparing their final push to the south, Stalin warned the Chinese Communists not to put socialism on the agenda:

some representatives of [opposition] parties will have to be incorporated in the Chinese people's democratic government, and the government as such [will have] to be proclaimed as coalition ... It should be kept in mind that after the victory of the people's liberation armies of China – at least, in a postvictory period for which the duration is difficult to define now – the Chinese government, in terms of its policy, will be a national revolutionary-democratic government, rather than a Communist one. This means that nationalization of all lands and cancellation of the private ownership of land, confiscation of properties from the whole, major and petty, industrial and trade bourgeoisie, confiscation of properties from not only large, but middle and small landowners, who live together with their hired labor, cannot be effected yet.[57]

Even during the victorious Mao Zedong's visit to Moscow in 1949–50 Stalin persisted in treating the Chinese Communists as representatives of a "national revolutionary-democratic government, rather than a Communist one." Uncertain about the long-term viability of a Communist leadership in Beijing, Stalin aimed at getting a treaty that was conducive to Soviet security, rather than an alliance between two Communist-led states. It took concerted and courageous intervention by his key advisers to get him to offer the Chinese something that would give them the recognition they craved as revolutionaries from the head of the world Communist movement. But even after the Sino-Soviet Treaty of Friendship, Alliance, and Mutual Assistance was signed, on 14 February 1950, Stalin kept his doubts about the authenticity of the Chinese Communist leaders. If they were genuine Communists, the *vozhd* explained to his coterie, they would not last long in power in a country at China's level of development. If the Beijing government seemed secure, that in itself was evidence of its non-Marxist character.

Stalin's last Third World adventure, the Korean War, testified to how far down the road toward theoretical tautologies the Boss came during his final years. Seeing socialism in only the northern part of Korea as unviable in the long run, in spite of the new Democratic People's Republic of Korea under Kim Il Sung being contiguous to the Soviet Union and receiving aid from it, Stalin by early 1950 claimed that "the South was determined to launch an attack on the North sooner or later and it was important to forestall this aggression." In giving Kim the go-ahead to attack the US-supported regime in South Korea, Stalin also pointed to "the significant strengthening of the socialist camp in the east: the victory of the Chinese revolution, the signing of an alliance between the USSR and the PRC, and the USSR's acquisition of an atomic bomb," as well as "the obvious weakness of the reactionary camp: the shameful defeat of America's intervention into Chinese affairs, Western troubles in Southeast Asia, and the inability of the South Korean regime and its American masters to improve the social, economic, and political situation in South Korea." For Stalin, indirect support of Kim's war would also be a way of getting back at "the dishonest, perfidious, and arrogant behavior of the United States in Europe, the Balkans, the Middle East, and especially its decision to form NATO."[58]

It was pessimism and not optimism about the future of the Korean revolution that led Stalin to accept Kim's plan for reunification by military force. As many of the Communists who were in charge of Soviet foreign policy realized, the Korean War showed that Stalin had left behind any hope that social processes in the Third World by themselves would lead toward socialism. Even under the best of geographical and political circumstances – such as in North Korea – the primary objective of Third World Communism should be to serve Soviet purposes in the global Cold War, because the defined circumstances under which they themselves could carry out a successful social transformation were so narrow as to be almost nonexistent. It was as if Stalin – having started the climb toward socialism in one country – was deliberately kicking away the ladder for others to follow.

The Soviet rediscovery of the Third World (1955–60)

Stalin's last known in-depth comments on Third World problems are in his secret instructions to the Indonesian Communist Party (PKI) from January 1951. After having criticized the Indonesian party for their "leftism" both during the failed 1948 rebellion against the nationalist independence movement under Sukarno and during the subsequent gradual reestablishment of the party under Chinese tutelage, the Boss went on to show the impossibility of an Indonesian Communist revolution. Even building on the Chinese model would not work:

they [the Chinese] at last found a good way out, when they moved to Manchuria and found a solid rear [base] in the friendly Soviet state. Characteristically, only after [the] Chinese comrades got a solid rear base in Manchuria and after they began leaning against the USSR as against their own rear, the enemy lost the chance to encircle them and the Chinese Communists found an opportunity to wage a planned offensive against Chiang Kai-shek's army from north to south. Can we suppose that the Indonesian comrades, after they have gained a guerrilla-liberated area, will have the opportunity, as the Chinese comrades did, to lean against frontiers as against their own rear [base] and thus deprive the enemy of the opportunity to encircle them? No, we cannot say that, as Indonesia represents a group of islands encircled by seas, and the Indonesian comrades could not lean anywhere.[59]

To the Soviet Communists who took over after Stalin's death in March 1953, the Boss's Third World policy seemed self-defeating. In spite of serious disagreements as to the future of socialism, they all agreed to end armed interventionism, such as in Korea, and to emphasize the government-to-government links that could be built not only with self-declared socialist regimes – such as China – but also with radical bourgeois regimes ("Jacobins," in Comintern terms), such as Sukarno's Indonesia, Nasser's Egypt, or Nehru's India. The new party leader, Nikita Khrushchev, underlined the new policies by making a trip to Beijing in 1954, his first major visit abroad, and by traveling to India, Burma, and Afghanistan the following year. During his trip to South Asia, the new first secretary of the Soviet Communist Party (renamed the Communist Party of the Soviet Union, CPSU, in 1952) stressed Soviet willingness to cooperate with the "national development" of nonsocialist countries in the Third World both in economic and military terms. The common enemy, the Soviets stated, was colonialism and imperialism on a worldwide scale.

For Khrushchev – an intelligent but unschooled peasants' son who had made his way up Stalinism's slippery slope by boundless enthusiasm for hard work – visiting India was just the beginning of a much broader campaign for gaining influence in the Third World. As he solidified his grip on power within the Soviet state, Khrushchev attacked Stalin's policies toward Asia, Africa, and Latin America in two different directions. On the one hand, the *vozhd* had neglected the Third World, by focusing too narrowly on those national-bourgeois movements that by themselves had sought friendship and cooperation with the Soviet Union, and by not attempting "actively" to forge links with others. On the other hand, Stalin had failed to see that transitions to socialism could take many different forms, and that more assistance to Third World workers' parties was needed, even if some of these parties had no chance of gaining power on their own in the short run. Khrushchev's big fear was that Stalin's policies had nearly made the Soviet Union miss the train in the new and historical departure away from colonial empires and toward the establishment of independent states. In 1956, at the 20th Congress of the CPSU, Khrushchev – after sensationally condemning Stalin's general behavior as "vile," "monstrous," and "terrorist" – declared that

The new period that Lenin predicted in world history when peoples of the East take an active part in settling the destinies of the whole world and become a new, powerful factor in international relations, has arrived ... In order to create an independent national economy and to raise the living standards of their peoples, these countries, though not part of the world socialist system, can benefit by its achievements. They now have no need to go begging to their former oppressors for modern equipment. They can obtain such equipment in the socialist countries.[60]

Typically for Khrushchev's regime, the new leadership – while condemning Stalin – were unable to move away from much of the dogmatism that the Boss had bequeathed to Soviet ideology. In its Third World policies, this meant that the narrow thinking about "stages of development" was still in place, as was the Soviet-centrism of Moscow's perceptions of the outside world. What did improve was Soviet knowledge about the Third World, through a full-scale revamping of the institutions that provided the information upon which the leadership could act. In its self-criticism after the twentieth party congress, the Academy of Sciences' Institute of Oriental Studies declared that its work had "been greatly harmed by a failure to understand the nature and the depth of the contradictions existing between the forces of imperialism and internal reaction, on the one hand, and those of national progress in the nonsocialist Eastern countries on the other."[61] The institute's work was expanded, and new institutes for the study of Africa and Latin America were set up in 1960 and 1961 respectively. The Soviet intelligence services were reorganized, and both the Committee for State Security (Komitet gosudarstvennoi bezopasnosti, KGB) and military intelligence (Glavnoie razvedivatelnoie upravleniie, GRU – Chief Intelligence Directorate of the General Staff) were given specific geographical briefs relating to Third World information gathering. Most important of all, the Central Committee reorganized its international work, setting up two new departments, the International Department (Mezhdunarodnyi otdel, MO) and the Department for Relations with Communist and Workers' Parties of Socialist Countries (later called the International Liaison Department). Both departments were under the control of Comintern veteran Boris Ponomarev, who was also made a member of the Secretariat.[62]

Of all the big tasks Khrushchev foresaw for the Soviet Union in the Third World, building the alliance with China was by far the most important. Not just the First Secretary, but the whole party leadership was convinced that the socialist transformation of the most populous country on earth was a task that the Soviet Union had to engage in – it not only confirmed their Marxist worldview, but also highlighted the universal centrality of the Soviet experience in building socialism. The assistance program carried out under the Sino-Soviet Friendship Treaty was the Soviet Union's Marshall Plan – already in May 1953, two months after Stalin's death, Moscow agreed to increase aid to China sevenfold over two years, and the total cost of the program up to 1960 was about twenty billion roubles in export prices, something which the historian Sergei Goncharenko estimates as equaling 7 percent of Soviet national income for the period. It was a massive attempt at stamping Soviet socialism on China – in every department of every ministry, in every large factory, in every city, army, or university there were Soviet advisers, specialists, or experts who worked with the Chinese to "modernize" their country and move their society toward socialism. Their achievements changed the Chinese economy forever and – unbeknown to the Soviet experts or their Chinese comrades – were to lay the foundation for the Chinese capitalist revolution of the 1980s and 1990s.[63]

Out of the increasingly close cooperation, Khrushchev saw developing a future international socialist community – with the Soviet Union at the center – that replicated many of the functions the capitalist world economy had (*sans* capitalism, of course). International distribution networks would supply standardized and unified production lines from Berlin to Shanghai, research and training would be shared between socialist countries, as would innovations in technology, defense, and planning, and ideological questions would be decided at international congresses. In the Chinese case, however, the problem with increasing integration was that the basic acceptance of the Soviet model – which underpinned all of Khrushchev's project – was beginning to be questioned by the late 1950s. Mao Zedong wanted "more, faster, better, and cheaper" socialism, and by designing "The Great Leap Forward" in 1958 he broke decisively with all Soviet advice about caution and stages. At the same time, through its conflict with India and its criticism of Soviet *détente* with the United States, China broke with the key concept of Moscow setting the tune for the "socialist camp" in international affairs.

By 1959 the Sino-Soviet relationship was in crisis. The personal diplomacy that Khrushchev engaged in by visiting Beijing had little effect. Mao Zedong saw the Soviet slogan of "peaceful competition" with the West as class treason, and Moscow's alliance policies with nonsocialist Third

World regimes as directed against China. Khrushchev tried to defend his new line as tactics – "Nehru," he said, "may go over to the United States. He is among our fellow travelers who go with us when it is to their advantage. When we delivered assistance to Nasser, we knew that he might turn against us. Had we not given him this credit, Nasser would have ended up in America's embrace."[64] But Mao could not be mollified, and in the summer of 1960 Khrushchev reacted to the steady pinpricks of criticism coming from Beijing by abruptly withdrawing most Soviet experts from the PRC. The First Secretary and those working with him failed to understand that for Mao Zedong the real issue was the future of the Chinese revolution – by sticking too closely to the advice the Soviets gave, the rapid advance toward socialism that the Chairman envisaged would simply not be possible. By 1962 Khrushchev had condemned the Chinese as careless, ungrateful, and chauvinist peasants, and although it took up to 1965 for the final remnants of the alliance to vanish, the increasingly heated public polemics between Moscow and Beijing convinced the Soviets of the future problems the confrontation with Chinese socialism would pose.

The difficulties with China presented the Soviet leaders not only with new security issues and with increased competition for influence in the Third World. It also posed a formidable challenge to Soviet foreign policy ideology. The relationship to China had been lauded as the ultimate proof of socialism's applicability to the Third World, and, up to 1958, Soviet experts had held the People's Republic of China up to the North Vietnamese and the North Koreans as the near perfect application of Marxist political theory in "oriental" countries. With the alliance in tatters, Moscow had to explain what had gone wrong and to stake out the road ahead. On the one hand, the wrecking of the supposedly irreversible gains made in China was explained by the wrongheadedness of the "Mao-clique," which had come to power due to the Chinese party's lack of "proletarian experience." On the other hand, the combination of immense disappointment and no proper cause for failure led many Soviet leaders to racist explanations: the Soviet effort in China was failing because of the inborn deviousness and selfishness of the Chinese.

Just like the United States in the 1950s, the Soviet Union in the 1960s made no attempts to learn from the its failure in China. On the contrary, the former alliance became a taboo area of Soviet foreign policy, rarely touched on in official or unofficial discourse. The many advisers who had served in China, and whose experience could have benefited future Soviet Third World policy, instead became the "lost generation" in foreign affairs, rarely allowed near international relations in any form again. Those who were put in charge of what Khrushchev envisaged to be a full-scale attempt at competing with the United States in the newly liberated countries in Africa and Asia were mostly young people with very little experience abroad. Their main frame of reference was *not* China but the successes the Soviet Union had had in technology and production in the 1950s. It was Soviet modernity that would win people for Communism abroad, as socialism – freed from Stalin's shackles – showed its full productive potential. Two key projects that would inspire Soviet assistance to the Third World were the Virgin Lands campaign and the space program. The attempt at bringing into cultivation 32 million acres of previously uncultivated land in Kazakhstan and southwestern Siberia, begun in 1954, was a flagship of the new and intensive growth phase that the Soviet Union claimed to have entered. Using massive amounts of irrigation and chemical fertilizers to develop the barren plain, Khrushchev's leadership assumed that they had devised a new way of intensifying food production. The launch of the first space vessel, the Sputnik, in 1957 and the first manned space flight by Iurii Gagarin in 1961 convinced most Soviets that they had the upper hand over the West in technology and science. Together, Soviet know-how in agriculture and industry would revolutionize production at home and make it possible for countries moving toward socialism to move faster and with fewer conces- sions to the West. In his speech to the United Nations in 1960, Khrushchev saw the joining of national liberation in the Third World with socialism's productive potential as symbolizing the future:

Everyone knows that the economics of the colonies ... are at present subordin- ated to the mercenary interests of foreign monopolies, and the industrialization of these countries is being deliberately impeded. Imagine that the situation has changed and that these countries and territories, having become independent, are in a position to make ample use of their rich natural resources and to proceed with their industrialization, and that a better life has begun for their peoples. This would ... no doubt have a beneficial effect, not only on the economic develop- ment of the countries of the East but also on the economies of the industrially developed countries of the West.[65]

To his audiences within the party and the international Communist movement, such as at a closed meeting on political theory and propa- ganda in January 1961, Khrushchev stressed the same idea in more ideological terms:

Bourgeois and revisionist politicians claim that the national-liberation movement develops independently of the struggle for socialism waged by the working class, independently of the support of the socialist countries, and that the ~~~~ ~~~~lists themselves bestow freedom on the peoples of the former colonies. The ~~~~ these fabrications is to isolate the newly independent states from ~

camp and to try to prove that they should assume the role of a "third force" in the international arena instead of opposing imperialism. Needless to say, this is sheer humbug. It is a historical fact that prior to the victory of the Great October Socialist Revolution the peoples failed in their attempts to break the chains of colonialism. History proves that until socialism triumphed in at least a part of the world there could be no question of destroying colonialism.[66]

By the early 1960s Soviet ideology had already reached a stage where the competition for influence in the Third World was an essential part of the existence of socialism. As in the United States, the Soviet elites saw their mission as part of a world-historical progression toward a given goal. Their view of their own role in that process was conditioned not just by Marxist-Leninist political theory but also by Russian exceptionalism and by the experiences of the Soviet leadership since 1917. In spite of setbacks and retreats the Soviet elite firmly believed that socialism would replace capitalism as the main international system within a generation. Stalin's successors held that the transition could be managed without global war only if the imperialists became convinced that they could not successfully intervene against social revolution outside their own borders. The Soviet Union's role was to help make the world safe for revolution and thereby to assist in the progress of humankind.

3   The revolutionaries: anticolonial politics and transformations

From the mid-nineteenth century up to 1920 more than 450 million people in Africa and Asia came under direct colonial rule.[1] Britain, France, Russia, the Netherlands, and Portugal – the old European colonial powers – were followed by the newly formed Germany and Italy, by Belgium, and, in a somewhat hesitant manner, by the United States. Even Japan – itself a victim of imperialist expansion at the beginning of the epoque – joined the club of aggressors. While the capacity for expansion arose from the changes in technology, organization, and communication that took place in the nineteenth century, the motives varied from the search for markets and raw materials to religious zeal and national pride. By the early twentieth century most people in the capitalist countries had stopped asking for motives: imperialism to them had become the natural order of things, just like the Cold War would be two generations later.[2]

In spite of the vigorous defense put up in many Third World areas, it often took decades after the attacks before the victims were able to organize comprehensive resistance to colonial rule. The brutality of the invasions and occupations were fearful – one recent estimate is that the direct and indirect death toll from the colonial wars was around five and a half million. In addition, as Mike Davis has shown, famines set off by global droughts reached catastrophic proportions in Asia and Africa in the late nineteenth century in part because the attacks had undermined social structures that in times past might have ameliorated the suffering. The new colonial territories were vast and the population – even before decimation – was usually sparse. When the occupiers began imposing some form of order, the colonies they established often did not match the colonized peoples' own states, identities, or organizations, something that gave plentiful opportunities for "divide and rule." Organized counterattacks were also held back by the many varieties of colonial government, as we have already seen in the American and Russian cases, from enforced cultural assimilation to extermination and genocide.[3]

The period of successful resistance against colonial rule began in the aftermath of World War I, just as the Cold War was in its infancy. In the

1920s and 1930s the struggles between empires and their opponents was also a battlefield for ideas of social revolution or capitalist development. As the powers in Europe completed their self-destruction in World War II, most revolutionary movements in the Third World were coming of age. And the revolutions that gave most Third World countries their freedom happened after World War II, when the Cold War had already become a fully-fledged international system. In other words, the forming of anti-colonial revolutionary movements and of new Third World states is inextricably linked in time to the Cold War conflict and to Cold War ideologies. Though the processes of decolonization and of superpower conflict may be seen as having separate origins, the history of the late twentieth century cannot be understood without exploring the ties that bind them together.

Colonialism and its effects

One of the key objectives of colonization was the destruction of established worldviews among the colonized peoples. The claim to racial superiority that was built into the imperialist project meant that those subject to colonization were intended to see themselves as having less value than their superiors and to believe that their indigenous cultures were doomed to extinction. The proof of the proposition was in the European takeover of the colonial territories themselves: *because* the colonizers possessed such a surplus of arms, technology, and organization they had succeeded in taking control of the world, and their possessions – both material and territorial – showed their supremacy. As if power was not enough, the colonized were subjected to relentless propaganda – often through Christian missions – about the justness of the new order and the bankruptcy of their own ideals and beliefs.

The degree to which this intended destruction of indigenous culture and organization succeeded in the Third World is still hotly debated. Depriving a group totally of its previous identity usually took projects of mass extermination, such as in the cases of the American Indians or the Australian Aborigines. In most cases, what began emerging at the end of the nineteenth century – at least at elite levels – were indigenous and colonial hybrids, with a distinctly modern twist. The initial cooptation of non-European administrators and the advent of colonial education meant that groups emerged that were as dedicated to such staples of modernity as technology and systematization as were the colonial authorities themselves. To administer the colonies without these intermediaries would have been impossible, since the number of foreign administrators was miniscule compared to the vastness of the territories they were supposed to control. Later on, as we shall see, it was often from this group of intermediaries – or rather their sons and daughters – that the first nationalist organizations emerged.

The colonial projects that had developed during the nineteenth century were extremely diverse in character. While the British were often happy to rule through non-European forms of organization and therefore allowed a wide variety of local systems to emerge, the French (and later the Americans) were much more assimilationist, attempting to spread their own culture and institutions to the peoples they had conquered. The presence or absence of European colonists also played a crucial role in shaping the colonial systems – bringing such groups in or allowing them to settle intensified the conflict between the imperial center and the colonized peoples, as the Southern African or Algerian cases show. Finally, the minor colonial powers – such as Belgium and Portugal – had neither the instruments nor the resources to impose an effective administration or other aspects of modernity on the territories they controlled. Their rule therefore remained crudely exploitative – more similar to the defunct Spanish empire of the seventeenth and eighteenth centuries than to the French or British of the late nineteenth and early twentieth.

The state organizations that colonized peoples encountered at home were therefore not of a kind and led to different responses as the anticolonial resistance took shape. The general characteristics they did have in common were a lack of local legitimacy, a fear of subversion, and a predilection for big projects. The colonial state was always the representative of the imperial center and of the colonists, never of any indigenous group, however collaborationist such a group may be. As such, the state therefore emerged as something extraneous to indigenous peoples, even at the elite level. The "foreignness" of the state led to a constant need for policing at all levels, even in the most assimilationist of colonies. And the lack of local knowledge, the availability of labor, and the abundance of resources led to the inauguration (but not always the completion) of grand projects, intended both to deliver raw materials to the empire and to show the indigenous peoples the efficacy and superiority of the colonial state. It is no wonder that the colonized often described their existence as living within a giant prison.

The height of the colonial era, around 1900, coincided with a period of reform within many of the imperialist powers themselves. Just as criticism intensified over the exploitation of workers at home, over the lack of hygiene and education, and over corruption and inequality in state services, the attacks on standards in the running of the colonies also grew. The result was, on the one hand, an increase in education and in health services available to non-Europeans, and, on the other, attempts at extending the reach of the colonial state into areas in which it had so far had little control. Whole new educational institutions were set up in the imperial centers to train a better sort of future colonial administrator, including an increasing number of young men from the indigenous elites.[4] Upon their arrival in Africa or Asia, these representatives of the colonial project were charged with penetrating geographical regions or areas of society into which the early colonial system had barely reached. Instead of raw materials and trade, the new slogans of imperialism at around 1900 were progress and development, both for the imperial powers and for the colonies.

Most enterprises that the authorities undertook or supported toward the end of the colonial era were carried out on an even bigger scale than before, in part because the vastness of the new colonial territories invited "big thinking" and in part because many of the social and ecological complexities of the territories they controlled simply were not visible to the foreign heads of administration. Projects such as the Suez and Panama Canals, the Gezira irrigation scheme in Sudan, or the Cabora Bassa dam in Mozambique demanded massive amounts of labor, drawing tens of thousands of workers into a new economy. In some cases, such as the equally massive agricultural projects undertaken from the late nineteenth century on, labor had to be imported from other colonies in order to make up for an indigenous shortfall. Almost always based on one cash crop, such as tea, sugar, or tobacco, these schemes not only replaced local polycultural growing patterns but also transformed the demography of some colonies, bringing, for instance, Indians to Fiji and Chinese to Malaya (where the new immigrants in both cases came to make up around half the population).

However multiform the structures of the colonial photostates were, their central fact for the colonized was that they were blatantly constructed to represent the interest of the imperial power and, in some cases, the colonists, not those of the colonized peoples themselves. In spite of the advantages sometimes given to the local elites, the colonial state could never be fully *their* state – it represented a foreign power whose local legitimacy continued to be based on force, not on consent. After 1900, when larger numbers of young people from Africa, Asia, or the Caribbean began traveling to the imperial centers – mostly for education – the^ egan contrasting their and their parents' lack of influence ie gradual expansion of public participation in government imperialist countries. If European workers could have te parties, and aspire to political influence, why were without political rights in their home countries?

Reporting on the wealth and energy of the imperial capitals, many young Third World travelers naturally began suspecting that some of this pan-European exuberance was the result of imperialist exploitation. But they also deplored conditions within their own societies, which they saw as standing in the way of modern progress. One of the founders of the Indonesian nationalist movement, Sutan Sjahrir, wrote in his biography *Out of Exile*:

For me, the West signifies a forceful, dynamic, and active life. It is a sort of Faust that I admire, and I am convinced that only by a utilization of this dynamism of the West can the East be released from its slavery and subjugation. The West is now teaching the East to regard life as a struggle and a striving, as an active movement to which the concept of tranquility must be subordinated . . . Struggle and striving signify a struggle against nature, and that is the essence of the struggle: man's attempt to subdue nature and to rule it by his will.[5]

At the top of the ladder – reached through incessant struggle – were the imperial megalopolises, where all the force and dynamism of imperialism had solidified into a system of power, stability, and permanence. Walking toward London's Hyde Park sometime in the 1920s, the Indian writer Nirad Chaudhury had "an impression of solidity so strong that if I had had a hammer in my hand I should have walked along unconsciously tapping the houses with it, and in a mood of impatience, which endless rows of bricks and stone often generate, I should have involuntarily thought of a battering ram."[6] European expansion, and the ideologies this expansion produced, furnished ideas of transformation and resistance in roughly equal amounts.

Within the colonies themselves resistance against colonial occupation continued from the moment of the invasion up to the end of the colonial empires. After the shock of the first defeats subsided, rebellions and disobedience campaigns were commonplace and increasingly well organized. Already from the mid-nineteenth century onwards the diffusion of technology meant that non-European groups were able to defend themselves better against the imperialists. The problem was often the lack of a *united* resistance – there was a constant possibility that the colonial power could mobilize one ethnic or religious group against another, since Third World contenders for power were always aware of the strategic value of having well-armed foreigners on their side. There was also the divide between the rural and the urban, between indigenous elites and the common people, who often had distinctly different experiences of the colonial process. While for most groups the fight against colonialism was a desperate struggle to avoid being conscripted, plundered, or taxed, and thereby to protect the minimal surplus that for subsistence farmers was the difference between life and death, many of the elites, as we have seen, slowly began subscribing to the ethos of progress that was inherent in the late colonial project.[7]

These splits in colonial society made what Karl Deutsch refers to as "social mobilization" – the creation of organizations, movements, identities – very difficult, at least until parts of the elites started appealing to legitimacy from below in order to challenge the colonial state. In those Third World countries that avoided formal colonization, the divides were as visible as within the empires themselves, but in these cases the indigenous elites could appeal at least to the toleration of their countrymen in order to better resist colonial aggression. It was probably this toleration that enabled a diverse group of states, such as Japan, Thailand, Afghanistan, and Ethiopia, to begin defensive modernizations that, together with their fighting skills, kept them out of the grasp of the imperialist powers. China in the early twentieth century also came up with the minimum of societal cohesion and military ability to avoid being carved up fully, although the large areas that were under imperialist control in or around the foreign concessions, or in Manchuria, meant that the most populous country on earth was kept in a form of semicolonial status.

While more than half of Asia was under direct colonial rule around 1900, and more than 90 percent of Africa, less than 30 percent of Latin America was formally colonized. In economic terms, however, most of the continent was dominated by European or US capital, in forms that varied from total economic control – as in the case of Central America – to exceptional influence, such as in Mexico, Brazil, and Bolivia. Although the major South American countries experienced high economic growth in the first part of the twentieth century, their economies and their trade became increasingly bound up with the United States, in ways that gave the US government substantial influence on their politics and the decisions of their governments. For many Latin Americans, resistance against the Giant of the North took the form of anticolonialism, in spite of the lack of a formal empire to resist.

The new imperialism of the late nineteenth and early twentieth centuries created a world in which, for the first time, actions taken by the main European states had truly global consequences. As ideas of reform and progress became key parts of the colonial ethos, increasing numbers of local elites were drawn into the protostates that the imperialists were establishing, while the basic political injustice of the colonial projects began appearing in a sharper light than ever before. In part as a response to this contradiction, the late colonial regimes became, as the anthropologist James Scott has pointed out, sites of extensive experiments in social engineering, in many ways similar to the revolutionary regimes that were to succeed them. The ideology of "welfare colonial-ism," combined with the authoritarian power inherent in colonial rule, encouraged ambitious schemes to remake Third World societies, both through grand projects and through general policies of resettlement and mechanization.[8]

The anticolonial revolutions

World War I signified the starting point for the modern resistance move-ments against colonial rule and semicolonial oppression. The carnage that European powers engaged in on their home turf – and to a lesser extent in the colonies – was observed by large numbers of non-European conscripts (1.4 million from India alone), and undermined any faith they, or the indigenous elites, may have had in European superiority. The Great War was an acute crisis in the colonial system, especially since it came at the end of a period of rampant imperialist expansion, in which some 8.6 million square miles in Africa and Asia had been acquisitioned by Europeans in the name of "progress" and "humanity." No wonder that members of the indigenous elites – often emerging from within the colonial systems – believed that the time had come to build a non-European alternative to imperial rule. With European self-esteem in tatters, these leaders wanted to conquer modernity for themselves.

As during the Cold War, some Third World leaders saw the European war as an opportunity for support from their enemies' enemies. Germany, and later the Soviet Union, stood out as such options, as did – for a short period – the United States, not least because of President Woodrow Wilson's rhetoric about self-determination and democracy. One anti-colonial leader whom we have already met, the young M. N. Roy, chided the Americans for not understanding why some supporters of Indian independence opted for an alliance with Germany:

Germany could be for India what France was for the American colonials. The rebellious colonials of North America addressed themselves to France in their search for help because, in spite of the apparent peace, France was the potential enemy of England. In the present conflict, the Indian people saw in Germany an ally whose interests were identical and in harmony with their own. In the same way as your ancestors sent the Franklin mission to France in order to make an alliance, we have tried to arrive at an agreement with the power that could serve our interests and immediate needs. To blame us for exercising our legitimate right when we proceeded in this way would mean to condemn the conduct of your great patriots, Washington, Jefferson and Adams.[9]

After the Russian revolutions of 1917, and especially disappointments many anticolonial leaders felt w powers refused to honor the slogans of self-determination at the postwar peace conferences, the new Soviet Union became a focus for Third World attention. Not only did the Bolsheviks condemn colonialism and offer alliances to those who resisted it, but they also showed the way, it was believed, toward a nonexploitative form of modern society. Roy's countryman Jawaharlal Nehru noted in 1919 that

today the spectre [of Communism] has materialised and is holding the western world in its grip. Russia and Hungary have ended the age-long domination of the capitalist and the owner of property ... Horrible excesses are ascribed to the Bolshevists in Russia ... But if this is so then it is difficult to imagine how millions of human beings should prefer this terror and degradation and should voluntarily labour to bring it into existence ... We are a communal people and when the time comes perhaps some form of communism will be found to suit the genius of the people better than majority rule. Let us prepare for that time and let our leaders give thought to it.[10]

For India and for the Third World at large, Roy and Nehru could symbolize the two main ideological directions of the anticolonial resistance – Communism and nativism (albeit in Nehru's case a nativism tinged, as the years passed, with a remarkable degree of Anglophilia). They are also typical of the generation and background many anticolonial leaders came out of. Born in 1887 and 1889 respectively, Roy and Nehru both came from prominent families within their communities, and from an early age came to think of themselves as leaders of their people.[11]

Mahabhendra Nath Roy first studied in a local English-language school and then at the Bengal Technical Institute in Calcutta.[12] He joined a Bengali revolutionary group at 18 and in 1915 fled abroad to seek German support for Indian independence. From 1916 to 1918 he lived in the United States, where he married a Stanford graduate and began his interest in Marxism. In 1918, claiming police harassment, he left for Mexico, where he cofounded the Mexican Communist Party and became its delegate to the first congress of the Comintern and later – as we have seen – a key operative in the Communist International. For Roy, the key element in the Indian revolution was rapid social change, and he believed strongly that without a socialist revolution, Indian independence would be an empty shell.

Coming from a much wealthier background, Nehru studied at Harrow and at Trinity College, Cambridge, became a lawyer and served in the colonial high court in his home town of Allahabad. In 1918 he joined the Indian National Congress, which he, together with Mahatma Gandhi, formed into the main Indian independence party. Imprisoned several times by the British, Nehru remained an admirer of the Soviet Union, even though he as India's first postindependence prime minister argued for reform-oriented domestic change and a nonaligned foreign policy. In development policy Nehru was a state-oriented pragmatist who argued that

[the] idea of unrestricted private enterprise is out of date ... The State has to come in the picture in a big way. We cannot with our limited resources allow people just to go in any direction they like. We have to plan and planning has to include both the public and the private sector, leaving a great deal of room to private enterprise. The Plan is a national plan of all our activities, public or private.

Nativists and Marxists in the resistance movement were divided by their views of their countries' pasts as well as their futures. While the Marxists generally saw little to admire in the precolonial era and – on the whole – blamed the "treason" of indigenous elites for the ease with which the imperialist countries had taken over, the nativists thought their history and, often, their religion, were weapons against colonialism that would also determine their peoples' future direction after the struggle for independence had been won. For most anticolonial leaders, these constructed pasts mirrored their imagined futures. The nativists saw rebuilding the economic, social, and military strength of their countries as the key objective, which could be achieved by honoring indigenous traditions and by strong leadership. The Communists saw the strong state as a product of social revolution and wanted to copy models directly from the only successful noncapitalist power, the Soviet Union.

Both trends of thought were modern, in the sense that their leaders wanted to conquer new technologies and new organizational methods for their own purposes. Even those who saw the word of God as the basic message of liberation – such as the powerful Islamic anticolonial resistance – did not want to return to a society without the material advances that were available to increasing numbers of people within the colonial centers. In many cases, just as in the European and American phases of intense social transition in the nineteenth century, idealized images of the past became a framework for envisioning new and thoroughly modern societies, in which the return to "the roots" (or "the scriptures") showed a new preoccupation with social justice, "national" organization, or racial uniqueness. Ironically, those who worked for a revolution in the colonies were often helped by European "orientalist" images, which sought to impose a "tradition" on colonized societies in order to better separate them from their own supposedly more advanced civilizations. Eventually, these largely imaginary "traditions" could be turned against the oppressors and help the revolutionary movements recruit adherents based on concepts of identity or nation.

The Marxist and nativist labels used here are of course only crude and imprecise pointers to movements that emerged on different continents and among widely varying cultures. While Chinese Marxism had something in common with Marxism, say, in Cuba, there was also much that separated them. Worse, from an analytical point of view the two general trends were often present in the same people at different points in their careers – for instance, Nehru was a Hindu particularist who at Bandung became a spokesman for Third World internationalism, while Roy was a Communist who later became an individualist and a humanist. And, finally, there is the uneasy equilibrium that for generations existed between the opponents of colonialism and its collaborators. Based on their personal position, indigenous leaders often passed from representing the colonial power *vis-à-vis* the colonized to representing their own people *vis-à-vis* the metropolis, or the other way around. Were these people adherents or infiltrators, revolutionaries or counterrevolutionaries? In the colonial situation, ideological or organizational identities were often as fluid and uncertain as the framework for the colonial protostate itself.[13]

Still, declaring oneself a revolutionary took not only considerable personal courage, but also a strong faith in possessing an alternative that one's "people" would choose over the existing colonial reality. In most cases, of course, it was a losing proposition – most revolutionaries in most places of rebellion against an established state (colonial or not) ended up either dead or in prison. What drove them seems, as in most cases of human endeavor, to have been a mix of the push and the pull: witnessing state violence or the repeated humiliation of themselves, relatives, or friends because they belonged to the "wrong" ethnic group or class pushed people into organized opposition. Brutal imperial interventions into the affairs of a Third World country could win even those who admired European culture over to the role of revolutionaries. In convincing a person to confront a mighty state that could do untold damage to oneself, one's family, and one' s community, the sense, as the sociologist Jeff Goodwin has put it, of having *no other way out* must have played a key role. But there was also, as we have seen, the attraction of revolutionary ideologies and the growing understanding, especially after World War I, that local elites could do better than foreigners in solving the many problems that confronted Third World societies.

Combined, these incentives led many leaders born around the turn of the century to turn to revolution as their instrument for changing their countries (and the world). Within a colonial setting, it was almost given that some form of revolutionary change was necessary if colonialism was to be abolished; imperialist control, by its very nature, refuted any legitimate change of government, and – until after World War II – offered no opportunities for indigenous leaders to rise to the top of the local political leadership. But even in countries that were not colonized – such as China and most of Latin America – the rhetoric of anti-imperialism furnished key ideas and concepts to those who wanted to change their societies and their states. "Since the great call for world revolution, the movement for the liberation of mankind has pressed forward fiercely, and today we must change our old attitudes toward issues that in the past we did not question, toward methods we would not use, and toward so many words we would have been afraid to utter," the 25-year-old schoolteacher Mao Zedong – not yet a Marxist – noted in 1919. "Question the unquestionable," he exhorted his countrymen. "Dare to do the unthinkable. Do not shrink from saying the unutterable. No force can stop a tide such as this."[14]

For the young Ho Chi Minh, three years Mao's senior, the years immediately after World War I were crucial for his future course. Having appealed in vain for US support for democratic freedoms and political autonomy in Vietnam at the Versailles Peace Conference, the 30-year-old photo retoucher living in Paris became bitterly disappointed with Wilsonian diplomacy and turned toward Marxism as a solution to his country's ills.[15] "The hydra of Western capitalism has for some time now been stretching its horrible tentacles toward all corners of the globe, as it finds Europe too restricted a field of action, and the European proletariat insufficient to satisfy its insatiable appetite," Ho explained to the congress of the French Socialist Party at Tours in 1920.[16] Criticizing the French socialists for not doing enough for the liberation of the colonies, Ho voted for the party to join the Communist International, and later became an itinerant agent for the Comintern in many countries in Europe and Asia before leading the Vietminh – the Communist-led Vietnamese resistance movement – in the 1940s.

Like Ho Chi Minh, the Indonesian leader Sukarno spent time in prison for his efforts to liberate his country from colonial rule. At his trial in 1930, Sukarno had explained why he had not become a Marxist. "We are nourishing that fervor for freedom," the 29-year-old Sukarno told his judges, "[but] we promote it not so much through class consciousness ... [as] through an awareness of nationality through nationalism ... In the colonial country it is not primarily the resistance of the laborer to the capitalist or a class conflict which we experience. It is the conflict between black and white, East and West, colonizer and colonized."[17] For a nativist like Sukarno, the "old" values – Islam included – of the new country he wanted to create would also guide the future state after liberation. At his trial, the future Indonesian president's key point of defense was that the best in

Fig. 2   Sukarno the orator: addressing supporters in 1950.

Indonesian traditions were in line with the European values of democracy and liberalism. By putting him on trial, Sukarno argued, the Dutch were judging their own political system more than his revolutionary movement.

As much as in Asia and Africa, Latin American revolutionaries of the interwar period directed their rhetoric against outside forces, and not just against problems in their own societies. The fact that most of their countries were *not* formal colonies contributed to the need to identify a foreign oppressor. For the Nicaraguan revolutionary leader Augusto César Sandino – like Sukarno a nativist, not a Marxist – it was US economic control and its repeated military interventions that were responsible for his country's predicament. In the florid language of Latin American revolution, Sandino declared his willingness to fight US influence to the death (which he eventually achieved in 1934, aged 39, at the hands of the US-supported Somoza dictatorship):

I am not Mary Magdalene, to beg on bended knee forgiveness from my enemies, the enemies of Nicaragua, because I believe no one on earth has the right to be a demigod. I will await you, standing firmly on my own feet at the head of my patriot soldiers, unconcerned with your number. But remember that when that happens the destruction of your grandeur will shake the Capitol in Washington, and the dome that crowns the famous White House, the den where you plot your crimes, will be reddened with your blood.[18]

The personal experiences of many of those who became leaders of Third World revolutions were formed through long periods in prison or exile. Much of their concept of the organizational methods they wanted to use and the states they wanted to create was formed through reading or through conversations with people far away from their homelands. Their sense of responsibility for their own communities was usually strengthened by the personal sacrifice they had to make and by seeing members of their immediate family or close friends being tortured or killed for the sake of their common cause. In many cases, the feeling of purpose and urgency that such experiences created made Third World revolutionary leaders willing to take great risks on behalf of gaining power or of securing the rapid development of their new states. They believed strongly in their mission, and knew that success, whatever its ultimate cost, would not come cheap.

To many revolutionary leaders, the violence committed against them and their countries by the European powers justified a willingness on their own part to use violence to rid the Third World of foreign domination.[19] The Martiniquan Frantz Fanon, who trained as a psychiatrist before becoming a key supporter of the Algerian liberation struggle, went as far as to argue that "violence is a cleansing force. It frees the native from his inferiority complex and from his despair and inaction; it makes him fearless and restores his self-respect."[20] Fanon's countryman Aimé Césaire also attacked the Europeans' attempts at conquering the moral high ground for the themselves in the conflict with Third World revolutionary movements:

They talk to me about progress, about "achievements," diseases cured, improved standards of living. I am talking about societies drained of their essence, cultures trampled underfoot, institutions undermined, lands confiscated, religions smashed, magnificent artistic creations destroyed, extraordinary possibilities wiped out. They throw facts at my head, statistics, mileages of roads, canals, and railroad tracks ... I am talking about millions of men torn from their gods, their land, their habits, their life – from life, from the dance, from wisdom ... I am talking about millions of men in whom fear has been cunningly instilled, who have been taught to have an inferiority complex, to tremble, kneel, despair, and behave like flunkeys.[21]

Even those who rejected a socialist revolution and wanted to see forms of capitalist development take hold in their countries – leaders such as Syngman Rhee (born 1875) in Korea, Mustafa Kemal (born 1881) in Turkey, or the Shah of Iran, Mohammed Reza Pahlavi (born 1919) – emphasized the need for their countrymen to shake off their sense of inferiority and build a new self-confidence based both on an understanding of the past achievements of their countries and of the weaknesses in their past economic, cultural, and political behavior that had led to these countries falling under foreign domination. In terms of the future direction they wanted to take their countries in, these antisocialist nativist leaders were as revolutionary as their socialist or Marxist opponents. Mustafa Kemal – later known as Atatürk (the father of the Turks), the general who headed the first modern and secular Turkish state and who saw the name of his first party, the Young Turks, used the world over as synonymous with a new generation of modernizing elites – argued that in the new Turkey one "should judge the measure of time not according to the lax mentality of past centuries, but in terms of the concepts of [the] speed and movement of our century.

We shall raise our country to the level of the most prosperous and civilized nations of the world. We shall endow our nation with the broadest means and sources of welfare. We shall raise our national culture above the contemporary level of civilization … We shall perform greater tasks in a shorter time … because [we] hold the torch of the positive sciences.[22]

The late colonial era endowed the Third World with a set of profound processes of change that were all carried over into the post-World War II construction of new decolonized countries. First and foremost, it could be said that colonial rule created Third World nationalisms through providing both their subject – the nation – and their primary object – the modern state. Many features of the colonial protostate were to be found in the successor regimes, not least the predilection for big projects, mass mobilization, and the basic concept that continuous economic development is possible and desirable. But while the empires taught local elites to think big, they also left a legacy of warped, one-sided economies, rigid social stratification, and racism. And, as in an evil circle, the effectiveness and legitimacy of the new states that had to deal with these problems were often hampered, more than anything, by their very origins in the colonial system.[23]

Creating new states

As World War I had helped to create the local resistance movements against colonial rule in the Third World, so World War II helped to destroy the colonial system as such. While it could be argued that much of both the ideological and the economic justification for having colonies had come under pressure in the metropolis during the interwar crisis years, there is little doubt that it was the second war in Europe that destroyed both the will and the ability of European elites to keep their colonial possessions. The processes of decolonization – in some cases, forced through bloody wars; in others through simple and quick withdrawals – began in the 1940s and lasted up to the 1970s. But already in the immediate postwar years, as the Cold War became the dominant international feature, the *direction* of future developments was becoming increasingly clear: the era of colonial rule in the Third World was quickly coming to a close.

From the perspective of the colonized elites, the fact that the Europeans for a second time in a generation were engaged in fratricidal warfare was yet more proof of their unsuitability to rule others. But at the start of World War II, in addition to the renewed indignities that Europeans were capable of inflicting on themselves, there were also the defeats the Western empires suffered at the hands of Japan – the only non-European power to have developed a strong and independent military force. The fall of Singapore – the citadel of British imperial power – and the subsequent Japanese takeover of all the British, French, American, and Dutch colonial possessions in Southeast Asia in one grand sweep in early 1942, convinced many Asians that European colonialism was on its last leg, whatever the outcome of the war. In spite of the general image of Japan in Asia as a colonial oppressor in the worst style of the Europeans, there were among some nationalists the somewhat naïve idea that Japan would grant independence to the colonies if it won the war against the West. Much more widespread, though, was a certain pride that the Japanese, after all, were Asians too, and that their victories against the Europeans showed what Asian arms, organization, and dedication could achieve. The majority of Asian nationalists, especially of the nativist kind, simply saw the Japanese expansion as another potential ally against the colonial power that oppressed them – in the style of "my enemy's enemy is my friend." When war broke out, the Indian leader Subhas Chandra Bose – prominent in the Indian National Congress alongside Gandhi and Nehru – went first to Germany and then, in 1943, to Japan, where he set up a government-in-exile and raised a 40,000 strong Indian army to fight alongside the Japanese against the British in Burma and eastern India.

Bose died in a plane crash in Taiwan in August 1945, as the Japanese empire itself was coming crashing down under the weight of American military might. But for other Asian nationalists, be they nativist or Marxist, August 1945 – when Japan's power was gone and the European powers seemed unable to resurrect their empires – was the moment of opportunity. Sukarno, who had spent two years in a Dutch jail and more than eight years in exile after his trial, had hailed the Japanese as liberators and promoted himself as their chief adviser on Indonesian affairs. On the 17 August 1945, on the steps of his house in Jakarta, Sukarno

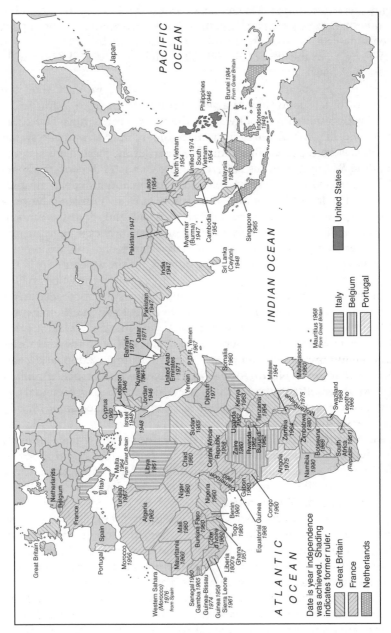

PACIFIC OCEAN

Japan

Philippines *1946*

North Vietnam *1954*
Unified 1974
South Vietnam *1954*

Laos *1954*

Pakistan 1947

Myanmar (Burma) *1947*
Cambodia *1954*

India *1947*

Brunei 1984
From Great Britain

Indonesia *1949*

Malaysia *1963*

Singapore *1965*

Sri Lanka (Ceylon) *1948*

INDIAN OCEAN

Pakistan *1947*

Bahrain *1971*
Qatar *1971*

Kuwait *1961*
United Arab Emirates *1971*
Yemen   P.D.R. Yemen *1967*

Cyprus *1960*
Lebanon *1946*
Israel *1948*
Jordan *1946*

Somalia *1960*

Djibouti *1977*

Mauritius 1968
From Great Britain

Madagascar *1960*

Malawi *1964*

Sudan *1956*

Uganda *1962*
Kenya *1963*
Tanzania *1964*
Zambia *1964*

Swaziland *1968*
Lesotho *1966*

Central African Republic *1958*

Zaire *1960*
Rwanda *1962*
Burundi *1962*

Mozambique *1975*
Zimbabwe *1980*
Botswana *1966*
Namibia *1990*
South Africa (Republic of) *1961*

Libya *1951*

Chad *1960*

Angola *1975*

Malta 1964
From Great Britain
Italy

Netherlands

Belgium

France

Tunisia *1957*

Niger *1960*

Nigeria *1960*

Cameroon *1960*
Gabon *1960*
Congo *1960*

Equatorial Guinea *1968*

Algeria *1962*

Mali *1960*

Burkina Faso *1960*

Benin *1960*
Togo *1960*
Ghana *1957*
Côte d'Ivoire *1960*

Morocco *1956*

Western Sahara (Morocco) *1976*
from Spain

Senegal *1960*
Gambia *1965*
Guinea-Bissau *1974*
Guinea *1958*
Sierra Leone *1961*
Liberia *1800's*

Mauritania *1960*

Great Britain

Portugal   Spain

ATLANTIC OCEAN

Date is year independence
was achieved. Shading
indicates former ruler.

Great Britain

France

Netherlands

United States

Italy

Belgium

Portugal

Map 3   Decolonisation in Africa and Asia since 1945.

unilaterally declared Indonesia's independence. Two weeks later, Ho Chi Minh declared Vietnam's independence in Hanoi. Ho began by quoting from the 1776 American Declaration of Independence:

"All men are created equal. They are endowed by their Creator with certain inalienable rights; among these are Life, Liberty, and the pursuit of Happiness" ... In a broader sense, this means: all the peoples on the earth are equal from birth, all the peoples have a right to live, to be happy and free.[24]

For a Marxist revolutionary, it was a rather surprising performance. But then Ho and all other rebels against the colonial order knew that the only country that could effectively aid their enemies in the postwar period was the United States, which together with the Soviet Union was the main victor of World War II, both in Asia and in Europe.

The main transfers of power from colonial to indigenous rule took place during the first two decades of the Cold War. Both in the cases of Sukarno and Ho Chi Minh, as well as those of numerous other independence leaders, there was no easy walk to freedom – the colonial powers often attempted to come back from the grave to reassert themselves in the immediate postwar era, as we will see in the next chapter. France, the most assimilationist of empires, tried perhaps for that very reason longer than others to cling on to its colonies by force. Already on the very day that France celebrated its own liberation from Germany, 8 May 1945, French forces fired on an independence rally in the town of Setif in Algeria, killing hundreds of civilians.[25] By the time the last French soldiers withdrew from North Africa, in 1962, more than half a million people had been killed, almost all on the Algerian side. In Vietnam, the French had continued to fight against the Vietminh forces up to 1954.

For the Vietnamese, the Algerians, and all others who attacked the colonial system after 1945, the existence of two superpowers, who both were eager to disassociate themselves from European colonialism, opened up new possibilities for aid and support. Very different from the nineteenth-century system of states and from the process of colonial expansion, the Cold War was bipolar to the point of exclusivity, meaning that if one's enemies were supported by *one* superpower, there was always the chance of getting aid from the other. As we will see, the availability of powerful outside backers later became a key element of instability within Third World states – it helped to create lasting rebellions and insurgencies after decolonization. But in those relatively few cases where the road to independence was a long and open war, military aid – most often from the Soviet Union and its allies – became vital during the 1950s and 1960s.

For the great majority of colonized areas, especially in Africa, liberation was a stunningly quick process. In the five years from 1957 to 1962 alone, twenty-five new states were created, in most cases after only a few years of preparation. Very often the postcolonial elite moved directly into the state that the colonial power had set up; as the historian David Abernethy puts it, government, the shelter the colonists had built, was for the first time available for new occupants.[26] Institutions and practices transferred directly from the metropolis during the colonial era were at the heart of these new states after independence, often with a functioning indigenous bureaucracy inherited from the past, such as in India or in Nigeria. The whole entity that the new leaders were trying to fill with their own content was a colonial construct: its borders, its capital city, its official language. It was from the beginning, as the French sociologist Bertrand Badie has pointed out, an "imported state."

The problem, of course, for the new leaders was their sense that the empires had not only been oppressive and unjust, but that they had failed in bringing the kind of modernity to the Third World that local elites aspired to. The colonial state, which they had inherited, was therefore a symbol of failure to many of them, and constrictive in terms of the new and bold programs that they envisaged. There was also the suspicion – quite correctly held, in some cases – that the colonial bureaucracy still served two masters; that the officials who had been appointed by the old regime served as agents for the political and economic interests of the former metropolis. Since the colonial power often attempted to keep some of its key investments – especially in the exploitation of raw materials – after decolonization, the reconstruction of the functions of the state stood near the top of the priority list of all the new Third World countries.

The main capital on which the postcolonial leaders could bank was the almost boundless enthusiasm of the younger urban generation. "The day of independence," one young Kenyan intellectual recalled, "was unforgettable. When I saw the flag, I broke down crying. This was what we had waited for, what we had fought for, during so many long and hard years. For the first time ever I felt like a complete human being, because from now on we would no longer be ruled by others, but by ourselves only."[27] Few of the supporters of independence had any doubt that in all respects they could do better than the Europeans within their own countries. And many outside observers tended to agree with that conclusion, at least as far as long-term development was concerned, especially in those many new countries where plentiful natural resources could be harvested by a large generation of young people who were willing to work hard under the guidance of the new authorities.

As we have already seen, a reconstructed and powerful state remained the main aim of the postcolonial elites, whatever their political background, during the struggle for independence. The reason for emphasizing the state was the sense that only through a massive mobilization of manpower and resources could Third World countries break out from what was increasingly, in the 1950s, termed "underdevelopment" – an economic and social situation under which countries in Africa, Asia, and Latin America were less productive and therefore had less to offer their citizens in material terms than the European countries. "Once freedom is gained," the new leader of the former British colony the Gold Coast, Kwame Nkrumah, told his countrymen, "a greater task comes into view.

The dependent territories are backward in education, in agriculture, and in industry. The economic independence that should follow and maintain political independence demands every effort from the people, a total mobilisation of brain and manpower resources. What other countries have taken three hundred years or more to achieve, a once dependent territory must try to accomplish in a generation if it is to survive. Unless it is, as it were, "jet-propelled," it will lag behind and thus risk everything for which it has fought.[28]

This "jet propulsion" into modernity that Nkrumah hoped for in the new country he called Ghana turned out to be elusive, not just in West Africa, but all over the Third World. While in 1950 Western Europe's real gross national product per capita was five times greater than that of Africa and Asia, by 1970 – toward the end of the decolonization process – the gap had grown to about 8:1 for Africa and 8.5:1 for Asia.[29] The struggle for development proved an uphill battle for many Third World countries, primarily – it could be argued – because they were forced to compete within an international system that was geared to the interests of the former colonial centers. As a result, Third World leaders found that they would need an ever more intensive effort within their countries to break through what they themselves by the late 1960s had begun referring to as "the development barrier."

As the buoyant optimism of the first years of independence began to wane, many Third World leaders concluded that they needed a more radical approach in order to reach their aims. Within the state, colonial holdovers would have to be replaced as officials by "new" men who were politically trustworthy, while the political leaders would need to get more authority at all levels. And in society at large the state would need to obtain an ever increasing role in organizing production in order to better make use of the scarce resources available. Since the foreign investments that many new Third World governments were hoping for did not generally materialize – often for the very good reason that the new regimes were busy nationalizing the foreign investments that already existed – economic planning often turned toward self-sufficiency and import substitution. According to Nkrumah, who had learnt much of his political creed from Harold Laski at the London School of Economics,

Capitalism is too complicated a system for a newly independent nation. Hence the need for a socialistic society. But even a system based on social justice and a democratic constitution may need backing up, during the period following independence, by emergency measures of a authoritarian kind. Without discipline true freedom cannot survive.[30]

A key reason for the radicalization of many Third World regimes in the 1960s was their leaders' discovery of the immense poverty in which most of their countrymen lived. Those who had not spent time in rural base areas during a war for liberation – a Nkrumah, say, compared to a Ho Chi Minh – often discovered the depth of destitution in the countryside when touring the country in their official cars after independence. On the one hand, having spent most of their lives in the cities, in exile, or in prison, they were genuinely shocked by what they saw and felt a need to improve the lot of their countrymen. But social justice was also, for most leaders, a promise built into the decolonization process itself: they had appealed for the support of the peasants in creating a nation, and – at least believing that they had received it – they now needed to deliver on their own promises of a better life for all.

Because of the global distribution of power and because of the Cold War ideological division, there were two hegemonic models of development on offer when the new states were being created. One, symbolized by the United States, promised intensive urban-based growth in both the private and the public sectors, the import of advanced consumer products and the latest technology through joining a global capitalist market, and an alliance with the world's most powerful state. The other, that of the Soviet world, offered politically induced growth through a centralized plan and mass mobilization, with an emphasis on heavy industry, massive infrastructural projects, and the collectivization of agriculture, independent of international markets. The US model was tainted by the association of US capitalism with the capitalism of the colonial oppressors. The Soviet model suffered from the image of the Soviet Union as the "secondary" superpower and from what was often seen as second-rate Soviet products and technology. Both, however, offered a road to high modernity through education, science, and technological progress.

While, as we have seen, Soviet political alliances with Third World countries developed only slowly, the Soviet model of development became increasingly influential as Third World regimes were forced to the left in the first years after independence. The main reasons for the leftward trend was the sense that the Soviet model was more in line with the state-centered and justice-oriented ideals they themselves had for the development of their new countries, allied with a belief that the Soviet Union was advancing more rapidly than the United States. While the number of Marxist-led states remained a small though growing minority, countries from Zambia to Algeria, and from Syria to Indonesia, were headed by leaders who believed in learning from the Soviet experience. India's Nehru, while battling the Communist Party at home at independence, told a visiting Soviet delegation in 1947 that

> For many years past we have looked with very great interest toward the Soviet Union for many reasons, but more especially because of the tremendous achievements of the Soviet Union during the last quarter of a century or so ... You have been pioneers in many fields and you have transformed the vast tracts of your country before our eyes with a speed that has astonished humanity. Inevitably, when we want to produce great changes in India, we want to learn from your example. We want to know what you have done and how you have done it. Among the many things that you have done is this tremendous flowering of science in the Soviet Union and the application of that science to the betterment of human beings who live in those vast territories.[31]

Science and education were at the heart of the project to build modern states in the Third World, not least since thirty-four of the new chief executives had themselves been trained at universities in the former metropolis.[32] Through government programs, the postcolonial countries went through an education revolution in which the rate of secondary school enrollment more than quadrupled, while higher education figures on average increased more than sevenfold from 1960 to 1990. Even the poorest countries sent thousands of students to study abroad, to the United States, Europe, or the Soviet Union. But in many cases the investment in education seemed not to pay off in terms of economic development, and often highly qualified students returned to low-paid government jobs or to unemployment. While there is no clear direction in terms of the political ideas that this postcolonial generation picked up while abroad – some who trained in Western Europe or the United States returned as Marxists, while quite a few of those who went to the Soviet Union became critical of Soviet Communism – there is a clear connection between radicalization and returning to un- or under-employment at home. Many of the radical regimes of the late 1960s and 1970s, especially in Africa, were fuelled by the visions of disgruntled intellectuals with too much time on their hands.

The building of industry was another great aspiration of the postcolonial regimes, and one where the differences in outcome between different countries was most striking. Already in the 1960s a great gulf had started appearing between the few Third World states that had some existing domestic industrial and capital base, that targeted and gained access to international markets, and that carried out concerted export-oriented industrial, trade, and technology policies, and the countries that did not. While some East and Southeast Asian economies began to grow fast, the growth in the states that emphasized self-suffiency and import substitution, especially in Africa, was much slower. There are, of course, a whole host of reasons in addition to domestic policy choices why some economies grew faster than others – a few of these causes, such as the availability of US support, depended to a high degree on the Cold War – but the main issue for our purpose is that by the late 1960s there was a growing sense in many Third World countries that the first postcolonial leaders had failed in their development efforts. This argument contributed to increased political instability and, in some cases, to a total rejection of the political institutions that had been set up at independence.

The most contested area of policy making in postcolonial states was generally land reform. The key promise that the elites who led the anticolonial movements had made to the peasants in order to mobilize them for a "national" struggle was their acquisition of land as soon as the struggle had been won. Land reform was therefore both about paying back political debts as much as it was a part of the search for increased productivity, social justice, and alleviation of rural poverty. In many cases, however, the promises turned out to be difficult to keep without disastrous effects for the economy. In North Vietnam, where most farmers with anything more than holdings of a few acres saw their land confiscated in 1955–56, the result was a stream of refugees to the south and a loss of productivity for the Communist government.In Egypt a much more moderate reform instituted in 1952, touching only about 12 percent of arable land, still had significant consequences, because it reduced the commercial output in agriculture by up to 50 percent through abolishing the larger and most productive farms. For most Third World regimes themselves, however, the economic effects were less important than the political: land reform was good, the new leaders thought, because it destroyed "feudalism" while securing support among poor peasants for the new government and the state it was creating.[33]

While it could be argued that most land reforms could have brought a generally beneficial effect over time – at least in those cases where the peasants' pride of ownership had not been destroyed by forms of collectivization and lack of investment – it is more difficult to see much long-term good coming out of the nationalities policies of most new regimes. The fiction that an inclusive "nation" existed within the mostly haphazardly drawn borders created by the colonial powers led to untold misery for those who did not recognize themselves as part of that entity. In Iraq,

Kurds and Shia Muslims found no place within the new Baathist state. In Algeria, the Berbers resisted the Arabification of the postcolonial regime. In Zimbabwe, the minority Ndebele were forced to accept a state based on the interests of the majority people, the Shona.And in Rwanda and Burundi – the most unsuccessful of all states created in the postcolonial Third World – different state- and nation-building projects led to genocidal wars between the main population groups, the Hutu and the Tutsi.

The need to create an effective and integrationist state – which in some cases substituted for the nonexisting "nation" – led many Third World leaders to exacerbate preexisting ethnic tension instead of relieving it. The extension of the reach of the state beyond what was seen in colonial times led to resistance – mostly by peasants – against attacks on their identities and, often, their religions. But for most new regimes this often brutal extension was a necessity for the kind of modernity they wanted. The leaders felt that the odds were against them at independence, because of poor communications, illiteracy, and – as they saw it – colonially induced apathy. They also feared – rightly in some cases – that the imperialist powers would use forms of separatism to destroy their government. Creating a nation was a trial of strength that had to be won. Julius Nyerere, founder of the Tanganyika African National Union (TANU) and first president of independent Tanzania, used to say that while some nations were trying to reach the moon, TANU was still trying to reach the villages.[34]

The battle against the influence that religion had on people's lives was a key postcolonial enterprise. While science and organization were the foundations of the "good" state, "religion" and "tribalism" were the evils of the past. Religion – both in the form of "imported" and "native" forms of belief – was a particularly pernicious enemy, since it competed with the new state for the loyalty of its citizens. Kemal's new Turkish state was aggressively secular, to the point of refusing Muslims the right to wear religious garb outside of mosques and madrasas. For Mao Zedong, his country's religious beliefs were the very symbol of China's backwardness. For the leader of the Partido Africano da Independência da Guiné e Cabo Verde (PAIGC), Amílcar Cabral, the influence of religion was a question of power – its practices were attempts by feudal and *petit bourgeois* leaders "to reestablish their complete cultural and political domination of the people."[35]

The battle to gain ideological control of one's population was made more difficult by what postcolonial leaders saw as their continued economic dependence on the West through foreign control of the exploitation of raw materials, thorough foreign loans, or through development aid. In many cases, such as the Congo (minerals), Nicaragua (coffee), or Iran (oil), big European and American companies clung on to the giant profits they were making in extracting the wealth of the Third World, often by trying to buy the political and economic collaboration of the local regimes. Nationalizing these businesses – as often happened – made sense politically, but led far too often to a sharp decline both in productivity and profitability, since Third World states lacked the technological skills and the knowledge of international markets that were needed to make nationalized businesses successful. By the mid-1970s most Third World regimes had become massively indebted to international lending institutions and to corporate banks – countries such as Egypt and Tanzania owed sums well above half of their annual GDP. Since the loans had been taken out by the state, and the state's income was crucial both to jobs and welfare in most Third World countries, many regimes weakened themselves politically by having to siphon off money directly from their budgets to scheduled debt repayments.

During the Cold War the availability of aid from one of the superpowers or their allies was therefore a welcome rescue package for many Third World countries. But very little aid – *none* in the case of the Soviet Union and the United States – came without strings attached. While some Third World leaders became experts in political coat-turning, dependent on where the aid was coming from, most felt that the foreign countries that provided the aid were out to interfere with the domestic and international direction their state moved in. The "experts" that most often came with the aid were resented because they created a social sphere over which the recipient country had little control, even when they came from countries with which the regime had close relations, such as Soviets in Angola or Americans in Iran. Furthermore, the aid packages turned out to be too much of a quick fix for some states, since they delayed the need for Third World leaders to begin questioning their own ideological motives in domestic development or governmental system.

The difficulties in constructing viable states led to increasing political instability in the Third World in the first two postcolonial decades. The opposition to the first postcolonial governments came mainly – though not exclusively – from the Left, and often from Marxist or Marxist-inspired movements. Domestic development problems contributed significantly to the process. Another key reason was the on-going struggle for decolonization in some areas, such as the Portuguese-held territories in Africa, in Zimbabwe, or in South Africa – the internationalism inherent in Marxism appealed to many young people in the postcolonial states. Meanwhile, Vietnamese resistance to US intervention reminded many of their own anticolonial revolutions, and helped make domestic forms of

Western capitalism seem even more unattractive than before. And, for some movements, there was the increasing availability of Soviet support, as Moscow turned its attention to the Third World.

In spite of the obvious causes of dissatisfaction, it would be completely wrong to see the creation of a new generation of Third World revolutionaries as disassociated from the general leftward trend of the 1960s. As historian Jeremi Suri has pointed out, on a global scale the decade saw many different rebellions against established orders, and these rebellions in many cases sought both moral and intellectual sustenance from each other. For African, Asian, and Latin American revolutionaries the general leftist trend among intellectuals in Europe and the United States in the 1960s contributed significantly to convince them of the righteousness of their cause. With the explosion in communications and travel during that decade, the discourses of North and South began to blend, in ways that often took little notice of the social and economic situations the intellectuals operated in. Often, Third World students brought back new and big ideas to their home countries, where they found confirmation of their faith among radical First World voluntary aid workers.

Bandung and the Nonaligned Movement

For the new Third World states, there were as many problems with finding one's way in international affairs as there were with creating successful domestic development strategies. To begin with, domestic difficulties clearly dominated the policy agenda – very few of these countries had much of a clear foreign policy when they came into being. There were, however, foreign policy orientations and sentiments that had been created during the anticolonial struggle. In some cases these were ideologically based connections with other countries, through politics or culture. In most new states, however, it was more a sense of Third World internationalism that had been created by the colonial enterprise itself (or, in the case of Latin America, the sense of having common problems in confronting the United States). The Barbadian writer George Lamming's 1953 novel *In the Castle of My Skin* shows how someone from his islands, after witnessing anticolonial protests elsewhere in the Caribbean, "starts to think of Little England [Barbados] as a part of some gigantic thing called colonial."[36] If the revolutionaries who had defeated the colonial enterprise were a diverse lot, they at least had in common the problems left behind by the imperialists.

That the new states were offered membership in d
organizations set up by the former colonial power, su
Commonwealth or the French Union, did little to re

sense of Third World solidarity. While the Commonwealth succeeded – after initial difficulties – in creating at least a forum for discussion between the former metropolis and its former colonies, the French version failed, mainly because it was set up in 1946 as a blatant attempt at staving off full-scale decolonization by agreeing only to limited sovereignty. Its successor, the French Community (La Communauté, created with the Fifth Republic in 1958) fell into oblivion during the 1970s, again largely because of French attempts at keeping a right to interfere in the domestic or regional affairs of the former colonies. Some new states – such as Guinea in West Africa and Burma – refused to have anything at all to do with the imperialist powers, within or without the commonwealth-type organizations.

The sense of community among Third World countries was reinforced by attempts by the former colonial masters to get them to choose sides in the Cold War, as British Prime Minister Harold Macmillan did in his famous "Wind of Change" speech in Cape Town in 1960. Most Third World leaders saw such efforts as aimed at diluting their independence, and resisted them vigorously, in spite of their political sympathies. Already in the immediate postwar years some had begun fearing that their countries would become future pawns in the Cold War, as the Tunisian leader Habib Bourguiba made clear in 1946: "North Africa is one of the best [assets] in the eyes of the Anglo-Saxon world: key to the central Mediterranean and an ideal base of operations against a Europe on its way to Bolshevization. It is not therefore for our beautiful eyes that the Anglo-Saxons interest themselves more and more in our fate."[37]

Already in the first part of the twentieth century there had been several attempts at forging international ties between the anticolonial movements – some, as we have seen, through the Comintern, and others through pan-African or pan-Asian conferences.[38] The first pan-African conference was held in London in 1900, and four more were held between 1919 and 1927, with prominent African Americans – such as W. E. B. Du Bois – as key organizers. The fifth pan-African conference, held in Manchester, England, in 1945, had ninety delegates, with twenty-six from all over Africa, including Nkrumah, Hastings Banda (later president of Malawi), and Jomo Kenyatta (later president of Kenya). The conference stressed that the liberation of Africa, of the Caribbean colonies, and of African Americans were part of the same struggle. It also underlined that all African liberation struggles were connected and should be supported collectively by all Africans, until full independence had been gained by colonized territories everywhere. In spite of being held outside Africa, the Manchester conference pointed toward the All-African People's

Conference in Accra in 1958 and the founding of the Organization of African Unity in 1963.

The April 1955 Asian–African conference in Bandung, Indonesia, had its origins in an initiative taken by the leaders of five Asian states – Indonesia, India, Pakistan, Burma, and Sri Lanka – but during its preparation the conference developed into the biggest and most influential gathering of Third World leaders held during the colonial era. Part of the importance of the Bandung conference was its timing: coming right after the French withdrawal from Indochina and at a time when several African countries seemed headed for independence, the conference caught the moment of greatest hope and expectation in the anticolonial struggle. It also came at a point in the Cold War when the Soviet Union – after Stalin's death and the end of the Korean War – was engaging in a major offensive for peace and *détente*. The latter changes allowed China – a close ally of the Soviets at the time – to participate in the conference alongside leaders whom Mao had earlier denounced as lackeys of imperialism. The new optimism in superpower relations also set part of the agenda for the conference – as Nehru and Sukarno underlined, the countries represented at Bandung, with their population of more than 1.5 billion people, had a responsibility for making the European powers see sense in their relations among themselves.

The African American writer and former Communist Party member Richard Wright was among those who witnessed the opening of the conference.

I'd no sooner climbed into the press gallery and looked down upon the vast assembly of delegates, many of them clad in their exotic national costumes, than I could sense an important junction of history in the making. In the early and difficult days of the Russian revolution, Lenin had dreamed of a gathering like this, a conglomeration of the world's underdogs, coming to the aid of the hard-pressed Soviets ... [But] from a strictly Stalinist point of view, such a gathering as this was unthinkable, for it was evident that the Communists had no control here ... Every religion under the sun, almost every race on earth, every shade of political opinion, and one and a half thousand million people from 12,606,938 square miles of the earth's surface were represented here.[39]

The image of the torch of civilization being passed to new continents outside Europe was omnipresent among the Third World leaders at Bandung. Nehru, especially, spoke of responsibility and sacrifice in ways that lent as much credence to his years at a British public school as to his new position as India's prime minister.[40] But at the heart of the efforts of the nativist leaders at Bandung lay an attempt to create some form of common ideology which, eventually, could supersede the Cold War system, at least as far as the Third World was concerned. In his great opening speech at the conference, Sukarno globalized his own aim of integrating nationalism, Islam, and Marxism into a new, moral ideology within Indonesia:

Perhaps now more than at any other moment in the history of the world, society, government and statesmanship need to be based upon the highest code of morality and ethics. And in political terms, what is the highest code of morality? It is the subordination of everything to the well-being of mankind. But today we are faced with a situation where the well-being of mankind is not always the primary consideration. Many who are in places of high power think, rather, of controlling the world.[41]

The only way, Sukarno claimed, in which morality could be regained within international relations was through the efforts of the Third World, which, having suffered the indignities of colonialism, could understand such aims better than the European societies. But such efforts demanded Third World unity:

All of us, I am certain, are united by more important things than those which superficially divide us. We are united, for instance, by a common detestation of colonialism in whatever form it appears. We are united by a common detestation of racialism. And we are united by a common determination to preserve and stabilise peace in the world ... Relatively speaking, all of us gathered here today are neighbours. Almost all of us have ties of common experience, the experience of colonialism. Many of us have a common religion. Many of us have common cultural roots. Many of us, the so-called "underdeveloped" nations, have more or less similar economic problems, so that each can profit from the others' experience and help. And I think I may say that we all hold dear the ideals of national independence and freedom. Yes, we have so much in common. And yet we know so little of each other.[42]

But in order for the Third World countries to fulfill their destiny of getting to know each other and thereby putting the world in better shape, avoiding nuclear war between the superpowers was crucial.

What can we do? We can do much! We can mobilise all the spiritual, all the moral, all the political strength of Asia and Africa on the side of peace. Yes, we! We, the peoples of Asia and Africa, 1,400,000,000 strong, far more than half the human population of the world, we can mobilise what I have called the *Moral Violence of Nations* in favour of peace. We can demonstrate to the minority of the world which lives on the other continents that we, the majority, are for peace, not war, and that whatever strength we have will always be thrown on to the side of peace.[43]

Finding ways of dealing with the Cold War also dominated the sessions of the Bandung conference. While agreeing that the superpowers were states that in their essence had "sprung from Europe," as one delegate put it, the delegates also understood that both Washington and Moscow were special forms of European powers, which in both cases ideologically had a troubled relationship to colonialism. In his opening speech, Sukarno quoted Longfellow's poem "Paul Revere's Ride" and his own conviction that the global anticolonial struggle had begun 180 years ago in America.[44] Nehru, on the other hand, resisted attempts by Western-oriented Third World states – led by the Baghdad Pact countries Iraq, Iran, and Turkey – to condemn the Soviet Union for colonialism in Eastern Europe. "However much we may oppose what has happened to countries in Eastern Europe and elsewhere, it is not colonialism ... It seems to me rather extraordinary that we should discuss nations as such whose people we have recognised in the capacity of sovereign nations and then say that they are colonial territories."[45]

Being forced to spend a great amount of time at the conference dealing with Cold War issues probably pushed the main nativist states closer together in their determination to create principles of nonalignment. The attitude of the Chinese delegation, headed by Premier Zhou Enlai, helped by seeing nonalignment and the revived Communist slogan of peaceful coexistence as highly compatible.[46] Zhou told the conference that

the Chinese delegation has come here to seek common ground, not to create divergences ... The great majority of Afro-Asian countries and peoples have suffered and are still suffering from the disasters of colonialism. If we unite in order to do away with these sufferings, then it will be very easy for us to achieve mutual understanding and respect.[47]

In a speech to a closed session of the conference, Nehru formulated what to him was the core of the nonalignment principle:

So far as I am concerned, it does not matter what war takes place: we will not take part in it unless we have to defend ourselves. If I join any of these big groups I lose my identity; I have no identity left, I have no view left ... If all the world were to be divided up between these two big blocs what would be the result? The inevitable result would be war. Therefore every step that takes place in reducing that area in the world which may be called the "unaligned area" is a dangerous step and leads to war. It reduces that objectivity, that balance, that outlook which other countries without military might can perhaps exercise.[48]

To the majority of delegates at the Bandung conference the unfinished struggles for liberation formed key parts of their concern. Many of the liberation movements were represented, and, though stopping short of endorsing armed struggle, the meeting called on France to recognize the right of the North African peoples to self-determination and independence. It also called for an end to racial discrimination in South Africa and the implementation of the UN resolutions on Palestine. But the delegates could not agree on much in terms of practical support for those territories that were still under colonial domination.

Neither did the meeting spend much time discussing what "freedom" meant in terms of political rights for the citizens of the countries represented. Instead, Nehru used the poorly developed safeguards for personal liberties within many Third World states as an argument to avoid criticizing the lack of freedom in the socialist countries – "if we examine the state of freedom, the state of individual or national freedom, the state of democratic liberties or democracy itself in the countries represented here, well, I feel many of us are lacking, terribly lacking."[49] Knowing full well the limited legitimacy of many of the governments represented at Bandung, Nehru did not want debates on democracy to overwhelm the fragile unity he and the other organizers had created. It was a move that would return to haunt the nonaligned movement throughout its existence.

The main focus of the conference's final communiqué, passed by the twenty-nine states represented, was on economic and cultural cooperation. There were high hopes that the more technologically advanced Third World countries could help the others reach their development aims, so that dependence on "outside forces" could be reduced. The communiqué particularly stressed Third World cooperation on raw material exports, and recommended, for instance, that "common policies" be adopted on "matters relating to oil" – an initiative that led to the creation of OPEC in 1960. But the main significance of the statement was the ten basic principles listed at the end that were intended to govern the relations between Third World states:

1. Respect for fundamental human rights and for the purposes and principles of the Charter of the United Nations.
2. Respect for the sovereignty and territorial integrity of all nations.
3. Recognition of the equality of all races and of the equality of all nations large and small.
4. Abstention from intervention or interference in the internal affairs of another country.
5. Respect for the right of each nation to defend itself, singly or collectively, in conformity with the Charter of the United Nations.
6. a. Abstention from the use of arrangements of collective defense to serve the particular interests of any of the big powers.
   b. Abstention by any country from exerting pressures on other countries.
7. Refraining from acts or threats of aggression or the use of force against the territorial integrity or political independence of any country.
8. Settlement of all international disputes, by peaceful means, such as negotiation, conciliation, arbitration of judicial settlement as well as other peaceful means of the parties' own choice, in conformity with the Charter of the United Nations.
9. Promotion of mutual interests and cooperation.
10. Respect for justice and international obligations.[50]

Bandung Conference

In his final speech at the conference, Nehru appealed to the superpowers to respect the principles of the Bandung declaration and start to formulating similar rules for their own interaction. "We have," the Indian prime minister told his audience,

this great opportunity, [this] unique opportunity of playing a constructive, peaceful role in the world today in a friendly way. Not that we like everything that happens in the Soviet Union or in America. [But] we should not increase the feeling of dislike and hatred. If you do things in the right manner, people will respond, and you will have good results ... [even though] the results may not be there immediately ... I submit therefore that the policy that this Conference should pursue is that of friendly coexistence.[51]

While inspiring a new sense of closeness among African and Asian countries, the Bandung conference raised grave concerns both in Washington and Moscow. To the Eisenhower administration the meeting symbolized the drift toward the Left among the neutral countries, and Secretary of State John Foster Dulles toyed with the idea of a US-sponsored "reverse Bandung" conference, in which the Western-oriented Third World countries would have the upper hand. In all, the Secretary concluded, the newfound ability of Third World countries to act in unison meant that "the scene of the battle between the free world and the Communist world was shifting."[52] In Moscow, Khrushchev welcomed the general political trend of the conference, but many of his key aides worried that too much independent international organizing among Third World leaders could make it more difficult for both the Soviet Union and local Communist parties to gain influence. In other words, while nonalignment was good if it meant breaking away from imperialism, it was bad if it meant the preservation of bourgeois rule –as in the case of the host country, where Sukarno's emphasis on Third World solidarity effectively sidelined the Indonesian Communist Party.[53]

Soviet worries increased in the summer of 1956, when Nehru, Egyptian president Gamal Abdel Nasser, and Yugoslav leader Josip Broz Tito met at the island of Brioni in the Adriatic.[54] Although Khrushchev was doing his best to woo Tito back into the international Communist movement (from which he had been ejected by Stalin in 1948), the Soviet party chief knew that the Yugoslavs were set on a course that implied both political and ideological independence from Moscow. As one key aide put it, "the idea of having a whole set of T̶ ̶ ̶ ̶ ̶ ̶ ̶ ̶ the Third World was not very palatable from the Krei̶ tive."[55] From a Third World perspective, howev̶ meeting was first and foremost a sign of how the person between its leaders were developing: when the young Egyptian leader had stopped in New Delhi on his way back from Bandung, he and Nehru had spoken not just of international affairs but also about how to deal with issues of governance and legitimacy. In his account of the meetings, the Indian prime minister had noted, with a tinge of regret, Nasser's question "What exactly was this democracy?

> In most of the Arab countries where there were parliaments and the like, there was complete corruption ... What then was he to do? It was perfectly true that at present the government of Egypt consisted of ten members of the revolutionary group. They could do what they liked, within reason of course, because the army was supporting them. He realised that this was not a satisfactory state of affairs and he would like to change it. But he just did not see what change he could bring about without a reversion to all the evils of the past ... Colonel Nasser thought that as soon as parties came in, they would be bought up by foreign powers and financed by them as they used to be financed previously. Newspapers were similarly financed by foreign powers and also individuals.[56]

One of the big disappointments in the period following Bandung was that so little happened in terms of trade and economic cooperation between Third World countries. In spite of many political attempts by governments to get such exchanges going, there were three main reasons why little came of these efforts. One was the similarity, rather than the complementarity, of most Third World economies. What these countries wanted to import was mostly available in the industrialized countries, not in other Third World states. Second, there was little obtainable credit for trading with other countries in the South, since all the main international banks centered on trade involving the capitalist countries of the North. And, third, governments themselves hindered South–South trade by insisting on barter agreements, so as not to deplete their limited reserves of hard currency. Together these and other factors made economic links between Third World countries have only limited influence on their relations during the Cold War.

Making certain that Third World states had the necessary power to defend themselves against attack and help others liberate their countries became a key issue after the 1956 Suez Crisis, which we will hear more about in the following chapter. Nasser's July decision to nationalize the Suez Canal was already discussed during the Brioni meeting, and although the precipitating event for the timing of his action seems to have been the British and American reversion of an earlier promise to finance the Aswan Dam, there is no doubt that for the Egyptian leadership the takeover of the canal was a matter of nationalist pride. The Egyptians were particularly enraged that the Western decision on the

Aswan Dam came in response to Nasser's weapons' supplies from the Eastern Bloc. The failed British, French, and Israeli invasion that followed the nationalization of the canal further underlined to many Third World leaders the need to be prepared for future imperialist interventions, if need be by seeking weapons from the Soviet Union and its allies.

The Suez intervention also sparked a much more direct Egyptian involvement in the liberation struggles in North Africa in the late 1950s. As historian Matthew Connelly has put it, the Algerian War – in part because of its international dimensions – constituted a "diplomatic revolution," in the dual sense that a liberation movement, the Algerian Front de Libération Nationale (FLN), became treated as a de facto government by much of the Third World, and that even in Europe the discourse about colonialism and state control began to shift from its previous emphasis on power, rationality, and progress to a new underlining of self-determination and human rights. At a time when the Soviets were doubtful about a direct involvement – both because Moscow did not rate the FLN's chances highly and because of it hoped to woo France in a more neutralist direction in Europe – Ahmed Ben Bella and the other leaders of the FLN found that most of their support came from Egypt and that country's newfound friends among the nonaligned, including Yugoslavia.

By 1960 the war in Algeria had become the primary symbol of Third World unity and, for many Third World leaders, a clear sign that the West was not willing to accept the full liberation of their continents from imperial domination. As Nasser explained to Tito at Brioni, there were always the best areas, the juiciest pieces of Africa and Asia – such as Algeria, Southern Africa, and Malaya – that the imperialists hoped to hang on to. During the 1960s the key task of the newly liberated countries would be to show solidarity with the countries still "imprisoned by imperialism." For leaders such as Nasser, Sukarno, and Nehru the future of the territories still under colonial control was first and foremost an issue for the Third World itself – they would welcome support from elsewhere, but it was Third World solidarity with the local resistance that in the end would force the imperialists out. The theme of solidarity with oppressed peoples also echoed in the younger generation of Europeans, especially among intellectuals and students, who were eager to make up for Europe's colonial past and thought they could do so through identifying themselves with a Third World that seemed new, vigorous, exciting, and socialist. In his preface to Fanon's *The Wretched of the Earth*, the French philosopher Jean-Paul Sartre saw Europe – through the lens of the Algerian War – as a "fat, pale continent." The future, Sartre argued, belonged to the Third World.[57]

During the 1960s the idea of the Third World as the future – in political and moral, if not economic, terms – linked the European and American "New Left" to the politics of Africa, Asia, and – increasingly – Latin America. Dubbed *tiermondiste* (thirdworldist) in French, the approach did much to internationalize both the liberation struggles and the debates over development. Its primary function, though, was as a mirror for the criticisms that some young Westerners had of their own countries as undemocratic, racist, and elitist. What they particularly were looking for in the Third World was a sense of unity of purpose, of mobilization from below, and – first and foremost – of radical action. The Cold War stability of the countries of the North disgusted them – even the Soviets were criticized for being slow, dull, and very white, especially when it came to their perceived failure in assisting Third World liberation movements effectively enough. The Port Huron statement, issued by the US Students for a Democratic Society in 1962, held up the Third World as an example: "While weapons have accelerated man's opportunity for self-destruction, the counterimpulse to life and creation are superbly manifest in the revolutionary feelings of many Asian, African and Latin American peoples. Against the individual initiative and aspiration, and social sense of organicism characteristic of these upsurges, the American apathy and stalemate stand in embarrassing contrast."[58]

After the new Algerian state was set up in 1962, its capital Algiers became a focus point for Third World radicals and for the African liberation movements, which all set up offices there. In some cases the new Algerian government, under Ben Bella's leadership, also offered weapons and military training facilities to these movements.When FLN troops had marched in victory through their main foreign base in Morocco in 1962, Nelson Mandela had been there to see them. And when those same troops had entered Algiers in triumph, Yasser Arafat had been cheering among the crowd. Both the ANC and al Fatah would later draw significant support from independent Algeria, as would the liberation movements in Angola and Guinea Bissau. Ben Bella became a key spokesman for Third World unity. At the founding meeting of the OAU in Addis Ababa in 1963, journalists described his vow to participate in an all-out effort to liberate Africa:

Pushing his notes aside, pounding the podium with both hands, very pale, the Algerian leader made an impassioned appeal in a breathless voice for aid to the Angolan rebels, reminding the assembly that Algeria's experience showed that only shared sacrifice would force open the gates of freedom. His homage to the Tunisians, Moroccans, and Egyptians who had died for Algeria provoked an emotional response ... I do not think that I have ever had such a profound sense of African unity as when I listened to Ben Bella, tears in his eyes, visibly moved, urge his listeners to rush to the assistance of the men dying south of the equator.[59]

Alongside India, Indonesia, Egypt, Ghana, and Yugoslavia, Algeria became a key member of the Non-Aligned Movement (NAM), founded in Belgrade in 1961 on the principles of self-determination, mutual economic assistance, and neutrality outlined at Bandung. Twenty-five countries participated at the first conference, but by the second head-of-state meeting, in Cairo in 1964, that number had almost doubled.[60] The key political content of the Belgrade meeting was to underline the solidarity of the member states, to warn the superpowers against spreading the Cold War into the Third World, and to appeal to all countries to forego war as a means of settling international disputes. The preamble to its first declaration concluded: "Aware that ideological differences are necessarily a part of the growth of human society, the participating countries consider that peoples and Governments shall refrain from any use of ideologies for the purpose of waging cold war, exercising pressure, or imposing their will."[61] Meeting in Belgrade as the 1961 Berlin Crisis was peaking, all heads of state present sent identical personal letters to Khrushchev and Kennedy, in which they warned against the threat of war and appealed for a peaceful solution. Lecturing the superpowers on the conduct of international relations was a powerful sign that the Third World was coming of age.

In spite of the continued organizational growth of the Non-Aligned Movement, 1962 – the year when Algeria finally won its independence – also saw the beginning of the unraveling of the spirit of Bandung. The Sino-Indian border war was a devastating blow to the Bandung promise of peaceful negotiations, and removed much of the authority India had had as a Gandhian arbiter of international disputes. Its war with another founding member of the NAM, Pakistan, over Kashmir three years later meant that Moscow and Washington had to step in as peace brokers, and that India increasingly leant toward the Soviets for its security needs. The 1967 Middle East crisis was another setback for the nonaligned idea – while Nasser had hoped that Third World solidarity would strengthen his hand, it was Soviet support that he had to fall back on as his armies were crushed by the Israelis. By the end of the 1960s all the initiators of Bandung were gone from the scene; Nehru died in 1964, Sukarno, Ben Bella, and Nkrumah were overthrown in military coups in 1965/66. Nasser died, with his hopes of Arab and Third World unity unfulfilled, in 1970. That same year the NAM finally was able to arrange its third conference, in the Zambian capital Lusaka, but with much of the initial optimism long gone.

By the late 1960s the lack of representativeness and the economic difficulties that produced domestic political instability also frustrated the work that the NAM and the OAU had pledged to do in support of the liberation movements. The leaders of some of these movements, such as the PAIGC's Amílcar Cabral, began claiming that many new regimes were instruments of "neocolonialism"; more preoccupied with their good relationship with European and American bankers and investors than in mobilizing the masses for revolutionary action at home or abroad. In his speech at the deposed Ghanaian leader Kwame Nkrumah's funeral in Guinea in 1972, Cabral cited Nkrumah's work *Neocolonialism – the Last Stage of Imperialism,* published the year before he was overthrown, as evidence of how the father of African nationalism had turned toward Marxism in his later years. "How much of the [army's] successful betrayal of Ghana was linked to questions of class struggle, contradictions in social structure, the role of the Party and ... the armed forces?" Cabral asked.[62] His own answer was clear: these were the links that counted, and Nkrumah – in spite of his heroic stature – had discovered them too late. Only through the instruments of Marxism–Leninism could a new generation of Third World leaders set up states that were truly independent, internationalist, and economically viable.[63]

By the late 1960s much of the wind had left the ideological sails of the Bandung generation's radical nativist elite. Either they had been kicked out by the military forces they themselves had been so eager to establish – such as in Ghana, Indonesia, or Algeria – and replaced by authoritarian and mostly nonideological dictatorships. Or their native forms of socialism had come under pressure from a new and more radical generation with Marxist ideals, such as in Julius Nyerere's Tanzania. In some states, as we will see in later chapters, parts of the military itself was radicalized in a Marxist direction. This turn toward Marxism in some Third World states was possible because of the practical failings of the *tiermondiste* approach (which even so was able to hold out as an ideal in Europe and to a lesser degree in America well into the 1970s) and because Marxist theory was offering exactly those qualities that the person-oriented, charismatic, and amorphous *tiermondisme* was seen as lacking. In the eyes of many in the postindependence generation, Marxism, in its Leninist form, was valuable because it was structured, defined, and first and foremost scientific.

The turn toward Marxism among some Third World elites and within the liberation movements had significant implications for the Cold War. While the Soviet rediscovery of the Third World in the late 1950s and had been based on limited but strategically important alliationalist forces, some of the new relations that were developing between Moscow and the Third World from 1970 on were based on a common political theory, and were therefore intended to be more comprehensive and pervasive. The broader ideological developments in the Third World were, of course, not the only background to this turn; as we shall see, the US war in Vietnam and the international effects of the Cuban revolution also played significant roles. But the overall disappointment with the paths chosen by the first postindependence leaders both domestically and internationally was a key reason why so many of the new power holders, especially in Africa, turned toward the Soviet model in the 1970s.

4   Creating the Third World: the United States confronts revolution

In the aftermath of World War II the United States intervened repeatedly to influence the processes of change that were taking place throughout the Third World. In some quarters in Europe (and often in the Third World itself) it became usual to speak of America replacing the European colonial powers in their struggles against anticolonial radicalism. But, as we shall see, these interventions were generally grounded in US perceptions and beliefs, and were not primarily attempts at helping out bankrupt and war-weary European powers. At the core of American Third World involvement stood the Cold War anti-Communist agenda and the exceptional interventionist capabilities that the United States possessed after the Second World War ended, a war which had made it, for the first time in its history, the dominant capitalist power, economically and militarily, as well as ideologically.

In economic terms, the US dominance was absolute, both as a reflection of American growth and because of wartime destruction elsewhere. In 1950 the US gross domestic product (GDP) was higher than all of Europe's put together, and possibly equal to that of Europe plus the Soviet Union. Its annual average growth rate since the outbreak of World War I had been almost three times that of Britain or of France, its GDP per capita was twice that of Western Europe, and productivity was almost three times the European average. And even though most of its economic growth was still concentrated at home, by 1950 the United States was by far the world's leading exporter and foreign investor.[1]

The modern Third World was created in the shadow of American predominance, and many of the leaders of the newly independent countries looked to the United States for support and direction. At the same time, the US gaze was firmly turned toward Europe – there was no Marshall Plan for the countries that emerged from colonialism, and American support for independence was increasingly tempered by its fear of Communism. US postwar policies therefore helped to give birth to the extreme inequality that has existed between the developed capitalist states and the Third World over the past two generations, both in terms of power and economic resources. This relegation did not take place because American policy makers lacked the will to globalize its model of development – as we have seen, that drive existed as a significant element of their ideology, both in Europe and in the Third World. It was, rather, the combination of ideological predilections, racial stereotyping, and Cold War political and strategic aims that made America become part of the Third World's problem.

Why did the United States intervene in the Third World as often as it did during the Cold War? One obvious reason was its capabilities, another its taking on of the responsibility for a global capitalist system. Very often, as we shall see, US involvements were perceived in America as *defensive* interventions, mainly against left-wing or Communist movements. Still, Washington always remained preoccupied with structural solutions to the Communist challenge, meaning – in the language of the 1950s – *development*, or becoming more like America. The political scientist Douglas Macdonald is therefore right when he calls US Cold War interventions "interventions for reform." But the American perceptual dilemma was that in a Cold War setting, Third World domestic political conditions often needed to be changed first, before US-inspired reform could begin to take hold. Such change generally meant the defeat of radical attempts at controlling the political order, and it was in order to produce such a result that most US interventions took place, even when military strategy, economic gain, or favors to friends also played a role in the decision making.

In overall terms, the US Cold War mindset was implemented only slowly with regard to the Third World. The late 1940s was a period of transition. Even NSC 68 – the most consciously ideological of all foreign policy documents from the Truman administration – saw the American objective as "with our allies and the former subject peoples to seek to create a world society based on the principle of consent. Its framework cannot be inflexible. It will consist of many national communities of great and varying abilities and resources." But the same document also gave the United States a special responsibility for imposing order:

In a shrinking world, which now faces the threat of atomic warfare, it is not an adequate objective merely to seek to check the Kremlin design, for the absence of order among nations is becoming less and less tolerable. This fact imposes on us, in our own interests, the responsibility of world leadership. It demands that we make the attempt, and accept the risks inherent in it, to bring about order and justice by means consistent with the principles of freedom and democracy.[2]

The United States and the first postcolonial crises

The revolutionary situations that existed at the end of the war in many parts of Asia constituted the first crises of US interventionism during the

Cold War. Where, as we have already seen, Stalin had detected no hope for successful Communist revolts, the Americans were getting increasingly fearful that such events were on the horizon in a vast area stretching from Korea to Iran. Soviet policy toward Qavam's government in Teheran – and especially the delayed withdrawal of the Red Army from the northern parts of the country in 1946 – aroused the Truman administration's suspicions of Soviet plans to get control of Middle Eastern oil supplies, helped by local radicals. And even though US assurances of support for the young shah, Mohammed Reza Pahlavi, coupled with diplomatic threats against the Soviets, assisted Teheran in withstanding Moscow's pressure, the fear still remained in Washington that the Soviets could use future nationalist upheavals in the region to cut off the oil supplies that could fuel an economic resurgence of Europe and Japan.

The situation in China was even more of a challenge for US policy in the early Cold War period. American distaste for the domestic situation in China after they themselves had helped Jiang Jieshi's forces take control of the country in 1945 led to a decision-making dilemma that lasted until the Communist victory in the civil war was obvious in early 1949. On the one hand President Truman feared Soviet influence in China and was prepared to resist it. On the other hand he detested the inefficiency, corruption, and brutality that he saw in Jiang's Guomindang regime. As had been the case during World War II, US postwar policy toward China centered on forcing the regime to reform along the lines postulated by its American advisers, while increasing military aid to the same regime as it dug itself deeper into political and strategic trouble. One US problem in China was that the Chinese Communists – Jiang's chief opponents – represented many "modern" values that the Americans admired: organization, discipline, self-sacrifice. At the same time the Communist Party was increasingly seen as closely allied to Moscow and therefore a threat not only to US aims in China, but also to American policies elsewhere in East and Southeast Asia. The schizophrenic US aid policy toward Jiang's regime – increasing the amount of aid while doubting the survivability of the state – set a pattern for future problems in US policy, not least in Indochina.

But US ire was not just raised against Third World partners gone bad. It was also directed against those Western Europeans who did not understand that their clinging on to the colonial enterprise might endanger the US mission to battle Soviet Communism. As we have seen, there had been scant sympathy for European imperialist programs in the United States even in the early twentieth century. But after World War II any attempts to defy local nationalism by bankrupt, inefficient European governments under threat from Communism at home (and therefore dependent on American aid there) simply did not make sense to Washington. The only exceptions were cases in which the immediate alternative to colonial government was Communism, such as in the British colony Malaya, where the returning imperial forces were fighting a Communist-led insurgency. But even there the aim would have to be the gradual building of a real nationalist alternative to colonial rule.

Elsewhere in Asia the Truman administration was less charitable of imperial designs. NSC 51, a report on US policy toward Southeast Asia presented to the National Security Council in March 1949, made it clear that "19th century imperialism is no longer a practicable system in SEA [Southeast Asia] excepting in the short run in Malaya ... Colonialism is successful where the subject people are unsophisticated and acquiescent, as in the case of certain South Pacific islanders. Once the dependent people, even if a small minority of them, acquire a degree of worldly wisdom and personal ambition, complications set in. Discontent, resistance and political psychoses develop." But while the United States – in the Philippines – and Britain – in India and Burma – had treated these symptoms with the only possible remedy – independence under a local non-Communist leadership – "French and Dutch imperialism have, however, tended to undo the salubrious effect created by enlightened American and British policy ... Thus, the short-sighted blunders of two members of the Atlantic Community have done much to cancel out the progress made on behalf of the whole community by its two principal members."

Although remarkably thin on concrete policy proposals, NSC 51 refuted claims that the United States should refrain from facilitating Asian processes of decolonization because of the domestic political effects the loss of the colonies would have within Europe. Such a proposal, the report found,

has its roots in ideological negativism. Now the essence of our struggle with the USSR is ideological. And the crucial issue in SEA is clear-cut – colonial imperialism versus militant nationalism. In such circumstances to attempt evasion of an obvious ideological issue is (1) objectively, to yield much of the field of conflict to our adversaries, and (2) subjectively, to subvert our own ideological integrity – that is, to deny subconsciously the heritage and philosophic concepts which are inner reasons that we are, for all our shortcomings, not only great but good, and therefore a dynamic force in the mind of the world.[3]

The conflict in Indonesia was, for the Truman administration, a key example of the chaos that misguided attempts at reimposing European colonialism could lead to in Asia. The United States had, through the CIA, developed excellent contacts with some of the Indonesian independence leaders, including Sukarno, and especially after the Indonesian Communists tried – unsuccessfully – to challenge the nativist leadership in September 1948, the United States felt that a handover of power to the Indonesians could not happen fast enough. When the Netherlands government instead attempted to crush the nativist independence movement in December 1948, the CIA reported serious concern: not only had the operation weakened the prestige of the United Nations, where the United States had taken the lead in achieving a peaceful solution, but it would undermine political and economic stability both in Indonesia and in the Netherlands, while providing the Soviets with a powerful propaganda tool. Even worse,

the Dutch action has precipitated the emergence of a Pan-Asian bloc which ... may follow an independent path. While it is not aligned with the USSR, this Pan-Asian bloc may become strongly antagonistic toward the US because of US identification in Far Eastern minds both as champions of a discredited regime in China and as a sponsor of continued control by Western colonial powers in Southeast Asia. A Pan-Asian bloc under Indian leadership, even though unsympathetic to the USSR, might become an effective instrument of Soviet policy.[4]

In the case of the Netherlands – a small and insignificant European ally – the Truman administration was quick to pull the plug on whatever aspirations its government may have had to settle its colonial problem by force. Even though the administration had been reluctant to threaten the government in the Hague directly as long as Dutch–Indonesian negotiations were taking place, the 1948/49 "police action" by the Netherlands' colonial authorities forced Washington's hand, and in March 1949 Secretary of State Dean Acheson told the Dutch that they would lose both Marshall Plan funding and military support under the NATO plans if their opposition to a negotiated settlement was not "promptly removed."[5] Having the fighting continue was a risk the United States was not willing to take. The Dutch government had no choice but to give in and sign an agreement recognizing the new Indonesian regime under Sukarno. As NSC 51 had noted that same month, "19th century imperialism is no antidote to Communism in revolutionary colonial areas. It is rather an ideal culture for the breeding of the Communist virus. The satisfaction of militant nationalism is the first essential requirement for resistance to Stalinism."[6]

The exception to this rule was, as we have seen, the British colony of Malaya, primarily because Washington believed that the only short-term alternative to the reimposition of control from London was a takeover by the Malayan Communist Party (MCP). The United States supported the British strategy of attempting to gain support for the war against the MCP – dominated by Malayan Chinese – among the Malay population, while slowly preparing the country for independence. The plan, wrote the

American Consul in Kuala Lumpur, was "excellent in conception but weak in implementation" – the United States complained that Britain was not willing to send in the necessary resources to win a military victory.[7] This concern increased after the Korean War broke out in June 1950, when Washington began fearing the MCP – even when driven on the defensive – acting as a bridgehead for PRC expansion into Southeast Asia. As in Indonesia, the Americans therefore attempted to build contacts with non-Communist Malayan nationalists, even though they were not enthusiastic about some of the British favorites, such as Tunku Abdul Rahman, the later prime minister of Malaysia, whom the American consul in Penang saw as "a small and weak man."[8]

Inspite of its prewar decision to grant independence, the United States faced similar problems in its own Southeast Asian colony, the Philippines. The first elected president of the Philippine Republic, Manuel Roxas, had been a close collaborator of the Japanese occupation regime, and in spite of his willingness to give the Americans the terms they wanted in order to withdraw (including economic access and military bases), he was less than ideal from the US perspective, especially after his government increasingly appeared hostage to the interests of large landowners and to the Catholic Church. Roxas' attempts at crushing the popular Communist-led People's Anti-Japanese Army (in Tagalog, Hukbo ng Bayan Laban sa Hapon, or Huk for short) backfired, and in 1947 the Huk rebellion spread all over central Luzon. By 1948 the alarm bells had begun to go off in Washington, and the US-led Joint Military Advisory Group began receiving more support in terms of weapons and advisers. Roxas' convenient death in April 1948 helped the US begin to design a counterinsurgency strategy, assisted by the young officer Ramon Magsaysay, a US-trained former military governor of Zambales. The key to the US strategy was the recognition that social problems were at the heart of the rebellion. Major Edward Lansdale, one of the chief US military advisers, wrote in his diary that

most of the Huks are now youngsters under twenty with 'old men' in their early thirties as leaders. Most of them believe in the rightness of what they're doing, even though some of the leaders are on the communist side of politics. And, there is a bad situation, needing reform, which still exists in central Luzon. Agrarian reforms still seems to exist only on paper and I suppose armed complaint is a natural enough thing after the guerrilla heritage of most of these people.[9]

With Magsaysay installed as Secretary of Defense, the US counter-insurgency campaign went into high gear in 1950, after the Communist victory in China. The Huks had hoped to launch an offensive against the capital, Manila, toward the end of the year, but the capture of most of the

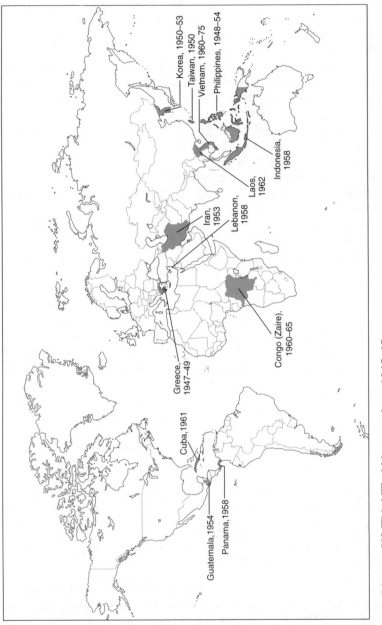

Map 4   US Third World interventions, 1945–65.

Korea, 1950–53

Taiwan, 1950

Vietnam, 1960–75

Philippines, 1948–54

Indonesia, 1958

Laos, 1962

Iran, 1953

Lebanon, 1958

Congo (Zaire), 1960–65

Greece, 1947–49

Cuba, 1961

Guatemala, 1954

Panama, 1958

Huk leadership in a US-led intelligence operation put an end to the offensive plans – instead, a reorganized and expanded Philippine Army, funded and trained by the United States, began taking the fighting to the areas controlled by the guerrillas. Supported by airpower and – for the first time – the use of napalm, the Philippine Army made considerable gains against the Huks between 1951 and 1953. But the reason the rebellion collapsed was more political than military. The Huk leaders – including the Philippine Communists – could not agree between themselves on a strategy to follow, and Manila, belatedly, came up with a real program for defeating its opponents, including promises of land reform, anticorruption measures, and improving the behavior of its troops. It also offered enticements to get guerrillas to defect, such as land grants to those who surrendered and cooperated with the authorities. Most importantly, Magsaysay's successful campaign for the presidency in 1953 convinced many people that the period of authoritarian and oligarchic rule was about to pass, and that active resistance against the government was no longer necessary.

Washington's – and especially the Pentagon's – reading of the end of the Philippine rebellion stressed the US-led counterinsurgency operation and not the changing political realities. Lonsdale and his men were credited with finding exactly the right mix of the carrot and the stick to defeat a popular Communist guerrilla movement. Lonsdale's second in command, Charles Bohannan – who later, like his boss, would go on to staff the US Military Advisory Group in South Vietnam – stressed the qualities of the US personnel who served in the operation as preconditions for success:

a. They were, or had been, officers of the US Army.
b. They knew, had worked and fought with hundreds of Filipinos, had gained their respect . . .
c. They knew their business . . .
d. They had top-level US backing stateside, and tolerance or cooperation from local US authorities. (Note well, this cannot be assumed in future situations, it must be mandatory [that] . . . top local US authorities . . . at least cooperate with such a team.)
e. They were feared by the local chief of state, they had the full cooperation of the leader of the effort (the Sec. Def.).
f. They were ingenious, adaptable, rather unscrupulous bastards, and one, the senior, was a master salesman.[10]

In spite of the successes that many in the State Department, the Pentagon, and the CIA felt that the United States were having in Southeast Asia, the failed US policy in China had a very negative effect on the domestic policy debate with regard to the Third World. Public rhetoric about its friendship with the Jiang Jieshi regime and the increasingly anti-Soviet hysteria in the United States caught up with the Truman administration in 1950 in a very US-centered debate on the "loss of China." But while those who had been in charge of Truman's China policy were being hounded out of the State Department by the McCarthyite Right and also while the Korean War led to a sense of the United States being at war with "global" Communism, Washington's policies on Third World issues hardened considerably. In the Senate, Joseph McCarthy condemned all attempts at making peace with Third World nationalism as weakness: "We must not fight under the leadership of perfumed, dilettante diplomats. We cannot fight successfully under the leadership of those who are either half loyal or disloyal to what we are fighting for."[11] But even General Dwight D. Eisenhower – serving in 1950 as the president of what the senator would undoubtedly have seen as a rather "perfumed" university – feared that the United States was in deep trouble in the Third World. Already before the outbreak of the Korean War, the general confided to himself that "I believe Asia is lost with Japan, P[hilippine] I[slands], N[etherlands] E[ast] I[ndies] and even Australia under threat. India itself is not safe!"[12]

Until 1950 many US officials had felt that the retrograde policies of some European colonial powers were as much of a problem as the revolutionary aspirations of Third World leaders. With the Communist victory in China and under pressure from domestic public opinion, such attitudes were gradually replaced by a stress on ideological commitment and military strategy, in which the whole world was seen as divided between two camps. The best example of the gradual dilution of the postwar approach is Washington's policy on French attempts at regaining control of its colonies in Indochina. While the Truman administration in 1948 had despaired of France ever realizing the pervasive depth of nationalist feeling in the Third World, by 1950 Vietnam had become a security issue, in which the threat posed by Ho Chi Minh's Communism outweighed French intransigence in providing real self-government to Indochina. The United States therefore recognized Bao Dai's "State of Vietnam," fully aware that the majority of his countrymen viewed the former emperor as a tool of the French. It was, Washington admitted, an interim solution, while waiting for "true" nationalists – untainted by the Communist brush – to emerge.

But by 1952 it was fast becoming clear that it was French patience with a costly and unproductive war that was wearing thin, in spite of increased military and financial support from the United States. "It is questionable," noted the British ambassador to Paris, "how long the French, not a notably disinterested people, will continue to ruin themselves in a cause which they do not now regard as primarily their own."[13] The new Eisenhower administration, coming into office in 1953, therefore saw the French military's plans to force the Vietminh on the defensive through a series of large and spectacular military operations as a godsend, since battlefield victories would stiffen French resolve and encourage anti-Communist nationalists to step forward to join in government. The president agreed to provide $500 million per year for the purpose. He also sent Vice President Richard Nixon to visit Vietnam in December 1953. Upon his return, Nixon let a national television and radio audience know that "if Indochina falls, Thailand is put in an almost impossible situation. The same is true of Malaya with its rubber and tin. The same is true of Indonesia. If Indochina goes under Communist domination the whole of Southeast Asia will be threatened and that means that the economic and military security of Japan will be inevitably endangered also."[14]

The vice president's worries about Japan could be extended to Europe as well, and possibly – as we will see later in this chapter – further afield. By the early 1950s the United States had taken over a role as protector of the international capitalist market and therefore extended its universal ideological resistance against Communism into the global strategic sphere. The domino theory was a fixation that covered not just Southeast Asia: by subsuming under Communism any resistance to Third World governments that swore allegiance to capitalism, democracy, and an alliance with the United States, Washington wilfully reduced its potential for real alliances with popular nationalist movements. It was this self-inflicted isolation from associations of the more syncretic kind that forced the US to intervene repeatedly in the Third World during the height of the Cold War.

Jakarta Axiom

Iran, Suez, and the new American role

The 1948 "Jakarta Axiom" – the idea that radical Third World nationalism of the nativist kind could be of long-term advantage to the United States – was ultimately defeated in Teheran in 1953. The new Eisenhower administration saw the nativist policies of the Iranian government, and especially its nationalization of the country's oil production, as a threat to US positions in the Middle East and as a possible prelude to a Communist takeover. If such a revolution happened, Secretary of State John Foster Dulles told the president, "not only would the free world be deprived of the enormous assets represented by Iranian oil production and reserves, but the Russians would secure these assets and thus henceforth be free of any anxiety about their petroleum situation. Worse still, Mr. Dulles pointed out, if Iran succumbed to the Communists there was little doubt that in short order the other areas of the Middle East, with some sixty percent of the world's oil reserves, would fall into Communist control."[15]

The development of an oil industry exploiting the giant reserves around the Persian Gulf in the 1930s had given a completely new strategic significance to the Middle Eastern region. American companies had begun investing in the area before World War II, and in the postwar period the US-operated Arabian American Oil Company (ARAMCO), operating out of Saudi Arabia, had become by far the largest exporter of oil to Europe. For the al Saud royal dynasty the link with the Americans was a godsend, in spite of the spread of US cultural influence that the Sauds – as conservative Wahhabite Muslims – tried to contain as best they could. American money enabled the regime to fasten its grip on the huge territory that it claimed to control without having to give concessions to opposition groups. For Washington, significant strategic benefits came out of American economic involvement in the Gulf, especially after the Truman administration had forced ARAMCO to split its revenues equally with the Saudis in 1950. While the British influence in Iraq and Iran was coming under pressure from local nationalists – in 1948 there had been rioting and demonstrations in Baghdad against the renewal of the Anglo-Iraqi treaty – Washington saw its own relations with the House of Saud as a partnership in which local needs were taken into consideration.

The problem the United States had faced in Iran ever since it began intervening in that country's affairs during World War II was not dissimilar to decolonization conflicts elsewhere. Since the 1920s the Anglo-Iranian Oil Company (AIOC) – later British Petroleum – had run the southern parts of the country very much as a colonial power, exporting huge profits to its stockholders in London. The wartime allied occupation and the Iranian government's dependence on postwar Western support to stave off Soviet pressure made the AIOC's political position stronger than it had ever been, and the new British Labour government seemed as disinclined as its predecessors to force the company to begin sharing its profits with the Iranians. Meanwhile, the workers in the oilfields around Abadan lived in misery, receiving on average less than fifty cents per day, with no vacations, no health care, and no insurance provided by the company. In hastily constructed shantytowns where people lived without electricity or any form of sanitation, the Iranian Communist Party – the Tudeh – was making a rapid political comeback in spite of being persecuted by the Shah's police.

As in Southeast Asia, the United States faced a difficult balancing act in Iran, with concern over British insensitivity to local demands on the one hand and increasing worry over Soviet designs on Iran on the other. Iran shared a 1,600-kilometer border with the Soviet Union and Stalin had made his long-term plans clear in 1946, Truman thought. While the United States itself was largely self-sufficient in oil and petroleum products, Moscow could exploit political chaos in Iran to take control of the energy supplies that Western Europe and Japan depended on for their reconstruction. Unlike in Malaya, where Washington admired London's stand, British blockheadedness in Iran was playing right into the hands of the Communists. Sent by Truman on a special mission to Teheran in mid-1951, Averell Harriman reported that the "situation that has developed here is a tragic example of absentee management combined with world-wide growth of nationalism in underdeveloped countries."[16] It was a challenge that the United States had to take up.

The only point of light for Washington in a rather dire situation in Iran was the young shah, Mohammed Reza Pahlavi. By the late 1940s the shah had begun to put aside his playboy reputation and take what he saw as his God-given right to rule seriously. His model for reforms was the United States – he had visited the country in 1949 and came away profoundly impressed with American industry and standard of living. He liked the dynamism he found in the United States and its emphasis on education and rapid progress, comparing it favorably with the "backwardness" he saw in his own country. He was also impressed with the reception that was accorded him (especially, it is said, by having been made the honorary captain of George Washington University's football team). Back in Teheran, he was increasingly looking to the United States for help with overcoming those he saw as responsible for the country's internal ills: reactionary clerics, power-hungry feudalists, left-wing rabble-rousers, and foreign imperialists.[17]

The situation in Iran reached crisis proportions after the shah in 1951 was forced to accept the parliament's (Majlis) choice for prime minister, Mohammad Mossadeq, and his plan to nationalize the concessions of the Anglo-Iranian Oil Company. Mossadeq was born in 1880 into Iran's feudal elite and was educated at the Ecole Nationale des Sciences Politiques in Paris and later in Switzerland, becoming the first Iranian to earn a European Ph.D. After World War I he became a proponent of Iranian nativist nationalism, lambasting the monarchy as sellouts to foreign interests and advocating a return to true Iranian values. A man with a strong emotional appeal to many Iranians because of his rhetorical style and his principled and largely secularly based opposition to the Pahlavi family, Mossadeq's government became a rallying point for both left-wing and nativist nationalists. Even some of the Shia religious leaders supported him, although the Islamists – such as Ruhollah

Khomeini – from the beginning denounced him and his government as infidel.

While the Truman administration had attempted to mediate in the oil dispute between the Iranian and the British governments, the new Republican leadership in Washington saw Mossadeq as playing into the hands of the Communists and the Soviets. Even though John Foster Dulles knew that it was the British embargo – imposed in response to the oil nationalization – that more than anything was responsible for the deteriorating social and economic situation in Iran, he was unwilling to take the risk of Mossadeq remaining in power. The Iranian premier was, according to the new US ambassador in Teheran, Loy Henderson, "lacking in stability," "clearly dominated by emotions and prejudices," and "not quite sane."[18] Even with President Eisenhower wondering aloud at an NSC meeting on 4 March 1953 why it was not possible "to get some of the people in these down-trodden countries to like us instead of hating us," his administration was edging closer to taking up a British plan for the overthrow of Mossadeq's government in alliance with a few high-ranking military officers and the shah.[19] The go-ahead for Operation AJAX – the first postwar US attempt at removing a legitimate Third World government – was given by the White House on 14 June 1953.

To begin with the whole plan seemed to go terribly wrong for the CIA team in Teheran and their British partners. In spite of his links to the Americans, the shah was reluctant to take part in overturning the Iranian constitution. On 15 August, the day the coup was to have been carried out, the Pahlavi prince was on his way out of the country "for a vacation" instead of facing up to Mossadeq. Worse, the colonel who was going to spearhead the coup was arrested by forces loyal to the government. For a few days power hung in the balance, but in the end the US strategy of manipulating public opinion through staged attacks on religious figures, through massive bribery of local leaders and of the press, and through helping to organize anti-Mossadeq rallies bore fruit. After four days of increasing chaos in the streets, the military sided with the man the shah had named as his new prime minister, General Fazlollah Zahedi, who during the riots had been in hiding with the CIA station. Mossadeq was arrested. The operation, the CIA later concluded, had not been based on the wrong assumptions, but "upon the principle of strong, positive action to make the assumptions come true."[20]

The Iranian coup was in many ways a new departure for US foreign policy in the Third World, except, of course, toward Latin America. For the first time Washington had organized in detail the overthrow of a foreign government outside its own hemisphere, and – as the CIA post-mortem made abundantly clear – the results were to its satisfaction. Not only had Iran been steered away from chaos and a possible Communist takeover, but Washington had also shown its hesitant and uncertain European allies that hard decisions sometimes had to be taken when confronted with Third World crises. Most importantly, however, Iran after the coup had been set on the course toward a stable economic and political development under the shah's leadership, many in Washington thought. On the latter point, however, the Eisenhower administration was to be disappointed. Not recognizing the balance the shah had to strike in pursuing a revolution from above – with regard to local power holders, the army, the clergy, as well as an increasingly threatening regional situation – Dulles was disappointed that the Iranian authorities did not pursue an even more radical policy. "We still take a gloomy view of the Shah's future unless he can be persuaded to undertake some dramatic reforms," the secretary told Eisenhower in mid-1958.[21]

By the late 1950s, however, potential trouble in Iran had slid down the list of Washington's priorities compared with real trouble in the Arab world. In 1952 nativist revolutionary officers had taken power in Egypt, abolishing the monarchy and setting the most populous Arab state on the road to radical reform. Two years later a coalition led by the vaguely socialist and strongly pan-Arab Baath Party had won elections in Syria. A secular form of nationalism seemed to be strengthening all over the region, with anticolonialism and Arab unity as its primary aims. The Baath – certainly the strongest proponent of this political direction – was founded in 1943 in Damascus by Michel Aflaq and Salah ad-Din al-Bitar, with the former as its key ideological leader. Aflaq – a Syrian from a Greek Orthodox family, educated at the Sorbonne – saw a single Arab nation artificially divided by European imperialists. The mission of the Baath Party was to restore a unified state, along with the greatness of the Arab people. The revolutionary process, Aflaq claimed, would be headed by a pan-Arab Baath high command, operating within a strongly authoritarian organizational structure, borrowed in part from European Communist and Fascist parties of the 1930s. The Baath ideology claimed to transcend divisions of class, religion, and culture, and in the 1950s focused much of its anger on Middle Eastern Communists and Islamists who were seen as the spoilers of the pan-Arab idea.

The new Egyptian strongman, Colonel Gamal Abdel Nasser, was born in 1918, the son of a postman with a fascination with Arab culture and history. Already as a teenager Nasser began seeing himself as chosen to rescue the Arab people from foreign domination. After the unity of the Arabs had been restored, and Cairo had become the headquarters of the Arab revolution, it would be the duty of the new power to assist in the liberation of the Muslim world and of Africa, both of which looked to

Egypt for inspiration. Showing his reading of European literature as well as Arab mythology, Nasser wrote in 1953:

For some reason it seems to me that within the Arab circle there is a role, wandering aimlessly in search of a hero. And I do not know why it seems to me that this role, exhausted by its wanderings, has at last settled down, tired and weary, near the borders of our country and is beckoning to us to move ... When I consider the 80 million Muslims in Indonesia, and the 50 million in China, and the millions in Malaya, Siam [Thailand] and Burma, and the nearly 100 million in Pakistan, and the more than 100 million in the Middle East, and the 40 million in the Soviet Union ... I emerge with a sense of the tremendous possibilities which we might realize through the cooperation of all these Muslims, a cooperation going not beyond the bounds of their natural loyalty to their own countries, but nonetheless enabling them and their brothers in faith to wield power wisely and without limit ... And now I go back to that wandering mission in search of a hero to play it. Here is the role. Here are the lines, and here is the stage. We alone, by virtue of our place, can perform the role.[22]

The military government that Nasser led was, however, aware that it had to solidify its own power before it could move against British influence in Egypt which it so detested. In a series of meetings with Dulles in May 1953, Nasser had insisted that it was British imperialism, not Soviet Communism, that threatened the region. In the Arab countries, he told the secretary of state, "the match is between two teams, Communism and nationalism. And if *you* insist on playing, you are going to spoil the game for the others."[23] What Nasser wanted was for the United States to stand aside while Arab nationalism defeated its external and internal opponents.

But in order to defeat these enemies – especially after the Iranian coup of 1953 – Nasser realized that he had to create a wide network of allies. As we have already seen, Bandung was a watershed for Nasser, who attended as head of the Egyptian delegation. From 1955 onwards his links with the nonaligned countries were strong and lasting, with an especially close relationship with Tito's Yugoslavia. In Moscow, too, Nasser saw an potential ally, albeit one that would have to be handled with great care. He explained to Tito in July 1956, when meeting with him and Nehru at the Yugoslav island of Brioni, that buying weapons and other supplies from the Soviets was a way of increasing one's options. Based on the Iranian precedent, Nasser knew that the Americans were unlikely to help with getting rid of the British Suez bases and returning the Palestinian refugees to their homeland, the two problems that were increasingly at the forefront of the Egyptian leader's priorities. But he was still hopeful that the United States would eventually provide some of the economic assistance that Egypt badly needed for its development projects.

By the time of the Brioni meeting, Nasser had already made up his mind for the first step in what he envisaged to be a long campaign to drive imperialism out of the Middle East: He would nationalize the Suez Canal to show Arabs everywhere that he was serious about confronting the Europeans and to force the Americans to reconsider their refusal to provide aid, communicated to him in the wake of the Soviet–Egyptian arms deal. Only if he showed himself as a man of action would the superpowers take him seriously, Nasser thought. After nationalizing the canal on 26 July 1956, Cairo immediately started talks with the Soviet Union concerning further aid and weapons assistance, while making certain that both the British and the Americans knew what was going on. Egypt was playing for high stakes for control of its territory and for its position within the Arab world.[24]

For the Eisenhower administration, the Suez Crisis came at a particularly unfortunate moment. Not only were there US presidential elections coming up in November 1956, but Washington was also working hard to score propaganda victories from Soviet troubles in Poland and Hungary. If Britain and France – the European coproprietors of the canal – intervened to protect their position, their American ally would be put on the defensive *vis-à-vis* the Soviet Union and would also lose any chance of prying Nasser loose from Moscow's grip through appeals to his nationalism. In other words, in spite of Washington's growing concern over Cairo's leaning toward the Soviets, Eisenhower and Dulles did not want a hasty intervention against a popular, determined, and reasonably capable Arab regime, which was set to remain in place whatever happened to the Suez Canal. Eisenhower warned the new British prime minister, Anthony Eden, that if an intervention did take place, "the peoples of the Near East and of North Africa and, to some extent, all of Asia and all of Africa, would be consolidated against the West to a degree which, I fear, could not be overcome in a generation and, perhaps, not even in a century, particularly having in mind the capacity of the Russians to make mischief."[25]

When the British and the French, joined by the Israelis, in late October disregarded US pressure and invaded Egypt, Washington was caught in a quandary. While sympathetic to the aims of the invaders, the president was furious at the way he had been treated by his British allies. "We should let them know at once," Eisenhower bristled, "that we recognize that much is on their side in this dispute with the Egyptians, but that nothing justifies double-crossing us."[26] A week later, after a ceasefire had been established, the United States used economic means – pressure against the value of the British currency and reduction of US oil deliveries to Europe – to ensure a swift withdrawal of foreign forces from Egypt.

Having lost militarily, Nasser kept control of the canal and gained the status of a hero in the eyes of most Arabs. His response to the European attempts to gain control of the canal was taught to schoolchildren all over the Middle East:

I am speaking in the name of every Egyptian Arab and in the name of all free countries and of all those who believe in liberty and are ready to defend it. I am speaking in the name of principles proclaimed by these countries in the Atlantic Charter. But they are now violating these principles and it has become our lot to shoulder the responsibility of reaffirming and establishing them anew.[27]

One of the key reasons why the United States had reacted so angrily to the invasion was Soviet attempts at using the Suez Crisis to increase their influence among Arab nationalists and to portray their own crushing of the Hungarian rebellion in a better light. In Communist Party Presidium (Politburo) discussions and also in his communications with Washington, Khrushchev proposed a joint US–Soviet peacekeeping intervention, under UN auspices, and threatened to send Soviet forces "to enforce the peace" in the Middle East even if the Americans did not join in. Dulles felt that the United States was being "forced to choose between following in the footsteps of Anglo-French colonialism in Asia and Africa, or splitting our course away from their course," so as to better confront Soviet policies.[28] In deciding to pull the rug from under London's and Paris's actions in Egypt, the Eisenhower administration knew that they were effectively ruining both the power and the will that the European countries had to defend their colonial possessions in the future. America would replace them as the major Western force all over the Third World, with a policy based on its own strategic and economic priorities.

From 1956 up until the Arab-Israeli War of 1967 the direct influence of the United States in the Middle East took on new proportions. It soon found that its Cold War priorities led to as deep a conflict with Arab nationalism as the European powers had had prior to the Suez Crisis. After having invoked the right (and the support of Congress) for what became known as the Eisenhower Doctrine – US willingness to intervene unilaterally in the Middle East to support its friends and allies against Communism – the president in 1958 sent US Marines to Lebanon to rescue the pro-Western regime of Lebanese president Camille Chamoun from its challengers. The same year a revolution in Iraq had begun removing that country – hitherto a close British and US ally through the Baghdad Pact – from the Western orbit. Instead of being deterred by the US intervention in Lebanon, the new Iraqi regime of Abdel Karim Qassim set up a close alliance with the Iraqi Communist Party and

[margin handwritten note: Eisenhower Doctrine]

began negotiations with Moscow on a whole range of issues, including military aid. In Jordan, the British sent their troops – this time with Washington's overt blessing – to rescue the throne for King Hussein, when he that same year was challenged by pan-Arabic nationalists. The Soviets concluded that the whole Middle Eastern situation was unravelling for those local rulers who stood in the way of Nasser-style nationalist revolutions. "Apparently," Khrushchev told the CPSU Presidium, "both in Lebanon and Jordan the rulers don't have the support of their people anymore. Being afraid of them [their own people], not able to rely on their army, which cannot support the regime, which does not respond to the interests of these countries, they decided to rely on the forces of interveners – the United States and England."[29]

In spite of their optimism regarding the political turnarounds in the Middle East, the Soviets warned local Communists that they had to proceed cautiously in their alliance with the nativist revolutionaries who seemed to take hold of the region in the late 1950s and early 1960s. The Kremlin's warnings soon turned out to be all too relevant: by the end of 1959 both Nasser and Iraq's Qassim had turned on their countries' Communist parties in a brutal show of who was in charge, and even though the Iraqi leader kept zig-zagging in his relationship with the Communists up until his overthrow by the Iraqi Baath Party in 1963, the US concerns about Communist takeovers seemed increasingly unfounded. Still, the alliances that had developed between Arab nativist revolutionary regimes and the Soviets in the 1960s continued to give Washington plenty of cause for concern.

A major reason for the development of these Soviet–Arab alliances was the increasingly close US relationship with Israel. When the Israeli state in Palestine set up by the UN as a Jewish homeland in 1948, both the United States and the Soviet Union had been supportive of the proposal. To Stalin, the main advantages were tactical: since the Arab states were reactionary feudal regimes, supported by Western imperialism, the creation of a Zionist state in their midst could, over time, enhance the growth of a genuine Arab nationalism. If threatened by their neighbors, left-wing Zionism could end up turning to the Soviets for protection – such alliances had been created before in Europe. But Stalin also saw his support for the creation of Israel as a means of taking attention away from his own growing anti-Semitism at home. For the Americans, and for many postwar European leaders, Israel was first and foremost expiation for the Holocaust – an easy way of atoning to Jews for not having done enough to save them from Hitler's policy of extermination. But, especially in Washington, the implantation of a European state in the Middle East was also seen as a way of exporting civilization and democracy to the region. In both East and West, the UN plan for the partition of Palestine was seen as taking a tricky problem off their hands, and as a potential benefit for their side in the Cold War, in spite of their awareness – as Truman put it in February 1948 – that "the situation is not solvable as presently set up."[30]

The Zionist victory in the civil war in Palestine in 1948, and the Arab refugee problem that followed, created massive resentment against Israel all over the Middle East, and anti-Zionism became a staple of Arab nationalism in the 1950s. Conscious that the Arabs had had imposed "upon them the major initial cost of attempting a solution to the international problem of Zionism," and preoccupied with securing access to vital Middle East oil, Washington at first tried a hands-off policy in the Arab-Israeli conflict.[31] We know today that it was the nascent alliances between Moscow and radical Arab nationalist regimes that made the United States a reluctant supporter of Israel from the mid-1950s on, in spite of Eisenhower's anger at Tel Aviv's involvement in the Suez Crisis. What drove American policy was more the attraction of Israel's growing strength and political stability than it was the quest for domestic Jewish votes: the Zionist state could, over time, act in conjunction with the United States in fighting to keep Soviet influence out of the Middle East.[32]

But the Middle East was just one area for the 1950s US ideological construction of a Third World ripe for intervention. Another area was Southeast Asia, where the Eisenhower administration found that the limited interventionism of the Truman years was not enough. Deeply worried about the development in Indochina and the left-wing turn of nationalist regimes elsewhere in the region, the president hoped to use US influence to change the future of the region before the Soviet Union was able to gain footholds. As a result, the United States intervened in Burma, where it kept 15,000 Chinese troops – remnants of the Guomindang armies that had been defeated in 1949 – under weapons in order to challenge Communist China and put pressure on the left-wing nativist regime in Rangoon. In Cambodia, the administration sponsored rebellions against Prince Sihanouk's regime, because of the prince's willingness to work with the domestic left-wing and with the People's Republic of China. In Laos and South Vietnam, the United States footed the complete bill for the build-up of the armies in an effort to counter the growing influence of leftist forces. But it was in Indonesia – the biggest and most influential Southeast Asian state – that the Eisenhower administration launched its most ambitious program of intervention, in effect trying to change the future political direction of the world's most populous Muslim country.

As we have seen, under Truman the United States had attempted to work with the first postcolonial nativist Indonesian regime, led by the mercurial Sukarno. But by the mid-1950s the relationship was in trouble, both because Washington was becoming less tolerant of Sukarno's brand of neutralism, typified by his hosting of the Bandung conference, but also because Sukarno himself was moving toward the left in his domestic policies and, increasingly, wanted to strengthen his contacts with the Soviet Union and the PRC. The Indonesian leader was dissatisfied with his country's slow economic progress and with a parliamentary political system that, in his opinion, gave far too much room for established elites and for separatist groups. The Dutch retention of Irian Jaya and American support for the British colonial presence in Malaya – both areas that Sukarno saw as natural parts of a greater Indonesian federation – also angered the nationalist leaders in Jakarta, and made them look for allies elsewhere.

Having taken care to visit Washington first, Sukarno in late summer 1956 visited both Moscow and Beijing, and on returning home praised the development of the Chinese economy, from which he thought Indonesia had much to learn. In 1957, after having been turned down by the Americans, Sukarno obtained a $100 million credit from Khrushchev for military purchases. The same year the Indonesian leader proclaimed that his goal was a "guided democracy," where a cabinet composed of all four major parties, the Indonesian Communist Party (PKI) included, should steer the state under his own guidance, without relying on Parliament. Faced with open rebellions by Muslim separatist forces in Sumatra and Sulawesi, Sukarno and his head of the General Staff, the anti-Communist General Abdul Nasution, declared martial law in an attempt to preserve the territorial integrity of Indonesia and Sukarno's own power.

In Washington, Eisenhower and Dulles were increasingly wondering whether it was exactly the extent of territorial control that Jakarta held that was the problem, at least as long as Communism was seen as being on the rise. Already in 1953, Dulles had told his ambassador-designate to Indonesia that "as between a territorially united Indonesia which is leaning . . . towards Communism and a break up of that country into racial and geographical units, I would prefer the latter."[33] By late 1957 the NSC had concluded that the United States should "strengthen the determination, will and cohesion of the anti-Communist forces in the outer islands, particularly in Sumatra and Sulawesi, in order through their strength to affect favorably the situation in Java."[34] The president sanctioned a major covert operation, headed by the CIA, to supply weapons and communications equipment to the rebels, and soon US Air Force pilots, joined by Guomindang Chinese and Philippine air force personel, were flying combat missions for the Sumatra-based rebel regime. It was the biggest covert operation the United States had ever carried out. In December 1957 Dulles told his deputy that he would like to "see things get to a point where we could plausibly withdraw our recognition of the Sukarno government and give it to the dissident elements on Sumatra and land forces to protect the life and property of Americans; use this as an excuse to bring about a major shift there."[35]

But the secretary's plans for the break-up of Indonesia did not succeed. Faced with an open rebellion and a large-scale foreign intervention, Sukarno was able to recreate – albeit for a short time only – the coalition of mainstream Muslims, Communists, and nativist officers that had brought his republic into being in the 1930s and 1940s. To the Indonesian military, a unified country and an integrationist domestic policy was its *raison d'être*, and the US policy of supporting the rebels made even the most anti-Communist of the main army leaders swing back toward Sukarno. As their offensive against the rebels began, the Jakarta regime was also helped by their capture of a US pilot, shot down while on a bombing mission for the rebels.[36] This clear evidence of US involvement meant that even anti-Communists, such as General Nasution, began arguing for Indonesia receiving military aid from Moscow. As the rebel armies fragmented, Sukarno postponed the 1959 elections indefinitely and declared the introduction of "guided democracy." The Eisenhower administration decided against a direct intervention to help their Indonesian clients, but continued to give some support to guerrilla remnants in North Sumatra, as these began moving toward an Islamic more than a regionalist identity.

By the late 1950s the United States had established an interventionist policy with a global reach. Only regimes that accepted the American hegemony in foreign policy and in development strategy were seen as viable, and some of the "unviable" states were condemned for voluntarily or involuntarily opening up for Communism, and thereby provoking a US intervention. Even in cases such as Indonesia, where Washington's strategy did not work out, there were few regrets. To the Eisenhower administration it was more important to spoil the chances for a successful left-wing development strategy than it was to impose its own version of development on newly independent countries. While opposed to heavy-handed old world imperialist interventions – such as Suez – and tolerant of neutrality as long as it meant leaning toward the United States and holding any domestic Communist party in check, Eisenhower created a record of US covert interventions that put America on a direct collision course with nationalist sentiment outside Europe. Through its strategies, it did much to create the Third World as a conceptual entity: seen from America, these were areas to be intervened in; and seen from the South, areas that had a common interest in resisting intervention.

The United States and African decolonization

The African revolutions and the decolonization that accompanied them were low on the American list of foreign affairs priorities until the 1960s. Still, the encounter between US foreign policy ideology and the African freedom movements in the early decades of the Cold War set the pattern for a troubled set of interactions, which were to reach their high point in the Cold War confrontation over the decolonization of the Portuguese empire in the 1970s. As we have already seen, the United States in the aftermath of World War II found itself caught between genuine antipathy toward the European colonial projects and increasing fear of the rise of Communism. But in Africa, as in Asia, the ideological and strategic perspectives created by anti-Communism soon got the upper hand in US foreign policy. By the late 1950s, when most of the continent was getting ready for the setting up of new, independent states, Washington's greatest preoccupation was with avoiding a growth in Soviet influence, while securing the continued access of the West to strategic raw materials.

As could be expected in a country where a large part of the 25 million African Americans were still not enfranchised, there was a strong division of opinion about whether Africa – now or in the future – belonged in the realm where freedom could flourish. In note after note, both the Truman and the Eisenhower administrations wondered about the viability of African states, while being – in principle – in favor of decolonization. "Rather than slow down the independence movements," Eisenhower instructed his NSC in 1958,

[I] would like to be on the side of the natives for once . . . We must believe in the right of colonial peoples to achieve independence . . . [but] if we emphasized this right too strongly, we created a crisis in the relations with the mother countries . . . why we could not foster education and religion, leaving the mother country to prepare the colony for independence . . . Mr. Randall [chairman of the Council on Foreign Economic Policy] felt that more emphasis should be placed on education *in* Africa; there were risks in bringing Africans to the United States to be educated.[37]

Throughout the late 1940s and the 1950s Washington worried about the effect African decolonization would have on its European allies, and especially the weaker ones among them, such as Portugal or Belgium. "Our policy," Gerhart Niemeyer of the State Department's policy planning staff noted, "should be based on the general premise of the right to self-determination ... Obviously, so long as the present world tensions prevail, our national interest is closely bound to precisely those countries which still to [a] greater or lesser degree carry the stigma of colonial imperialism. When these tensions safely subside, other considerations will become valid."[38] But with the Cold War in full swing, those "other considerations" took a long time to emerge, and the United States kept focusing much on the European side of African affairs. It was a dual policy with a "theory" of anticolonialism and a practice of support for colonial elites very much like the Soviets' nationalities policy: support for national self-determination "in principle," but only as long as the exercise of that right did not override the ideological predilections of the state.[39]

Even so, most of the European colonial powers saw the United States as a fickle ally at best in African affairs, and in some quarters there was deep resentment against what was seen as American attempts to replace European influence, politically and economically. Still, no European elite after 1945 was in doubt that it needed US support in order to keep its influence in Africa, and that it therefore needed to work with, and sometimes on, the Americans. "One must not forget ... that the American education in African affairs has long been neglected and one runs the risk, in discussing the problems at too elevated a level, of losing all but a small part of the audience," sneered French ambassador Henri Bonnet.[40] From a European perspective, the United States sometimes stood out as the real "dark continent" as far as Africa was concerned.

Even worse from the perspective of many colonial administrators was the fact that the United States – however much its elites tried to hide or neglect it – was itself a multiracial society. In World War II, Native Americans, Asian Americans, African Americans, and Hispanics had fought in all branches of the US armed forces, and as the military slowly stumbled its way toward full desegregation in the 1950s, more and more non-European Americans appeared abroad when it was necessary to defend their country's interests.[41] European colonialists had seen early on that having to deal with black Americans would explode some of the racial stereotypes they had conscientiously cultivated in their colonies. Felix de Muelenaere, an adviser to the Belgian Governor-General in Congo, had tried to explain the effects to the African American diplomat Ralph Bunche in 1942: black American soldiers "would have a bad effect on the Congo natives, especially on the detribalized native clerks ... The Congo native would begin to think that he should have the same privilege as the highly developed American blacks who are college graduates, doctors, and professors."[42]

During the early Cold War South Africa was the only independent country – besides the United States itself – where racial segregation was a matter of law. It was also by far the most important African country to the United States, in part because of its strategic location and in part because of its natural wealth. The problem for Washington was that while the US federal government had begun, slowly, to abolish institutionalized racial oppression, Pretoria was moving in the opposite direction after the victory of the National Party in the (all-white) elections of 1948. But the introduction of *apartheid* – enforced racial segregation in all areas – did not lead to a breakdown of the US–South Africa relationship. The US elites believed that the white South Africans would eventually follow the American lead on racial relations – in fact, the American underlining of how much the two societies had in common became stronger during the 1950s – and, besides, South Africa was far too important to discard because of a difference of opinion on the treatment of Africans. It was "possible, even likely," the US consul in Durban reported, "that we would act in the same manner if we endeavored to govern as a white race among a black population five times as numerous."[43]

While the CIA kept warning about the increasing radicalization of the African majority – especially after the young Nelson Mandela and others got the African National Congress to adopt a "Program of Action" in 1949 – US relations with apartheid South Africa became closer during the 1950s. American investments increased, as did South African exports – including uranium for the nuclear industry – and military cooperation. State Department Assistant Secretary George McGhee, a Texan, praised "the progressive spirit and dynamism of the Johannesburg businessmen," whose skyscrapers and factories had developed "an atmosphere more like Chicago than Africa."[44] By 1960 the Eisenhower administration had got so used to cooperating with the National Party regime that when news of the police massacre of Africans at Sharpeville reached Secretary of State Herter, his first reaction was fury over an earlier statement from his own department that "regretted the tragic loss of life." The statement was "a breach of courtesy between nations," the Secretary said, and both he and the President apologized to the South African government.[45]

But in spite of the apology – and in spite of the aging President Eisenhower's insistence that "one could not sit in judgment on a difficult social and political problem six thousand miles away" and that "they have to make progress their way" – Sharpeville became a watershed in US–South African relations.[46] The intelligence organizations stepped up their warnings that inside South Africa "the years ahead will be characterized by increasing tension, culminating eventually – probably after considerable bloodshed – in the end of white domination."[47]

The problem, the CIA had warned before, was that US policy left the field of resistance against apartheid to the Communists, internally and externally, and that more had to be done to court "moderate" members of the African opposition.

As the civil rights movement advanced in the United States, the Cold War in Africa became more acute. While most US political leaders up to the early 1960s had thought of Africans as children who were destined to remain children, the Kennedy administration began seeing Africans as adolescents, in the process of growing up, as witnessed by the creation of new states and political movements. The anti-Communist argument was no longer that socialism did not fit "the African tribal mentality" or the "languid and quiescent" African Americans, but the fear that Communists might seduce adolescent African leaders. In other words, moving Africans inside the realm of potential freedom increased the danger that they could move toward an "incorrect" form of modernity. Freedom for Africans, both at home and abroad, meant that the United States had to open up a new offensive in the Cold War.

Both the Kennedy and the Johnson administrations conducted that offensive with vigor and determination, even if it broke with political precedents and paid few dividends in the short run. The Soviet determination to make inroads for its ideology in Africa had to be broken. In the Portuguese colonies of Angola and Mozambique, both administrations operated covert links with two of the nascent African liberation movements through CIA-funded support for Holden Roberto's National Front for the Liberation of Angola (Frente Nacional de Libertação de Angola; FNLA) and through secret meetings with Eduardo Mondlane, the head of the Mozambique Liberation Front (Frente de Libertação de Moçambique; FRELIMO), whom Averell Harriman described as a "well-balanced, dedicated, [and] serious man."[48] America's Portuguese allies were, understandably, furious.[49]

The biggest challenge for Washington was how to handle the newly independent states that suddenly burst into being all over Africa in the early 1960s. "We live in a hazardous and dangerous time," the newly elected John F. Kennedy told his audience in 1961.

We live in a world which has changed tremendously in our lifetime – history only will secure a full perspective on that change. But there is Africa, which was held by Western European powers for several centuries, now independent – which holds within its countries masses of people, many of them illiterate, who live on average incomes of 50 or 60 or 75 dollars a year, who want a change, who now are the masters of their own house but who lack the means of building a viable economy, who are impressed by the example of the Soviet Union and the Chinese, who – not knowing the meaning of freedom in their lives – wonder whether the Communist system holds the secrets of organizing the resources of the state in order to bring them a better life.[50]

As long as direct Communist influence was kept out, the Kennedy administration attempted to practice "restraint" when African leaders – such as Ghana's increasingly radical president – criticized US policies. "Nkrumah is continuing to lose ground as a political force and is likely to become increasingly isolated from the mainstream of African politics," Chester Bowles noted after a visit to Africa in 1962. "Our policy in Ghana should therefore be one of restraint. By denying Nkrumah a demagogic issue ... we will help to assure his increasing isolation."[51] The problem with Kennedy's approach was that African leaders often saw US Cold War policies in Africa as diametrically opposed to their own interests, in spite of the economic assistance that America could offer. They also watched the African American struggle for civil rights and saw little for Africans to admire in the response of white America.

Already during the battles over the desegregation of Southern schools in 1957, John Foster Dulles had noted that "this situation was ruining our foreign policy."[52] The pictures of white mobs spitting at black school-children in Little Rock or police setting their dogs on peaceful black demonstrators in Selma shocked African leaders and made US efforts to portray their country as a friend much more difficult. As the American civil rights movement gained ground in the 1960s, even the most right-wing African groups and regimes made their solidarity with the African Americans known, all over the continent. For presidents Kennedy and Johnson the US segregationists became a Cold War liability and their removal from power in the American South a necessity, not least because of the damage their rhetoric did to the international anti-Communist crusade at home and abroad. As the radical civil rights leader Malcolm X put it in his 1964 critique of the Johnson administration:

I read in the paper yesterday where one of the Supreme Court justices, Goldberg, was crying about the violation of human rights of 3 million Jews in the Soviet Union ... How in the world are you going to cry about problems on the other side of the world when you haven't got the problems straightened out here? How can the plight of 3 million Jews in Russia be qualified to be taken to the United Nations by a man who is a justice in this Supreme Court and is supposed to be a liberal, supposed to be a friend of Black people, and hasn't opened up his mouth one time about taking the plight of Black people down here to the United Nations?[53]

Preaching to others while not having one's own problems "straightened out" also hampered Kennedy's efforts to pry France lose from its colonial war in Algeria, a conflict which – as we have already seen – was a key reason for the radicalization of Third World anticolonialism in the early

1960s. Kennedy's problem was that the French government of General de Gaulle seemed too weak domestically to survive an immediate withdrawal from North Africa. The CIA warned that de Gaulle might be unseated in a military coup if he tried to settle the conflict with the Algerian nationalists. "Our sympathy," Kennedy explained to his staff, "continues to be with the nations throwing off the bonds of colonialism; but the cause of anticolonialism will not be helped by the overthrow of de Gaulle."[54] The Algerians' successful strategy of bringing their grievances to the United Nations, where the US alliance with France brought little but embarrassment for Washington, proved to be one of their best weapons. Meeting in New York, many African and Asian diplomats at the UN drew parallels between what they saw as the US federal government's weak response to the American civil rights struggle and its inability to condemn colonial violence abroad.

The UN as an anticolonial battlefield was in itself a problem for the United States, which attempted to keep the focus of world condemnations on the Communist states. Since its foundation, Washington had thought of the UN as an extension of its own power, symbolized by the war in Korea, where US troops officially fought against the Chinese and Korean Communist forces on behalf of the United Nations. But the advent of new, independent Third World states began already in 1960 to change the role of the United Nations into a more diverse forum, less susceptible to American influence than before. The five-year conflict over the decolonization of Congo showed how the UN developed from being viewed by many as an arm of US intervention abroad to being an altogether different organization, in which the strengthened position of the nonaligned countries was perhaps the most visible characteristic. The Congo conflict also became the most intense of American interventions into the 1960s decolonization process in Africa, and the one where the stakes were by far the highest both for the United States and its rivals.

"Belgian" Congo – one of the biggest and most resource-rich of all African colonies – was also the least developed. Established as the personal possession of Belgium's King Leopold II in the late nineteenth century, Congo had been taken over – somewhat reluctantly – by the Belgian state in 1908, who thereafter proceeded to neglect most aspects of development in the colony except the exploitation of its wealth. It was only in the post-World War II period that Belgium began the same kind of development schemes in Congo as Britain and France had started a generation earlier in their colonies, and – as a result – Congo in the late 1950s, when agitation for independence peaked, was without a professional elite that could take control of the political movement. Instead, during 1959, when it suddenly became clear that the Belgians were on their way out, most of the organizations that appeared were local or regional, owing their allegiance to one or several of the more than two hundred ethnic groups in the colony. The Belgians, who believed that their continued economic presence in Congo was better served by local strongmen than by any central government, did little to oppose the fragmentation.

There was only one political party in Congo that did have at least some support in most parts of the country: the Congolese National Movement (Mouvement National Congolais; MNC), headed by Patrice Lumumba. Lumumba was born in a small village in southwestern Congo in 1925 and was educated at a Protestant missionary school. He became a postal clerk – one of the few positions in the colonial bureaucracy open to Congolese, applied for Belgian citizenship, and began to write articles for the local press, mostly on how Congo could develop under Belgian guidance. In 1955 he became regional president of the first Congolese trade union and began bringing cases of gross exploitation of workers to the attention of the authorities. The following year he was arrested for embezzlement from the post office – a dubious charge at best – and sentenced to one year's imprisonment. After his release from prison, Lumumba moved to the left politically and helped set up the MNC, and in 1958 he visited Accra for the first all-African People's Conference. Independent Ghana made a great impression on him, and it was on Kwame Nkrumah's example that Lumumba based much of his political practice.

In the May 1960 elections in Congo the MNC became the largest party and Lumumba the prime minister designate, in spite of Belgian attempts at blocking him. On independence day, 30 June, Lumumba spoke of the indignities that had been imposed on the Congolese by the colonial system, but he also promised that "all this is over and done with now . . .

We are going to institute social justice together and ensure everyone just remuneration for his labor. We are going to show the world what the black man can do when he works in freedom, and we are going to make the Congo the focal point for the development of all of Africa. We are going to see to it that the soil of our country really benefits its children. We are going to review all the old laws and make new ones that will be just and noble. We are going to put an end to the suppression of free thought and see to it that all citizens enjoy to the fullest all the fundamental freedoms laid down in the Declaration of the Rights of Man.[55]

To the United States, Lumumba's new Congolese government seemed to be another left-wing threat in the Third World, a threat that was made worse by Congo's immense natural wealth, which included the uranium that had been used to develop the first US nuclear weapons. Although the United States was no longer dependent on Congolese uranium, Washington was determined to avoid Congo's minerals coming under the control of the Soviet Union. Lumumba, the NSC thought, was exactly the kind of figure who could serve as a conduit between his country's mines and Moscow's wishes. Lumumba "was irresponsible, had been charged with embezzlement, was now being offered bribes from various sources and was supported by the Belgian Communists," CIA director Allen Dulles had told President Eisenhower already in May 1960. The president, while expressing his surprise that there was so much political activity before the elections since "he did not know that many people in the Congo could read," had still authorized American payments to prevent Lumumba's election.[56]

Already in the week that followed independence day in Congo it became clear that Lumumba's visions for his country were dimming fast among his countrymen. With no state institutions in place, Congo began to fragment both at the social level and the political level, harvesting the terrible fruits of the tensions sown by the colonial regime. By mid-July large numbers of Africans and Europeans had fled to the cities for safety. The southern province of Katanga, also known as Shaba – holding more than half of the country's known mineral resources – had seceded, well helped by the Union Minière, the Belgian company that controlled the mining in the region. Lumumba asked the UN to intervene to help put down the rebellions and evict the remaining Belgian forces from the country, and – when the UN force turned down his request to take over Katanga – the prime minister in desperation let it be known that he considered seeking Soviet assistance. Washington was appalled. "In Lumumba we were faced with a person who was a Castro or worse," Allen Dulles told the NSC at the end of July. The Congolese premier's background was "harrowing," according to Dulles; it was "safe to go on the assumption that Lumumba has been bought by the Communists; this also, however, fits with his own orientation."[57] Lumumba's own oft-repeated statement that his government was not "Communists, Catholics, or Socialists" but "African nationalists [who] reserve the right to be friendly with anybody we like according to the principles of positive neutrality" did not make much of an impression in Washington.[58]

But Lumumba himself did make an impression when, to the State Department's surprise, he showed up at the UN in New York in August. Requesting a meeting with the president, he was flown to Washington to meet with Secretary of State Herter and Under-Secretary C. Douglas Dillon, who later became Kennedy's and Johnson's Secretary of the Treasury. In spite of the Dillon's later testimony that the Congolese prime minister had appeared "irrational, almost 'psychotic' " during the interview, the declassified record of the conversation makes it clear that it was Lumumba's determined defense of his country's sovereignty and integrity that posed a problem for the Americans.[59] Despite praising the US role in the world, he demanded the immediate withdrawal of all Belgian troops from Congo, refused to rule out military action against the separatist regime in Katanga, and confirmed his country's right to ask for support from whatever side they wished.[60] On his arrival back in Kinshasa, Lumumba criticized Swedish UN Secretary-General Dag Hammarskjöld – an American favorite – for not giving the support of the UN forces in Congo to his government, but instead preventing the forcible reincorporation of Katanga into the new republic. The challenge to its UN policy was a problem for the United States. In an NSC meeting on 18 August Allen Dulles "suggested that if the assets of Katanga could be retained, the economy of the Congo could be throttled. The Soviets would have to throw a lot of money into the rest of Congo to keep it viable in such a case." Eisenhower even suggested that "the UN might recognize Katanga."[61]

As the political and economic situation in Congo deteriorated, the US Joint Chiefs of Staff insisted that "in addition to United Nations actions, effective or otherwise, the United States must be prepared at any time to take appropriate military action . . . to prevent or defeat Soviet military intervention."[62] The president hoped, though, that things would not go that far – the key point was to get rid of Lumumba. While Dulles instructed the CIA station in Kinshasa on 26 August that the prime minister's "removal must be an urgent and prime objective," the CIA director had to admit to the president a couple of weeks later "that it was not easy to run a coup in the Congo."[63] While pushing for a takeover by the Congolese military, headed by the former journalist, now general, Joseph Mobutu – a "completely honest [and] dedicated" man, according to the US ambassador – Washington also gave the go-ahead for a top-secret plan to assassinate Lumumba.[64] On 19 September an agent – known to his Kinshasa CIA colleagues as "Joe from Paris" – showed up in the Congolese capital with poison that could be used to kill the prime minister.[65]

We still do not know whether the CIA tried to kill Lumumba but failed, or whether Mobutu's *coup d'état* in mid-September beat the Americans to the post. With Mobutu in charge of a ramshackle anti-Lumumba alliance, and with the elected prime minister seeking refuge with the UN, US efforts switched to buoying up the new regime and making sure that orders were issued for the eviction of Soviet and Eastern Bloc embassies and advisers. But in spite of getting rid of the East Europeans and the Chinese, and – through US help – getting at least a tacit cooperation with the UN troops, by November Mobutu's regime seemed to be in trouble. The problem was both that other African countries refused to have anything to do with the new government in Kinshasa, and that Lumumba's persistent calls for a general uprising against those who had plotted the coup seemed to be working, at least in some parts of the country. As Averell Harriman – now the president's self-appointed emissary to Kinshasa – reported: "Lumumba will continue to cause difficulties in the Congo whether he is in control of the government, in jail or released. He is a rabble-rousing speaker, a shrewd maneuverer with clever left-wing advisers ... He is obsessed with his mission to unify the Congo."[66]

The lucky break for Mobutu and the Americans came on 1 December, when Lumumba was captured by Congolese soldiers as he attempted to leave Kinshasa for the eastern city of Kisangani, where his supporters were still in control. Desperate to get rid of the prime minister, but unwilling to have Lumumba's blood on his own hands, Mobutu decided to hand him over to his archenemies in Katanga. A US correspondent witnessed the prime minister's arrival in Lubumbashi:

Swedish United Nations guards at the airport, tall and tough, stood by, shadow figures in the background, as Lumumba, blindfolded with a grimy bandage, his hands tied behind him, and roped to two of his political lieutenants, was directed down the steps of the plane. Within sight of a large airport billboard proclaiming "Welcome to Free Katanga," the trembling, stumbling Lumumba and his fellow prisoners fell to the ground in a hail of savage baton, rifle-butt and fist blows and kicks from a gauntlet of snarling Katangese.[67]

After being tortured for five hours, Lumumba was murdered, with Katangese "ministers" and Belgian officers in attendance throughout.[68]

While the prime minister's death removed the most immediate problems for US policy in Congo, the long-term issues of opposition to the regime and lack of economic development remained. The incoming Kennedy administration continued Eisenhower's support for Mobutu, but forced him to install a civilian government and make peace with the Katangese leader Moise Tshombe, giving the latter and his Belgian partners a free hand to plunder the region's mineral resources. At the same time, the United States made sure that the unruly Belgian military contingents left the areas controlled by the Kinshasa regime and replaced them with US advisers. When Mobutu visited Washington in May 1963 – where he informed the president that his highest wish was to undergo "parachute training for four weeks at Fort Benning" – Kennedy was full of praise. "General," the president commented intimately during a walk in the White House Rose Garden, "if it hadn't been for you, the whole thing would have collapsed and the Communists would have taken over."[69] But Kennedy was also aware that the social and political conditions in

Fig. 3   "Nobody in the world had done more than the General
to maintain freedom against the Communists" – Kennedy
and Mobuto at the White House in 1963.

Congo were worsening, not improving – "we are hanging on to a bankrupt policy at the moment," as George McGhee had put it in a NSC
meeting in December 1962. The Congolese regime, the US ambassador
conceded, was "obscurantist, arbitrary, primitive, totalitarian, willful,
and irresponsible."[70]

As happened in so many other areas, Kennedy left unfinished business
in Congo for his successor to sort out. When the government in Kinshasa
began collapsing in the fall of 1964, under pressure from left-wing and
regionalist rebels in the north and east, President Johnson faced the tough
decision of whether to intervene with US forces. Coming right after
Johnson had decided to step up the US involvement in Vietnam after
the Gulf of Tonkin incident, the president was understandably reluctant.
While telling his NSC that "time is running out and the Congo must be
saved," LBJ resisted pressure from the Joint Chiefs of Staff and the
ambassador to send a much larger number of US military advisers to
the country.[71] The president told the State Department that he did not
"want to get tied in on the Congo and have another Korea, another
Vietnam, just because of somebody wandering around searching for
'Jesus Christ.'"[72] The Americans in Congo would have to learn to work
with the local power holders. "We'll just need to watch it a little bit,
because we are going to be investigated and we are going to be murdered ...
you're going to get those Africans and those Muslims raising hell ... [and

the] FBI shows that [Martin Luther King] is getting ready to go international," Johnson told Dean Rusk in late November.[73]

What Johnson would agree to, however, was intervening to free
Europeans who had been captured after the rebel takeover of
Kisangani. "We couldn't just let the cannibals kill a lot of people," the
president commented after airlifting five hundred Belgian paratroopers
into the city on 24 November 1964.[74] But the successful paratroop drop
was also a cover for a much more extensive US-supported military operation against the rebels, carried out by Western mercenaries paid and
organized by the CIA. Assisted by a CIA-operated airforce piloted by
anti-Communist Cuban pilots, the mercenaries and Mobutu's forces
were able to retake Kisangani and slowly, over the span of a year, crush
the rebel strongholds in eastern Congo. The brutality of the operation
was astonishing, even to seasoned European observers. One mercenary
recounted the takeover of Boende, a town in the northern Équateur
province: "After the looting came the killing. The shooting lasted for
three days. Three days of executions, of lynchings, of tortures, of screams,
and of terror."[75]

In his report to Washington as the final rebels were being rounded up or
disappeared into exile along Congo's eastern and northern borders, the
US ambassador in Kinshasa G. McMurtrie Godley II searched for the
reasons for the American victory. "The insurgency itself never developed
here to the same extent [as] we have seen it elsewhere in the world. [The]
rebellion in 1964 got ahead of its Communist supporters who apparently
never had the materiel nor the trained personnel on the spot to exploit it
as successfully as they did elsewhere in the world. Also, GDRC's
[Congolese regime's] more recent military actions against [the] insurgents, supported by GOB [Government of Belgium] and USG, nipped a
developed insurgency in the bud." But the success was also due to
the weaknesses of the people the United States intervened to save:
"Congolese individual is not good insurgent or counterinsurgent.
He does not have the moral or physical fiber or courage to sustain
protracted guerrilla actions or their countermeasures ... Non-Africans
have been required despite obvious political drawbacks and their presence required at least for immediate future." But the dependence on
European mercenaries to keep the population in check was no hindrance
for the modernization of Congo, according to Ambassador Godley: "We
believe we are in nation building aspect here where seeds of future
insurgency must be eliminated by improving local administration, and
security and economic well-being of [the] little people ... There is no rpt
no disagreement in [the] country team in these objectives and we are
continuously groping to find ways [of] achieving this objective."[76]

As the United States government helped the Mobutu dictatorship reestablish itself, other people were drawing other conclusions. Che Guevara, who – unbeknownst to the Americans – had gone to Congo with a Cuban team to assist the rebels (see fig. 5), believed he learnt much about the weaknesses of counterinsurgency strategies, as we shall see in the next chapter. African leaders – shocked at the brazenness of the intervention – denounced US objectives in Africa. Tanzanian president Julius Nyerere, who had his own difficulties with the Congolese rebels, sent a letter to Johnson which the US ambassador to Dar-es-Salaam described as full of "emotionalism, suspicions, and fear," and even pro-Western leaders – such as Kenya's Jomo Kenyatta and Morocco's King Hassan II – registered their strong opposition to the use of mercenaries and the alliance with Tshombe, whom they regarded as "a walking museum of colonialism."[77]

And in a forewarning of how the Vietnam War would split America apart a few years later, Malcolm X connected the struggle for African American rights directly to the role the United States was playing abroad:

The racial sparks that are ignited here in America today could easily turn into a flaming fire abroad, which only means it could engulf all the people of this earth into a giant race war. You cannot confine it to one little neighborhood, or one little community, or one little country. What happens to a Black man in America today happens to the black man in Africa. What happens to a Black man in America and Africa happens to the black man in Asia and to the man down in Latin America. What happens to one of us today happens to all of us.[78]

Latin America: Sandino to Castro

While the US domination of Latin America was, as we have seen, developing out of processes that began well before 1945, the Cold War gave shape and direction to attempts at the systematic subordination of the states on the southern half of the continent to the will of the United States. But in spite of the conformity with its overall Cold War policies that the US system of control and intervention developed in Latin America, it does not make sense here to see the late 1940s as a starting point; rather, the Cold War system of domination was superimposed on nineteenth- and early twentieth-century trends, especially as far as Central America and the Caribbean are concerned. The core causes of US hegemony were its growing economic supremacy and the weakness of the state in most Latin American countries, while the causes of direct US interventions were mostly ideological or strategic. As postulated in the Monroe Doctrine and reformulated many times since, most US leaders believed it was part of their country's mission to lead the peoples of Latin America and the Caribbean to democracy and capitalism, while keeping out foreign influences that could "seduce" the southern part of the hemisphere away from the path of "Americanization." By the early twentieth century the US–Latin American relationship had begun resembling an informal empire, where decisions taken in Washington would be carried out by local power holders who in multiple ways were tied into a subservient relationship with the United States.

The basis for US power in Latin America and the Caribbean was economic. From the turn of the century onwards the United States was the most important import and export market for the region, and by World War II the United States had surpassed Britain as the leading investor. In the independent states of the Caribbean and Central America the US economic dominance was in place already by 1900, while the bigger economies of the southern part of the continent developed their dependence on the United States more gradually up to the early Cold War years. By 1945 US preeminence was clear and visible all over the continent, from the import of consumer goods and movies to the export of tin, copper, fruit, coffee, and sugar.

Just as the European powers discovered in Africa and Asia, the United States found in Latin America that the developing of a system of political subservience was far more complicated than achieving economic predominance. Beginning already right after the war of conquest against Mexico, the United States was forced to intervene directly against local resistance to foreign control, such as in Nicaragua in the 1850s. In the 1890s the pattern of intervention widened, as we have seen in the case of Cuba and other countries in the Caribbean and Central America. Richard Olney, President Grover Cleveland's Secretary of State, in 1894 stated what was obvious to most Americans, that "today the United States is practically sovereign on this continent, and its fiat is law upon the subjects to which it confines its interposition."[79]

The Mexican revolution of 1910–11 was a watershed in US–Latin American relations. Not only did a major Latin American country for the first time go through a political upheaval in which many leaders aimed for profound social change, but the postrevolutionary situation was also inherited, on the US side, by President Woodrow Wilson, who saw the Mexican revolutionary leaders as having sinned against the virtues of democracy and therefore in need of being set right by the force of the United States. The Mexican president, General Victoriano Huerta – characterized by one of Wilson's advisers as "an ape-like old man, of almost pure Indian blood" – bore the brunt of Wilson's ire, and when he refused Washington's order to resign, Wilson invaded the Mexican port of Veracruz in April 1914 and began an extensive program of military support for Huerta's opponents.

By the end of the year Huerta was out and so were the US forces, but Washington's direct interventions in Mexican affairs continued up to the late 1920s, when the Partido Revolucionario Institucional (Institutional Revolutionary Party, PRI) did exactly what its name implies – institutionalized the Mexican revolution in the form of an elite that were more than happy to reestablish links with the giant northern neighbor.[80]

One of those who were inspired by the ideals of the Mexican revolution was the Nicaraguan leader Augusto César Sandino. Born in 1895 in a rural village, Sandino was the offspring of a landowner and a peasant woman in his employ. In 1921 he fled to Mexico after killing a political opponent. Working in the oilfields in Tampico, he learnt about the radicalization of Mexican politics, but also came into contact with Christian religious sects and the organized Left, including the Communist Party. In 1926 he returned to Nicaragua and joined the rebellion against the US-sponsored regime, soon becoming the most celebrated and most radical of the rebel commanders. But in spite of their military prowess, Sandino's forces were not able to defeat the government and the US Marines sent to protect it. In 1933, after the withdrawal of US forces, Sandino gave up the military struggle and settled in Nicaragua, while still declaring himself to be the center of a new anti-US Central American movement. The following year he was taken prisoner by the commander of the National Guard, Anastasio Somoza, and executed alongside his most prominent supporters.

Sandino's ideas were a form of millenarian socialism: he identified himself in an almost physical sense with his Indian ancestors who had fought against foreign domination and, increasingly, believed he was the incarnation of God's truth and light. On the other hand, he believed strongly in a united Central America, rid of foreign influence, and where the peasants and workers would rule through their organizations. He ridiculed other Latin American governments for not seeing the ultimate purpose of US domination:

Do the Latin American governments think perhaps the Yankees would be content with the conquest of Nicaragua alone? Have these governments perhaps forgotten that among twenty-one American republics six have already lost their sovereignty . . . and become colonies of Yankee imperialism? . . . Today it is with the peoples of Spanish America that I speak. When a government does not reflect the aspirations of its citizens, the latter, who gave it power, have the right to be represented by virile men with concepts of effective democracy, and not by useless satraps whose lack of moral valor and patriotism are a disgrace to a nation's pride.[81]

During World War II Washington's fear of revolution in Latin America merged with its fear of authoritarian governments of both the Left and the

Right. In Argentina the rise of Juan Peron – an army colonel who was inspired by European Fascism – gave rise to a new sense of threat, although most US advisers thought that Peron's movement could be controlled after it had taken power. The real threat of the first years of the Cold War lay in a possible Soviet challenge in Latin America, both the Truman and the Eisenhower administrations believed. Even though it was skeptical toward the chances that local Communist parties had for taking power, the CIA concluded in 1947 that "Communist undercover penetration of strategic sectors of the various economies is already such as to permit the USSR, by merely giving the necessary orders, (1) to withhold from the US its normal peacetime flow of strategic raw materials from Latin America, and (2) to precipitate economic crises in several key Latin American countries."[82] The US strategy became to prevent the Soviet Union establishing what it called "footholds" in Latin America.

The first direct US intervention of the postwar period took place in Guatemala in 1954. While the CIA had been warning for years against what it saw as the rise of "isolationist and nationalist opinion" in Latin America, the Guatemalan regime of President Jacobo Arbenz seemed a much more immediate and direct threat.[83] Since the removal of the US-supported dictator Ubico in 1944, Guatemala had been a thorn in Washington's side, especially since the elected governments of Juan José Arévalo and then Arbenz stressed social justice and cooperation with the labor unions, as well as an independent foreign policy and control of foreign capital. The US United Fruit Company, which dominated Guatemala's economy through large investments in banana plantations, railroads, ports, and shipping, complained that it expected its holdings to be confiscated by the government. Most important of all to Washington, the Guatemalan government legalized the Communist Party and allowed it to operate freely throughout the country.

Jacobo Arbenz was only 38 years old when he was elected president of Guatemala in 1951. The son of a Swiss pharmacist who had emigrated to the country, Arbenz was trained as a military officer and had been a key participant in the overthrow of Ubico in 1944. As president, he made agrarian reform the centerpiece of his administration – in Guatemala, landless peasants constituted more than half of the population, while 91 percent of arable land was controlled by big landowners or, directly or indirectly, by foreign companies. Arbenz wanted to expropriate unused portions of landholdings in excess of a specified acreage and distribute them among the landless.[84] At his inauguration, he stressed the land reform program first and foremost as a component of social justice:

All the riches of Guatemala are not as important as the life, the freedom, the dignity, the health and the happiness of the most humble of its people. How wrong we would be if – mistaking the means for the end –we were to set financial stability and economic growth as the supreme goals of our policy, sacrificing to them the wellbeing of our masses ... Our task is to work together in order to produce more wealth ... But we must distribute these riches so that those who have less – and they are the immense majority – benefit more, while those who have more – and they are so few – also benefit, but to a lesser extent. How could it be otherwise, given the poverty, the poor health, and the lack of education of our people?[85]

By early 1953 Arbenz's increasing cooperation with the Guatemalan Communist Party (Partido Guatemalteco del Trabajo, PGT) was sounding alarm bells in Washington. The CIA's warnings about increasing unrest in Latin America had forced the State Department to take the region more seriously, and, as historian Piero Glejeses has pointed out, the White House had reasonably good information about events in Guatemala. President Eisenhower did not like what he saw and ordered the CIA to organize, arm, and train Guatemalan opposition groups based in neighboring Honduras, a military dictatorship firmly under American control. The State Department official charged with justifying US hostility to Arbenz, Louis Halle – later a prominent Cold War historian – had already in 1950 tried to explain why US problems with Latin America were bound to rise in the future: it had, Halle, explained, "a tradition of political behavior marked by intemperance, intransigeance [sic], flamboyance and the worship of strong men," all of which testified to political immaturity, "characteristic of adolescence." The problem in Guatemala, Halle argued in May 1954, was that "the Communist infection" could "spread over much of Latin America." That same month Washington used the arrival in Guatemala of a Swedish freighter, the *Alfhem*, with about 2,000 tons of artillery, antitank mines, and light weapons from Czechoslovakia to introduce a full naval blockade of the country. The CIA used the *Alfhem* episode to justify its earlier claim that

Russia is intervening in the affairs of a Latin American republic ... The purpose of this intervention is to establish, first in Guatemala, and later in other countries of this hemisphere, a form of democracy entirely foreign to the American tradition. Socialism, and not democracy, is the goal of the Communists, and by that we mean that the real purpose of the Communists is to secure for the imperialistic movement of Russia the complete subservience of the peoples of the western world, and the resources therefrom.[86]

In spite of what the CIA believed, one of Arbenz' problems as US pressure mounted was the lack of interest by other powers, including the Soviet Union, and the lack of preparedness of the Guatemalan Left and the trade unions in defending his government. As the political agitation, sabotage, and rumor campaigns orchestrated by the CIA began to take their toll on the general popularity of the Arbenz government in the spring of 1954, the Guatemalan president seemed uncertain how to respond. In July 1954 US-trained troops under the command of Colonel Carlos Castillo Armas, a émigré officer based in Honduras, began an invasion of Guatemala, but were at first defeated by the Guatemalan Army. Leading army officers began to have second thoughts, though, about fighting a force that was so obviously backed by the United States. The CIA's covert message, distributed widely by agents in the Guatemalan capital, reminded the officers that "if they are unhappy about being in the US sphere of influence, they might be reminded that the US is the most generous and tolerant taskmaster going, that cooperation with it is studded with material rewards, and that the US permits much more sovereignty and independence in its sphere than the Soviets."[87] After President Eisenhower permitted the use of US aircraft in attacking Guatemalan military bases, the army deposed President Arbenz in a bloodless coup on 27 June 1954, and after a week of confusion – enough for many Communist leaders to escape – the US ambassador was able to install Castillo Armas as the new president.

The Guatemalan operation – codenamed PBSUCCESS – was indeed a success for the CIA, although not in the way the Agency had at first expected. The important thing, though, for Washington was that Communism had been "rooted out" in Central America; the fact that Guatemala had been handed over to a military dictatorship that through its reactionary policies laid the foundation for unending unrest mattered less. In fact, for the rest of the 1950s and at important junctures later on, US leaders found that dictators were the only form of leadership that "worked" in "adolescent" Latin American states threatened by Communism – "they are the only people we can depend on," as John Foster Dulles put it after the Guatemalan coup. But it was not only those who believed that the United States would bring democracy to Central America who were surprised in the aftermath of the overthrow of Arbenz. The United Fruit Company – useful to the US government during the operation – was brutally brought to heel in its aftermath, in part through antitrust action that spelled the beginning of its end. As the CIA put it in one of its internal directives, the position of the company in Guatemala ought to be curtailed, since its search for profit through dominance was "harmful to the over-riding American political interest."[88]

The anti-US attitudes of Latin American and Caribbean nationalists and left-wingers were, understandably, maximized by the overthrow of Arbenz. When US Vice President Richard Nixon was sent to visit

Latin America in 1957, he was greeted at the airport in Caracas by a huge rally chanting "Go away, Nixon!" "Out, dog!" "We won't forget Guatemala." Later, an angry mob attacked his motorcade in Caracas, broke the windows of the official car, and spat at the vice president.[89] Some Latin Americans drew the conclusion that only armed revolution and a complete "decapitation" of the old regime would be enough to secure a revolutionary victory. A young Argentinian doctor, Ernesto Guevara de la Serna – called "Che" by his friends – was in Guatemala City when the invasion took place, after arriving to witness the radical changes that were taking place in the country under Arbenz. Having sought refuge in the Argentinian embassy from the killings that followed Castillo Armas's victory, the 26-year-old Che wrote to his mother that the Arbenz strategy had failed: "Although Korea and Indochina are there as examples, he did not think to himself that a people in arms is an invincible power. He could have given arms to the people, but he did not want to – and now we see the result."[90]

The young Che escaped to fight another day – having made it safely to Mexico, he told his mother that he was much minded to join the Communist Party after having seen its heroism in Guatemala, but he wanted to wait until he had traveled to Europe and, he hoped, New York City. As we know, Che in the end opted for what he called a "real" revolution, in Cuba, instead of the cafés of Paris or the neon of Times Square. The Cuban challenge became a dividing line in US Third World policy; as we shall see in the next chapter, Fidel Castro's victory increased the urgency of an American counteroffensive in the Third World. But some of the methods of US intervention remained. As one CIA analyst observed later: "The language, arguments, and techniques of the Arbenz episode were used in Cuba in the early 1960s, in Brazil in 1964, in the Dominican Republic in 1965, and in Chile in 1973."[91] In a striking parallel to the role of Angola in the developing Soviet patterns of intervention in the 1970s, Guatemala was seen in Washington as a template for future success, even after the interventionist strategy had failed in quelling the Cuban revolution in 1961.

A major US covert intervention against the Brazilian nationalist regime of President João Goulart ten years after Guatemala showed how persistent Washington's perceptions of Latin American politics were. Coming after the Kennedy administration's attempts at coupling an anti-Communist strategy with a strategy for development through the Alliance for Progress, the US problem with Brazil in 1964 was that President Goulart had undertaken a program that included land reform, control of foreign capital, and the recognition of Cuba and other Communist countries. President Lyndon Johnson's view, paralleling that of Eisenhower in 1954, was that Goulart was a dangerous radical who should be removed by any means possible. But Washington knew that Brazil was a big and powerful country with a strong nationalist sentiment, and that direct intervention was therefore out of the question, except in the case of an attempted Communist takeover. Instead, LBJ's administration concentrated on destabilizing Brazil's economy, while encouraging a military coup against a government that already had enough domestic enemies on the Right to last it a lifetime. By early spring 1964, as there were signs that the Brazilian Left and the trade unions were getting ready to defend the government, Washington stepped up the pressure by promising the military plotters immediate aid and recognition in the case of a successful coup against Goulart. In a hastily called meeting on 28 March 1964 Johnson's National Security Adviser McGeorge Bundy told his colleagues that "the shape of the problem [in Brazil] is such that we should not be worrying that the military will react; we should be worrying that the military will not react."[92]

When the Brazilian military did "react" by ousting President Goulart three days later, the first reaction in Washington was joyful. In a telephone conversation with President Johnson, then at his ranch in Texas, there is an audible sense of relief in George Ball's voice when informing the President that the coup was underway.[93] Although much of the US materials on the coup are still secret, it is clear that Washington kept worrying for more than a week that President Goulart might not choose to go voluntarily, or that the Left would stage a countercoup. As a precaution, Johnson ordered US naval units to deploy off the Brazilian coast and made sure that the rebel forces could be supplied with fuel.[94] When the US ambassador, Lincoln Gordon, first called on General Castelo Branco to congratulate him with his new office of president, the ambassador "presented him [a] book on [the] White House, recently published Portuguese translations of [the] LBJ biography and collection of speeches, and [a] Kennedy half-dollar. All were graciously acknowledged."[95]

In spite of its pro-US orientation, General Castelo Branco's new regime disappointed those within the Johnson administration who had phantasized about a chance to implement a US-directed reform program in a major Latin American country. Even though the influx of American advisers and assistance became one of the biggest in the Third World, the CIA's expectations that "the regime's economic program represents a major, coordinated effort to remove the wreckage left behind by the Goulart regime and make a start on national recovery" came to nought.[96] Far too busy carrying out a civil war against the poor and those who opposed the military regime, Castelo Branco and his successors had little time to worry about reform. In the first month of the "new order" more than 50,000 people were arrested, in the start of a "dirty war" that would last up to the overhrow of the military dictatorship in 1985. Brazil remained the most socially inequitable country on earth, in which even today the poorest 40 percent of the population receive less than 7 percent of the total income.[97]

In strategic terms, however, the new Brazilian military dictatorship became a close ally of the United States in intervening elsewhere in Latin America.[98] Before the elections in Uruguay in 1966, the US embassy made it clear that a leftist victory could lead to a Brazilian invasion.[99] The Brazilians also helped the United States invade the Dominican Republic in 1965. The Dominicans had seen the first elected government in their history overthrown in 1963 . When parts of the army rebelled in order to reinstate the constitutional order two years later, the Johnson administration feared that the leftist forces among the "constitutionalists" could get the upper hand, with or without the elected president's support. "It is clear," the CIA wrote, "that [Bosch's] return to his former position would be highly undesirable ... He will in large measure be indebted to the Dominican Leftists and Communists for bring [sic] about the conditions which permitted his return." For that reason, Washington encouraged the military power holders to stay on, even when recognizing that their leader was "an unpopular figure."[100]

With fighting increasing in Santo Domingo and the military leadership in retreat, the United States first sent Marines in to protect US citizens and then decided on a full-scale invasion, but only after much soul-searching. Reflecting on the international consequences of an invasion, Johnson sighed that he was "in a hell of a shape either way. If I take over, I can't live in the world. If I let them take over, I can't live here."[101] What finally convinced the president was the alleged Communist involvement. "CIA says that this is a completely led, operated, dominated – they have got men on the inside of it – Castro operation," Johnson told McNamara on 30 April.[102] "I am seeing the pattern and I just cannot be silent," he told Bundy. "What they are doing in La Paz, Bolivia, what they are doing in Mexico City and what they are doing in Vietnam and the Dominican Republic is not totally unrelated."[103] The problem for Johnson was that the Dominican constitutionalists were ready to defend their gains even after 23,000 US troops had taken control of the country – they were "not yet prepared [to] let reason flow," as Bundy told Washington after his arrival in Santo Domingo to dictate a political solution to the crisis. Abe Fortas, whom Johnson sent to Puerto Rico in an attempt to get President Bosch's agreement to step down, was also without luck. "This fellow Bosch is a complete Latin poet-hero type and he's completely devoted to this damn constitution," the Supreme Court justice-to-be reported back to Washington.[104] The end result in the Dominican Republic was a compromise, where the constitutionalists agreed to surrender their left-wing allies and accepted new elections against a promise of the withdrawal of US forces.

As Johnson had expected, international condemnation of the US invasion was swift, even among America's allies. Alberto Lleras – the former president of Colombia and first secretary-general of the Organization of American States – complained that the Cold War was becoming a hot war in Latin America.[105] In Europe, French president de Gaulle told the American ambassador "that he thought the US, as ... all countries that had overwhelming power, was coming to believe that force would solve everything but that was not the case and we would soon realize it."[106] But to president Johnson himself, the Dominican intervention was a benchmark for similar operations in the future – even if he berated those who had provided him with faulty intelligence when very few "Cuban-trained Communists" were among those arrested in the anti-leftist purges in Santo Domingo, he still believed that the United States had to intervene in similar ways in the future whenever Communism threatened.[107] This so-called "Johnson Doctrine" worried many American policy makers in a world that seemed increasingly to turn against the United States. In mid-1965 Deputy National Security Adviser Robert Komer thought that "we're in for a troubled time abroad – with few successes in the offing.

Vietnam will indefinitely remain at best a messy problem. Indonesia is quietly slipping out of our hands ... On the Afro-Asian front, only Africa looks better in general and even there the pressing issues of Southern Africa could put us behind the eightball again. And Latin America being what it is we could easily have a few more revolutions even if we get San Domingo patched up. Let's face the fact that the things we have to do in Vietnam and elsewhere are a heavy burden for us to bear in the Afro-Asian world as well as Europe ... So my sense would be to offset it by more forthcoming policies elsewhere – to compensate for, and divert attention from ... the impact of Vietnam and Santo Domingo ... how many problems do we want to tackle at one time – shouldn't some at least be put on the back burner?[108]

The Third World and the Cold War economic system

At the beginning of the Cold War era the institutions of the world economic system were redesigned to fit American purposes of defeating Communism and promoting capitalist growth. Influenced by the effects of two world wars and the Great Depression, American thinking on world economic affairs in the twenty-five years that followed its victory in Europe and the Pacific included a bigger role for the state than had ever been envisaged before (or since, for that matter). The view among many was that some element of state and interstate planning was needed in the service of markets and in the defense of freedom against authoritarian regimes. The institutions that were set up to service these needs at the international level – the World Bank and the International Monetary Fund – came to have signal importance for the way the Cold War was fought in the Third World, and the trade regime that accompanied them was to be the determining factor for the economic development of most Third World countries.

The Bretton Woods system – named after the place in New Hampshire where the allied powers met in 1944 to charter the course of the world economy after the war – was strongly influenced by Keynesian ideas of cooperation between governments instigated to avoid future crises of the 1930s sort. The core concept was to make American capital available as cheap public loans to those governments that chose an open economy and the development of capitalist markets – Keynesianism used for ideological purposes, in a way. After the Soviet Union and the countries it controlled opted out, the new institutions could be set on a path that guaranteed American hegemony, dammed up Soviet influence, and contributed to the growth of international capitalism. The International Bank for Reconstruction and Development (IBRD), later the World Bank, was to make long-term capital available to states urgently needing such foreign aid. The International Monetary Fund (IMF) was to finance short-term imbalances in international payments in order to stabilize exchange rates. The latter, it was felt, was necessary to help out regimes under threat by political or economic unrest. The condition for membership in the IMF, however, was to peg one's currency to the US dollar, in effect linking one's overall monetary decisions to those of the US government.

Even though they were set up primarily to service the needs of the industrialized countries, the World Bank and the IMF had a significant effect for the Third World. At the outset, loans and short-term credits helped some colonial powers – notably France and Portugal – to fight antiliberation wars that they otherwise would not have been able to undertake. Then, as new Third World states were set up, the international economic institutions favored those countries that chose a market-oriented and open economy over those that did not, and as a result provided loans primarily to anti-Communist regimes and those in which Western investments already existed. The US control of the World Bank and the IMF was a potent weapon in the Cold War, in many cases determining which countries could receive international loans and credits and which could not, even as far as loans from individual governments and private banks were concerned.

While the international economic institutions grew in importance after the postwar period of reconstruction had ended, their intended role as global economic regulators declined in popularity in the United States as the growing role of the American state itself came under increasing domestic criticism in the late 1960s and early 1970s. By 1971, when US President Richard Nixon effectively ended the Bretton Woods system by refusing to sell gold at the price stipulated by the IMF, the idea of regulation was under pressure and the concept of unfettered markets ascending. For the Third World, the collapse of Bretton Woods initially meant better access to international credit, even if the conditions set for such borrowing were still in place. But as the amount of Third World loans increased, the inequities of the other half of the postwar economic system – trade conditions – came more sharply into focus.

All dominant powers have set their own trading regimes, which they often presented as "logical," "necessary," or "in the common interest." During most of the nineteenth century, for instance, Britain insisted on international free trade for its own products and services, thereby employing its advantage in techology and productivity to the maximum benefit for itself. Compared to Britain, the United States in the late twentieth century to a much higher extent emphasized the advantage that the export of its economic *model* would have for other countries. Because of its ideology and the Cold War confrontation, the economic benefit of the dominant power was not enough – the Americans wanted to create a world economic system in which both the international rules and the domestic markets conformed to the image of what had served the United States. As with other ideologies, the US market ideology of the late twentieth century often disregarded its own past – conveniently forgetting, for instance, how well measures of protectionism had served the development of US industries in the nineteenth century. But the conviction that the US model would serve the world was still genuinely held, first referred to as "Americanization," and then, as the United States was winning the Cold War, as "globalization."[109]

As we have seen in chapter 3, there were many domestic historical and political causes why most development projects in the Third World did not work out as intended. But the key obstacle that Third World countries had to contend with was a world trade system that set low prices for their raw materials and high prices for the products, the technology, and the skills that they wanted to import. The international trade negotiations, conducted primarily through the General Agreement on Tariffs and Trade (GATT), while setting a low threshold for the import of Third World semimanufactured goods and textiles to the North, did nothing to involve itself in influencing prices of raw materials, thereby allowing the strong fluctuations in prices that markets and technological progress in the North dictated. Overall – totally against Washington's stated intention – the international trade regime created divergence, not convergence, between rich and poor economies, because the terms of trade for raw materials got worse and worse as technology improved. The typical foreign income of a Third World country was enough to sustain a small elite and enough – added to domestic income – to run a state, but created an economy with little capital and even less will to invest in one's own country.[110]

The general terms of trade since World War II show a gradual decline in value for Third World raw materials compared to that of manufactured goods, presumably because technological change greatly reduced both wastage and the amount of materials needed for a single product.[111] For primary commodities, the export of which some of the poorest Third World countries depended upon, the price zigzagged from 1950 to around 1977 and then declined sharply as high-technology production took off in North America, Europe, and in the newly industrialized countries of East Asia. As prices declined, many Third World countries were forced to intensify production just to keep up their profits, thereby causing severe environmental damage and making their economies non-sustainable in the longer term, since their key natural resources were depleted faster than they could be replenished or converted to human resources at home. Together with population growth and failed agricultural development plans, these enforced strategies created soil erosion and deforestation on a scale unimaginable before, especially in areas where production was dependent on a single crop for export. Local property rights were also eroded, since large-scale production demanded confiscations or resettlement.

As could be expected given the ideological background that already existed in most newly liberated states, the unfavorable terms of trade stimulated the belief in state socialism; if there was no way out within the system – as some "dependista" economists predicted – it was better to opt out of the system altogether. Still, as we have seen, few managed to do so. Instead, during the 1960s and 1970s most Third World countries tried to limit the damage to their own economies by high protective tariffs, restrictions on imports, foreign exchange controls, ceilings on interest rates, a minimum wage, set prices for vital commodities, and restrictions on private investment. A few countries were able to use such autarkic methods to their advantage, at least for a while, but for most they instituted unnecessary barriers against private enterprise, while doing little to keep control of their resources. Instead, autarky benefited the privileged few, whether they represented an avant-garde party or a cleptocratic state.

The same could be said for many development aid programs, instituted first by the United States and then gradually by other capitalist countries, often as a way of compensating for the raw deal that the Third World was given in world markets, out of remorse for the effects of colonialism, or out of straightforward humanitarian concerns. While most US aid was tied to buying American products or was given as an accompaniment to military aid, some of the European aid – for instance from the Scandinavian countries – was given unconditionally. In both cases the aid contributed to allieviating poverty, but usually only in the short term. Much development assistance was squandered because it was spent on ectopic projects, often big and prestigious infrastructural plans, in the worst tradition of colonial development schemes. Also, receiving aid from donors far away readily stimulated corruption and other forms of malpractice in Third World countries.

As in the case of its Soviet opponents, most of the American aid was channeled for political or strategic purposes. Israel was by far the largest recipient, with $81 billion received since its creation, and Egypt number two with $53 billion (all of it since the early 1970s), testifying to the importance Washington gave to the Middle East region. South Vietnam received $24 billion during its relatively short existence, while the grand total for all of sub-Saharan Africa since 1945 is $32 billion.[112] The Foreign Assistance Act of 1961 was explicitly intended to use aid to fight the Cold War. "The ability to make long-range commitments has enabled the Soviet Union to use its aid program to make developing nations economically dependent on Russian support – thus advancing the aims of world Communism," President Kennedy concluded in presenting the act to Congress. "These new nations need help for a special reason. Without exception they are under Communist pressure. In many cases, that pressure is direct and military. In others, it takes the form of intense subversive activity designed to break down and supersede the new – and often frail – modern institutions they have thus far built." American aid would show that "economic growth and political democracy can develop hand in hand," Kennedy claimed.[113]

The one exception that existed to declining raw material prices and increasing dependence on loans and aid was in the oil-rich Third World countries, where increasing petroleum production provided a buffer against poverty. The continued economic growth of Western Europe and Japan, and increasingly also the United States itself, depended on the chances to exploit the world's primary oil fields, all situated in the Middle East. Some thinly populated countries, such as Saudi Arabia and the small sheikdoms in the Persian Gulf, became very rich indeed, especially after the Saudi-sponsored Organization of Oil Exporting Countries (OPEC) made use of the instability of world markets and the resentment of many of its member states against the West after the 1973 Arab–Israeli War to quadruple the price of crude oil. Washington had to play along, even if the Nixon administration did – at first – consider a military takeover of the oilfields.[114] Saudi Arabia, along with Iran, the main anti-Communist state in the Middle East, was too important to lose, even if the bill for keeping it stable rose sharply through the 1970s.

For most other Third World countries, the early 1970s was mostly about borrowing to keep the state afloat. The huge debts that began to be incurred around 1970 were created both because many Third World states needed to borrow and because credit was easily available. While banks generally had high liquidity, there was a slack in demand for credit in the North, accompanied by increasing inflation and negative real interest rates. In other words, many banks were just too happy to lend to Third World regimes, including in cases where the bank directors knew that their chances for recovering all of the loan were slim. American banks especially expected their own government to support them if things went wrong and in the meantime hoped to draw benefits in other areas from helping out Washington's favored Third World allies, such as Zaire's Mobutu. The result was a borrowing bonanza, in which many Third World elites willingly mortgaged their states' futures in order to secure the short-term survival of their regimes, or, in some cases, their own corrupt gain.

By around 1970 the United States had done much to create the Third World as an entity both in a positive and negative sense. Through its policies of confronting revolution, Washington had helped form blocks of resistance and a very basic form of Third World solidarity. Ironically, its interventionist policies had also contributed to radicalizing many Third World regimes, including some that were distinctly uncomfortable with any association with the Soviet Union, although – as we have seen – there was more than one reason for the leftward direction that came into full bloom in the 1970s. On the other hand, through the world economic system that it created, the United States had helped prolong the time that was needed for most countries to break out of poverty. This in itself increased the appeal of the Left in most areas of the Third World. But, as we shall see in the next chapter, US pressure was only one reason for the increasing antagonism between the Third World and the West. The apparent successes of socialist regimes – the availability of an alternative to capitalism and an alliance with America – also played a key role in radicalizing many Third World regimes, parties, and movements.

5   The Cuban and Vietnamese challenges

The dynamic of Cold War confrontation in the 1960s and 1970s depended to a high extent on the policies of the new revolutionary states. Cuba and Vietnam challenged not only Washington in defense of their revolutions; they also challenged the course set by the Soviet Union for the development of socialism and for Communist interventions abroad. In launching their defiance of the Cold War as it had developed up to the 1960s, the two countries provided inspiration for a range of left-wing states and movements in the Third World (and some groups in Europe and America). As often happens in history, this inspiration was – in most cases – more indirect than direct, and at times based on a very superficial knowledge of the Cuban or Vietnamese revolutions themselves, what could be called – if one wants to be charitable – creative misunderstandings. What mattered most, however, to the Third World movements that raised the banner of Che Guevara or Ho Chi Minh was that the example of these revolutionaries implied a license to take action for and by themselves, in spite of US military dominance or Soviet political dogma.

The Cuban and Vietnamese challenges to the Cold War would have been impossible without the early 1960s Sino-Soviet split in the international Communist movement. That Mao Zedong – himself, as he was fond of pointing out, the head of a Third World country – could claim to speak of Marxist-Leninist theory with an authority that he denied the Soviets, meant more room to maneuver for Marxists elsewhere. Mao's claim of criticizing Moscow from the *left* was particularly useful for Third World revolutionaries – even if very few of them wanted to adopt Chinese models of development or follow the vagaries of Chinese foreign policy – because it implied that they, too, could claim to have found ways of speeding up socialist construction. The Sino-Soviet split opened up great opportunities and great dangers for Communist parties in the Third World; it made it possible to tack between the two self-proclaimed centers of Communism and get support from both, but it also signaled an internal split in many parties, which in some cases reduced them to political irrelevance (if not infantility).

For the Soviet Union, the Sino-Soviet split and increasing Cuban and Vietnamese activism outside their own borders meant that its Third World policy came under increased pressure just at the moment when decolonization opened up opportunities for the advancement of socialism outside Europe. Both for Khrushchev, and for the troika of Brezhnev, Kosygin, and Podgornyi who succeeded him in October 1964, three aspects dominated their thinking on the Third World in the 1960s. They were increasingly obsessed with their conflict with China (and after 1966 also by the Chinese threat to Soviet security). They had begun a slow but positive reevaluation of the party's views on the potential for socialist revolution in the Third World. And they were impressed – in equal measure, it seems from their documents, irritated and awed – by Cuban and Vietnamese willingness to confront the United States. All made for a long period of uncertainty in Soviet Third World policy – a time of euphoric engagement between 1958 and 1962, followed by an era of doubts and disappointments up to the end of the 1960s, leading to a renewed activism from around 1970 onwards.

US policy toward the Third World showed more consistency, even as it came increasingly under the shadow of the Vietnam War. Ironically, as the United States became militarily mired in the Vietnamese civil war from 1964 onwards, some of the sense of immediate danger, bordering on hysteria, with regard to Third World developments that had existed in late Eisenhower and Kennedy administrations began to abate. The main reason for this lowering of the tone was political events in the Third World in the mid-1960s, which seemed to set a path away from dangerous alliances with the Soviet Union. Military coups in Congo, Indonesia, Algeria, and Ghana – all key countries in the battle for the Third World – seemed to take these states out of the Soviet embrace and toward some form of engagement with the United States (although varying in form from the full support of the Indonesian, Ghanaian, and Congolese dicators to the more moderate but still socialist policy of the Algerian junta headed by Ben Bella's former defense minister, Houari Boumedienne). Most important for the Johnson administration, these "victories" had come without large-scale overt or covert American interventions – small CIA-led operations combined with a lot of patience seemed to be the recipe for success, except, of course, in countries where the Soviet Union or China had the operational capability to intervene directly in support of its allies, such as in Vietnam.

The successes of the mid-1960s were not, however, paralleled during the final years of the decade. The sense of accomplishment and the can-do attitude which some of Johnson's policy advisers took from the anti-Communist coups (and which had such a disastrous effect with regard to Vietnam) did not hold up as insurgent movements began gaining ground elsewhere. As the US Secretary of Defense Robert S. MacNamara put it, "it soon was like having too few fingers to tighten the dike" – Washington got the sense of having to hold the line, rather than making progress. Much of that feeling, undoubtedly, had to do with the long US nightmare in Vietnam, which people like MacNamara only began waking up from at the end of Johnson's tenure. The fear of "Vietnams" happening elsewhere in the Third World became, for the United States, a form of self-fulfilling prophesy – becoming increasingly alienated from large numbers of Third World political activists because of its war in Vietnam, the American obsession with Indochina held back the administration's initiatives to ameliorate poverty and revise trade conditions for the Third World. In the Third World – just as at home – the Johnson administration's own policy choices made it synonymous with war and repression rather than with the social reforms that the president so fervently sought to implement.

The Sino–Soviet split and the Third World

For Nikita Khrushchev and the Soviet leadership the Sino-Soviet split meant a new departure in their Third World policies. While continuing to hope, at least up to the 1966 outbreak of Mao's Cultural Revolution, that the two countries could rejoin in some form of alliance, the Moscow leaders also felt that it was liberating not having to look over one's shoulder at China whenever an initiative was put forward. What puzzled them, however, were the *causes* for the split – Khrushchev had explained to Mao again and again that Soviet maneuvers for a *détente* with the United States were tactical and did not imply a neglect of the international class struggle. The Soviet leader cited the increase in Soviet activities in the Third World as proof – the purpose, he said, of Communist Bloc involvement both with revolutionary parties and with left-wing regimes was to undermine the American position in Africa, Asia, and Latin America while pursuing the *détente* tactic in bilateral relations and in European affairs.

But not all Third World leaders were able to understand the tactical aspects of *détente*, Khrushchev complained. He recounted to the Central Committee a conversation with Cuban leader Fidel Castro in 1963:

He is getting upset. He says: They [the Americans] are such sons of bitches. I told him: Listen, they are not sons of bitches, they are simply capitalists, they carry out a policy of their class. He says: They are sending us [counterrevolutionaries]. I told him: What do you expect them to send you? Presents? ... When we were born, they also sent [forces] against us ... But, looking from the opposite side, between us, if we find where we could send someone, if there is a hole somewhere, we also get in there. Now, this is peaceful co-existence.[1]

To the Soviets, the violent and public Chinese objections to this policy – both in terms of *détente* and in terms of engaging non-Communist left-wing regimes – testified to Beijing's neglect of Marxism and its "national-chauvinist attitude," especially as far as its criticism of Moscow – friendly relations with India was concerned. Gradually, in the early 1960s, the Soviets became convinced that Mao's real aim was to replace the Soviet Union as the international Communist superpower and that its avenue for doing so was through its links with the Third World.

The Soviets were both right and wrong in emphasizing Chinese nation-alism as a cause for the split. As the Chinese documents we have available today show, Mao's main purpose in terminating the form of alliance which had existed in the 1950s was to regain full autonomy for China's own policies. But the Chairman's focus was on his country's *domestic* development rather than on foreign policy. True, Mao wanted to oppose the United States in international affairs more vigorously than the Soviets did, at least in words. But his obsession was with the direction the Chinese revolution itself had been taking since the foundation of the PRC and the start of the Sino-Soviet alliance in 1949–50. He discovered a drift within his own party toward setting Chinese society into forms where bureaucrats and planners had the upper hand, not the revolution-ary initiative of the people. Increasingly, in the late 1950s, the CCP chairman began to regret the wholesale copying of Soviet models that had taken place in China, because it did not allow the country to progress rapidly enough toward socialism and, ultimately, Communism. When his instrument for doing away with centralized planning and relying on the mass action of the people – the so-called "Great Leap Forward" – ended in dismal failure in 1959, Mao suspected that some of his party comrades had deliberately been holding the people (and himself) back, and that his opponents had the support of the Soviet Union. The main causes on the Chinese side for the split were "nationalist," but they were primarily domestic, not international, and they were most definitely linked to Mao's own idiosyncratic form of Marxism.

With the split openly visible after the confrontation between Soviet and Chinese delegates at the Romanian party congress and the subsequent withdrawal of most Soviet advisers from China in the summer of 1960, both sides began a frantic search for allies within the international Communist movement. The Chinese thought it unlikely that European Communist parties – except Albania – would support their views and focused most of their propaganda efforts on the Third World. Mao's view was that Soviet society under Khrushchev was going through a counter-revolution, in which it was gradually becoming more like the Western imperialist states, leaving its Leninist and Stalinist roots behind. While in reality projecting his fears for China on to its northern neighbor, Mao also during the early 1960s began seeing the Soviets as returning to a pre-revolutionary state, in which their *cultural* affinity with the West was determining their international political positions. The Soviets were part of the self-centered and complacent Western culture, while revolutionary China fought on against imperialism, helped by other Third World countries. The so-called "three worlds theory" – a variation on a Stalinist theme that Mao first put forward in 1964 – placed the United States and the Soviet Union within the First World as hegemonic super-powers, while the other industrialized countries, over which the two superpowers exerted their hegemony, constituted a Second World. China and the poor countries of the South made up a Third World, which were making revolution against the superpowers and would become the future center of international developments.[2]

During the 1960–66 period – when China's Third World activism was at its peak – Chinese Communists seemed initially to do well in their campaign to link other parties and countries to their cause. Mao's identification of the Third World as the united international proletariat battling against imperialism – so reminiscent of Sultan Galiev's positions in the 1920s – was attractive for many Third World Communists and left-wingers. The mass mobilization strategy, the insistence on the creative powers of "the people," who would make up for a lack of technology through effort and enterprise, the sheer voluntarism of Maoism, projecting Communism from the distant future to the here and now, had a distinct appeal as a general development model both to Marxist and nativist revolutionaries. To some of the radicals whom we met in chapter 3, Mao's thinking seemed indeed to be socialism applied to the Third World. As the head of the mighty Indonesian Communist Party (PKI) Aidit noted in January 1964, "those countries which try to build Communism, with the existence of imperialism in the world, will become 'rich, fat cats' at the expense of the backward countries and will lose their revolutionary spirit ... You only have to look at the Soviet Union where there has been built a higher standard of living and you will find that the Soviets have lost their revolutionary fervor."[3]

The most obsessive phase of the Third World competition between the Chinese and the Soviets came as the Sino-Soviet alliance finally collapsed during a series of abortive talks in Moscow in the summer of 1963. At the Moscow meetings, Deng Xiaoping – the chief Chinese spokesman – accused the Soviets of attacking China in "increasingly sharp, increasingly extreme form, in an increasingly organized [way], on an increasingly large scale, trying, come what may, to crush others ... using such methods is a habitual affair for you."[4] The foreign visits of Chinese president Liu Shaoqi and premier Zhou Enlai, who – between them – visited twenty Third World countries during 1963, including the radical nativist regimes in Indonesia, Burma, Egypt, Algeria, and Ghana, helped project a China that was on the offensive in the Third World. Beijing began extending cheap loans and sending advisers abroad on a much larger scale than before, including military experts. The most visible example was the Chinese funding – and in part building – of a new railway linking land-locked Zambia to the Tanzanian coast. In Vietnam and Indonesia, as we shall see, China became the closest international ally for their Communist parties.

But while Beijing seemed to be making progress in its campaign to replace the Soviet Union as the main inspiration for Third World socialism, it was already from the beginning working under considerable handicaps, some of which increased over time. The Sino-Indian border conflict, starting with skirmishes in 1959 and culminating in a brief war between the two countries in 1962, did much harm to China's pretensions to be a leader of the Third World. True, many Third World politicians resented Nehru's arrogance, but China's own aims and its behavior in the conflict were seen as narrow-minded and nationalistic. The real problems in China's Third World policy, however, ran deeper than the conflict with India. Very few Chinese Communist leaders had any experience whatsoever in working with foreigners, and their reference points were their own experiences and their ideology, just as in the cases of the United States and the Soviet Union. The onset of the Cultural Revolution – Mao's final attempt at catapulting China into the socialist modernity that he envisaged to be his greatest legacy – took Sinocentric attitudes to new heights, with the Chinese insistence that all other Third World countries would have to learn from Maoism if they were to be successful. By the end of 1966 many countries, parties, and movements had had enough of Chinese preaching and what they considered unwarranted interventions in their own affairs.

The advent of the Cultural Revolution also meant that China increasingly turned inward and upon itself. Mao's highly successful emissaries Liu Shaoqi and Zhou Enlai were, in Liu's case, hounded to death, and in Zhou's reduced to playing the sad role of mouthpiece for a dogmatic and self-defeating policy that was abhorrent to him. By 1967 Chinese foreign policy had by all practical measures ceased to exist, as Red Guards occupied and ransacked the Foreign Ministry, while most ambassadors were recalled to Beijing for political education. The British embassy was attacked, and the Soviet embassy was laid under siege by youthful Maoists for several months. Even China's closest allies backed away. The North Korean leader Kim Il Sung called the Cultural Revolution "unbelievable madness." China's Maoist Red Guards, on their side, condemned North Korea as revisionist.[5] In a speech to a Korean party conference on 5 October 1966 Kim obviously referred to Beijing when he said that "it is ... wrong only to shout against US imperialism without taking concrete actions to stop US imperialist aggression. In particular, one should not cause difficulties to the anti-imperialist forces taking practical measures for dealing blows in unity at the US imperialist aggressors."[6] The Chinese insistence on not cooperating in any way with the Soviet Union, even in facilitating aid to Vietnam, was for Kim enough to interrupt his long-standing relationship with Beijing.

To the Soviets, the breakdown of the alliance with China not only destroyed the great anti-US compact that they had put together with so much effort, investment, and hope during the 1950s. The increasing challenge from China soon became a key international diplomatic priority for the USSR and – from the mid-1960s onwards – a security threat. Already in May 1963, in preparation for the abortive Moscow talks, the Soviet ambassador to China, Chervonenko, sent a long report to Mikhail Suslov, the Politburo member who headed the working group that dealt with the relationship to China. In his report the ambassador made it clear that "there are no doubts any longer ... that the current policy of the Chinese leadership in practice serves to undermine the unity of the fraternal parties ... [the] vanguard aspirations of the Chinese leadership, which developed on the soil of the Great Han nationalism, [aimed at] world leadership [through] undertaking a major subversion of the international Communist movement [and] rudely compromising the CPSU." In particular, Chervonenko pointed to Beijing's aim of "establishing unchallenged political influence in Asia and Africa," but he was also concerned that China could destabilize Soviet control in Eastern Europe and over West European Communist parties. What the ambassador reported – and which Suslov to a high degree took to heart – was not only an all-out Chinese onslaught on the Soviet position in the world, but also that China's attack had good chances of succeeding, at least in the Third World.[7]

By late 1963 the Soviet Foreign Ministry was reporting a large and coordinated Chinese campaign to push Third World countries away from cooperating with the Soviet Union in any area, claiming – among other accusations – that the "Russians" were Europeans, and that people of the Third World had to stand together against European influence. Even long-time Soviet allies were feared to be susceptible – North Korea seemed to Moscow to be solidly in the Chinese camp already from late 1962, and North Vietnam at least from the fall of 1963. According to a top-secret Soviet Foreign Ministry report, the Chinese "spare[d] neither

funds nor time, [did] not shun away from the most unworthy methods –
blackmail, flattery, bribery, [while] using the services of splitters and
renegades."[8] The Soviet embassy in Algeria complained about the
"tons of propagandistic literature" imported from China and decried
Moscow's lack of "appropriate countermeasures."[9] The Soviet embassy
in Burundi anxiously reported that the Queen covertly received sixty
thousand dollars from Chinese representatives.[10] And from Port Louis,
the CPSU embassy representative related with trepidation how the
Chinese had attempted to bribe the chief of the Communist Party of
Mauritius to support the CCP in international forums.[11] By 1965 a major
portion of all Soviet efforts in the Third World were aimed at countering
Chinese measures in even the smallest and most remote countries in
terms of Moscow's interests.

After Chinese foreign policy self-destructed with the advent of the
Cultural Revolution, Soviet security worries increased, even while the
fear of a Chinese takeover of the Third World slowly abated. In 1967
Soviet Prime Minister Kosygin told both US and British leaders that he
considered the Chinese and not the West the greatest threat to world
peace. "Imagine," he told his British counterpart Harold Wilson, "if they
[the Chinese] deprive themselves of everything, if they devote themselves
to militarization, to building up their armed forces, they can be a great
force."[12] According to President Johnson, during their summit meeting
at Glassboro, Kosygin showed "an obsession on China, and just said we
better understand that they are very dangerous people."[13] The Sino-
Soviet border issue, which Mao Zedong used deliberately in order to
heighten tension with the Soviets before the Cultural Revolution, was to
Moscow the most frightening of all foreign policy questions. Mao's
statements in July 1964 to a visiting delegation of Japanese socialists
that "about a hundred years ago the area east of Baikal became Russian
territory, and since then Vladivostok, Khabarovsk, Kamchatka and other
areas have become territories of the Soviet Union. We have not yet," the
Chairman continued, "presented the bill for this list."[14]

For the Soviets, the double tragedy of the split with China was that it
originated at a time when Moscow genuinely believed the world situation
to be decisively turning in its favor. Within the Soviet Union itself,
de-Stalinization and the remarkable technological progress of the late
1950s created a renewed enthusiasm for serving one's people and, at least
in some quarters, for the socialist idea. The dank cynicism of the late Stalin
era and the period of post-Stalin squabbles within the leadership seemed
gone; living standards were on their way up and there were great projects –
such as the Virgin Lands scheme – to join in. Alongside this renewed
domestic confidence – and helping to sustain it – came the process of

decolonization in the Third World and the fact that so many of the new regimes wanted to learn from the Soviet experience. It all amounted, as Khrushchev put it, to a "world historical opportunity" for the Soviet Union, which pointed directly to the creation of a world community of socialist states and, eventually, to revolutions in the imperialist countries.

At the center of this new and enthusiastic approach to the Third World was the party leader himself, Nikita Khrushchev. Very much like his US counterpart in the early 1960s, John F. Kennedy, Khrushchev came to identify his time in power with the era of the breakthrough of liberation in the Third World. To him, decolonization had created a new world in which the Soviet Union could operate:

The renovation of the world along the principles of freedom, democracy and socialism, in which we are now taking part, is a great historical process wherein different revolutionary and democratic movements unite and interact, with social-ist revolutions exerting the determining influence. The success of the national-liberation movement, due in large measure to the victories of socialism, in turn strengthens the international positions of socialism in the struggle against imperi-alism. It is this truly Leninist concept of the historical processes that is the basis of the policy of the Communist Parties and socialist countries, a policy aimed at strengthening the close alliance with the peoples fighting for independence and peoples that have already won it.

Khrushchev's impatient hailing of a new dawn in the Third World meant that Soviet political theory would have to find an explanation for why this was happening and determine a new outline of what the future for Asia, Africa, and Latin America would be like. Stalinist dogmatic determinism, in which one era followed another in human society in a pattern that was set for all countries and continents, was already on its way out in the late 1950s, along with the finding that socialism was a theoretical oxymoron in the Third World. The mood in Moscow was in many ways similar to that in Beijing: a strengthening of the voluntaristic aspects both of public policy and of foreign policy. Mao's Great Leap slogan "Build more socialism: faster, better, and more economically" could as well have belonged to the intensifying Soviet propaganda around 1960.

Alongside this renewed enthusiasm for building socialism at home, the Soviet leadership began a broad reevaluation of the character of Third World social change, with great implications for Soviet policy. Much like in the United States, it was social scientists with links to the world of politics who spearheaded the reevaluation. And just like American mod-ernization, theory meant breaking away from past doubts – in part of a racial character – of whether "development" was really available to all, the beginning changes in Soviet Marxist theory on the Third World empha-sized the potential of Third World peoples *themselves* to carry out rapid and successful revolutions, pointing the way toward socialism in spite of their "backwardness" in relationships of production. That backwardness, the new generation of Soviet social scientists explained, was due primarily to foreign exploitation. If the exploitation was removed, and the forces of production were given a free rein, the relationship between the classes could develop rapidly, making countries ready for socialism much more quickly than the time needed in countries that had not been laboring under artifical impediments to the development of their productive forces.

Much of the emerging Soviet optimism with regard to the Third World was based on studies of what Soviet social scientists called "new groups active in society." These educated Third World elites, be they in the civil service or in the military, had – ideologically speaking – nowhere to go except toward a socialist consciousness. The capitalist system itself implied collaboration with the former colonial masters, and even those who viewed Communism with suspicion would not like to go down that path again. Some of the military elites, because they spearheaded the defense that the new countries constantly had to prepare in order to defend themselves against imperialist aggression, would become increasingly susceptible to Communist propaganda. In other words, elites in postcolonial states were *inherently* drawn toward socialism, even if they themselves had not discovered the scientific appeal of Marxism.

The new thinking on the Third World – which had its first heyday for a short period in the early 1960s – also began employing Lenin's concept of the working class as in some cases having to be infused with class consciousness from the *outside*. For Africa, Asia, and Latin America this meant that Marxist members of the new elites could – with aid from the Soviet Union – be able to instill a sense of unity and revolutionary potential into the emerging working class. What really mattered for making a breakthrough, some advisers observed, was a small group with a dedication to a scientific Marxist-Leninist theory of society and with an "internationalist" attitude to the Soviet Union. While Stalin had implicitly assumed that the Soviet Union was unique (and tried to obfuscate the realities of the November 1917 coup and the Soviet party's lack of a working-class base), most new leaders believed that the Soviet experience provided a very practical pattern for social change in other countries, albeit in a broad sense and under different circumstances. Interestingly, the early enthusiasts for a more activist Soviet Third World policy included at least a few who were willing to rethink the Soviet experience in a more factual direction and who would later come to play key roles in the reform programs of the 1980s.

This second phase of Soviet enthusiasm for a direct involvement in the Third World – the first one having been the early Comintern period in the 1920s – lasted a few years at most. Already by the early 1960s the Kremlin's fascination with the potential Soviet contribution to social change in Africa, Asia, and Latin America was on the wane. There were several reasons for this, some of which are obvious. The split with China set cooperation with Third World countries in a distinctively negative light: the massive Soviet aid program seemed a waste of money and effort, which had only led to ingratitude and downright hatred from the Chinese. The Cuban Missile Crisis, in which a conflict over Soviet nuclear weapons installed by stealth on the island had led the superpowers to the brink of war, reminded Moscow leaders of the dangers involved in intervening in conflicts that could not be easily controlled far from home. As we will see later, the refusal of the Cuban leaders to put a good face to the Soviet climbdown over the missiles scared many of the Kremlin leaders and meant that there was opposition to getting directly militarily involved in Third World affairs for some time to come.

In addition to the conflict with China and the missile crisis, there were also less visible concerns on the Soviet side that had started to grow well before Khrushchev left office. Events in Congo showed the sheer difficulty of Soviet operations far from its own borders – when Lumumba had called for Soviet aid, the Red Army had very few options at its disposal had it been ordered to launch a large-scale operation. The Soviets did not have naval vessels that could move fast into a far-off conflict area, carrying out amphibious landing operations or parachute drops from helicopters. Neither did they have a system of landing rights for their aircraft in the Third World, not to mention bases from which their soldiers could operate. Congo reminded the Soviet leadership of their limited capabilities in most of the Third World, and they knew that it would take a long time to develop this forward potential, because much of it depended on the general strengthening of its military forces. The latter could only be done by further increases in a military budget that already took up more than a quarter of the Soviet GDP. The uprisings against Soviet rule in Novocherkassk and elsewhere had reminded Khrushchev of the dangers involved in squeezing the civilian parts of the budget further, and even if his successors proved more willing to invest in expanding the military, Soviet interventionist capabilities would continue to lag far behind those of the Americans for the rest of the Cold War.

The military coups of 1965–66 also reminded the Soviets of the fragility of many radical Third World regimes. To many Central Committee advisers, the lessons of the defeats in Ghana, Algeria, and Indonesia were that a breakthrough for socialism in the Third World had to be based on the development of Communist parties, rather than on vague radicalism. Such parties would have to be built from the moment real independence was achieved and be consciously patterned on the Soviet Communist Party and its experiences. The reason why Vietnam and Cuba had held, while the others had not, was precisely the existence of such revolutionary vanguards of a distinct "internationalist orientation." It would be wrong for Moscow to assume the existence of such trends in former colonies where the bourgeoisie – even in its radicalized form – had the hegemony in the liberation front. But, on the other hand, it would be equally wrong to write off Marxist nuclei that had secured the leading role for themselves within larger movements, even if these "internationalists" were only a small group of the total. The judgment on which were which of these situations was, of course, Moscow's, and that duty would have to be carried out with greater discrimination and more diligence than before, the International Department claimed.

Both the Foreign Ministry and the two international departments of the Central Committee found it difficult to present their complex arguments to the new heads of the party and the state. Leonid Brezhnev, the general secretary of the Central Committee and increasingly the leading figure in the Politburo, had very little foreign policy experience, and veered between different positions presented by his advisers on most matters except his heartfelt desire for recognition of Soviet power by the West. He told his chief foreign policy adviser, Aleksandrov-Agentov, that "my life worked out in such a way that I worked all my childhood in a village, [spent] my youth at a factory, and then – party committees, and for the entire war – the army. I never had anything to do with this damn foreign policy and know nothing of it."[15] Other leaders, such as head of the KGB (from 1967) Iurii Andropov or the party secretary in charge of the international departments of the Central Committee, Boris Ponomarev, only gradually began concentrating on key developments outside Europe. Several key party foreign policy advisers recall how difficult it was to get the leadership's ear for any affairs not connected to the United States, Europe, or China up to the late 1960s.

By 1968 a major reason why this inattention to the Third World began to change was the situation in Vietnam. Up to the aftermath of the Tet Offensive (which the Soviets initially interpreted as a North Vietnamese defeat), Moscow's main concern with Indochina had been its role as a barrier against *détente* – as long as the Americans were fighting in Vietnam, the Soviets could not envisage major advances in reducing international tension overall. It was only after American public opinion started to turn against the war because of its costs to the United States that some Soviet leaders began entertaining the prospect of a Vietnamese victory, and it was not until Nixon pledged his new administration to a speedy withdrawal from Vietnam in 1969 that Third World activists within the Central Committee started using Indochina as an argument for increasing the attention paid to Asia, Africa, and Latin America. If the United States was willing to gamble with the future of South Vietnam – one of its key Third World allies – then the prospects for the survival of revolutions elsewhere seemed infinitely better than what they had been only a few years ago. It was an opportunity that many Soviet leaders were willing to try to exploit, even though to begin with they had few concrete ideas of how to do it.

Cuba as revolutionary example

The Cuban revolution, which was to inspire radicals all over the Third World, began as a nativist rebellion and only gradually developed into a Marxist experiment. Fidel Castro – the key leader of the revolution – turned against the regime of Fulgencio Batista in Cuba because he saw it as allied with US exploitation of the island and as being incapable of carrying out the social and economic reform that Castro thought neces-sary. The promise of the Cuban revolution was that Cubans – and eventually all Latin Americans – could by themselves overthrow US control and create truly independent states. The young Castro – he was 32 when he came to power – combined his anger at his own country's backwardness with a strong sense of being a vanguard for future revolu-tions elsewhere on the continent. "America," he told a rally in Havana in 1959, "is the victim of ambitious men, military caudillos, military castes.

How much America and the peoples of our hemisphere need a revolution like the one that has taken place in Cuba! How much America needs an example like this in all its nations. How much it needs for the millionaires who have become rich by stealing the people's money to lose everything they have stolen. How much America needs for the war criminals in the countries of our hemisphere all to be shot.[16]

Fidel Castro was born in 1926 in Mayari in the easternmost part of Cuba, the son of a well-off sugarcane farmer who had immigrated from Spain. Castro came to prominence as a student leader and fiery orator in the early 1950s, seeking an outlet for his intense nationalism in traditional Cuban politics, but remaining dissatisfied with the way the opposition resisted the increasingly dictatorial Batista. In 1953 Castro led an unsuc-cessful attack on an army post in Santiago de Cuba and was imprisoned. Released on a general amnesty in 1955, he went to Mexico along with his brother, Raúl, and a small group of followers. It was in Mexico that Castro began to see his planned expedition against the Batista regime as an opening salvo in a general Latin American rising against US domination. He also – through his brother and the Argentinian physician Ernesto Che Guevara, whom the brothers met in Mexico – began a gradual exploration of Marxism, but there are few indications that Fidel Castro began seeing himself as a Marxist or a Communist before coming to power.

Castro's intense anti-US feelings increased after his small band of revolutionary fighters made it back to Cuba to start a guerrilla war in December 1956. The Cuban dictator they were fighting against, Batista, had received weapons from the United States in spite of the Eisenhower administration's increasing concern over his repressive misrule. The State Department's feeling – widely reported at the time – was that Batista may be a son-of-a-bitch, "but at least he is *our* son-of-a-bitch."[17] The revolutionaries that Castro led were an untested bunch, as Washington saw it, with many advisers who were Marxist-oriented. For Castro, the US supplies to his enemy became a signal of battles to come. In 1958, after an attack by the regime's US-equipped airforce, he wrote to his lover, Celia Sánchez,

When I saw the rockets being fired at Mario's house, I swore to myself that the Americans would pay dearly for what they are doing. When this war is over a much wider and bigger war will begin for me: the war that I am going to wage against them. I know that this is my real destiny.[18]

After Fidel Castro's forces defeated Batista and took over Havana in January 1959, Washington began sensing a real danger to its Caribbean policies. Castro was not just another vaguely romantic military strong-man without any special political program. He was under the influence of the Communists and he had a hemispheric plan for revolution. Castro, the CIA soon concluded, could not be brought over to the US side. He would have to be contained or removed. In October 1960 the United States prohibited most exports to Cuba, cutting off the country's economic lifeline. The CIA started training Cuban exiles in camps in Guatemala the same year and encouraged them to begin hit-and-run attacks along the Cuban coast. By the time John Kennedy entered the White House, the United States had broken diplomatic relations with Cuba and the preparations for an invasion were already underway. In spite of his doubts about the readiness of the mostly exiled Cuban invasion force, Kennedy decided to let the CIA's plans go ahead. Castro's revolution was a direct threat to the president's plans for reforming the US–Latin American relationship. Kennedy also felt that he could not be seen as being "soft on Communism" during the first weeks of his presidency as this would risk both his relationship with Congress and with the American public.

The invasion began on 16 April 1961 on and near Playa Girón on the southern coast of central Cuba. The area had been handpicked by the Kennedys as a good landing area, lightly defended. But the invasion soon turned to disaster for the United States and its Cuban allies. Already by the second day of fighting it became clear that the invaders could not hold their own against Castro's forces without direct US air support, something President Kennedy was unwilling to provide. By the end of the third day most of the 1,300-strong invasion force had surrendered. Still, the Kennedy administration was not willing to give up its efforts to remove Castro. "The alternative to the steps that were taken this past week would have been to sit and wait and hope that in the future some fortuitous event would occur to change the situation," Robert Kennedy wrote to his brother, the president. "The immediate failure of the rebels' activities in Cuba does not permit us ... to return to the status quo with our policy toward Cuba being one of waiting and hoping for good luck. The events in the last few days makes this inconceivable."

Castro's response to the continued threats from Washington was equally clear:

[Kennedy] says his patience is coming to an end. Well, what about our patience, with all the things we have had to endure? The imperialist powers use the method of surprise attacks, the same method of Hitler and Mussolini. We wish they would reconsider things, take a cold shower or a hot shower, anything. Let humanity, let history end a system which is now outdated. Imperialism must pass, just as feudalism did, just as slavery did.[19]

As Castro's rhetoric makes clear, the victory of his forces in early 1959 had set off a gradual but rapid leftward trend in his thinking. From some of his own key advisers – such as his brother and Che Guevara – Fidel took over both Marxist phrases and at least some elements of Marxist thinking. The Cuban Communist Party – with whom relations had been cool up to the revolution – supplied much-needed proposals and plans for the building of a new type of state. Lastly, there was Castro's increasing admiration for the Soviet Union, which he had developed since he first met Soviet representatives in Mexico. To Fidel Castro, the Soviets represented that "other" kind of modernity – emphasizing social justice – that he hoped to build in Cuba, even if he had no plans to replicate all of Moscow's models.

Convinced from the outset that the United States would try to snuff out his revolution, Fidel Castro already in 1959 set out to encourage support from other countries, including the Soviet Bloc. In February 1960 a member of the top Soviet leadership – Anastas Mikoyan – came to Havana to sign a trade agreement and open a Soviet exhibition (Mikoyan had also handled the first Soviet man-to-man contacts with

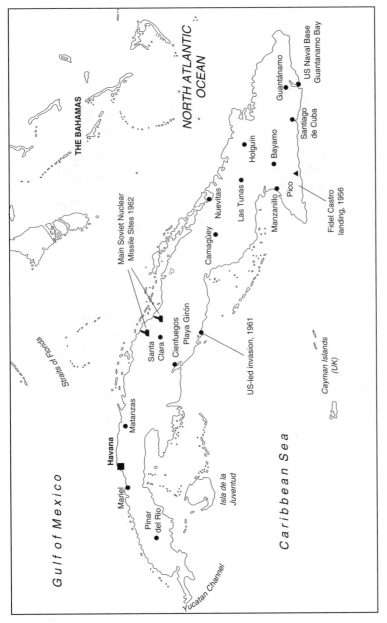

Map 5   The United States, the Soviet Union, and Cuba.

Fig. 4   "I felt as though I had returned to my childhood" – Mikoyan with Fidel Castro and Che Guevara in Havana, 1960.

Mao Zedong back in 1949). Castro saw his Soviet contacts as stimulating the Cuban revolution and as an important economic link.[20] But first and foremost it provided security against a US attack, Castro believed. By March 1960 the Soviet leadership had granted a Cuban request for arms and military advisers. Castro had impressed the veteran Bolshevik Mikoyan as "a genuine revolutionary, completely like us. I felt as though I had returned to my childhood."[21] Khrushchev was equally convinced after meeting the young Cuban revolutionary at the UN in September 1960. During a much-publicized meeting at the hotel where the Cubans were staying in Harlem, the pudgy Soviet leader locked Castro in an awkward embrace, telling reporters that he did not know if the Cuban was a Communist, but he knew that he himself was truly a Fidelist.[22]

While the Soviets in 1960–66 increasingly wedded themselves to the defense of the island in case of an all-out US attack, there was substantial skepticism in Moscow toward taking on too many financial guarantees for Castro's survival. When the Cubans in the fall of 1960 wanted to become "permanent observers" in the COMECON – as a cover for real membership in the Soviet economic bloc – Moscow demurred, and the Cubans had to mobilize East German and other Eastern European support for their cause.[23] The Cubans – and Castro in particular – resented what they saw as Soviet closed-fistedness and less than total dedication to their revolution. And while Fidel told his comrades already in November 1960 that "I have been a Marxist from my student days," that Communists should occupy "all of the key positions ... in the government, the cultural apparatus, the army, and the state economy," and that "Moscow is our brain and our great leader," in March 1962 he purged leading old Communists from the leadership and stressed that Cuban Communism would revolve around *his* ideas and those of the "guerrilla generation."[24]

The fateful Soviet May 1962 decision to place nuclear missiles in Cuba had as one of its key purposes to convince Castro that Moscow had made a strategic decision to defend and assist his revolution against its enemy. The Soviet climbdown, after the missile crisis in October, infuriated Castro and convinced him that in spite of the ideological closeness to Moscow, Cuba would have to develop its own revolutionary strategy. The "concessions on the part of the Soviet Union produced a sense of oppressiveness," the Cuban leader told Mikoyan, who came calling to explain the Soviet decision in November.

Psychologically our people were not prepared for that. A feeling of deep disappointment, bitterness and pain has appeared, as if we were deprived of not only the missiles, but of the very symbol of solidarity. Reports of missile launchers being dismantled and returned to the USSR at first seemed to our people to be an insolent lie. You know, the Cuban people were not aware of the agreement, were not aware that the missiles still belonged to the Soviet side. The Cuban people did not conceive of the juridical status of these weapons. They had become accustomed to the fact that the Soviet Union gave us weapons and that they became our property.[25]

The Cuban leadership's disappointment with the Soviet capitulation during the missile crisis – unperturbed by the fact that the only alternative seemed to be nuclear war – led Havana to seek new directions for its foreign policy. While Castro's main emphasis up to 1963 had been the survival of his revolution and, as part of that program, an ever closer link with the Soviet Union, by the mid-1960s Cuba had developed a much more aggressive policy of assistance to other Third World movements as part of its defense of the principle of revolution. Given what he saw as Soviet timidity – which Castro in his mind connected to its Europeanness – the Cuban support of the revolutions of other Third World peoples was not just a duty and an historical necessity, but also a forward defense against an American attack on Cuba. As the tide of revolution rose around the world, the Cuban leader believed, the United States would have to remove some of its obsession with his small Caribbean island. Meanwhile, Cuba would carry out its great historical mission to help sow the seeds of revolution elsewhere.

As the Sino-Soviet conflict intensified in 1964–66, Castro appealed for socialist unity, but did not expect to achieve it, at least not anytime soon. Instead he lauded the Cuban and Vietnamese experience:

we small countries, which do not entrust ourselves to the strength of armies of millions of men, which do not entrust ourselves to the strength of atomic power – we small countries, like Vietnam and Cuba, have enough instinct to calmly see and understand that no one more than we, who are in a special situation 90 miles from the Yankee empire and attacked by Yankee planes, are affected by these divisions and discords that weaken the strength of the socialist camp.[26]

But the discord among socialist states should not lead to a defensive attitude in fighting imperialism. On the contrary, Castro proclaimed in 1965,

could we exchange the right of other people to their future for our rights to the future? No. Could we be happy knowing that other peoples do not have the same rights as we have? No. That is the reason we concern ourselves with the fate of the other peoples. That is the reason we express solidarity with nations fighting such as Vietnam, the Congo, Venezuela, any nation fighting imperialism ... We know that there is an enemy standing in the way of all peoples here in America, as well as in Asia and Africa. That enemy is imperialism, especially Yankee imperialism. That is the enemy that must be defeated here, and in Asia and Africa. Aggression against any nation, any continent must be considered as an aggression against us. It should hurt us as though aggression was committed against us. Furthermore, we must understand that if a nation can be attacked in Asia it can also be attacked in Africa and in America. What we must liquidate is the right of imperialism to commit aggression against nations. What we must establish is that any nation attacked by the Yankee imperialism will have the aid of the rest of the nations, the rest of the nations fighting against imperialism.[27]

This reverse doctrine of intervention was slowly put into action by the Cubans from 1963 onwards. To begin with, the focus was on Latin America and the Caribbean, from where the Cubans trained at least 1,500 guerrilla fighters up to 1964. But, as the historian Piero Glejeses explains, the Cuban Latin American strategy ran into trouble from the very beginning. The Soviets advised caution. The Latin American

Communist Parties resented Cuban interference and lecturing. And the immediate chances for waging a successful guerrilla war of the type Castro was looking for seemed weak in most countries. After a secret meeting of Latin American Communist Parties in Havana in November 1964, where Fidel Castro was criticized for interfering too much with the strategies of other parties, Cuban attention changed to Africa, an option the Cuban leaders had been studying since early 1963.

The Cuban preoccupation with Africa was ideological, strategic, and emotional. Havana had absorbed much of the Soviet and East European preaching from the late 1950s and early 1960s on the ideological significance of decolonization, in which the competition for ideological hegemony in the new states was seen as crucial for the global conflict between socialism and capitalism in the longer run. Supporting African liberation movements was also seen as hitting at one of the weak spots of American imperialism and one area where the United States least expected the Cubans to be involved. Finally, all Cubans were aware of the links that connected their island to Africa, through the 800,000 slaves that had been brought there up to the nineteenth century and who had created a nation in which today one-third of the people are of African descent. Helping African liberation was solidarity with long-suffering relatives, it was paying back a debt to Cuba's African ancestors.

The Cuban involvement abroad centered around Che Guevara, whom Castro had put in charge of the overall program of aid to foreign revolutions from 1961 onwards. Guevara was born in Argentina in 1928, into a wealthy family that helped him train as a doctor and funded his early travels through the continent. It was when hiking through the Andes that Guevara's mind first started centering on the problems of social oppression and poverty. Always sickly and often bedridden in his youth, Guevara was an obsessive reader who gradually began to see Marxism as providing an explanation of the injustices he witnessed. In 1955, having escaped to Mexico after having observed firsthand the US intervention in Guatemala, he wrote to his mother:

There are two ways of arriving at what you so much fear: a positive way of direct persuasion, and a negative way of complete disenchantment. I arrived by the second way, but immediately convinced myself that it was necessary to continue by the first. The manner in which the gringos treat the American continent aroused my growing indignation, but at the same time I studied the theoretical explanation for what they do and found that it was scientific.

The science of Marxism became Guevara's faith and the *foco* (center) of rebellion, his favored theory of social change. A daredevil and egomaniac, Che wanted – like Castro, with whom he linked up with in exile in

Mexico – to transform the world according to scientific guidelines, but with a significant place in that transformation set off to heroic action with himself at its center. Having joined in the Cuban revolution and fought with great bravery and brutality, Guevara summed up his experience in the 1960 book *Guerrilla Warfare*, which became something of a bible to revolutionaries elsewhere in the 1960s and 1970s. In the book Che stresses that "it is not necessary to wait until all conditions for making revolution exist; the insurrection can create them."[28] In other words, the slow and class-based strategy of the Latin American Left should be exchanged for a strategy of spontaneous insurrections, set off by small bands of guerrillas under the leadership of the Communist Party. This, Guevara claimed, was the way victory had been won in Cuba and the only method that would work when faced with overwhelming US power and lacklustre support from the socialist countries.

In 1965 Che Guevara was 37 years old. He had served as president of the Cuban National Bank and as Minister for Industry in his new home-land, and he had traveled incessantly, to Eastern Europe, China, and Africa. Increasingly restless, he requested Castro's permission to secretly lead a force of Cuban advisers going to fight with the Congolese rebels against the US-supported regime. Unsuccessful in Congo, as we have seen, Guevara moved back to Cuba and then traveled through South America to Bolivia – the area where his social consciousness had first been awakened – where he hoped to set off a general rebellion against a repressive government. There, in October 1967, his small band of Bolivian and Cuban fighters were tracked down by the Bolivian Army and the CIA. Guevara was summarily executed, and his body paraded in front of television cameras to make sure that the world knew he was dead. Walt Rostow reported to President Johnson that the killing of Che Guevara "marks the passing of another of the aggressive, romantic revo-lutionaries like Sukarno, Nkrumah, Ben Bella – and reinforces this trend … It shows the soundness of our 'preventive medicine' assistance to countries facing incipient insurgency – it was the Bolivian 2nd Ranger Battalion trained by our Green Berets from June–September of this year, that cor-nered him and got him."[29]

However much he frightened the CIA, Guevara's (and Castro's) polit-ical and military philosophy had only a limited impact on the Third World. As Guevara himself noted in self-critical mood after the Congo debacle,

what had we to offer? We did not give much protection, as our story has shown. Nor did we offer any education, which might have been a great vehicle of com-munication. Medical services were provided only by the few Cubans there, with inadequate medicines, a fairly primitive system of administration, and no sanitary

Fig. 5   Che Guevara in Zaire (Congo), probably June 1965.

organization. I think that some deep thought and research needs to be devoted to the problem of revolutionary tactics where the relations of production do not give rise to land hunger among the peasantry.[30]

But Che Guevara's real aim in his post-Congo report to Fidel was to show the inadequacies of the material he had been given in order to carry out modern revolution:

The soldiers are of peasant stock and completely raw, for whom the main attraction is to have a rifle and a uniform, sometimes even shoes and a certain authority in the area. Corrupted by inactivity and the habit of ordering the peasants around, saturated with fetishistic notions about death and the enemy, devoid of any coherent political education, they consequently lack revolutionary awareness or any forward-looking perspective beyond the traditional horizon of their tribal territory. Lazy and undisciplined, they are without any spirit of combat or self-sacrifice.[31]

The fact of the matter is that Guevara's *foco* theory was not even valid for the Cuban revolution, on which it was ostensibly modeled. Like the Soviets and the Americans, the Cuban interventionists created a myth of their own development that others were supposed to follow. When they did not, such as in the cases of Congo or Bolivia, it revealed to Havana the inadequacies, follies, and general backwardness of the local population. What made an impression on other Third World leaders by the late 1960s and early 1970s onwards was not, therefore, first and foremost the Cuban theories of revolution, but rather their spirit of dedication and self-sacrifice in providing aid to African and Latin American movements. This aid was military, medical, and educational. Cuba as a revolutionary example, as a small country that defied the United States and was willing to help in far-away places without asking for anything in return, was the Cuba that others saw as an inspiration for their homegrown revolutions. And it was in this sense that the killing of Che marked the beginning rather than the end of America's trouble with Cuba in the Third World.

Vietnam and Southeast Asia

The superpower conflict over Vietnam had not been eagerly sought by either Moscow or Washington, but had been brought about by the interventionist mindset of both powers in responding to the dynamics of the Vietnamese revolution. After the Korean War the United States had made it clear that it would not accept a unified Vietnam under Communist leadership, and that it would rather intervene than see Ho Chi Minh succeed in his aims. Viewing Ho's Hanoi government as an extension of Soviet and Chinese power in Southeast Asia, both the Eisenhower and Kennedy administrations believed that the fall of the weak South Vietnamese state – set up after the 1954 Geneva Accords and completely dependent on US support – could set off a domino effect through which not only neighboring Laos and Cambodia, but also the much more important states of Thailand, Malaya, and Indonesia would face successful challenges for power by their Communist parties supported by an aggressive Chinese regime. Although preventing the unification of Vietnam – even through nationwide elections – was not in itself an aim for either Eisenhower or Kennedy, it became the *sine qua non* of US policy since the only force powerful enough to unify the country by the ballot or the bullet was Ho's Communist-led Worker's Party of Vietnam. By the early 1960s the prospect of a direct US intervention loomed increasingly large on the horizon, as the South Vietnamese government seemed both unwilling to follow US prescriptions for internal reform and incapable of containing the left-wing rebellion spreading on their side of the supposedly temporary 1954 demarcation line.

Judging from the new sources we now have access to, the American view of South Vietnam's role in Communist thinking within Southeast Asia was largely correct. After 1954 and especially after the rebellion in the south started in 1960, Vietnam became a benchmark for what other Communist parties could hope to achieve domestically and what kind of support they could hope to receive from Moscow and Beijing. The 1954 division of Vietnam sent the signal that the immediate prospect for extending the pattern of socialist revolutions was not good. US intervention in the Korean War, China's war-weariness symbolized by Zhou Enlai's careful diplomacy, and the Soviet post-Stalin mixture of theoretical dogmatism and *détente* toward the West had created a sense of retrenchment among many Communist leaders in Southeast Asia.

This attitude was perhaps best exemplified by the Malayan Communist Party's leader, Chin Peng, who remembers that by 1953–55 "neither Moscow nor Peking saw value in an armed struggle dragging on in Malaya. A military victory ... it had been decided for us, was out of the question."[32] At the same time, the Indonesian Communist Party began feeling its way toward an electoral and parliamentary involvement in its country's politics – a strategy which, by the late 1950s, had proved spectacularly successful, to both Beijing's and Moscow's surprise.

The 1959–66 VWP decision to give its blessing to an armed rebellion in the south was the clearest indication that this period of caution was over. Hanoi's decision was its own, but it was taken after much pressure from southern Communist cadre and, as we shall see, against advice from both Moscow and Beijing. The northern-based party's new-found determination to reunify the country by force first and foremost came out of desperation with the lack of any international or country-wide process that pointed in the direction of the reunification promised at Geneva. On the contrary, the US-supported regime of Ngo Dinh Diem seemed at least in economic terms to be entrenching itself in the south.[33] As is so often the case in revolutionary situations, it was fear that the existing regime would improve its fortunes that forced the revolutionaries to take action. The southerners in the VWP leadership were instrumental in shaping a strategy that saw a 10,000 Communist cadre from the north infiltrate the south during the year 1960, with the aim of helping to organize a broad-based National Liberation Front (NLF) inside the Republic of Vietnam.[34]

But while the contemporary US view may be right about the influence Vietnamese decisions had within Southeast Asia in the late 1950s and early 1960s, it was certainly wrong about the roles Moscow and Beijing had in shaping Vietnamese strategy. To the Soviets the aim in the 1950s had been to help build a viable socialist state in the northern half of Vietnam, which – in due course – would be economically successful and politically and militarily strong. When Hanoi had adopted the necessary (Soviet) models of development and harvested the fruits from them, then the people in the country as a whole would "opt for socialism." This strategy for "socialism in half a country" was the only possible solution for Vietnam, Soviet advisers insisted in the 1950s, and was the only one Moscow was willing to support. The problem was the "independent Vietnamese friends, working in South Vietnam, who believed it was necessary to organize separate attacks against the Diem regime as a means of inspiring the masses to fight. This manifested an oversimplified, un-Marxist approach to the situation and to the question of armed insurrection," the Soviet leadership complained to their Chinese colleagues in 1957.[35]

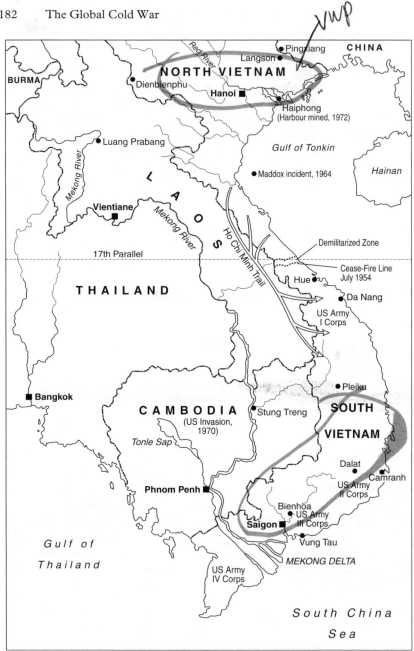

Map 6   The US war in Indochina, 1960s.

When representatives of the VWP met with the Soviets and the Chinese in Moscow in May 1960 to prepare the upcoming 3rd Congress of the Vietnamese party, both of its big allies warned against an "insurrectionist" policy in the south. Even so, the VWP Congress sanctioned – in broad outline – the policy of armed struggle that the party leadership had decided on the previous year, while covering the new policy in phrases about eventual "peaceful reunification" that would be close to the Soviet heart. It was therefore the Vietnamese decisions – not the Sino-Soviet split, as often claimed – that broke the Geneva stalemate and set the country on course for war. New Chinese evidence shows that even after the beginning of the open split with the Soviets in the summer of 1960, Beijing remained lukewarm to the idea of a war of liberation in South Vietnam, while increasingly providing it both with rhetorical and military support. Mao's problem was that although he wanted to assist the Vietnamese party – no other foreign revolution was as important to Mao as that in Vietnam – the timing for a war in the south was exceptionally bad from a Chinese perspective. The self-inflicted wounds of the Great Leap Forward had left the Chinese economy severely weakened, while leaving behind sores that would continue to fester in Chinese politics for years to come. Chairman Mao wanted to deal with the problems through dramatic political changes within China. While the support of revolutionary parties elsewhere was part of that agenda, having a full-blown war and a possible US intervention next door to China was not.

The Sino-Soviet split was therefore a setback and not an advantage for the Vietnamese Communists. They attempted assiduously to stem the tide of dissolution in the world Communist movement, even to the point of trying to get Ho Chi Minh to mediate in the conflict in person. Consultations between the North Vietnamese, the North Koreans, and the Mongolians up to 1965 show that all of the three smaller Asian socialist states viewed the split as a potential threat to them, even though Hanoi and Pyongyang were substantially closer to Beijing in ideological terms than was Ulaanbaatar. When the conflict between Moscow and Beijing intensified in 1963, North Vietnam found itself sharing many positions with the Chinese, while still vying for Soviet support in waging a civil war against South Vietnam. Mao's stress on Third World solidarity, on revolutionary action, and on short, massive campaigns appealed to the Vietnamese leaders, as did his strong anti-imperialist rhetoric. By late 1963 Moscow saw Hanoi as firmly in the Chinese camp as far as ideology went, and Soviet diplomats reported that it was just a question of time before Hanoi would come out openly as an ally of Beijing.

Given the high hopes the Soviets had for the development of socialism in Vietnam, and also their substantial investments of time and money there, Hanoi's Chinese leanings shocked the Kremlin almost as much as the collapse of its relations with Beijing had done a few years earlier. Both before and after the fall of Nikita Khrushchev in October 1964, the Soviet party leadership attempted to rationalize Hanoi's political direction. Sadly, their conclusions were often racial rather than political: both being "orientals," the Chinese and the Vietnamese would naturally draw together in their views and their policies, many Soviet leaders thought. This fundamental misunderstanding of the Chinese–Vietnamese relationship clouded Soviet policy during the crucial 1964–66 period in Vietnam, and gave rise to policy recommendations – both during Khrushchev's regime and after – that made Moscow steadily lose influence in Hanoi. When the US military intervention in 1964 convinced a majority within the new Soviet leadership that they would have to dramatically increase their aid to Vietnam, they did so without having much of a hope of influencing Hanoi's military or political strategy, at least in the short run. To the Soviets, their aid to Vietnam was an ideological duty and a response to US aggression, as well as an answer to China's and Vietnam's rhetoric.

To Mao Zedong, the Johnson administration's bombing raids and its sending of US ground troops to Vietnam came as a surprise. Since the late 1950s the Chairman had been preaching that the United States was a superpower in decline, afraid of taking on new involvements in the Third World and increasingly incapable of maintaining its hegemony over the capitalist countries. Indeed, much of Mao's domestic and international policy had been based on this assumption, including the break with the Soviet Union. By 1964–66 there were many voices within the CCP that felt China to be dangerously isolated at a time when its southern neighbor was coming under attack from the United States. But Mao's response, as was often the case when under pressure, was to take a step to the Left: only if China carried out a "continous revolution" that would purge it of "rightists, revisionists, and all kinds of traitors" could the country face up to its external challenges. The Chairman realized, however, that while this cultural revolution was going on, China should attempt to avoid a war with the imperialists. The PRC's foreign policy in the mid-1960s was therefore high on rhetoric but low on action: even though Mao had decided to respond militarily to an all-out US ground attack across the 1954 demarcation line, China's continued involvement in Vietnam was the exception that confirmed the rule. As we have seen, China's general direction during the Great Proletarian Cultural Revolution was inward and away from engaging foreign revolutions.

In spite of Washington's views to the contrary, there was around 1965 a strong sense both in Moscow and Beijing that things were not going well in their conflict with imperialism. The initial euphoria over decolonization had worn out and the United States seemed to be resurgent, confronting the Soviets over Cuba, intervening in Vietnam, and dealing with some of its domestic problems, such as poverty and race. The new leadership in Moscow was disappointed over the fate of many of its potential Third World allies, which had been replaced through military coups in the mid-1960s, and seemed to turn away from most increases in its involvement in Third World affairs, except as far as Vietnam was concerned. Ironically, the Soviet and Chinese reluctance (for differing reasons, as we have seen) to step up their aid to other countries may have been a blessing for the Vietnamese revolution, concentrating the assistance to one country at the time when it was most needed – even if neither Moscow nor Beijing thought that Hanoi could win militarily against the Americans. One particular reason for this rising preoccupation with assisting the Vietnamese Communists was the brutal crushing of the Indonesian Left in 1965, perhaps the greatest setback for Communism in the Third World in the 1960s and – seemingly – a signal victory for US abilities to influence Asian affairs.

By the early 1960s Sukarno's regime in Indonesia was as much a puzzle for Moscow and Beijing as it was for Washington. While welcoming the Indonesian leader's increasingly strident anti-Western rhetoric and his willingness to confront the remnants of colonialism in Southeast Asia, the Soviets worried about Indonesia's economic decline, about the regime's and the Indonesian Communist Party's (PKI's) closeness to China, and about what they saw as Sukarno's unpredictability. Mao Zedong, on his side, was becoming increasingly intolerant of "bourgeois" Third World regimes, even when they tried to be close to China, and suspected Sukarno of trying to use Beijing to achieve his own hegemony in the Southeast Asia region. While Beijing welcomed the PKI's public support for its ideological positions, it viewed the Indonesian party as such as throughly infected with revisionist practices. Ironically, while moving into its ultra-left mode, Beijing also resented what they saw as bad treatment of the Chinese in Indonesia (who, of course, in most cases were badly treated because they were merchants or capitalists).

But if the Communist states saw trouble brewing in Indonesia, their alarm was nothing compared to Washington's views. "The road ahead for Indonesia is a troubled one of domestic deterioration, external aggression, and overall Communist profit," a US national security estimate concluded in July 1964. In spite of President Johnson's unwillingness to cut all ties with Sukarno – and thereby with the Indonesian military, whom the president saw as a counterweight to the PKI – he had concluded that the leader of the fifth most populous country in the world was a threat to the stability of the whole region. "I don't trust him. I don't think he is any good," the Texan confided to Senator Richard Russell. By mid-1964 the covert operations program against Communist influence in Indonesia – originally sanctioned by President Kennedy in December 1961 – had moved into high gear. Although we still do not know precisely what methods the CIA used or who their Indonesian collaborators were, the aims were clear:

Portray the PKI as an increasingly ambitious, dangerous opponent of Sukarno and legitimate nationalism and instrument of Chinese neo-imperialism. Provide covert assistance to individuals and organizations capable of and prepared to take obstructive action against the PKI. Encourage the growth of an ideological common denominator, within the framework of Sukarno's enunciated concepts, which will serve to unite non-Communist elements and create cleavage between the PKI and the balance of the Indonesian society. Develop black and grey propaganda themes and mechanisms for use within Indonesia and via appropriate media assets outside of Indonesia in support of the objectives of this program. Identify and cultivate potential leaders within Indonesia for the purpose of ensuring an orderly non-Communist succession upon Sukarno's death or removal from office.

A key cause of US concern was Sukarno's policy of confrontation – *konfrontasi* – with neighboring Malaysia, a country that he regarded with some right as a British neocolonial creation, set up to prevent the unification of all Malays in one Indonesian state. In 1963 and 1964 Jakarta dithered on the brink of war with Malaysia and its British ally, while the Johnson administration tried to defuse the tension so as not to strengthen the PKI and its allies.[36] But for Sukarno the US attitude was one of betrayal. In his view, while the Kennedy administration had helped Indonesia gain possession of Dutch-occupied Irian Jaya, its successor now schemed to keep Malaysia under British control. Confronted with Washington's threats of cutting off all aid to the faltering economy, Sukarno responded in characteristic style:

All I have really wanted from America was friendship ... Maybe she didn't see how our revolution parallelled hers? OK, America. Don't try to win my heart. But don't try to break it either ... Don't publicly treat Sukarno like a spoiled child by refusing him any more candy unless he's a good boy because Sukarno has no choice but to say "to hell with your aid."[37]

With the economy in free fall, mainly because of his regime's financial incompetence, and with internal unrest on the rise, Sukarno moved to the left politically. In a speech on independence day, 17 August 1964, he stressed who his supporters were:

There are still people who accuse Sukarno of "taking sides," who accuse Sukarno of "favoritism." Sukarno taking sides? Taking sides with whom? If it is against imperialism, feudalism, and the enemies of the revolution in general, yes! Certainly Sukarno has favorites, that is, he sides with the people and he sides with the revolution itself ... I have been accused of bringing advantage to one group only among our big national family. My answer is also, yes. Yes, I am giving advantage to one group only, namely – the revolutionary group! I am a friend of the nationalists, but only of the *revolutionary* nationalists! I am a friend of the religious group, but only the *revolutionary* religious group! I am a friend of the Communists, because the Communists are *revolutionary* people.[38]

In October, during the Non-Aligned summit meeting in Cairo, Sukarno explained to Tito that his current purpose was to drive all of Indonesian politics to the left and thereby to neutralize the "reactionary" elements in the army that could be dangerous for the revolution. He did not intend to give up the long-term alliance between nationalists, religious progressives, and Communists, but to ensure that the alliance, as he put it, "would be able to defend itself."[39]

The end of Sukarno's year of living dangerously came in September 1965. In the overheated political atmosphere in Jakarta, where rumors of plots and coups circulated daily, a group of young radical officers attempted to crush the army leadership, whom they claimed were against Sukarno and the revolution. In spite of killing six of the leading generals and – belatedly – getting the support of the PKI Politburo, the so-called "30 September Movement" failed to seize control of the country. After a day of chaos, during which Sukarno refused to commit himself to either side, the army and its Islamic and nationalist allies struck back furiously. With the head of the Army Strategic Reserve, General Suharto, in command, more than half a million Communists and left-wing sympathizers were massacred in an orgy of violence during the months that followed. Sukarno's political project was also dead – the "great leader of the revolution" was repeatedly humiliated by the generals and forced to resign, ignominiously, in 1967.

The end of the Indonesian revolution came as a shock to the Soviets, who blamed Chinese scheming and the PKI's ineptness for the defeat of the Left. Already in January 1964, PKI leader Aidit had charged Moscow with building capitalism and claimed that some day it "would fully revert back to capitalism."[40] Moscow's relationship with the PKI leadership had been deteriorating fast since the beginning of 1965, with the main Indonesian Communist newspaper accusing the Soviets of being part of the NEKOLIM (neocolonialist, colonialist, and imperialist) forces that Sukarno and the PKI so detested.[41] The Soviet embassy, on its side, increasingly found its main contacts among officers and moderate nationalists rather than in the PKI. In a 1964 report to Moscow on the Chinese hold on the PKI, the embassy even quoted the heads of the Islamic

Nahdlatul Ulama Party as saying that the "PKI is working against the Soviet Union and the Soviet Union is a friend of Indonesia. Therefore PKI should be taken care of."[42] The Soviet ambassador's postmortem on the 30 September events accused the PKI leaders of having been held hostage to events rather than trying to steer them, and thereby having brought disaster upon themselves. The ambassador suspected Chinese complicity in the coup, especially since it was directed against the army chief of staff, Nasution, with whom the Soviets had been on increasingly good terms.[43]

For the United States, the crushing of the coup, the sidelining of Sukarno, and the gradual imposition of General Suharto's pro-US dictatorship was a result of the Indonesian political crisis that was almost too good to be true. Granted, something along these lines was what the Americans had been working toward since the early 1960s, but only twelve months before Suharto's coming to power the US embassy's prediction had been that the army's "strength and unity of purpose under non-Communist leadership will inevitably erode."[44] In November 1965 the CIA advocated US support for the army's efforts to exterminate Communism:

Now that it has seized upon the fortuitous opportunity afforded by PKI's error in the 30 September affair and is asking for covert help as well as understanding to accomplish that very task, we should avoid being too cynical about its motives and its self-interest, or too hesitant about the propriety of extending such assistance provided we do so covertly, in a manner which will not embarrass them or our embarrass our government.[45]

Even though the full extent of US support for Suharto and Islamist groups in hunting down the Communists in 1965 and 1966 is not known, it is clear that the United States – as well as Britain and Australia – provided the Indonesian Army with lists of members of the Communist Party, and that they thereby, at least indirectly, became complicit in mass murder of monstrous proportions.[46]

For the main advisers in the Johnson administration, what mattered most after the military takeover in Indonesia was the effect it would have on the rest of the region. "It is hard to overestimate the potential significance of the army's apparent victory over Sukarno," Robert Komer wrote to the president in March 1966. "Indonesia has more people – and probably more resources – than all of mainland Southeast Asia. It was well on the way to becoming another expansionist Communist state, which would have critically menaced the rear of the whole Western position in mainland Southeast Asia. Now ... this trend has been sharply reversed."[47] In the National Security Council, Johnson's ambassador to South Vietnam, Henry Cabot Lodge, claimed that "the recent overthrow of the Communists in Indonesia is a direct result of our having taken a firm stand in Vietnam."[48] In Moscow – while crying few tears for the PKI leadership – many key foreign policy advisers felt "a sense of shame" for not having done more for the Indonesians. For the Soviets, too, the overthrow of Sukarno increased the importance of Vietnam – if the Communist Party lost there, then Soviet positions would have been forced out of Southeast Asia altogether.

After late 1966 both China and the Soviet Union began changing their estimates of North Vietnam's endurance, the Communists' fighting abilities in the south, and the Johnson administration's political ability to increase the intensity of US warfare up to a point that would make Hanoi amenable to a return to *status quo ante*. For China, this change in its Vietnam estimate did not mean much in terms of foreign policy, since the country was already consumed by the Cultural Revolution (although it did prepare the ground for Mao's normalization of relations with the United States after 1969). For Moscow, the unexpected successes for Vietnamese arms and the ensuing difficulties for Lyndon Johnson presented opportunities for a great victory, but also conjured up the danger of a Hanoi that would go too far and a United States that would respond by increasing pressure against other socialist states, including those in Europe. The Kremlin therefore viewed itself increasingly as a peacemaker, willing to bargain for the best possible settlement for North Vietnam (but at the same time desperately afraid that others would uncover its real lack of decisive influence within the VWP leadership). The American insistence on trying to deal with Hanoi through Moscow was therefore a particular comfort to Brezhnev and Kosygin – not only did it confirm in their own minds that Moscow was at the head of a world revolution, but it also provided the Soviets with leverage in other areas of world politics.

Within Vietnam's immediate neighbors, Laos and Cambodia, which had shared its fate as part of the French colonial empire, the beginning military successes of the Vietnamese Communists against the United States emboldened the Left to launch offensives of its own. In Laos, where renewed civil war between the Communist-led Pathet Lao and the neutralist government broke out in 1963, North Vietnamese military support (at first against the wishes of the Soviet Union) led to increasing successes for the Pathet Lao toward the end of the 1960s. At the same time the Laotian Left came increasingly under Vietnamese direction and control. In Cambodia, however, the main radical party – an intensely nationalist group known in French as Khmer Rouge – had an uneasy relationship with Vietnam from its inception in the early 1960s. Their chances of success seemed slim in a country led by a prince – Noroddom Sihanouk – who not only had allowed the North Vietnamese and the NLF to set up supply bases on Cambodian territory, but who, in 1965, had broken diplomatic relations with the United States. But the start of US bombing of Cambodia, in 1969, and the brief US ground invasion the following year completely changed the picture. Prince Sihanouk was overthrown in a coup, while the Khmer Rouge began attracting a large following based on its strange mix of Marxist and nativist ideas. While condemning Vietnamese interference in his revolution at every turn, the Khmer Rouge leader Saloth Sar – calling himself Pol Pot – began receiving military aid from Hanoi from 1969 onwards in order to help defeat the Americans and the Cambodian military regime they supported.

During its war against the United States, Vietnam never engaged in the kind of socialist internationalism outside its own immediate region that we see in the case of Cuba. The Vietnamese revolution therefore became an indirect inspiration for others in the Third World, and – as we shall see – in the pan-European world as well. Vietnam became a symbol of successful resistance to the United States, of revolutionary heroism, of David battling Goliath. For many *tiermondistes* – especially those who had begun their journey toward disillusionment over corruption and mismanagement in newly independent states – Vietnam was a shining example of the good guerrilla (sufficiently far away geographically for most of them that the real consequences of the Vietnamese revolution would not have to be taken into account). Che Guevara, just back from a humbling defeat in Congo and working his way into an even more disastrous defeat in Bolivia, sent a message to the 1967 Tricontinental Conference in Havana where he cried out for two, three, many Vietnams:

What greatness has been shown by this people! What a stoic and courageous people! And what a lesson for the world their struggle holds ... The peoples of three continents are watching and learning a lesson for themselves in Vietnam. Since the imperialists are using the threat of war to blackmail humanity, the correct response is not to fear war. Attack hard and without let-up at every point of confrontation – that must be the general tactic of the people.

But Che also chided those who had not done enough to help the Vietnamese:

The solidarity of the progressive world with the Vietnamese people has something of the bitter irony of the plebeians cheering on the gladiators in the Roman Circus. To wish the victim success is not enough; one must share his fate. One must join him in death or in victory ... guilty are those who at the decisive moment hesitated to make Vietnam an inviolable part of socialist territory – yes, at the risk of a war of global scale, but also compelling the US imperialists to make a decision. And also guilty are those who persist in a war of insults and tripping each other up, begun quite some time ago by the representatives of the two biggest powers in the socialist camp.

For Che and for many other leftists around the globe – including, as we shall see, some in the industrialized countries – Cuba and Vietnam contributed to inspiring a New Left, which saw both the Soviet development model and Soviet foreign policy as too dogmatic, too self-satisfied, and too timid. Often claiming to criticize the Soviets from a more radical Marxist position, a small number of these groups and parties viewed Maoist China as a new lodestar, but far more claimed that Cuba and Vietnam were showing the way to a more comprehensive and quicker victory over imperialism. While the Cubans engaged some of these movements directly, both in Latin America and Africa, the Vietnamese served as example more than support. Hanoi's military and political success against the US, especially after the 1968 Tet Offensive, created a revolutionary resurgence in Southeast Asia, in which parties claimed to have learnt from the North Vietnamese and the NLF how to wage a new form of revolutionary guerrilla warfare. Since very few of their leaders had studied the actual Vietnamese experience (not to mention its military tactics, which tended to be increasingly conventional forms of warfare), one may talk of these "Vietnam-inspired" rebellions as a form of creative misunderstanding, often led by intellectuals worshipping the heroic peasant guerrilla.

Malaysia, Thailand, and the Philippines all saw revolutionary upswings led by such groups in the wake of the North Vietnamese offensives against the United States and the South Vietnamese government. In Malaysia the Communist guerrilla movement of the late 1960s was based on the MCP remnants and took over many of that party's weaknesses, including remaining an almost exclusively ethnic Chinese movement. As a result, the Malaysian Communists remained isolated, without any real chance of challenging the Malay establishment, which struck back by in effect disenfranchising the whole Chinese community in 1969. After China cut off its support in 1974 the Malaysian party quickly became defunct. In Thailand the 1971 and 1976 military coups – which the military juntas claimed were undertaken in response to ethnic and student unrest – drove left-wing activists underground, from where they for a time seemed set to launch a successful guerrilla war against the government and against US bases. But the Thai Left soon fragmented, under pressure from a massive US aid program to the government. With no viable military strategy of their own and without support either from Vietnam or China, the majority of the movement's leaders soon found their way back to the cities, abandoning the peasants and ethnic minority groups they had claimed to lead to the fury of the Bangkok military junta.

In the Philippines, the New People's Army (NPA) and the Communist Party of the Philippines (Marxist-Leninist; CPP [m-l]) followed a somewhat different trajectory. Originally a China-oriented breakaway from the Soviet-oriented Communist Party, the CPP (m-l) group began assassinating officials of Ferdinand Marcos' dictatorship in 1970 and acquired weapons by ambushing troops around its original base in northern Luzon. By the mid-1980s the NPA had an army of more than 20,000 men organized in guerrilla groups throughout the Philippine archipelago and underground party cells in many small towns and villages. Its leader, Jose Maria Sison, was an intellectual who has studied not only Marxism–Leninism, but also Western theories of revolution. Coming from a family of big landowners in Luzon, Sison was inspired by the example of leaders such as Lumumba and Castro, and – like many New Left intellectuals in the West – came into conflict with the authorities for the first time when protesting against the Vietnam War. Having studied in Indonesia in the early 1960s, Sison believes that the PKI failed because its underground organization in the countryside was too weak, and he has been determined not to repeat the same mistake in the Philippines. But while the rural strategy may have helped the CPP to survive up to today, it also isolated it from the main opposition groups in the cities. When the Marcos dictatorship fell in 1986 the CPP was unable to take advantage of the political changes and became increasingly marginalized toward the end of the Cold War, as a more pluralistic political system took hold in the Philippines.[49]

Vietnamese resistance to the United States inspired not only Third World radicals but also – for the first time – made the Cold War in the Third World a central part of left-wing mobilization within the pan-European world itself. The Western European and American students who demonstrated in the streets and occupied their universities in the late 1960s found the "old" Left – both socialists and Communists – too timid on domestic reform and too placid in dealing with the problems of the Third World. Only "direct action" from below, through an alliance of students and workers, could break the impasse in Western politics, the New Left radicals believed. The NLF or Che Guevara – or even China's Cultural Revolution – became symbols of the impassioned action demanded by student protesters. "The Third World taught us the concept of an uncompromising and radical policy, different from the shallow, unprincipled bourgeois *Realpolitik*," Hans-Jürgen Krahl, one of the leaders of the West Berlin student revolt, told his judges from the dock in 1968.

Che Guevara, Fidel Castro, Ho Chi Minh, and Mao Zedong are revolutionaries who teach us the political ethics of the uncompromising policy, which enables us to do two things: first, to reject the policies of peaceful coexistence, such as is being conducted as *Realpolitik* by the Soviet Union, and, second, to see clearly the terror that the United States, assisted by the Federal Republic [of Germany], is carrying out in the Third World.[50]

Placing the "new anti-imperialism" at the heart of the struggle for change in the West may have been a popular view among student protesters, but it infuriated some West European socialists such as the German author Günther Grass, who accused the students of solidarizing themselves with the Third World while forgetting Communist oppression inside Europe itself. Protesting the Soviet invasion of Czechoslovakia in August 1968 was less attractive to the students than attacking US behavior in Vietnam, he argued. To the students of Berlin or Paris, Grass claimed, "the attempted reform in Prague proved to be sketchy and unattractive.

Or in other words: Alexander Dubcek's attentively formulated programme for democratic socialism could not compete with the cult of Che Guevara. A sober process, hampered at the time by the necessary compromises, interrupted today by power politics, drowned in the rhythmic clapping and the argument-less cheers for Ho Chi Minh.[51]

The New Left in the end had only a limited influence on West European or US politics, but the protests they organized did help convince many within the American elite that the Vietnam War could not be won at an acceptable cost – at home and abroad. When Lyndon Johnson declared that he would not seek reelection in order to open the way for a peaceful settlement of the Vietnam conflict, opponents of US policy, be they in New York, Paris, Moscow, or in the Third World, were truly astounded. For the first time a conflict in the Third World had brought down an American president and imposed limits on what only a few years before was seen as an unbound – if not boundless – pattern of intervention. And while Johnson's successor, Richard Nixon, in no way subscribed to a noninterventionist foreign policy, he too soon realized that the war in Vietnam was unwinable, and chose to withdraw (although only after copying the North Vietnamese in expanding the war to Cambodia). The slow end to the Vietnam War was a watershed in Cold War history, from which lessons were drawn that, in the 1970s, came to implicate the Third World more, not less, in the global conflict between the United States and the Soviet Union.

Ironically, the end to the war *inside* Vietnam, when it finally came in 1975 – two years after the Paris Peace Accords and the US withdrawal – was a highly conventional military offensive by the North, patterned more on the Soviet victory over German forces at Kursk in 1943 or the CCP's offensive across the Yangzi in 1949 than on slogans of "people's war." South Vietnam saw no bloodbath in defeat, but rather a slow strangling of the southern non-Communist forces that had cooperated with the Hanoi regime as part of the NLF. From the late 1970s onwards hundreds of thousands of people fled by sea, or, in the strangest of twists, across the border to China to escape from a doctrinaire northern regime that seemed to offer few opportunities for those who were not in the service of the Party. By 1979 Vietnam found itself at war not only with a genocidal Khmer Rouge regime in neighboring Cambodia (which the Vietnamese themselves had helped to power), but also with its former Chinese allies, with whom relations had been deteriorating since the beginning of China's Cultural Revolution. To Washington and Moscow – whose fear of Beijing's influence in Hanoi had motivated much of their Vietnam policy – the Third Indochina War ought to have served as a *memento mori* for their Third World policies overall. But, as we shall see, superpower interventionism did not receive a profound setback through the Vietnam War and its aftermath. Their only impact was on the form such interventions were to take in the 1970s.

The Cold War and superpower *détente*

The period of superpower *détente*, lasting from 1968 to 1975, was in many different ways a direct response to America's debacle in Vietnam. The war had put pressure both on US government finances and on its alliance system, first and foremost in Western Europe, where the war had long been unpopular – seen as a crime by the Left and as an unnecessary distraction by most conservatives. Even at home, where the war had turned into a moral issue that severely weakened the faith many people had in America's political institutions, a significant part of the elite had come to believe that the United States needed a respite from international crises and that such a truce between America and the world could only be achieved through some form of agreement with Moscow and possibly even with Beijing. It is ironic that the same misunderstanding that led to the many abortive searches for peace in Vietnam – that Hanoi's behavior could be decisively influenced through Moscow – also created one of the fundamentals for *détente*: the concept that the global disorder of the late 1960s could be dealt with through an understanding with the other superpower and be based on an implied recognition of its "interests."

From the Soviet perspective, *détente* was the culmination of a policy that its leaders had tried to implement since the mid-1950s – the idea of peaceful coexistence and a recognition by the West of the Soviet Union as the other genuine superpower with global involvements of its own. Vietnam, Moscow concluded, had demonstrated to the US and West European leaders how the Soviet Union could assist an ally even over long distances and contribute decisively to his victory. Coming at the same time as the division line between East and West in Europe seemed settled – President Johnson, obsessed with Vietnam, had barely bothered to protest the 1968 Soviet invasion of Czechoslovakia – Moscow hoped to use its relationship with the Nixon administration to reduce overall defense expenditure, while concentrating on dealing with the Chinese threat in Asia. For Leonid Brezhnev, who had become the key member of the Soviet collective leadership by the late 1960s, both these issues seemed crucial: he wanted his legacy to be a better life for the Soviet people and security against Mao's China, which he had come to see as a direct and major threat, especially after border clashes in 1969 brought the two countries close to war.

While the Soviets never intended *détente* with Washington to include an end to Moscow's support for movements and regimes in the Third World – quite the opposite, as we shall see below – the Nixon White House saw major gains to be had in all areas of the US–Soviet relationship through the negotiations with the Brezhnev leadership. By the time he finally gained the US presidency, after eight years as vice president under Eisenhower and a narrow loss in the 1960 campaign against John Kennedy, Nixon had become a believer in the need to create a regularized US foreign policy environment. To a much higher extent than any US president before or since (and, in many cases, significantly different from his chief foreign policy adviser, Henry Kissinger), Nixon thought of the United States as the major power in a world of rising powers, where some order could be found only by agreements based on narrowly defined self-interest. Nixon's tendency to see the United States as a "normal" state within an international system was rare among American leaders and, of course, in direct conflict with the view of the world that most of the US elite held dear. His views were to a large extent the result of the Vietnam War, which had left him disillusioned with the inconsistency of support for the Cold War at home and the dominance that a "peripheral issue" had gained in US policy. By nature distrustful and secretive, Nixon believed that the full extent of his initiatives toward the Soviet and Chinese leaderships had to be kept secret from the American public in order to avoid a backlash at home. By the time of the trumphant signing of the first Strategic Arms Limitation Treaty in 1972, many Americans had come to believe that Moscow had signed up to across-the-board cooperation with the United States, largely on US terms.

Nixon viewed the Third World first and foremost as a source of disorder in international relations, which only counted to the super-powers if its internal squabbles were made use of by one superpower to threaten key interests of the other, especially with regard to access to raw materials. Believing in a strict racial hierarchy between nations, Nixon was disdainful of plans to further democracy in the Third World as part of

America's mission abroad. Before becoming president, in July 1967, he lauded the economic "success stories" of Thailand, Iran, Taiwan, and Mexico.

Thailand has a limited monarchy. Iran has a strong monarchy. Taiwan has a strong President with an oligarchy. Mexico has one-party government. Not one of these countries has a representative democracy by Western standards. But it happens that in each case their system has worked for them. It is time for us to recognize that much as we like our own political system, American-style democracy is not necessarily the best form of government for people in Asia, Africa, and Latin America, with entirely different backgrounds.

The key to US Third World policy, as far as Nixon was concerned, was that "what happens in those parts of the world is not, in the final analysis, going to have any significant effect on the success of our foreign policy in the foreseeable future."[52] Making too much of sporadic Third World crises would only take attention away from the crucial competition with the Soviet Union. Kissinger's assistant Marshall Wright, when charged with developing a statement on the administration's Third World policy, reported to his boss in despair:

both in Africa and in the UN our policy is essentially defensive. Neither is central in any way to US foreign policy operations or interests. We deal with them because they are there, not because we hope to get great things out of our participation. We aim at minimizing the attention and resources which must be addressed to them. What we really want from both is no trouble. Our policy is therefore directed at damage limiting, rather than at accomplishing anything in particular.[53]

Contrary to his self-cultivated image as the ultimate realist in international affairs, the newly declassified documents of the Nixon administration show that Henry Kissinger remained much more influenced by concepts of modernization and American mission that did the president. Cynical he could be, but when push came to shove Kissinger preferred the traditional means of aid, political and economic pressure, and – in the final instance – intervention to keep Third World countries in line with US Cold War strategies. While noting, in his crucial October 1969 report to Nixon on changes in international politics since World War II, that "the increased fragmentation of power, the greater diffusion of political activity, and the more complicated patterns of international conflict and alignment that have emerged over the past decade have limited the capacity of the US and the USSR to control the effects of their influence and have revealed the limits of their capacity to control the actions of other governments," Kissinger ended his report by stressing the significance of America for the world: "The US exerts immense and growing influence in the world through a broad range of international activities conducted by nongovernmental individuals, enterprises, and organizations. While the direct influence of the US Government over its international environment has been restricted in one way or another, the scope and reach of American commercial, technical, and cultural influence has continued to expand."[54] A main problem, according to Kissinger, was that while the United States remained the model for the world, the Americans themselves were increasingly unwilling to take up the leadership role that naturally had fallen to them.

One of the areas where Nixon's and Kissinger's perspectives agreed was on the need to reduce direct American intervention in the Third World in the wake of the Vietnam disaster. Instead of using American power in crises, regional "policemen" would have to take responsibility – with US support – for keeping Communism contained in their regions. These Third World policemen states – Brazil, Turkey, South Africa, Iran, and Indonesia – would receive assistance and training from the United States, while Washington would interfere as little as possible with how they solved their "local" Communist problems. The United States would continue to support Israel, not because of any sentimental attachment, but "for the reason that Israel is the current most effective stopper to the Mideast power of the Soviet Union."[55] Japan would be required to build a military power of its own and gradually take on the role of a counterbalance to Chinese influence in Asia. Even more than Kissinger, Nixon believed that US public opinion in the long run would not stand for a high level of foreign involvement, perhaps not even in Europe. His self-proclaimed "Nixon Doctrine" was an attempt to counter the fallout of the wars in Indochina: "[a]s far as our role is concerned, we must avoid the kind of policy that will make countries in Asia so dependent upon us that we are dragged into conflicts such as the one we have in Vietnam."[56]

Such a reduced role in the Third World – as an overseer, not an intervener – was both a necessary accompaniment to *détente* and a vital limitation in order to keep the American people's support. In his long, rambling conversations with Kissinger, the president stressed his own role in holding the fort against American left-wingers, peaceniks, and isolationists.

The US – what it will be like for the next 25 years depends on whether we have the guts, the stamina, the wisdom to exert leadership, will determine whether the future of the country ... that is really what the facts are. People may want to put their heads in the sand; they may want to clean up the ghettos. All right, we will get out of the world. Who is left? The two activists, Russia and Communist China.[57]

While originating in the rise of tension between Israel and its Arab neighbors, the two Middle East wars of 1967 and 1973 were both test cases for the superpower relationship, and especially for the principles of nonintervention.[58] In 1967 Soviet support for Egypt and Syria led Nasser to believe that he could step up the pressure on Israel. Instead, he provoked an Israeli attack that the United States knew was coming but did little to prevent. Its victory in the Six-Day War left Israel in control of large areas of Arab territory, which it seemed reluctant to give up. The military force of the Arab states was crushed and Nasser's faith in the value of Soviet support dramatically reduced. The Egyptian leader thought it was time that Moscow showed its real inclinations in the Middle East: was it willing to help the Arab states liberate their territories, or were all the declarations of solidarity just empty talk? After escalating skirmishes with Israeli forces in 1969, Nasser paid secret visits to Moscow in December 1969 and January 1970, asking for the assistance of Soviet military forces. "Let me be quite frank with you," he told Brezhnev. "If we do not get what I am asking for, everybody will assume that the only solution is in the hands of the Americans."[59]

Brezhnev, while willing to help Nasser reconstruct his military force, was unhappy with the Arabs' fighting prowess. "Our military equipment was once again squandered," he told a gathering of Eastern Bloc heads of state in July 1967. "The Arabs are counting on us, they want to drag us into war. In Vietnam we are in fact already involved, but [at least] there is a political platform." The Soviet leader continued:

Why has the UAR suffered a defeat? A total carelessness, a lack of understanding of what an army is under modern conditions, an inability to deal with modern military techniques. It is a fact and it needs to be told straight: this is a feudal country, which suddenly got in touch with modern weapons, the newest tanks, rocket-launchers, etc., with weapons which can be handled only by a man having at least secondary-school education and 2 years of training with such weapons. Now Nasser is doing self-flagellation, but we are not feeling better ... In terms of morality and prestige we suffered a defeat. Not every one of our workers understands why 2 million Israelis defeated so many Arabs, equipped with our weapons? It is not easy to explain.[60]

The Soviet resupply program for the Egyptians had already by late autumn 1967 replaced free of charge 80 percent of Egypt's aircraft and tank losses in the war.[61] The decision of early 1970 to send regular Soviet artillery, air defense, and air force units to participate in the fighting was a significant step up by the Politburo, reflecting both concerns over the long-term survival of a key Third World ally but also a more activist approach to Third World affairs in general. Deputy Foreign Minister Vladimir Vinogradov recalls that

disagreement arose only over the technical details of the proposed action. Nasser insisted that the entrance of Soviet forces be overt. At worst, it could be explained to the world that only volunteers were involved. Brezhnev opposed this, arguing that no one would believe the Soviet leadership as it was impossible that so many volunteers could be raised in a few days for a war in a foreign country. Finally it was agreed that the operation would be top secret and without unnecessary "noise."[62]

More than 20,000 Soviet servicemen served in Egypt for longer or shorter periods in 1969–70, Soviet pilots engaging Israeli jet fighters and Red Army artillery shelling Israeli positions.[63] Tel Aviv's decision to agree to a ceasefire in October 1970 was much influenced by the Soviet support for the Egyptians. Still, Nasser's successor Anwar Sadat proved too cautious to place all his eggs in one basket. Insulted by what he saw as increasingly overbearing behavior by the Soviet military advisers, he asked Moscow to withdraw them in 1972, hoping that Washington could be convinced to lean on the Israelis to effect a withdrawal. Sadat had no qualms with presenting his motives directly to the Soviets. In a meeting on 11 July he explained to Vinogradov that he had received a message from Nixon through the Dutch foreign minister, saying that the United States would engage itself more strongly in a solution to the Middle East crisis only if Soviet military advisers left Egypt. While obviously insulted, the Soviets attempted to put a good face on the expulsion of their officers by telling their allies that it would strengthen Sadat's political and diplomatic position and could therefore open possibilities for nonmilitary solutions to the conflict.[64]

Nixon, however, was reluctant to pressure his Israeli ally too far. When Israel remained unmoved, Arab forces attacked in October 1973, briefly putting its opponent on the defensive before Israel struck back decisively. With Egypt's Third Army trapped and the country on the verge of collapse, the Soviets first tried negotiating a solution with the Americans within a *détente* framework, agreeing to a joint ceasefire proposal that was immediately passed by the UN Security Council. But the Israelis ignored the ceasefire and – with the secret blessing of Washington, the Soviets thought – continued their counteroffensive. When Sadat called for US and Soviet forces to enforce the ceasefire, Brezhnev personally stated that Moscow might send troops unilaterally if Washington continued to ignore Egypt's pleas. Nixon, already engulfed by the Watergate Crisis at home, responded with heightening the alert of US strategic nuclear forces. The Soviets again backed down. No Soviet forces would be sent to Egypt except after a decision in the Security Council, Brezhnev assured Nixon in a personal telegram on 25 October.

The Arab defeat in the Yom Kippur War was a reminder to the Soviets that the United States, in spite of *détente*, still considered itself to be more "super" than the other superpower in the Third World. While the basic declaration of cooperation that the two powers had signed in May 1972 refuted "any efforts to obtain unilateral advantage at the expense of the other, directly or indirectly," Yom Kippur had shown that Washington only cooperated with Moscow as far as its own immediate interests went. To Brezhnev and the Politburo this attempt at excluding Soviet influence – *not* the *détente* framework – was Nixon's main legacy to his successors with regard to Third World policy. It was a lesson the Soviet leadership would remember in future crises. For the Middle East, the result of the Yom Kippur War was that Egypt moved closer to the United States in its search for a peace agreement with Israel. The Soviet Union, meanwhile, came to concentrate its support on Syria and Iraq, both "progressive" military regimes that condemned both US domination and all attempts at finding a negotiated solution with the Jewish state. It also increased its aid to the Palestinian Liberation Organization (PLO) and its leader Yassir Arafat.

From a Soviet perspective, its relationships with the PLO, Syria, and Iraq constituted very complex alliances, because of the character of the Baath regimes and the Palestinian leader's use of terrorism in his fight against Israel. Both Damascus and Baghdad brutally suppressed the local Communist parties, while the Soviets lectured Iraqi and Syrian Communists – in exile in Moscow or East Berlin – about the virtues of building a united front with the Baath parties. Since the Baathists had the support of the masses, the MO claimed, their regimes needed only to be infused with socialist ideas in order to move to the left. The PLO, meanwhile, was a jumble of different groupings, with Arafat's Fatah the clear Soviet favorite. The MO hoped to move the PLO away from terrorism abroad and on to a joint political and military strategy, and provided the organization with significant amounts of money, arms, and training. It also realized, as Arafat himself put it in a 1974 conversation with the East Germans, that the "PLO prevents the Arab bourgeoisie from making arrangements with imperialism" – as long as the Palestinian issue dominated Middle Eastern politics, even Arab conservatives would have a troubled relationship with Israel's main backer, the United States.[65]

The Nixon administration's closeness to the other non-Arab "policeman" in the Middle East, Iran, was in part motivated by the need to develop a staunch regional ally *outside* the immediate setting of the Arab-Israeli conflict. Even if Nixon through intelligence reports realized that the furious modernization drive that the shah had entered into in the 1960s was in trouble, Iran was too important to the United States – strategically and financially, as well as ideologically – for the administration to back away. On the contrary, Nixon praised Mohammed Reza Pahlavi for providing "strong, effective support of the United States," and

Kissinger reiterated, after conversations with the shah in mid-1972, that "decisions on the acquisition of [US] military equipment should be left primarily to the government of Iran."[66] By 1973 Iran was the most important recipient of US weapons in the Third World and the key in Nixon's strategy for controlling Middle Eastern oil supplies without a need for direct US intervention. When the shah ferried 1,200 Iranian commandos to Oman that year to help the sultan break his left-wing opposition, Washington applauded.

But while Nixon's "policeman" concept seemed to be working well in the Middle East, it was in trouble in Latin America and Southeast Asia. Much as Kissinger had predicted, Brazil and other Latin American right-wing dictatorships were reluctant to act on their own when Chile in September 1970 elected a socialist president, Salvador Allende, with a program of radical income redistribution, nationalizations, and an independent foreign policy. Having concluded right after the Chilean election that an Allende regime in Chile "was not acceptable to the United States," Nixon asked the CIA "to prevent Allende from coming to power or to unseat him."[67] He was "not concerned with the risks involved" and ordered the Agency to "save Chile" through putting its "best men" on the job.[68] Kissinger at the same time insisted that "what happens in Chile ... [will have an effect] on what happens in the rest of Latin America and the developing world ... and on the larger world picture, including ... relations with the USSR."[69] The CIA's undermining of Chile's elected president took almost three years to produce a result, however, and would probably have failed outright if the Chilean socialists had been better at managing the economy. As it was, the military struck against the government on 11 September 1973, producing Chile's first military coup ever. The military regime of General Augusto Pinochet – in spite of its atrocious human rights record – was welcomed by the Nixon administration, which resumed economic aid to Chile in the aftermath of the coup.

In Southeast Asia Nixon's program of Vietnamization of the Indochina War failed because the South Vietnamese regime was too weak to stand up to its Communist opponents after the US withdrawal. Nixon, however, was never in doubt about what was most important for his administration. When South Vietnamese President Thieu protested a peace agreement that would leave North Vietnamese troops in place inside South Vietnam, Kissinger told his envoy to Saigon to "remind Thieu – as he is no doubt aware – that withdrawal of US forces will continue in any event ... under the Vietnamization track."[70] Thieu and the South Vietnamese regime would be left to fend for themselves, and to collapse in 1975, two years after the Paris Peace Accords allowed the United

States to withdraw its troops. To Washington, the defeat in Vietnam was a setback, but not one that would force a basic reconsideration of its Third World policy. On the contrary, the collapse of South Vietnam helped undermine support for *détente* at home and, over time, lent credence to the right-wing's claim that the Soviet Union was going on the offensive in the Third World.

While Moscow watched in disbelief the mounting US difficulties in Indochina, some of the internal Soviet arguments from the late 1950s and early 1960s for a more active Third World policy had begun reappearing. Many of the Kremlin advisers with whom this renewed activism originated in the late 1960s had been reform-oriented during the Khrushchev era and deplored the domestic retrenchment that had taken place under the new leadership from 1965 onwards. They saw the victories of the Vietnamese and the radical turn in many liberation movements as creating an international arena in which their zeal for socialist transformation could be realized – as an outlet for energies they were not fully allowed to employ at home. Mostly intellectuals and often trained in the area studies institutes of the Soviet Academy of Science in the post-Stalin period, they had found employment during the 1960s in the departments of the Central Committee or in the analytical branches of the KGB, and had maintained close links with the academic institutions where they had done their postgraduate work. By 1969 their arguments started coming into the open, first and foremost in inner CPSU party publications and in academic journals, and they began gaining the ear of some of their bosses.

The arguments these advisers put forward for a broader Soviet engagement in the Third World were based on many different aspects of ideology and political strategy, and were not always mutually reinforcing. One such argument – often, as we shall see, put forward by the KGB and its military counterpart, the GRU – was mostly opportunistic: the Soviet Union by the late 1960s had the capabilities to intervene quickly and decisively in support of revolutions elsewhere, and the West would be taken by surprise by such assistance. The substantial advances in Soviet military and infrastructural capabilities during the late 1960s – the Soviet navy, the development of a large fleet of long-distance transport planes, training facilities, and global communications – all made interventions easier.[71] Because of its own failed intervention in Vietnam, the United States would be unwilling to commit in a large-scale fashion to counter Soviet support for foreign revolutions or progressive regimes. An opportunity existed that should not be wasted for supporting the global trend toward socialism. While most key advisers were rather dismissive of such pseudostrategic arguments – even when specific "opportunities" were pointed out – they may have played a role in convincing the top leadership that the Third World could be worth the investments that they had been unwilling to commit right after taking over in 1964.

An argument where the opportunistic and the ideological positions met was in pointing out that most of the competition between capitalism and socialism as systems in the immediate future would necessarily take place in the Third World, since the division lines in Europe had stabilized. Interestingly, the argument that Western Europe would only turn to socialism after a long and protracted struggle through parliaments and trade unions – the view which some younger Soviet advisers had taken over from the Italian Communist Party, for instance – helped push the argument that Moscow would have to reorient some of its attention toward the Third World. It also helped convince some ambitious CPSU cadres that making their own mark as promoters of socialism and the Soviet position abroad could better be done through centering on events *outside* Europe than through interactions that were increasingly becoming routine measures taken by Foreign Ministry bureaucrats.

A key argument for most of those who campaigned for a broader Soviet Third World engagement was their Marxist analysis of historical trends in Africa and Asia. After the first period of decolonization, this argument went, the imperialist powers and Western capitalists were able to dominate the former colonies economically. But during the 1960s – and much faster than Soviet economists had predicted – a national bourgeoisie had arisen and begun supplanting foreign interests, helped by states over which they increasingly held sway. Because of the many levers the imperialists could pull – including direct and indirect intervention – the only way this national bourgeoisie could assert itself fully was through some form of collaboration with the working class and progressively minded peasant leaders. Since the latter had already or were in the process of organizing Communist parties or Communist-led fronts, such alliances could bring a country under the real dominance of progressive organizations. And because some of the leading members of the national bourgeoisie were realizing how weak they really were in the competition with foreign interests, they might accept a socialist system that would minimize their profits but secure their market share against foreign competition.

Without admitting it, of course, these advisers and academics had taken the orthodox Marxist position and turned it upside down. Instead of the slow progression of society through social stages toward socialism and eventually Communism, they were arguing that the very weakness of an exploited country could help it toward socialism by forcing the bourgeoisie to submit itself to control through a progressive state. Third World countries could therefore – in exceptional cases, such as shown in Vietnam or Cuba – begin advancing toward socialism without having gone through a prolonged phase of capitalist development *if* the right policies for sustaining such social alliances and defending the revolution against foreign interventions were put in place. Some of these revisionist intellectuals were smart enough to realize that what they were really doing was bringing the Soviet view of postcolonial societies more into line with the actual development of the Russian revolution and the Soviet state than the mythical version that the Stalinists had developed to make it conform to Marxist orthodoxy.

The external causes of these unexpected possibilities for socialism in the Third World were increased competition between imperialist powers and the growing strength of the Soviet example. With the temporary stabilization of the fronts between socialism and capitalism in Europe, and the decolonization in the Third World, the postwar phase of US hegemony had come to an end. Instead of being able to institute their control further, the Americans had met a strong barrier – revived economic competition from Germany, Japan and other capitalist powers that were unwilling to submit to the US hegemony that they had suffered under after World War II. At the same time the domestic advances of the Soviet Union had drawn widespread attention from the Third World, and people of all classes who opposed US control now knew that in the Soviet model there was a successful (and powerful) alternative to foreign domination. The International Department of the CPSU CC reported frequently on the desire of "progressive elements" from different non-Communist parties in the Third World to study the Soviet socialist experience.

Finally, some of the advisers who advocated a renewed Soviet Third World strategy were influenced both by the conflict with China and, in a different way, by Cuba, Vietnam, and Western radicals. The fervent hatred of the Chinese mockery of internationalism in the Cultural Revolution spurred many young leaders (especially in the MO) on to argue for a more activist Soviet position in order to rebut Chinese charges and counter Chinese propaganda. Quite a few of the midranking cadre in the international departments had been trained to deal with China in the 1950s and were therefore understandably focused on the Chinese challenge. But even more important were the open and secret accusations by Havana, Hanoi, and the European Left that Moscow was too timid in its global conflict with the United States, that it had lost its appetite for assisting revolutions elsewhere. By 1969, when the conflict with China was at its peak and after the ignominious Egyptian defeat in the Six-Day War, it had become crucial for many Soviet decision makers to show that in spite of *détente* the Soviet Union would do what was in its power to assist and protect revolutions abroad.

It would be wrong, however, to see these younger advisers – people such as Vadim Zagladin (born 1927), Georgii Shakhnazarov (born 1924), and Karen Brutents (born 1924) – as believers in unlimited Soviet intervention.[72] On the contrary, they stressed the need to be careful and to evaluate each situation on its own premises. The setbacks of the mid-1960s were still very much on the Soviets' minds and each of the influential advisers were aware of the overriding importance of not having one's name associated with such failures. Most also kept the conviction developed during the Stalin era that only by learning directly from the Soviet experience – and first and foremost the lessons in party-building – could foreign revolutions be made secure. The Leninist concept of "vanguard parties" was very much at the forefront of their minds: all future development depended on the creation of such a party of dedicated local Marxist-Leninists, who could make the right tactical decisions and steer the complicated processes of building alliances, instituting social reform, and furthering socialist education. These vanguards – even when much further developed than the class they represented – were the lodestars around which the whole concept of revolution in poor countries revolved.

Within the context of a rapidly evolving political situation – influenced, decisively, by the vanguard party – the march toward the goal of revolution could take many different paths. Karen Brutents – by far the most important theoretician among the heads of the MO – argued in his *Revolutions of National Liberation Today: Some Theoretical Questions*, published in 1974, that tension would continue to exist for a long time within the anti-imperialist fronts, even after they had taken power. One reason for these "struggles within the struggle" was the mixed class composition of the liberation fronts. Another was the subversive activities of the imperialist countries, first and foremost the United States. There would be no easy victories for the "progressive" forces, even if imperialism was weakened on a global scale. On the contrary, the chances of failure were substantial, especially if the local Communists did not apply Leninist models of organization and alliance-building.[73]

The emphasis on the primacy of the Communist Party and its collective leadership in the post-Khrushchev era facilitated the rise of the MO to a position of influence that its predecessors had had only in the very early Soviet period. Soviet leaders of the Brezhnev era tried to promote younger Communists who had a firm grasp of political theory and whose background very often was in the party rather than in the state apparatus. While not always listened to, their prominence grew in the 1970s and up to the set-in of the final sclerosis of the system at the very end of the decade, around the time of the Afghanistan intervention. The influence of the CC departments on foreign policy was also helped by the

Foreign Ministry being led by a group of – even for the Soviet era – exceptionally unimaginative politicians, who were slow in responding to the Politburo's wishes and who were seen as being far too preoccupied with diplomatic routine involving other great powers. The result from the early 1970s onwards was a kind of division of power, in which Foreign Minister Gromyko's supremacy as the main interpreter of Brezhnev's *détente* policies was kept intact, but where an increasing amount of policy initiatives *outside* the immediate *détente* framework were left to the CC departments and the KGB. None of them, of course, could act independently of sanction from the Politburo, but as Politburo oversight began to wane, especially as a result of Brezhnev's increasingly acute health problems from 1974 onwards, the different centers of foreign policy activity were left with substantial leeway in interpreting their instructions from above.[74]

For a while, it could be said, two parallel tracks of Soviet foreign policy were being formed, roughly at the same time. The one that had central importance for the leadership was the policy of *détente* toward the United States and Western Europe, mostly carried out by the Foreign Ministry. But at the same time political advisers who generally supported the *détente* process put down the foundations for a more activist approach to the Third World. The Soviet system of decision making – and the fact that the proponents of each policy were to be found mostly in different sectors of the bureaucracy – meant that it took a very long time before the Politburo realized that one policy could endanger the other. For most leaders, including Leonid Brezhnev himself, the two were both correct responses to a changing world, based on the best of Soviet political theory. In practice, the end of the American intervention in Vietnam had shown that Moscow could stand by its allies while negotiating *détente*. And if the Soviet Union were to make use of its power in the future to support other friends in the Third World, it would still be a "little interventionist" compared to the United States, as Brezhnev saw it.

6   The crisis of decolonization: Southern Africa

From the mid-1960s onwards it was clear to both Washington and Moscow that the focus for Cold War competition in Africa was shifting from North and Central Africa to the southern part of the continent, where both the remnants of the Portuguese empire – in Angola and Mozambique – and the white supremacist states of South Africa and Zimbabwe (Rhodesia) were confronting guerrilla wars by African nationalist movements. Much of the leadership of these movements belonged to the second and more radical generation of African nationalists – some were Marxists and most were critical of the failings of the first African postindependence leaders to set their countries and the continent on a course toward more unity, more equality, and less European influence. Many were inspired by what they considered to be the lessons of the wars in Vietnam and in Cuba, believing that guerrilla warfare and mass political mobilization would defeat their enemies, while preparing their societies for the postwar building of a socialist state. The increasingly important international role of the Soviet Union made many radical African leaders see Moscow as the global socialist counterweight to the United States, both providing a balance in international affairs that would help their revolutions and also assisting their movements with training, weapons, and supplies. It was the Marxist orientation of many Southern African liberation movements that made both Moscow and Washington take notice of their significance – to the United States, they threatened radical, Soviet-oriented regimes taking power in the Third World; to the Soviet Union, they hailed the beginning of a new stage of Third World social development, in which African leaders acknowledged the superiority of "scientific Marxism."

As we shall see, it was not easy for liberation leaders in Southern Africa to force a Marxist analysis on their understanding of the societies in which they operated. But Marxism – especially in its Leninist form – had one great advantage in countries where the authorities increasingly used different forms of racist ethnic categories to split the population and perpetuate their own rule. By subdividing people into their productive roles, as peasants, workers, or intellectuals, rather than into Zulu, Xhosa, Ndebele, Shona, or Ovambo, Marxism helped create at least the perspective of a united front against the regimes. It also fueled the hope of creating future states that were modern and just – without racial oppression, but with the advantages that the Europeans then enjoyed available to all. With the immense natural riches that Southern Africa held, it was no surprise that most liberation leaders felt that the fundamental problem in the region was one of social justice – if a nation was constituted to include *all* inhabitants within one nondiscriminatory state, then want of all sorts would be a thing of the past. And, finally, the turn toward Marxism helped non-African leaders of the liberation movements – of whom there were many – to justify their roles and positions; if ethnicity was not the main issue, then they could help lead revolts that in essence were carried out by Africans.

Southern African liberation and superpower Cold War

Throughout the 1960s and 1970s South Africa was the main arena in the conflict for power in Southern Africa. Its racist regime, established under the Afrikaaner-dominated National Party from 1948 onwards, used a policy of segregation – *apartheid* in Afrikaans – to split the country along ethnic lines and to allow the European minority of around 13 percent to control the economy, the military, education, and politics. Africans (around 75 percent of the population) were required to carry passbooks for entry and exit into the European areas where they worked, but where they could not live or go to school. As the European areas expanded, Africans and other non-Europeans were forcibly removed, often to what the apartheid regime called "homelands" or "Bantustans." These areas, about 14 percent of the country, were to be set off as distinct regions for African ethnic groups as defined by the regime, and, as a result, people who had never thought of themselves as Tswana or Zulu became not only removed from the areas where they lived, but forcibly incorporated into a "homeland" for "their" tribe. "Apartheid," South African Prime Minister and Afrikaaner chief ideologue Hendrik Verwoerd proclaimed, "comprises the political sphere; it is necessary in the social sphere; it is aimed at in Church matters; it is relevant to every sphere of life."[1]

The South African economy – and especially the crucial mining industry – was dominated by international companies in which the Afrikaaners themselves had only a minor stake. Completely dependent on cheap African labor, dutifully delivered by the apartheid regime, the South African mining industry was not only extremely profitable, but also important to both the strategic and economic interests of the West.

As we have seen, these economic links did not prevent the deterioration of South Africa's political relationship with the West, and especially with the United States during the Johnson era. The president had thought that South Africa's refusal to reform its racial policies along the lines he had set out in the United States would be its undoing, and that America should use any means at its disposal (short of breaking the economic and military links with Pretoria) to influence the South African government. By the late 1960s South Africa was finding that it had fewer and fewer friends in the pan-European world who were willing to overlook its institutionalized racial oppression in the name of white solidarity or economic profit.

As we have seen, the main South African liberation organization, the African National Congress (ANC), from its inception opposed all forms of racial discrimination and allowed both Europeans and Asians to join its ranks. While its leadership was a mix of all ethnic groups in South Africa, Africans dominated the rank and file, especially through the significant African trade unions that the ANC had helped to build. The South African Communist Party had its members join the ANC and by the 1960s much of the nascent military organization – created after the banning of the party in 1960 and the arrest of much of its leadership – was dominated by Communists. The ANC's military challenge to the apartheid regime had been difficult to get started, however: the country was surrounded by friendly regimes and Pretoria held a considerable sway over African ethnic and clan leaders, who discouraged young people from joining the military resistance. By the late 1960s the ANC military units, the Umkhonto we Sizwe (Spear of the People), consisted of a couple of thousand youths who had made it to faraway Tanzania, mostly lacking in training and weapons, and badly suffering in morale.

The situation for the liberation movements in the Portuguese colonies of Angola and Mozambique, located on the borders of South Africa and the South African-occupied Namibia, was very different. In spite of its NATO membership, the Portuguese dictatorship found it increasingly difficult during the 1960s to man, supply, and finance its colonial wars. Its European NATO partners considered Lisbon's wars to keep its colonies a diversion at best and a disgrace at worst, and the Johnson administration was hardly won over by Portuguese dictator Salazar's arguments that Portugal's mission in Africa was to fight Communism. But in spite of Washington's internal concerns over Portuguese "incompetence" and "bungling," it was not able to disentangle itself from indirect support of Portugal's colonial wars. As Secretary Rusk attempted to explain to Salazar's successor, Marcello Caetano in 1968, "the US was not leading a crusade on the African question and had no interest in the disappearance of the Portuguese presence from Africa ... we had to express our views, which were not always the views of our Portuguese friends ... A great deal depended on the expression of the authentic views of peoples in areas like Angola and Mozambique."[2]

As we have seen, the Mozambican liberation movement FRELIMO was not only reasonably united in its struggle but it also had strong secret links to the United States. In spite of Mondlane being a dedicated socialist, he believed that a broad united front both domestically and internationally would be for the best of the cause of liberation, even if it might slow down the processes of social transformation. But in Angola – the much more strategically and economically important Portuguese colony on the southwestern coast of Africa – three liberation movements, divided both by ideology and ethnicity, split the loyalty of the anti-colonialists between them. In the early 1960s the biggest of these movements was the Frente Nacional de Libertação de Angola (FNLA; National Front for the Liberation of Angola) led by the colorful Holden Roberto. The FNLA ideology was a strong African nativist nationalism – anti-Communist and anti-Western in equal amounts. Holden Roberto, an authoritarian and inflexible leader whose position depended very much on his leadership of the Bakongo ethnic group in the north, also had secret links with the CIA and was dependent on Mobutu's Zaire for bases and support.

The leadership of the Movimento Popular de Libertação de Angola (MPLA; Popular Movement for the Liberation of Angola), on the other hand, consisted of Europeans and mestizos as well as Africans. Headed by Antonio Aghostinho Neto – an mild-mannered, but rather egocentric doctor and poet – the MPLA had become a Marxist-led front by the mid-1960s, stressing the need for social revolution and the adherence to its purposes of all of Angola's peoples. While hoping for Soviet Bloc assistance, Neto, however, remained an independent-minded Marxist, with as strong an intellectual inspiration from the European Left – through the Portuguese Communist Party – as from Moscow. His role in the Angolan liberation struggle was as much inspirational as political, with many of his lieutenants directing the military activities both within Angola and abroad. In his poetry, Neto encouraged his countrymen to

> Start action vigorous male intelligent
> which answers tooth for tooth eye for eye
> man for man
> come vigorous action
> of the people's army for the liberation of men
> come whirlwinds to shatter this passivity.[3]

The third of the Angolan liberation movements, the União Nacional para a Independência Total de Angola (UNITA; National Union for the Total Liberation of Angola), had been established in the mid-1960s by Jonas Savimbi, in protest against what he saw as military inactivity and general lack of vigor of the other parties. By far the most charismatic of the Angolan leaders, Savimbi was a political opportunist whose ideology placed him in the nativist camp, but who received support and training from China. He criticized the MPLA for being dominated by Europeans and the FNLA for its Bakongo links, preaching self-sufficiency and national unity as his key aims. But at the same time he depended on support from his own ethnic group, the Ovimbundu of central and southern Angola, and was willing to strike deals with everyone else (including, occasionally, the Portuguese) in order to strengthen the position of his party.

The increasing radicalization of the MPLA and, to a lesser extent, FRELIMO, by the mid-1960s owed much to the leader of the liberation movement in the third Portuguese colony in Africa, Guinea-Bissau on the western coast. Amilcar Cabral, the head of the Partido Africano de Independência da Guine e Cabo Verde (PAIGC; African Party of Independence of Guinea and Cape Verde), who had been waging a guerrilla war against the Portuguese since 1959, had spent time in Angola in the 1950s and knew the leaders of the other liberation movements well. He had become a Marxist when studying in Lisbon and was a forceful voice for the need to link national liberation to social revolution all over Africa. He was also a champion of the need for African liberation movements to ally themselves more closely with the Soviet Union. While the Soviets themselves came to regard Cabral as an inconvenient, free-thinking Marxist, his message was heard all over Africa, and especially in the Portuguese colonies. In 1965, at a conference of all the left-wing parties fighting the Portuguese, Cabral defended his position: "Those who do not like to hear us talk of the aid of socialist countries, what have they been helping us do? They aid Portugal, the fascist and colonialist government of Salazar. It is no longer a secret to anyone that Portugal, the Portuguese government, would not be able to lead a struggle against us if it did not or could not have access to help from its allies in NATO." On the same occasion, Cabral presented the 1960s liberation struggle in Africa as being directly in conflict with the United States:

our hearts [beat] in unison with those of our brothers from Viet Nam who give us a unique example in fighting the most scandalous, the most unjustifiable imperialist aggression of the United States of America against the peaceful Vietnamese people ... We are with the Blacks from America, we are with them in the streets of Los Angeles, and when they are denied any possibility of a decent life, we suffer with them.[4]

While Cabral and the revolutionaries of Lusophone Africa identified themselves with American radicals, the United States under Richard Nixon entered into a closer relationship with the archenemy of the African liberation movements, apartheid South Africa. Convinced of the need for a strong, Western-oriented power to play the role of policeman in the region, the White House began pulling closer to Pretoria in 1969, by foiling African attempts at isolating the apartheid regime and reactivating the intelligence-sharing and naval coordination programs that had been suspended by the Johnson administration. The administration's preferred alternative outlined in an NSC study in December 1969 was to

maintain public opposition to racial repression but relax political isolation and economic restrictions on the white states. We would begin by modest indications of this relaxation, broadening the scope of our relations and contacts gradually and to some degree in response to tangible – albeit small and gradual – moderation of white policies ... We would be more flexible in our attitude toward the Smith regime [in Zimbabwe]. We would take present Portuguese policies as suggesting further changes ... At the same time we would take diplomatic steps to convince the black states of the area that their current liberation and majority rule aspirations in the south are not attainable by violence and that their only hope for a peaceful and prosperous future lies in closer relations with white-dominated states.[5]

After 1970 US–South African relations improved rapidly, even though many of the outward limitations for US investment in and cooperation with the Afrikaaner minority regime stayed on the books. The administration's view was that South Africa would not face any form of significant inner change soon and that it had proven to be an important ally of the United States in a strategically significant area. Henry Kissinger told the South African foreign minister at a meeting in October 1973 that "we face a tragic situation in a world that reverberates with shibboleths of political and social doctrines ... I will curb any missionary zeal on the part of my officers in the State Department to harass you."[6]

But it was not only the United States who was looking for allies in Africa. As we have seen, even before the Bolivian disaster and Che Guevara's death, Cuban attention had been drawn to the continent. Some of the Cuban troops who had gone to Congo had begun training MPLA guerrillas and already in 1965 some Cubans had crossed with Angolan fighters into the northern enclave of Cabinda. From 1966 onwards the Cubans staffed training schools for the MPLA in Congo-Brazzaville and organized the reentry of MPLA troops into Angola proper, on a dangerous journey across territory held by Neto's deadly enemies, Zaire's Mobutu and Holden Roberto of the FNLA. The early Cuban support for the MPLA was crucial for the Angolan movement, even though it was a very limited investment for Havana in terms of men and money. From Castro's perspective, it established a relationship, even if his evalution of the fighting capacity and the political preparation of the MPLA in the mid-1960s was fairly negative.

By 1967 most of the Cuban attention had passed from Angola to another Portuguese colony, Guinea-Bissau, where it found both the revolutionary movement – the PAIGC – and the terrain more conducive to the kind of guerrilla strategy Cuba proposed. The PAIGC leader, Amilcar Cabral, had visited Havana for the Trilateral Conference in 1966, where, according to the Cuban commander Jorge Risquet, "everyone was struck by his great intelligence and personality. Fidel was very impressed by him."[7] The new Cuban envoy to Guinea-Conakry, Oscar Oramas, was put in charge of managing a substantial amount of Cuban aid to the PAIGC: weapons, military instructors, doctors, teachers, technicians, and civilian supplies. The presence of the Cubans in Guinea was no secret – Cabral's brother remembers that "it soon became public knowledge that the men who were driving the PAIGC trucks were Cubans; they were the only people in Conakry who smoked cigars!"[8] But as historian Piero Gleijeses has shown, Washington to begin with worried little about the appearance of a few Cubans in Guinea, believing both that the energy had gone out of Cuba's foreign programs after the death of Che Guevara and that Guinea was too small and too remote to figure in the bigger picture.

American complacency began to change in the early 1970s, when it became clear that the PAIGC was defeating the Portuguese in Guinea, thanks in part to the Cuban assistance. While the liberation movements in both Mozambique and Angola seemed to be stumbling, Cabral's organization by early 1973 had an army of 8,000 strong and controlled nearly two-thirds of the country. It had built up an effective civilian administration, which continued to function well even after Amilcar Cabral was assassinated in January 1973. But what really got Washington's attention was the sudden appearance late that spring of newly developed Soviet surface-to-air missiles among the rebels – the CIA reported that such weapons would make the war almost impossible to win for the Portuguese, who so far had relied heavily on their air superiority. Even more importantly, Moscow's willingness to supply such weapons implied a new dedication to support African liberation movements in forms that so far had not been seen.

Unbeknown to the Americans, the Soviet investment in the PAIGC had much to do with the improvement in Cuba's relations with Moscow, which had been at a low ebb up to late 1968. There were three major reasons for this change. First, the death of Che Guevara and the end of the Cuban offensives in Latin America removed an irritant in the relationship – the Soviets had seen Cuban policy as adventurist, while Castro had criticized the Soviets for their timidity and for their trade links with right-wing regimes on the continent.[9] Second, the Cuban economy had nosedived in the late 1960s and was in need of increased Soviet support. Third, the prospect of Richard Nixon – an avowed enemy of Castro's Cuba – winning the US elections in the fall of 1968 reminded Havana of how dependent they would be on Soviet support in case of an American attack. Some of the alternatives to Moscow seemed also to have evaporated for Havana: by late 1967 Castro had condemned both the Chinese for attempting to carry out Cultural Revolution propaganda in Cuba and the Yugoslavs for their ideological compromises at home. The Soviets were understandably pleased with the new Cuban direction – after Castro showed his loyalty by defending Moscow's invasion of Czechoslovakia in August 1968, both military and economic aid to Cuba started to increase.[10]

By the early 1970s Cuban–Soviet (and sometimes East German) coordination of efforts to assist Third World liberation movements were well under way. Berlin, whose Communist Party had served as a conduit between Havana and Moscow, reported in 1971 that while the Cuban party had never given enough priority to "political and ideological work," now Havana was more willing to deal with theoretical problems and to learn from the Soviet experience. Berlin also noted, thankfully, that Castro had become tougher on dissident Marxism, at home and abroad. "Cuba's relations to the socialist countries are now stable and solid; there will be no further setbacks," Raul Castro told visiting East Germans in June 1973. "We will not allow mines to be placed under the bridge that connects us to the Soviet Union."[11] The Soviets were grateful to Castro for sending Cuban tank crews to Syria in the aftermath of the 1973 Yom Kippur war, a move which the Soviets had asked for and which they saw as yet another example of Cuban loyalty. The Soviet supply of heavy weapons to the PAIGC took place, according to the recollections of Moscow officials, after a Cuban request. But, as both the Cubans and the East Germans concluded, it would not have happened if the Soviets themselves had not come to focus more clearly on the African continent.[12]

The new Soviet African strategy had been developed mostly by the KGB and got the Soviet leadership's – and in particular Leonid Brezhnev's – support in the summer and fall of 1970. The KGB reports to Brezhnev emphasized that the regimes and liberation movements of Southern Africa were searching for international allies, and underlined the "simplistic" approach most African regimes had had to world affairs in the past, understanding neither the conflict between the two camps nor the nature of US imperialism. The leaders of the independence movements belonged to a new generation, the KGB claimed. The new political leaders of Southern Africa felt that their attempts at getting US support had failed, and that the Soviet Union was the only major power that could assist them in reaching their political, social, and economic goals.[13]

The Portuguese colonies – Angola, Mozambique, and Guinea-Bissau/ Cape Verde – were particularly interesting from a Soviet point of view, both for political and strategic reasons. The KGB noted the Nixon administration's renewed alliance with Portugal and South Africa, and the military setbacks for the Portuguese forces in their wars, especially in Guinea. KGB Deputy Chairman Viktor Chebrikov explained that Angola and Guinea-Bissau had potential strategic importance for the Soviet Union, and that both the United States and China were trying to increase their influence with the liberation movements in these countries.[14] The intelligence organizations saw Soviet rivalry with China over influence in Africa as a major element behind their policy recommendations. The main military intelligence bureau – the GRU – reported that China was targeting countries and movements that already received aid from the Soviet Union. China, the GRU stressed, would use its resources to the maximum in order to attract African supporters, and could, within a few years, build its position sufficiently to control large parts of Africa in a sort of loose coalition with the United States.[15]

Iuri Andropov, the KGB chairman, also had other reasons for recommending an increase in Soviet involvement in Southern Africa. Summarizing a report on Western estimates of Soviet policy in Africa, Andropov stressed that Western experts believed that although the Soviet Union would strive to strengthen its position in Africa, "in the coming years [it does] not plan a 'broad offensive,'" limiting itself to "securing positions [already] achieved." These Western estimates, Andropov found, were by themselves good reasons why the Soviet Union should step up its African operations.[16] But there was also a need to block Chinese attempts at "subverting" the African liberation movements, attempts that Moscow had to expect to see increase when China passed out of the trauma of the Cultural Revolution.[17]

By far the most important Soviet ally in Southern Africa was the South African ANC. The ANC leadership under Oliver Tambo was trusted by the Soviets, who kept up a close relationship with the South African leaders through Moscow's embassy in Zambia, where the ANC had its exile headquarters. Perhaps surprisingly, the documents show that Soviet closeness to the ANC developed in spite of, rather than because of, the South African Communist Party's strong influence within the Congress.

The International Department, which – alongside the KGB – was the key Soviet institution in developing the links, disliked and mistrusted many of the leading South African Communists, among them the political head of the ANC military wing, Joe Slovo, for their emphasis on independence and their suspected fondness for Euro-Communism. Tambo and some of the non-Communist Africans who worked with him, on the other hand, seemed more trustworthy to the Soviets and were, the MO believed, in a better position to lead the South African revolution because of their ethnic origin. The ANC's multiethnic composition was among the chief problems of the organization, the Soviets believed, and contributed – as Aleksei Kosygin put it in a conversation with a visiting ANC delegation already in 1969 – to make the struggle in South Africa "probably the most difficult in the world."[18]

1969 had been a watershed year for the ANC. Before its conference at Morogoro in Tanzania, younger members, such as Chris Hani, had written of "the frightening depth reached by the rot" inside the organization and demanded a more activist policy inside South Africa itself. Sanctioned by the conference, the military wing of the ANC began preparations for refiltrating some of their fighters back into South Africa, but ran into problems when the Tanzanian authorities, on whose territory the ANC bases were located, wanted to scale down its military activities. By the end of 1969, instead of bringing the war to the Afrikaaners, the Umkhonto we Sizwe was forced to evacuate its main units three and a half thousand miles north from Africa to the Soviet Union, where the CPSU arranged camps for them, mostly around Simferopol in the Crimea. More than 1,500 young South Africans left Tanzania on board Soviet Iliushin-18 planes from the Red Banner Special Purpose Air Brigade. Many of them would spend years in the Soviet Union and receive most of their education and training there.[19]

The new emphasis on Africa in Soviet foreign policy was also put into practice in the case of Angola. After a number of unsuccessful MPLA appeals for increased support in the spring of 1970, Agostinho Neto was startled by the roundhandedness of what the Soviets had to offer in mid-July. Soviet Zambian ambassador D. Z. Belokolos proposed a series of plans for Moscow to assist the MPLA in terms of military hardware, logistical support, and political training. In addition, the Soviets were willing to offer political support for Neto's movement in its difficulties with the neighboring African states – Zambia, Zaire, and Congo.[20] The MPLA leadership responded with enthusiasm toward their Soviet alliance. In his meetings with Belokolos, Neto downplayed MPLA relations with "capitalist countries and social-democratic parties," and stressed that the Soviet Union was the party's main international ally. Neto especially wanted the Soviets to know that he saw no grounds for working closely with China. The Soviet ambassador, in his communications to Moscow, believed that the MPLA leadership's positions reflected the general sentiments in the movement – that the Soviet Union was their only probable source of major military support.[21]

In spite of their new-found enthusiasm for African affairs, Soviet leaders in the period 1971–73 found it increasingly difficult to work out effective ways of collaborating with their favored Southern African liberation movements, and particularly with the MPLA. The Soviets found that Neto's movement had more than its fair share of the poor communications, bad organization, and widespread factionalism which, as seen from Moscow, characterized all the liberation movements in Southern Africa – with the possible exception of Moscow's favorite partner, the South African ANC.[22] The International Department viewed some of Neto's demands – such as his December 1972 request to come to Moscow "to sign an agreement on cooperation and [issue] a joint communiqué" to be somewhat excessive.[23] By early 1974 the MPLA had split into three factions – the Tanzania-based leadership under Agostinho Neto, the Zambia-supported group of Daniel Chipenda (known as Revolta do Leste [Eastern Revolt]), and a Congo-based faction calling itself Revolta Activa (Active Revolt). As historian John Marcum has pointed out, the discord was not as much due to doctrinal differences as to "faulty communication, military reverses, and competing ambitions."[24] The MPLA had never, even at the best of times, been a well-organized movement. Coming under pressure from Portuguese counteroffensives, ethnic tensions and challenges to Neto's leadership split the party. Chipenda, typically, drew most of his support from his own Ovimbundu ethnic group in the central and eastern parts of Angola.

The Soviet envoys spent much time and effort trying to restore unity to the MPLA and creating a liberation front between it and the main nativist independence movement, Holden Roberto's FNLA. The Soviets held on to Neto as their main Angolan connection, securing a trickle of military and financial support for the besieged leadership. More importantly, Moscow invited an increasing number of Neto's associates to the Soviet Union for military and political training. Still, the Soviets also gave some assistance to Chipenda's group, and continued to invite Chipenda for "confidential" conversations at their Lusaka embassy up to 1974.[25] But as Soviet critizism of Neto's lack of flexibility in the unity talks increased, their support for his movement gradually declined. In March 1974, just a month before a Lisbon military coup suddenly threw the political situation in Angola wide open, the Soviet ambassador in Brazzaville drew a bleak picture of the situation in the MPLA. For all practical purposes the movement had stopped functioning, and there was little hope of Neto bringing it back together again. The only bright spot was the existence within the MPLA of a number of "progressively oriented activists" who wanted close relations with the Soviet Union.[26]

As the Moscow leadership developed its links with the liberation movements, it created African expectations of further support as well as a sense of commitment in its own ranks. This sense of commitment was particularly strong with the cadre of the CPSU CC International Department, who handled most of the contacts with African organizations. In addition, the Cuban leadership viewed the early 1970s Soviet involvement as a harbinger of a much wider Eastern Bloc engagement on the continent. The enthusiasm was also high in Berlin, where the newly installed leadership under Erich Honecker saw Third World involvements both as a way of proving the advanced position of East Germany within the Bloc and as a means of avoiding superpower *détente* becoming too cozy, possibly at the GDR's expense. As Neto underlined during his visit to Berlin in November 1971, "we are fighting against the same enemy, whom you will find both at the Brandenburger Tor and in Angola."[27]

Still, a larger Soviet involvement in Africa was slow in coming. Moscow's ideologically inspired attempts to influence the policies of the local revolutionary movements complicated the building of stable alliances with these groups, and often frustrated Soviet foreign policy aims. The links that the Soviets – often wrongly – assumed existed between many African militants and China contributed to Moscow's caution. It was not until Soviet and Cuban leaders agreed on their military plans in Angola in late 1975 that the Soviet Union finally made a major investment in one of its Southern African alliances, and thereby made the MPLA a regional ally second in importance only to the South African ANC.

The collapse of the Portuguese empire

Portugal – the first and last of the European colonial states – was a rapidly changing society at the beginning of the 1970s. Economically, its entry into the European Free Trade Agreement (EFTA) in 1961 meant that its own colonial markets were becoming increasingly marginal. Politically, a large segment of the population – across social divides – was beginning to oppose the dictatorship of Marcelo Caetano. Militarily, the wars against the liberation movements seemed to be going nowhere, with Portuguese casualty rates increasing and unrest brewing among junior officers. The leadership of the army was becoming concerned that the wars in Africa, which consumed 40 percent of the government's budget and more than 5 percent of the country's GDP, would not only undermine the legitimacy

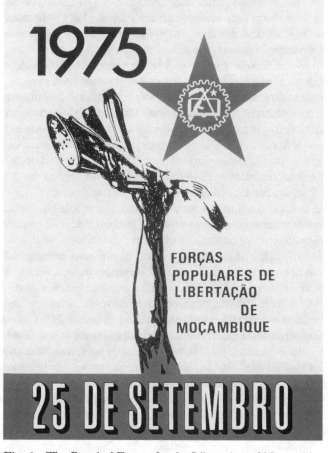

Fig. 6   The Peoples' Forces for the Liberation of Mozambique,
FRELIMO's army, celebrates victory in 1975, on the eleventh
anniversary of its founding in 1964.

of the corporatist New Order established by Salazar, but pave the way for a
left-wing takeover. In early 1974 two of Portugal's leading generals,
Francisco de Costa Gomes, head of the General Staff, and António de
Spínola, former commanding general in Guinea-Bissau, called for a political solution to the conflict in the colonies. Both were quickly dismissed
from office, but the book Spínola published on the same topic sold 50,000
copies in a few days and was a sensation among the public.[28]

On 25 April 1974 junior officers across the country struck against the
government. The Movimento das Forças Armadas (MFA; Armed Forces

Movement) carried out a bloodless coup, installing General Spinola as president, abolishing censorship, surveillance, and the secret police. The first item on the new government's agenda was to solve the colonial problem; Guinea-Bissau was granted independence soon after the April coup and negotiations began for the independence of Angola and Mozambique. Meanwhile, the Portuguese revolution drifted toward the Left. Spinola resigned in September 1974 because he opposed what he saw as aimless and hasty decolonization. The influence of the Communist Party and the left-wing of the MFA increased, and in some cases left-wing Portuguese officers began cooperating openly with the radical liberation movements in the remaining colonies, even before any decisions had been taken on a transfer of power. What was clear to everyone was that very soon the Portuguese empire would cease to exist.[29]

For the Nixon administration, who had significantly increased US relations with Caetano's regime and was in the middle of sensitive negotiations over the future of the US base on the Portuguese Azores islands in the Atlantic, the Lisbon coup came as an unpleasant surprise. In addition to the immediate issue of the Azores base, Washington had two main concerns with regard to the Portuguese revoluton: avoiding Soviet involvement in the decolonization process and preventing the creation of a neutralist Portugal that could split NATO and work as a magnet for other Europeans who were dissatisfied with Washington's policies.[30] By autumn 1974 Kissinger had mobilized both Spain and the NATO allies to try to influence the political situation inside Portugal. In an October meeting with Franco's foreign minister, the US secretary of state claimed that "the [Portuguese] Communists will try to move quickly because they've learned from Chile that if they move too slowly we will do something ... it's suicide just to let events take their course ... You have to do something. You have a border, and friends there who speak a similar language."[31] But all outside attempts at influencing Portugal in the run-up to the spring 1975 elections seemed to backfire – the MFA stuck to its leftist convictions and its alliance with the Communist Party.

The Alvor Agreement, signed between Portugal and all the Angolan liberation movements in January 1975, promised full Portuguese withdrawal by 11 November and a transfer of power to a coalition government. In the meantime, Angola would be ruled by a Portuguese high commissioner and a transitional government with representatives of all parties, and the integration of the armed forces of the Angolan movements would be begun under the auspices of a joint General Staff. Very soon, though, the Alvor Agreement started fragmenting as clashes between the Angolan movements became more frequent. On 23 March

Fig. 7   MPLA supporters listening to a speech by Neto in Luanda,
September 1975. The movement had both African and European
members in the capital.

the FNLA attacked the MPLA headquarters in Luanda, accusing Neto of
planning to take power on his own with the assistance of sympathetic
Portuguese officers in the transitional government. As the civil war began
spreading to all parts of the country, Portuguese settlers fled in large
numbers, contributing to the general sense of chaos. The colonial officers
in charge did little to intervene, especially after the April elections in
Portugal had delivered a crushing blow to the Communists and their
allies, who together got less than 20 percent of the votes.

By spring 1975 foreign intervention in the Angolan civil war was in full swing. On the US side, the CIA had in January finally won the battle to increase aid to Holden Roberto and the FNLA (though the full program still only constituted around $300,000 for nonmilitary items). Coming just a week after the Alvor Agreement, the US decision was a strong signal that Washington was more interested in keeping the MPLA out than in preserving the peace. It took, however, several months before Kissinger himself began to focus on Angola in a major way – the fall of Saigon and other events far overshadowed what was happening in Africa. It took a combination of pressure from African governments – first and foremost Zaire and Zambia – intelligence on the growing Soviet involvement, and the failure of the first FNLA/UNITA offensive against the MPLA, for the new Ford administration to step up US involvement in the summer of 1975. On 18 July the decision to help FNLA and UNITA win the Angolan civil war was taken in Washington – against the advice of most experts in the State Department. The subsequent operation became sizable. Over the span of a month nearly $25 million was authorized for the CIA's covert intervention in Angola, an operation called IAFEATURE, intended to show that even after the Vietnam debacle, the United States could change events in the Third World according to its will.

While the outline of US actions to perpetuate the Angolan civil war are reasonably well known, the Soviet moves have been far less studied. Soviet documents show that the April 1974 overthrow of the Caetano regime by radical Portuguese officers sent Moscow's Africa policy into high gear. Already in May the Kremlin was convinced that the Portuguese colonial empire would soon collapse. On Angola, the Soviet policy was to strengthen the MPLA under Neto's leadership, thereby making the movement the dominant partner in a postcolonial coalition government. Disregarding previous reports on the situation in the MPLA, the CPSU International Department and the Moscow Foreign Ministry instructed the Soviet embassies in Brazzaville, Lusaka, and Dar-es-Salaam to "repair" the damaged liberation movement.[32]

This salvage operation turned out to be exceedingly difficult. The MPLA factions' views of each other did not change much with the waning of Portuguese power. Soviet ambassadors tried their best in meetings with Neto, José Eduardo dos Santos, Chipenda and other MPLA leaders – promising substantial Soviet support to a united MPLA – but to little avail. The "unification congress," held near Lusaka in mid-August, broke down when Neto's supporters walked out of what they considered a staged attempt at removing the party leadership.[33]

In the meantime, the MPLA's rivals had substantially strengthened their positions in Angola. Roberto's FNLA, having received supplies,

Fig. 8   The first years of independence were difficult for all the former Portuguese colonies: a poster from Mozambique from 1976, marking the first anniversary of independence, proclaims a general political and organizational offensive on the production front.

weapons and instructors from China, moved its troops across the northern border from Zaire and started operations in the northern provinces. The youngest of the liberation movements, Jonas Savimbi's UNITA, signed a ceasefire with the Portuguese in June and started recruiting large numbers of Angolans for military training in their base areas in the east. In spite of its diplomatic efforts, the Soviet Union seemed to lose out in the battle for influence in postcolonial Angola.[34]

In October 1974, as the Portuguese revolution was moving to the Left, the Soviets decided to drop the idea of forcing the MPLA factions to unite, and threw their weight squarely behind Neto's group. According to what the Soviet ambassador to Brazzaville, Evgeni Afanasenko, told the MPLA's José Eduardo dos Santos, there were two main reasons behind this decision. First, Neto had in late September managed to convene a rump congress inside Angola, in which the main MPLA guerrilla commanders took part. The political manifesto passed by the congress was to the Soviets' liking. Second, the new head of the Portuguese military administration in Angola, Admiral Rosa Coutinho, was a left-winger who openly sympathized with Neto's views. But whatever way Afanasenko presented the Soviet change in attitude, Neto's people must have been aware that if Moscow wanted to maintain some influence in Angola, they had little choice but to support the "reconstructed" MPLA.[35]

The events of the last two months of 1974 seemed to indicate that Moscow had made the right move. The Soviets, belatedly, got support for their new Angolan policy from the Portuguese Communist leader Alvaro Cunhal. On 21 October the MPLA signed a ceasefire with Portugal, and on 6 November large crowds greeted the MPLA veteran Lúcio Lara when he arrived to open an office in Luanda. About the same time forces of the newly organized MPLA military wing – the FAPLA (Forças Armadas Popular para Libertação de Angola) – took control of most of the oil-rich enclave of Cabinda in the north. In the main Angolan cities the MPLA organizers, now free to act, started setting up strong paramilitary groups in populous slum areas, drawing on the appeal of their message of social revolution.[36]

Moscow in early December drew up an elaborate plan for supplying the MPLA with heavy weapons and large amounts of ammunition, using Congo as the point of transit. Ambassador Afanasenko got the task of convincing the Congolese of their interest in cooperating. This was not easy. Congo had never been a close ally of the Soviet Union – in the ruling military junta there were many who sympathized with the Chinese – and it had for some time sponsored both Neto's MPLA rivals and a Cabinda separatist group. The latter issue was particularly problematic, and Agostinho Neto had on several occasions criticized the Congolese leader

Marien Ngouabi for his support of Cabindan independence. Still, on 4 December Ngouabi gave his go-ahead for the Soviet operation.[37]

Though noting the flexibility of the Congolese government, Afanasenko knew that the job of reinforcing the MPLA would not be easy. In a report to Moscow he underlined the problems the MPLA faced on the military side. Both the FNLA, now joined by Daniel Chipenda's MPLA rebels, and UNITA were in strong positions and would be equipped further by the Americans and the Chinese. In the civil war which the ambassador predicted, the "reactionaries" would initially have the initiative, and the MPLA would depend on "material assistance from progressive countries all over the world" just to survive. Politically, however, Neto's group, as the "most progressive national-liberation organization of Angola," would enjoy considerable support. On the organizational side, one should not think of the MPLA as a vanguard party, or even as a party at all, but rather as a loose coalition of trade unionists, progressive intellectuals, Christian groups, and large segments of the petty bourgeoisie, Afanasenko reported.[38]

In spite of the skirmishes, which had already begun between MPLA and FNLA forces in late 1974, African heads of state succeeded in convincing the three Angolan movements that they had to join in negotiations with Portugal and thereby attempt an orderly transfer of power in Luanda. These negotiations led to the 15 January Alvor Agreement, which the Soviets – like the Americans – claimed to believe in, but then did their best to undermine. The Soviet position after Alvor was that a coalition government was to be preferred, but that such an alliance could only be based on a position of strength by the MPLA, since both the other parties wanted to take power militarily. Only through a further strengthening of Neto's MPLA could more long-term peace stand a chance, the CPSU International Department claimed.[39]

The Soviet Union was also aware of the increase in the CIA's covert support for the FNLA starting in late January 1975. The Soviet embassy and the KGB station in Brazzaville concluded that the American assistance would lead Holden Roberto to make an all-out bid for power very soon. The embassy experts realized that there was little the Soviet Union could do to assist the MPLA in resisting the initial attacks by Roberto's forces. Their hope was that the further increase in Soviet "technical, military, and civilian assistance," which the Brazzaville ambassador promised José Eduardo dos Santos on 30 January, would arrive in time. But in addition to their material assistance, the Soviets also tried to push the MPLA to mend its negotiation strategy. Moscow now hoped that a new alliance between the MPLA and Savimbi's UNITA could get their Angolan allies out of the difficult spot they were in.[40]

Moscow was joined in its wish for an anti-FNLA alliance by many of the independent states in Southern Africa. Tanzanian president Julius Nyerere attempted to get the Soviets to increase the pressure on the MPLA leadership to make the necessary concessions to forge such an alliance. Nyerere – sympathetic to the political aims of the MPLA – was exasperated with Neto's unbending demands in the negotiations. The Angolan leader was "a good poet and doctor," Nyerere told the GDR ambassador, but "a bad politician." Nyerere also warned the Soviets against direct involvement in the Angolan conflict. African countries would react sharply against any form of foreign intervention, Nyerere said.[41]

By early summer the FNLA troops had mounted limited offensives against the MPLA both along the coast and in the northern part of Angola. Then, in July, as another African-brokered attempt at negotiations broke down, the MPLA counterattacked. By the middle of the month local FAPLA forces were in control of Luanda and MPLA troops began attacking FNLA strongholds in the north. The Soviets had not foreseen the MPLA military success, although in April the Brazzaville embassy had foreseen an improvement of FAPLA fighting capabilities because of the Soviet aid. However, the embassy did not expect a full-scale civil war to break out before Angola got its independence in November, and even then such a development could be forestalled through political negotiations.[42]

Moscow now seemed to have the recipe for success in Angola. By a limited supply of military equipment, it believed to have had secured for the MPLA the upper hand in the fighting. As the date for independence approached, Moscow expected that the rival movements, or at least UNITA, would return to the negotiating table and become part of an MPLA-led coalition government. The Soviet experts did not believe that the United States would stage a massive intervention, nor did they give much credence to MPLA reports of direct South African or Zairean involvement. Their main worry was with the Chinese, who had stepped up their FNLA assistance program from bases in Zaire. It was particularly disturbing for Moscow that the Chinese were joined as instructors in these camps by military personnel from Romania and North Korea.[43]

The Chinese involvement in Angola began in the late summer of 1974. Although it is very difficult to get access to Chinese information, it is clear that Beijing wanted to prevent an MPLA victory in Angola not so much because of a growing interest in the region itself, but because it thought that with Neto installed in Luanda the Soviet Union would have substantially increased its position in the Third World. Mao was concerned that the Americans were losing out to Moscow in conflicts in Asia and Africa. He believed that a more powerful Soviet Union in the Third

World could lead to the Kremlin putting more pressure on China. As the chairman saw it, the real Soviet aim was not Third World reactionaries or even the United States; it was to snuff out Chinese socialism and to destroy the only existing socialist state in the world. The Soviet Union had become the main imperialist power, the one that all other countries had to ally against.

About three hundred Chinese instructors served with the FNLA in Zaire. Beijing also recruited about fifty North Koreans and Romanians, mostly technicians and artillery specialists, through its contacts in Pyongyang and Bucharest. From early 1975 the Chinese used US supplies, but there was little coordination with the CIA in the field. Increasingly, however, during 1975 the United States and China discussed Angola in Beijing, where the Chinese pushed for a greater US involvement to aid FNLA and UNITA.[44]

The Soviets, on their side, were prodded in their widening commitment to the MPLA by the Cuban leaders. Cuba had supplied the MPLA with some material support since the mid-1960s, and Havana had increasingly come to regard Agostinho Neto as one of its favorite African liberation leaders. As historian Piero Gleijeses – the only scholar so far who has had access to Cuban documents – shows, Havana's involvement in Angola came out of its own links with Africa and its relationship with the MPLA. In the fall of 1974 the Cubans told Moscow that Neto would not, and should not, accept sharing power with the other movements. The Portuguese revolution meant an opening for the colonized countries not only to shake off foreign rule, but also to begin their social transformation. Cuba would itself concentrate more on Africa (i.e., Angola) in its foreign policy, and expected the Soviets to upgrade their support for the MPLA. Moscow would not be bettered by Havana. Afanasenko told the Cuban ambassador to Brazzaville that "the Central Committee of the CPSU is attentatively watching the development of events in Angola and reiterates [its] unity with the progressive forces, in order to smash the cherished adventures of foreign and domestic reaction."[45]

Watching attentively was good enough for Fidel Castro, but only up to a point. While Cuba did little to assist the MPLA directly in the immediate wake of the Alvor Agreement, it kept up its pressure on Moscow and the Eastern Bloc countries to do more. The Alvor Agreement would not hold, the Cubans reported in mid-February, and the socialist countries had to be prepared to do more to help the MPLA. By mid-spring both the South African ANC and the Namibian liberation movement the South West African People's Organization (SWAPO) – with whom the Soviet embassy in Lusaka kept in close touch – were promoting the same message.[46]

The Angolan civil war

The Ford administration was, however, not willing to let Neto's MPLA force a solution to the nascent civil war in Angola. As we have seen, in mid-July the president authorized a large-scale covert operation in support of the FNLA and UNITA. Over three months the CIA was allocated almost $50 million in total to be used to train, equip, and transport anti-MPLA troops. IAFEATURE involved some of the same components as the operation in Zaire ten years earlier: training programs, weapons and communication equipment, and air drops to FNLA and UNITA forces inside Angola. John Stockwell, the head of the program, who later published a book harshly critical of the Agency's involvement, claims that CIA officers also operated inside Angola. But the key instrument, just as in Zaire, was deemed to be the recruitment of mercenaries to help organize the Angolan troops, especially those of FNLA, whom the CIA found to be a complete shambles.[47]

We searched the world for allies who could provide qualified advisers to put into the conflict, or better yet, regular army units to crush the MPLA and deliver the country to Roberto and Savimbi. We canvassed moderate friends – Brazil, Morocco, South Korea, Belgium, Great Britain, France, and even Portugal, without success. South Africa eventually came to UNITA's rescue, but the Zairian commando battalions in northern Angola were only slightly better than the FNLA forces they joined. Mercenaries seemed to be the answer, preferably Europeans with the requisite military skills and perhaps experience in Africa. As long as they were not Americans, the 40 Committee approved. We began an exhaustive search for suitable candidates ... Portuguese were already being recruited in small numbers by the FNLA, Colonel Castro, Captain Bento, and their men. We decided to expand this effort by recruiting three hundred Portuguese Angolans to support the FNLA ... The French intelligence service introduced CIA case officers to onetime Congo mercenary Bob Denard, and for $500,000 cash – paid in advance – he agreed to provide twenty French mercenaries.[48]

The South African government had been observing the collapse of the Portuguese positions at their border – or, in the case of Angola, on the border of South African-occupied Namibia – with considerable trepidation. Some of the leaders of the army argued for an early intervention to forestall an MPLA victory, but had few concrete ideas about how to carry it out with the desired effect. The National Party right wing, in ascendance since the early 1970s, was strongly opposed to South African interventions outside its own borders. Its favored model was to concentrate on "reform" at home – that is, the deportation of all Africans to the Homelands and the creation of a secure, all-white state. South Africa had

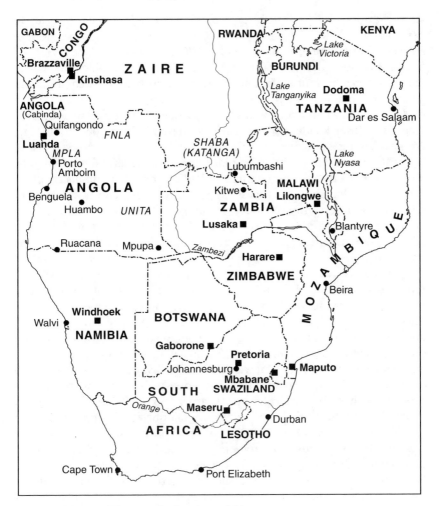

Map 7   The wars in Southern Africa.

no mission, the right-wing claimed, in civilizing Africans in other parts of the continent, and its spokesmen were deeply suspicious of prime minister John Vorster and his assumed weakness for cooperation with America.[49]

Vorster therefore had every reason to move carefully when confronted with the deepening Angolan crisis in early 1975. His ambassador to Washington, J. S. F. Botha, reported Donald Easum, the Assistant Secretary of State for African Affairs, in January as saying that the administration had "so little interest that it would take a major sales job to persuade any American agency to become involved in a new program in Africa."[50] The Bureau of State Security (BOSS) – whose director, General Hendrik van den Bergh, was strongly opposed to intervening in Angola – used US leaks of South African intelligence information as an argument against cooperating with Washington on the matter, in spite of CIA director Colby's abject apology for one such incident in March, when the DCI "regretted [the] incident, particularly in view of the co-operation [the] Agency has received from South Africa."[51] In late May Vorster asked both BOSS and the military for full reports on the situation in Angola, but it was clear that the prime minister had still not made up his mind.

It is not evident from the accessible South African archives why Vorster decided for intervention in July 1975. A BOSS memorandum from September, highly critical of the United States, indicates that the South African government responded to American pressure in the matter. The increasingly alarmist reports from South Africa's consul-general in Luanda, E. M. Malone, must also have played a role. In June Malone repeatedly conveyed Holden Roberto's requests for assistance and asked Pretoria for urgent instructions. The same message came from Jonas Savimbi, whom the South Africans had been supporting with light weapons and ammunition since October 1974. According to South African sources, Savimbi also claimed that "Zambia would support South African military action in Angola – if it was kept secret." Still, as late as April 1975 Vorster turned down Savimbi's urgent requests for more assistance.[52]

After receiving the reports from the army and intelligence in late June, which predicted an MPLA victory in Angola but which stopped short of recommending South African intervention to prevent it, Vorster on 4 July sent the army's director of operations, General Constand Viljoen and van den Bergh's deputy at BOSS Gert Rothman to Kinshasa to meet with Savimbi, Roberto, and Mobutu. On their return they recommended a dramatic increase in South African assistance to the two Angolan movements: mortars, rocket launchers, landmines, vehicles, armored cars, and helicopters. Vorster approved all, except the helicopters, and ordered van den Bergh to purchase everything abroad, so that the supplies could not be traced back to Pretoria. By August small South African military teams were operating inside Angola, and on 15 September the first South African training camp for UNITA troops was operational at Mpupa. In mid-October, as the fighting in Angola intensified, Vorster ordered regular South African forces to invade, setting a limit of 2,500 troops and 600 vehicles. Operation SAVANNAH, as Pretoria termed it, was under way.[53]

The political aims of the South Africans with regard to Angola were unclear. Some of those who planned the operation claimed that the real purpose was to split the country into semi-independent regions along ethnic lines – a bit like South Africa's Homelands – and thereby to secure a UNITA-controlled buffer zone against both the MPLA and against the Namibian liberation movement SWAPO. But it is also clear that Pretoria expected great returns from the Americans for – as they saw it – helping the Ford administration out in Angola. The four main items on Vorster's wish list were US acceptance of his plans for "independence" for the Homelands, an end to the US weapons embargo, no US interference with the rapidly accelerating South African nuclear weapons program, and American support for Vorster's scheme to get rid of Ian Smith's regime in Zimbabwe and replace it with an African coalition government beholden to South Africa.[54] The immediate priority for the South African Defense Force, however, was to crush FAPLA, the MPLA's armed forces, in a lightning offensive toward the north.

In addition to its flagging fortunes on the battlefield, the MPLA ran up against increasing problems in securing a Soviet lifeline through Congo. The flamboyant and independent-minded Congolese leader Colonel Marien Ngouabi had been angered by Neto's persistent criticism of Brazzaville for sheltering Cabindan separatist groups. In an irate message to the Soviet ambassador, Ngouabi informed Moscow that he would no longer accept for Neto to "on the one hand, demand assistance from Congo, [and] on the other make accusations against us." By early August the Congolese had informed Afanasenko that they would not accept Soviet plans for large-scale support of the MPLA through Congolese territory.[55]

It was the threat to the "Congo connection" which, in early August, prompted Moscow to ask Fidel Castro – who had close connections with the Congolese leadership – to act as a facilitator for assistance to the MPLA. The Soviet leaders got more than they bargained for. The Cubans had, since early spring, tried to get Moscow to support an armed strategy on behalf of the MPLA. Already in February the Cuban ambassador to Dar-es-Salaam had told his Soviet colleague that "the choice of the socialist road in Angola must be made now ... In October it will be too late." In late summer Castro used the new Soviet request as a prompt for launching his own plan for the intervention of Cuban forces in Angola.[56]

Very little is known about the Cuban involvement in Angola up to August 1975, and historian Piero Gleijeses' magnificent account of Cuba's role in Africa throws little light on the topic. We know from Soviet documents that Cuba kept a considerable military mission in Congo-Brazzaville, and that instructors from this mission had helped to train MPLA fighters for several years before the collapse of the Portuguese colonial empire. By early summer 1975 these advisers numbered about two hundred and fifty, and – in spite of not participating in combat – they played an increasingly important role in planning the MPLA operations. By May the Cuban officers functioned as a form of general staff for Neto and the MPLA leaders. Through their operational training Castro's instructors supplied the necessary knowhow that the Angolan forces lacked, especially on communications, supply lines, and coordinated operations.[57]

On 15 August Castro sent a message to Leonid Brezhnev arguing the need for increased support for the MPLA, including the introduction of Cuban special troops. The Cubans had already developed a fairly detailed plan for transporting their troops to Luanda (or Congo), for supplies, and for how the Cuban soldiers would be used on the ground in Angola. Castro wanted Soviet transport assistance, as well as the use of Soviet staff officers, both in Havana and Luanda, to help with planning the military operations. The Cubans underlined to the Soviets the political strength of the MPLA and the threat which foreign assistance to the FNLA–UNITA alliance posed to socialism and independence in Angola.[58] The head of the Décima Dirección of the Cuban armed forces (responsible for foreign military assistance), Commandante Raúl Díaz Argüelles, arrived in Luanda as Castro's emissary on 3 August. He reported back to Raúl Castro:

We wanted to clarify what aid we should offer, given the FNLA's and Mobutu's aggression against the MPLA and the possible course of events before independence in November. We knew that the forces of reaction and imperialism would try with all their might to prevent the MPLA from taking power because it would mean a progressive government in Angola. Therefore we were bringing Neto the militant solidarity of our Commander in Chief, our party, and our government, and we gave him the $100,000. In the course of this conversation the Angolans complained about the paucity of aid from the socialist camp ... [and] also complained that the Soviet Union stopped helping them in 1972 and that the military aid it is now sending is paltry, given the enormity of the need.[59]

The Cuban initiative was coordinated with the MPLA leaders, who now in turn tried to put pressure on the Soviets to get involved with the Cuban plan for direct military intervention. Lúcio Lara, the senior MPLA underground leader in Luanda, had already on 17 August appealed to Ambassador Afanasenko for the dispatch of Soviet staff officers to the MPLA General Command, which had just moved from Brazzaville to Luanda. "The MPLA Command needs qualified advice on military questions at the strategic level," Lara said. Afanasenko, however, could only promise technical experts, but agreed to invite the MPLA's defense minister designate, Iko Carreira, to Moscow in late August for talks with the CPSU International Department, the Defense Ministry, and the

Armed Forces General Staff. Meanwhile Díaz Argüelles arrived back in Luanda on 21 August to head the Cuban Military Mission there.[60]

In spite of their policy to support Neto's MPLA, Soviet leaders were not pleased with the content of the Cuban plan. First of all, they objected to the use of Soviet officers and even Soviet transport planes in Angola prior to independence. They worried that such a move would be going too far and would damage the policy of *détente* with the United States. They also knew that most African countries, including some of those close to the Soviet Union, would react against a direct Soviet involvement, as would some of their political friends in Portugal, both inside and outside the Communist Party. Second, the Cubans were, in the Soviet view, not sufficiently aware of how even a Cuban intervention could upset superpower relations, since the new Ford administration would see Cuban forces as proxies for Soviet interests. Third, Moscow was still not sure that the military situation in Angola warrented a troop intervention in support of the MPLA.[61]

In spite of their displeasure, Soviet leaders found it difficult to make their objections known to Castro. Moscow knew that the Cuban leader was weary of the Soviet policy of *détente*, and their experience with Havana told them to tread carefully so as to avoid episodes such as the near break between the two allies in the late 1960s. Still, Brezhnev flatly refused to transport the Cuban troops or to send Soviet officers to serve with the Cubans in Angola. The Soviet General Staff opposed any participation in the Cuban operation, and even the KGB, with whom the policy of paying increased attention to Africa originated, in August 1975 warned against the effects of direct Soviet intervention on US–Soviet relations.[62]

Havana would not be deterred by the Soviet hesitation. After having sorted out most of the logistical problems of an Angolan mission with Congo's Ngouabi, who visited Cuba in mid-September, the first Cuban soldiers arrived in Brazzaville and Luanda in early October on board several aircraft and rebuilt prerevolutionary Cuban cruise ships. The five hundred Cubans immediately fanned out into FAPLA units in the Angolan countryside, and took charge of much of the fighting against the MPLA's enemies. But the infusion of Cuban troops was not enough to sustain the MPLA conquests from early summer against the new onslaught of its combined enemies.[63]

In September the MPLA continued its retreat, hard pressed by Zairean and mercenary-led FNLA troops in the north and UNITA forces, supported by men and materiel from South Africa, in the south. Savimbi's incongruous alliance with Pretoria had given his military units the equipment they badly needed, and they could now exploit their substantial ethnically based support in central and eastern Angola. The MPLA, meanwhile, was by mid-October entirely dependent on the support it received in the western Luanda–Mbundu regions and in the cities. It controlled less than one-fourth of the country and was losing ground, in spite of its Cuban reinforcements, who participated in fighting for the first time on 23 October.[64]

The foreign alliance policies of the MPLA, and thereby its possibilities for winning the struggle for power in Angola, were saved by Pretoria's October decision to launch an invasion. Moscow knew of the South African plans in advance of their implementation in mid-October, and the Kremlin leadership discussed how to respond. The CPSU International Department considered the new stage of anti-MPLA operations in Angola a joint US–South African effort, and believed the Soviet Union had to come to the aid of its ally. In the third week of October Moscow decided that it would start assisting the Cuban operation in Angola immediately after the MPLA had made its declaration of independence, on 11 November. The Soviet aim was to get enough Cuban troops and Soviet advisers into Angola by mid-December to defeat the South Africans and to assist the MPLA leaders in building a socialist party and state.[65]

The Soviet perception of the widening role of the CIA in assisting FNLA forces from bases in Zaire also played a role in Moscow's reevaluation of its Angolan policy. The KGB station in Brazzaville supplied vital information on the dramatic increase in US assistance, and Iurii Andropov believed that the Americans had a long-term strategy of equipping large groups of Angolan, Zairean, and Western mercenary troops, to be sent into Angola. It was also likely, the KGB said, that US "experts" would increase their own cross-border activities.[66]

The reaction of most African countries to the South African invasion led the Soviets to believe that it would be less dangerous than before to intervene in the Angolan conflict. Julius Nyerere, an African leader whom Moscow respected in spite of his often blunt criticism of its Africa policies, told the Soviet ambassador on 3 November that in spite of deploring the war in Angola, Pretoria's intervention had made outside support for the MPLA necessary. He hoped that many African countries would now aid Neto's movement. Still, he warned against a too open Soviet support for the MPLA, and hoped that Moscow would channel the bulk of its aid through African governments. The Soviet ambassador, untruthfully, responded that this was indeed their intention.[67]

Soviet military preparations for the airlift of Cuban troops to Angola intensified in early November. The CPSU secretariat met on 5 November and decided to send Soviet naval units to areas off the

Angolan coast. In Brazzaville, in a striking reversal of roles within less than two months, the Soviet ambassador now exhorted his Cuban colleague to "intensify" Havana's preparations for combat in Angola. "But a Cuban artillery regiment is already fighting in Luanda," the Cuban ambassador responded, somewhat incredulously.[68]

Agostinho Neto declared the independence of the People's Republic of Angola on 11 November , just as the MPLA was fighting for its very existence only a few miles north of Luanda. In the Battle of Quifangondo Valley the Cuban artillerymen proved to give FAPLA the crucial advantage over its FNLA–Zairean opponents. Soviet-supplied BM-21 122 millimeter rocket launchers devastated the attacking forces and sent them on a disorderly retreat toward the northern border, giving the MPLA and the Cubans a free hand to turn on the South African and UNITA forces approaching from the south. The Quifangondo battle in effect destroyed the credibility of the FNLA military challenge. The CIA officers, the South Africans, and the mercenary leaders, who all had assisted in mounting Holden Roberto's failed attempt to take Luanda, decided that unless progress was made by their UNITA partners in the south, FLNA would be a spent force. All attention passed to Jonas Savimbi, who had spent the day before independence in Pretoria, meeting secretly with John Vorster.[69]

Soviet, Cuban, Western, and South African information gives conflicting versions of the Cuban build-up of troops in Angola. Cuban sources claim that up to late December, when there were four thousand Cubans in Angola, all transport had taken place on Cuban ships and aircraft. Soviet archival documents give a different story, which is – at least in part – corroborated by information from other countries. During the week before independence large groups of Cuban soldiers had started arriving in Luanda on board Soviet aircraft. The Soviets had organized and equipped the transports, although the operation was technically directed by the Cubans themselves. Moscow had made it clear that the primary objective of these forces was to contain the South Africans along the southern border, and that they should not be used for general purposes in the civil war. For the same reason the Soviet General Staff ordered about sixty of their own officers to join the Cuban forces from Congo. These men started arriving in Luanda on the evening of 12 November.[70]

The ensuing two weeks saw the rapid advance toward Luanda of the UNITA army led by about three thousand regular South African troops. By late November these forces had reconquered all the territory that Savimbi had lost to the MPLA over the preceding months. They had occupied every major port south of the capital except Porto Amboim, taken control of the Benguela railway, and were attempting to set up their own civilian administration in Huambo. Both the Soviets and the Cubans concluded that if the MPLA regime was to survive, the Cuban forces would have to attack in the south as soon as possible.[71]

After the creation of the MPLA regime the Politburo authorized the Soviet General Staff to take direct control of the transatlantic deployment of additional Cuban troops, as well as the supplying of these troops with advanced military hardware. The massive operation – the first Soviet effort of its kind – transported more than twelve thousand soldiers by sea and air from Cuba to Africa between November 1975 and mid-January 1976. In the same period it also provided FAPLA and the Cubans with hundreds of tons of heavy arms, as well as T-34 and T-54 tanks, SAM-7s, antitank missiles, and a number of MiG-21 fighter planes.[72]

It is still not possible to chart in any detail the logistics of the Soviet operation. What we do know is that the governments of several African countries accepted to assist the enterprise. Congo was the main staging ground for personnel and arms arriving from Cuba and the Soviet Union (although in some cases An-22 transport planes flew directly from the southern USSR – mostly from Odessa – or from Cuba). Algeria, Guinea, Mali, and Tanzania cooperated with the efforts in different ways, even if the Soviets on some occasions had to push hard to get their cooperation. Moscow also had to push some of its East European allies to rush to the defense of "African liberation and global anti-imperialism" by supporting the MPLA.[73]

The critical phase of the war was in November and the first part of December 1975. Holden Roberto, whom the CIA had hoped would take Luanda by independence day, 11 November, never regained much ground after the rout in Quifangondo Valley. By the end of November the Cubans had stopped the South African-led advance on Luanda, and in two battles south of the Cuanza River in December the southern invaders and their UNITA allies suffered major setbacks. Pretoria then decided to withdraw toward the border, partly because of its military problems and partly because the US Senate voted to block all funding for covert operations in Angola on 19 December. Pretoria would not accept being left in the lurch by Washington, with its own men held hostage to a conflict they no longer believed they could win. The shock at the American decision struck deep inside the South African government, in spite of Kissinger's attempts to explain the differences between the views in the administration and in Congress. Some South African observers claim that the US betrayal of Vorster over Angola severely weakened the prime minister's position within his own party and thereby helped the more right-wing defence minister P. W. Botha to replace him two years later.[74]

Just as it had opened the gates for African acceptance of Soviet–Cuban aid to the MPLA, the by now defunct South African intervention also paved the way for African diplomatic recognition of the new Angolan regime. By mid-February most African states had officially recognized Neto's government, as had the Organization of African Unity (OAU), in spite of attempts by its chairman, Ugandan president Idi Amin, to have the decision postponed. Soviet diplomatic efforts contributed significantly to this development, for instance in the case of Zambia, where President Kenneth Kaunda switched over to the MPLA's side after substantial Soviet pressure.[75]

In terms of control of the central regions, the Angolan war was over by early March 1976. The capital of the anti-MPLA forces, Huambo, fell to FAPLA on 11 February. Holden Roberto had already in January returned to exile in Zaire, and the FNLA had given up its military activities. Jonas Savimbi had retreated to the bush areas of southeastern Angola with about 2,000 guerrillas and their US and South African advisers, and although he was to fight his way back to international prominence by the early 1980s, in 1976 Savimbi himself realized that he could not effectively challenge FAPLA and the Cubans.[76]

In the spring of 1976 the Soviet leaders felt – with a high degree of certainty and self-congratulation – that they had won the Angolan war. The leadership was impressed that the logistics of the operation had worked well – over five thousand miles from Moscow, the Soviet Union had conducted a campaign in support of its allies against the power of the United States and its strong regional supporters, and come out on top. For Brezhnev himself, Angola became a benchmark for "active solidarity with the peoples of Africa and Asia" and evidence that the Soviet Union could advance socialism in the Third World during a period of *détente* with the United States.[77]

The Ford administration, understandably, was dejected. Not only had the Angolan intervention failed, but it had given rise to unprecedented anti-interventionism among the American public. At the same time the failure in Angola had made the administration look weak in the Cold War conflict over influence in the Third World and prepared the ground for attacks from the domestic right-wing and from America's Chinese partners. The relationship with apartheid South Africa, a key "policeman" in Kissinger's estimate, was on the rocks. In a meeting with the South African ambassador on 15 May, after the last South African troops had left Angola, Kissinger had little comfort to give Pretoria.

He said I [Amb. Botha] should know what the political situation in the USA is and under the present circumstances he and the president are trying their best to keep the Russians out of Africa. He left no stone unturned in his attempts to find funding to keep the Russians out of Angola. He was convinced that the Russians could be contained, but Congress made that impossible. It is an awful situation and ultimately the Russians will be able to ride the momentum of the victory in Angola to defeat the powerful leaders in Africa, resulting in total victory in Africa ... Kissinger said I should know that the American people in certain situations become divided, like with Vietnam, and then there will be no action taken by them. We therefore cannot count on them. He wanted to be open and truthful with me. He acknowledged that they could not commit to us. They realize our dilemma.

After Ford lost the 1976 election to Jimmy Carter the relationship deteriorated further. According to one foreign policy adviser to the South African prime minister, writing in 1977,

We have more to fear from the United States than from the Soviet Union. The Soviet Union showed by its action in Angola in airlifting 15,000 Cubans and providing $300 million worth of logistical support that it was prepared to take extraordinary risks with its *détente* with the United States to achieve objectives which it regarded as valuable ... It is the United States, with its volatile swings in opinion, its unassuaged yearnings for what it thinks of [as] idealistic action, its new administration with its debt to black votes, its growing belief that white rule in Southern Africa may be doomed, and its fear that the Soviet Union will take advantage of it if the United States doesn't act, that is the truly unpredictable and potentially revolutionary force.[78]

What did the Soviets believe they had learnt from the Angolan conflict? From reports coming into the CPSU International Department the most important lesson at the time seems to have been that the United States could be defeated in local conflicts under certain circumstances. First, the Soviet armed forces must be capable of and ready to provide, at short notice, the logistics for the operation required. These tasks were primarily assigned to the navy and the air force, both of which were commended for their efforts in Angola. Second, the Soviet Union must be able to organize and control the anti-imperialist forces involved (unlike in Vietnam, where, Soviet leaders felt, disaster had struck again and again because of the Vietnamese leaders' inability to follow Moscow's advice).[79]

The Soviet cadre in Angola were, by 1976, very satisfied with the way both Angolans and Cubans had respected Moscow's political primacy during the war. According to the embassy, Neto realized his dependence on Soviet assistance and, equally important, that it was Moscow, not Havana, who made the final decisions. Even though the embassy still did not trust Neto fully, they admitted that he had performed to their liking during these battles. In the spring of 1976 he continued to press for more Soviet military instructors, an attitude which the chargé d'affaires in

Luanda, G. A. Zverev, held up as a sign of the Angolan president's dedication to the new alliance, even if Neto had not yet consented to request permanent Soviet military bases.[80]

As to the Cubans, Soviet representatives often expressed a certain degree of surprise to Moscow over how harmonious relations were with the small Caribbean ally. Soviet–Cuban "close coordination in Angola during the war has had very positive results," Zverev told his superiors in March. Soviet diplomats and officers lauded the Cubans for their bravery and for their ability to function as a link between Moscow and Luanda, while "respecting" the paramount role of the CPSU leadership. The overall Cuban–Soviet relationship improved significantly in the wake of the Angolan operation, up to a point that had not been reached since the 1962 Missile Crisis.[81]

Moscow and Havana also agreed on strategy in Angola after the main battles ended in spring 1976. Both countries wanted to wind down their military involvement as soon as possible, to "avoid broad military clashes with South Africa and attain their goal by means of political and diplomatic struggle."[82] In May Raúl Castro told the Soviet General Staff that he wanted to start withdrawing Cuban troops right away, and that he expected almost fifteen thousand Cubans (out of a total 36,000) to have left by late October. The Cuban leaders asked Moscow to inform Pretoria of their intentions, well knowing that such a demilitarization of the conflict – albeit with a MPLA government in place – was what the Soviets had wanted all along. Havana knew how to placate the superpower, although, as we will see below, they exacted their price for doing so.[83]

The second lesson the Soviets believed they had learnt from the Angolan adventure was that the Soviet Union could and should rebuild and reform local anticapitalist groups in crisis areas. The MPLA, local Soviet observers postulated in 1976, was saved from its own follies by advice and assistance from Moscow, which not only helped it win the war, but also laid the foundation for the building of a "vanguard party." The Angolan movement had earlier been plagued by "careerists and fellow-travellers," but, due to Soviet guidance, the "internationalists" were in the ascendance. These new leaders – men like Lopo do Nascimento and Nito Alves – understood that the MPLA was part of an international revolutionary movement led by Moscow and that they therefore both then and in the future depended on Soviet support.[84]

It was these "internationalists" whom Moscow wanted to assist in building a new MPLA, patterned on the experience of the Soviet Communist Party. Noting the poor state of the MPLA organization in many areas, Soviet party-building experts suggested that this was the field in which Nascimento, Alves and others should concentrate their activities. By taking the lead in constructing the party organization, they would also be the future leaders of a Marxist-Leninist party in Angola.[85]

The Soviets supplied very large amounts of political propaganda to be disseminated among MPLA supporters and used in the training of cadres. The ordinary embassy staff sometimes found the amounts a bit difficult to handle – a plane-load of brochures with Brezhnev's speech at the 25th CPSU Congress, two plane-loads of anti-Maoist literature – but in general the embassy could put the materials to good use (or at least they so claimed in their reports to Moscow). By summer 1976 they had run out of Lenin busts, and had to request a new supply from the CPSU Propaganda Department.[86]

The transformation of the MPLA turned out to be an infinitely more difficult task for the Soviets than the dissemination of Lenin busts. Neto's independence of mind and his claim to be a Marxist theoretician in his own right rankled the Russians and made it increasingly difficult for them to control the MPLA as soon as the military situation stabilized. Some of the Angolan leaders whom Moscow disliked, for instance FAPLA veteran commander and defense minister Iko Carreira and MPLA general secretary Lúcio Lara, who was strongly influenced by the European left, strengthened their positions after the war was over. According to the embassy, the influence of such people delayed both the necessary changes in the MPLA and the finalization of the development plans on which the Soviets and the Cubans were advising.[87]

Differences between the Soviet and the Cuban perceptions of the political situation in the MPLA did not make things easier for Moscow. Part of the price which Castro exacted for his general deference to the Soviets on the Angolan issue was a right to argue for Angolan political solutions that were to his liking. Preeminent in Castro's political equation was the leadership of Aghostino Neto – whom he considered a brilliant man and a great African leader, as well as a personal friend. The Cubans therefore missed no opportunity to impress the Soviets with their view that the MPLA president was the only solution to Angola's leadership problems, well knowing Moscow's suspicions of him. "We have the highest regard for President Neto," Raúl Castro told Soviet Vice Minister of Defense I. F. Ponomarenko. "Cuba wants to strengthen Neto's authority," the head of the Cuban Communist Party's International Department, Raúl Valdés Vivó, told the Soviet chargé d'affaires in May.[88]

The Cubans were, however, always clever at sweetening their tough position in support of Neto by underlining that the Soviet Union of course was Angola's primary international ally. "Relations with the Soviet Union will become a more important aspect of Angolan foreign policy in the future," Raúl Castro told his Soviet colleagues.

He instructed Risquet to "on all questions inform the USSR embassy in Angola and maintain close contact with the Soviet comrades." Castro also castigated some of the Angolan leaders whom the Soviets distrusted; Lúcio Lara "displays a certain restraint on questions [of] broadening the collaboration with the socialist countries. He is reserved and not frank ... [and] has avoided us," Castro told Ponomarenko.[89]

But even such measures could not always convince the Soviets of Cuban loyalty. Reporting on Neto's visit to Havana in July 1976, the Soviet embassy noted with disapproval that Fidel Castro had told the Angolans that Cuban troops would remain in Africa "as long as they are needed," and that Neto had asked for Cuba's assistance in building a Marxist-Leninist party. Even worse, Castro had spoken of Angola, Cuba, and Vietnam as "the main anti-imperialist core" of the world. That the Cuban president had also mentioned the "central role" of the Soviet Union was not sufficient to please the Soviet observers, particularly since Castro coupled his statement with an endorsement of Neto's own "paramount role" in the MPLA.[90]

The Cold War in Africa and the decline of superpower *détente*

Recent memoirs and Moscow's own declassified documents show that the MPLA victory in Angola, together with Hanoi's victory in Vietnam, gave rise to unprecedented optimism in Soviet Third World policy – "the world," according to one of their high officials, "was turning in our direction."[91] The commonly held view among officials both in the party and in the government was that large sections of the Third World yearned after socialism, which, they recognized, was the only remedy to their problems. Together with the recognition their country achieved through Nixon's and Kissinger's *détente*, and through *détente* in Europe, the socialist offensives in the Third World gave many Soviets a renewed sense of pride in their own achievements and a conviction that the Soviet Union could contribute decisively to breakthroughs for socialism elsewhere. Even members of the Politburo, the top Soviet leadership, who were generally advanced in age and had had little experience with any part of the world outside Europe, got caught up in the excitement. During the preparations for the CPSU's 25th Party Congress in February 1976 the younger advisers of the International Department got unprecedented access to the top leaders themselves, including Leonid Brezhnev, who expressed their direct approval of Soviet involvements in the Third World. At the congress Brezhnev lauded the advances for socialism in Africa and Asia, and stressed the close Soviet alliance with Cuba and Vietnam.

While the events of 1975 helped to bring the Third World to the forefront of Soviet thinking, the highly ideologized version of what had really happened in Southern Africa and in Southeast Asia produced by the Moscow leadership set the direction for policy. Instead of the gradual and hesitant build-up of Soviet involvement, with decisions taken very much under the pressure of events over which Moscow had little or no influence, the 1976 version saw a purposeful Soviet policy, in which advisers and experts had "correctly" interpreted local events based on instructions received from the Politburo and the general theoretical line of the party. Crucially, both the turn to socialism in the Third World and the success of Soviet assistance was based on the structural crisis of US hegemony and the international capitalist system. In other words, advances in the Third World were symptoms of a much more general change in the balance of power between socialism and capitalism. The former colonies were the weak spots of international capitalism, and it was therefore not surprising that the first manifestations of these crises would occur there, many Soviet policy makers thought.

Curiously, this swing toward optimism in Moscow's Third World policy took place at the same time as some important symptoms of weakness started to appear in the Soviet economy. While the economy as such throughout the 1970s would have a growth rate that more or less paralleled the one in the West – albeit a West in crisis, as the Soviets themselves pointed out – the year 1975 saw a sharp decline in agricultural production, making the Soviet Union dependent on foreign grain imports (a dependence that would stay in place up to the end of the Soviet era). While the CPSU – with some right – blamed climatic conditions, what many observers found interesting was that the Soviet economy did not seem to have the flexibility to deal with the effects of this setback except through cuts in other areas – in other words, the command economy failed to deliver in the key field of resource allocation. Eager, as all politicians are, to focus on good news rather than bad, the Soviet leadership came to focus more than they otherwise would have done on the political advances for socialism in the Third World, because it served to obscure problems at home.

A key theme in the Soviet evalution of Angola and Vietnam was that these revolutions had succeeded because they were led by a Marxist core. The discipline that the Communists had shown in the face of adversity had, in the end, enabled them to gain victory. This argument worked two ways. One the one hand it underlined the significance of Leninist discipline and party-building: the VWP and the MPLA had survived a military onslaught by imperialism, while non-Marxist radicals such as Sukarno and Nkrumah were gone. On the other hand it reemphasized the role of the Soviet example: what Moscow had to contribute – even more important than its military might – was its experience of building socialism. Since socialism was what the masses wanted, it was those parties that could show a practical and well-founded approach to how to construct it that would get the adherence of the masses. It was, in other words, their socialist know-how that had saved both the Angolan and the Vietnamese revolutions.

One example of the new Soviet approach after Angola was its increased support for the South African ANC. This new emphasis was in part practical and in part ideological. The MPLA regime in Angola presented new opportunities for educating ANC soldiers and cadres near South Africa itself – already by summer 1976 most of the ANC's training camps had been relocated to Angola. But there was also a sense in Moscow that South Africa itself was approaching a revolution. The ANC and SACP leadership remained extremely cautious about the future – a 1975 SACP note complains that "the Party has ceased to exist as an organized force in South Africa. We are no longer in touch with members at home."[92] The MO, however, attempted to argue that the liberation of Portuguese Africa would necessarily have an effect inside South Africa itself. The spontaneous outbreak of the Soweto uprising in the summer of 1976 – which came after South African police had massacred more than forty schoolchildren at a protest meeting – seemed to confirm that the Soviets were right. The resulting exodus of young refugees created a fertile ground for ANC recruitment. By 1977 the camps in Angola were filling up and Cuban and Soviet instructors were training young South African soldiers, some of whom were successfully sent back home for military operations against the apartheid regime.

Both the Soviets and the ANC were aware, however, that Mozambique – directly bordering South Africa – would have been a better staging ground for attacks. The Mozambican leadership was, understandably, skeptical to ANC military operations from its territory: their capital, Maputo, was right on the border, and South Africa would strike back with terrible consequences for the new FRELIMO regime. But the Mozambicans were also critical of the ANC's close relationship with the Soviets. In 1974 the FRELIMO president Samora Machel told Oliver Tambo that "for its own safety, the ANC had to be watchful of the activities of the SACP. He also stated that the USSR and the CPSU were not genuine friends of the African people, were racists and were interested in dominating Africa." This advice, the ANC report noted, came at the same time as Machel "admitted the decisive importance of Soviet aid for the Mozambican struggle."[93] Obviously, while the Soviets had come to see themselves as the champions of African radicals, that view was not shared by all the new and radical African leaders.

While the role of the Cubans in Angola was almost airbrushed out of the internal Soviet version of events, Fidel Castro celebrated his first major victory against the Americans. For him, Angola was to a very high extent payback time – for American attacks on Cuba, for Che's death in Bolivia. It was also a test of how far the Cubans were willing to follow him in promoting international revolution. In July 1976, when Aghostino Neto visited Cuba, Castro proclaimed:

This attitude of our country, willing to fight, to help, on one terrain or another, is a good way to measure its maturity and its revolutionary conscience. That is why the imperialists always make mistakes with Cuba; because they have no equipment to measure these moral attitudes. They have no way of measuring the spirit and morale of a people. They made a mistake at the Bay of Pigs. And now, when they planned the invasion of Angola, they again made a mistake. They could not conceive that, at a distance of 10,000 km, Cuba would be able to give Angola the cooperation that it did ... Because they thought that the blockaded people, the people they have tried to sink and ruin, were not able to give this type of aid. And they made a mistake. Our combatants were there on the front line ... The most important thing about a country is not its wealth. The imperialists have a lot of wealth, but they do not have morale or spirit. The most important thing about a country, a society, is its morale and its spirit.[94]

Castro also took pride – although in a more quiet fashion – that the Soviets had had to rely on Cuban forces and Cuban advice in order to solve the Angolan crisis. He was never in doubt about where that placed his Cuban commanders inside Angola – as we have already seen, the Cubans in Luanda may have praised the Soviet leading role, but they themselves made the crucial decisions on security matters. The spectacle of the May 1977 coup attempt against Neto, when Nito Alves – a Soviet favorite – found his bid to oust the president blocked by Cuban tanks, testifies fully to this.[95]

The Communist victory in Indochina and, especially, the Soviet–Cuban intervention in Angola, made even the most ardent US supporters of *détente* doubt whether the future for US foreign policy lay in seeking cooperation with the Soviet Union. The problem for many within the American elite was that Moscow seemed to outdo the United States in bidding for power in the Third World, exploiting US weakness after Vietnam and Watergate and mocking the "spirit" of *détente*, which many took to encompass a lessening of Soviet–American rivalry outside Europe. While some in the administration stuck to the view that Angola was a cost rather than a benefit for the Soviets, even Henry Kissinger, who knew the limitations of *détente* better than anyone, began publicly to accuse the Soviets of breaking *détente* through their actions in the Third

World. With 1976 being an election year, both Ford and Kissinger realized that the concept of *détente* was on the verge on being unusable for getting in votes.

Some of the harshest international criticism of the Angola debacle came from America's new-found Chinese allies. In a series of meetings with the ailing Mao Zedong and the man who would eventually become his successor, Deng Xiaoping, in Beijing in December 1975, Ford and Kissinger had promised to step up their help if China would reenter the Angolan fray. Mao had commented: "You do not seem to have many means." "Just before I left Washington," Ford had responded, "I approved another $35 million to help the two other forces [FNLA and UNITA]. This is a solid indication [sic] to meet the challenge of the Soviet Union and defeat the MPLA." Only a few days later Congress had effectively ended the US covert program. The Chinese were furious. To Beijing the administration's claims of powerlessness over Angola were yet another example of American defeatism and deviousness when confronted with Soviet power. It taught Mao's successors not to depend on the United States cooperating effectively in the battle against Moscow in the Third World. Kissinger fumed to his staff:

We are going to lose big. The President says to the Chinese that we're going to stand firm in Angola and two weeks later we get out ... the Department leaks that we're worried about a [Soviet] naval base and says it [Angola] is an exaggeration or aberration of Kissinger's. I don't care about the oil or the base but I do care about the African reaction when they see the Soviets pull it off and we don't do anything. If the Europeans then say to themselves if they can't hold Luanda, how can they defend Europe? The Chinese will say we're a country that was run out of Indochina for 50,000 men and is now being run out of Angola for less than $50 million.[96]

Instead of moving his attention somewhere else – as he would have done in better times – and pulling US press attention with him, Kissinger in the spring of 1976 kept soldiering away at shoring up resistance to what he saw as Soviet penetration of Africa. He told the NSC in early April that

We must keep our eye on the strategic concepts, our Africa policy is one thing but the surrogate Soviet action could come through North Viet Nam as well as Cuba. If this principle is accepted, it will be very dangerous for us. In time, there will be a real problem if the Cuban presence remains in Africa. In the period 1970–73 we successfully frustrated the Soviets in the Middle East so the Arabs finally had to turn towards us. We will try to identify with the aspirations of the black nations in Africa, but not in response to Cuban pressure.[97]

In April Kissinger even went to Africa himself – a first visit in his seven years as National Security Adviser and Secretary of State. His main aim with the trip was to seek an internal, negotiated settlement to the conflict in Zimbabwe, in order to prevent a similar situation from developing as the one in Angola. "If the Cubans are involved there," he had told the president before leaving, "Namibia is next and after that South Africa itself. We must make the Soviets pay a heavy price. If the Cubans move, I recommend we act vigorously. We can't permit another move without suffering a great loss."[98] During his trip, Kissinger met with the most important African leaders, including Tanzania's Julius Nyerere, who obviously sensed his guest's almost personal discomfort with the situation post-Angola. "We want pressure on the regime in Rhodesia [Zimbabwe]," Nyerere said.

We want pressure on Vorster regarding Namibia, and ultimately for change in South Africa. We can't live with South Africa as it is. As to what you can do, sometimes the things we ask are extravagant for you within the limits of the old system. You might not be able to give us arms, but what can you give us? We hope you will answer that question, within the limits not of your power, but of your system.[99]

Remarkably, Kissinger's response to the pleas from African leaders, after he returned to Washington, was to attempt to reactivate his link with South Africa. An incredulous John Vorster, under attack at home for having trusted the Americans over Angola, began receiving requests through his Washington embassy for Pretoria's cooperation on Zimbabwe. This time Kissinger tried to sweet-talk the South Africans by pointing out that the United States and South Africa had the same problem with native populations, "although employing different tactics." He assured the South African ambassador, Pik Botha, "that if he was in my position he will also not allow one man one vote." He tempted Vorster with "solving the Transkei independence problem through statecraft ... with all the problems between black and white being such that the political situation can be controlled."[100] With the Soweto uprising under way, Vorster tried to use Kissinger to regain some of his lost internal stature by agreeing to meet with the Secretary three times in mid-1976 to discuss the issues of Zimbabwe and Namibia. What Vorster sought was an internal solution in Zimbabwe on South Africa's premises and Kissinger went far in promising Vorster that during their talks with Rhodesian leader Ian Smith in Pretoria in mid-September. But by then time was running out for Kissinger, who was uncertain whether he would be kept on even if President Ford should win the US election on 2 November.

Only in one region did the "policeman" strategy help the Americans in preventing radical change after the collapse of the Portuguese empire. When the former Portuguese colony of East Timor, in Southeast Asia near Indonesia, declared its independence under the left-wing liberation organization Revolutionary Front of Independent East Timor (FRETILIN; Frente Revolucionária de Timor Leste Independente), Indonesia immediately threatened to intervene. Unlike during Sukarno, when the United States had opposed Indonesian expansion, this time around Ford and Kissinger saw the right-wing dictator Suharto's plans as a godsend. Asked by the Indonesian dictator in December 1975 – when visiting Jakarta on their way back from the less than successful summit with Mao in Beijing – for US "understanding if we deem it necessary to take rapid or drastic action, President Ford replied: "We will understand and will not press you on the issue. We understand the problem you have and the intentions you have." Kissinger added: "It is important that whatever you do succeeds quickly. We would be able to influence the reaction in America if whatever happens happens after we return. This way there would be less chance of people talking in an un-authorized way ... We understand your problem and the need to move quickly, but I am only saying that it would be better if it were done after we returned."[101] The Indonesian Army did move in mid-December, crushing FRETILIN and incorporating East Timor into Indonesia. Kissinger – increasingly despondent and inefficient in office – saw the invasion and annexation of East Timor as a sign that some of his Cold War policies were working, even when his role was coming under increasing pressure both abroad and at home.

The US domestic attacks on *détente* in 1976 came from several different angles. The new Secretary of Defense, Donald Rumsfeld, and the Pentagon began questioning some of the provisions of the SALT II treaty that President Ford had already signed up to at his summit meeting with Leonid Brezhnev in Vladivostok in November 1974. In the process leading up to the Republican presidential nomination in August, Ford was challenged by the neoconservative California governor Ronald Reagan, who based much of his campaign on a radical critique of *détente* as practiced by Nixon and his successor.

Our nation is in danger, and the danger grows greater with each passing day ... Now, we are told Washington is dropping the word *détente*, but keeping the policy. But whatever it's called, the policy is what's at fault ... Now we must ask if someone is giving away our own freedom. Dr. Kissinger is quoted as saying that he thinks of the United States as Athens and the Soviet Union as Sparta. "The day of the US is past and today is the day of the Soviet Union." And he added, " ... My job as Secretary of State is to negotiate the most acceptable second-best position available." Well, I believe in the peace of which Mr. Ford spoke as much as any man. But peace does not come from weakness or from retreat. It comes from the restoration of American military superiority.[102]

Ford survived the nomination battle, only to lose the election to Jimmy Carter, a Southern governor with even less foreign policy experience than the incumbent president himself. While Ford and Kissinger had to answer increasingly critical questions about *détente* from the press, Carter had tried to position himself on both sides of Ford on the issue, claiming both that his opponent "tried to start a new Vietnam in Angola, and it was only the outcry of the American people and the Congress when their secret deal was discovered that prevented our involvement in that conflagration which was taking place there." But on the other hand Carter complained that "we've become fearful to compete with the Soviet Union on an equal basis. We talk about *détente*. The Soviet Union knows what they want in *détente* ... and we've been out-traded in almost every instance."[103]

Carter's election opened a period of uncertainty in superpower relations. The new president wanted to improve relations with the Soviets and to focus on a more moral foreign policy, not least with regard to the Third World. Deeply suspicious of covert operations as an instrument of policy, Carter wanted to emphasize human rights and what he saw as American ideological principles in combating Communism and other forms of authoritarian government. The Soviets did not know what to expect and – after eight years of Nixon and Kissinger – many Third World leaders remained deeply suspicious of American motives. Carter's main foreign policy advisers, Secretary of State Cyrus Vance and National Security Adviser Zbigniew Brzezinski, were at loggerheads almost from the moment the administration was sworn in. Vance, a somewhat old-fashioned genteel politician with experience both from the Kennedy and Johnson administrations, preferred focusing on continuing and expanding *détente* with the Soviet Union, especially in the areas of arms control and Europe. Brzezinski, a Polish émigré intellectual who became a US citizen in 1958, favored a much more hard-headed approach to the Soviets and to Communism in general. Brzezinski was particularly concerned about Moscow's intentions in the Third World. Already in a 1976 memorandum to Carter, the future national security adviser had warned the future president that

the Soviet leaders have openly stated that the *détente* is meant to promote the "world revolutionary process," and they see American–Soviet *détente* not only as a means of preserving peace, but also as a way of creating favorable conditions for the acquiring of power by Communist parties, especially given the so-called aggravated crisis of capitalism ... [We must make] it unmistakably clear to the Soviet Union that *détente* requires responsible behavior from them on fundamental issues of global order and it is incompatible with irresponsible behavior in Angola, the Middle East, and the UN.[104]

7 The prospects of socialism: Ethiopia and the Horn

By the mid-1970s, after the economic decline of many Arab states and their defeats in the 1967 and 1973 wars against Israel, the political atmosphere all over the Middle East went through a period of intense radicalization. The postcolonial regimes of the region came under pressure from below, from left-wing socialists and Islamists, and responded either by increased repression – such as in Egypt and Iran – or by transforming their regimes in a more radical direction, such as in Syria or Iraq. In spite of their hatred for each other, both Baathist regimes ended up as close allies of the Soviet Union and as the main recipients of Soviet aid in the region, especially after Egypt in 1977 began a separate peace process with Israel. The Soviets and their allies hoped that the leftward trend in Syria and Iraq, and within the PLO, could be speeded up by local Communists working *within* the established leaderships. The CPSU International Department believed that Sadat's treason and America's reinvigorated alliances with Israel and Iran could be turned to Moscow's advantage, by letting radical Arabs know that they had nowhere else to go for support than to the Communists and to the Soviet Union.

In reports to the top Soviet leadership in the mid-1970s, the International Department often pointed to Iraq as the best example of how Communists could gain influence within the government through an alliance with radical bourgeois nationalists, such as the Baath Party. But while Iraq, Syria, and the PLO were headed by Soviet-leaning front governments, the former British colony of South Yemen, on the southern tip of the Arabian peninsula, had moved beyond that stage and declared itself to be the People's Democratic Republic of Yemen (PDRY). The Soviet advisers who arrived in the early 1970s liked what they found in South Yemen – granted, it was the poorest state in the Arab world, but its leaders were dedicated Marxists who wanted to solve the country's problems through social transformation, following the Soviet model. While some of their East European allies were highly skeptical of the South Yemeni regime and the Yemen Socialist Party – first under Salim Ali Rubayyi and then, from 1978, under Abd al-Fattah Ismail – the Soviets were less concerned with the political instability of its new-found friend than with the potential to help guide a successful socialist revolution "right under the nose of the imperialists," as one MO adviser put it.[1]

The PDRY's strategic position at the entrance to the Red Sea and not far from the Persian Gulf worried many US military planners, especially in the aftermath of the Angolan crisis. Already right after he had taken over as president in 1977, Jimmy Carter had become concerned that the Soviets were positioning themselves to control the West's access to raw materials – and especially oil – through interventions in Africa and the Middle East. Much helped by his National Security Adviser Zbigniew Brzezinski, Carter began seeing a pattern of Soviet activities that conformed to this picture. While the president remained convinced that an improved Soviet–American relationship in other areas – such as arms control and trade – could prevent what he termed "regional crises" from spilling over on to the superpower relationship, Carter remained sensitive to any Soviet action that would be seen to threaten the Gulf region, directly or indirectly. When the Soviets in 1978 intervened to support Ethiopia, its new ally on the Horn of Africa, in the war against Somalia, the US president had therefore already been primed to see Moscow's decision as a dramatic stepping up of international tension.

The Ethiopian revolution was the most important Marxist-inspired transformation in Africa during the Cold War. Because it took place in the only major African country that had defeated the European colonialists, many people on the continent saw the new regime in Addis Ababa as embodying the leftward trend in African nationalism. While the 1960s had belonged to African socialists such as Tanzanian president Julius Nyerere, the 1970s, many argued, belonged to Marxist-Leninists such as Ethiopia's leader Mengistu Haile Mariam. Only through the science of society and the state, tested out in the Soviet Union, could a socialism with foundations strong enough to withstand internal decay and future imperialist offensives be constructed. And, as the Angolan war had shown, if imperialism attempted to strangle a homegrown revolution in its cradle, then only an alliance with Moscow would be strong enough to withstand the attack.[2]

For the Soviet Union, the alliance with Ethiopia became by far its most important intervention in Africa. The air bridge that supplied Mengistu's forces during the war against Somalia showed that Moscow could project its military power in a direct rivalry with the United States thousands of miles from its own shores, and come out victorious. The alliance also meant that in a strategic sense the Soviet Union had become a direct influence both in the Indian Ocean and in the Red Sea area, through its access to Eritrean ports such as Massawa and Assab. Just as during the

Fig. 9   Mengistu Haile Mariam, who became the leader
of the Ethiopian revolution.

Ogaden War, from March 1977 to May 1978, it is estimated that the
Soviet Union delivered weapons to the value of roughly $1 billion to
Ethiopia.[3]

But the Soviets and their Cuban and East European allies not only
supplied and trained Mengistu's armies. They also set the ideological
direction for the development of the Ethiopian state, joining the new
leadership in a massive attempt at fundamental social and economic

reforms that promised to turn the country toward modernity. Before collapsing in 1991, in the wake of ecological disaster, mass starvation, and ethnic rebellion, the Ethiopian regime was an experiment that on a gigantic scale attempted to prove the validity of the Soviet experience for Africa, in a manner similar to the US civilian effort in Vietnam.[4]

Archival access shows that the Soviet leaders, after initial doubts, decided to ally themselves closely with Addis Ababa in 1976 for three main reasons. First, they were influenced by the local Soviet representatives in Ethiopia, who took an increasingly favorable view of the new regime. Second, the Soviet–Cuban victory in Angola in the spring of 1976 encouraged Moscow to intervene further in Africa. Third, the language and symbols of the Ethiopian revolution matched the ideology of the Kremlin leadership, creating the belief that Moscow's Ethiopian alliance would be a viable long-term investment. For the aging Soviet Politburo, the Ethiopian revolution was further proof that the Third World was turning toward socialism and that their experience would be crucial in securing and fostering that world historical turn.

The Ethiopian revolution and its opponents

Ethiopia in 1974 was an old Christian state with a regime that under two remarkable rulers (Menelik II, who set himself up as emperor in 1889, and Haile Selassie, in power since 1930) had not only avoided European colonization, but had expanded its power and territories in the Horn of Africa. Traditionally led by Christian Amharas – about 25 percent of the population living in the northern and central highlands – by the 1970s the other main groups in the motley Ethiopian empire were the mostly Muslim Oromos and Somalis in the south, 40 percent and 8 percent respectively; the northern Tigrinya, 12 percent; and the Eritreans – inhabitants of the former Italian coastal colony – around 8 percent. In the early twentieth century the imperial elite became dominated by a group that proposed defensive assimilation to Western technology and organizational methods. In Ethiopia this group was called the *Japanizers* – the example Japan had set from the 1860s onwards in staving off European expansion, improving skills and education, and while keeping its imperial form of government had made a profound impression among the elite in Addis Ababa. Haile Selassie brought in European and American experts to train the army and to begin developing the country's industries. Still, Ethiopia remained predominantly agricultural – by the time of the revolution there were only around 50,000 workers in a population of more than 35 million.[5]

The end of the World War II Italian occupation and the return of Haile Selassie from exile in Britain increased the prestige of the emperor and made him intensify his attempts at modern development. Hundreds of new schools and academies were set up after 1945, and, although they trained only a miniscule portion of the population, the Ethiopian elite was transformed from the aristocracy of the past to a segment that sought its legitimacy in education and skills. An increasing number of the younger members of that elite went abroad to seek further education. Many educated Ethiopians served with international organizations and, after its creation in 1963, with the Organization of African Unity (OAU), which had permanent headquarters in Addis Ababa. But while the aging emperor in the 1960s sought to be portrayed as the father of African independence, an increasing number of Ethiopians began to regret the lack of opportunities in their own country, the backwardness of its rural areas, and the corruption and inefficiency in Haile Selassie's administration. For many, the famine that hit parts of Ethiopia in 1972–73, and the lack of a coordinated response from the government, symbolized the collapse of the emperor's attempts at modernization.[6]

During the 1960s Haile Selassie had increasingly looked to the United States for assistance in developing his state and society. While never completely giving up his principle of seeking help from many sources – India, Israel, Scandinavia, and the Netherlands all gave both civilian and military assistance – it was the Americans who could make a difference both in terms of security and economic development. With regard to his country's international position, it was the conflict with the Arab world – especially since the independence of neighboring Somalia in 1960 and the simultaneous outbreak of a rebellion in Eritrea; both supported by radical Arab regimes – that topped the emperor's agenda. "Somali irredentism supported by massive Soviet military aid" would be a problem in the future, Haile Selassie predicted to US president Lyndon Johnson in February 1967.[7] Meanwhile, the emperor was pushing for increased US assistance for what the CIA called his "program of painfully gradual economic and social reform."[8]

Ironically, the main ideological influence on young Ethiopian radicals in the early 1970s came neither from the Soviet Bloc nor from China, but from inside the United States and Western Europe. The many students who went abroad during the 1960s often returned home profoundly impressed by the radical student movement in the West, which not only showed that the intelligentsia and students had a role to play in politics, but that they could provide an alternative focus of power to that of the government. For a significant minority of Ethiopian students Marxism came to symbolize the alternative focus, both for future development plans and for theory explaining why the current regime could not fulfill the people's aspirations. The correctness of radical views among the intelligentsia in Ethiopia was confirmed through young Westerners – often sponsored by the US Peace Corps or European variants thereof – who brought their own radical thinking to the country and who were sincerely shocked by the government neglect and mass poverty they found in Ethiopia around 1970.[9]

There were two main reasons why Haile Selassie's rule began to crumble in early 1974. As a result of the global oil crisis, the Ethiopian state was experiencing severe difficulties with its balance of payments, and, as a result, tried to cut down on its expenditure at home. While prices, especially for imported goods, went up, salaries in the public sector declined, and fewer graduates were hired for government jobs. Added to the economic problems, the emperor's age was preventing him from the kind of resolute action he had shown to overcome crises in the past; it became easy to accuse him and his government of a lack of response to people's concerns. As unrest increased, students, teachers, and other groups began taking to the streets to protest against the emperor's policies.[10]

Civilian opposition to the regime could by itself probably have been overcome rather easily by the imperial government. The activism that by the beginning of 1974 was spreading among junior officers in the military was much more difficult to handle. Already in January the privates and NCOs in the southern city of Negele had mutinied as a result of a lack of response to their demands for better clothing and food. When the commander of the Ethiopian ground forces was sent to meet with them, he was taken prisoner and only released after the emperor had sent a personal letter promising to look into their demands. By late February the soldiers of the elite units stationed near the capital sent representatives to see the emperor and demand pay rises for themselves as well as political and economic reform in the country. The emperor had to agree to substantial handouts to the troops in order to stave off their political demands.[11]

With the government on the wane in the military and with soldiers refusing to obey orders in many areas, by April 1974 the situation in the cities was getting out of hand for the Ethiopian state. Strikes spread to the ministries and key public services, such as transport and telecommunications, and the government was afraid to call on the army to intervene, since key units might disobey orders, even if they came from the emperor himself. With power hanging in the balance, the NCOs of the armed forces in and around the capital set up a coordinating committee in June that for the first time, on behalf of the soldiers, publicly linked demands for democracy with support for the civilian antigovernment opposition. Soldiers proclaiming their support for the Coordinating Committee began randomly arresting ranking officers, government ministers, and members of the aristocracy. By the end of June the committee (or *Derg* in

Amharic) was in control of the capital and had assembled a national meeting of soldiers' delegations. Gradually, up to its formal emergence as a government in September, the Derg took over the functions of the emperor's various ministries and agencies. With all communications in the hands of the rebels, there was little resistance to their orders.[12]

The first national meeting of the Derg in mid-1974 showed that while the soldiers could agree on the need for reform, they disagreed on most matters more specific. The policy they declared, under the slogan "Ethiopia First," was a mixture of loyalty to the empire, punishment of corrupt officials, and general improvement of people's living conditions. But under the influence of Marxist advisers whom they brought into government, the majority of the Derg moved to the Left during the fall of 1974. Those who could not, or would not, follow them on that road were dealt with harshly; the emperor was deposed in September and later strangled in prison, while the first chairman of the Derg, Lieutenant-General Aman Andom, was killed together with sixty others in November.[13] By the end of the year the Derg was arresting both members of the old elite and those within the former opposition who challenged its authority to rule, including a few leaders of the Left mainly associated with the Marxist Ethiopian People's Revolutionary Party (EPRP).

While the way in which the old regime had died showed that it had lost the confidence of most urban Ethiopians, the new military regime at the beginning had very few adherents of its own outside the barracks. With a vague program and obvious inability to understand some of the critical issues facing the country, the junior officers' coup could be said to raise more questions than it solved. What the fall of the imperial government did do, however, was to open Ethiopian urban society to a new climate of debate and fervent, almost frenzied, political activity. Almost all observers agree that most of this activity came from below. "Addis Ababa became a permanent seminar," recalls one of them.

Everything was discussed, everything examined closely, nothing escaped the rolling fire of criticism. But what had been intended only as a safety valve [lifting press censorship] became a catalyst. Drunk with their freshly acquired liberty, all the social forces began to raise the horizon of their demands.[14]

The sense of everything being under debate was true for the political conditions within the Derg as well, although – with the future of the country at stake – the consequences were often severe for those who lost the debates. The man who more than anyone else drove the Derg toward the Left and who gradually emerged as leader of the radical wing of the new regime by late 1974 was Major Mengistu Haile Mariam, who had arrived in Addis that summer as a delegate from the Third Army Division stationed in the south. Born in 1937, Mengistu was an Amharic-speaking servant's son, whose dark skin indicated to the northern elite that he had his family origins in the colonized south. He was a graduate of Holeta Military Academy, whose only criteria for admission had been the skill to read and write the official language and basic arithmetic, and his only visit abroad was an artillery course he had attended in the United States in 1971. It was first and foremost Mengistu's ability to think about the future of the Ethiopian revolution that made it possible for him to turn these disadvantages into strengths. His humble background appealed to those among the officers who wanted profound change, but also to the urban poor and the formerly disenfranchised national minorities. At the same time, his fervent Ethiopian nationalism gave legitimacy to his increasingly radical socialist thinking.[15]

While the majority in the Derg in the first months after the revolution was satisfied with vague declarations of "Ethiopian socialism" – patterned roughly on Nyerere's Tanzania – Mengistu by early 1975 had adopted at least some of the thinking of his Marxist student advisers about "scientific socialism." His greatest political success in the first year of the revolution was pushing through a set of comprehensive socioeconomic reforms, by far the most important of which was a land reform campaign that regularized the land-holding patterns in what had been a complex, localized, and mostly feudal system. The Derg declared all rural land "the property of the Ethiopian people," while dividing it up for cultivation by those who were willing to join in cooperatives or peasants' associations. Alongside land reform went a massive campaign for social equality and literacy in the Ethiopian country-side, and especially in the south. Thousands of students in the cities joined the "brigades" that the government sent to rural areas to improve conditions. Their enthusiasm gave the Derg its first mass following.[16]

But, as they penetrated deeper into the lowland regions in which the Ethiopian state earlier had had little influence, radical activists from the cities began running into trouble. Promoting land reform as a principle was not particularly difficult. Breaking up local patterns of power and social customs placed the students at great risk, mostly provoked by their own behavior. In Maale, in the south, they met with disaster:

In an act of calculated effrontery the semi-divine and normally secluded *geramanja* [a local leader] was unceremoniously paraded in the streets of a provincial town ... Just what happened [later] is not clear, but several accounts agree that the students deliberately desecrated the *geramanja*'s sacred eating utensils and. after dinner, seated a low-caste *manjo* on his special horse. The outraged followers of the *geramanja* waited until the students had assembled in a school building in the neighborhood. The building was surrounded and put to the torch. According to reports ... all the students died in the blaze or were shot as they fled.[17]

Map 8   The Ethiopian revolution and the Ogaden war.

By late 1975 local power holders in areas all over the country had declared war on the regime, and it was only by using the army that the Derg gradually began to regain control over the situation. In the cities, at the same time, the government came under pressure from leftist organizations that criticized it for not going far enough in reform or for not having legitimacy from the working class. After unsuccessful attempts at incorporating all the leftist movements into a Provisional Office for Mass Organizational Affairs (POMOA), the Derg in April 1976 lost patience with its leftist critics. Declaring those who were not willing to join POMOA enemies of the revolution, the head of the Derg, Teferi Bante, and his deputy, Mengistu, started an intense persecution of leftist critics, most of whom were arrested, executed, or driven into exile.[18]

While splitting the Left and maximizing its number of enemies among the moderates and in traditional Ethiopian society, the Derg continued on its radical trajectory. Taking up many of the ideas of the Marxist-Leninists, in 1976 it replaced "Ethiopian socialism" with what the leaders called the National Democratic Revolution Program of Ethiopia. The Derg now declared that its aim was "the complete elimination of feudalism, bureaucratic capitalism and imperialism from the country, to build a new People's Democratic Republic of Ethiopia on solid foundations through the concerted collaboration among anti-feudalist and anti-imperialist forces and to pave the way for [a] transition towards socialism."[19] It was a program based on the Soviet experience, couched in a language that was immediately recognizable in Marxist terms, but which had little resonance with most Ethiopians.

The move to the Left did nothing to help the Derg with the nationalities issue, which fast became a key problem in 1976–77. Foremost among the many separatist movements that challenged the Ethiopian regime was the Eritrean People's Liberation Front (EPLF), a Marxist group that had received substantial support from South Yemen, the GDR, Cuba, and the Soviet Union. With the left wing within the Derg steadfastly refusing to compromise on "one inch of national territory," as they called it, the EPLF gradually took control of most of rural Eritrea, leaving only the main cities in the hands of the Ethiopians. For Mengistu, especially, no negotiations with the Eritreans or other national movements were possible until they had recognized the "leading role of the national government." When the foreign affairs spokesman for the Derg, Sisay Habte, had the courage to suggest otherwise, Mengistu had him purged and shot.[20]

After the execution of Sisay in July 1976, the regime seemed to be dissolving from within. Because of his willingness to sacrifice others for the cause of socialism, Mengistu began losing the confidence of some of his longtime associates within the Derg. At the same time armed attacks against the government by separatists, left-wing dissenters, and by representatives of the old regime intensified. By the end of the year few observers in Addis believed that the Derg could stay in charge much longer. Mengistu's response was to take complete power within the committee. In a firefight at government headquarters in early February 1977 Teferi Bante, the head of state, was killed with five of his key supporters. Thereafter Mengistu unleashed what he unabashedly called the "Red Terror" – an attempt to kill as many as possible of the regime's real or imagined enemies, and thereby to force the population in the areas held by the Derg to obedience.

Although Mengistu would never have believed it, it was the Red Terror that led the United States to its final break with his regime. In the words of Paul Henze, who served in the US embassy in Addis and later on President Carter's National Security Council staff, the United States in the early 1970s had "stood aside as Haile Selassie's authority eroded."[21] That the emperor's fall coincided with the Watergate crisis and the collapse of US-supported regimes in Indochina did not help those in Washington who called for a more activist US approach to the Horn of Africa. During the Ford presidency, Kissinger's policy on Ethiopia had been to attempt to work with the new regime in Addis. Convinced that the Ethiopians for security reasons could not endanger their relations with the United States as long as the Soviet Union was supplying their enemies in Mogadishu and in Eritrea with weapons, the Secretary of State repeatedly intervened to keep the flow of military assistance to the Derg flowing.[22] Brent Scowcroft, Kissinger's chief military aide, had Ethiopia earmarked as one of six countries that should receive increased military assistance after the fall of Cambodia. Such aid, Scowcroft wrote, coming at a time when threats from Somalia and the Eritrean separatists were growing, "will help maintain our influence in Ethiopia in the face of the new government's suspicious attitude toward the US."[23] "Our friends in Africa were frightened by Angola, that the US had withdrawn from Africa, and that they faced Soviet domination," Kissinger told President Ford in May 1976. Only increased support to Washington's "traditional friends" on the continent could reverse that trend, the secretary thought.[24]

To the Carter administration, with its emphasis on human rights as a guiding principle in foreign policy, the Ethiopian regime stood out as a sore spot from the moment the new president entered the White House. Receiving plentiful CIA information about the intensification of the Red Terror, the president immediately ordered a review of US links with Mengistu's regime, including Kagnew, the sensitive US-operated communications base at Asmara, Eritrea. "There is a case to be made for taking advantage of the closing of Kagnew to convey the political message to the Ethiopian military regime that we are disengaging from them," Henze reported to Brzezinski in March 1977.[25] A month later, having received intelligence reports that the Derg was preparing – for its own reasons – to throw the Americans out of Ethiopia, the president decided to withdraw all US personnel – to "move to preempt their moves."[26] By June Brezezinski had suggested to the president that the United States might consider giving aid to Somalia in its confrontation with Mengistu's regime. To Brezezinski, the deteriorating Ethiopian human rights record and the consolidation of Soviet positions in the country went hand in hand.[27]

In mid-June, in a rather farcical meeting with the long-shunned Somalian ambassador to Washington, Carter signaled a strong US shift toward support for the Mogadishu regime. As he was to do later with

regard to the Chinese invasion of Vietnam, Carter on the one hand
"hoped that the problems with Ethiopia could be worked out peacefully,"
while one the other told the ambassador that "we are eager to understand
your needs more clearly" and – while not promising US weapons – let the
Somalians know that the US government had discussed with its
European friends and the Saudis "how important it is to have [Somalia]
associated with us as a democratic country." Listening to Ambassador
Addou's new-found convictions that "Somalia's people are deeply democratic by nature" and "we must either resist Soviet pressure or succumb,"
President Carter at the end of the conversation left the room and reap-
peared with a volume of US intelligence satellite photography of the Horn
as a farewell present to the Somalian ambassador. Carter's message was
clear: the United States would not get directly involved in the ongoing
war, but was willing to support Somalia covertly and by proxy.[28]

In late summer 1977, as Washington became increasingly convinced
that Mengistu's regime was collapsing under pressure from the Somalians
and internal opposition, it adopted a dual strategy of indirect support for
Somalia and covert attempts at overthrowing the Ethiopian government,
and set the country "back on the path to constructive political evolution in
association with the Free World." Henze in August suggested that the
United States make use of Mengistu's renewed attempts at dialogue with
Washington to assist the domestic opposition to carry out a coup.
Predicting that the Somalians could "march right on to Addis and push
Mengistu out of his chair," the NSC's Ethiopia expert opined that any
sensible leader in Addis would want to preempt that situation by getting rid
of Mengistu, turn toward the United States, and thereby rescue what could
be rescued of the Ethiopian state.[29] According to Washington, time had
run out for the revolutionary experiment in Ethiopia, and it wanted to be in
on picking up the pieces, at least if that could help driving the Soviets out.

The emergence of the Soviet–Ethiopian alliance

Back in 1974, the Soviet embassy in Addis Ababa had had little sympathy
for the Ethiopian radicals. Commenting on the disturbances that preceded the ousting of the emperor, the embassy had cautiously commented that it "was not ready to characterize these events as a revolution."
Since the Soviet Union and other socialist countries had limited possibilities of influencing the situation, particularly because of the "absence of
ieverage in the army," Moscow should "take an extremely circumspect
position, preserve loyal ties with the Emperor and, at the same time, not
alienate the new forces."[30] Believing that the old and the new regime both
represented the traditional ruling class, the embassy wanted to strengthen

the political positions of the Soviet Union in Ethiopia whatever outcome the political struggle would have.[31]

The overthrow of Haile Selassie did not do much to change the embassy's perspective. In a comprehensive report in early fall 1974 the Addis embassy worried primarily about a potential growth in Chinese influence in the area, as a result of the unstable political situation and the Soviet alliance with Somalia. The embassy feared that the Horn would be a first-class area of cooperation between the United States, China, and local anti-Soviet and antisocialist forces. The Chinese ambassador in Addis Ababa, the embassy warned, could not conceal his satisfaction with the course of events in Ethiopia.[32]

Unaware of the Soviet reluctance to involve itself in the Ethiopian revolution, the Derg took the initiative to organize a first meeting with embassy officials on 21 and 22 September. The delegate of the coordinating committee was Enio Fereda, who met with the counselor of the Soviet embassy Sergei Sinitsin. This meeting primarily provided the Soviets with useful information. According to Fereda, a considerable part of the Derg, about sixty to seventy of its members, shared ideas of "scientific socialism," but since there was a number of conservative members in the committee the progressives preferred to conceal their convictions, at least temporarily, and "not proclaim openly [that they] consider, as their principal task, the elimination of the divide between rich and poor, [and] the social and economic progress of Ethiopia under the aegis of a republican Constitution."[33] Ultimately, Fereda said, one would have to do battle with the conservatives in the committee. "But under the present circumstances, the Committee does not have its own ideology or a concrete political program."[34]

The meeting between Fereda and the Soviet embassy counselor was the Derg's initial probe. The next meeting, in November 1974, was seen by both sides as much more important.[35] The participants were on the Ethiopian side Fessek Gedda, chief of the Public Relations Division of the PMAC, and, on the Soviet side, First Secretary of the Soviet Embassy Viktor Romashkin. The official pretext for the meeting was the screening, at the Soviet embassy, of a film about Castro's Cuba. But in the talks Fessek went through in detail the political situation in the Derg and the political aims of its left wing. He told Romashkin that Mengistu Haile Mariam was the real leader and organizer of the revolution and that Mengistu himself and a number of his close associates in the council considered a "socialist orientation" the only appropriate position for Ethiopia.[36]

Although Fessek's statements created some ideologically based optimism among local Soviet representatives, they did not change the generally cautious position of the embassy. In its 1974 annual report the embassy labeled the political changes in Ethiopia an "antifeudal revolution" and emphasized the transitional character of the period. Even Mengistu himself appeared in the report as a representative of the "tendency of *petit bourgeois* democracy." "The peculiarity of the internal situation in Ethiopia," the report stated, "is that it is still difficult to predict definitely an inevitable and complete victory for the revolutionary-democratic tendency in the movement of army officers and, thus, the establishment in Ethiopia of a regime similar to those of progressive African countries."[37]

The Kremlin had few positive reports from its representatives in Addis Ababa to build on when the PMAC in January 1975 approached the Soviet Union in search of military assistance. During a conversation that month between Soviet Ambassador Anatolii Ratanov and head of the Provisional Military Administrative Council Teferi Bante, Teferi opened by declaring that "Ethiopia counts on the political, economic, and military assistance of the Soviet Union – the great power whose policy and ideology coincide with the policy and ideology of Ethiopia." The Ethiopian leader then explained that his regime hoped the Soviet Union would support Ethiopia in her relations with the West, in her quest for territorial integrity under pressure from the Eritreans and the Somalis, and in the development of the economy and education. The key problem for the new Ethiopian leaders was military assistance. Teferi Bante explained that the aims of the Ethiopian revolution would cause difficulties with the United States, which had so far been the principal supplier of arms to Ethiopia. The PMAC, Teferi noted, did not trust the Americans, who were now trying to undermine the new regime. It was therefore essential for Ethiopia to obtain Soviet military support.[38]

Teferi's request posed a serious problem for Soviet policy makers. They were no doubt willing to improve relations with Ethiopia – in fact, activism on the Ethiopian issue would square well with the new Soviet African policy, which had been emerging since 1970. But they could not engage in relations with Addis in a way that would seriously damage the tie between Moscow and Mogadishu. Starting out with a military commitment to the Derg was a sure loser with Siad Barre, and might have meant the end to Soviet bases on the Somali coast. The only solution for Moscow would be to maintain some kind of relations with both countries, which for the time being could mean only limited relations with Addis Ababa. When the Soviets met Ethiopian representatives at the Congolese Workers' Party's Second Congress in Brazzaville in early 1975, they had been "extremely cautious and reserved," according to the report of the Italian party delegate.[39]

On 11 February Soviet Ambassador Ratanov met with the leaders of the PMAC and read a statement on behalf of the Soviet government in response to their request. In the statement the Kremlin assured the PMAC of the Soviet people's sympathy toward its building of a new progressive society in Ethiopia and said that there was a need to develop thorough contacts between the two countries. "In principle," the Soviet government was ready to receive a PMAC delegation in Moscow, but it was still too early to set a date for such a visit. As for as military cooperation was concerned, the statement expressed Soviet consent to send a military delegation to Addis Ababa "to study this question."[40]

The meaning of the Soviet statement, with its cautious and subjunctive phrases, was lost on the Ethiopian leaders. Instead of playing softly on Moscow's local representatives, the Derg decided to present them with a comprehensive list of Ethiopian wishes. In his letter of 11 March, Teferi Bante, referring to the consent of the Soviets to send a military delegation to Ethiopia, told Ratanov that the Ethiopian leaders hoped that the delegation would arrive within the coming seven to ten days and include high-ranking representatives of the army, the air forces and the navy. The mission should be "strictly secret." After initial discussions in Addis, Ethiopia would send a delegation to Moscow to work out a final agreement.[41]

Why did the new Ethiopian regime decide to push so hard for an alliance with the Soviet Union? One reason was the wish to lessen the dependence on the United States in terms of military supplies. In the eyes of the radical wing of the Derg the relationship with the United States was closely associated with the policies of the old regime, and, as we have already seen, they suspected Washington of supporting counterrevolutionary groups. Mengistu and the radicals also identified the United States with Western imperialism, which they viewed as a threat to socialist movements across the African continent. This view became particularly pronounced as US criticism of the Ethiopian government mounted in the wake of the first purges within the Derg in late 1974.

Achieving an alliance with the Soviet Union would also provide the Derg with much needed legitimacy among its potential domestic supporters.[42] By signing agreements with Moscow, the Derg leaders hoped to get an external confirmation of the correctness of their statist development strategy, and thereby the means to deflect criticism of the ruling elite. Being seen as having Moscow on its side could help Derg radicals stave off other left-wing movements, which challenged the socialist credentials of the young army officers.

While the Soviet alliance did not materialize, however, the Derg was happy to work out new plans for military support from the United States, as long as the Americans did not try to block its plans for social transformation. Between mid-1974 and the fall of 1976 Washington supplied Addis Ababa with $180 million worth of arms, in spite of the political problems beteeen the two countries. The Ford administration, and Henry Kissinger in particular, argued that the United States had to support Ethiopia because of continuing Soviet support for Somalia and because of the importance of the US communications base at Asmara. To the extent that the Ethiopian relationship to the Soviets "does not lead to systematic opposition to the United States, it still leaves ample opportunity for continued cooperation," the State Department argued as late as mid-1976.[43]

But the other side to the Derg's alliance policies was its leaders' conviction that the Soviet Union would offer the kind of assistance they were seeking. The Soviet embassy understood this attitude – and the kind of leverage it gave Moscow over the new Ethiopian regime. The ambassador also noted the political effects of the abolition of the monarchy in March 1975, comparing it with the fall of the Romanov dynasty in Russia in 1917, and seeing it as indicating a dramatic turn to the Left. He emphasized the "sensitivity" of the new regime with regard to Soviet political interests in the region, for instance in Eritrea. "The development of Soviet–Ethiopian cooperation in the military sphere," the embassy noted, "gives us the opportunity to strengthen the position of the Soviet Union in this strategically important region and to exercise our influence both in Ethiopia and in Somalia and in other countries of the Red Sea basin in the directions profitable for us." A Soviet rejection of the Ethiopian offer, the embassy warned, could mean the destruction of the revolutionary-democratic wing of the PMAC and a danger of American or Chinese penetration of Ethiopia.[44]

Based on the embassy's recommendations, Moscow decided to send a military delegation to Addis, and even scrambled to get it in place by the time Teferi Bante had requested. The secret mission, which arrived on 20 March 1975 and was headed by Lieutenant General Skorikov, was met with far-ranging demands from the Ethiopian side. The Addis regime aimed at no less than a complete reorganization of the armed forces within a five-year plan, primarily with the help of Soviet military advisers and Soviet and East European shipments of arms and equipment. The purpose of the plan, according to the Ethiopians, was to free Addis Ababa of its dependency on the United States.[45]

The Ethiopian delegation that left for Moscow in April brought with them a top-level message from the Derg for the Soviet leadership. In this message the Ethiopian leaders presented their concrete suggestions for military cooperation. Some needs, they said, were urgent, because of their wish to reduce Ethiopia's military dependence on the United States and to change the positive views junior officers had of America. The amount of weapons needed in the initial period was "comparatively modest." A total revolution in the army was necessary, however, in the longer term. While the principal task for the first period was to avoid "a possible lack of weaponry that would be destructive for the fighting efficiency of our armed forces," the more long-term goal was the socialist transformation of the army. "Submitting our request," the Derg emphasized, "we have considered thoroughly the question of lessening the possible risks in the transitional period, which could lead to a dangerous vacuum. We also propose a coexistence of [military] systems that demands a reasonable combination of military doctrines not interconnected with each other." While opting for socialism, the Derg, in other words, foresaw a short-term coexistence of Soviet and American military aid for their regime. Being military men, and with their power held up by bayonets, they knew that they could not afford to neglect the immediate aspirations of their colleagues for increased access to more advanced weaponry.[46]

Even after the Moscow negotiations, which the Ethiopians characterized as a breakthrough in their relations with the Soviets, military aid was not immediately forthcoming. In leaving the Soviet Union, the representatives of the Derg received only a promise that their proposals would be answered in a month's time.[47] The Soviet leadership remained hesitant. Although the prospect of a development toward socialism in both countries on the Horn of Africa was attractive, the uncertainties as to the political situation in Ethiopia outweighed the possible dividends. Besides, Moscow found the PMAC's request for military assistance excessive. In his conversation with Teferi Bante on 15 July 1975, Ambassador Ratanov underlined that Moscow realized the "necessity" of future Soviet–Ethiopian military cooperation. "However," Ratanov argued, "the amount of weapons [you] demand is very large." The ambassador made it known that the Soviet Union normally reached such high levels of military cooperation with other countries only after the development of a fifteen-year relationship – or more. But Teferi again pressed the ambassador, saying that the modernization of Ethiopia depended on having a modern army with which to defend the revolution.[48]

Moscow, however, could not make up its mind on whether to supply weapons to Ethiopia. Month after month went by after the intitial two delegations, and Addis heard nothing more about the Soviet weapons that the Ethiopian regime had expected to arrive soon after the return of its people from Moscow. The summer and fall of 1975 were disappointing for the Ethiopian leaders in terms of foreign relations. They did not understand why the Soviet Union did not respond to their requests, and on several occasions went to see the Soviet ambassador with their complaints and misgivings. On at least one occasion, the chairman of the Derg's Political Committee, Sisay Habte, pointed out to Ratanov that there were "alternative" ways to reorganize the Ethiopian Army.[49]

The Derg's impatience in getting Soviet support was understandable in terms of the situation in Ethiopia. The Eritrean insurgents viewed the fall of General Andom as a sign of weakness in the regime, and started new offensives against government troops. In Ogaden, the predominantly Somali region in the east, there was also new unrest. Relations with Washington seemed to be souring, in part because of US reactions against the socialist proclamations of the new regime and against its human rights record. Under these circumstances the Ethiopian regime risked finding itself "between two chairs," as an Ethiopian official put it – to lose US support and to fail to obtain new ties with the Soviets.[50]

When Addis finally got a response from Moscow, on 15 November 1975, the Derg deemed the proposed plans for cooperation much too limited. The new regime had gambled much of its foreign policy – and a certain portion of its domestic legitimacy – on a Soviet alliance. What Moscow offered was a trifle: assistance with military training and the delivery of communications equipment both for military and civilian use. The Derg's leaders concluded that the Soviet Union was too focused on its alliance with Somalia to deliver military equipment that really mattered to the Ethiopians. In the Soviet–Ethiopian negotiations in Addis Ababa in January 1976 the PMAC seemed ready to go for make or break: if a comprehensive agreement could not be signed, then Addis was not willing to sign any agreement at all. The head of the Soviet delegation, V. E. Kuznetsov, gave the Ethiopians a draft agreement of 3.5 million roubles of communication and engineering equipment along with 16.5 million roubles of other technical equipment. The PMAC formally rejected the agreement. Its representative Addis Tedla noted icily that the Ethiopian side understood that the difficulties of the Soviet Union stemmed from its obligations toward "the other country of this region" (i.e., Somalia) and suggested that the negotiations be broken off for the time being. Relations between Addis and Moscow had been put in the deep freezer.[51]

The Soviet reluctance to deliver arms to Ethiopia made the PMAC continue to honor the agreements it had already signed with the United States. But the Soviet embassy knowingly or unknowingly read the wrong message out of the continued American arms sales: it reported to Moscow that the PMAC had rejected the Soviet proposal of limited military cooperation because of the fear of US sanctions against Ethiopia, which could result even from a low level cooperation with Moscow. The embassy also reported on increased Ethiopian contacts with Israel and China.[52] Ever since the spring of 1975 the embassy had been doing its best to prove to Moscow the reliability of the Ethiopian regime and its leaders, first of all Mengistu Haile Mariam. Soviet Military Attaché Viktor Pokidko had emphasized that there was a faction in the PMAC which was serious about socialist reforms in Ethiopia and that the influence of this faction was rising. Pokidko tried to dissipate the Kremlin leaders' suspicion toward the regime's slogan of "Ethiopia Tikdem" (Ethiopia First). According to Pokidko, the members of the progressive faction of the council "understood that socialism cannot be 'Ethiopian,' 'Tanzanian' or of any other kind. It can only be real scientific socialism."[53]

While warning about the effects of a Soviet refusal to sell advanced arms, Ratanov had continued to push the credits of left-wing leaders of the Ethiopian regime. It noted that Major Mengistu Haile Mariam was the most influential member of the Provisional Military Administrative Council and that he was supported by the majority of the Derg. This majority was striving for progressive reforms in Ethiopia and was seeking close relations with the socialist countries. At the same time it was ready "to fight seriously [against] its political enemies." The embassy emphasized that it was Mengistu who had insisted on the execution of fifty-nine "reactionaries" in November 1974, thus showing himself to be a leader not inclined to compromises or half-measures.[54] The aim of the ambassador was clearly to prove to Moscow that the regime in Ethiopia was becoming more reliable and manageable.

By early 1976 Ambassador Ratanov and his military attaché also underlined to Moscow the strategic use of Ethiopia for Soviet military purposes. Ratanov stressed the opportunity for the Soviet Union to increase its influence in the whole region (Ethiopia, Somalia, and Sudan) and the operational possibilities for the Red Navy in the Red Sea. He also held up the specter of greater influence of the United States and China, if Moscow did not respond positively to the Ethiopian leaders' overtures. Building solely on relations with Somalia would be dangerous, Ratanov felt – if the other powers got into the "vacuum" Moscow could risk loosing its positions in Somalia as well.[55]

In his conversations with the PMAC leaders, Ambassador Ratanov was obliged to defend the Soviet position of dragging out the final decision on military support, not to mention a military alliance. He stressed that the Soviet Union was in favor of military cooperation but that the Ethiopians had asked for too much too quickly.[56] But toward his Moscow superiors Ratanov continued to suggest compromise solutions. After the failure of the Kuznetsov visit to Ethiopia with the proposals of limited cooperation, Ratanov suggested presenting a much broader proposal for Soviet military assistance by arming the Ethiopian Navy, its anti-aircraft defence forces, and the new militia. Moscow accepted this suggestion and put it forward during the visit of an Ethiopian delegation in June 1976. But to the Soviets' surprise the PMAC rejected this offer too.[57]

It seems very likely that the visible stubbornness of the PMAC in the negotiations was due to their confidence in a favorable outcome. The Soviet embassy suspected that both Cuban and East European representatives had hinted to Mengistu that Moscow would eventually come around. In its letter after the July negotiations in Moscow the embassy argued that Ethiopian "hesitations" with respect to the conclusion of a military cooperation agreement with the Soviet Union resulted from fear that the Soviets would not agree to the *complete* rearmament of the Ethiopian Armed Forces, that is, doubt that after the consent to render assistance to the navy and anti-aircraft defense the Soviets would not be ready to rearm the air force and to deliver tanks to Ethiopia.[58] The embassy's clear indication was that the Soviet Union ought to think big in establishing its relations with the new regime. To the Addis embassy, it was the *political* content of the Derg's rule that mattered.

The left wing of the Derg, led by Mengistu Haile Mariam, wanted to use their links with the Soviets both to get political assistance and to convince Moscow of their trustworthiness. They stressed their wish to learn from the Soviet practice in "building socialism" and organizing society. From his very first conversations with the Soviet ambassador, Mengistu had asked for programs for sending young Ethiopians to Moscow for education and political training. The candidates should study the theory of CPSU activities as well as the activities of trade unions and youth and womens' associations. They should also study Marxism.[59] To the Soviet ambassador the April 1976 Program for the National Democratic Revolution, which became the charter of the new political leadership, seemed an oath of loyalty to Soviet ideas. It reflected a basic policy for the gradual development of scientific socialism by a vanguard party of "revolutionary democrats," and contained no references to "Ethiopian" or "African" socialism, unlike the Derg's earlier proclamations.[60]

In its annual report for 1976 the Soviet embassy told Moscow that "the important practical results of the Program has been the introduction, on the orders of the PMAC, of obligatory study of the theory of scientific socialism in the army, police, governmental institutions, factories, and large farms." In addition, discussions and publications in the press on the questions of socialism became a usual practice. "All this," the embassy proudly declared, "has led to a considerable growth of interest in the theory of Marxism – Leninism and in its practical realization in the Soviet Union and other socialist countries, which [again] has created the bases for a strengthening of our ideological influence." The Ethiopian regime, in the Soviet embassy's view, had all the hallmarks of wanting to develop a state of socialist orientation.[61]

The Soviet ambassador also found Mengistu Haile Mariam's ruthless removal of political rivals to be to his liking. In mid-July 1976, on the eve of the visit of the Ethiopian delegation to Moscow, Mengistu's most prominent opponent in the Derg, Sisay Habte, was purged and executed with eighteen of his supporters. By eliminating his enemies Mengistu became a "resolute and uncompromising leader," in ambassador Ratanov's view. Watching the activities of Mengistu's supporters within the Derg with approval, local Soviet representatives noted the similarity with the early revolutionary experience in Russia with rooting out enemies of the people. And although they noted that Mengistu's enemies still had a foothold within the Derg, they now expected the "Ethiopian revolutionary forces" and their agenda of social justice to gain the upper hand. By the end of 1976 the Soviet embassy no longer had any words of approval for the regime's left-wing critics.[62]

Based on the embassy's reports, Moscow during 1976 gradually became convinced that extensive aid for the Ethiopian regime could not be put off any longer. On 14 December the two sides signed the first "basic" agreement on military cooperation between the Soviet Union and Ethiopia. This agreement was a breakthrough not only for the PMAC but also for the Soviet leaders in their views of the region. They must have seen the possible consequences the signing might have for Soviet relations with Somalia and for the regional situation as a whole. But by 1976 the Soviets had already started to doubt the reliability of the regime of Siad Barre in Somalia. Already the previous summer, when commenting on the situation in Eritrea, the Addis embassy had observed that some Arab countries were trying to make the Red Sea an "Arabian lake," something which would be "a loss for other countries" [read the Soviet Union]. The embassy had argued that the influence of oil-rich "reactionary" Arab countries such as Saudi Arabia and Kuwait on the positions of other Arab countries and on Somalia was on the increase.[63]

However, even after the signing of the Soviet–Ethiopian agreement on military assistance the Moscow leaders were not ready to sacrifice their alliance with Mogadishu. Under the 1974 treaty of friendship and cooperation with Somalia the Soviets had sent $30 million worth of arms, equipping the Somali Army with hundreds of tanks and dozens of modern fighter aircraft. On its side, the Soviet Union had built some of its largest naval facilities abroad at Berbera and Mogadishu.[64] In the winter of 1976/77 Moscow focused its energies on finding ways of preserving its relations with its old ally, while beginning to build a stronger and ideologically based connection with Addis Ababa. At the end of January 1977 Leonid Brezhnev sent a personal and urgent request to Siad Barre that he reconsider the Somali position on Ethiopia and refrain from exacerbating the conflict.[65]

The International Department and the Foreign Ministry held several crisis meetings on the situation in the Horn in early spring 1977. The reports coming in from both Addis and Mogadishu that regular Somali units had joined the Western Somali Liberation Front and other rebel groups fighting in the Ogaden made Moscow fearful that it would not be able – even in the short term – to balance its old and new alliances in the region. "By providing support to Eritrean separatists, Somalia ... is expecting that the separation of Eritrea from Ethiopia will lead to the collapse of the multinational Ethiopian state, which will facilitate the unification of the Ogaden territory with Somalia," the Foreign Ministry noted. "Arab reaction supports and heats up the aspirations of the Somalis, with the goal of putting pressure on the progressive Ethiopian leadership." The Soviets had initially been skeptical of a December 1976 joint Cuban–South Yemeni mediation initiative, because of the outspoken Ethiopian resistance to it during the signing of the Soviet–Ethiopian agreement. But by February 1977 the situation in the Ogaden had deteriorated to such an extent that Moscow saw no other way out than to join Fidel Castro's initiative.[66]

The real turning point in Moscow's approach to the region was Mengistu's coup on 3 February 1977, during which he assassinated most of his remaining rivals within the Derg. Although not informed in advance, the Soviets viewed the coup as a giant step forward in its relations with Ethiopia. On the morning of 4 February a representative of Mengistu contacted the Soviet ambassador and requested an urgent meeting. They met that evening. Mengistu set forward his version of the events in the Derg headquarters the previous day and assured Ratanov that his actions would strengthen the Ethiopian revolution. He asked for the support of the Soviet Union and socialist countries. Ratanov promised such support, without mentioning the killings and the reign of terror in the capital. Just a few days later the Soviet government issued an appeal to Arab countries and Somalia with the blessing of the Ethiopian leadership.[67] Mengistu's putsch had reinforced Soviet confidence in the regime.

Right after taking power, Mengistu also appealed to other socialist powers for urgent assistance. In a letter to the GDR's Erich Honecker,

Mengistu tried to portray events in Ethiopia as a counteroffensive by imperialism:

During the past ten years, the oppressed peoples of Latin America, Indochina and Africa have succeeded in overcoming imperialism ... Now, [imperialism is] making a final but desperate assault in order to reverse the revolution of the oppressed people of Ethiopia and liquidate progressive revolutionaries ... We hope that you will respond urgently to our call for assistance in arming the Ethiopian masses, so that this young revolution on the African soil can forge ahead.[68]

While keeping up its attempts at mediation, the Soviet government in early spring 1977 began to pour arms and military equipment into Ethiopia. In March Ambassador Ratanov told his Ethiopian counterpart that Moscow had agreed to send Soviet tanks from South Yemen. In April Mengistu received a number of advanced Soviet helicopters.[69] Right before his visit to Moscow in May 1977 Mengistu told Ratanov that he would request a wider military agreement, which would oblige the Soviets to deliver T-55 tanks and MIG-21 jet fighters to Ethiopia. In addition, the Ethiopian leader asked for Soviet and Cuban advisers, and for the transport of Cuban regiments from Angola to his country.[70] According to Western estimates, by mid-April more than one hundred tanks and armored personal carriers were delivered from the Soviet Union. During his May visit to Moscow Mengistu obtained from the Soviets a commitment for between $350 million and $450 million of arms.[71] In the spring of 1977 Moscow had overcome its former hesitance with regard to the Ethiopian regime, in spite of continued advice from its other friends in the region – such as Iraq's Saddam Hussein – that the Ethiopians were not to be trusted.[72]

The Mengistu regime, now confident of its own power, acted immediately to bring Ethiopian foreign relations in line with Soviet wishes. On 23 April the PMAC announced that five American organizations in Ethiopia: the Asmara base, the American consulate in Asmara, USIS offices throughout the country, the US Military Assistance Advisory Group office and the US Navy's medical research center should be closed forthwith. In its report to Moscow the Soviet embassy noted with satisfaction that "these steps of the PMAC are its most important political action directed against US interests in Ethiopia ... [which shows] the deepening of the revolutionary processes in Ethiopia after the events of 3 February and the intensification of the struggle against internal reaction supported by imperialism as well as the beginning of a broad cooperation of Ethiopia with the Soviet Union, Cuba, GDR and other socialist countries, particularly in the area of military affairs."[73]

The Ogaden war

The Ogaden is a rocky desert in southeastern Ethiopia. Its waterholes are essential for nomads in the area, most of whom are of Somali origin, although there are also others, mostly groups of Oromo. During the imperialist carve-up of the Somali territories in the late nineteenth century the Ethiopian empire secured Ogaden for itself. After the former British and Italian possessions at the Horn became independent and joined as the new state of Somalia in 1960 there had been several Somali–Ethiopian border wars over control of the Ogaden. In 1975, in the aftermath of the Ethiopian revolution, Siad Barre's regime in Somalia had set up the Western Somali Liberation Front (WSLF) in an attempt to wrest control of the disputed territory from the new government in Addis Ababa. Having established itself inside the Ogaden, the WSLF found broad support in the area, both because of Somali ethnic solidarity and as a reaction against the upheavals the revolution had brought. The stepping up of Somali support for the WSLF during 1976, and the participation of regular Somalian forces in the fighting, led Ethiopia to claim in early 1977 that it was under attack by its eastern neighbor.[74]

The Somalian regime of the Italian-trained soldier Mohammad Siad Barre, who had taken power through a coup in 1969, turned toward Egypt and eventually to the Soviet Union for military and economic assistance. But in spite of training and equipping Siad's armies, the Soviets were kept at arm's length with regard to Somalia's internal development. While impressed with Soviet and East European technological prowess and skilled in Marxist-Leninist rhetoric, Siad realized that the complicated network of clan patronage on which he depended for political survival simply could not stand large-scale social reform, at least not until his state was more firmly entrenched in Somali society. After Egypt's defection from its Soviet alliance in 1972–73, Somali–Soviet relations became more distant. A Muslim country and a member of the Arab League, Somalia began to repair its relations with Saudi Arabia and other conservative Arab states, while continuing its import of weapons from the Soviet Union. Most important for the Soviets, it kept the naval and missile base the Soviets had built at the Somalian port of Berbera.

To Moscow, the conflict over the Ogaden complicated its approach to an area in which there were already many difficult challenges. Increasingly, during 1977, key policy makers, such as head of the International Department Boris Ponomarev, saw Ethiopia as an ideological ally, while Somalia would remain an ally of convenience. This analysis went above Ponomarev's personal dislike and distrust of Siad Barre; it was fed on almost a daily basis by the positive reports coming in from Addis Ababa. From March 1977, all of the key reports of the Soviet embassy in Ethiopia were routinely circulated to the Politburo, confirming the new-found importance that the region had achieved in Moscow.

The changed attitude of the Soviet representatives in Addis Ababa toward the Ethiopian regime is clear from Ambassador Ratanov's political reports to Moscow. In an August 1977 memorandum the ambassador presented his overall views of the situation within the Military Council, emphasizing that the key question was who supported and who opposed Mengistu. "There are hidden enemies of Mengistu in the Military Council," Ratanov wrote, "and the extent of their influence is difficult to ascertain since they do not come out openly." Among "right-wing" officials Ratanov also included Minister of Defense Ayalew Mandefro, who was shipped off later that year to become ambassador to Washington. Deputy Chairman of the Derg Atnafu Abate was suspected by the Soviets of being influenced more by social-democracy and "even Amharic nationalism than by Marxism – Leninism in his political and ideological positions." Atnafu was purged and executed, along with forty-six other officers, in November 1977. The "defiant" behavior of the anti-Mengistu forces led Ratanov to believe that they received support from the imperialist West. Mengistu's tactics in dealing with real or perceived enemies received Ratanov's full approval, however. "The Ethiopian leader knows [who] the representatives of the right wing [are], but abstains from an open attack," providing them an opportunity to "show their political face" and then "strike a blow." In spite of his admiration for Mengistu, the Soviet ambassador admitted, however, that such tactics might be dangerous since "the enemies" could organize their supporters.[75]

While Moscow politically was drawing closer to Ethiopia, attempts at mediation still continued through spring and early summer 1977.[76] On his own initiative, Fidel Castro had become mediator-in-chief, alongside South Yemeni leader Ali Rubeya, on behalf of the socialist states. A face-to-face meeting in March, when Castro brought both Mengistu and Siad Barre to the negotiating table in Aden, failed to reach any results, but the Cuban reporting of the meeting contributed further to Soviet determination to aid Ethiopia. "Siad Barre was very arrogant and severe; maybe he wanted to intimidate us," Castro reported to Erich Honecker. "I have made up my mind about Siad Barre, he is above all a chauvinist. Chauvinism is the most important factor in him. Socialism is just an outer shell that is supposed to make him more attractive." Mengistu, on the other hand,

strikes me as a quiet, serious, and sincere leader who is aware of the power of the masses. He is an intellectual personality who showed his wisdom on

3 February . . . A very consequential decision was taken on 3 February in Ethiopia. The political landscape of the country changed, which has enabled them to take steps that were impossible before then. Before it was only possible to support the leftist forces indirectly, now we can do so without any constraints . . . I declared that we could not possibly agree with Siad Barre's position. I said that Siad Barre's position represented a danger to the revolution in Somalia, endangered the revolution in Ethiopia, and that as a result there was a danger of isolating the PDRY [South Yemen]. In particular I emphasized that Siad Barre's policies were aiding the right wing in Somalia itself in its efforts against socialism, and delivering Somalia into the arms of Saudi Arabia and imperialism.

The Cubans had decided to send advisers to Ethiopia, Castro declared.

In Africa . . . we can inflict a severe defeat on the entire reactionary imperialist policy. One can free Africa from the influence of the United States and the Chinese. The developments in Zaire are also very important. Libya and Algeria have large national resources, Ethiopia has great revolutionary potential. So there is a great counterweight to Egypt's betrayal. It might even be possible that Sadat could be turned around and that the imperialist influence in the Middle East can be turned back.

"This must all be discussed with the Soviet Union. We follow its policies and its example," Castro told Honecker in early April.[77]

As late as 4 August 1977, when the situation in the Horn was discussed at a meeting of the ruling Politburo, some Soviet leaders thought that their country ought to refrain from direct involvement in the region. Kirilenko, who chaired the meeting in Brezhnev's absence, stressed that "the situation which we have here with these two countries is extremely complicated. We have no reasons to quarrel with either the Somali side or the Ethiopian side, but we have only limited capabilities to influence their mutual relations."[78] Kirilenko and other skeptics, as well as Brezhnev and KGB chief Andropov, all hoped they would not have to make a choice after Somalian vice president Samantar visited Moscow in early June, and promised no aggression toward Ethiopia.[79] Following a personal appeal from Brezhnev in late July, Mengistu also promised he would "continue the dialogue with Somalia."[80] There was also doubt in Moscow as to whether Ethiopia could meaningfully use an increased amount of Soviet military equipment. Cuban chief military adviser Arnaldo Ochoa reported from Addis that he had told the Ethiopians in no uncertain terms that they had "not yet prepared their cadres for work with the technology they were receiving from the Soviet Union according to the agreements signed earlier. Arnaldo Ochoa told Mengistu that such a light-headed approach to serious business might undermine the prestige of the Military Council." The Cuban reported that he "had the feeling that Mengistu understood what he meant."[81]

For the Ethiopian leader, however, the situation was getting increasingly desperate. In late summer the last remaining left-wing civilian movement, the All-Ethiopia Socialist Movement (whose Amharic acronym was MEISON), broke with his government. Mengistu's response was to have some of their leaders assassinated, while unleashing a wave of terror against their supporters and against all real and imagined enemies within Ethiopian society. On 1 September the key eastern city of Jijiga fell to Somali forces, in spite of the Derg's call for general mobilization against the enemy a few days before. By early October all departments in Moscow had concluded that the Ethiopian regime would not survive unless there was a massive influx of aid from the socialist countries. Key policy makers were also enraged that Siad had not kept his word to Leonid Brezhnev, and instead kept up his offensive, in part with Soviet weapons he had received at the beginning of the year. "We had not expected," Mengistu lamented publicly in Addis, "that one of the main towns in Ethiopia ... and the revolutionary workers in it would be bombed by tanks and artillery produced by socialist workers."[82] With regular Somalian forces less than 200 km from Addis Ababa, other "progressive" African states, such as Angola, Mozambique, and even Nyerere's Tanzania, pressed for more aid to the Ethiopians.[83] Advised by Mengistu and the Cubans that an immediate and spectacular show of Soviet support was needed in order to save the regime, Ambassador Ratanov on 19 October stated publicly in Addis that the Soviet Union had stopped arms supplies to Somalia and instead were providing Ethiopia with "defensive weapons to protect her revolution."[84] For the Somalian leader Siad Barre, already in touch with the Americans, this was the final straw. In early November Barre announced that his government had decided to break relations with Cuba, expel all Soviet and Cuban military personnel and close down the Soviet naval and air stations at Berbera and Mogadishu.

Although a defeat for Soviet diplomacy, the break with Mogadishu meant that Moscow could engage in a large-scale operation to save the Ethiopian revolution.[85] Via an air bridge starting in September 1977 and lasting for the following eight months, the Soviets sent more than $1 billion worth of military equipment to Ethiopia. In late September two South Yemeni armored batallions arrived to take part in the fighting. Fidel Castro sent 11,600 Cuban soldiers and more than 6,000 advisers and technical experts, who were crucial in defeating the Somalian advance. Most spectacularly of all, almost one thousand Soviet military personnel went to Ethiopia in 1977–78 to help organize the counteroffensive. By early 1978, when the tide of the war turned in favor of Mengistu's regime, General of the Army Vasilii I. Petrov, deputy commander of USSR ground forces, was in charge of Ethiopian military planning.[86] Altogether, it was the most important Soviet-led military operation outside the area of the Warsaw Pact since the Korean War.

Both in Moscow and in Havana, planning of the Horn of Africa operation was necessarily a rushed affair. From the beginning the chief military leaders of both countries insisted that this time they would be in control, unlike in the case of Angola, where many soldiers felt that the "intrusions" of Soviet diplomats – not to mention Angolan politicians – had come in the way of the effectiveness of the operation in the early phase. During his visit to Moscow at the end of October, Mengistu had to promise that the military strategy of the counteroffensive would be controled fully by the Soviets and the Cubans. In no case would Soviet and Cuban soldiers be under the command of local officers, even when – as in the case of some Soviet tank crews and fighter pilots – they operated materiel that was technically Ethiopian. A quick victory was essential, the Soviet Defense Ministry thought, as was the need to minimize losses among foreign troops.

The Soviets and their Cuban allies saw their duty in Ethiopia as being not only rescuing a revolution from foreign intervention, but also helping the country along politically and socially. While in Moscow, the Ethiopian leader received "as comradely advice … ideas in favor of the accelerated creation in Ethiopia of a party based on the principles of Marxism – Leninism, which would further the mobilization of the masses to defend revolutionary conquests and to promote the revolution." The Soviets would send experts to Addis Ababa to help with the process. Mengistu also got stern warnings from Brezhnev to "adopt practical measures to resolve the nationalities question in Ethiopia" – Moscow would not intervene again to help the government defeat dissidents. The message Mengistu received was very clear: the Soviets and their allies would help defeat the Somalians, but after that the Ethiopian leaders had to set their own house in order.[87]

One of the biggest problems the Soviet adviser corps were up against after their arrival in 1977 was Ethiopian overconfidence. "One has to convince the Ethiopian side that it is an illusion to be able to create a monolithic party from the start … It has to develop on the basis of social conditions," Ratanov complained to a visiting East German diplomat in December.

The PMAC presently has about 80 members. 30 of them are a burden. These members hardly have any education and can easily become victims of the counter-revolution. Mengistu intends to send them to the USSR, Cuba, and the GDR to turn them into revolutionaries. Only 25 to 20 men belong to the active inner circle. It is therefore necessary upon the establishment of the party to add to the leadership other capable forces from outside. There will be a fight about the leadership positions within the central committee of the party. If the forces around Mengistu do not succeed in this fight, then the CC will not be an improvement in quality over the present PMAC. The Ethiopian leadership has lately devoted much attention to the establishment of the party. There still exists great confusion with respect to ideological questions as well as strategy and tactics. For example, they have only diffuse ideas about the class basis.[88]

A key task of the Soviet advisers was to reduce the violent factionalism within the Derg and among Ethiopian left-wing groups, as well as the regime's brutal treatment of opponents. The head of the Soviet International Department "Comrade Ponomarev expressed his concern over the extremes in the Ethiopian Revolution. In talks with Mengistu, [Cuban] comrade Raúl Valdés Vivó has already stated that such events as the mass executions of prisoners led by the 'Red Terror,' which would not be advantageous to the Revolution, are incomprehensible," Ponomarev told his East German counterparts in February 1978, as the Somalian forces were being driven out of the Ogaden.[89] But as military victory drew near, Mengistu began to stall on internal reform: "Mengistu apparently has no concept of cooperation with the advisers" on party building, Ratanov exclaimed.[90]

On 5 March 1978 Jijiga was recaptured for Ethiopia by Cuban and Ethiopian soldiers led by Soviet and Cuban officers. After that the conventional war against Somalia was practically over, although guerrilla resistance in the Ogaden persisted for several years (as late as 1980 most of the desert territory was controlled by the WSLF and other Somali groups). Without massive outside assistance, the Somalian Army had no chance against its combined enemies. Politically as well as diplomatically, Siad Barre had also overstated his case. In spite of the ravages of the Ethiopian revolution, the Somalians had not been received as liberators outside the core Somali ethnic regions of the Ogaden – the expected general rising of other nationalities inside the Ethiopian empire did not occur. In diplomatic terms, Somalia became isolated from all countries in non-Muslim Africa, while even North African countries such as Algeria and Libya thought Siad's actions to be madness.[91]

For the Soviets and the Cubans, the initial effect of their intervention within the African continent was positive. Seen by many African leaders as a follow-up to the successful operation in Angola, the events in the Horn established Moscow as a major power in African affairs and a useful balancer of US and West European influence. What mattered for most African leaders was that the Soviets had intervened *in favor of* existing borders and for a black secular progressive regime against what they suspected to be an Arab and Muslim attempt to expand its positions in Africa.

In Moscow, the CPSU leadership was impressed at the ease with which the Ethiopian operation had been carried out. To many Soviet leaders of the World War II generation, it was the successful intervention in the Horn of Africa that established the Soviet Union as a real global power – a power that could intervene at will throughout the world with decisive consequences. While Angola had set the pattern of how such interventions could be carried out, it had done so haphazardly, without any real coordination and planning. The General Staff thought that the Soviet–Cuban alliance had got lucky in Angola, especially in the fighting against the South Africans. Ethiopia was different. Not only had the Soviet military planned and commanded the operation, it had made use of Cuban infantry almost as a form of auxiliary troops. The main difference from Angola was that in the Horn the Soviet Union had become the arbiter and, ultimately, the decider of the relationship between sovereign states in a far-away conflict; it had taken for itself the position that first Britain and then the United States had had in international relations. It had, in other words, become a complete superpower – a global alternative to the United States.

For the Soviet embassy in Addis Ababa and for most of the advisers who came to the country in 1976 and 1977, Ethiopia also had all of the excitement of a revolution in the making, a revolution that could influence the political fate of all of Africa. For some Soviets, the country already had a fair number of connotations; not only was it the only African state that had withstood colonization, it was also an area that had attracted numerous Russian travelers and explorers in the nineteenth century, and it was an empire in which the old elite confessed to a form of Orthodox Christian religion. But the most exciting aspect of all for many of those who directed Soviet foreign policy was that the Ethiopian revolutionaries themselves wanted to pattern their revolution directly on the Soviet experience. For a Moscow leadership who thought of revolution in narrow terms, who were always seeking parallels with their own development, and who deemed progress a consequence of following Soviet models, Ethiopia seemed a very suitable grand challenge for the transformational powers of socialism.[92]

Soviet interventionism and the collapse of *détente*

From the fall of 1977 onwards the number of civilian Soviet advisers in Ethiopia increased dramatically. By early 1979 the combined number of experts – civilian and military – from the socialist countries had reached more than seven thousand; the single largest foreign assistance program the Soviets ever undertook after China in the 1950s. In a process coordinated by chief advisers working in part out of the Soviet embassy, foreign experts were in place in all ministries and departments, attempting to oversee and influence the direction that the building of socialism in Ethiopia would take. In some parts of the government bureaucracy, such as water supplies, energy, and transport, Soviets, East Germans, Bulgarians, and Cubans were carrying out most of the work with the help of interpreters (mostly from English), while suitable Ethiopian personnel were being trained in Eastern Europe or the Soviet Union. In Moscow the International Department was working overtime to supply the kinds of experts the Ethiopians needed – one official remembers sending off half the workers from a chocolate factory in Armenia to satisfy the needs of the Ethiopian revolution for the immediate construction of a confectionery industry.

The chief priority for the Soviet political advisers in Addis Ababa was the construction of a Marxist-Leninist party that could take charge of the Ethiopian revolution. While soldiers could set the country on the road toward socialist transformation, Mengistu was told, there needed to be a party to complete it. Mengistu heartily agreed. "A shortcoming of the Ethiopian revolution is that it has no political organization which, either in secret or openly, has been tested in struggle and which, equipped with working-class ideology, would give it direction," Mengistu declared when announcing the setting up of a Commission for the Organizing of the Workers' Party of Ethiopia in 1979. But the problem with setting up a party, as the Soviet advisers well knew, was that the Derg had already executed, purged, or driven into exile most Ethiopian Marxists. The Soviets and the Cubans wanted Mengistu to make peace with some of the surviving leaders and to allow them to return to help set up the party. Mengistu, understandably, refused. By the end of 1979 Soviet advisers were telling the Derg that the foundations for constructing a Marxist-Leninist vanguard party simply did not yet exist in Ethiopia, and that much effort was needed to raise the consciousness of the workers to the point that such a party could be brought into existence. As a result of the stalemate that ensued, it took another five years – up to 1984, when Soviet influence was on the wane – before the Workers' Party of Ethiopia was founded. Until then, the Organizing Committee was run as a government department.[93]

The other big headache for the Soviet advisers in Addis Ababa was the Derg's ongoing war against the separatist movements in the northern coastal province of Eritrea. This conflict, which had lasted ever since imperial Ethiopia took control of the former Italian colony in the 1950s, was particularly troublesome to the Soviets because the leaderships of both the Eritrean People's Liberation Front (EPLF) and the Eritrean

Liberation Front (ELF) were avowedly Marxist. Furthermore, the EPLF had received Soviet funding and been trained by the Cubans up to 1975. But piling pressure on Mengistu and the EPLF to find a peaceful solution simply did not help. The Soviet position – that Eritrea should remain a part of Ethiopia with extensive autonomy – was unacceptable to both sides. The Eritreans claimed that their former friends were pressing them to give up their fundamental goal of independence.[94] Mengistu, privately, told Moscow that any deal on Eritrea "would throw him to the nationalist wolves."[95] Already during the Ogaden War Karen Brutents tried to enlist Cuban, East German, and Palestinian assistance in working out some form of compromise – Mengistu responded by making a formal request that his allies also send forces to Eritrea.[96] Cuban vice president Carlos Rafael Rodriguez reported in February 1978 that

> Comrade Fidel Castro and all the members of our Politburo are of the opinion that we cannot afford to make any mistakes in our handling of the Eritrean question. A wrong move now could endanger our entire policy and important positions in Africa. We would be confronted by the majority of African states, the Arabs, international organs, probably also the countries of the Non-Alignment Movement, and others. Therefore we continue to oppose a military intervention in Eritrea.[97]

The two sides met several times, unsuccessfully, in East Berlin in the spring of 1978 to find a solution. Honecker attempted to get Soviet support in dictating a compromise to the Eritreans and the Ethiopians, but the Moscow International Department refused.[98] Instead the East Germans learnt in early April that Soviet advisers had begun participating in the offensives against Eritrea and that advanced Soviet weapons had been supplied to the northern front.[99] "All steps and initiatives on the part of the CPSU, the CP Cuba, and the SED must be put forward extremely tactfully and carefully not to cause any protests," Ulianovskii explained to the East Germans in May. "Frankly," he admitted, "the problem lies to a certain degree in the fact that we all attempt to square the circle."[100]

Already by summer 1978, a few months after the decisive victory in the Ogaden, Soviet enthusiasm for Mengistu's regime had begun to deteriorate. The continous infighting among the Ethiopian Left infuriated Moscow's local representatives, who were reduced to writing extensive reports on conflicts such as the one between the "Ethiopian Marxist-Leninist Revolutionary Organization" and a group calling itself "The Revolutionary Flame."[101] In a July 1978 meeting of the Politburo, Maltsev complained that in spite of all the help the Soviets had given them, the Ethiopians could get neither the Eritrean nor the Ogaden situation right. Kirilenko, who chaired the meeting, saw Mengistu as a "sensible person," whose main problem was his lack of experience. "Therefore it is just necessary to educate him, to teach him," Kirilenko concluded. Andropov and Ponomarev, who both had invested much in the Ethiopian connection, reminded the Politburo of "the importance to show Mengistu that we are on his side." While several members worried about being able to stay in control of the situation, including managing the alliance relationships involved, Ponomarev stressed that "Cuba will not undertake to do anything in Ethiopia without prior agreement with the Soviet Union."[102] In Moscow's view, Ethiopian socialism itself was in the process of being reduced to a troublesome charge.[103]

While the Soviet leaders had been agonizing over their options in the Horn of Africa, Moscow's intervention in the region had further antagonized the Carter administration. Coming at the same time as the president realized that there would be no quick breakthrough in the negotiations over nuclear arms limitation, Carter was increasingly sensitive to political pressure from the Right, which claimed that he was making too many concessions to the Soviets in order to rescue *détente*. But while the White House was already leaning toward a tougher policy in late 1977, it was the Soviet intervention in the Horn of Africa that created a crisis in the relationship, to the extent that Carter's national security adviser, the hawkish Zbigniew Brzezinski, concluded in his memoirs that "*détente* lies buried in the sands of the Ogaden."[104] During a tense meeting with Soviet Foreign Minister Andrei Gromyko in May 1978, after the Ethiopian victory, Carter told him that the United States was strongly concerned "over Soviet efforts to increase Soviet influence in Africa by supply of weapons and by encouragement of Cuban involvement." The president asked Gromyko to "report to President Brezhnev that we considered this to be an alarming development, one that is still in progress."[105]

During the Horn of Africa crisis, Brzezinski's views of Soviet policy had clashed sharply with those of Secretary of State Cyrus Vance. While Vance believed that the Soviet intervention in Ethiopia – however deplorable it was – should not be allowed to create trouble for the much more important strategic arms negotiations, Brzezinski held that "they must understand that there are consequences in their behavior. If we do not react, we are destroying our own posture – regionally and internationally – and we are creating the conditions for domestic reaction." Cyrus Vance opposed the proposals for reacting by increased support for Siad Barre, moving a US naval task force to the Horn, issuing a joint Sino-American condemnation, and canceling space and trade talks with the Soviets. "This is where you and I part," Vance told Brzezinski. "The consequences of doing something like this are very dangerous."[106] Although the US reaction in the end was limited, the crisis helped Brzezinski win the president's ear for his claims of what drove Soviet behavior. In a June 1978 speech Carter claimed that "to the Soviet Union, *détente* seems to mean a continuing aggressive struggle for political advantage and increased influence in a variety of ways. The Soviet Union apparently sees military power and military assistance as the best means of expanding their influence abroad." And when finally agreeing to send Brzezinski to Beijing that summer, the president's first request to the Chinese was for them to provide aid to Somalia.[107]

For the US right wing, Carter's measures were too little, too late. Ronald Reagan, certain to launch a campaign for the presidency at the next election, viewed Moscow's activities in the Horn in almost apocalyptic terms:

If the Soviets are successful – and it looks more and more as if they will be – then the entire Horn of Africa will be under their influence, if not their control. From there, they can threaten the sea lanes carrying oil to western Europe and the United States, if and when they choose. More immediately, control of the Horn of Africa would give Moscow the ability to destabilize those governments on the Arabian peninsula which have proven themselves strongly anti-Communist . . . in a few years we may be faced with the prospect of a Soviet empire of protégés and dependencies stretching from Addis Ababa to Capetown.[108]

In 1978 most policy makers in Moscow were unaware of the profound effects their Third World policies were having on American perceptions of the future of the *détente* process. To Leonid Brezhnev and to the majority of his colleagues, the principle of superpower equality that they felt had been established in their negotiations with the Nixon administration not only entitled them to intervene in areas where local revolutions were coming under threat, but also to keep their Third World policies separate from the bilateral relationship to the United States. The Americans, after all, had not asked Moscow before they intervened against Allende's government in Chile or against other leftist movements elsewhere in the world. What had changed in the early and mid-1970s, the majority in the Politburo felt, was that the overall political trends in the South had turned toward the Left, and that the Soviet Union had been able to protect, assist, and guide some of the Third World radical movements through the crucial stages of erecting revolutionary institutions and beginning to form new states. The Americans may protest these developments, the Soviets felt, but in the end Washington would not risk wrecking the overall process of *détente* because of developments in poor countries far away from the key strategic areas of the world.

It would take several years before the Soviet leadership began understanding how determined the US political elite was to resist the Soviet

Union competing globally as an equal. But well before Moscow began realizing the damage its Third World policies had done to its most cherished international aim – *détente* with the United States – opinions started to diverge within the Kremlin on the merits of Soviet involvement in the South in terms of Marxist-Leninist political theory. Spurred by the inability of Soviet advisers to influence the course of the Ethiopian revolution after miltary victory had been won, a few senior experts in 1978 began questioning the character of some of the national-democratic revolutions in the Third World. The burning issue was the degree to which a military regime such as Mengistu's could initiate the transition to socialism without itself being transformed through class-based action from below. In other words, did the Soviet Union and its allies through their support for such regimes risk standing in the way of the next stage in the revolution?

Among a small group of influential academics – mostly centered around the Institute of the Economy of the World Socialist System (IEMSS), headed by Oleg Bogomolov, and the Institute of Oriental Studies (IOS), headed by Evgenii Primakov – these questions were taken even further. Did some "progressive" regimes in the Third World, through their inability to form united fronts with the local bourgeoisie, represent a "Bonapartist" road *away* from the economic and social change that was needed to develop the working class? If that was the case, the Soviet Union might not only be risking its own position in these countries by supporting regimes that were by their very nature fickle and untrustworthy, but it might also be hindering the natural social development that at some stage in the future could begin move these countries toward socialism. While these more radical Marxist perspectives were limited to small groups of intellectuals, there is no doubt that by the end of 1978 the broader disenchantment with Soviet Third World interventionism had spilled over to the key institutions of the government, such as the International Department and the KGB.[109]

Within the institutions, it is striking how many in the mid-1970s had been enthusiastic supporters of further Soviet involvement in the Third World – and especially of the Angolan and Ethiopian interventions – yet by the end of the decade found themselves among the skeptics. Boris Ponomarev's deputy in MO, Karen Brutents, who had started campaigning for a more activist Soviet Third World policy in the early 1970s and who had personally overseen a number of the key connections to movements in Africa and the Middle East, became one of the dissenters. In a series of devastating memoranda that he sent his boss between January and June 1979, Brutents argued that the building of socialism in the Third World had become too much of a *Soviet* project, while the *local* input stayed minimal. The reason, according to the deputy head of the MO, was that several of the newly established regimes were led by petit bourgeois or by militarists, who simply had no class interest in the victory of "real" socialism. It was not just that they were hard to teach. They did not want to be taught, and through its continued involvement with them the Soviet Union was encouraging – at great expense to itself – fantastic projects that bore no relation to the current stage of development of the countries.

In addition to Ethiopia, Brutents used Iraq and South Yemen as cases in point. While Soviet support for the Baath regime had increased in the late 1970s, the Baathist leadership had stepped up its attacks on the local Communist leadership as well as on left-wing Kurdish groups. By 1978 the East Germans, who had very close contacts with the Iraqi Communist Party (ICP), appealed to the Soviets for help in order to prevent the complete destruction of the ICP, and East German leader Erich Honecker wrote personal letters to Iraqi president al-Bakr pleading with him not to execute imprisoned Communists. Soviet and East German attempts at mediation between the two Iraqi groups came to nothing. In January 1979 Saddam Hussein told the leaders of the ICP that the "relationship is over." "The ICP," Saddam said, "had shown itself to be incapable of participating in governing Iraq. The reason is that the ICP carries out its own campaigns within the armed forces." Saddam "deplored certain excesses [by his security forces], but the Baath Party's counterattack had been necessary." Thousands of Iraqi Communists were executed or died in jail.[110]

In South Yemen the political situation was not progressing much better from a Soviet perspective. In the summer of 1978 the two main wings of the ruling Yemeni Socialist Party clashed violently after the party's leader Salim Ali Rubayyi had been implicated in a coup attempt in neighboring North Yemen. After having Rubayyi executed, the PDRY's new boss, Abd al-Fattah Ismail, tried to shore up his faltering legitimacy by drawing even closer to the Soviet Union, proposing a treaty of friendship that gave Moscow the right to station troops in Aden. In spite of warning noises in the International Department and the KGB, the Politburo regarded the alliance with the PDRY as too important to lose, and a twenty-year treaty was signed in October 1979. Likewise, in Iraq the Soviets and their East German allies also took steps to improve relations after the low point of 1978–79. The SED International Department noted in May 1980 that it was high time to "restart" the relationship with Saddam Hussein's regime. Iraq, the SED leaders noted, was the most important ally the GDR had in the Middle East or in Asia, and the Baath Party should "not be lost to the imperialists."[111]

Much of the bitterness and disillusionment among some Soviet policy advisers undoubtedly came out of their personal encounters with the Third World. Up to the mid-1970s very few Soviet party leaders had had much personal experience with longer stays in Third World countries. The exceptions, of course, were Cuba and Vietnam, but the difficulties they encountered there could easily be brushed under the carpet in view of the frontline position these countries held in the battle against imperialism. The unwillingness to take Soviet advice among its new allies – Angola, Mozambique, Somalia, Ethiopia, South Yemen, Afghanistan – was quite another challenge. Soviets who served in these countries invariably reported back on the inefficiency, superstition, and dirt that were everywhere in society, and which only a methodical and theoretically correct transition to socialism could overcome. In light of the urgency with which a "Soviet" solution was needed, the obstinacy and bad will with which local leaders often met the proposals of their foreign advisers appeared disheartening, and made some of the visitors lose taste for the whole project or at least want to curtail it. Rarely stopping to consider *why* their plans met local resistance, or contemplating the fact that local leaders may have understood the political complexies of their own countries better than the Soviets, the chief advisers tended to veer between recommendations of retrenchment or solidification of Soviet control as remedies for their troubles. For more junior experts, analysts, and agents in the field, the best course was simply to avoid difficulties by filing reports showing the fulfillment of the plan, just as they had been used to doing when living in the Soviet Union.

In Moscow a clear majority both in the Politburo and among its key advisers continued to support a Soviet involvement in the Third World at the end of the decade. For most party leaders, their country's newly acquired positions in the South were welcome proof of its superpower position and of its capacity to guide foreign revolutions. While some members of the Politburo – such as Aleksei Kosygin and Andrei Kirilenko – were ruing the costs to the Soviet economy, their position was not new, and did little to threaten the overall involvement. On the contrary, some advisers in the MO and in the Foreign Ministry – for once, acting in conjunction – began fielding plans for how these costs could be overcome through an increased burden-sharing among the developed socialist states. While the critics generally kept their positions, their recommendations did not circulate outside their departments. As long as the composition of the Politburo did not change, nobody among its members wanted to take the initiative for an overall reevaluation of Soviet foreign policy. After all, the same people who only a few years ago had voted for these interventions – on the advice of the departments – were still in power. By the end of the decade both supporters and critics of 1970s interventionism agreed that only a dramatic shift in the fortunes of Soviet foreign policy or a fundamental top-down reconceptualization of that policy's aims could shift the balance within the Politburo.[112]

For the peoples of the Horn of Africa the war and the interventions of the late 1970s would beget apocalyptic consequences. On the losing side, the very existence of the Somalian state came under threat as Siad Barre's regime declined. By defecting from Marxism, Siad had gambled on receiving Arab and Western aid after the war – when very little was forthcoming, he tried to increase the government's income by introducing levies and taxes in the provinces, thereby reigniting much of the clan sentiment that the government had outlawed in 1973. With Ethiopia fomenting resistance against the government, and Siad's legitimacy in free fall – this was the man, after all, whom all Somalians had first been taught to revere as part of the socialist trinity of Comrade Marx, Comrade Lenin, and Comrade Siad – the whole Somalian state structure began to shake. When, in 1988, Siad tried one final desperate twist by allying himself with Mengistu's regime, all the Somali clans had had enough of him. Since Siad had effectively undermined any positive need that any Somali might see in a centralized state, the result of his fall was not regime change but civil war and clan rule. Any attempt – including that of the United States in the 1990s – of putting the Somalian state back together again has so far ended in utter failure.

In Ethiopia the victory and the Soviet support led Mengistu to intensify his attempts at transforming state and society. The nationalization of land and the setting up of collective farming, which initially had increased productivity somewhat, provided fewer and fewer returns after 1979. The Derg's answer – with the help of its international allies – was to impose more intensive farming methods to increase short-term output. Together with the nationalization of forest areas – which led to a free-for-all by peasants in need of firewood – the introduction of intensive farming led to massive soil erosion in the early 1980s. When the regime tried to push production to the limit in order to feed the army and the cities – and, hubristically, to begin exporting agricultural products – a crisis was in the making. With a difficult harvest and peasants in some areas keeping their products away from the market in order to prevent government confiscation, agricultural supplies collapsed. In 1984, in Wollo province alone, 500,000 to 750,000 people died of hunger. It was, in the words of the regime's own chief relief commissioner Dawit Wolde Giorgis, a famine that never needed to have happened. It devastated Ethiopia and, with it, the dreams the regime had for the introduction of socialism in the Horn of Africa.[113]

8   The Islamist defiance: Iran and Afghanistan

While the 1970s marked the high point of Cold War confrontation in the Third World, it was also the decade in which the hegemonic presumptions of US and Soviet ideologies began to be challenged. The Iranian revolution of 1978–79 broke with the pattern that revolutionary insurgencies against the established order came mainly from the Marxist-inspired Left – on the contrary, after the overthrow of the shah, the Left was soon pushed aside by revolutionaries who found their inspiration in the Holy Koran, the Prophet, and, ultimately, in God. By the 1980s many of the social groups in the Islamic world from which left-wing parties had recruited in the past – especially students and intellectuals – had begun to provide cadres for political Islamic, or *Islamist*, parties and movements. At the same time, many of these parties also recruited from among those who had supported a Westernized form of development in the past, but who no longer felt that the meager economic results could weigh up the loss of cultural autonomy that such development implied.[1]

Islamism as a political ideology has its origins in the resistance to colonial domination in the Middle East at the beginning of the twentieth century. Searching for a modern, often pan-Islamic state that would base its ideas and structures on the teachings of the Holy Prophet, the early Islamist leaders envisaged something akin to the European Reformation of the sixteenth century: a return to the original promise of their religion and the incorporation of religious laws into the foundation of the state. Like Communism, political Islam underlined justice as a key concept in its message – without the reestablishment of an empire of righteousness, a new caliphate to replace that which had been destroyed by Western imperialism, Muslims would not find their way back to God.[2] Persecuted first by the colonial powers and then by the secular regimes – Left and Right – that succeeded them, the Islamists in many countries went underground, adopting a form of organization similar to left-wing revolutionary movements. By the mid-1970s, with the secular regimes under pressure from population increase, economic imbalances, and Israel's victory in two Middle East wars, the Islamists hoped that their time had come. Still, it is unlikely that they would have become a potent and powerful political force without two events largely external to their own key focus: the revolution by the Shia sect in Iran, and the Soviet invasion of Afghanistan.

The Iranian revolution and the Cold War

Since the US-supported overthrow of the Mossadeq government in 1954, Iran had become America's closest and most powerful ally in the region. The autocratic regime of the monarch – Shah Mohammed Reza Pahlavi – made sure that the crucial deliveries of Iranian oil to the West continued, while US assistance with weapons and training gave the shah the most advanced military machine in the Middle East. Cooperating with the United States and Britain, the shah's regime became the guarantor of the security of the smaller conservative states in the region and of the sea-lanes that connected the Arabian peninsula to the Western oil markets. By the early 1970s Iran was a key US regional ally, one of those regimes – along with Brazil, South Africa, and Indonesia – that the Nixon administration viewed as instrumental in preventing a turn toward Communism in the Third World.[3]

But the shah's own key aims were not concentrated on foreign affairs. Having, as a very young man, suffered through outside interventions and the carving up of his country into zones of influence for foreign governments and their oil companies, Mohammed Reza was determined to recreate Iran as a modern state, capable of rational government, economic growth, and military preparedness. His inspiration was first and foremost the United States, which after John Kennedy's election responded by embracing Iran as one of the key countries undergoing successful modernization, and launching significant programs of support and advice in the civilian sector as well as extending aid to the military. "During recent months the Shah has launched and pushed with boldness and determination a reform program, drastically and irrevocably altering the political situation and prospects of Iran," reported the State Department's executive secretary William Brubeck in January 1963. "Much of the earlier context and background of Iranian politics has disappeared, and the political process has moved into a new background, with new forces operating within new parameters."[4]

The shah's "White Revolution" was one of the most ambitious attempts at non-Communist modernization in the Third World. The plans, worked out with the help of Western economists and social scientists, stressed large-scale construction of heavy industry and power plants. They also emphasized the effectivization of Iran's export industries, especially textiles; the import of new technologies; and the opening up for foreign investment. In agriculture, in which the majority of Iranians still worked, the "White Revolution" promised better conditions – mainly through government-provided irrigation schemes and the import of better seeds and fertilizers. But the shah also wanted a dramatic change in social conditions among the peasantry, through land reform, education, literacy campaigns, and women's emancipation. The White Revolution aimed at social transformation as much as economic progress.[5] As the shah put it in a 1968 speech at Harvard University, to which he had been invited to receive an honorary doctorate:

Why should we put up with the present evils in our society? As opposed to the society we are visualizing, the present one can be described as a diseased one ... there are facts which, being dependent on science and technology, are in the process of change, and indeed must change with the forward march of technology and science. Evolutionary progress is irrevocably associated with these changes ... [L]ike, for instance, land reform or participation of workers in up to 20 percent of the net profit of the factories where they work, or the creation of compact organizations which we have collectively called "The Armies of Iran's White Revolution." These consist of conscripts who perform their national service in the Literacy Corps, the Health Corps, and the Development Corps ... These young men go to the Iranian villages to educate the illiterate, to improve the health services, or generally to reconstruct the district concerned. They take with them the newest ideas and principles of progress and civilization.[6]

To both the Kennedy and the Johnson administrations, the shah's message was a welcome one, dovetailing their own emphasis on modernization as a prerequisite for development and security. After members of the Islamic clergy protested against the reforms in the summer of 1963, Kennedy wrote a personal letter to the shah: "I share the regret you must feel over the loss of life connected with the recent unfortunate attempts to block your reform programs. I am confident, however, that such manifestations will gradually disappear as your people realize the importance of the measures you are taking to establish social justice and equal opportunity for all Iranians." "I also know," warned Kennedy, "that you would agree that a vigorous and expanding economy would provide the best backstop for the basic reform program you are undertaking."[7] He then went on to lecture the monarch on the advantages of the US economic model. Neither Kennedy nor Johnson heeded the warnings that the shah's modernization program was isolating him from his former conservative supporters and from the clergy. "The Shah now speaks for an even smaller proportion of the ruling elite than was the case here two years ago," wrote William R. Polk of the State Department's Policy Planning Council to his boss Walt Rostow after a visit to Teheran in

December 1963. "I do not believe that we are in a better position today than we were two years ago. To the contrary I believe that we may be in a considerably worse situation."[8]

It was indeed the Shah's perceived weakness during the launch of the White Revolution in 1963 that encouraged Islamic religious leaders to start speaking out against him. While the clergy of the Shia sect, dominant in Iran, had had little or no contact with Islamist thought, the majority still believed that their leading figures – the ayatollahs – should be able to frame official policy. Moreover, the shah's White Revolution seemed a direct challenge to the influence and the beliefs of the clergy. One of the ayatollahs, the 63-year-old Ruhollah Khomeini – hitherto known mostly as an expert on Islamic mysticism – during the 1963 rebellion began publicly warning the shah that he was compromising Islam and Iranian sovereignty:

You wretched, miserable man, forty-five years of your life have passed. Isn't it time for you to think and reflect a little, to ponder where all this is leading you ...? You don't know whether the situation will change one day, nor whether those who surround you will remain your friends. They are friends of the dollar. They have no religion, no loyalty.[9]

Khomeini's reward for lecturing the shah was fourteen years in exile, first in Turkey, then in Iraq and ultimately in France. During his time abroad the ayatollah became a proponent of political Islam, picking up Islamist inspiration as well as organizational ideas promoted by the left-wing opposition to the shah. What Iran needed, Khomeini had concluded by the early 1970s, was an Islamic revolutionary movement aiming at the ovethrow of the monarchy and the establishment of an Islamic republic based on Sharia – Islamic law – and guided by religious experts. "The fundamental difference between Islamic government and constitutional monarchies and republics is this," Khomeini preached: "whereas the representatives of the people or the monarch in such regimes engage in legislation, in Islam the legislative power and competence to establish laws belongs exclusively to God Almighty."[10] In other words, accepting a secular state – any secular state – for Muslim countries amounted to sacrilege, and could under certain circumstances necessitate a holy war – a *jihad* – against infidels in order to liberate the Muslims.

For Khomeini and his followers the shah's link with the United States was proof of the hopelessness of his reforms. In his final salvo against the monarch before being evicted from Iran, the ayatollah had asked:

What use to you are the American soldiers and military advisers? ... I don't know where this White Revolution is that they are making so much fuss about. God knows that I am aware of (and my awareness causes me pain) the remote villages and provinces, of the hunger of our people and the disordered state of our agrarian population ... Let the American President know that in the eyes of the Iranian people, he is the most repulsive member of the human race today because of the injustice he has imposed on our Muslim nation.[11]

But Khomeini's warnings went unheeded by the shah and by the Americans. By the 1970s Iran was the most important regional ally of the United States – more important, it could be argued, than Israel, with whose government the shah had begun to coordinate his resistance to Arab radicalism. The main target for the US–Israeli–Iranian coordination was Ahmad Hassan al-Bakr's and Saddam Hussein's Baathist regime in Iraq, a left-wing secular government allied with the Soviet Union. During his visit to Teheran in late May 1972, on his way back from a summit meeting in Moscow, President Nixon explained to the shah that the United States would strive to tip the balance in the region in its favor "by demonstrating that neither Arab radicalism nor Soviet arms could achieve Arab aims."[12] In Iraq the main vehicle for the US destabilization plans were the Kurdish separatists in the north, headed by Mustafa Barzani's Kurdistan Democratic Party (KDP), which received weapons and training from Iran, the United States, and Israel, including Soviet weapons taken from Egypt by the Israelis in the 1973 war. But the Soviet-supported Iraqi counteroffensive in late 1974 proved too strong for the Kurds, and in 1975 the shah preferred striking a deal with Baghdad, which gave him territorial concessions and an Iraqi curb on Iranian exiles – such as the ayatollah Khomeini – in return for abandoning the KDP. With the Iranian border closed to them, the Iraqi Kurds faced disaster. "Our movement and our people are being destroyed in an unbelievable way with silence from everyone," Barzani wrote to Kissinger.[13] But the Kurdish leader's desperate pleas for help from his CIA minders went unanswered by an Indochina-focused US administration unwilling to cross the shah.[14]

By late 1976 it was clear that the Shah's White Revolution was in trouble. The government had taken the country through a stupendous economic expansion founded on the increase in oil prices of the early 1970s. But while nonoil GDP doubled between 1972 and 1976, and per capita income tripled, public expenditure saw a more than sevenfold increase – the aims of the 1973–78 Development Plan were adjusted upwards to match the new estimates of oil income. The result was that more money and investment were pumped into the economy than Iran could possibly absorb; by 1975 inflation was rampant, corruption and economic inequity on the rise, and speculation in land undermining the effects of land reform. When even the massive oil revenues did not satisfy the shah's needs for government investment, taxes were increased and the 1960s pattern of foreign borrowing restarted on a grander scale than ever before. At the same time the government set minimum wages in order to avoid labor unrest, instituted price controls as a campaign against the "irresponsible rich or the parasites of our nation," and cracked down on middle-class tax evaders.[15]

The result of the new policies was that the shah's state, and the revolution he represented, maximized the number of its enemies – by the late 1970s it was not only the Left, the clergy, and the big landowners who saw the Iranian state as exploitative, brutal, and unjust, so also did large numbers of workers, the new middle class, shopkeepers, and industrialists. In mid-1977 the shah finally took the advice of Washington and his Western-trained economists and began to slow down growth. But when oil prices stabilized soon afterwards, the decline in government spending led to a severe recession, which hurt all layers of Iranian society. Many younger members of the new middle class felt cheated by the state, which had educated them for public sector jobs that were no longer available. As unemployment grew, so did outspoken criticism of the shah's repressive regime, and the monarch's attempts at buying off his opponents by liberal political and judicial reforms did not work. By the end of 1977 Mohammed Reza – seriously ill with cancer – faced the biggest crisis of his reign since Mossadeq's premiership in the early 1950s.[16]

Jimmy Carter's new US administration was also painfully aware of the parallels with earlier crises in Iran. Elected the year after the fall of Saigon, President Carter emphasized the responsibility of the United States for the spread of liberal democracy and American values, but without the overt interventionism that his Democratic predecessors had cherished. As a result, the new administration's Third World policies were almost schizophrenic from the beginning: while introducing codes of behavior for Third World states that wanted weapons or loans from America, the president was convinced that the United States should confront the spread of Communism in the Third World. The best way of doing so, Carter thought, was through the spreading of American ideals. The former governor of Georgia, who had no foreign policy experience – his 1975 visit to Japan was nearly canceled because none of the Carter campaign staff had a passport – lectured the shah in November 1977 on the need to institute further reforms. The shah, who had met every US president since Franklin Roosevelt, understood that American support for a harsh military crackdown on the opposition would not be forthcoming.[17]

Carter's biggest mistake on Iran may have been his decision to pay the shah a return visit in January 1978 – a trip reportedly instigated by Mrs. Carter, who thought it would be nice to spend New Year with their new friends, the Emperor and Empress. It was perhaps the worst possible moment for a presidential visit; just as the shah needed to shore up his nationalist credentials to confront the opposition, the US President landed in Teheran, praising Mohammed Reza's leadership and noting the "respect and the admiration and love" that the Iranians felt for their leader. In mid-January riots broke out in Teheran and other cities, with slogans condemning the shah as a traitor and upholding the exiled ayatollah Khomeini as an example of patriotic rectitude. Although the shah's police temporarily regained control, in September 1978 further demonstrations in Teheran, during which hundreds were killed by the police, made it clear that the state was losing control of the streets. The September rallies also showed that the leftist, moderate Islamic, and Islamist opposition had joined forces against the shah, with Khomeini as their foremost symbol.[18]

Among American Iran experts the Left, not the Islamists, was still held to pose the greatest threat to US positions, and there was little faith in the two directions coming together. As the State Department had concluded during the last major crisis in 1963, "Communist propaganda has been antireligious and tolerant of the Shah's reforms; mullahs are traditionally hostile to Russia and to Communism."[19] Washington therefore saw the Iranian revolution within a broad Cold War framework, in which the Iranian Communist Party – the Tudeh – stood to gain from any threat to the shah's regime: it represented an alternative form of modernity and was capable of governing, unlike the "reactionary" Islamists, who were a purely negative force. While attempting to set up links with both the moderate Islamic opposition and the Islamists – attempts strongly rebuffed by Khomeini – the CIA and the US embassy concluded that the United States really had no other alternative than supporting the shah.

Booted out of Iraq by Saddam Hussein's regime – an insult he never forgot – Khomeini in the autumn of 1978 began issuing instructions for the Iranian opposition from his new exile in Paris. Spread by audio- and videotape, and in leaflets within Iran, the ayatollah's messages called on the people to continue their strikes and rallies, and on the military to rebel against the infidel government. Khomeini also began setting out a broad political agenda, in which terms such as "independence," "democracy," and "freedom" figured prominently, although mostly with the preface "Islamic" as a modifier. Opposition figures of all political inclinations started to flock to Khomeini's side in Paris, helping to create the impression that the ayatollah headed a broad resistance to the shah. But Khomeini's own thoughts about the state he wanted to construct were little influenced by his new associates; on the contrary, their secularism often appalled him, and he admonished them to return to the true path of Islam. Only that way, Khomeini believed, could they become an integral part of the revolution.[20]

The shah's government collapsed in December 1978, as nearly a million marched in Teheran demanding the removal of the monarch and the return of Khomeini. The marches were held during Ashura, the two most important days of the month of Moharram, during which the Shias remember the seventh-century martyrdom of Imam Hussain. The protester's slogans were filled with symbolic significance, centring on the need for sacrifice and purification – exactly the vocabulary Khomeini wanted to see, in contrast to the economic and political demands that had dominated earlier demonstrations. The Moharram marches were a powerful symbol of the growing dominance of the Islamic discourse in the opposition, while showing the impotence of the shah's government. On 16 January Reza Pahlavi left his country, never to return, while the final government he had installed, led by Shahpur Bakhtiyar, a Mossadeqist nationalist, increasingly ceded its powers to an Islamic Revolutionary Council appointed by Khomeini. On 1 February the ayatollah returned to Teheran in triumph, being hailed by many ordinary Iranians as the *Imam*, the descendant of the prophet who had returned to redeem his people.

The Iranian revolution signified a shift in Third World opposition to superpower domination. While the Left had been the main force in confronting the United States since World War II, Khomeini's return to Teheran and the Islamic Republic he proceeded to set up visualized the existence of an alternative focus of opposition, in which temporal justice derived from the word of God and not exclusively from the decisions of men. Islamism provided an ideology centered on the Third World itself, through which *both* Western projects of modernization could be condemned.[21] As put by a student activist in Teheran interviewed at the height of the revolution:

Imperialism exploits us and dominates the whole world. Imperialism wants to make everyone its lackey, and wants to be the master of all. America would like the country and the people of Iran to be its business. The Islamic republic on the other hand favours all free and independent governments which are for justice. It is the kind of government that people wanted and that they have created themselves; this government is the friend of freedom and the enemy of imperialism, Communism and all the rest. Countries like America do not give any freedom to those that need it and favours only the class that has taken possession of them.[22]

However, while condemning *Western* modernity, Iranian Islamists were careful not to write off the technology and organizational methods that modernity implied. Khomeini kept repeating that Muslims had to improve their access to and understanding of modern development, while not letting material things have dominion over their thinking. The advances of science had to be harnessed to the service of Islam. The ayatollah's hatred of the orthodox clergy was as great as his hatred for the superpowers – his son, Ahmad, questioned whether Khomeini's "greatest art [was] to set up the Islamic Republic? No. What made him the Imam and led to the historic and victorious Islamic movement was the fact that he fought the backward, stupid, pretentious, reactionary clergy."[23]

For Khomeini's new regime, the confrontation with the United States and – especially after its invasion of Afghanistan – the Soviet Union was a key confirmation of its revolutionary and religious correctness. In a message to pilgrims about to set out for Mecca in September 1980, Khomeini appealed both to international solidarity and to the believers' willingness to sacrifice for their faith:

Neutral countries, I call upon you to witness that America plans to destroy us, all of us. Come to your senses and help us achieve our common goal. We have turned our backs on the East and the West, on the Soviet Union and America, in order to run our country ourselves. Do we therefore deserve to be attacked by the East and the West? The position we have attained is an historical exception, given the present conditions in the world, but our goal will certainly not be lost if we are to die, martyred and defeated.[24]

In spite of Khomeini's strident anti-American rhetoric, many in the Carter administration continued to believe that some kind of *modus vivendi* could be found with the new Iranian regime. Expecting the main challenge to the agenda the United States had been promoting to come from the Left, the CIA and area experts in the National Security Council kept trying to set up channels for communication with Khomeini's inner circle right up to the occupation of the US embassy by a group calling itself "Students Following the Line of the Imam." It was when Khomeini openly supported the takeover and the subsequent holding of US embassy staff as hostages in response to the arrival of the shah in the United States, that it dawned on Washington that the Islamists were both more implacable and more successful enemies of America than the Tudeh Party and the rest of the Iranian Left. Carter's failed military rescue mission confirmed the impotence of the United States in Iranian affairs after the revolution, and gave Khomeini a golden opportunity to sideline all of his domestic rivals for influence in the name of an external threat to the revolution.

The Soviet view of the Iranian revolution as it unfolded in many ways mirrored that of the Americans. Iran had since 1945 been near the top of the list of countries ripe for revolution in the eyes of the CPSU

International Department. The Soviet Union had cultivated close ties not only with the Tudeh and the Iranian Left, but also with the moderate Islamic opposition to the shah. Moscow first expected the outcome of the 1977–78 crisis to be the replacement of the shah's autocracy with some form of nationalist constitutional government of the Mossadeq type. Then, when at the end of 1978 it became clear that Mohammed Reza had to go and the strikes intensified, the International Department began believing that the Tudeh could have a real opportunity to influence future Iranian politics, well helped by the reports from Nureddin Kianuri, the Communist Party's secretary. The strategy Moscow recommended and which the Tudeh clung to was a close identification with the ayatollah as a revolutionary leader. In a statement the Tudeh leadership denied any intention to "build socialism at once" but stated they were planning to "consolidate the anti-imperialist gains." "It is quite obvious that anti-imperialist forces are active under the leadership of Khomeini," the statement continued. "That is why the most important Left forces [and the] Tudeh of Iran ... are behind Khomeini."[25]

By mid-1979 two very different approaches to the Iranian question had developed in Moscow. The gradualist approach, championed by the head of the International Department Boris Ponomarev and commanding a majority in the Politburo, held that the Iranian revolution was an anti-imperialist movement that in time would turn to the Left for political guidance. In the meantime what mattered was to avoid a US-inspired counterrevolution, as had happened in 1953. The other main approach, promoted by KGB chief Iurii Andropov, held that the mullahs would keep their grip on Iranian politics for the foreseeable future, and that the Tudeh was too weak and too disunited to gain significant influence. The best that the Soviet Union could hope for was some form of compromise with Khomeini, in which the Iranian leader would dampen his rhetorical attacks against the Soviet Union, refrain from intervening against the Communist government in neighboring Afghanistan, and not create "difficulties" for the "anti-imperialist policies" of the main Soviet allies in the region, Iraq and Syria. The arrival in Teheran of KGB veteran Major General Leonid V. Shebarshin as *rezident* was intended to ensure both that the Soviet leadership had enough intelligence to decide between these two approaches, but also, as Shebarshin pointed out in his first reports to Andropov, to understand that the positions held in Moscow were not necessarily contradictory. What divided them was first and foremost the degree of optimism with regard to Soviet short-term opportunities in Iran.

The duality of opinion with regard to the Iranian revolution among his advisers also influenced the views of the General Secretary of the CPSU,

Leonid Brezhnev. In a conversation with East German leader Erich Honecker in early October 1979, Brezhnev stressed "tendencies of a not particularly positive character" in Soviet–Iranian relations, and noted that "our initiatives with regard to the development of good neighborly relations with Iran are currently not gaining any practical results in Teheran." He also regretted the ayatollah's campaigns against the Left and the oppression of national minorities. "We know all that," said Brezhnev.

But we also understand something else: the Iranian Revolution has undercut the military alliance between Iran and the United States. With respect to a number of international problems, particularly with respect to the Middle East, Iran is now taking anti-imperialist positions. Imperialism tries to regain its influence in the region. We are trying to counter these efforts. We are patiently working with the current Iranian leadership and moving them to develop cooperation on an equal and mutually beneficial basis.[26]

Following the November 1979 hostage crisis, Shebarshin's reports to Moscow turned increasingly negative. While the Soviet ambassador to Teheran Vladimir Vinogradov interpreted Khomeini's approach to the Soviet Union as inimical but cautious, fearful of getting into conflict with both superpowers at once, the KGB rezident saw it as increasingly hostile. His reports foresaw three scenarios: that the Americans would successfully intervene against the regime, that the reactionary followers of Khomeini would take over and patch up their differences with the United States, or that the ayatollah would stay in power, but become increasingly anti-Soviet, encouraging Muslim rebellions against Communism all over the region. In order to keep tabs on Iranian politics, the KGB asked their agents as well as other contacts to provide increasing amounts of information, particularly concerning the Revolutionary Council.

Both Vinogradov and Shebarshin were proven right, after a fashion. While sticking to his public condemnation of Communism and the Soviet Union as "the other Great Satan," Khomeini made sure that open conflict with the Soviets was avoided. All the positive goals Moscow had for Iran proved chimeras, in part because of the Soviet Union's own policies. Moscow's failure to prevent its ally Saddam Hussein from attacking Iran in September 1980 made sure that the Soviet wish for a regional anti-imperialist front remained unfulfilled. And the KGB's assiduous information gathering contributed to disaster for the Tudeh Party. In 1983, on the pretext of its members being Soviet spies, the party was crushed by the Islamists. Several thousand Communists were arrested and hundreds executed. Probably as a gesture to the Soviets, the lives of the main party leaders were spared, but, as a sign of the ideological bankruptcy of Iranian Communism, a large number of them converted to Islam while in prison. General Shebarshin was expelled, but soon given a chance to expound his anti-Islamist agenda as head of KGB foreign intelligence in Moscow.[27]

The Iranian revolution was a watershed for both superpowers in their encounters with the Third World. For the United States it meant that Communism was no longer the only comprehensive, modern ideology that confronted American power. While it would take the war in Afghanistan and, eventually, the collapse of the Soviet Union for Washington to begin seeing Islamism as a main challenge, the increased dangers of American interventionism in Muslim countries were plain to see. For the Soviets, Khomeini's victory meant that the Marxist theory of Third World revolutions had encountered significant problems: the Left was supposed to supplant "clerical reaction" as the alternative to imperialist exploitation, not the other way around. Moreover, the pronounced Islamic internationalism of the ayatollah's revolution spread apprehension in Moscow, since it was a direct challenge to the rise of leftist nationalist and anti-imperialist movements throughout the region and the Third World. But, in the early 1980s, Soviet Marxists still preferred to view the emergence of political Islam as being in its "main trends" "objectively" allied to Western imperialism. Eventually, most policy makers in Moscow believed, regimes such as the Iranian would end up in bed with the Americans, because of their shared anti-Communism.

The Soviet Union and the Afghan revolution

The domestic policies of Mohammed Daoud's regime in Afghanistan during the mid-1970s were in many ways a shadow of those of the shah in neighboring Iran. Having come to power in a bloodless coup against his cousin and brother-in-law King Zahir in 1973, Daoud was a modernizer in the mold of the interwar Afghan royal family, who had attempted to develop agriculture, build communications, and establish a centralized state. Operating in one of the world's poorest countries, with steep-sloped mountain ranges separating areas with distinct ethnic or clan-oriented populations, Daoud's task was a difficult one, which bore few fruits except growing resentment against the state's interference in local affairs. By 1977 Daoud was in a political bind, criticized by technocrats in his own government for not moving fast enough, and by local power holders, including the clergy, for attempting to overturn ethnic and religious customs.

Different from the shah, Daoud sought the main inspiration for his modernization campaign in the Soviet Union, not in the United States, though he was flexible (and needy) enough to receive aid from both power blocs. The Soviets had been involved in assistance to Afghanistan since the 1920s, believing that a nationalist regime in Kabul could serve as a buffer for their southern border, preventing imperialism and its local allies – during the Cold War era, Iran and Pakistan – from spreading their influence. But while the Soviets saw their Afghan involvement as an experiment in how friendly assistance over several generations could help a backward society move gradually toward socialism, the promodernization Afghan elite viewed the Soviet Union as an immediate and direct example – they wanted to transform their economy and their state along Soviet lines, but preferably without class struggle or the dictatorship of the proletariat. Soviet aid – and the technology it provided – convinced many urban Afghans that Moscow's model of industrialization was a key to Afghanistan's future, just like Soviet support was a key to Afghan security against rapacious and US-assisted neighbors, Pakistan and Iran.

The opposition that Daoud worried most about was not the rural antimodernization forces – with his background in the royal family, he thought he had enough experience in manipulating and buying off local power holders to deal with them effectively for a very long time. Rather, the challenge was from the urban-based Communist and Islamist movements. The Communists seemed the most dangerous threat: there were a number of Communist sympathizers both in the civilian administration and in the army, and several prominent Leftists had helped to stabilize Daoud's regime during its first years in power. In 1977 the "founder, president, and prime minister of the Republic," as he liked to term himself, began a wave of purges against the Left.

When the repression began, the Afghan Communist Party – the People's Democratic Party of Afghanistan – was a fairly recent creation, having been formed in 1965 by two small left-wing study groups. The oldest of these groups – later to be known as Khalq (the Masses) after the name of their journal – was headed by Nur Mohammad Taraki, born in 1921, a mild-mannered poet from a poor rural family. As a politician, Taraki proved doctrinaire and authoritarian, believing himself to be the natural leader of the Afghan Communists. His closest associate, Hafizullah Amin – described as "clever, energetic, and hard-working" – was born in 1929 as the son of a low-ranking civil servant in a village close to Kabul.[28] Amin had studied in the United States, where he became a Marxist, and viewed himself as the main organizer within his party. Amin's ambition led to early conflict with Babrak Karmal, who organized a competing Marxist study group in the early 1960s. Karmal, who was the same age as Amin, was a gifted orator and popular student leader whose family belonged to the old Pashtun aristocracy. His group, Parcham (the Banner), thought Amin reckless and brutal, and believed the PDPA could only succeed through broad alliances with other parties.[29] Until Daoud's repression brought them closer together, the two factions understandably continued to lead mostly separate lives.

Like Communism, Afghan Islamism was a latecomer within the Muslim world, having emerged as a movement in opposition to Daoud's reforms in 1973, but with intellectual antecedents dating back to the late 1950s, when the first group was formed at Kabul University. Burhanuddin Rabbani, a northern Tajik born in 1941, was the first significant Islamist student leader, heading a group that would later be known as Jamiat-i Islami Afghanistan (Afghanistan Islamic Society). Though directed by radical Islamists, Rabbani's group believed in making alliances with other groups in society in the transition to an Islamic state in Afghanistan. Rabbani's chief rival for influence was the young Gulbuddin Hekmatyar, a radical Islamist born in the Ghilzai Pashtun area in the north in 1949. Before joining the Islamist movement while a student of engineering at Kabul University, Hekmatyar had been attracted by the Communists, from whom he borrowed many of his organizational ideas. While continuing to operate underground cells at schools and at the universities in Kabul and Jalalabad, the main Islamist leaders fled to Pakistan after a failed coup attempt in December 1973. Their calls for general uprisings against Daoud's regime were not heeded by many, but caused widespread repression against their sympathizers inside Afghanistan, with almost six hundred Islamists killed.[30]

To their surprise, the Afghan Islamists found that not only were they welcome in Pakistan, but that Zulfikar Ali Bhutto's highly secular government was willing to provide support for their cause. While Bhutto's motives were purely practical – he wanted to use the presence of the Islamists to counter Daoud's increasingly Pushtun-nationalist rhetoric, which was also finding a hearing among Pushtuns on the Pakistani side of the border – there were also Islamists in the Pakistani military and in its intelligence services who saw assistance to the Afghans as being in the common cause. After General Zia ul-Haq's military coup in July 1977 Pakistani support for the Afghan Islamists intensified, making them a force to be reckoned with, in spite of their limited recruitment inside the country.

While generally happy with the overall direction of Daoud's regime, the Soviets had kept in close touch with the Afghan Communists since the formation of the early study groups, supplying them with money, using their information for intelligence purposes, and encouraging them to widen their influence within the Afghan state. By 1977 the Soviets were worried that Daoud's crackdown on the Left might be a sign of weakening relations with Moscow, especially since the KGB detected signs of a relaxation of tension between Kabul and Pakistan. In response, the Soviets increased the emphasis on the PDPA in its Afghan policies, on several occasions using KGB facilities to help Communists escape from Daoud's agents. But in spite of the repression, the Soviets still made it clear to Babrak Karmal and other representatives of the Parcham – Moscow's favored faction within the PDPA – that they expected the Communists to find some form of accommodation with Daoud over time. Even after Daoud's arrest of several of the PDPA's top leaders on 25 April 1978, the Soviets insisted on accommodation, even though the embassy warned Moscow that their advice may not be heeded: "there is a danger that among the members of the PDPA Central Committee still at liberty there may be some who will take extreme measures. They may be incited to do this by provocateurs from the government's special organs. In our view such extreme action in the present situation could lead to the defeat of the progressive forces in the country."[31]

The successful 27 April 1978 Khalq coup in Kabul was therefore as much a surprise to Aleksandr Puzanov, Soviet ambassador since 1972, as to other diplomats in the Afghan capital.[32] In his first comprehensive report to Moscow after the coup, Puzanov gave a sober assessment of the new regime and its coming to power. The coup had been badly prepared, Puzanov explained, and its main figures – Taraki and Amin – were both given to ultra-left initiatives. Still, the PDPA did represent the interests of the "laboring masses" against former President Daoud's regime, which had become increasingly bourgeois. The new government will be "more sympathetic toward the USSR," Puzanov said, "further consolidating and strengthening our positions in Afghanistan." The revolutionary leadership seemed to have all provinces under its control, and had "taken measures" against Daoud's supporters.[33]

The main trouble with the new regime, according to Puzanov, was bound to be the endless factional infighting within the PDPA itself. The ambassador explained to his superiors in Moscow that the two main factions of the party – the Khalq and the Parcham – were more like two separate parties, and that years of mutual suspicion and animosity divided the leaders of the two groups. The "revolution" had not eliminated these divisions – particularly since all the main leaders of the new regime represented Khalq. Puzanov, however, promised Moscow that he would immediately "take steps to overcome the differences in the Afghan leadership."[34]

These "steps" led Puzanov on a path which he followed for his remaining nineteen months in Kabul. It proved to be a thorny track, leading not to harmony in the PDPA but to the murder of two Afghan presidents and to the Christmas invasion in 1979. The PDPA was too divided, too set against itself, to ever become a functioning political unit. The Parcham claimed that Khalq and its leaders Taraki and Amin were revolutionary dreamers, with little understanding of Afghan politics. The Khalqis, on the other hand, viewed Babrak Karmal and other Parchamis as "royal Communists," and condemned their early alliance with Daoud.

The two groups had been jockeying for Soviet support for years, and their competition continued after the April coup. Amin, who had become vicepremier and foreign minister, clandestinely contacted the Soviets to press the positions of his faction. Making no secret of the Khalq dominance in the new government, Amin stressed that it would be "easier for the Soviet Union to work with the people from Khalq, [since] they are brought up in the spirit of 'Sovietism.' If the leaders of Khalq and Soviet comrades disagree, the Khalqis will say without a moment's hesitation that the Soviet comrades are right." "In such a situation," Amin added wryly, "the Parchamis will say that *their* leaders are right."[35] The foreign minister then passed on the Soviets his own plan for reorganizing the PDPA – a plan which would exclude the other faction from any position of real influence.[36]

Puzanov's first official conversations with Taraki show how the Khalqi leaders expected to build close relations with Moscow. In his first meeting with Puzanov on 29 April, Taraki opened by stating that "Afghanistan [will] follow Marxism – Leninism [and] will embark on the road of building socialism and belong to the socialist camp." The PDPA president felt, however, that this policy had to be pursued "with care," and that the party would for a while have to withhold its real intentions from the people. Taraki offered to cooperate closely both politically and economically with the Soviet Union, but added that he saw no necessary conflict with the West – only with "reactionary Muslim countries."[37] In his meeting with the ambassador on 17 May, Taraki asked for Soviet assistance in building the party and securing its position, particularly in the armed forces. Taraki underlined the need for Soviet experts on "state security," whom Puzanov promised to send promptly.[38]

The Parchamis were also trying to get Moscow's support. In a conversation with the Soviet ambassador on 11 June, Nur Ahmad Nur – minister of the interior and Karmal's closest collaborator in Parcham – warned Puzanov that Amin was usurping Taraki's position and was preparing a purge of Parchamis from government. "In the Politburo everybody fears Amin," Nur said. Without Soviet support, nobody could stand up to Amin, not even Babrak Karmal, who now filled the inconsequential post of Vice Premier without Portfolio. "There is one leading force in the country – Hafizullah Amin," Nur said.[39] A week later Puzanov met with Sultan Ali Keshtmand, another of Karmal's closest allies. Keshtmand told the ambassador that the political crisis inside the PDPA was now acute. "Unfortunately," Keshtmand said, "some people believe that the party organs are themselves and nobody but them." "These people," Keshtmand stated (aiming without doubt at Amin and Taraki), view "the strengthening of ties with the USSR as a temporary policy, or as a tactical device." Both Nur and Keshtmand appealed to Puzanov to save Babrak Karmal.[40]

The Soviet ambassador agreed. The next day he met with President Taraki to discuss Karmal's position. Puzanov told the president of his recent conversation with Karmal, who had praised Taraki and Amin, and had said that it was "his duty toward the revolution not to create problems." Taraki, however, was adamant. He seemed set on reducing the influence of the Parchamis, and told Puzanov that "the party is united and its unity is being strengthened." And he added angrily that "we will run over those who oppose unity with a steam-roller."[41]

The purge, which was initiated by Amin and agreed to by Taraki, was announced on 1 July. Karmal, Nur, and Keshtmand were removed from their cabinet posts, and Karmal was named ambassador to Prague – virtual exile for someone who regarded himself as a leader of the revolution. But Karmal could probably thank Puzanov and the Soviets for not having fared much worse. Late at night the day the purges were announced, Karmal, fearing for his life, sought refuge with his family in the apartment of one of his Soviet friends. Afraid of being put squarely at the center of the conflict, Puzanov refused the Parcham leader's insistent request for a meeting in the early morning. After having considered the situation for some hours, the ambassador even called Amin to inform him of Karmal's whereabouts. The Soviets still used their leverage to save Karmal's neck and to see him safely off to Czechoslovakia.[42]

But Puzanov was to get no peace from PDPA factional infighting. Having reported to Moscow his successful intervention in the June crisis, Puzanov in August had to inform Foreign Minister Andrei Gromyko and head of the CPSU International Department Boris Ponomarev that the Khalqis had launched an all-out purge of Parchamis in government. Upon claiming to have discovered a plot organized by Karmal's followers to unseat the Khalqi regime, Taraki and Amin arrested Keshtmand and several other PDPA leaders. In the weeks that followed the regime ran a witch-hunt throughout the country for Parchamis and suspected Parcham sympathizers.[43]

Moscow had always been substantially closer to Karmal and his group than to the Khalqis. Even so, the Soviet ambassador knew that for the time being the Parchamis had been utterly routed, and that it would not pay for Moscow to intervene on Karmal's side.[44] He therefore did not protest openly in his meetings with Taraki or Amin, limiting himself to questioning just a few of the arrests and executions which took place in the fall of 1978.[45] He did, however, on instructions from Moscow, tell Taraki that "when there is a difficult situation in the country of our close friends we have a time-honored practice of sending one of our leaders, a member of our Politburo, on an unofficial visit." The Afghan president had little choice but to welcome Puzanov's suggestion.[46]

The emissary from Moscow was Boris Ponomarev, head of the CPSU Central Committee International Department for more than two decades and a key Soviet decision maker on foreign affairs. Ponomarev came to Kabul to ask Taraki and Amin to stop the purge. "This confrontation worried us," Ponomarev later recalled. "It was clear that nothing good would come of it ... He [Amin] might have had reasons for punishing the others, but not in such a drastic way. It made the revolution itself seem unattractive."[47] As if this was not enough, Ponomarev had before his departure got a report from the KGB suggesting that Amin had ties with US intelligence services.[48] To Moscow, the Afghan party seemed "a fine mess."[49]

Ponomarev's visit did not result in any changes in Kabul. "He [Taraki] agreed that my displeasure was justified, [and] thanked me for my advice. And everything continued as before."[50] Moscow had to accept the Khalqi regime, and in late fall and winter 1978 Puzanov was instructed to discuss a limited extension of both military and economic aid with Taraki and Amin, in preparation for the signing of the Soviet–Afghan Friendship Treaty in Moscow in December.[51] The Parcham leaders remained in prison or in exile in Eastern Europe.

In Puzanov's discussions with the PDPA strongmen on aid to Afghanistan, the Afghans often pushed for more supplies and technical assistance than the ambassador was prepared to recommend to Moscow. In one case, when Taraki asked for a major training program for officers and border guards, Puzanov bluntly told him that he regarded the request as inflated, and that if the president insisted, Taraki would have to take it up with Moscow himself. The Afghans pushed back, with Amin in mid-November telling the ambassador that the Khalqi regime was "seeking actively to attract other socialist brother countries to wider cooperation, as well as other friendly states which will give us such support." "But," he added, "the Afghan leadership in such matters naturally counts primarily on the Soviet Union."[52]

Taraki's and Amin's visit to Moscow in mid-December 1978 was a watershed in Soviet relations with the Khalqi regime. As the conversations between Puzanov and the Afghan leaders after their return to Kabul show, the increased Soviet emphasis on cooperation had much to do with the development of the Iranian revolution, which in late 1978 and early 1979 was in its decisive phase. The Khalqi leaders returned from Moscow convinced that Brezhnev personally supported their case. They immediately came up with new requests for assistance to be discussed with the Soviet ambassador. Some of the new programs were designed in view of the changes taking place in the region. On 28 December Amin explained to Puzanov why he had asked for 20 million roubles for "special assignments." It was, Amin said, "to cover the expenses of the organs of security and intelligence services abroad" – first and foremost in Iran.[53]

Puzanov had his doubts about the results of the Soviet leadership's new eagerness to enter into long-term agreements with the Khalqi state. On 30 December he complained to Taraki that Soviet–Afghan cooperation was not efficient. For instance, many applications for economic support were sent to the embassy "with great delay" and their figure-work was so confusing that much time was lost. "One could," he reported to Moscow, "feel that Taraki did not understand these issues and [that he] cannot imagine how complex decision making is on the Soviet side."[54]

The Kremlin no longer shared the ambassador's caution. In a meeting of the Politburo on 7 January, Aleksei Kosygin proposed new instructions for Puzanov, ordering him to put increased emphasis on developing plans for military and economic assistance to Afghanistan.[55] Many of the new programs of support were finally agreed to during Vice Premier Ivan Arkhipov's visit to Kabul in late February. The plans agreed to by Arkhipov constituted a major increase in Soviet aid to Afghanistan, and made the country a top receiver of Soviet foreign assistance. Taraki still pressed for more: he now wanted to suspend some of the development plans in order to use the assigned sums for defense. He also asked for more loans directly to the Afghan Ministry of Defense.[56]

For most of the time since the April coup the PDPA leaders had been preoccupied primarily with the party's own internal problems, and done little to strengthen the regime's position in the provinces. The Soviets had repeatedly tried to get the party to do more to win adherents in the countryside – go easy on local customs, invest more in building ties with nonparty local leaders. By late February 1979 it was becoming apparent even to the regime that the armed Islamist groups that challenged them along the Iranian and Pakistani borders could become a serious military threat.[57]

The civil war and the split in Afghan Communism

The threat became obvious to anyone – outside or inside Afghanistan – after the rebellion in and around the western city of Herat, which started in the morning of 15 March 1979. An alliance of townspeople, Islamist guerrillas, and defectors from the local garrison fought for four days against the best troops of the Afghan Army and their Soviet advisers. The fighting left 5,000 people dead, among them some Soviet experts and their families, around fifty in all, who were massacred by enraged Heratis. Most of the dead were Afghan civilians who lost their lives when Soviet aircraft bombed the city on Amin's orders.[58]

The crisis in Herat was a symptom of the increased confidence of the Afghan Islamist opposition in the year since the Communist coup. The Islamist movements had begun to spread their influence in most parts of the country and, in the case of both Rabbani's and Hekmatyar's organizations, to gain adherents from different clans and ethnic groups, thereby placing themselves in a position where they could be seen as coordinating the struggle against the Communists. Ideologically, too, the Islamists were making progress. Their key idea – that the Communist coup had come as a result of the corruption, injustice, and immorality of the Daoud and Zahir eras – began appearing more likely to many rural Afghans as the Communists intensified their efforts at penetrating local communities with programs that seemed like overblown versions of those of the previous regimes. It is not surprising, then, that the need for an Islamic state became a reasonable cause even to Afghans who mostly cherished their local customs in spite of any dissensions between those and Islamic law.

Still, as the Herat example shows, the opposition was most effective in those cases where the Islamists were willing to coordinate their efforts with local power holders. In 1978–79 that often meant that the emissaries from Peshawar were dependent on locally organized groups – often with a clan-based leadership structure – in order to carry out military raids against the government. What had changed with the Communist coup was that the Islamists now were generally welcomed in areas where they, as outsiders with a distinct political message, probably would have been chased away only a few months earlier. Their presence gave the local resistance a sense of being part of a larger anticentralist and anti-Communist movement, and the weapons and gifts that the Islamists brought in strengthened those groups who were willing to resist the PDPA. On the other hand the biggest of the Islamist parties, Rabbani's Jamiat Islami, was willing to accept strong local leaders such as Ismail Khan in the Herat area and Ahmad Shah Massoud in the Panjshir Valley, who were only nominally subordinate to Rabbani's command. It was a small price to pay, the Islamist leaders felt, for the ability to proselytize freely within large areas of Afghanistan.

The Iranian revolution provided important inspiration for the Afghan Islamists. In spite of the doctrinal differences – Afghanistan has only a small and often persecuted Shia minority – most educated Afghans read Persian and could therefore follow Khomeini's ascent to power at first-hand. The slogans and the worldview of the Iranian Islamists, purged of its Shia vocabulary, fitted the purpose of the Afghans well: the creation of an Islamic state, the stress on Islamic internationalism, and the condem-nation of the godlessness and materialism of the superpowers gave a larger purpose to what might have been an incongrous alliance between traditionalist mullahs and clan leaders on the one hand and Islamists on the other. Their immediate target, however, was the Communist regime in Kabul and the reforms it had instigated.

The PDPA's economic and social reforms were, in form, a version of the party's maximum program from its brief period of unity before the 1978 takeover, stressing literacy, secular education for men and women, land reform, and state-led industrialization. But very few of these initia-tives became more than empty slogans and ineffective laws. The Afghan state was weak, lacking income and trained personel. The reforms met with resistance among broad groups of the Afghan people. And the PDPA responded to that resistance, almost from its first day in power, with attempts at creating compliance through coercion. In a country where more than 85 percent of the population lived in rural areas, the Communists naturally concentrated their early efforts on the agricultural sector, including reform of rural mortgages and debt (decree number 6), reform of marriage and the bride price (decree number 7), and land reform (decree number 8). All of these measures were resented by the traditional elites in the countryside, and contributed greatly to the recruit-ment of fighters for the resistance movement.[59]

The Herat rebellion added to the fears Soviet advisers in Kabul had for the future of the Afghan Communist revolution. On 19 March, the day the uprising was put down, Soviet ambassador Puzanov met with President Taraki. The ambassador was accompanied by a group of Soviet officers who had served with the Afghan troops. Together they tried to show the president just how bad the security situation was in the countryside, and urged the PDPA leaders to change their policies. At the end of the meeting Puzanov "tactfully" advised Taraki to take urgent steps, "with the same energy as in the conduct of the armed struggle, to develop education and propaganda in order to attract the population to their side."[60]

The Herat rising was a rude shock both to the PDPA and to Moscow. The CPSU Politburo and Secretariat met in emergency sessions to dis-cuss how to strengthen the PDPA – including the option of a Soviet military intervention – and Puzanov's direct criticism of Taraki and Amin became more acute. The ambassador was particularly worried by the Khalqis' insistence that the rebellion had occurred because of Iranian "interference." He warned Taraki not to provoke an open Afghan–Iranian conflict, and told him that Moscow would attempt to take "new initiatives" with Khomeini. Puzanov thought that the president instead should become more preoccupied with stopping the flow of Soviet arms from government units to the guerrillas, and should improve the Afghan Army's knowledge of how to use the equipment that Moscow supplied.[61]

In spite of the ambassador's blunt criticism, Moscow decided to increase its Afghan investment. Seeking an increased military commitment, including the use of Soviet forces, Taraki flew to Moscow for a secret meeting with the Soviet leadership on 20 March. He met with Kosygin, Gromyko, Ustinov, and Ponomarev late in the afternoon. Kosygin started the meeting by criticizing Taraki for already depending too heavily on Soviet support in his conflicts with domestic and foreign enemies. The Soviet premier reminded Taraki of how Vietnam had defeated both the United States and China by mobilizing its own people. "The Vietnamese themselves steadfastly defended their country against aggressive encroachments," Kosygin said. Soviet troops in Afghanistan was out of the question, primarily because of the negative international reactions to such deployments. Besides, Kosygin argued, even if Iran wanted to force a conflict with Kabul, the Iranian leaders were at the moment unable to do so because of the political chaos in Teheran.

On the other hand, the Soviets told Taraki very bluntly that the Herat rebellion had been bad for his regime's image at home and abroad, and that it could not be repeated. Kosygin and Ustinov presented a detailed plan for Soviet assistance to the Afghan Army, with the aim of preventing further mutinies. Their proposal gave Taraki everything he had come to Moscow to get, except the commitment of Soviet troops and a public security guarantee against Iranian and Pakistani attacks.[62]

In his meeting with Leonid Brezhnev on the evening of 20 March, Taraki received a new set of lectures on how to govern Afghanistan. In his patronizing and spoon-feeding manner, Brezhnev continued to browbeat the Afghan president with the need for a "patriotic front" and a loyal army. The Soviet leader underlined recent examples of how armies could be used to develop socialism in Asian and African countries – at one point he hinted that armies by their nature contained "particular conditions" for the growth of socialist ideas. Brezhnev urged Taraki to strengthen the political work among the masses, patterning his efforts on the experience of the Soviet Union in the period immediately after the October Revolution.[63] The Afghan president returned to Kabul with a whole series of new Soviet commitments in his pocket. The Soviet leaders had promised the Afghans to support them politically and militarily in case of aggression from Iran or Pakistan, to speed up air deliveries of weapons, to postpone indefinitely all payments on loans, and to supply Kabul with 100,000 tons of wheat. Taraki gleefully informed Puzanov that he was very satisfied with the Soviet response.[64]

Alongside their increased involvement in Afghanistan, the Soviets attempted to reduce the tension between that country and its neighbors. In addition to the initiative toward Iran, Moscow also tried to improve relations between Afghanistan and its eastern neighbor, Pakistan. After Aleksei Kosygin met with Pakistani foreign minister Yakub Khan in Moscow, Puzanov stressed to Taraki the need to seek an arrangement with Islamabad. He warned the president against implementing a massive Afghan plan for operations on Pakistani territory, and "tactfully" urged Taraki to follow Moscow's lead.[65]

After the Herat rebellion, the conflict between the Afghan government and the Islamist opposition developed into a full-scale civil war. From the start the war went badly for the government forces; thousands of men defected to the guerrillas, and the army started losing minor battles with the Islamist groups. In the west and in the eastern provinces of Kunar and Paktia the army was slowly forced on the defensive, limiting itself to defending its major strongholds. Even in Kabul itself the situation deteriorated rapidly for the government, as the opposition started operating underground cells in parts of the old city.[66]

The Soviet Politburo reviewed the situation in Afghanistan in its meeting on 12 April. Gromyko, Andropov, Ustinov, and Ponomarev presented a joint report, underlining the seriousness of the situation in Kabul to their Politburo colleagues. "The flare up of religious fanaticism in the Muslim East" and "the actions and events in Iran [serve as] incitement for the activization of antigovernment inclined clergy in Afghanistan," the group told the meeting. So far the opposition to the PDPA was not well organized, but it had a substantial recruitment potential in the countryside. The Khalqi regime had outmaneuvered its rivals in Kabul, but would face severe difficulties unless it strengthened its position. Dissatisfaction in the army was running high, and there was a risk of new mutinies during summer. The four suggested a ten-point plan of action in Afghanistan. They wanted first of all to strengthen the army – both militarily and politically – through training programs and deliveries of arms. They called for extending the economic support programs, and, in particular, developing new programs for rural areas. Finally, they would ask the CPSU International Department and the Kabul embassy to devise a plan for enlarging the political base of the Afghan government.[67]

The Soviet embassy responded to the call from Moscow and the visible decline in the fortunes of the Khalqi regime by seeking to set up a new coalition government, including several Parchamis and members of the old regime. According to Vasilii Safronchuk, the embassy counsellor in charge of "political assistance," the Soviets even contemplated including representatives for some of the Islamist groups in these talks. But the regime refused to budge, and vetoed the Soviet initiatives.[68] "We are among enemies," Amin told Puzanov. "We must be vigilant."[69]

The Soviet attempts to force the Khalqis to accept members of Parcham and even nonparty representatives in government was followed by a plan to stimulate the rivalry between the two top leaders of Khalq, Taraki and Amin. After listening to Amin's complaints that he was excluded from the military leadership and that the president was increasingly concentrating powers in his own hands, Puzanov in late July suggested that Taraki "retire" from day-to-day military affairs and set up an emergency leadership group headed by Amin. Since the ambassador regarded Amin as a dangerous man, it is likely that his suggestions were intended primarily to stimulate Taraki's suspicions of his ambitious deputy, whom the KGB already in June had concluded was trying to seize complete power for himself. The Soviet aim was to get Taraki to purge Amin from the Afghan leadership.[70]

Puzanov also took two other initiatives in late summer 1979 in order to get Taraki to listen more to his suggestions. He asked Moscow to send two Soviet battalions to be placed respectively at Kabul airport and at the old castle, the center for the Khalqi government. At its meeting on 28 June, the Politburo decided on a modified version of this plan, agreeing to send a battalion to Bagram Airforce Base outside Kabul and "special detachments" of the KGB and GRU to Bagram and to the Soviet embassy compound. Puzanov also arranged for yet another visit by Boris Ponomarev in late July. But Ponomarev was again unable to impress the need for change on Taraki.[71]

Instead of the Afghan leaders realizing that the only way out was a broadening of the regime's power base, the Soviet embassy in August received information that Amin was planning to have Keshtmand and other imprisoned Parchamis executed. Puzanov made his strongest appeal to Taraki. These men, the ambassador said, were "prominent leaders of the revolution, members of the PDPA and of the Afghan leadership. The leaders of the Soviet Union draw Taraki's attention to the necessity of caution in carrying out repressions, in particular against leaders of the party."[72]

In addition to Puzanov's efforts, Moscow organized two special military missions to Kabul in order to put pressure on Taraki. The first, which arrived in mid-April and was led by General Aleksei Epishev, head of the Main Political Administration of the Soviet Army, came up with a series of suggestions for how to improve the fighting capacity of the Afghan troops. The second, headed by Vice Minister of Defense Ivan Pavlovskii – the man who in 1968 had commanded the Soviet task force sent to invade Czechoslovakia – arrived in Kabul on 17 August and stayed for almost two months. Pavlovskii was authorized to push for a full reorganization of the Afghan Army, and to threaten to withhold military assistance if Taraki did not respond positively.[73]

By late August Taraki seemed to have gotten the message. After the KGB representatives in Kabul had made it clear to the Afghan president that Amin's arrest was the only way of saving Soviet–Afghan relations, Taraki was ready to act. The chairman of the KGB reported to the Politburo in Moscow on 1 September that a series of emergency measures had to be taken with regard to Afghanistan, including Amin's removal, the release of political prisoners, and the creation of a broad "democratic coalition government." But the KGB also asked – and was granted – permission to begin putting together a 'fall-back' leadership of the PDPA "in case the crisis situation in the country deteriorates." On 9 September Taraki arrived in Moscow on his way back from the nonaligned summit in Havana. Brezhnev and Gromyko promised him increased Soviet military assistance if he would soften his regime's approach to land reform and educational reform and make changes in his government, getting rid of Hafizullah Amin and appointing a number of prominent Parchamis to cabinet posts. Taraki agreed. On his return to Kabul, however, the Afghan president got cold feet. Seeing that Amin had prepared his countermoves, the president again refused to make the changes Moscow demanded of him.[74]

Moscow lost patience. Acting on a urgent message from Gromyko, Puzanov, General Pavlovskii, and the heads of the Soviet military and KGB missions to Kabul sought out Taraki at his home in the evening of 13 September. The Soviets demanded an immediate meeting with him and with Amin. Amin, who was already in the palace, came to Taraki's rooms and listened while Puzanov read out a long list of charges of military inefficiency, political incompetence, and outrageous personal ambition. When the ambassador had finished, Taraki looked at him and said calmly: "Tell our Soviet friends that we thank them for their concern and agree with their views; everything will be all right." Amin joined in: "I agree with dear comrade Taraki ... If I have to depart this life, I will die with the word 'Taraki' on my lips."[75]

But the charade of unity led nowhere. The next morning, after learning of the inconclusive result of the meeting, several of the top PDPA leaders who supported the dismissal of Amin went into hiding at the Soviet embassy. After finding that Amin had asked for support against Taraki from several generals in the Afghan Army, the president appealed to the Soviets for help. "He spoke in a bitter tone about Amin, making the same charges which we had made earlier without any result," Puzanov remembered later.[76] In the afternoon of 14 September the two Afghan leaders had arranged another meeting at Taraki's residence, attended by the Soviet representatives. As Amin made his way into the building, the president's guards opened fire and killed two of the prime minister's assistants. Amin escaped unharmed. When meeting with the Soviets later that day, Amin "said that the revolution in Afghanistan could clearly develop without him, as long as it had the help of the Soviet comrades. But the point was … that Taraki's orders were not carried out at the moment by the armed forces, whereas his were."[77] Puzanov and the other Soviet representatives claimed to have had no knowledge of the murder plans. However, Amin's foreign minister, Shah Wali, assembled the ambassadors from the socialist countries immediately afterwards and told them that the Soviets had guaranteed Amin's safety when visiting Taraki, and that they had failed to deliver on their promise.[78]

After his escape Amin had military units loyal to him surround the palace. He called a meeting of the Politburo which duly expelled Taraki and made Amin the new head of the PDPA. When the Soviets attempted to get him to withdraw Shah Wali's version of the assassination attempt, Amin's response was: "Can I be mistaken? Can my mistake cause damage to the world Communist movement? And if the Politburo of the CPSU Central Committee thinks so, then I will accept their advice."[79] But instead of taking any Soviet advice, Amin immediately started a new purge, directed both against Taraki's supporters and against other political enemies. A number of prisoners from Daoud's regime and the Parchami wing of the PDPA were executed. Taraki himself was executed in prison on 9 October, in spite of Soviet appeals for his life to be spared.[80]

The Soviet scheming to get rid of Amin had backfired completely. They were now left with Amin as the head of both the party and the state. To make things worse, Amin – who in the early days of the regime seemed genuinely to admire the Soviet leaders – now with good reason distrusted Moscow and hated its local representatives, telling his followers that "when Ambassador Puzanov lied to me directly … then I cannot stop myself from saying everything I think about this person. I do not wish to meet him or talk to him. It is difficult to understand how such a liar and tactless person has been ambassador here for so long. I find it unpleasant that the Soviet ambassador (at this point Amin swore volubly) tries to depict the events of 14 September in a different light and asks me to confirm this untruth. I shall never do this."

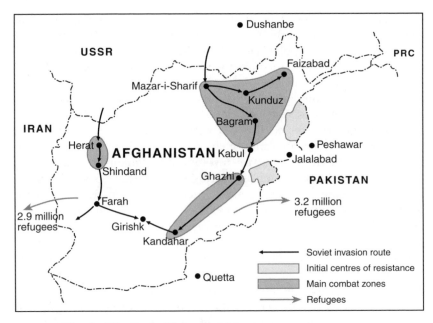

Map 9   The Soviet Union in Afghanistan.

In Moscow a top leadership group was formed to report to the Politburo on Afghanistan. The group, which consisted of Ustinov, Iuri Andropov (head of the KGB), Gromyko, and Ponomarev initially recommended a wait-and-see attitude toward Amin, combined with an increased Soviet military presence in Afghanistan. In Kabul relations between Amin and Puzanov remained frosty. In a meeting on 27 October the ambassador tried to force Amin to reduce his campaign of terror by threatening to withhold Soviet assistance. After this meeting Amin formally requested that Puzanov be recalled to Moscow. The ambassador also realized that his time in Kabul was over, and asked Gromyko to be transferred.[81]

Before leaving the Afghan capital Puzanov called on almost everyone in a position of power in the Khalqi government. The purpose of these meetings was primarily to impress on the PDPA leaders the extreme dependence of their regime on Soviet support. The Minister of Finance was told that Moscow worried over the costs of assisting Kabul in the year to come. To the Minister of Planning Puzanov stressed the need to learn from the experience of a developed socialist country – the Soviet Union. The head of the General Staff received promises that the Soviet Union would consider more direct assistance to officers and would also consider wider programs for Afghans to train in the Soviet Union. The message was clear: only if relations with Moscow improved could these leaders expect to receive the favors they depended on.[82]

Hafizullah Amin knew that the bonds that tied him to Moscow were wearing thin. He made almost desperate attempts to improve his position by opening relations with the Americans and, at the same time, appealing to the Kremlin to accept the new PDPA leaders – apparently not grasping how difficult such a combination of initiatives was in the Cold War conflict of the late 1970s.[83] In Moscow, Ustinov, Andropov, and Gromyko – the leaders who managed foreign policy for an increasingly frail Leonid Brezhnev – repeatedly refused to see Amin. In his final conversation with Puzanov, on 19 November, the Afghan leader kept underlining how much had been achieved in his country in terms of cooperation with the Soviet Union. But the ambassador *non grata* had no departing present for Amin.[84]

The Moscow leaders realized that the situation in the region was going from bad to worse for the Soviet Union. The Iranian–American hostage crisis did not dispel Soviet fears that Iran would turn increasingly hostile toward Moscow. The KGB reported in mid-October that the Iranian leaders were convinced that "the Soviet Union will not give up the ideological struggle and its attempts to set up a leftist government in Iran." The aims of the Islamic Republic were, according to Soviet intelligence, to weaken the Afghan regime, exert influence on the Muslim republics in the Soviet Union, and prevent the spread of Communism in the region.[85]

In Afghanistan itself the realization of the latter of these Iranian aims seemed to be moving ever closer. The Islamist rebels improved their positions considerably in October and November, as the morale of the Afghan Army was undermined by the coup and by Amin's relentless persecution of his enemies. The Kremlin started receiving unauthorized reports from Soviet commanders in Afghanistan on how bad the situation really was. V. P. Kapitanov, the chief Soviet military adviser to the Afghan 12th Army Division, then in Paktia province, wrote that the opposition was militarily on the offensive, that the brutality of the Afghan officers antagonized the local population, and that Soviet military equipment was routinely destroyed or sold.[86]

The new Soviet ambassador, Fikrat Tabeev, arrived in late November, as Soviet plans for an armed intervention were finalized in Moscow. Tabeev, a Tatar and a member of the CPSU Central Committee, had his first and last meeting with Amin on 6 December. Amin insisted that he had to go to Moscow, that there were vital issues concerning the long-term cooperation between the PDPA and the CPSU that he had to discuss with Brezhnev. Tabeev held him off. As he saw it, the situation in the country was verging on disaster, the ambassador later recalled. "Kabul was weakened. The army was deprived of a head after Amin's purges and reprisals. The clergy was against [the regime]. The peasants – against. The tribes – who had to endure much from Amin – against. Around Amin there were only a few lackeys, who like parrots repeated after him all kinds of nonsense about the 'build-up of socialism' and the 'dictatorship of the proletariat.'" Tabeev left Kabul on 10 December 1979.[87]

The Soviet decision to intervene

When the introduction of Soviet troops had first been discussed in March 1979, after the rebellion had erupted in western Afghanistan, the Kremlin leaders had hesitantly concluded that "in no case will we go forward with a deployment of troops." Aleksei Kosygin and Andrei Kirilenko, who until the end remained opponents of a Soviet invasion, had argued that the Afghan Communists themselves were to blame for the rebellion. "We gave it everything," Kirilenko had told the Politburo. "And what has come of it? Nothing of any value. After all, it was they who executed innocent people for no reason and told us that we also executed people in Lenin's time. You see what kind of Marxists we have found."[88]

It was President Taraki's murder by his second-in-command Hafizullah Amin in October which set the Soviet leadership on the course to intervention. In light of past Soviet support for Taraki, the KGB suspected Amin of planning what General Shebarshin called "doing a Sadat on us": a wholesale defection from the Soviet camp and an alignment with the United States, which would allow the Americans to place "their control and intelligence centers close to our most sensitive borders."[89] The KGB closely monitored Amin's meetings with US officials in Kabul in late October, believing that Washington was eyeing for a replacement for its lost positions in Iran.

Although no political orders had yet been issued concerning a possible intervention, the military chiefs of staff in late October began preparations and some training for such a mission. These orders reflected the increased concern of Defense Minister Dmitri Ustinov over the Afghan issue, and his sensing that proposing an intervention may soon be politically acceptable to his colleagues. In the not-too-subtle game of who would succeed Brezhnev – which by the fall of 1979 was in full swing within the Politburo – a premium was placed on both caution and enterprise: "recklessness" or "being a Napoleon" were deadly epithets to use against a politically ambitious defense minister, while

(a)   (b)

(c)   (d)

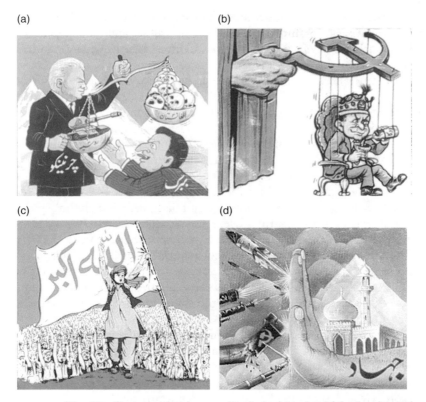

Fig. 10 Propaganda pictures distributed by the Afghan resistance on
the back of matchboxes, 1983–85. From top left: (a) Karmal receiving
Soviet weapons from Chernenko in return for dead Afghans; (b) Karmal
as Russian puppet drinking wine; (c) the people supporting the Islamic
resistance; (d) and the strength of Islam resisting Soviet weapons.

"forcefulness" and "looking after our interests" could be used as arguments in his favor.

Ustinov's colleague, collaborator, and sometime rival KGB chief Iuri
Andropov also started leaning toward military intervention in late 1979.
The KGB had been in charge of several Soviet bids since September to
remove Amin from the Afghan leadership, including at least one
attempted assassination. None of these efforts had succeeded, a fact
that cannot have pleased the ambitious Andropov and may have weakened his political position.[90] Already in mid-October the KGB had
begun working with PDPA exiles in Czechoslovakia and Bulgaria.
Sometime in early November the KGB took the most prominent of

these exiles – Babrak Karmal as leader of Parcham and anti-Amin Khalqis such as Sayed Muhammad Gulyabzoi and Asadullah Sarwari – to Moscow, where they formed a political coalition, whose general political platform was formed with the help of the Soviet International Department, and plans were drawn up to remove Amin from power with the help of the KGB.[91] In late November, after Amin had demanded the replacement of Soviet Kabul ambassador Puzanov, Andropov and Ustinov decided that the only way to solve the Afghan issue was the combination of a Soviet military intervention and the physical elimination of Hafizullah Amin. Amin's persistent calls for increased Soviet military aid, including Soviet troops, enboldened them and made it easier for them to present their suggestions to the Politburo.

The increasing strains in the East–West relationship – including in the essential field of arms control – over the last months of 1979 may have influenced Andropov and Ustinov's decision, and certainly made it easier for them to convince some of their colleagues. The NATO decision to deploy a new class of medium-range nuclear missiles in Europe, and the increasing reluctance in the US Senate to ratify the SALT II agreement, removed the concerns of some Politburo members over the effects a Soviet intervention may have on *détente*. As Anatoly Dobrynin later put it, "by winter of 1979 *détente* was, for most purposes, already dead."[92] The bleak outlook of the diplomatic arena helped carry the day with Foreign Minister Andrei Gromyko – at the best of times a somewhat pusillanimous participant in Soviet high politics, who had opposed intervention in March only after being sure which way the wind was blowing in the Politburo discussions.

The heads of the KGB and the Ministry of Defense had two remaining obstacles to overcome in their determination to send Soviet troops to Afghanistan. First, they had to narrow the field of participants in the decision-making process to an absolute minimum, to make sure that the decision was not delayed by the formal submission of reports from various departments and ministries to the Politburo. In this effort they were assisted by Mikhail Suslov and Brezhnev's chief adviser on foreign policy, Andrei Aleksandrov-Agentov. Karen Brutents, deputy head of the Central Committee International Department, remembered getting a telephone call from Alexandrov-Agentov. "First, he asked me what I was doing. When I told him I was writing a report on Afghanistan, he asked, 'And what exactly are you writing there?' When I told him that I was going to write a negative opinion, he said: 'So, do you suggest that we should give Afghanistan to the Americans?' And he immediately ended the conversation."[93] Brutents' report was not in the materials prepared for the Politburo members at the conclusive meetings.[94]

The same happened to dissent within the military. Major-General V. P. Zaplatin, the senior military adviser to the head of the Chief Political Directorate of the Afghan Army, was deemed too close to Amin and therefore recalled to Moscow for "consultations" in early December. While there, he received a secret message from his friend, senior military adviser to the head of the political department of the Afghan central army corps in Kabul, Colonel E. N. Kapustin. Kapustin wrote that "[KGB General] B. S. Ivanov was planning some venture in Afghanistan which Kapustin and other advisers considered rash and foolish" and begged his friend to report immediately to the top leaders. Unfortunately for both Zaplatin and Kapustin, the messenger chosen was a KGB informant. In order not to reveal his cover to the military, the informant was allowed to deliver Kapustin's message personally to the general, but the KGB made sure that Zaplatin never met with anybody of consequence when he was in Moscow.[95]

The last obstacle on the way to intervention was to win over, or at least neutralize, those Politburo members who throughout the crisis had been vocal opponents of the sending of Soviet troops, men like Kosygin and Kirilenko. Ustinov and Andropov realized that only way to make sure that a proposal for intervention would carry the day in the Politburo was to convince Leonid Brezhnev of the need to strike fast. The party head – by temperament a cautious and circumspect man on international issues – was persuaded by arguments much connected to his personal status on the world stage. According to General Aleksandr Liakhovskii, after Amin's coup "Brezhnev's attitude to the entire issue had changed. He could not forgive Amin, because Brezhnev had personally assured Taraki that he would be able to help him. And then they disregarded Brezhnev completely and murdered Taraki. Brezhnev used to say, 'how should the world be able to believe what Brezhnev says, if his words do not count in Afghanistan?'"[96]

In a remarkable personal handwritten letter to Brezhnev in early December, Iuri Andropov summed up the case for intervention:

We have been receiving information about Amin's behind-the-scenes activities which may mean his political reorientation to the West. He keeps his contacts with the American chargé d'affaires secret from us. He promised tribal leaders to distance himself from the Soviet Union ... In closed meetings he attacks Soviet policy and the activities of our specialists. Our ambassador was practically expelled from Kabul. These developments have created, on the one hand, a danger of losing the domestic achievements of the Afghan revolution, and, on the other hand, a threat to our positions in Afghanistan. Now there is no guarantee that Amin, in order to secure his personal power, would not turn to the West.

But Andropov could provide Brezhnev with the remedy for his troubles:

recently we were contacted by a group of Afghan Communists residing abroad. In the process of consultations with Babrak Karmal and Sarwari we found out – they informed us officially – that they had worked out a plan for moving against Amin and for forming new state and party organs. However, Amin began mass arrests of political opponents; five hundred people were arrested, and three hundred of them were killed. In these circumstances Babrak Karmal and Sarwari, without changing their plans for an uprising, appealed to us for assistance, including military assistance if needed. We have two battalions stationed in Kabul, so we can provide certain assistance if there is a need. However, just for an emergency, for extreme circumstances, we need to have a group of forces stationed along the border. If such an operation is carried out, it would allow us to solve the question of defending the achievements of the Afghan revolution, resurrecting the Leninist principles of state and party building in the Afghan leadership, and strengthening our positions in that country.[97]

Although agreeing with Andropov concerning the political purpose of the use of Soviet troops, Defense Minister Ustinov was not willing to accept a limited operation along the lines recommended by the head of the KGB. General Valentin Varennikov, who headed the operational planning in the General Staff, remembered that Ustinov wanted 75,000 men for the operation for two main reasons: first, he wanted to make sure that the toppling of Amin's regime could be carried out smoothly, even if some of the Afghan Army groups in Kabul decided to resist. Second, he believed that Soviet forces should be used to guard Afghanistan's borders with Pakistan and Iran, thereby preventing outside support for the Afghan Islamist guerrillas. On December 6, Andropov accepted Ustinov's plan.[98]

Around noon on 8 December the two met with Leonid Brezhnev and Andrei Gromyko in the general secretary's office in the Kremlin. In addition to the concerns Andropov had raised with Brezhnev earlier, he and Ustinov now added the strategic situation. Meeting two days after vital German support for NATO's double-track decision, "Ustinov and Andropov cited dangers to the southern borders of the Soviet Union and a possibility of American short-range missiles being deployed in Afghanistan and aimed at strategic objects in Kazakhstan, Siberia, and elsewhere."[99] Brezhnev accepted the outline plan for an intervention that the heads of the Defense Ministry and the KGB presented to him.

Right after their meeting with Brezhnev, Ustinov and Andropov met with the head of the General Staff, Marshal Ogarkov, in the Walnut Room, a small meeting-room adjacent to the hall where the Politburo usually met. The two informed Ogarkov of their conversation with Brezhnev. Ogarkov – who together with his deputies General Varennikov and Marshal Akhromeyev had earlier warned Ustinov against the effects of an intervention – once again listed his reasons why Soviet troops should not be sent in. Ustinov overruled him, and in the evening called a meeting of the senior staff of the Defense Ministry and told them to implement preparations for the intervention. The decision to send in troops was certain to come, Ustinov said.

By early December the infiltration of KGB special forces into Kabul was already well under way. A *Spetsnaz* unit had been positioned at Bagram air base north of the city, and other KGB units were in place near the presidential palace, the PDPA headquarters, and the main radio station. The purpose of the KGB's "Operation Agat" was to remove Amin and assist a takeover by Karmal's group. The deputy heads of the Soviet Foreign Ministry, the Defense Ministry, the KGB, and the Central Committee's International Department met at least twice in Moscow to sort out some form of coordination between their different areas of responsibility with regard to the planned intervention, but without much success, primarily because of unwillingness both on the side of the KGB and the military to divulge details of their operational plans.

On 12 December the Politburo met and formally ratified the proposal to intervene. Gromyko chaired the meeting, after having cosigned the proposal together with Ustinov and Andropov. Konstanin Chernenko wrote out, by hand, a short protocol accepting the proposal – entitled "Concerning the Situation in 'A'" – and had all Politburo members present sign their names diagonally across the text. Aleksei Kosygin – who almost certainly would have opposed an intervention – was not present. Andrei Kirilenko signed after some hesitation. Brezhnev, who entered the room after the brief discussion was finished, added his name, in quivering handwriting, at the bottom of the page.

Two days later the General Staff operative team, headed by Marshal Sergei Akhromeyev, was in place in Termez, not far from the Afghan border. A group from the operative team arrived at the Bagram Airforce Base outside Kabul on 18 December. The main operation started at 3 p.m. sharp on Christmas Day – airborne troops from the 103rd and 105th Air Divisions took off for Kabul and Shindand in western Afghanistan, and units from the 40th Army's 5th and 108th Motorized Rifle Divisions crossed the border at Kushka and at Termez. Just before nightfall on 27 December more than seven hundred members of the KGB's special units attacked Amin's residence at Dar-ul-Aman Palace, and, after having overcome stiff resistance from the Palace Guards, summarily executed the president, several of his relatives, and his closest aides.[100] Babrak Karmal, who was flown into Kabul with a KGB unit as the attack on the palace started, proclaimed himself Prime Minister and General Secretary of the PDPA the following day, heading a leadership that consisted mostly of leaders who had returned from exile with him. During the first days of the occupation Babrak spent much time interrogating those leaders of Amin's regime who had been captured alive, berating them for having endangered the connection between the Soviet Union and the Afghan revolution. "We and the Soviet comrades considered you a true Communist," he told the veteran party member Ghulam Dagastir Panjshiri. "You betrayed the interests of the Soviet comrades who spoke to you in Moscow."[101] Still, the Soviets forced Babrak to release most of the Communists arrested in the days following the invasion, and in some cases have them join the new government in senior positions, all in the name of party unity.

In the late 1970s and early 1980s the Soviet invasion of Afghanistan was viewed in the West – and not just in the United States – as ultimate proof of aggressive intent. Among the policy elite in Moscow, however, the intervention was seen as defensive, as a policy of last resort. Why, then – in spite of their preponderance in military power, international influence, and technical prowess – did the Soviets not succeed in forcing a change in Khalqi policies by any means short of armed intervention, with large-scale damage to their international position as a result? Why, in the end, did they have to intervene *against* a regime that they had spent so much effort and money to protect? The answers must be sought both in the contents of Soviet foreign policy ideology and in the actions of Moscow's local representatives, neither of which did well when confronted with the Afghan civil war and with revolutionary Islam.

Puzanov and his assistants in Kabul saw their mission as helping the Afghans to turn away from domestic feudal oppression and dependence on the West, and to develop a socialist state and a socialist economy. The furthering of these aims would also strengthen Soviet security and improve Moscow's position in the region. The PDPA "revolution" could, with the infusion of aid from north of the border, become a "cheap" victory for socialism and for the Soviet state. In order to be recognizable to the Soviets, however, the process toward socialism in Afghanistan had to contain a rather narrow set of symbols and events. The sequence and language of the "April revolution" would have to be patterned on the "October Revolution" – or rather on the late 1970s image of that cataclysm. Likewise, independence from the West to Puzanov and his colleagues meant being closely allied with the Soviet Union. "Socialism" equaled the Soviet society the advisers knew – and especially the role of the party in that society.

The Soviet advisers in Kabul from the very start found little to "recognize" in Taraki's regime. The faction-ridden party leadership, the unruly countryside where the "revolution" became just another element in age-old ethnic and clan rivalries, the touch-and-go reform plans which included Western as well as Soviet ideas – none of this contributed to Soviet sympathy for the regime, and all of it was dutifully reported back to Moscow. But in spite of the visible failings of the Afghan party under Taraki and Amin, its rhetoric helped convince the Soviets that there would, ultimately, emerge from within the PDPA a "true socialist" leadership. Until this happened the Soviet embassy, the political and military advisers, and the technical experts were the custodians of Afghan socialism. They would have not only to plan its development but also to direct the implementation of the plans.[102]

The embassy's frank reporting from Kabul must have left Moscow in no doubt that after the summer of 1978 Soviet aims in Afghanistan were becoming less and less attainable. As the Afghan leaders repeatedly acted contrary to Soviet advice, the strain could be felt in both capitals. It is possible that the continued feuding between Puzanov and the Khalqis would have led Moscow to curtail or end its aid to Kabul in late fall 1978, had it not been for the dramatic international changes in the region.

The Iranian revolution led Moscow to place increased emphasis on its Afghan policy. Even if it had little faith in a left-wing takeover in Iran, the Kremlin did not expect the Islamists to form the core of the new government. Already by March or April 1979 the Soviet leaders had come to view Teheran as a potentially dangerous challenge to its regional security. The Soviet presence in Afghanistan thereby acquired a new significance; Kabul had increased both its strategic value and its usefulness as a listening post and a spy center. The primacy of regional considerations increased in mid-1979, as Moscow viewed developments in Teheran with increasing alarm. The negative Soviet assessment of the Islamic revolution and of the consequences the revolution could have on the Soviet position in the wider region led Moscow to increase its aid to the Khalqi regime. "The deterioration of the situation in Afghanistan must be viewed as a result of the events in Iran," the KGB Center reported to its stations after the intervention.[103] The new Soviet "investments" – starting already in early 1979 – increased Moscow's stake in the survival of the Kabul regime, but did little to increase its leverage.

The Soviet preoccupation with foreign policy gave Taraki and Amin an opportunity to use their own conflicts with Iran and Pakistan to press for further Soviet assistance. Neither Puzanov nor his advisers seem to have understood the historical and cultural bases for Khalq enmity toward their country's neighbors. Taraki and Amin had both been influenced by Pushtun nationalism in their early years, and hopes for control of the Pushtun minority in Pakistan, as well as fear of Iranian influence with the Afghan Shia minorities, were among their political staples.

In conversations with the Soviets, however, the Khalqi leaders would play up Iranian Islamist radicalism and Pakistani links with the United States in order to press for increases in Moscow's military support.[104]

In addition to the lack of understanding of traditional Pushtun foreign policy aims, the Soviets also lacked sensitivity as to how Afghan local elites perceived Moscow's involvement in PDPA politics. The haughty and often confrontational style of the Soviet advisers – including Puzanov, whose behavior earned him the nickname "the Little Czar" – contributed to the erosion of the regime's hold on local loyalties.[105] The opposition did not have to work miracles in order to exploit local resentments of "foreign" dominance. In part as a consequence of their indifference to local resentment of foreign power, Soviet representatives consistently overrated their influence with the PDPA. Even when able to appeal to a large group of Afghan leaders, Puzanov's ardent but dour proclamations were no match for the passionate pleas of a Hafizullah Amin, who could draw on personal and political loyalties developed over decades. In spite of its promises to Moscow, the embassy could therefore stop neither the purge of the Parchamis in the fall of 1978 nor the toppling of Taraki a year later – both events which the Soviets rightly predicted as stepping-stones to disaster for the PDPA regime.

At the outset, in 1978, Moscow's representatives to Kabul did *not* think of Soviet support to Afghanistan primarily in terms of arms and military training. Technical assistance and, even more importantly, education formed the base for the aid programs in Puzanov's recommendations to Moscow. In this respect Afghanistan poses an interesting contrast to what seems to have been the pattern of Soviet support for Marxist regimes in the Third World. The reason may be that the embassy in Kabul, the KGB station, and the International Department all believed that increased military support would tempt the regime to alienate the population further through a radicalization of its reform programs. When Taraki asked for arms, he most often got lectures from Puzanov about the need to build the party and strengthen its alliance policies.[106]

The Soviet reluctance to provide large amounts of military support disappeared in early 1979. The Islamist threat to the regime's survival and the events in Iran led Moscow to decide on greater military involvement in the Afghan civil war. But as the Epishev and Pavlovskii missions show, the Soviet general staff perceived the substantial increase in assistance in terms of more military hardware, field advisers, training, and participation in "special operations" (including air strikes) – not as the introduction of Soviet ground forces.[107]

The alternatives to armed intervention, as the Kabul embassy, the military advisers, and the KGB perceived them in late 1979, were either to negotiate a settlement between the Khalqis and some of their enemies, or to draw closer to Hafizullah Amin and support his ruthless but energetic conduct of the war. Some of the Soviet representatives, most notably Safronchuk, attempted to get negotiations going, including not only Parchamis and supporters of Daoud and the former king, Zahir, but also groups belonging to the moderate Islamist opposition. Safronchuk, however, found the initiative blocked by Khalqi intransigence and by lack of support from Moscow. The Amin option was discarded primarily because of the ambassador's and the Kremlin leaders' strong personal antipathy toward the new Afghan leader. As one of them put it, "Taraki's ghost was in the way."[108]

Although none of the chief Soviet representatives in Afghanistan recommended a massive military intervention, Soviet officials differed on how to force the Afghan regime to change. Puzanov and the embassy advisers toyed with the idea of deploying Soviet armed units at key positions in order to underline their "suggestions" to Taraki, but their main conclusion was that political pressure in the end would carry the day. The KGB, headed in Kabul by Boris Ivanov and Aleksandr Morozov, seem to have been skeptical of increased military involvement, and recommended a Soviet-engineered *coup d'état*, which would bring the Parchami leaders to power. The heads of the military missions and General Leonid Gorelov, the Soviet military attaché, believed that with Soviet military training and equipment the Afghan Army would ultimately become powerful enough to set the political mistakes right.[109]

For the Moscow Politburo, however, the gradual worsening of relations with Washington during the Carter administration made it easier to accept Andropov's and Ustinov's insistence that the United States was seeking to undermine the Soviet position in Afghanistan by secret contacts with Hafizullah Amin. It was this perceived US challenge – coming on top of a regional Iranian-led Islamist challenge – that increased the urgency of a solution to the Afghan crisis; the situation in Kabul went from being "unstable" to "demanding a Soviet response." The aging Soviet leadership saw no other way to respond than through a military intervention.[110]

The Politburo did not foresee the strength of the international reaction to the events in Kabul and grossly underestimated the extent of the US response. Brezhnev himself seemed to have genuinely believed that the intervention would be a "limited operation" and that "it would be over in a few weeks' time."[111] Since the main purpose of the operation was to remove the Amin leadership, Brezhnev expected that the situation in Afghanistan would begin to stabilize as soon as that aim had been achieved. With the advent of the "real Communists" in Kabul, the visible

Soviet role could be minimized, and Brezhnev was willing to bear the international costs of seeing that happen.

But Afghan Communism had self-destructed already by the end of summer 1979, well ahead of the Soviet invasion. Confronted by a far more potent and popular revolutionary force – the Afghan Islamists – and unable to reshape its domestic and foreign policies in such a way as to gain stable alliances of any kind, the regime could not win the civil war. The basic policy failure of the Soviet Afghan intervention was the belief that foreign power could be used to secure the survival and ultimate success of a regime that demonstrably could not survive on its own.

The Islamist response

The Soviet intervention provided new impetus for the Afghan resistance groups headquartered in Peshawar, and especially for the Islamists. According to one of their leaders, Gulbuddin Hekmatyar, the resistance had had few successes after Herat, in part because of the severity of PDPA reprisals and in part because of disagreements among the seven main parties on strategy and areas of operation. While the recruitment of sympathizers continued, the number of military operations actually declined between summer 1979 and the arrival of Soviet troops in January 1980. But with increasing evidence of Soviet participation in the rounding up of local guerrillas, the Islamists had little trouble linking up to those resistance groups that remained at large. The months immediately after the Soviet invasion proved a breakthrough for the Pakistan-based parties, with a dramatic increase in local support and external supplies.

Why did many local commanders – the majority of whom had originally been skeptical of the Islamists – begin cooperating with the Hezb-i-Islami and other parties after the Soviet invasion? The main reason was the improved access to weapons and other supplies that these parties could provide. With increasing Pakistani, and after a few weeks also US, support, the exile groups were the only available source of the hardware that the resistance groups so badly needed. Also, there was an increasing sense among Afghans of all ethnic groups that with the open participation of Soviet troops on behalf of the government, the whole idea of a secular state had come into disrepute. What the Islamists offered was a distinctly Islamic government, even though the specifics of their recipe for what that government should do was not especially attractive to most Afghans.

The Islamists were also strengthened by increased ideological training, often provided by outsiders or by Afghans who had studied in the *madrasas* – religious schools – in Egypt, Saudi Arabia, or Pakistan. For some of the

(a)   (b)

(c)   (d)

Fig. 11 Propaganda pictures distributed by the Afghan resistance on the back of matchboxes, 1983–85. From top left: (a) Andropov with a stranglehold on the Afghan Communists; (b) Karmal's flag: Communist on one side, Islamic on the other; (c) Karmal kowtowing before Chernenko, with the two Soviet "great Satans," Brezhnev and Andropov, pictured on the wall; (d) Karmal pretending to be a muslim, with Marx's *Das Kapital* under one arm and Lenin up his sleeve.

leaders of the Afghan resistance fighters – the Mujahedin, or holy warriors, as they had begun referring to themselves – advisers who had strong links to puritanical Islamic sects in the Middle East became increasingly important from 1980–81. While careful in bringing these men into Afghanistan itself, where it was thought they could cause controversy because of their strict interpretation of Islamic practices, Islamist leaders such as Gulbuddin Hekmatyar, Mohammad Younus Khalis, and Abdul Rasul Sayyaf soon began drawing on these advisers in their search for a political strategy and a vision of the future. They were encouraged to do so by their supporters in Pakistan, who sympathized with the

"Arabs" – as these advisers were often known, whatever their ethnic background – and liked the funding and international connections they could bring to the Afghan resistance.

For hard-liners in the Carter administration, and especially for the National Security Adviser, Zbigniew Brzezinski, the Soviet invasion of Afghanistan provided much welcome proof of Soviet aggressive intentions in the Third World. In his report to Carter on the day of the invasion, Brzezinski noted that "both Iran and Afghanistan are in turmoil" and that "the age-long dream of Moscow to have direct access to the Indian Ocean" was in the process of being fulfilled.[112] While the president himself had been sliding toward a more alarmist interpretation of Soviet actions at least since the Horn of Africa crisis, it was Brzezinski's portrayal of Brezhnev's Afghanistan policy as a naked act of aggression and as a first step in challenging US positions in the Gulf area that won Carter over to seeing the Soviets as implacable enemies and the invasion of Afghanistan as the gravest threat to world peace since 1945.[113] When the National Security Council met to discuss US countermeasures, the president surprised even his National Security Adviser by supporting all proposals that were on the table, including a prohibition on US grain exports to the Soviet Union and a boycott of the 1980 Moscow Olympics, both measures that would do little good to the embattled president's chances of reelection. But for Carter, the need to get back at the Soviets and, as he saw it, deter further Soviet aggression was stronger than even his political survival skills. "Soviet actions over the next ten to twenty years will be colored by our behavior in this crisis," the president said. "We should ... try to do the maximum, short of a world war, to make the Soviets see that this was a major mistake."[114]

In spite of the president's sense of shock and outrage, the invasion in no way came as a surprise to Washington. US signals intelligence – both air surveillance and intercepts – had shown Soviet forces being readied for action in Afghanistan since late November 1979. Also, the United States had begun a program of direct financial and material support for the Afghan anti-Communist opposition in July 1979, which was stepped up as the year progressed. By early September Admiral Stansfield Turner, Carter's director of central intelligence, had asked for several "enhancement options" to be worked out, including one that would provide "funds for the Pakistanis to purchase lethal military equipment for the insurgents, and ... a like amount of lethal equipment ourselves for the Pakistanis to distribute to the insurgents."[115] But US planning was soon overtaken by events in Afghanistan itself.

In February 1980, barely six weeks after the Soviet invasion, Zbigniew Brzezinski went to Pakistan, where he discussed an expanded covert action program with General Zia and traveled to the Afghan frontier, where he was photographed waving a khalashnikov rifle roughly in the direction of the border-line. On his way home, Brzezinski stopped in Saudi Arabia, where he agreed a Saudi matching contribution for the Mujahedin to anything the Americans would provide. Well before Carter had been defeated by Ronald Reagan in the US presidential election in the fall of 1980, there was agreement within the administration that Afghanistan could, and should, be made into a "Soviet Vietnam."[116] The final adherent of a more cautious line, CIA Director Turner, had already in March admitted defeat. In a note to Brzezinski he admitted that "how assertive the Soviets will be in the future will very likely depend upon how 'successful' the Soviet leadership views their intervention in Afghanistan to have been."[117]

By then a number of new US programs to counter "radical Marxist governments" in the Third World were well under way, including Yemen, Angola, and the tiny Caribbean island state of Grenada. For Brzezinski, South Arabia became a high priority issue after war broke out between the Soviet-backed People's Democratic Republic of Yemen (PDRY) – the former British colony of Aden – and the Northern Yemen Arab Republic in February 1979. The Soviets had used the port of Aden to stage its intervention in Ethiopia, and supported the PDRY's new and ultra-leftist leadership in its aims to foment a rebellion in the north. But instead of reunification between the two Yemens, the immediate result of the border war was further fragmentation in both states. The Soviets pushed for ceasefire, which was achieved in late March. But for Washington the events in Yemen were further proof of Soviet advances in the Third World, and for President Carter it seemed as if another segment of what Brzezinski claimed was an "arc of crisis" – from Southern Africa via the Horn to the Middle East – had been put in place by Moscow. The CIA supported immediate US action to prevent the PDRY "from fomenting a Marxist revolution throughout the Arabian peninsula." On 6 April 1979 the NSC agreed on a program of covert assistance to North Yemen, while attempting to "create dissension" in the Marxist south – a "quite forward leaning" plan, according to the CIA's deputy director, Robert Gates.[118]

The beginning US offensive in the Islamic world became much easier because of the Muslim reaction to the Soviet invasion of Afghanistan. Moscow's decision not only made many nationalist regimes turn against it – the Islamabad meeting of thirty-five Islamic nations in January 1980 condemned "the Soviet military aggression against the Afghani people" – but it also delegitimized the Left and made it easier for Islamist agitation to find an audience in the Middle East, North Africa, and even in Muslim Southeast Asia.[119] For many Islamists, especially new recruits to the cause, the Soviet Union and Communism became the main enemy, and the United States a tactical ally in deed, if not in word. For the Saudis, the US support for the Afghan Mujahedin was essential. "We don't do operations," the head of the Saudi General Intelligence Department, Prince Turki al-Faisal told his CIA allies. "We don't know how. All we know how to do is write checks."[120]

In spite of the intensity of conflict with the United States during the hostage crisis, even the new Iranian leadership made Soviet intentions one of its main worries after the Afghanistan invasion and the Iraqi attack in 1980. Already two days after the Soviet invasion, Ambassador Vladimir Vinogradov had met Khomeini in Qum and tried to explain his country's actions. Moscow would assist Teheran in its conflict with the United States, Vinogradov said, but "counted on understanding of the action it had been forced to take in Afghanistan." The ayatollah saw no such meeting of minds. "There could," Khomeini said, "be no mutual understanding between a Muslim nation and a non-Muslim government."[121] His message, which Iranian pilgrims brought to Mecca in 1980, gave no quarter to either Washington or Moscow:

Repel the treacherous superpowers from your countries and your abundant resources. Restore the glory of Islam, and abandon your selfish disputes and differences, for you possess everything! Rely on the culture of Islam, resist Western imitation, and stand on your own feet. Attack those intellectuals who are infatuated with the West and the East, and recover your true identity. Realize that intellectuals in the pay of foreigners have inflicted disaster upon their people and countries. As long as you remain disunited and fail to place your reliance in true Islam, you will continue to suffer what you have suffered already. We are now in an age when the masses act as the guides to the intellectuals and are rescuing them from abasement and humiliation by the East and the West. For today is the day that the masses of the people are on the move; they are the guides to those who previously sought to be the guides themselves.[122]

9 The 1980s: the Reagan offensive

The election of Ronald Reagan to the presidency of the United States in 1980 signified a change in method rather than aims in American Third World policies. Jimmy Carter's last two years in office, especially, had pointed directly to the key priorities of the new administration – stepping up the pressure against radical regimes and gaining new allies among indigenous anti-Communist movements. But while Carter – a hands-on president if there ever was one – had at first been held back by moral reservations and disagreements among his advisers, Reagan from the out-set gladly left both policy implications and policy execution to others. The result was a host of new and sometimes contradictory initiatives, all carried out with the blessing of the president, that sought to target Third World regimes seen as closely allied to the Soviet Union, such as Nicaragua, Afghanistan, and Angola. The president wanted to see Soviet defeats and an internal change of political direction in these countries, because such changes would confirm Reagan's own conviction that his country was on the side of history and that socialism was a thing of the past. But even as he strove to overcome the effects of the Vietnam War, Reagan was aware that he had to do so without risking the US losses that conflict had produced. The renewed dedication to interventionism implied finding allies who were willing to do the fighting. Reagan was not looking for regional policemen of the Kissingerian type – he, or rather his ideologically driven advisers, were looking for revolutionary movements of the inverse kind, those that for their own reasons were willing to let left-wing regimes bleed.[1]

The Reagan approach was in many ways a continuation of the policies and methods developed by Carter's National Security Adviser Zbigniew Brzezinski and his staff. Already well before the Soviet invasion of Afghanistan, Brzezinski had – with Carter's consent – begun implemen-ting what some referred to as a "counterforce strategy" in the Third World, meaning an emphasis on supporting whatever opposition could be mustered to Soviet allies in Africa and Asia. The aid to Siad Barre's regime in Somalia – characterized by one of Brzezinski's assistants as "remarkably unsavoury and untrustworthy" – was a turning point in that respect: a

Fig. 12   US President Jimmy Carter attempted to contain the Nicaraguan revolution – here greeting a skeptical Daniel Ortega in Washington in 1979.

US administration that in its first months had been agonizing over arms supplies to long-term allies with blemishes to their human rights record by 1978 was willing to launch a major operation of support for one of the bloodiest dictators in Africa, in order to bail him out of a war he himself had started.[2] By 1980 Barre was in the company of the Cambodian Khmer Rouge and the Afghan Mujahedin as recipients of US aid to fight pro-Moscow regimes.

This remarkable turning away from even the mildest form of skepticism with regard to the qualities of the movements that directly or indirectly received American backing can only be explained by the great concern that US elites by the late 1970s had begun attaching to the new wave of revolutionary change in the Third World and to Soviet interventionism. While in part connected to the domestic rise of the New Right and the critique of liberalism in America, the emphasis on a Third World challenge was also related to seeing revolutions as the *result* of Soviet involvement rather than a cause of it. The concept of "totalitarianism" – promoted by Brzezinski and other social scientists in the early 1960s – developed the Rostowian theories of modernization by postulating that as soon as a country's "natural" development had been perverted by a socialist revolution then only outside support could relaunch that country's trajectory toward democracy and capitalism.[3] In other words, it was dependent on

Fig. 13   Ronald Reagan meets with Afghan Mujahedin commanders
in the Oval Office, 1983.

America to reestablish order in the natural development of "newly independent states," which the Soviet Union had been perverting at will during
the *détente* era. If unsuccessful, not only would the fates of these countries
be sealed, but the United States itself would, in time, be in mortal danger.[4]

While impervious to any of its theoretical underpinnings, Ronald
Reagan had from the mid-1970s onwards become one of the main critics
of American "inaction" in the Third World, and by far the most eloquent
spokesman for US interventionism. During the 1976 campaign, running
for the Republican nomination against the incumbent president, Gerald
Ford, Reagan took aim at the whole concept of *détente*:

"Wandering without aim" describes United States' foreign policy. Angola is a case in
point. We gave just enough support to one side to encourage it to fight and die, but too
little to give them a chance of winning. And [mean]while we are disliked by the winner,
distrusted by the loser, and viewed by the world as weak and unsure. If *détente* were the
two-way street it is supposed to be, we could have told the Soviet Union to stop its
troublemaking and leave Angola to the Angolans. But it didn't work out that way.[5]

By 1980 – with the Carter administration's slow debilitation in a battle
against revolutionary Islam handing him the presidency – Reagan happily
conflated all threats to American security under a common heading:

"Let's not delude ourselves, the Soviet Union underlies all the unrest that is going on. If they weren't engaged in this game of dominoes, there wouldn't be any hot spots in the world."[6] There was, Reagan firmly believed, a grand design in Soviet foreign policy that was diametrically opposite to all that America stood for – its antithesis, the evil version of empire.

Third World fragmentation and the origins of the Reagan offensive

Outside of the United States, by the early 1980s the very concept of a Third World – united by similar historical memories of imperialist oppression and similar challenges in building a new state and a new economy – was beginning to fragment. Though in straightforward political terms there had always been more that divided than united, as late as the mid-1970s many Third World regimes had still been ready in the UN and through the Non-Aligned Movement to project a semblance of unity. The oil boycott after the 1973 Middle East war and African support for the MPLA regime in Angola had been two cases in point. The turn in the late 1970s toward emphasizing economic demands through a so-called New International Economic Order (NIEO) – first passed as a UN General Assembly resolution in 1974 – can be seen as a sign of the increasing lack of political identification among Third World countries. Even though NIEO included many demands that were political as well as economic – for instance, compensation for damage done during colonial rule – the main message was to underline a Third World primary identity as that of producer of raw materials. The message did little to stem the return to diversity in the self-images of Third World elites. On the contrary, economic demands sharpened the distinction between industrializing and nonindustrializing Third World countries.[7]

During the 1970s economic growth in some Third World countries in Asia and Latin America had intensified. South Korea, Taiwan, Singapore, Hong Kong, Brazil, and Mexico had an average economic growth per year of about 7.5 percent during the decade.[8] The growth of their manufactured exports was even more impressive, increasing by an average of more than 13 percent per year in a period when the economies of most Western countries seemed to stagnate. By 1979 these six newly industrializing countries supplied the West with almost 40 percent of its clothing imports and were beginning to compete for market shares in car and ship building, as well as in consumer electronics. Even though large areas of poverty remained, especially in Latin America, and the exploitation of workers and the environment was rampant, the successes of the export-led model of development posed a direct challenge to the collectivist orientation of so many Third World regimes. When China in the early 1980s quickened its ideological transition from socialism to market-driven reform, an increasing number of Third World elites began questioning whether collectivist ideologies could deliver the economic progress they so desperately needed.[9]

For many of the left-wing revolutionary states that had come into being in the 1960s and 1970s, the early 1980s proved to be a time of disappointments and severe setbacks. None of them could present a comprehensive alternative to capitalism in their internal policies, relying in most cases on models imported from Eastern Europe that were badly suited to their own social and economic conditions. Except where an infrastructure existed to bring valuable raw materials to international markets, the programs of nationalization proved economically unsuccessful, and usually led to an exodus of those parts of the local bourgeoisie which possessed the most important knowledge and technical skills. In Ethiopia, for instance, two-thirds of the educated elite left between 1974 and 1980.[10]

The lack of an integrated nationally based economic model led to increasing political friction within the regimes themselves, and to intensification of the conflict between them and their domestic enemies. When a state that used a newly coined national identity as its main legitimacy notably failed to deliver in economic terms, it is rather obvious that some groups would begin opposing *both* state policies and the identity that these policies represented. In many Third World countries, beginning in the early 1980s, local prenational identities gained ground at the expense of the postcolonial nation. This conflict was most intense in countries of a socialist orientation, because these regimes ideologically refused to recognize the existence of domestic identities beyond their own, thereby precluding negotiations, and because local rebels here could count on foreign support, thereby stirring civil wars. By the mid-1980s most of the non-Islamist internal challenges to leftist Third World regimes came from movements with an ethnic background.[11]

The challenges posed by struggles over policies and identities were exacerbated by the sharp economic downturn at the end of the 1970s. Already cut off from Western official aid and of little interest to private trade and investment both because of their policies and because of the attraction of East Asia, the recession put enormous pressure on left-wing regimes in the Third World. With over 90 percent of their exports being raw materials, countries such as Angola, Ethiopia, South Yemen, and Nicaragua were hard hit by declining prices, which in some cases cut the state's income in half between 1979 and 1982/83. The lack of flexibility in their economic models made the crisis worse, leading to severe drops in living standards and to a lack of ability to handle the consequences of natural disasters, such as the 1983 drought and mass starvation in Ethiopia.[12]

Many of the same global trends that caused a series of crises within its Third World allies also contributed to stagnation within the Soviet Union itself. From 1979 onwards there was a significant reduction in growth for the Soviet GDP, from a projected increase of more than 3 percent for that year to a real result of around 0.7 percent growth, according to CIA figures. The Soviet economy, US intelligence said in a report for the president, had "slowed to a crawl."[13] While the overall causes of Soviet economic stagnation are beyond the scope of this book, it is important to note that the sharp drop from 1982 onwards in the international price of oil – the commodity on which a large part of Soviet foreign exports depended – contributed significantly to problems in the economy and further reduced Moscow's room for maneuver in economic terms, both at home and abroad. The global role that the Soviets had taken on meant that both military expenditure – already in the late 1970s just slightly less than 25 percent of GDP – and support for socialist states continued to increase into the 1980s, although it was clear to the leadership that the additional shortages this created at home were socially harmful and unpopular.

The increasing discrepancy between Moscow's international aims and the means available to achieve them would have been easier to adjust if there had been a younger and more energetic leadership. As it was, the median age in the Politburo in 1981 was almost 70, and the top level of the Communist Party consisted mostly of the same leaders who had initiated the new Third World offensive in the early 1970s. Both factors conspired to make any adjustment more difficult, even where individual members of the leadership realized ("*objectively,*" as they would have said) that policy changes would be useful or even necessary. Iurii Andropov, who took over as General Secretary after Leonid Brezhnev's death in November 1982, sensed the dangers of "overstretch" in part because he as KGB Chairman had had unique access to intelligence information.[14] Facing the anti-Sovietism of the Reagan administration, Andropov was particularly preoccupied with reducing Soviet enmity with other countries, especially China and Western Europe, but also Japan and Southeast Asia.

But the leadership had no solutions to offer to the Soviet predicament. The discussion at the Politburo meeting on 31 May 1983 is typical for the times. After informing members of yet another funeral in the inner circle, the General Secretary went on to complain about the overall Soviet position in the world.

If you look at the events that are taking place in the Western countries, you can say that an anti-Soviet coalition is being formed out there. Of course, that's not accidental, and it's highly dangerous ... We should consider some sort of compromise in our relations with Japan. For example: we could think about joint exploitation of those small islands [which] have no strategic importance. Maybe there will be other suggestions. I, personally, think that Japan could initiate more active cooperation with the Soviet Union in the economic sphere.[15]

Similar high-flying ideas were broached in 1983–84 with regard to a number of countries, but they all came to nothing since Moscow was unwilling to touch the key issues that had led them into conflict with these countries in the first place. Japanese premier Nakasone Yasuhiro, for instance, had no incentive to arouse Washington's wrath by cooperating with Moscow in any area, including trade, as long as any discussion of sovereignty over the northern islands was anathema to the Soviets.

Andropov had no remedy for an international environment that turned increasingly hostile to the Soviet Union, except extolling prudence among Soviet foreign beneficiaries and hard work at home. The same ideologically based interventionist mindset that had led the Soviet Union into conflict with so many of the newly developed countries that it could have developed a closer economic relationship with – for instance South Korea or the countries of Southeast Asia – now prevented the adjustments that were needed to overcome its international isolation. While its Third World allies proved the Soviet role as a superpower, they were more like millstones when the Soviet aim was to move towards reducing tension with capitalist states.

While Ronald Reagan and some of his advisers were convinced that the Soviet Union by necessity was on the losing side of history, no one in the new administration understood how dramatically perspectives had changed within the Soviet leadership itself. Moreover, while united in its rhetorical condemnation of Soviet behavior, the administration was divided between moderates and radicals in the debate over how far the United States could go in confronting the Soviet Union without the risk of war. But to those many in the United States and in Europe who believed that any incoming US administration would have to moderate its rhetoric when coming to power, the first months of the Reagan administration became a bit of a shock: from day one it was the radicals – for instance, those who believed in a strict monetarist agenda in the economy or the need to roll back Soviet influence in the Third World – who created the administration's agenda, even though they were mostly dependent on establishment figures such as Reagan's two secretaries of state, Alexander Haig (1981–82) and George P. Shultz (1982–89) to implement it. The radicals' strength was in their sense of mission and in their firm belief that they were fulfilling the mandate the president had been given in the election. Reagan's own occasional involvement with policy making also seemed to confirm that he supported the radical options over the more moderate ones that came from the bureaucracy at the Pentagon and the State Department.[16]

The main reasons why it still took most of the president's first election period to work out some basic principles for a more interventionist US Third World policy were the policy inexperience of the radicals, disagreements among Reagan's top advisers, and resistance from well-established officials. Looking back, some of the radicals refer to 1981–82 as "the lost years," because so little concrete action was taken to join the battle against Soviet-supported Third World regimes.[17] Radicals such as Richard Perle and Fred Iklé at Defense, and Richard Pipes in the NSC, were frustrated at finding their ideas ridiculed by more experienced officials, even when these same ideas in only slightly more moderate forms found their way into the administration's key policy statements. For some, memories of happier times criticizing the government from the *outside* led them to resign in disgust. Richard Pipes – the ideologically zealous history professor who had been made the NSC's top Soviet specialist – left the administration to return to Harvard in 1982.[18]

Meanwhile moderates such as the Secretary of State, Alexander Haig, attempted to use the Reagan rhetoric to instill fear into America's Third World opponents and get them to change their behavior. His approach was similar to the one he had recommended as Richard Nixon's chief of staff back in the early 1970s: make the opponent think the US president a "madman," who is capable of using extreme force to settle international conflicts. At the end of November 1981 Haig met secretly with Cuban Foreign Minister Rodriguez in Mexico City to put pressure on Havana.

In 1975 we were witnesses to a situation which subjectively led us to conclude that the Soviet leadership assessed the changes which took place in our country as changes of a geo-political character – I am talking about Watergate and the war in Vietnam. This was abundantly clear in the widening of activity in Africa, Southeast Asia and in Northwest and Western Asia. In this manner, there exists a tendency – correct or mistaken – to believe that an agreement exists between Moscow and Havana in connection with various international activities, at least a tacit one, if not expressed. All this has created a mood in the United States which brought Mr. Reagan to power.[19]

To the radicals, it was also important to point to the dangers Caribbean and Central American revolutions posed to the United States, since they knew that the president himself saw that area as a stepping-stone for Communist attacks against the United States. Already six weeks after coming to power, Reagan talked about what we've learned of the actual involvement of the Soviet Union, of Cuba, of the PLO, of, even Qadhafi in Libya, and others in the Communist Bloc nations to bring about this terrorism down there [in El Salvador] ... And I think it is significant that the terrorists, the guerrilla activity in El Salvador was supposed to cause an uprising, that the government would fall because the people would join this aggressive force and support them. The people are totally against that and have not reacted in that way.[20]

The problem with a widening US involvement in Central America was the president's political fear that the public would see it as the prelude to another Vietnam. From the very beginning, therefore, the American intervention would have to be primarily covert, relying on local forces to do the fighting. The initial focus had to be on El Salvador and, to a lesser extent, on Guatemala – the majority view inside the administration in 1981 and 1982 was that a rollback of revolution inside Nicaragua itself would be too costly, at least until the revolutionary movements elsewhere in Central America had been stemmed. But a minority spoke for the opposite conclusion: that only through the removal of the Sandinista regime in Nicaragua could the source of "instability" in the region be turned off. To the Reagan radicals, Central America was a gauge of the United States' global position: if it failed there, the Cold War in the Third World was lost.

The war in Nicaragua

US enmity toward their revolution was no surprise for the main leaders of the front that had taken power in Nicaragua in 1979. The Frente Sandinista de Liberacíon Nacional was named after Augusto Sandino, the radical guerrilla leader killed in 1934 by the US-supported National Guard. The Guard in the 1970s, as in the 1930s, was run by members of the Somoza dynasty – a family that had controlled Nicaragua for fifty years and operated it as their personal fiefdom. The main slogan of the Sandinistas – "Down with Somoza" – was at once a call for rebellion by the poor, an appeal for unity among different classes, and an indictment of years of US support for a spectacularly corrupt regime.

The Sandinista Front was one among many political movements in Latin America founded in the wake of the Cuban revolution and directly inspired by its example. The most radical of the Nicaraguan opposition movements, it was opposed by the liberal critics of Somoza and by the country's small Communist Party, both of whom were critical of the Sandinistas insistence on giving priority to armed struggle. Worse for the Sandinistas, they could not agree among themselves about how to carry out a revolution, being split into (at least) three factions, and as a result their various attempts at insurrections failed miserably in the late 1960s and early 1970s. With most of the original leaders dead or in prison, it fell to a group of younger people – mostly recruited from colleges and high schools – to save the movement.[21]

Unlike the more established actions within the Front, the Ortega brothers – Daniel and Humberto – who headed the new Tercerista faction, had no well-established or even very specific plans for how to overthrow Anastasio Somoza, the latest offshoot of the dynasty. As its name implies, the Ortega group's original aim had been to act as a "third alternative" and mediate between the factions, but – as often happens in left-wing organizations – it had ended up a tightly knit faction itself. By 1977 the decimation of the older factions had left the Terceristas by far the strongest contenders for leadership within the Sandinista Front, and their search for a strategy had landed them with a mixture of Leninist and populist positions that attracted support even from some of the older members of the movement.

In January 1978 the Terceristas got lucky. Somoza, whose reactionary incompetence had irritated both the Carter administration and the over-whelming majority of the Nicaraguan bourgeoisie, had one of his main liberal critics, Pedro Joaquín Chamorro, murdered in Managua. The assassination led to street protests and a general strike, which – although unsuccessful – was a sign of rapidly growing opposition to the Somoza regime. The Terceristas set up an opposition front – nominally headed by non-Sandinistas – that helped reduce the tension between the Left and the liberal resistance to the government. In August Sandinista guerrillas headed by Eden Pastora occupied the Nicaraguan parliament in the center of the capital Managua, and only released their hostages after most of the original leaders of their movement were released from prison. The success of the August raid led to uprisings against the government in the slums around Managua, revolts that Somoza tried to put down using his US-supplied airforce against the slum dwellers. By early 1979 it was clear to Washington that Anastasio Somoza was fast becoming a major obstacle to the policies of moderation in Central America, and the White House dropped its military assistance program and prohibited new eco-nomic aid projects in an attempt to force him from power. Venezuela and Panama – both headed by nonsocialist regimes – began supplying the Sandinistas with weapons and training.[22]

Throughout the Nicaraguan revolution the Carter administration was of two minds with regard to the outcome. One the one hand it had come to detest Somoza and wanted him to resign. On the other hand it wanted to avoid a radical socialist regime in Nicaragua, which – potentially – would ally itself with Cuba. By mid-1979, with the FSLN forces advancing on Managua, a member of the administration felt that "there was no point in talking anymore about getting Somoza out because there was no center (i.e. moderates) to replace him, and there was no point shoring him up because he was on a losing wicket."[23] At the NSC, Brzezinski argued for a direct US intervention, citing "major domestic and international implications [in] a Castroite takeover ... [The United States] would be considered as being incapable of dealing with problems in our own backyard." But the president could not make his mind up. With the United States recommending a ceasefire, a government of national reconciliation, and intervention by OAS forces – all to prevent an outright Sandinista victory – Managua fell to the FSLN in mid-July and Somoza fled to Miami. It was the first revolutionary victory in Latin America for more than twenty years, and the speed with which it had happened was a surprise not just to Somoza and the Americans, but also to the revolutionaries themselves.

The FSLN, when it came to power as the dominant part of a coalition government in July 1979, was in political terms a mix of a majority of strongly nativist and anti-US radicals and a smaller number of Marxists, such as the Ortega brothers (Daniel, who became the leading figure in the junta, and Humberto, its Minister of Defense) and Tomás Borge, who became Minister of Interior. Even the latter group, however, believed in a syncretic form of Marxism, where Sandino joined the pantheon alongside Marx and Lenin. All of the leading Sandinistas were internationalists, celebrating the assistance they had received from Cuba and proclaiming their willingness to help revolutionaries in other Central American countries, first and foremost El Salvador and Guatemala. But their main aim in 1979 was the rebuilding of a country where the war and Somoza's terror had left half a million people homeless and the economy in ruins. The Sandinistas' methods of achieving their aims were based on nationalization and land reform, policies that were popular among most Nicaraguans but ones that infuriated their former bourgeois allies and made them turn against the regime.[24]

The Sandinistas' foreign policies were also controversial within Nicaragua. While many Nicaraguans agreed with the new regime's willingness to help revolutionaries in other Central American countries, they were afraid of the effects it would have on Nicaragua, especially as a consequence of US countermeasures. Likewise, most Nicaraguans felt indebted to Cuba for the assistance it had given during the war against Somoza, but – at the same time – thought that the Sandinista leaders were a bit too close to Fidel Castro. Opinion was even more divided with regard to the Soviet Union and Eastern Europe. Having no knowledge of and little interest in "real existing socialism," most ordinary

Map 10   The Nicaraguan revolution and the Contra war.

Nicaraguans simply had no opinion on the issue. But for the bourgeoisie and for some intellectuals – nursed on years of US anti-Soviet propaganda – any relations with the Soviets were unacceptable, even to those who had supported the overthrow of Somoza.

To the Sandinistas, however, a policy of revolutionary internationalism and links with the socialist states was eagerly sought and was not to be deterred by opposition at home. It was part of their mission. As Tomás Borge explained, "this revolution goes beyond our borders ... Our revolution was always internationalist from the moment Sandino fought in La Segovia. With Sandino were internationalists from all over the world ... With Sandino was that great leader of the Salvadorean people, Farabundo Martí."[25] Already in the first weeks after taking over, the Sandinistas intensified their support for the Martí National Liberation Front (FMLN) in El Salvador. They also, publicly, announced their willingness to support other revolutionary movements that were fighting against injustice and oppression. Even Fidel Castro, who had sent advisers to Managua and to whom the Sandinista leaders were particularly close (Daniel Ortega had trained in Cuba), was worried about Nicaragua provoking a US response. But to Ortega – as to Castro twenty years earlier – this was much of what his revolution was about: through support for revolutions elsewhere, his country showed not only its internationalist solidarity with others, but – even more importantly – its independence and its sovereignty *vis-à-vis* the United States.[26]

When the new Reagan administration in August 1981 tried to pressure the Sandinistas into giving up their support for the El Salvadorean revolution in return for a less antagonistic policy from the United States, Daniel Ortega replied that Nicaragua was "interested in seeing the guerrillas in El Salvador and Guatemala triumph ... [It is] our shield – it makes our revolution safer."[27] When the US envoy, Assistant Secretary of State Thomas Enders, ridiculed the idea of Nicaragua standing up to a US invasion, Ortega responded that the Sandinistas had decided "to defend our revolution by force of arms, even if we are crushed, and take the war to the whole of Central America if that is the consequence."[28] But the Sandinista leader added that "we are not suicidal" and that Managua wanted to continue the dialogue with Washington.

The new regime in Managua was more cautious in approaching the Soviets and the East Europeans. Their caution coincided with advice from Castro and from Moscow itself – through meetings held in Cuba in 1979 and 1980 – that the Sandinistas would only provoke a strong US response by establishing too open and extensive relations with the socialist countries. Internally, as we can see from Soviet documents, Moscow's initial view was that the Nicaraguan revolution was an uncertain proposition, in which any Soviet direct assistance could turn out to be lost or counterproductive, or both. Coming at a time when the Soviet appetite for Third World involvements was on the wane, both the International Department and the KGB in 1979–80 recommended a wait-and-see attitude, during which most Soviet aid would come through the Cubans. Even though Castro agreed with a cautious approach – for tactical reasons – he still felt that the Soviets ought to do more in terms of support. The East Germans, with whom Havana was on especially good terms, also in 1980 argued for the need to do more for Nicaragua, and set up its own contacts with the Sandinista leaders.[29]

By mid-1981, with the new Reagan administration increasing the pressure on Nicaragua, the Sandinistas had had enough of Eastern Bloc caution. "The socialist countries, and especially the GDR, the USSR, and Cuba, are the true brothers of Nicaragua," member of the FSLN directorate Carlos Nuñez Téllez told the East Germans in July, wondering about why more assistance was not forthcoming.[30] While Managua had been receiving Soviet-made weapons since the early days of the revolution – mostly from Cuba – Tomás Borge pushed hard for increased military assistance during his visit to Moscow in August 1981. In November Humberto Ortega visited the Kremlin and got the first major military support agreement, including tanks, surface-to-air missiles, and helicopters. After his visit, Ortega also helped set up a complex system of arms deliveries, which included supplies by Algeria (an early supporter of the Nicaraguan revolution), Bulgaria, and Vietnam (which supplied captured US weapons), in addition to direct supplies from the Soviet Union, the GDR, and Cuba. "The kind of support that Cuba could give us was very limited when it came to building up our army, since they didn't manufacture armaments in the quantities that we required," Daniel Ortega explained in a later interview. "So we turned to Algeria and the Soviet Union for support."[31] By 1984, with the US–Nicaraguan conflict at its peak, its allies had supplied Managua with large amounts of heavy military equipment, enough to increase the cost of a US invasion substantially, even though the civilian assistance was far less than what the Sandinistas had been hoping for.[32]

From well before taking over as president, Ronald Reagan and his political supporters had seen the Central American revolutionaries as a direct threat to the United States. Though wary of a direct intervention against the Sandinistas – in spite of his rhetoric, Reagan was very adverse to seeing American losses in Third World conflicts – he was determined to contain the Nicaraguan revolution and prevent the Sandinistas from giving aid to other revolutionaries, first and foremost in El Salvador. "Without actually using Soviet troops, in effect, the Soviets are, you might say, trying to do the same thing in El Salvador that they did in Afghanistan, but by using proxy troops through Cuba and guerrillas," Reagan told CBS newsman Walter Cronkite in a March 1981 interview.[33] By 1984 the president's view of the Sandinistas had hardened into a caricature, in which "the Nicaraguan people are trapped in a totalitarian dungeon, trapped by a military dictatorship that impoverishes them while its rulers live in privileged and protected luxury and openly boast their revolution will spread to Nicaragua's neighbors as well. It's a dictatorship made all the more insulting, all the more dangerous by the unwanted presence of thousands of Cuban, Soviet, and radical Arab helpers."[34]

For many of the right-wing radicals in the Reagan administration, US Latin American policy became the preferred domestic battleground for imposing a new and more offensive approach to the Cold War, replacing what they saw as the moral emptiness of Kissinger and the moral confusion of Carter. The radicals, as Robert Kagan, then with the State Department, puts it, sought to win "the domestic battle for the American soul as well as the strategic battle against the Soviet Union" by getting support for fighting the war against Communism in Latin America. Jeane J. Kirkpatrick, who, as UN ambassador, was one of the leading neoconservative voices in the administration, lambasted Carter for not having understood US interests:

Because it failed to take account of basic characteristics of Latin American political systems, the Carter administration underestimated the fragility of order in these societies and overestimated the ease with which authority, once undermined, can be restored. Because it regarded revolutionaries as beneficient agents of change, it mistook their goals and motives and could not grasp the problem of governments which become the object of revolutionary violence.[35]

The breakthrough for a more offensive strategy against revolutionary regimes was the 1983 US invasion of the small Caribbean republic of Grenada, under left-wing control since March 1979. As the revolutionary leadership on the island self-destructed in an orgy of factional infighting in early October 1983, radicals within the Reagan administration saw a golden opportunity finally to score a victory in the Third World. On 25 October US troops invaded and within days secured control of Grenada's 100,000 inhabitants. While not even the most dedicated Cold Warrior would see the island as a major prize in the global contest, the success of the intervention was a boost for the radicals. "Grenada showed that it could be done," one of them said – it "proved that boldness and determination could defeat the Communists."[36] Grenada therefore contributed to the development of a counterrevolutionary strategy that was global in reach.

The secret war that the Reagan administration launched against Nicaragua was already under way in 1981. At first, the CIA supported and equipped anti-Sandinista forces, mostly from Somoza's former National Guard, who were trained by Argentinian officers in Honduras. Gradually, and against stiff opposition in the US Congress, the White House extended the war, through legal and illegal means, it was later found out, to arming, training, supplying, and directing a counterrevolutionary army of more than 15,000 men, the so-called Contras. With forces operating both inside Nicaragua and along its borders, this was the biggest CIA operation in Latin America since the Bay of Pigs in 1961, and was a cause that took on Crusade-like qualities for some Reaganites. "We do not seek a military defeat for our friends," declared Under-Secretary of Defense Fred Iklé, "We do not seek a military stalemate. We seek victory for the forces of democracy."[37] The administration did its best to convince the Sandinistas and its backers that it was serious: in 1984 the CIA even mined the main Nicaraguan harbors in order to prevent supplies reaching the government. By the mid-1980s, in spite of only limited military success, the Contra war was destroying domestic confidence in the Sandinista regime.

Given the military and economic power that was deployed against them, the main reason why the Sandinistas and their guerrilla allies in El Salvador held out as long as they did was the power of their political programs. Those who joined the revolutionary movements fought for their land and their dignity against outside oppressors, be they former landlords or interventionist armies. In her study of *campesino* participation in the revolution in El Salvador, the political scientist Elisabeth Wood quotes one such activist:

Before the war, we were despised by the rich. We were seen as animals, working all day and still without even enough to put the kids through school. This is the origin of the war: there was no alternative. The only alternative was the madness of desperation.[38]

A mid-level FMLN commander explained how that desperation fitted into the mobilization practices of the guerrillas:

We found a receptive response, and quite a lot of participation. One of the fundamental reasons was the unjust distrubution of land ... These resentments couldn't be expressed until guerrilla units appeared, making proposals for change. So a call to revolution was *heard*. We insisted that the *tarea* [the area of the coffee estate assigned to a worker to weed and prune] be decreased ... [As a result] it would have been impossible to arrest the wave of support for us.[39]

The savagery of the war on the tiny territory of El Salvador was made worse by the US refusal to push the right-wing government it supported toward negotiations. "We can no more negotiate an acceptable political solution with these people than the social democrats in revolutionary Russia could have talked Lenin into giving up totalitarian Bolshevism," Fred Iklé declared. "The guerrillas," Reagan found,

are not a group of peasants who just have taken their muskets in hand and wanted to stage a revolution because the government was tyrannical. They are trained military personnel, armed by way of the Soviet Union and Cuba, through Nicaragua, which has become a Communist base in this country [*sic*], by its own admission. One of the leaders of the guerrilla fighters the other day publicly stated, yes, they were a friend of the Soviet Union; yes, they intended to bring Communism to the Western hemisphere.[40]

In Nicaragua, the war limited the Sandinistas' political room for maneuver and made the leaders more doctrinaire and intolerant against anything that did not fit their social schemes. Among the minority Miskito population on the east coast, resistance against the new government grew, mostly as a result of intrusive and ill-considered plans for social and economic improvements. Among the majority of the population, war-weariness grew, especially after the mid-1980s. The Sandinistas reacted badly against all forms of skepticism toward their revolution. Tomás Borge, the authoritarian minister of the interior who had suffered more than most for his beliefs in the prerevolutionary era, already in 1982 referred to Communist experiences elsewhere in explaining the divisions the revolution would cause:

Experience tells us that on one hand, a certain number of elements belonging to these social groups cannot resign themselves to the new reality, and that even within the revolution, there are those who believe that ultimately the dreams of the workers and peasants would end in a nightmare and the dreams of the bosses as a class would end in paradise ... [The Sandinista front] had the wisdom and the courage to find the essence of the antagonistic contradictions between Nicaragua and US imperialism. It knew, and it will know, the role of the revolutionary classes in the process of the political and economic transformations of Nicaragua ... That is why the Sandinista front is the vanguard of our people; that is why the Sandinista front is the irreplaceable vanguard of the unity of the nation, a unity that must be based on the interests of the workers and on national patriotism.[41]

The effects of the Central American war for the region were dreadful. In Nicaragua it left 30,000 dead (as historian William LeoGrande points out, relative to the population this was more than the United States lost in the Civil War, the two world wars, and the Korea and Vietnam wars *combined*). The country had over 100,000 refugees and an economy with inflation out of control and massive unemployment. In tiny El Salvador the effects were even worse; 70,000 dead, death squads roaming the countryside, villages destroyed, lives shattered. While the brutality of the El Salvadorean civil war surpassed anything seen in the recent history of Latin America, US efforts at imposing change – with assistance costing around 1 billion dollars in military aid and three times as much in economic aid – had little effect: in 1990 more than 90 percent of El Salvadoreans still lived in poverty.[42]

Within the United States the wars also had serious effects, although not in terms of human lives. The Reagan administration's attempts at defying Congress in supplying funding to the Contras led to the Iran–Contra Affair, which hurt the neoconservative agenda with the public and inside the White House. The fact that Reagan's people had sold weapons to the Iranian Islamist regime (in the hope that they would put pressure on Lebanese Islamists to release American hostages) and used the proceeds of that transaction to fund the counterrevolutionary forces in Nicaragua was a bit too much even for Reagan's supporters to swallow. Together with the antiwar movement and Congressional resistance against the war, the Iran–Contra Affair contributed to a distinct reduction in the administration's appetite for foreign interventions toward the end of its final term in office. Its worldview, though, stayed intact: the Cold War was a conflict between good and evil, in which the United States was on the side of the angels.

The war in Afghanistan

For the Soviet Union, the invasion of Afghanistan had proven politically problematic and militarily messy from the very beginning. Even with the purges of the Amin-wing of the Khalq faction, the PDPA was far from a united party – on the contrary, senior Soviet Communist Party advisers who had moved in with the Red Army witnessed with apprehension how the increased potential for Soviet support invigorated the Afghan jockeying for position within the government. Already by early February 1980 a group of visiting Soviet dignitaries had to "speak sternly to" PDPA General Secretary Babrak Karmal in order to force him to get to grips with factionalism through finding some kind of balance in the leadership between the different "tendencies."[43] Also, Soviet advisers were working overtime at finding ways to "broaden" the regime by including non-Communist members in the government, but found very few candidates whom Karmal could accept. Several of those proposed by the Soviets had already fled Kabul for Mujahedin bases in Pakistan or gone into exile elsewhere. As their work proved more difficult than first assumed, the number of Soviet civilian advisers kept growing, numbering at least 8,000 by mid-1980.

In the months following the invasion, Afghan opposition to the PDPA regime inside Afghanistan was still dominated by supporters of the deposed king, Zahir Shah, and by ethnic or clan-based groups. But this picture soon changed. For the Islamist organizations, the Soviet invasion proved a golden opportunity to gain hegemony within the opposition by making use of their military potential – largely supplied by Pakistan – and by popular appeals for an Islamic and national *jihad* against the invaders. The hundreds of thousands of refugees who started crossing the border into Pakistan's Northwest Frontier and Baluchistan provinces were required to register with one of the seven exile groups headquartered in Peshawar in order to get relief supplies. By the summer of 1980 the Pakistan-based Islamist parties began to grow spectacularly, fueled by the recruitment of angry and desperate young men in the refugee camps and by supplies coming in from Pakistan, conservative Arab regimes, and from the United States.[44]

In 1981 and 1982 a strange pattern emerged within the Afghan opposition. While local groups – fueled more by the defense of their territory than by the hope of an Islamic revolution – carried out most of the fighting against the PDPA and the Soviets inside Afghanistan, these fighters gradually had to enter into some kind of subservient relationship with one of the Peshawar-based parties in order to get the supplies they needed. As a result, the supporters of Zahir Shah were increasingly marginalized, as were other traditionalist parties, such as the group headed by the prominent cleric Muhammad Nabi Muhammadi. Yet, on the other hand the relationship *between* the Islamist Mujahedin groups in exile was far from easy, with most of them having their background in some form of split or schism within the two main Pakistani-sponsored Afghan Islamist parties of the mid-1970s – Gulbuddin Hekmatyar's extremist Hezb-i-Islami (Islamic Party) and Burhanuddin Rabbani's Jamiat-i-Islami (Islamic Society). It took much pressure from General Zia ul-Haq, the Pakistani dictator, and the head of Saudi intelligence, Prince Turki al-Faisal, to force them into an uneasy cohabitation, which also included, at least in principle, Nabi's group and other traditionalists. The alliance relationship between the seven main parties was not formalized until 1984, and was even then as conflictual as it was cooperative.[45]

The "limited military contingent" that the Soviet Union sent in December 1979 had originally been intended primarily as back-up troops to the special forces that got rid of Amin and installed Babrak Karmal as Afghan leader. By early February 1980, however, Moscow – under pressure from Kabul – gave the Red Army units two main military objectives in addition to securing a change in the PDPA leadership. The first was to cut off foreign supplies to the Mujahedin and infiltrations from abroad during the interval in which Kabul's policies were "rectified." The second was to cooperate with the Afghan forces in securing the perimeters of main cities, roads, airports, and military training areas. Both objectives turned out to be difficult to reach for the Soviet military, even after reinforcements were sent in the two first months of 1980, bringing in the main part of the 40th Army – two motorized rifle divisions, an airborne division, an air assault brigade, and two separate motorized rifle regiments; 52,000 men in all.[46]

The two main military problems that the Soviets encountered were the rapid disintegration of the Afghan Army after the invasion and the readiness of villagers across Afghanistan to give food, shelter, and information to the Mujahedin. While Hafizullah Amin had been a ruthless but competent commander-in-chief, Babrak Karmal had no interest in and little understanding of military affairs. In the crucial first weeks after the Soviets arrived, almost nothing was done to shore up support among the lower ranks of the army, and, as a result, defections were rife and morale among those who remained was low. "Therefore," the official Russian history of the war concludes, "Soviet forces bore the brunt of the combat with the detachments of the armed enemy opposition."[47] Still, the badly equipped and poorly organized resistance could not have made a serious impact in the first years of the war if it had not been for the willingness of Afghan tribal society to support it. This was especially important for the main Islamist parties, which had few, if any, roots in the Afghan countryside. To many Afghans what mattered after December 1979 was that the explanation for what was wrong with the PDPA government had arrived: the regime was a tool of infidel foreign invaders. And the only way of destroying the regime was by killing as many Soviets as possible.

Seen in the light of the massive resistance within Afghan society to the Soviet presence, Moscow's attempts at emphasizing civilian assistance to Afghanistan may seem misplaced. But the documents we now have on the war show such plans for the betterment of the Afghans – and thereby for the strengthening of the Afghan regime – to have been of major importance to the Soviet mission. Of the roughly $3 billion that was transferred in non-military aid between 1980 and 1989, more than 30 percent was supposed to go to different forms of education, to create a new elite that supported the party and who could replace the many educated Afghans who had been killed or fled since the Saur revolution. Compulsory Russian replaced English in secondary schools, Soviet textbooks were used, and the teaching of Marxism constituted about 25 percent of the curriculum. With Soviet support, the regime introduced a massive literacy program and set up mass organizations at all levels, according to the East European model. Karmal particularly emphasized the participation of women in society as one of the government's aims. But most of these plans were stymied by a lack of trained personnel and by the opposition's deliberate targeting of school-teachers and educated women for intimidation or assassination.[48]

From the very beginning of the Afghan operation, the Soviet leadership was in doubt both with regard to its strategy and with its overall aims. Many Politburo members believed that what the general secretary had sanctioned in December 1979 was a quick intervention to facilitate a change in the regime. The troops were not intended to take part in direct combat against the Afghan opposition. On the contrary, even Brezhnev himself thought as late as early February that troop withdrawals could start in spring 1980 and be completed by late autumn. The arguments Defense Minister Dmitri Ustinov and the head of the KGB, Iurii Andropov, used to get sanction for a deeper Soviet involvement were the weakness of the Afghan regime and the opposition's deliberate targeting of Soviets, including civilians. The revolt in Kandahar over New Year, when more than fifty Soviet soldiers and civilians were killed – the KGB did not miss the opportunity to send the general secretary the gruesome details of how they died – were used as a reason to expand operations. While the pro-interventionists had to be more careful with the argument concerning Afghan weakness, it could still be used in terms of the Soviet presence in effect being a slightly expanded holding operation, until the Afghan Communists had reorganized and could fend for themselves.[49]

Given these uncertainties, it is understandable that Moscow from 1980 onwards tried to find an international solution to the presence of its troops in Afghanistan. Already in March 1980 the Politburo Afghanistan Commission suggested a Soviet withdrawal in return for a bilateral Afghan-Pakistani noninterference agreement guaranteed by the USSR and the United States. The problem was – as many Soviet policy advisers who privately were skeptical to the invasion realized – that both Moscow and Kabul clung to the definition of *all* antiregime activity inside Afghanistan as being foreign-inspired. In other words, for such a solution to work, it would not only require Pakistan to stop supplying the Mujahedin – something they were clearly unwilling to do – but also an end to guerrilla activity inside Afghanistan, something neither Pakistan nor anyone else could deliver, even if they had wanted to. As could be expected, the Soviet proposals had absolutely no political impact, even though they ultimately helped pave the way for UN-sponsored proximity talks to begin in Geneva in 1982. In the Cold War climate of the early 1980s, Afghanistan had become a signal issue: to many governments around the world the message it reflected was Soviet expansionism and the willingness of others to resist.

For Pakistan's military leader, General Zia ul-Haq, the Soviet invasion implied both opportunity and threat, though the former far outweighed the latter. Zia believed from very early on that the intervention meant a chance to let the Islamist movements that he sponsored become the internationally supported Afghan opposition. It also meant that Pakistan, in the eyes of the United States and Britain, could shed the stigma it obtained with Zia's coup, the execution of his civilian predecessor Zulfikar Ali Bhutto, and the burning of the US embassy in Islamabad by local Islamists in 1979. In other words, Zia could have it both ways: he could fulfill his dream of directing a jihad *and* receive Western support while doing so. Zia's plans were greatly helped by Third World condemnation of the Soviet invasion. The Islamic Conference denounced the invasion, as did the Non-Aligned Movement during its meeting of foreign ministers in New Delhi in February 1981, at which a Pakistani-sponsored resolution was passed over a much milder Indian version. Within the Muslim world, Iran and even Libya – not generally considered friendly to Zia's regime – were willing to cooperate with him in support of the Afghan Mujahedin.[50]

Within Pakistan, Zia left the organization of the support for the Afghan Islamists, and for the more than 1.5 million refugees who lived in camps on the Pakistani side of the border, to the head of the military Inter-Services Intelligence (ISI), General Akhtar Abdur Rahman. General Akhtar, an old classmate of Zia's, graduating with him in the last class of the British India Military Academy before independence, was known for his hatred of India and for his dedication to the concept of jihad. The system of supplies and political control that General Akhtar built put his own organization at the center, with Saudi Arabia and the United States as the main funders, and Egypt and China as the main deliverers of Soviet-type weapons. Akhtar also organized training camps for the Mujahedin, giving pride of place to recruits from Hekmatyar's Hezb-i-Islami. The instructors in these camps were Pakistanis, though American and British personnel were in place to train Pakistani officers in the use of the newly acquired weapons. From 1984 onwards the CIA helped run training centers for Afghan and foreign Mujahedin in Egypt and probably also in at least one of the Gulf states. Reportedly, General Akhtar visited the latter, but did not generally approve of these camps, since they took recruitment and training away from his immediate supervision.[51]

Up until 1983 the United States kept within the framework of aid to the Mujahedin established by the Carter administration. This meant that Washington paid for small amounts of weapons and other supplies that came to the Afghan resistance through third countries. The American aid – distributed through Pakistani agencies – was considerably less in total during the first two years of the conflict than that paid for by Saudi Arabia and other Arab countries. Both the State Department and the CIA still held relations with Pakistan to be too cool to envisage a major American effort through that country. There was also considerable resistance in the bureaucracy, especially at State, against confronting the Soviets too directly, especially since nobody seemed able to come up with a concrete plan of how any more extensive American involvement would figure out. But most important of all was the firm belief in the CIA and in intelligence organizations across the Western world that the Mujahedin could not, over time, inflict serious casualties on the Soviets. Investing in the Afghan resistance would therefore be a losing proposition. It would be far better to spend money and effort in reestablishing a relationship with Pakistan and thereby shore up the struggle against further Soviet encroachments in the region.[52]

Getting to know the general and what the administration called his "largely benign authoritarian regime" took a lot of money and a lot of effort.[53] In 1981 the United States provided Islamabad with a six-year $3.2 billion economic and military assistance program, including the delivery of forty F-16 jet fighters.[54] A US National Security Intelligence Estimate passed in November 1982 found, with a certain understatement, that "[the] US–Pakistani deal on economic aid and weapons' sales undoubtedly has strengthened the Pakistani international position and restored some of its self-confidence." During his visit to Washington the following month, General Zia pushed for more, including a tacit US acceptance of Pakistan's nuclear weapons program. Even though both Reagan and Shultz warned against the development of nuclear weapons, the secretary noted to the president that they "must also recognize that how we handle the nuclear issue can have a profound effect on our ability to continue to cooperate with Pakistan in supporting the Afghan freedom fighters."[55] In pursuit of further American aid, Zia also not too subtly stressed his "strong attachment to China," and hinted that the Chinese "remain faithful to their policies and agreements."[56]

The United States and the jihad

By 1983 a number of circumstances began coming together to form a more activist American approach to Afghanistan. Not only were relations with Pakistan improving, but a political alliance began to be formed at home on the Afghanistan issue, between administration radicals and activist members of Congress, both pushing for further US involvement in arming and supplying the guerrillas. Some of the key advisers at Defense – Iklé, Perle, and Perle's deputy Elie Krakowski – and two of the assistant secretaries of state – Elliot Abrams and Paul Wolfowitz – used the pressure for further aid coming from, among others, senators Paul Tsongas (D-Mass.) and Gordon Humphrey (R-N.H.) and congressmen Charles Wilson (D-Tex.) and Don Ritter (R-Pa.) to argue for more advanced weapons and further US training to be given to the "Afghan freedom fighters," in other words the Mujahedin.[57] Even US diplomats in Islamabad, who, together with the Assistant Secretary for Near Eastern Affairs Nicholas Veliotes, had been skeptical to increased US aid, now began to change their views. "It would be appropriate at this time to review our policies on Afghanistan," the ambassador wrote to Shultz in June 1983.

There is a good chance that our current set of policies will not take us where we want to go – bringing about the complete withdrawal of Soviet troops ... The

Soviets can afford to take casualties at the present rate interminably ... We have yet to demonstrate that we can increase the costs they have to pay ... The mujahideen may have fought the Soviets to a stalemate in Afghanistan, but over the long run the decisive factor will be [the] Soviets' staying power and the limited mujahideen resources.[58]

Both the declining Soviet threat to Pakistan and the interventionist enthusiasm created by the Grenada operation contributed to the victory of the radicals in the policy debate on Afghanistan in the fall of 1983. Still, the main reasons for the new approach were the fighting capability of the Mujahedin and the development – by White House and Pentagon staffers and by the CIA – of a plan for how to increase funding, arms shipments, and recruitment for the guerrillas. By 1983, three years after the war started, it was clear that the Mujahedin had not only survived, but in some areas was gaining ground on the Soviets and their allies. As the Reagan administration radicals were fond of pointing out, Afghanistan was not Hungary or Czechoslovakia; the Soviets could not achieve a political settlement after the invasion and military resistance would continue. A series of daring raids near Kabul in 1983, organized by the non-Islamist resistance leader Abdul Haq, got wide coverage and strengthened the sense that the Soviets were in trouble.[59]

It was the intervention of Director of Central Intelligence William Casey that tipped the balance in Washington. Casey had always been convinced of the need to "make the Soviets bleed" in Afghanistan. But in late 1983 he began believing that the Soviets could not only be contained but actually defeated in Afghanistan. To Casey – an archetypal Cold Warrior – such a victory would have momentous consequences. In early 1984 he told one of his assistants that "the Soviet Union is tremendously overextended and they're vulnerable. If America challenges the Soviets at every turn and ultimately defeats them in one place, that will shatter the mythology [of Communism as the future], and it will start to unravel."[60] Casey's first candidate for such a place was Nicaragua, but by 1983–84 Afghanistan stood out as maybe a better opportunity, given the domestic opposition to the US Central American interventions and the doubtful fighting capabilities of the Contras. "Here is the beauty of the Afghan operation," Casey told his colleagues. "Usually it looks like the big bad Americans are beating up on the natives. Afghanistan is just the reverse. The Russians are beating up on the little guys. We don't make it our war. The Mujahedin have all the motivation they need. All we have to do is give them help, only more of it."[61] Some time in January 1984 the CIA's Afghan Task Force, set up in late 1982, was charged with developing a new and more aggressive American strategy, including increased arms supplies, training, and more money for the Afghan resistance.[62]

For the first two years of the invigorated US assistance program, most of the arms that the Mujahedin received came from the so-called SOVMAT project, which relied on Soviet equipment captured elsewhere in the world and on supplies through former Soviet allies, especially Egypt. When, by early 1985, these forms of supplies began to run low, the CIA began buying weapons through Third World straw companies directly from Eastern Bloc countries (especially Bulgaria). In late 1985 the organization helped to set up a complete factory in Egypt designed to produce Soviet weapons for the Mujahedin. In 1984 a special training program had been organized for Pakistani ISI personnel and Afghan Mujahedin in the United States, run by the CIA at two US Army special training camps in Virginia, Camp Peary and Fort Pickett. The CIA also began channeling funds to Islamic charitable organizations that provided assistance to the Mujahedin. At least two of these organizations also recruited Muslim volunteers – mostly from North Africa – to fight in Afghanistan.[63]

By 1985 a very complex web of foreign support for the Mujahedin was in place, in which the United States cooperated closely with conservative Arab governments and voluntary organizations to jointly fund and operate key initiatives. Rapidly increasing amounts of money were available – not only were there major Arab donations, but Congress, pushed by the indomitable Charles Wilson (who, according to Bob Woodward, "wheeled the whole system") began appropriating extra money for the jihad.[64] By late 1985 Iran–Contra money was also earmarked for Afghanistan, although the overflow of Afghan funding by then made Casey want to divert some of these funds to "freedom fighters" in Cambodia and Ethiopia.[65] The CIA's favored bank for these operations was the Bank of Credit and Commerce International (BCCI), headed by the Pakistani Aga Hassan Abedi and with a number of prominent Saudis on the board.[66] Sometimes the contributions that came in could fill more than one purpose – money given by the Sultan of Brunei, for instance, was used both for Nicaragua, Cambodia, and Afghanistan.

In spite of the substantial increase in support for Afghanistan in 1984–85, some of the radicals in the administration and in Congress kept arguing that without high-tech Western weapons the Mujahedin would always be militarily inferior to the Soviets and their Afghan allies. As early as 1984 some officials, such as Clair George at the CIA, were arguing in favor of supplying the resistance with lightweight ground-to-air Stinger missiles, which – although untested in combat – were believed to give the Mujahedin a chance to hit back more effectively when attacked from the air.[67] The majority within the administration opposed sending the Stingers, mostly out of fear of the Soviet reaction and of what would happen if the advanced missiles fell into the "wrong hands." The Joint Chiefs of Staff opposed the move vigorously, as did most of Casey's advisers at the CIA. What tipped the balance was probably that George Shultz surprisingly sided with the radicals and argued in favor of the Stingers. Shultz was swayed primarily by reports of a Soviet stepping-up of the war in 1985, after Gorbachev came to office.[68] Reagan decided in April 1986 to send Stingers both to the Mujahedin and to the Angolan UNITA – in Africa they were used already that month against Cuban aircraft; in Afghanistan they were first used on 26 September, when, in one raid, three out of four Soviet helicopters approaching Jalalabad Airport where shot down.

For Pakistan and the ISI the increase in aid to the Mujahedin was a godsend. Since the great majority of the aid was distributed by Islamabad, it meant that Zia could claim credit for it and thereby form the political shape of the Afghan opposition almost at will. As General Youssaf, the head of the ISI Afghan bureau put it, "the CIA would arrange and pay for shipment to Karachi, notifying us of arrival dates. Once the vessel docked the ISI took over storage and distribution."[69] The ISI made sure that it was the Islamist movements – and especially Hekmatyar's Hezb – that received most of the aid, especially of the new weapons.[70] By 1986 Zia had already begun believing that the Soviets would have to withdraw sooner rather than later, and that the battle for control of post-Communist Afghanistan was already on. He was determined to keep the United States out of that equation as far as possible. Meanwhile Hekmatyar and other extreme Islamists began a campaign of terror both inside Afghanistan and in the camps against the more moderate groups of Mujahedin. The leaders of Hezb-i-Islami and other radicals – such as Abdul Sayaaf's Ittehad-i-Islami – also began telling their followers that they should condemn *both* Great Satans, America and Russia.[71] "We do not believe what the Americans believe," Hekmatyar told his visitors, even as the CIA stepped up its work to supply his movement with weapons and materiel.[72]

For the Soviet Union, Afghanistan proved very difficult to hold. From 1981 onwards the war turned into a bloody stalemate, in which more than 1 million Afghans died and at least 25,000 Soviets. In spite of well-planned efforts, the Red Army simply could not control the areas that were within their operational zones – they advanced into rebel strong-holds, kept them occupied for weeks or months, and then had to with-draw as the Mujahedin concentrated its forces or, more often, because its opponents attacked elsewhere. By 1985, for instance, the Soviets had already launched no less than nine offensives against Ahmad Shah Masud's bases in the Pansjir Valley, all without notable successes. The

Red Army was poorly equipped for such a limited and protracted war. Its operations were hampered by inadequate intelligence and by the need to defend its activities within a Marxist-Leninist framework. The 90,000 to 120,000 troops that the Soviet contingent comprised by the mid-1980s were often severely demoralized by the time they were rotated back home, bearing witness both to the inability of the army to succeed in Afghanistan and to the brutal way in which it treated its own recruits.[73]

The PDPA never reestablished itself as a political force in Afghanistan after the Soviet invasion. Even with a much better leader than the insecure and dreary Babrak Karmal, it would have taken a miracle to resurrect Afghan Communism – not, as is often believed, primarily because of a "nationalist" reaction within the party against the Soviet intervention, but because the last round of factional infighting simply had done away with most party members' belief in the building of a Communist Party as a viable project. There certainly remained dedicated Communists, but they tended to define themselves as helping the Soviets hold the fort against the onslaught of "reactionary" Islam rather than carrying out revolutionary changes. By 1985 a large number of former Communists – whether they remained within the PDPA or without – had taken refuge in ethnic identities that they hoped would form the framework for politics in a post-Soviet Afghanistan.

Aid, trade, and ideology

To many within the Reagan Administration, in the US neoconservative movement, and on the American Right in general, Third World left-wing radicalism was part of a global threat to the United States. It existed, however, mostly because previous US administrations had failed to confront it and stand up for American values. The Reagan supporters were tired of having their country denounced, especially at the UN, by what they saw as third-rate, bankrupt dictatorships, who cozied up to the Soviets and who had led their own populations into poverty and slavery. Why, many Americans asked themselves, should their country continue to give development aid to regimes that were anti-American; why should American taxpayers fund UN organizations whose very purpose – as they saw it – was to undermine US positions in the world? It was time, the American Right argued, to strike back against Third World regimes that opposed America's mission.

Confronting the Third World was part of the greater project to restore American power that the New Right movement had embarked on during the 1970s. It reflected a view of the United States as being under siege by cynical and self-serving Europeans, by brash and profiteering Japanese, and by irresponsible and corrupt Third World leaders. Instead of being accomplices in their moral degradation, the American neoconservatives thought, the United States needed to stand tall when condemning their behavior and holding itself up as the true model for world development. Then, and only then, could America gain real allies in its confrontation with the Soviet Union – "the empire of evil," in Reagan's terms – and have the necessary moral strength to prevail. For the Reaganites, the Cold War was an apocalyptic struggle that had to be won. According to the president, "we live today in a time of climactic struggle for the human spirit, a time that will tell whether the great civilized ideas of individual liberty, representative government, and the rule of law under God will perish or endure."[74]

The new US ambassador to the UN, Jeane J. Kirkpatrick, spoke for the neoconservative wing in the Reagan coalition with her distinct admonition to separate between "authoritarian" regimes – such as Pinochet's Chile – and "totalitarian" regimes – such as the Soviet Union, Cuba, and Hitler's Germany. The former could be reformed without war and intervention. The latter could not. Modernization theory had failed to separate the two.

Although there is no instance of a revolutionary "socialist" or Communist society being democratized, right-wing autocracies do sometimes evolve into democracies – given time, propitious economic, social, and political circumstances, talented leaders, and a strong indigenous demand for representative government ... The conceivable contexts [for US-sponsored change] turn out to be mainly those in which non-Communist autocracies are under pressure from revolutionary guerrillas. Since Moscow is the aggressive, expansionist power today, it is more often than not insurgents, encouraged and armed by the Soviet Union, who challenge the status quo. The American commitment to "change" in the abstract ends up by aligning us tacitly with Soviet clients and irresponsible extremists like the Ayatollah Khomeini or, in the end, Yasir Arafat.[75]

Reagan, chiding his predecessor for having "ceaselessly scolded authoritarian governments of countries that are friendly and ignored authoritarian and totalitarian countries that are not," was determined to speak out against what he saw as repressive left-wing regimes in the Third World. In terms of foreign assistance, he charged the Carter administration with having "operated under the assumption that the United States must prove and reprove and prove again its goodness to the world. Proving that we are civilized in a world that is often uncivilized – and unapologetically so – is hardly necessary," the new president found.[76] Reagan favored setting clear political conditions for all US foreign assistance, including that which went through multilateral organizations such as the UN institutions, the World Bank, or the International Monetary

Fund (IMF). From the outset the Reagan administration was much more intent than any previous US government had been in using economic warfare against its enemies through hitting at their trade, currency, and credit. "Make them scream," was a much heard slogan in the corridors of power, especially during Reagan's first period, when the administration's ideological militancy was at its peak.

Distrustful of the United Nations, the Reaganites turned their attention to the Bretton Woods institutions, the World Bank and the IMF, as instruments for US foreign economic policy. The problem with these institutions, however, was that in the past they had operated more or less according to Keynesian models of economics, and even if there had been a slow turn toward more conservatism in the late 1970s, this was not enough for the Reagan militants. Their aim was a complete reorientation of both institutions toward monetarism and market ideology, while – as far as possible – using their credit resources to serve US security objectives. Their slogans were *conditionality* – meaning a domestic and international change toward market solutions as a precondition for assistance – and *adjustment* – meaning an end to government quotas, subsidies, and very often social spending in the recipient countries under the guidance of IMF experts. The success the United States had in remolding both the World Bank and the IMF in two short years, between 1981 and 1983, testifies to its continued economic power in the early 1980s – something that was very different from what the neoconservatives had been claiming before the 1980 election, when they had seen a precipitous US economic decline. By 1983 the IMF managing director could exclaim in amazement that "adjustment is now virtually universal ... Never before has there been such an extensive yet convergent adjustment effort."[77]

The success of the United States within the Bretton Woods institutions, and even more its success in imposing the new economic standards worldwide, would not have been possible if it had not been for the global recession of 1981–82 and its effects. Coming at the end of the economic slow-down of the 1970s, the recession meant that most governments in the capitalist world were grasping for new solutions to their problems. The heavily ideological approach of the Reagan administration and the Thatcher government in Britain held out a hope for radical reform, which many leaders believed both their domestic economies and the world economy needed. At the same time, the recession contributed to – and in some cases probably caused – a sharp decline in the prices of raw materials that most Third World countries depended on for their exports, pulling the rug from under whatever domestic development plans they might have and leaving them at the mercy of international credit institutions.

The effects of the drop in raw material prices on Third World politics and international alliances in the 1980s were brutal and decisive. In the period 1980–82 alone prices fell on average by 40 percent. For a country like Tanzania, this meant that in order, to buy a truck – to use the sociologist Robert E. Wood's example – in 1981 the country had to "produce four times as much cotton, three times as much coffee, three times as many cashews, or ten times as much tobacco as five years earlier."[78] The poorest countries or those that were trying to carry out a comprehensive social transformation (and therefore needed a stable foreign income to sustain it) were the worst hit by the price drops. Together with indebtedness and, in some cases, mismanagement and corruption, the worsening terms of trade ended growth in the Third World during the 1980s, making per capita GDP decline by 4.5 percent in Latin America and 8.3 percent in Africa.

While both external and internal conditions for production declined, many Third World regimes were hit by the foreign debt that they, as we have seen, had taken on during the previous decade. Quite a few countries would have been hard pressed to repay their wildly exaggerated loans even if the overall conditions had remained as they were when the debts were first incurred. With Reagan's military build-up underway and US budget deficits soaring, interest rates increased dramatically in the early 1980s – from a negative interest, adjusted for inflation, of an average 7 percent in 1980 to a positive interest of nearly 22 percent at the end of 1982. There was no way Third World countries could pay back according to schedule, and some – especially those that had large sums due for repayment – were technically bankrupt. The Mexican default on its payments in August 1982 sent a shudder through the whole global economic system. The conditions set for the IMF to bail the Mexicans out accorded strictly with overall US purposes and sent a signal to all of the Third World that their economic room for maneuver was getting increasingly restricted.

While implementing the so-called Washington Consensus – the common purpose of the US government and the international financial institutions to force market-oriented change in the Third World – the Reagan administration itself was not exactly a pattern of fiscal responsibility and free-trade thinking. Not only did it, during its first term, implement measures against what it saw as unfair competition in US domestic markets that reeked conspicuously of protectionism, it also worked up the greatest government budget deficit in US history. In reality, the US government made the international debt crisis worse by sucking up most available credit for its own rearmament programs, but it also worked hard to keep the dollar high compared with other currencies, thereby making debt repayment – which mostly had to be made in US dollars – even more difficult for Third World countries. At the same time it took no political initiatives to deal with the debt crisis, making sure that Third World debts increased further in the 1980s. As a key survey of the international economy since 1945 notes, Reagan's policies were not only "predetermined and ideological," but "aggressively selfish."[79]

The model of development that the Washington Consensus prescribed to Third World countries – and which its emissaries forced the implementation of with near religious zeal – was considerably less flexible than the policies the United States allowed itself. In addition to budget austerity and devaluation, it consisted of price and trade liberalization, privatization, and – in some cases – the wholesale abolishment of public services. The IMF's star pupils – regimes such as Morocco, Côte d'Ivoire, Venezuela, and the Philippines – may have gone through a period of much needed economic readjustment, but at a terrible price in social terms: all of these countries saw a massive increase in poverty, which had or are now having disastrous effects on their political stability or even national cohesion. In a country such as Mali, one of the poorest African countries and among the first to implement IMF-imposed structural reform as a condition for further loans, the infant mortality rate – which had declined with more than 20 percent since independence – increased by more than 25 percent between 1980 and 1985. Much like the socialist experiments in Ethiopia at the same time (see chapter 7 above), the government's policy did not create hunger and malnutrition, but made the effects of these conditions much more difficult for the population to deal with.[80]

But it was not just their own economic inefficiency and pressure from the world financial institutions that made most Third World countries begin reorienting themselves toward a market economy in the early 1980s. The spectacular economic rise of the capitalist countries in East Asia and – especially – China's rapid and successful realignment with world markets helped undermine the faith in socialist solutions not just in the rest of Asia, but also in all of the Third World. With over 7 percent average annual growth for all nonsocialist economies in the region and an astonishing 9 percent annual growth for China, the economic results had to be taken notice of elsewhere. By 1984 many Third World leaders who only a few years earlier had expressed their interest in learning from Eastern Europe and Cuba – such as Jerry Rawlings in Ghana, Moussa Traoré in Mali, and Denis Sassou-Nguesso in the People's Republic of Congo – were claiming to study the East Asian miracle. What these Third World leaders ended up with was more often than not IMF-imposed solutions for their economies after they had decided to give up on socialism and economic planning in return for loans, but their pilgrimages to

East Asia at least made them feel good about the reasons why they had chosen to adjust to the international market.

China's reorientation was perhaps the most profound shock for many Third World politicians. Having became accustomed to being harangued by the Chinese for their lack of Marxist ideological purity, Third World socialists watched in disbelief as in the 1980s China itself embraced the market with almost pornographic enthusiasm. Most people in the Third World had believed that the Chinese alliance with America in the 1970s was a purely pragmatic step by Beijing, directed against their ideological archenemies, the Soviets. But by 1984 it was clear that China's decoupling from the Soviet Union had opened up a completely new social and economic system that accepted market values while keeping the one-party state and strict political controls. China's example made some Third World leaders believe that they could reorient their economies while keeping political power themselves. For many, having given up on fighting the international capitalist system and their own populations at the same time, the Chinese political model was as alluring as was its economic development.

For a country like Mozambique, mired in debt, with a containable but bloody domestic insurgency sponsored by South Africa, and with its infrastructure in tatters, it should be no surprise that it looked for a compromise with the United States. Increasingly impatient with the advice he received from his Soviet and East German aides – and in spite of his socialist convictions – Mozambican leader Samora Machel already in 1982 began a slow reconciliation with Washington. Machel was a pragmatic socialist, who had been instrumental in arranging the Lancaster House talks that led to independence for Zimbabwe in 1980 and who had advised the new Zimbabwean prime minister, Robert Mugabe, to avoid the dogmatic mistakes in constructing socialism that he himself had been guilty of. In 1984, under increasing pressure from the United States, Machel signed an accord with the South African government, in which both sides promised to stop aiding opposition groups in the other country. ANC activities in Mozambique were severely curtailed. The so-called Nkomati Accords became a watershed in southern African affairs, both because they were the first time a radical African regime had signed an agreement with South Africa, but also because they showed the limited benefit that socialist domestic policies and an alliance with the Soviet Union had left a country like Mozambique. In spite of South Africa's destruction of the accords two years later – and the death of Samora Machel in a suspicious plane crash inside South Africa in 1986 – Nkomati was a strong incentive for others, such as the ANC, to begin reorienting their own domestic and foreign policies.[81]

Long before the changes inside the Soviet Union, which began with the election of Mikhail Gorbachev in 1985, many radical Third World states were in the process of defecting from the ideals of Soviet-style Marxism – Leninism. With the exception of countries such as Afghanistan, Ethiopia, and Nicaragua, which were effectively cut off from the international economic system because of US pressure ("strategic nonlending," in Reagan speak), *all* Soviet Third World allies (North Korea excepted) had begun some form of market-oriented reforms prior to 1985. The East Asian "model" was, of course, as ill-suited to Third World needs as the other models that had been sought imposed on them during the Cold War. But as we have seen, there were both push and pull factors that caused this change. Many of the radical states had ended up with even worse economies than those of the regimes they replaced, with widespread suffering for their countrymen as a result. In some cases the leaders themselves had lost faith in planning and hoped to escape to a better economic model (while keeping some of their distributive policies in place). But even more important were the pull factors, through which the West made "structural reform" a condition for normal economic interaction. It was a dramatic extension of the Cold War into the global economy, and one that turned out to be very successful for the United States.

By 1983–84 many of the developments that pointed toward a dramatic reversal of fortune for the Soviet Union and for socialism in the Third World were beginning to come together. On the Soviet side, there was political and economic stagnation, and increasing international isolation as a consequence of the war in Afghanistan. On the US side, there was Reagan, rearmament and antirevolutionary interventions. On the side of the Third World, there was disillusionment with Marxist-inspired planning, and, under pressure from the West, a gradual move toward market-based economies. In many cases – such as that of Mozambique – the search for a new economic model was also a search for peace and reconciliation within a country's own borders; both populations and governments were tired of civil unrest, mass campaigns, and endless appeals for sacrifice and faith in the revolution. It was a form of capitulation and it happened unwillingly, but it seemed – just like revolution had seemed a generation earlier – to be the only way out.

10   The Gorbachev withdrawal and the end of the Cold War

The American offensive against Soviet positions in the Third World began just as Moscow's own doubt about its policies in Asia, Africa, and Latin America was intensifying. Initially, however, Reagan's attempts at spreading counterrevolution did not push the Soviets toward withdrawing – on the contrary, evidence indicates that at least up to early 1987 American pressure made it *more* difficult for Moscow to find a way out of its Third World predicament. While the debate on the prospects for socialism outside Europe continued among Soviet leaders during the post-Brezhnev *interregna* – though in a more stifled form than prior to the Afghan invasion – ideology, alliances, perceptions of threat, and inner-party rivalry held them back from radical new conclusions. But as Afghanistan in the early 1980s became predominant among Moscow's Third World concerns, the lack of political results there made certain that the South increasingly became a problem in Soviet foreign relations, and not the bountiful opportunity that it had seemed a decade earlier.

Prior to his accession to power, Mikhail Gorbachev thought about the Third World in roughly the same terms and in the same trajectory as large parts of the Soviet official intelligentsia, from elation in the mid-1970s to doubt in the mid-1980s. As he took the reins, Gorbachev was still torn between his general optimism for the global prospects of socialism and the caution that his Marxist reading imbued him with. He was also put on the alert by those of his key advisers who had experience with the Third World from the International Department of the party, several of whom had been among the originators of the critical debate on Third World socialism in the late 1970s. Still, Gorbachev at first believed that he could turn the Soviet relationship to its African, Asian, and Latin American allies around, just as he could reform its European alliances and, indeed, the Soviet Union itself. What it would take, Gorbachev argued, was the right mix of firmness and realism on Moscow's side, and – not least – the development of the "right leadership" within the countries heading toward socialism. Though others had been there before, Gorbachev set out to make his own lessons in the Third World.

Gorbachev's offensive

Mikhail Gorbachev's starting point for developing Soviet relations with Third World countries was a Marxist analysis of the capitalist world order. What he and his advisers saw in 1985–86 was a series of *temporary* setbacks for socialism in Asia, Africa, and Latin America, created by the economic upturn in the United States, the expansion of capitalism in East and Southeast Asia, and the successful integration of the local bourgeoisie in some Third World countries into a US-centered world economy. The *structural* situation for global capitalism remained unchanged from the crises of the 1970s: the United States was already facing increasing international competition from Western Europe and Japan, and the next economic downturn would therefore lead to conflicts not only between Washington and the Third World elites, but also, increasingly, to conflicts inside the coalition that the United States had put together after World War II. The "postwar era" had come to an end, Gorbachev was fond of proclaiming at the time of his accession, and the "middle-term" potential for socialism was improving.

However, the new general secretary and his advisers did not see the difficulties Third World socialism was having as being exclusively the result of objective causes. Both local parties and the Soviet Union had made mistakes that played into the hands of the imperialists. Of these mistakes, Gorbachev thought, the ones made by the Soviet Union were by far the worst, since Soviet leaders ought to have had the experience of class struggle and socialist construction that could have helped put Third World parties and states on the right path.

Gorbachev saw the failings of Soviet Third World policies as being linked to the failings of Soviet domestic policy. The most substantial error had been the lack of a clearly defined long-term path toward socialism based on "objective conditions" in each country. Gorbachev took up the critique first launched by the reformers of the late 1970s and early 1980s – some of whom now served as his assistants – that instead of encouraging sober analysis among revolutionaries in the Third World, Moscow had put aside important aspects of political theory due to vanity, carelessness, and undue haste. Instead of telling a leader such as Ethiopia's Mengistu that the construction of socialism in his country was a slow process that would take at least a generation, Soviet experts had been telling the Ethiopians and others that the advance toward a higher level of development could be achieved through "subjective" factors, such as "socialist consciousness" and "dedication to ideals." This subjectivism had existed, Gorbachev charged, because of the needs of "some" Soviet leaders to be personally associated with advances in the Third World.[1]

The lack of correct political theory in a Leninist sense had, according to Gorbachev, led to a number of ultra-left positions among socialist Third World leaders. The most problematic of these was the writing-off of a policy of alliances with other political and social groups. Instead of maximizing the number of domestic allies in the battle against imperialism and domestic reactionaries, some Third World leaders had deliberately minimized their number through radical economic and social policies that did not fit the present stage of development of their countries. The Soviets had allowed leaders in the Third World to misunderstand which stage of the road toward socialism countries such as Angola or Afghanistan were at: not the building of socialism, not even the gradual dismantling of capitalism, but a precapitalist stage in which broad alliances with the "progressive" bourgeoisie were not only natural, but necessary.

The Soviet policy mistakes had joined a series of mistakes by Communists and progressives elsewhere to help create the difficulties that the socialist world faced in the mid-1980s, Gorbachev claimed. In part because of their domestic failings, many Third World regimes were far too dependent on aid from the socialist countries, and especially from the Soviet Union. In spite of his willingness to continue to support progressive Third World regimes, Gorbachev already in early 1986 made it clear that such support would depend on "corrections" to local policies and increasing "coordination" between Moscow, the East European countries, and countries such as Cuba, where socialism was already established. In other words, only if the Third World parties did more for themselves, and if Moscow's allies chipped in, would the Soviet Union be able to continue its assistance at the levels of the mid-1980s.

But Gorbachev's views on the Third World – and his increasingly critical view of the Soviet domestic situation – did not at first signal a more defensive approach to Africa, Asia, and Latin America. The new leader and his advisers were critical of previous Soviet leaders' lack of will to defend "socialist gains," which in part, they charged, came out of the inability of the Brezhnev leadership to prioritize. According to Anatolii Cherniaev, Gorbachev's key foreign policy assistant, there were two different priority failures. One was not to give priority to important Third World countries – for instance India, Iraq, and South Africa – over less important states, such as Ethiopia or Guinea-Bissau. Another was not to react to imperialist advances with speed and decision. The relative lack of a Soviet reaction to the US invasion of Grenada in 1983, or to Mozambique's slide into the imperialist camp through its 1984 Nkomati accords with South Africa, were examples often used. Though these principles may seem somewhat in conflict – one main reason why

Moscow had not reacted more harshly to Reagan's Grenada adventure was precisely the sense that control of the "Island of Spice" did not much matter – they formed a useful platform for a new leader who wanted first and foremost to invigorate Soviet policies, especially at a time when he believed that the socialist camp faced an onslaught by the imperialist world.

Anatolii Cherniaev was perfectly suited to provide the new Soviet leader with advice on the Third World. A member of the International Department of the Central Committee since 1970, he had followed the ups and downs of Soviet relations with Africa, Asia, and Latin America closely and participated in the policy debates, although never as a main participant. In the late 1970s he had come to share many of the positions taken by Karen Brutents and other critics of Soviet interventionism, and in spite of his relative reticence and moderation, this association was enough to stall his career until Gorbachev came to power. In early 1986 Cherniaev was hand-picked by Gorbachev to replace Aleksandrov-Agentov as chief foreign policy aide to the General Secretary.

By 1985 it was clear to people like Anatolii Cherniaev and Karen Brutents that it was first and foremost the war in Afghanistan that had created a bottleneck in Soviet Third World relations. This was a view shared by many key officials in the Foreign Ministry, where the Soviet invasion had never had much real support. What was wrong with Afghanistan, in these people's minds, was not only that the intervention had failed militarily and that it was unpopular in the Third World and in Europe, but also that as long as the conflict was unresolved, the thinking that had led the Soviets into Afghanistan could not easily be challenged. Some of the leaders who had taken the 1979 decision were still in power-ful positions – Andrei Gromyko, foreign minster until summer 1985, was the president of the USSR, and Boris Ponomarev remained head of the MO until spring 1986. Most importantly, the decision to intervene was considered to be a collective decision that could only be undone through consensus within the party elite.

Gorbachev's first reaction to the Afghan morass he had inherited was to move to a more decisive and aggressive policy both in the war and in diplomatic dealings with the United States and Pakistan.[2] In the summer of 1985 Gorbachev's military advisers were instructed to work on plans to strengthen the regime and Moscow's military position in Afghanistan over the coming year, in preparation for a scaled withdrawal of Soviet troops beginning in mid-1986. The new leader had in no way given up on forcing a solution in Afghanistan. What he wanted was a time frame for advance in order to avoid the open-ended commitment his predecessors had made. But he was not willing to play into what he saw as a Western ploy to "bleed" the Soviets forever in Afghanistan, in case the new offensives did not work out. As he told US President Ronald Reagan during their first meeting in Geneva in November 1985, the West did not really want a short-term withdrawal of Soviet forces – "you want them there, and the longer the better."[3]

In a comprehensive meeting with Afghan leader Babrak Karmal in Moscow in early October, Gorbachev had laid out the new strategy to his ally. But although he had been disappointed with Karmal's incessant requests for increased aid since the spring of 1985, the Soviet leader knew that he had to be careful when presenting his long-term dilemma to the Afghans in order to avoid further infighting in Kabul or even the political collapse of the regime. Gorbachev's insistence on political and economic reforms in Afghanistan therefore had to be sweetened with further economic aid, in addition to the military offensive on the regime's behalf. To his Politburo colleagues, the General Secretary was considerably more blunt in describing what he had told Karmal:

by the summer of 1986 you'll have to have figured out how to defend your cause on your own. We'll help you, but only with arms, not with troops. And if you want to survive you'll have to broaden the base of the regime, forget socialism, make a deal with the truly influential forces, including the Mujahedin commanders and leaders of now hostile organizations. You'll have to revive Islam, respect traditions, and try to show the people some tangible benefits from the revolution. And get your army into shape, give raises to officers and mullahs. Support private trade, you won't be able to create a different economy anytime soon.[4]

Meanwhile, the war in Afghanistan expanded significantly, as the new Soviet general in charge of the operation, Mikhail M. Zaitsev, attempted a forward strategy to deal with the guerrilla problem. Six thousand GRU spetsnaz troops were sent to try to interdict Mujahedin supplies along the borders. Large numbers of regular Soviet and Afghan troops were moved closer to the Pakistani frontier for the same purpose and also to try to ambush guerrillas as they moved into Afghanistan. The Soviets also tried to intimidate Pakistan with increased airborne and artillery strikes across the border – the occurrence of such incidents *doubled* from 1985 to 1986, with the 1986 total at more than 1,400. Still, Zaitsev was under orders to reduce the involvement of Soviet troops in frontline positions during major engagements with the guerrillas in order to minimize battle casualties. The budget cost of the Soviet involvement in Afghanistan increased substantially in 1986 – by more than 30 percent according to CIA figures, particularly due to the intensified air warfare.[5]

At the same time, initiatives to end the war were made more difficult by several Mujahedin operations inside the Soviet Union, instigated by the Pakistani ISI, originally with the encouragement of Bill Casey and the

CIA station in Islamabad. We still do not know enough about these operations, but there were several conducted from late 1985 onwards. Many of those who crossed into Soviet territory did so as much to distribute copies of the Holy Koran and recruit Uzbeks and Tajiks for their cause as to carry out sabotage and ambushes. In April 1987, however, one of these teams attacked an industrial plant deep inside Soviet Uzbekistan, killing eight people and injuring more than forty. Gorbachev was furious. He threatened Islamabad with "serious consequences for the security and integrity of Pakistan" if the raids continued. The attacks provided political ammunition for those on the Soviet side who wanted to step up the war further and who refused to believe that any agreement on Afghanistan could be reached with the Americans and the Pakistanis.[6]

The treatment of captured Soviet soldiers held in Mujahedin camps in Pakistan also enraged Gorbachev. He protested several times to the Americans, but to no avail. In December 1986, after Soviet intelligence had discovered that nineteen Red Army personnel were held by Hekmatyar's forces near Varsak in Pakistan's Northwest Frontier Province, Gorbachev lost patience and had his new ambassador to the United States, Iurii Dubinin, deliver a sharp protest.

The responsibility ... is fully borne by the American authorities. We know that the representatives of the American special services present in the Varsak and other camps of the counterrevolution on the territory of Pakistan encourage the outrages the Soviet citizens are subjected to and try to induce the Soviet military men to betray their country. Such actions of the American representatives who have in fact assumed the functions of executioners and jailers are simply beyond the comprehension of the human mind; they are contrary to the most basic norms of morality.[7]

While Gorbachev and his advisers were struggling to find an end to the Afghan war, some party intellectuals – including a number of those who had been clobbered for their doubts about Third World policies in the late 1970s and early 1980s – in 1985 and 1986 had another go at convincing the leaders of the need for change. Though successful in gaining access to the new chief foreign policy aide, Cherniaev, and increasingly consulted by the experts of the International Department of the Central Committee (especially after long-time Soviet ambassador to the United States, Anatolii Dobrynin, replaced Ponomarev as head of the department in the summer of 1986), the critical intellectuals remained a distinct minority throughout the first two years of the Gorbachev epoch, even within their own institutes. An article on Third World affairs published in the summer of 1985 in the journal *World Economy and International Affairs* – put out by IMEMO, the institute in which most of the critical intellectuals had taken refuge – set the tone for the majority:

In the 1970s the internal contradictions of capitalist production once again became sharply exacerbated, which attest to a further deepening of the general crisis of capitalism ... The antihumane nature of the capitalist application of the accomplishments of the scientific and technological revolution, and the ruinous socioeconomic and ecological consequences of that application are manifesting themselves more and more vividly ... The real, actual transition to socialism is accomplished through the revolutionary breakup of the capitalist order. This takes place, as historical experience shows, through the successive defection of individual countries or groups of countries from the capitalist system.[8]

Gorbachev's own views – public and private – reflected this Marxist position. According to Cherniaev, "In the spring of 1986, Gorbachev was concerned about the problem of Third World debt. He demanded reports and calculations from specialists and got angry when, each time, they concluded that it was a complex problem of international economics that could not simply be chalked up to imperialist greed and exploitation." Even in his first one-on-one meeting with Reagan, Gorbachev pushed his understanding of Third World revolutions and their causes:

There had been those who considered that the *American* revolution should have been crushed ... Over a long period of time millions of people had engaged in such struggles – in India, Indonesia, in Algeria ... The Soviet Union did not consider that a way of life could be imposed if a society was not ready for it ... The US should not think that Moscow was omnipotent and that when he, Gorbachev, woke up every day he thought about which country he would now like to arrange a revolution in.[9]

"It is a natural [development] of Third World countries first pressing for political independence and then striving to gain control of their own resources and labor," Gorbachev told the Americans at Geneva when they were attacking the Soviet role in the Third World.[10]

One Third World issue on which the new General Secretary had been throughly briefed was Central America. Gorbachev viewed US behavior toward Nicaragua as typical imperialist aggression, and he was insistent that the Soviet Union do more to help Managua. During his first year in power, Soviet economic assistance to Nicaragua increased by more than 40 percent, partly in response to the US trade embargo launched in May 1985. Already during Daniel Ortega's visit to Moscow in May 1985 Gorbachev had agreed to supply Nicaragua with cheap Soviet oil. The new General Secretary also stressed to the Cubans that if the United States launched an all-out attack against the Sandinistas, then the Soviet Union would resupply and assist Cuba when it came to Nicaragua's aid. Under no circumstance would Moscow leave Nicaragua at the mercy of the imperialists, Gorbachev proclaimed.[11]

Gorbachev was also eager to improve relations with the West European Left on issues that concerned the Third World. He knew that the war in Afghanistan was deeply unpopular among European socialists and Communists, and instructed the International Department to conduct an "offensive" to explain why the Soviets were in Afghanistan. The main point in the Soviet propaganda was that the Red Army was helping the Afghan progressives defend themselves against the Islamists, who wanted to destroy schools, infrastructure, and cultural relics, while denying women and minorities the right to education and participation in society. The Italian Communists, who had been critics of Soviet Third World interventions since the mid-1970s, were not won over by Moscow's new arguments. What Gorbachev failed to understand was that by the mid-1980s the PCI and their Western European allies no longer regarded the Soviet Union as a positive force in international politics. The anger over Ethiopia, Afghanistan, and Poland, as well as the PCI's outspoken criticism of the Soviet human rights record, had opened up a chasm that Moscow's new propaganda efforts could not close.[12]

From early 1986 onwards, there was considerable tension between Gorbachev's basically Marxist understanding of Third World events on the one hand, and his wish for *détente* with the United States on the other. The Soviet leader knew well that already at their first meeting Reagan had placed "Soviet expansionism in the Third World" on top of the political agenda. A US National Security memorandum made in preparation for the Geneva talks presents as "basic message: we want countries to stop trying to expand their influence through armed intervention and subversion."[13] The Americans wanted to see the Soviets begin to give in in that area *before* other bilateral issues could be solved. It was, as Gorbachev recognized, a not too subtle strategy of blackmail. Still, he was willing to try to at least talk to the United States on what they called "regional conflicts" if the Americans would keep negotiating in areas that to Gorbachev were of much greater importance, such as arms control. Secretary Schultz was therefore able to tell the leaders of the NATO countries, whom he and Reagan met on their way back from Geneva, that the "Soviets [are] prepared to have regular meetings on regional issues" and "consider them important." Such a strategy was, as Norwegian Prime Minister Kåre Willoch put it at the meeting, an attempt "gradually to try to integrate the Soviet Union back into the mainsteam of European civilization through promoting East–West contacts."[14]

But Gorbachev in 1986 was far from willing to let himself be integrated, if that meant giving up the Soviet role in the Third World. Although he referred publicly to the war in Afghanistan as a "bleeding wound" at the crucial 27th CPSU Congress in the spring of 1986, he asserted to Cuban leader Fidel Castro in a meeting on 2 March "the necessity of maintaining control in Angola, Ethiopia, Mozambique, and other African countries that were 'taking the anti-imperialist path.'"[15] As he repeatedly told his colleagues, he could not understand why the Soviet Union should show restraint in the Third World when the Americans themselves were unwilling to do so. At the Politburo meeting on 15 April 1986, after US bombing raids on Libya, Gorbachev lambasted the Reagan administration: "We just cannot work with this gang. Shevardnadze will not go to Washington in May ... We should drop hints that we will not be able to solve serious problems with this administration."[16]

Out of Afghanistan

By late 1986 it became clear both to Gorbachev and to many of his key advisers that the invigorated Soviet strategy in Afghanistan was not working. American willingness to supply an almost unlimited quantity of arms to the Mujahedin, the improved organization of the guerrillas, and the participation of foreign fighters – mostly Pakistanis and Arabs – on the side of the resistance had upped the ante to a level where fighting for a better position prior to withdrawal seemed impossible. In February 1987 Gorbachev was close to desperation.

Of course we could leave Afghanistan quickly, without another thought, and claim that we don't have to answer for the mistakes of the former leadership. But we cannot do so. We hear from India and from Africa that if we just pack up and leave, it would be a blow to the authority of the Soviet Union in the national liberation movement – imperialism would begin [another] offensive in the Third World if we leave Afghanistan ... A million of our soldiers went through Afghanistan. And we will not be able to explain to our people why we did not complete [the war]. We suffered such terrible losses. For what? We undermined the prestige of our country, brought about so much bitterness. Why did we lose all those boys?[17]

First and foremost Gorbachev was preoccupied with the effects the war was having on the Soviet Union and on its international position. At Politburo meetings at the end of 1986 and the beginning of 1987 he stressed that "most importantly, the Americans must not get into Afghanistan."[18] But he was also aware of what the "alternative" – as Gorbachev himself put it – could be: "If we introduce 200,000 more troops, then our entire policy [i.e., *perestroika*] will collapse."[19] And "if we get stuck again, it would be bad for the country. And it is just what they want in the West – to see us get stuck, to fall. It is not our foreign policy that interests them, but what would happen with socialism."[20]

Fig. 14   Lieutenant General Boris Gromov, the last of the
Soviet commanders in Afghanistan, waves as he watches the Red
Army withdraw in 1989.

While Gorbachev was making up his mind, several of the conditions
that would ultimately allow him to withdraw were falling into place. After
the 27th Party Congress the general secretary's position within the CPSU
and the Soviet state was increasingly secure – if his political enemies
wanted to act against him, they would have had to do so before the
Congress, during which the general concepts of reform and restructuring

that Gorbachev stood for would be sanctioned. Slowly, his relations with the West were also being put on a firmer ground, especially through his contacts with West European leaders. Gorbachev understood that he would not be facing a direct threat of war with the West of the sort that he and some of his advisers had been fearing when they came into office. The general secretary's relationship with Conservative British Prime Minister Margaret Thatcher was particularly important – during her March 1987 visit to Moscow, Gorbachev had by far the most thorough discussion he had ever had of the issues that separated Western and Soviet perceptions. While still arguing for the social and economic causes of Third World upheavals, the head of the Soviet Communist Party now claimed that "never, at any time did we have a doctrine of spreading socialist revolution in the world."[21] Obviously on some issues Gorbachev's perception of what was "wrong" with the Soviet Union was moving closer to that of his former opponents.

Another reason why conditions in mid-1987 made a Soviet withdrawal easier for Gorbachev was the difficulties that the West was having over the American intervention in Central America. Never popular in Western Europe, in 1987 Reagan's war against Nicaragua was running into trouble in the United States as well. In November 1986 Reagan was forced to confirm that his administration had secretly sold weapons to Iran – presumably to secure the release of US hostages held by pro-Iranian groups in Lebanon – and that the proceeds from the sale had been used to fund the Nicaraguan Contras after Congress had severely limited such aid. The televised hearings on the scandal from May to August 1987 were followed closely in Moscow, and confirmed to many decision makers that the United States would be less eager to intervene directly in the future, including in Afghanistan.[22]

Finally, Moscow's successful replacement of the intransigent Babrak Karmal with the head of the secret police, the 38-year-old Najibullah, meant that the road was open for some form of phased withdrawal.[23] There was considerable nervousness in Moscow about this operation – many Soviet leaders remembered what had happened twice before when they had tried to engineer a palace coup in Kabul. But this time, in spite of demonstrations by Parchamis on his behalf in Kabul, the Afghan leader obeyed Soviet instructions and peacefully left the office of General Secretary of the PDPA "for health reasons" in May 1986. Still, it took Najibullah more than six months to get control of the party and the army. The Parchamis were split almost evenly between supporters of himself and of Karmal, and the latter kept some of his influence in the party even after he was also forced to resign from the largely ceremonial post of State President in November 1986. Only after Karmal in May 1987 had agreed to go back to the Soviet Union – from where Moscow's troops had brought him to Kabul eight years earlier – did some semblance of stability descend on the faction-ridden Afghan Communist Party.

At the meeting of the Politburo on 13 November 1986 Gorbachev had for the first time made it clear to his colleagues that in his view "we need to finish this process as soon as possible." While in late 1985 the emphasis in the Politburo discussion had been on "a combination of military and political measures," Gorbachev in the crucial November 1986 meetings insisted that the Soviet troops – whatever happened – would have to be brought home by the end of 1988. His colleagues largely supported his views. Marshal Akhromeev probably went furthest in saying that

there is no single piece of land in [Afghanistan] that has not been occupied by a Soviet soldier ... There is no single military problem that has arisen and that has not been solved, and yet there is still no result. The whole problem is in the fact that military results have not been followed up by political [actions]. At the center there is authority; in the provinces there is none. We control Kabul and the provincial centers, but on occupied territory we cannot establish authority. We have lost the battle for the Afghan people.

In early 1987 the Soviet strategy for a withdrawal finally began coming together. The strategy was set up by a Politburo-level special commission – headed by Foreign Minister Shevardnadze – that Gorbachev had charged with the withdrawal, but it was worked out primarily by the KGB. There were two reasons for this. Gorbachev felt that the state security committee was by far the best informed Soviet agency on what the political problems in Afghanistan really were and how they could be overcome. Second, Najibullah had been working closely with the KGB throughout his political career, not only when he headed Afghan state security, the KhAD, in 1980–87.[24] Vladimir A. Kriuchkov, the head of the KGB's First Main Directorate, was charged with helping Najibullah implement a new policy of moderation and alliance building in preparation for a Soviet withdrawal.

According to Kriuchkov, this new strategy was designed for the "level of development" that Afghanistan had at that moment, and was not based on dreams about what it could be in the future. Najibullah had to carry out "national liberation" in his country and needed allies for the purpose – the bourgeoisie, clerics, non-Islamist anti-Communists, even moderate guerrilla leaders and representatives of the former king, Zahir Shah. In their inner counsels, Najibullah and his foreign advisers derided not only the 1979 invasion, but even the Communist coup of 1978 (and on one occasion the participation of the Communists in the coup against the king in 1973) as "grievous mistakes" and "political errors." The new Afghan leader called a unilateral ceasefire in mid-January 1987 (not generally observed), called a "commission on national reconciliation," and offered the opposition seats in government. He also set up a *loya jirgah* – a supreme tribal council – that passed a new constitution, devoid of most references to socialism. But most importantly, at least by mid-1987, Najibullah – himself a Pashtun from the powerful Ahmadzai clan – began secret talks with Pashtun resistance groups based in Pakistan, appealing for an alliance on ethnic grounds.

The international negotiations between Afghan and Pakistani diplomats that the UN had tried to keep alive in Geneva since 1982 took on a new significance with Gorbachev's and Najibullah's policy changes. The Ecuadorian diplomat Diego Cordovez, who mediated in the talks, pushed for a solution based on international guarantees to accompany the beginning of a Soviet withdrawal – a solution remarkably similar to that taken by Iurii Andropov in 1982. But it was the direct diplomacy between the Soviet Union and the United States that now opened up the possibility for some form of concrete agreement to be arrived at. By mid-1987 Soviet diplomats had made it quite clear to their American counterparts that Moscow wanted to withdraw from Afghanistan as part of a wider pattern of understanding between the two concerning the Third World. But the Soviets were severely hindered in their diplomacy by Gorbachev's insistence – proclaimed publicly by Najibullah at the end of November 1987 – that the withdrawal would take place by the end of 1988. Both the Americans and their Pakistani allies – who increasingly favored the more radical of the Afghan Islamist leaders – knew that by holding out in the negotiations they could play against the self-imposed Soviet deadline.

The summit meeting between Reagan and Gorbachev in Washington in December 1987 showed to the Americans that the Soviets were ready to withdraw even with limited US and Pakistani guarantees of noninterference in support of the Mujahedin. Gorbachev framed his comments by referring to "increasing support for regional political settlements" in Third World conflicts, and then made his view of Afghanistan clear: "Afghanistan could not be considered a socialist country. There were too many non-socialist characteristics: a multi-party system, tribalism, capitalists, and clerical elements. The Soviets were realists. They did not want to try to make Afghanistan socialist." What Moscow needed was Washington's cooperation in moderating the increasingly tough pro-Islamist line that the Pakistani dictator General Zia ul-Haq was taking in the Geneva negotiations and also US willingness to stop supplying the Afghan opposition after the Soviet withdrawal got under way. Reagan's support "would help the Soviets judge American intentions regarding other regional conflict situations," Gorbachev added, indicating that the Soviet Union would stop selling arms to Nicaragua if other outside interference in Central America was reduced.[25] But instead of guarantees, what Reagan provided was a promise to continue supporting the Mujahedin whatever happened in Geneva.

Having realized that he would get little from the Americans, Gorbachev in a typical way decided on a gamble. He issued a statement on Soviet television on 8 February 1988 saying that agreement on Afghanistan had "almost" been reached, that a text would be signed in Geneva that spring, and that all Soviet forces would be out of Afghanistan within a year of the signing. In one way the gamble succeeded. In Kabul, Najibullah realized that he had to sign or get nothing but Soviet enmity. In Islamabad, Zia – at the advice of the Americans – came around to believing that he would lose nothing by signing. The result, however, was that the Geneva Accords of 14 April were meaningless with regard to peace in Afghanistan. The Soviets would withdraw by 15 February 1989. The Americans, however, would only stop aiding the guerrillas if and when Moscow abrogated their agreements with Najibullah's regime. The Mujahedin leaders, speaking with one voice – increasingly rare as the Soviet presence came to an end – condemned a peace process that they had not been part of. And Zia ul-Haq made it clear, to his colleagues, to Washington, and to the Mujahedin, that in his view the accords were not worth the paper they were written on. Pakistan's quest for an Islamic government in Afghanistan would continue even after Zia was killed in an airplane crash in August 1988.[26]

On the chilly winter morning of 15 February 1989 Lieutenant General Boris Gromov, the last commander of Soviet forces in Afghanistan, walked across the bridge over the Amu Darya River and back into Uzbekistan, from where the Red Army had come almost ten years before. To most Soviets Gromov's manner of departure from Afghanistan – a quick march and without looking back – symbolized their relationship to the intervention. In a society where new vistas had opened up as a result of Gorbachev's reforms, the last direction most people wanted to look was backwards. To the great majority of Soviets the involvement in Afghanistan had become a byword for an unloved and increasingly superfluous role that their government played in the Third World. To them, withdrawing from Kabul therefore meant the end of a failed intervention. By 1989 the common pride in the Soviet global role that had existed only a few years before was no longer there. It had been replaced not only by a lack of faith in the Soviet system, but also by a conviction that its leaders squandered their resources abroad while people at home lived in poverty.

While domestic public criticism of the Soviet Afghan adventure increased as a result of Gorbachev's *glasnost*, the Soviet leader himself had to fight throughout his remaining three years in power to prevent the elite within his own party from entering some form of reengagement with the Afghan morass. First, he had to stand firm during the last phase of the withdrawal, when Pakistan's blatant violations of the Geneva Accords led some army generals and high-ranking KGB officers to hope for a continued limited Soviet presence. Only a few weeks after Gromov's walk across the bridge, the Mujahedin siege of the city of Jalalabad and Najibullah's calls for assistance led to a strong coalition in the Politburo – Shevardnadze, Kriuchkov, and new Minister of Defence Yazov – calling for Soviet air strikes against the attacking forces. But Gorbachev had made his decision on grounds that were unrelated to the military situation in Afghanistan, and would not relent: "I am definitely against all bombings ... While I am General Secetary I won't permit anyone to trample the promise we made in front of the whole world."[27] In the end, Najibullah's regime survived longer than Gorbachev's, well assisted by Mujahedin infighting, Soviet arms supplies, and beginning American doubts about the wisdom of placing radical Islamist groups in control of Kabul. In early 1992, with the Soviet Union gone, the PDPA regime disintegrated. Four years later a Pakistani-sponsored offshot of the original Mujahedin – the Taliban – took over the capital, dragged Najibullah from his hiding place, tortured and killed him, and hung his mutilated body outside the palace where the Soviets had once installed him as president. Afghan Communism had reached the end of its short but bloody road.

The causes of the Soviet withdrawal

The ignoble Soviet exit from Afghanistan became a global symbol for the failure of Moscow's Third World policies. Not only did the Soviet Communists fail in perpetuating a left-wing regime in Afghanistan – a neighboring country where the Soviet Union had been closely involved in politics since the early 1920s – but through their intervention they undermined support for Soviet foreign policy at home and in the Third World. Most Soviets initially resented the costs of the war and the lack of results, rather than the policies that had produced that outcome. But since a substantial part of the CPSU regime's overall legitimacy was based on its superpower role abroad, the failure in Afghanistan became a deadly challenge to the key concepts of its foreign policy: Soviet military power and the global advance of socialism.

In the Third World the Soviet intervention in Afghanistan hastened the move among intellectuals and political leaders away from Communism and toward different kinds of other identities, most often nationalist, ethnic, or religious. In many Islamic countries the war opened a floodgate – just as the generation of the 1940s and 1950s had turned *from* Islam to secular socialism, the young of the late 1970s and 1980s turned from socialism to political Islam. In many cases the people involved stayed the same – *all* of the radical Islamist leaders in Afghanistan had been involved with left-wing groups in their youth. By the time Gorbachev shifted from emphasizing victory to emphasizing withdrawal, a majority of politically involved young people in the whole Muslim belt from North Africa to Indonesia had already shifted their gaze from Moscow to Mecca.

But while the war in Afghanistan in a domestic perceptual and international context may have done little more than advance the processes that were already underway, the decision to withdraw was a conscious choice by the Gorbachev leadership. In spite of the economic costs, the human losses, and criticism at home and abroad, there is little doubt that the Soviet Union could have held on to the 1985 status quo in Afghanistan for a very long time if it had so wished. But by early 1987 the general secretary had decided to withdraw the Soviet forces, and over the following two years the political direction was clear, although issues of means and timing were often confused and chaotic. Why did Gorbachev and his associates act the way they did?

Though the discussion here will concentrate on the immediate causes for Gorbachev's decision, there are of course a number of long-term and broader causes that need mention. The most important for the discussion is the change in Soviet thinking on the Third World since the late 1970s. Not only was much of what Gorbachev decided with regard to Afghanistan already there as an alternative in the early 1980s – arguably already at the end of the Brezhnev regime – but the inner-party critique of Soviet policies in Africa, Asia, and Latin America had never gone away after 1979. Also, Soviet economic difficulties played an important role with regard to Afghanistan, as indeed they did in all of Gorbachev's policies. The dramatic drop in its surplus income that the Soviet state experienced at the beginning of the 1980s – mostly as an effect of the drop in price of its main raw material exports – brought out the worst in a planned economy in which weapons expenditure played such a major part. The domestic and international criticism of the war in Afghanistan also played a key role. Before 1985 the most important critique – of the sort that was listened to in Moscow – came from West European Communists and from Third World radicals. After 1985 this disaffection was made even more visible by criticism within the Soviet Union; first in letters to the party leadership, then in the increasingly open mass media.

Still, it is in terms of its immediate causes that the decision to withdraw will have to be understood. In such a perspective, there were three main reasons for the withdrawal. The first was the Soviet critique of Third World socialism that found its way into the party leadership through Gorbachev's choice of advisers. The second was the Soviet hope that it could remove American hostility through making compromises in the Third World. The third was the ideological adherence to the principle of national self-determination that Gorbachev's reading of Lenin gave rise to, and which led the CPSU both out of Afghanistan and, eventually, out of the Kremlin.

Over the past few years we have been rediscovering the Marxist debate on the character of Third World revolutions that went on within the CPSU and within the research institutes in the late 1970s and early 1980s. The key critique of official policy centered on Moscow's misperception of the class content of revolutions such as those in Ethiopia, Angola, and Afghanistan. Instead of revolutions for national liberation lead by a Marxist "vanguard," the critics argued that some of these regimes – such as Mengistu's – were actually *holding back* the forces of development, representing "feudal" interests against the bourgeoisie. By supporting these regimes, the Soviet Union therefore ended up on the wrong side of history. Silenced to a large degree by the ongoing war in Afghanistan, this critique reemerged in the mid-1980s and formed a key background for Gorbachev's decisions.

The critique of Soviet interventions in the Third World was powerful because it was fundamentally Marxist and because – from late 1986 on – it was increasingly presented in public as a result of the glasnost policies. It also, of course, helped to explain what had gone wrong in Soviet policies, first and foremost with regard to Afghanistan, but increasingly also in terms of Third World interventions elsewhere. If the countries in question were not ready for socialism, then the whole basis on which Soviet policy had been erected was faulty. This was not an argument for a Soviet withdrawal in and by itself, but certainly indicated the need for a dramatic change of course from the strongly ideologically laden concept of solidarity with foreign comrades to a more limited concept of assisting Third World countries against imperialist attacks. Such an adjustment was, of course, nothing new in Soviet history, as we have seen from earlier transitions in the 1920s, the 1950s, and the 1960s. It was an adjustment that the Soviet Union could make rather easily and that would not have prevented it from continuing the Cold War in the Third World, although under a different strategic doctrine.

What was new was the number of Third World allies who depended on Soviet support, the uncontrolled and public venting of a diverse criticism of earlier policies, and the degree to which that criticism turned directly against the countries and movements the Soviets had supported. On the one hand Soviet stakes in the Third World were higher than before. On the other hand changes in Soviet society that Gorbachev had opened up invited non-Marxist as well as Marxist analyses of past (and increasingly present) policies. The result, from 1987 onwards, was a groundswell of criticism of Soviet interventionism and of the Third World recipients of Soviet assistance that went far beyond the boundaries of what Gorbachev had wished for. While paying lip service to the advances of socialism in Africa, Asia, and Latin America, many commentators found Soviet interventions too costly and asked embarrassingly frank questions about what had been achieved. "It has become practically a ritual," Rachik M. Avakov noted in the November 1987 issue of the leading Soviet journal on international affairs, "to substitute such sacramental phrases as 'they have encountered difficulties,' 'they have to overcome the resistance of the internal reaction and the consequences of colonialism,' and so forth, for real analysis of crises and other negative processes occurring in the countries of socialist orientation, including failures in their economies and their domestic and foreign policies."[28]

In a key article in the same journal, *World Economy and International Affairs*, the prominent Middle East expert Georgii Mirskii noted that "our scholarship, with its emphasis on the role of class factors, has shed no light on Asian and African peoples' internal ethnic and religious diversity." "Eastern" society, Mirskii noted, "is literally suffused with potential conflict on national, ethnic, religious, clan, and patronage-clientèle grounds."[29] The Soviet Union needed to revise its whole approach to the Third World and base it less on the way it *ought* to be than the way it really is, Mirskii and the well-known Third World expert Nodari Simoniia told leading members of the CPSU International Department at a seminar in late 1987. Their warning that some of the outcomes of Third World instability – such as extremism, terrorism, and civil war – could become dangers rather than opportunities for the Soviet Union did not fall of deaf ears in a department that after Ponomarov's departure itself had become a radical critic of Soviet Third World policy. While unwilling to give up the Soviet Union's Third World alliances, the International Department envisaged a reformed relationship, where Moscow supported internal changes through setting strict criteria for the use of Soviet aid.

The KGB also played an important role in creating a new climate for Soviet–Third World relations. Having been asked by the Center to provide evidence for corruption, mismanagement, and double-dealing (including getting the same projects financed by both the West and the

Soviet Union), the KGB *rezidents* supplied an endless stream of classified reports on such cases, quite a few of which ended up on the general secretary's desk from mid-1986 onwards. Gorbachev was furious. Some of the Third World leaders whom he had genuinely admired showed themselves to be morally depraved turncoats, the head of the CPSU told his advisers in private conversations. The question he asked was how the situation should be dealt with. Cherniaev – his key aide on this as on many other issues – was convinced already when he started working for Gorbachev in 1986 that the Soviets would have to withdraw from the Third World. But this was not the answer his boss wanted to hear. Gorbachev – as always – was looking for a way to take the offensive, to secure Soviet positions while advancing reform.[30]

The 1986 crisis in South Yemen was a turning point in Gorbachev's own view of the Third World and of the potential the Soviet Union had for influencing reform overseas. The Soviets had been the main allies of the People's Democratic Republic of Yemen (PDRY) – the only Marxist-Leninist state in the Middle East – for almost twenty years, and had provided large amounts of aid to it. In 1980 South Yemen was the fifth largest recipient of Soviet aid, after India, Ethiopia, Iraq, and Vietnam. Its ruling Socialist Party had leaders mostly trained in the Soviet Union or East Germany, and its pragmatic president, Ali Nasir Muhammad, had been a Soviet favorite since he outmaneuvered the more radical wing of the party in 1980. In spite of reports both from the MO and the KGB that underlined the ethnic dimensions of the rivalries within the PDRY leadership, the Soviet Politburo had chosen to believe that the country was relatively stable. When severe fighting broke out in Aden after a coup attempt in January 1986, the Soviets were wholly unprepared for how to respond. Gorbachev's first instructions were to evacuate Soviet citizens to get them out of harm's way as the civil war intensified. After a month of killing – in which more than ten thousand people died and the army used its Soviet equipment to raze much of Aden to the ground – the Kremlin was able to impose a semblance of unity on the Yemeni party. While Gorbachev offered aid to rebuild the country, his faith in Third World socialism had been severely tested. "What are we there for?," Cherniaev remembers him asking repeatedly in the wake of the Yemeni disaster.[31]

The civil war in Yemen shocked a large number of key Soviet allies, too. During a conversation with Mengistu in February 1986, the GDR's Erich Honecker found that "just like in Grenada, the events in Yemen show what leftist childishness can lead to." The difference between Gorbachev and other leaders, however, was that Gorbachev wanted to take steps to "clear up the mess," not just in Yemen but also in Soviet relations with the Third

World in general. He was even willing to consider increasing aid, but only if Third World leaders took his cue, admitted their past errors, and presented reform programs that included "national reconciliation" and respect for human rights. When none of the Soviet Third World allies came forward with such plans, Gorbachev showed his anger with their leaders quite openly, while criticizing them for what he saw as their endless demands on the Soviet Union. When meeting with Mengistu in April 1987 the general secretary told him to look for supplies elsewhere. Later the same year, when Nicaraguan leader Daniel Ortega told him that their economy was in decline and that the United States had just given $270 million to the Contras, Gorbachev spat out that he sincerely hoped Ortega was not asking him for 270 million. "Go ask elsewhere" was the uniform message Third World leaders got from Moscow from mid-1987 onwards.

In addition to the overriding preoccupation with Afghanistan – which in many ways set the schedule for Soviet withdrawal from other parts of the Third World as well – the increasing crisis in Ethiopia became part of Gorbachev's agenda from early 1988 onwards. In April 1988, with the opposition going on the offensive in Eritrea and in many of Ethiopia's provinces, Mengistu began sending frantic messages to Moscow for increased military assistance. Both Dobrynin and Foreign Minister Shevardnadze – who, for sentimental rather than political reasons found it difficult to abandon old allies – argued for extra aid, supported by the defense minister, Dmitrii Yazov. The chief of the general staff, Sergei Akhromeiev, argued against, with Cherniaev and others cheering him on from the wings. "Both at Politburo meetings and in public you're always urging people to make real political decisions," Cherniaev told Gorbachev in private. "And here we have the same old routine: a friend asks, and we immediately give. Our arms will not change anything, they'll only push Mengistu further into a hopeless undertaking – an attempt to solve everything by military force."[32] In the end Gorbachev provided only very limited amounts of aid to the Ethiopian regime. His personal distaste for Mengistu, having been briefed by the KGB on the human rights record of his regime, seems to have played a major part in the decision.

Just like its allies in Eastern Europe, many Soviet Third World allies were slow to understand that Moscow's policies were shifting in a fundamental way. Some tried to adjust their own policies to Gorbachev's bidding, but found that they were risking their own survival. Others resisted. "It's a hell of a story, when a big country begins to experiment with reforms that connect to so many other countries," Fidel Castro told an East German visitor in March 1987, especially when so many of its theoreticians "lack practical knowledge and experience."[33] Soviet "theoreticians" reciprocated Fidel's enmity. Cherniaev noted in his diary:

"The Bearded One" has destroyed the revolution and now he's destroying the country ... No one in Latin America takes Cuba seriously. It is not setting an "example" for anyone anymore. The Cuban factor has withered away ... If Castro breaks with us, he only hurts himself. And we will gain politically as well as saving five billion annually. Who'll protest? Dogmatists, sectarians in the "socialist camp," and dying Communist parties whose time is past.[34]

In spite of Gorbachev's increasing unease with most of his Third World alliances it took a long time before his government began to dramatically reduce its foreign assistance, and when it finally happened, in 1990, it was only after pressure from the increasingly powerful and independent national assembly, the Supreme Soviet. After the facts and figures of Soviet aid to the Third World were made public for the first time by Elena Erofeieva and other scholars in late 1989, the public backlash was considerable. Many people asked themselves why their government had outstanding and increasing debts from the Third World of 87.5 billion roubles, when their own country's economy seemed to be in free fall. As one commentator observed, the chances of getting any of this paid back were less than zero, since the model of development that the Soviets were helping to implement in these countries was exactly the same as that which had failed spectacularly in the Soviet Union itself. In mid-June 1990 – influenced by the first Gulf War – the Supreme Soviet ordered cuts in all forms of Soviet foreign aid, especially military, and Gorbachev, reluctantly, had to issue a presidential decree calling for a reevaluation of all existing assistance agreements.[35]

By 1990 disillusionment and cynicism among the population made further Soviet involvement in the Third World a difficult and dangerous political proposal at home. There is no doubt, however, that right up to the unsuccessful coup in August 1991, which in reality destroyed the Communist Party, Gorbachev used his inherited powers to intervene abroad where and when he thought necessary. The problem for Soviet Third World alliances was that the general secretary of the CPSU to a great extent *shared* the public's disappointment and preferred to disengage. Dmitrii Volskii, an influential foreign affairs commentator, had summed up the prevailing mood in December 1988:

It happened more than once that some African or Asian state turned out to be completely different from the way many of our press organs depicted it. True, this could only be established after the regime had fallen. Only then did it become known that "the national-patriotic forces," on coming to power, had behaved like feudal or even prefeudal princes, that "important industrial projects," created at the wave of a hand using the people's money, were needed only to indulge their vanity, that the country, after embarking on the path of "progressive transformations" and "strengthening national independence," had arrived at an economic catastrophe, and that its tired and indignant people had finally lost patience and overthrown their rulers.[36]

Himself convinced that the Third World was of little short-term importance to the Soviet Union, Gorbachev from mid-1986 onwards believed that he could use conflicts in Africa, Asia, and Latin America to find common ground with the United States and thereby improve his negotiating position on other issues, such as Europe, arms control, and trade. The critical view of Third World revolutions that he took over from his advisers eventually helped him adhere to the harsh demands of the Reagan and Bush administrations through the implication that Soviet policy prior to 1985–86 had been wrong and that the left-wing regimes should be able to survive on their own, albeit *if* they had the right of life in the first place. As the negotiations over Afghanistan neared a solution, Gorbachev hoped to use these talks as a model for solving what he now – picking up a US term – referred to as "regional conflicts." In his speech at the seventieth anniversary of the October Revolution, instead of underlining class struggle, the general secretary presented his view of an "interconnected and integrated world, one that calls for a balance of interest on an equal basis." In the Third World, he saw "a kaleidoscope of contradictory interests ... The liberation impulse, which operated during the stage of the struggle for political independence, it is growing weaker, of course ... The factors from which the [new] impulse is formed are diverse and heterogeneous."[37]

A young Soviet assistant deputy foreign minister, Andrei Kolosovskii, who had been involved in US–Soviet arms reduction talks, signaled a radical new approach to dealing with Washington on Third World affairs in a June 1988 article sanctioned by his boss, Eduard Shevardnadze:

We need a view of the developing countries that is to a considerable degree deideologized, and that recognizes the uniqueness of processes at work there, and their independence of the rivalry between the two socioeconomic systems ... [Experiences] demonstrate clearly that by no means does every regime that has quarreled with the Americans follow a course of social progress, justice and democracy ... The image of socialism will become immeasurably more attractive when the outside world sees that the criteria of democracy and respect for human rights are invariably present in our evaluation of events in other regions, and in our choice of friends and allies.[38]

Another Soviet Foreign Ministry official, Andrei Kozyrev, who later was to serve as Russian President Boris Yeltsin's first minister of foreign affairs, followed up in even more radical language in October 1988. The Soviet Union, Kozyrev said in the journal *International Affairs*, had no longer any reason to be in "a state of class confrontation with the

United States or any other country . . . The myth that the class interests of socialist and developing countries coincide in resisting imperialism does not hold up to criticism, firstly because most developing countries already adhere to or tend toward the Western model of development, and, secondly, because they suffer not so much from capitalism as from the lack of it."[39]

To the Americans, the shift in Gorbachev's own view of the Third World seemed almost to good to be true. Their exhilaration did not prevent them, however, from taking advantage of the new Communist leader's economic and political difficulties, as well as his idealism, generosity, and sometimes naïveté. During the Washington summit in December 1987 the Soviets offered to stop supplying Nicaragua with weapons if the United States would endorse the regional peace process set up by Costa Rica's President Oscar Arias. But the United States kept pressing Moscow for more concessions on Central America, especially after George Bush took over as president in 1989. Likewise, on Southern Africa, when Gorbachev during the Moscow summit in May–June 1988 offered to stop supplying the MPLA if the United States would stop its aid to UNITA, Reagan replied, rather lamely, that "Savimbi's only goal was the establishment in Angola of a government in which people could choose their own destiny." At the end of the first day's meeting Gorbachev gave Reagan a note he had written himself and that he hoped to get them both to sign:

Proceeding from their understanding of the realities that have taken shape in the world today, the two leaders believe that no problem in dispute can be resolved, nor should it be resolved, by military means. They regard peaceful coexistence as a universal principle of international relatons. Equality of all states, non-interference in internal affairs and freedom of socio-political choice must be recognized as the inalienable and mandatory standards of international relations.

Not surprisingly, perhaps, the US president was told by his advisers not to sign. Gorbachev burst out, in exaspiration: "The President had the choice, but seemed unwilling or reluctant to exercise the authority that was clearly his."[40] With his highly personalized style of foreign policy making, Gorbachev simply failed to understand that no American president could sign such an agreement without a basic reevaluation of his country's whole approach to the Third World, and that – unlike himself – neither Reagan nor Bush had any intention of fundamentally changing their approach.

Gorbachev and his advisers – especially Foreign Minister Shevardnadze, the later president of independent Georgia – developed an understanding of the significance of national self-determination that went beyond those of the leaders of any major power in the twentieth century. The Soviet president practiced what both liberals and revolutionaries had been calling for at the beginning of the century – a firm and idealist dedication to letting the peoples of the world decide their own fates without foreign intervention. This was a principle that Gorbachev held to, even when it was fully clear that the United States was not willing to abide by it. The power that that principle held in Gorbachev's Kremlin can only be understood through the president's own final months in office, when he – as the first head of state in history – resigned as a result of the constituent parts of a union republic voting that republic out of existence.

The end of the Third World

By the end of the 1980s the Third World had ceased to exist as a meaningful political or economic concept. The changes that started in the 1970s had driven different parts of Asia, Latin America, and Africa in different, almost opposite, directions. In terms of economics, some East and Southeast Asian countries were in the midst of a period of rapid capitalist growth, centered on access to world markets for their manufactured products. Latin America was stagnating, burdened by massive debt and increasing social imbalances. For most African economies the 1980s was a disaster, with sharp drops in national income and resulting impoverishment of their populations. Politically, Latin America moved away from military dictatorships, in the US-inspired belief that market growth and democracy came as one package. Some non-Communist countries in Eastern Asia moved in the same direction, albeit very slowly. In Africa, the Balkans, and parts of South Asia, ethnic identities overtook political ideologies as the main causes of conflict. In some of the Third World heartland – the Muslim belt from the African Atlantic coast to the Asian edge of the Pacific – political Islam confronted and sometimes replaced secular politics. At the end of the Cold War the Third World seemed to fragment.

Instead of Three Worlds – whatever way they had been imagined – the 1990s presented the concept of "globalization," or, to use a better term, "Americanization." Markets worldwide, and especially financial markets, were seen as being inextricably tied in to an expanding capitalist world economy with the United States – the only remaining superpower – at its center. Consumerism and liberal democracy were seen as the main values for the emerging global middle class. For Western-educated reformers, an adherence to free market capitalism was the only game in town, at least for a while. Outside "town," however, at the fringes of the electronic networks that defined the much lauded new global urban class, there were the many who had been the victims of the Cold War in the Third World. Most of them were peasants, whatever way one defines them, living inside or outside the city, in impoverished villages or in shantytowns where Americanization tended to be resented and resisted.

These new divides, which new patterns of conflict fed on, are well illustrated by the way the Cold War ended in some of the countries that we have been dealing with in this book. In Afghanistan, when the Najib regime finally collapsed in 1992, the radical Islamist Hezb-i-Islami seemed best poised to take over, but were opposed by ethnic and Islamist groups with less extreme positions on political and social issues. In the ensuing civil war much of Kabul was destroyed and the country began fragmenting along ethnic lines, until the new Pakistani- and Saudi-sponsored Taliban movement's rapid takeover in 1995–96. The Taliban won because they promised peace and security in a country where most people were desperately tired of war and disorder, and because many of their leaders were seen as traditionalists rather than radical Islamists. By 2001 the Taliban controlled more than 90 percent of the country's territory and Afghanistan seemed on the verge of getting a unified government for the first time since 1978.

As a reactionary, fundamentalist movement rather than a revolutionary Islamist one, the Taliban were unfortunate to inherit from their commanders' anti-Soviet war connections a link to the Saudi Islamist Osama bin Laden and his extremist group al Qaeda (the Base). Bin Laden had made his mark in the war against the Soviets as one of many young Arabs who had dedicated themselves to force the Communist invaders out of Afghanistan. Even though he then had been allied to their deadly enemy Gulbuddin Hekmatyar, some Taliban leaders felt that Afghanistan owed him a debt of honor, and when he returned to the country in May 1996 with some of his fellow veterans from the 1980s they gave him refuge, while he helped them take over Kabul and the northern cities. In the interim Islamists who had been recruited to fight the Soviets in Afghanistan through the shadowy networks set up in the 1980s by Islamist organizations, the Saudi government, and the CIA, had gone on to fight for what they considered their cause – the defense of the global Islamic *ummah* – in Bosnia, Chechnya, Algeria, and the Kurdish areas of Iraq. Mostly North Africans, Saudis, and Palestinians/Jordanians, in the 1990s some of these people had joined al Qaeda, attracted by bin Laden's fanaticism, his resources, and his willingness to strike directly at the remaining Great Satan of the non-Islamic world, the United States.

Many of those who sympathized with al Qaeda – in Afghanistan and among Muslims elsewhere – directed their rage both against their own corrupt and inefficient governments and also against Western influence in Islamic countries. While the big Islamist organizations became more politically moderate in the late 1990s, as they positioned themselves to take over from their archenemies, the secular left-wing governments of countries such as Algeria, Libya, Syria, or Iraq, al Qaeda moved in the opposite direction, preferring terrorism to political action. In part as a result of their activities, bin Laden and his followers became increasingly isolated among the Islamist movements, at least until the US occupations of Afghanistan and Iraq. While Islamism seems to be stagnating as a revolutionary ideology as it joins the political mainstream, there is enough resentment from the Cold War in the Muslim world to fuel terrorist groups like al Qaeda for a long time to come. In that sense, the situation is somewhat similar to that in Europe in the late 1970s, with the radical Left joining politics, leaving groups like the German Rote Armee Fraktion or the Italian Brigate Rosse behind.

For Indochina – a region which the Cold War had helped to destroy – there was a kind of settlement toward the end of the period, although a less comprehensive one than many had hoped for. Already in 1986 Vietnam had begun pulling its forces out of Cambodia, but Chinese, US, and Southeast Asian support for the Khmer Rouge and its allies made the withdrawal difficult. By 1988 the Vietnamese had made it clear that they would remove all their forces by the end of the decade, but Gorbachev's intense wish to reach an agreement with Beijing, and Hanoi's own hopes for an opening to the rest of Southeast Asia and its expanding economies, accelerated the speed of the withdrawal. Immediately prior to the Soviet leader's visit to China in May 1989 – the first by a head of the CPSU for thirty years – Vietnam declared that all its forces would be out by the end of September 1989. The United States, in response, increased its intervention, attempting – for the first time – to create a non-Khmer Rouge fighting front to confront the Cambodian government allied to Vietnam. By the end of 1991, however, the Association of South-East Asian Nations (ASEAN) – the regional integration organization that Hanoi and Phnom Penh hoped would rescue their devastated economies – had decreed a negotiated settlement under UN auspices. The war against the Khmer Rouge continued up until Pol Pot's death in 1998.

In Africa the changes at the end of the Cold War were even more intense. In Ethiopia, where Mengistu Haile Mariam's regime – as we have already seen – was in difficulties from 1987 onwards, Gorbachev's grudging continuation of Soviet aid postponed rather than prevented the outcome. Having responded to the oppositions' military offensives by renaming his country the People's Democratic Republic of Ethiopia (PDRE) and proclaiming his faith in Marxism–Leninism, Mengistu was drawing closer to Havana and Berlin in his search for allies. Neither did him much good. In May 1989, while on a visit to Berlin, Mengistu's army tried to unseat him. Although surviving the coup attempt, the regime faced economic meltdown, not because of reductions in Soviet aid but because of further reductions in the prices of its main exports. In desperation Mengistu turned to imperial Ethiopia's old ally Israel, who offered aid in return for the regime allowing the country's Jewish minority to emigrate. In early 1990 Mengistu dissolved communal farming and instituted market reforms, while proclaiming that he was ready to work with the United States. The Communist Party was renamed the Democratic Unity Party of Ethiopia, with the appropriate acronym DUPE.

But it was too little, too late, and too unconvincing for Mengistu's enemies. Having themselves shed their Marxist past, the opposition Tigray People's Liberation Front (TPLF) advanced on the capital, Addis Ababa, while the EPLF liberated almost all of Eritrea, isolating the Derg's main army of 200,000 men in Asmara. On 21 May 1991 the United States facilitated Mengistu's hasty removal to exile in Zimbabwe, while recognizing a new TPLF-dominated federal government in Addis. Two days later – following a pattern set in Eastern Europe – the people of Addis Ababa toppled the big Lenin statue in the center of the city, reputedly the most expensive Lenin statue outside the Soviet Union. While Eritrea got its independence in 1993, the Ethiopian nationalities were left with devastation and hunger as their prizes from the ruins of Mengistu's dream of socialism.

In Angola, the South African government interpreted Soviet–American *détente* and the renewed US support for Jonas Savimbi's UNITA as a renewed license to attempt to topple the MPLA regime. The right wing of the National Party, firmly in power under President P. W. Botha, hoped to see Angola disintegrate and the Cubans removed or beaten, so that it could arrange a similar settlement over Namibia as it had organized for the so-called "independent bantu homelands." Botha wanted to concentrate his efforts on destroying the ANC inside South Africa itself and preventing it from having bases at its borders. The MPLA, on its side, hoped to drive UNITA out, in order to reunify the country and prepare the ground for domestic reform and normalization with the United States. The MPLA and Cuban offensive ground to a halt near Cuito Cuanavale in southern Angola, when a force of more than 5,000 South African soldiers attacked across the border. By November 1987 the largest battle in Africa since the Ethiopian–Somalian war was raging around Cuito, with the FAPLA and Cuban forces cut off from the north by the attacking South Africans. To the horror of his Soviet

Fig. 15 "Botha, I'm fed up." South African anticonscription poster against the war in Angola, 1988.

advisers, Fidel Castro in January to March 1988 sent 15,000 of his best troops to Angola to launch a counterattack, signaling to Pretoria that Cuba was ready to begin fighting inside Namibia if the South Africans did not withdraw from Cuito Cuanavale.

While dismayed by Castro's actions, the Americans and the Soviets worked together to make use of the momentum for negotiations that the Cuban leader had created by his willingness to confront the South Africans. The number of South African soldiers killed at Cuito Cuanavale and at the Namibian border was increasing, and some of the leaders of the National Party and of the South African defense force began favoring a withdrawal. In July 1988 Angola, Cuba, and South Africa signed a ceasefire agreement in New York, with the United States as guarantor. In a final agreement, signed in December, Castro and the MPLA agreed to withdraw all Cuban soldiers within twenty-seven months. South Africa agreed to respect Angola's borders and negotiate a ceasefire with the Namibian liberation organization SWAPO, with a view to implementing UN Resulution 435 on Namibian independence. Ironically, the only outside power that reserved the right to continued intervention in the region was the United States, which doubled its aid to Jonas Savimbi's UNITA to $80 million in 1990. UNITA received more than $250 million worth of assistance in total from the United States between 1986 and 1991, including advanced weapons such as Stinger ground-to-air missiles.

However, with Nambia independent in 1991, the Soviets and the Cubans out, and the MPLA government scrambling to make up with Washington, time was running out for Jonas Savimbi. When he refused to recognize the result of the 1992 elections, which had given a majority to the MPLA, and restarted the civil war, the United States shifted its allegiance to the Luanda government. Savimbi had enough equipment to keep his rebellion going for another ten years, helped by his control of most of the Angolan diamond mines and his friends and associates in America and Europe. In February 2002, with the MPLA government working closely with Western multinationals in extracting the country's mineral wealth, and with rumors of US weapons supplied to UNITA showing up in the Middle East, Savimbi finally ran out of luck. FAPLA ambushed and killed him in a shootout near the Zambian border. Eighteen years after he had been received as Reagan's favored guest in the White House, Savimbi's bullet-ridden body was laid out for viewing under a tree in the village where he died. Stressing how the Cold War had come around since the Cuban revolution, the grisly display reminded some of how the Bolivian Army had shown off Che Guevara's body in 1967.[41]

For Angola, the effects of civil war and foreign intervention were truly disastrous. What could have been Africa's richest country was reduced to poverty and hunger. Public services and infrastructure had decayed because all government income had gone to fight the war. Politically, the MPLA had also decayed, becoming an increasingly corrupt and self-serving regime. In spite of the increasing income from oil and minerals for export after the civil war ended, it does little to help the population out of the destruction that the war has wrought. "Angola has one of the highest rates of landmine injuries per capita in the world," Human Rights Watch noted in a recent report. "Out of a population of about nine million, it has many thousands of amputees, the great majority of them injured by landmines. The most widely used figure is 70,000 people disabled by landmines. That would translate into 1,750,000 injured people in a country the size of the United States."[42]

One of the most remarkable transformations after the Cold War has been that of the African National Congress of South Africa. With the apartheid regime in retreat in the late 1980s, pressured by international sanctions, by increasing irrelevance to the United States, and by the military defeat in Angola, prominent white South Africans began informal talks with the ANC. In these talks the younger generation of ANC leaders, both inside and outside the Communist Party, made it clear that nationalizations and the rapid introduction of socialism were no longer their aim. Thabo Mbeki, in part trained in the Soviet Union, no longer quoted Marx and Engels, but assured white and black South African businessmen that their businesses would be safe under an ANC government. Instead of deriding "black capitalism" as the "confirmation of parasitism with no redeeming features whatsoever," as he had done to a Canadian audience in 1978, Mbeki made it clear that he wanted *more* black capitalists to compete with white capitalists in a market-oriented economy.[43] When P. W. Botha's successor F. W. de Klerk released Nelson Mandela and allowed free elections that the ANC won in 1994, Mbeki – as Mandela's chosen successor – became a guarantor for a stable, capitalist South Africa.

The ANC, however, had not forgotten all of its old debts. Upon his release, one of Nelson Mandela's first foreign visits was to Cuba, where he appeared together with Fidel Castro on a platform in Matanzas in July 1991, celebrating the thirty-eighth anniversary of the start of the Cuban revolution. To a cheering crowd, Mandela lauded Cuba's contribution to the liberation of South Africa. The battle of Cuito Cuanavale, Mandela told the Cubans,

is what made it possible for Angola to enjoy peace and establish its own sovereignty. The defeat of the racist army made it possible for the people of Namibia to achieve their independence. The decisive defeat of the aggressive apartheid forces destroyed the myth of the invincibility of the white oppressor. The defeat of the apartheid army served as an inspiration to the struggling people of South Africa. Without the defeat of Cuito Cuanavale our organizations would not have been legalized.[44]

For Cuba itself, though, the end of the Cold War meant no let-up in the hardship of its people. The US embargo stayed in place, as did most of the US attempts at isolating the country internationally. Castro was horrified with events in Eastern Europe in 1989, and had no wish to follow a road toward the extinction of Communism. After hard-line Czechoslovak General Secretray Milos Jakeš visited Cuba in January 1989, Gorbachev had noted that "Castro too cursed perestroika as a betrayal of Marxism–Leninism, revolution, socialism, friends, as opportunism and revisionism of the worst kind. And now, Fidel told Jakeš, Cuba is the last refuge of Communism and it will remain faithful to the end."[45] It did indeed. A fortnight before Erich Honecker was ousted as head of the East German party, and a month before the fall of the Berlin Wall, Castro sent him a personal message in which the Cuban leader reiterated "the firm and consistent solidarity of the Communists and all of the Cuban people against the machinations and the pressure that imperialism exerts against the GDR." "I embrace you like a brother," Castro told the embattled Honecker.[46]

In December 1989, as the last of the Communist regimes were collapsing in Eastern Europe and as other radical Third World regimes were busying themselves with making peace with their opponents and with the United States, Castro spoke to a memorial meeting for Cubans who had died in Angola.

Now imperialism wants the East European socialist countries to join in the colossal looting [of the Third World]. This apparently does not bother the theorists of capitalist reforms one bit. This is why in many of those countries nobody mentions the Third World's tragedy, and the unhappy crowds are geared toward capitalism and anti-Communism ... If events follow their present course, if demands are not made that the United States give up its concepts, what new ideas could we talk about? ... It is impossible to develop a revolution or a truly socialist rectification without a strong, disciplined, and respected party. It is impossible to carry out such a process by slandering socialism, destroying its values, discrediting the party, demoralizing the vanguard, relinquishing its leadership role, eliminating social discipline, and sowing chaos and anarchy everywhere.[47]

While Castro battled on, against increasing demands for political pluralism and market reforms at home, the Nicaraguan government sought a deal with its opponents within the format proposed by the Contadora peace process, organized by a group of Latin American countries. The bottom line of the agreement reached in February 1989 was that the Sandinistas promised to hold free and fair elections after one year if the Contras agreed to end their military activities. In spite of its continued military support of the Sandinista government the Soviet Union – itself pushed hard by the new Bush administration – pressed Daniel Ortega to stick to the timetable, even when it became clear that the Contras would not disband. When the head of the Latin America section of the Soviet Foreign Ministry, Iurii Pavlov, protested to the Americans that the Soviets – who had never themselves organized a democratic election – were unlikely teachers of democracy to the Nicaraguans, Washington persisted in applying what the Secretary of State termed Chinese water torture on Gorbachev. "We'll just keep telling them over and over – drop, drop, drop – that they've got to be part of the solution in Central America, or else they'll find a lot of other problems harder to deal with," Baker told President Bush.[48]

The Nicaraguan settlement came about for a number of reasons, both domestic and international. The Nicaraguan economy was in free fall because of US economic warfare against the country, while in military terms the Sandinistas had scored well against the Contras, who were in disarray in spite of the massive US assistance they had been receiving. The Iran–Contra scandal had made it difficult for the White House to push for further funding for its Nicaraguan allies, while US military exercises in Honduras (and, in December 1989, the US invasion of Panama) had convinced the Sandinistas that Washington might, after all, decide for a full-scale war. Gorbachev pushed for elections, mostly to please the Americans. Even Fidel Castro agreed that elections under international supervision would be a good idea, although he lamented the Sandinistas' decision to allow right-wing opposition media to reopen and to begin returning denationalized property to its private owners.

When the Sandinista Front lost the February 1990 elections, other left-wing movements in Central America moved to abandon the military struggle. In El Salvador the FMLN signed a UN-sponsored peace accord the following year, even though the right wing and the military stayed in control of the country. The peace accord did do away with the most flagrant violations of human rights in the country, and – through setting up the FMLN as a legal political party – allowed a voice for the Salvadorean poor and the peasants within the political system. One member of the guerrilla-affiliated land defense committees, interviewed in 1992, asked herself:

What was the war for? For the solution of the land problem. We feel something already, and we're sure that we will be free – that is a point of the war that we have won. Higher incomes? Who knows? But that we not be seen as slaves, that we've won.[49]

Her words sum up status at the end of the Cold War and at the end of the Third World. While many of the conflicts – political and economic – that have been dealt with in this book remain unresolved, many people in Africa, Asia, and Latin America have through their own actions begun to regain some of the human dignity that colonialism and the Cold War deprived them of. The melting away of the Third World concept – into a multitude of different positions, systems, and ideas – shows more than anything what has been achieved, and what the cost of it has been. In some places the dogmatic and unified certainties of the past give way to more tolerance and multipolarity. In others, old certainties are exchanged for new. But to have people not be seen as slaves is a uniform gain for all.

Conclusion: Revolutions, interventions, and great power collapse

The Cold War is still generally assumed to have been a contest between two superpowers over military power and strategic control, mostly centered on Europe. This book, on the contrary, claims that the most important aspects of the Cold War were neither military nor strategic, nor Europe-centered, but connected to political and social development in the Third World. I have argued that while the dual processes of decolonization and Third World radicalization were not in themselves products of the Cold War, they were influenced by it in ways that became critically important and that formed a large part of the world as we know it today. Some of these influences were coincidental, while others were brought about through direct interventions. Together they formed a pattern that had disastrous consequences for today's relationship between the pan-European states and other parts of the world.

In an historical sense – and especially as seen from the South – the Cold War was a continuation of colonialism through slightly different means. As a process of conflict, it centered on control and domination, primarily in ideological terms. The methods of the superpowers and of their local allies were remarkably similar to those honed during the last phase of European colonialism: giant social and economic projects, bringing promises of modernity to their supporters and mostly death to their opponents or those who happened to get in the way of progress. For the Third World, the continuum of which the Cold War forms a part did not start in 1945, or even 1917, but in 1878 – with the Conference of Berlin that divided Africa between European imperialist powers – or perhaps in 1415, when the Portuguese conquered their first African colony. Not even the conflict between the superpowers, or its ideological dimension, was a new element in this *longue durée* of attempted European domination. The powers that had intervened before had often been in conflict with each other, sometimes as a result of competing ideas. As Joseph Conrad put it in 1902 in *Heart of Darkness* – the most searing critique of colonialism ever published:

The conquest of the earth, which mostly means taking it away from those who have a different complexion or slightly flatter noses than ourselves, is not a pretty thing when you look into it too much. What redeems it is the idea only. An idea at the back of it; not a sentimental pretence but an idea; and an unselfish belief in the idea – something you can set up, and bow down before, and offer a sacrifice to.[1]

The tragedy of Cold War history, both as far as the Third World and the superpowers themselves were concerned, was that two historical projects that were genuinely anticolonial in their origins became part of a much older pattern of domination because of the intensity of their conflict, the stakes they believed were involved, and the almost apocalyptic fear of the consequences if the opponent won. Even though both Washington and Moscow remained opposed to formal colonialism throughout the Cold War, the methods they used in imposing their version of modernity on Third World countries were very similar to those of the European empires that had gone before them, especially their immediate predecessors, the British and French colonial projects of the late nineteenth and early twentieth centuries. These methods were centered on inducing cultural, demographic, and ecological change in Third World societies, while using military power to defeat those who resisted. With their founding concepts of social justice or individual liberty long atrophied into self-referential ideologies, the starting point was what the anthropologist James C. Scott, following David Harvey, has called *high modernism*, defined, in Harvey's terms, as

the belief in linear progress, absolute truths, and rational planning of ideal social orders under standardized conditions of knowledge and production ... The modernism that resulted was ... positivistic, technocratic, and rationalistic at the same time as it was imposed as the work of an elite avant-garde of planners, artists, architects, critics ... The "modernization" of European economies proceeded apace, while the whole thrust of international politics and trade was justified as bringing a benevolent and progressive "modernization process" to a backward Third World.[2]

As parts of the Third World rebelled against colonial control around the mid-third of the twentieth century, the revolutions that followed were often inspired by either the Soviet or the American form of high modernism. In a period of extreme global instability, it is not surprising that highly ideologized regimes such as the United States and the Soviet Union opted for intervention in what seemed to be a zero-sum game, unless there were strong domestic reasons against it. What is more surprising is the key role local elites played in abetting and facilitating these superpower interventions. Marrying their own domestic purposes to a faith in a common, international ideology, many aimed at some form of superpower involvement from the revolutionary stage onwards. A few of them set agendas – economic, political, military – that they knew could only be fulfilled through American or Soviet intervention. A large number waged war on their own peasant populations, attempting to force them – sometimes in conjunction with foreign interveners – to accept centralized plans for their improvement. Perhaps even more than the Cold War superpowers to which they were allied, these Third World elites viewed the modernization and ultimate abolition of the peasantry as a supreme aim, the pursuit of which justified the most extreme forms of violence.

Cold War ideologies and superpower interventions therefore helped put a number of Third World countries in a state of semipermanent civil war. In some cases there is likely to have been violent conflict at the end of the colonial period anyhow, but the existence of two ideologically opposed superpowers often perpetuated such clashes and made them much harder to settle. There were two main reasons for the perpetuation of war. One was the conviction among local elites that their aims were necessary and moral. Seeing the gulf that separated the lives of their populations from the lives led by those in the pan-European world, their agendas were fueled by the certainty that change was not just possible but necessary, and that almost any price was reasonable for defeating hunger, disease, ignorance, and injustice. Moreover, the moral imperative of progress that they appealed to was one that both superpowers shared, while the specifics for how to implement it were often inspired by one of them. It was not difficult, in other words, to find confirmation for agendas of change.[3]

Confronting the conditions under which the majority of the peasant population lived gave little room for moral equivalence between revolution and its opponents. As Che Guevara put it in his speech to the Afro-Asian Solidarity Conference in Algiers in 1965, entitled "The Death of Imperialism and the Birth of a Moral World,"

The struggle against imperialism – to be rid of colonial or neocolonial bondage – that is being carried on by means of political weapons or weapons of war ... is not unconnected with the struggle against backwardness and poverty. Both are stages in a single journey toward the creation of a new society that is rich and just at the same time ... We must win the battle of development by using the most advanced technology possible. We cannot start at the bottom of humanity's long ascent from feudalism to the atomic age of automation ... There must be a great technological leap forward ... in the great factories and also in a suitably developed agriculture.[4]

The Westernized elites generally engineered Cold War plans for progress – and the ensuing military interventions – for what they saw as the best of purposes. In its first major declaration, the Communist regime in Afghanistan told the population that its aims were land reform, "abolition of old feudal and prefeudal relations," "ensuring the equality of rights of women and men in all social, economic, political, cultural, and civil aspects," universal education, free health services, and the elimination of illiteracy and unemployment.[5] To believe in this as a realistic agenda for change in what was Asia's poorest country, with a literacy rate of 24 percent and an average life expectancy of 42 years, took a rather extreme effort of will.[6] But, as the Communist leader Hafizullah Amin put it in his first message as president,

People are the makers of history and it is the people who bring about the most important phenomenon of social evolution through victorious social revolutions. It is here that the Great Leader of the world's workers has said: revolutions are the festivals of the oppressed and exploited. In no other time except the time of revolution, are the masses in a position to actively go ahead as creators of a new social regime. In such times people can make miracles.[7]

Because of the bipolarity of the Cold War international system, Third World regimes and movements always stood a fair chance of gaining a superpower ally, however foolish their domestic plans were. Sometimes such alliances came about almost by default – in the style of "my enemy's enemy is my friend"; in other cases they were inspired by strategic considerations or by economic need. Most often, however, they were created by some sense of ideological cohesion, brought about by a reading of your ally's ideas and purposes as matching your own. In some cases such projections could lead to the most extraordinary meetings of minds, as when the authoritarian developmentalism of South Vietnamese elites found US modernization theory in a joint battle against Communism. The instruments they created, such as the strategic hamlet program (very similar, by the way, to the program used by Soviets and Communists against their peasant enemies in Ethiopia) were ecstatically modern. As one of Walt Rostow's young aides explained in 1961,

Over the years each of the ... villages could create its own subsidiary clusters. In the meantime a new agro-center could be constructed in the center of the "community compound." It would have a market place, bus terminal, stores, meeting hall, mid school, vocational training institute, landing strip, chopper pad [and] fair grounds. The agro-center would be completely modern – it would "futurize" village life without killing the old village.[8]

In a surprising number of cases peasants chose to fight back. Their resistance took different shapes and seldom conformed to the ideological patterns preferred by the high modernists. In most cases peasants were fighting for their villages, their beliefs, and their families. In a few cases, such as Vietnam or Algeria, large numbers opted for the form of modernity that seemed willing to give them some dignity and respect, while defending them from attack. But generally their battles were against centralized power, even when that power claimed to be representing "communal" values, such as in Ethiopia or Afghanistan. While their leaders sometimes chose to represent one imported ideology or another, there is little sign that the peasants themselves fought against anything other than a state – the "imported state," in Bertrand Badie's parlance – that was extending its grip toward their villages. Their battles were defensive, just as they had been in the colonial era, and just as they would be after their rebellions had helped to topple states of one ideological persuasion or another.

The wars fought in the Third World during the Cold War were despairingly destructive. Since they were, mostly, wars against the peasantry, the best way of winning them was through hunger and thirst rather than through battles and bombing. The methods of these wars were to destroy lives rather than to destroy property. In country after country – Kurdistan, Guatemala, Vietnam, Angola, Ethiopia – peasants were taken off their land and out of their villages, and given the choice between submission and starvation. Even after the battles were declared over, governments continued to wage war on parts of their peasant populations: much of what the IMF and the World Bank – in their twenty-twenty wisdom of the late 1980s – called mismanagement and indifference was in fact warfare intended to break the will of recalcitrant peasant communities through destroying water resources, irrigation systems, and pastures. The *cultural* violence was sometimes as bad as the physical: millions were forced to change their religion, their language, their family structure, and even their names in order to fit in with progress.

Already during the late colonial era the attacks on peasant communities gave rise to new forms of ideological resistance of the kind that may be called identitarianist – affirming other identities outside the immediate discourses of modernity. These were substitutes for enforced identities, programmed behavior, or patterns of obedience that were both meaningless and, often, without noticeable material reward.[9] As the appeals both of socialism and Americanization waned, ethnicity and religion – exactly those values that Cold War ideologies had attempted to deny – became central to many political activists in the Third World. Richard Wright sensed this already at Bandung, when he spoke of "a racial consciousness, evoked by the attitudes and practices of the West, [that] had slowly blended with defensive religious feeling; here, in Bandung, the two had combined into one: a racial and religious system of identification manifesting itself in an emotional nationalism which was now leaping state boundaries and melting and merging, one into the other."[10]

To some of the identitarianist movements that emerged out of the rubble that the Cold War left behind in the Third World, the pan-European West

is the enemy – a massive enemy, stretching around the globe in the northern hemisphere, with colonized outposts in the South: Australia, New
Zealand, even Latin America. Because few of these movements have
state power (yet) and they are generally less powerful than even their
local opponents, some use terrorism to state their case, as happened in
the United States on 11 September 2001. When they do set up states,
which some of them are bound to do, it is possible that the resentment and
anger that empower them will lead to some form of fascism, becoming a
new source of violence and instability both in their regions and elsewhere.
It is not a happy picture, but it is, I believe, a real one. Terrorism, in this
sense, may be the lesser part of the evils that come out of deprivation
and war.

For the winner and the loser of the Cold War contest – the United
States and the Soviet Union – the effects of the era defined their futures.
The losing state collapsed, ending both Soviet socialism and the Russian
empire. By the mid-1990s, with the non-Russian republics gone, the
economy in crisis, and a war in the province of Chechnya that Moscow
claimed was forced on it by intervening Islamists (but which Muslim
Chechens hailed as an anticolonial struggle), the former role of the
Soviet Union as a global superpower seemed like a strange dream to
most Russians. In the naïve cynicism that many of them put on in the
wake of the fall, trying to negate their past and show themselves as citizens
of the (capitalist) world, there were also solid portions of racism. Some
claimed that the Soviet Union had been taken advantage of by Third
World regimes and movements, who – aided by corrupt officials – had
helped themselves to the wealth created by the common Russian. Wild
rumors circulated on how much had been given to Nicaragua, to
Vietnam, to the PLO. The South African ANC was especially singled
out for criticism. After the Nobel ceremonies in Oslo in December 1993,
a commentator in *Izvestia* wrote that "one could understand if the
[Nobel] Peace Prize had been awarded to De Klerk three years ago,
when he single-handedly changed the course of the ship of state away
from apartheid. But what had Nelson Mandela to do with it? It was De
Klerk who released him from prison and provided the opportunity to
legalise the ANC."[11]

Whatever Russians believed they saw in the ruins of the Soviet Union,
the direct economic costs of foreign interventions were not the main
causes of the Soviet collapse. During its last ten years in power the
CPSU probably spent less than 2.5 percent of total state expenditures
on military and civilian assistance to the Third World. Although relatively
more than any other country at the time, one should remember that these
figures include most of the costs of the war in Afghanistan, which by itself

took up roughly half of the total. In real economic terms, the Soviet Union could almost certainly have continued its foreign interventions, even through a period of stagnation and decline, especially if a planned economy had continued to exist.

With regard to its economy, it was the total sum of the expenses of seeing itself as the other superpower that was too much for the Soviet Union to bear. Its colossal military establishment, which took up a third of total state expenditures, weakened the Soviet state by draining resources from productive areas of the economy. When overall economic growth slowed up, as it did from the late 1970s onwards, the CPSU regime's room for maneuver in budget terms became increasingly restricted, especially since the Soviet Union was dependent on strongly fluctuating raw material prices in the world market for most of its foreign currency income. The state's ability to respond to pressure from its own population – never great by any standards – declined at the same time as democratization made certain that such pressure would increase.[12]

This is where its Third World interventions figure in the main discourses at the time of the Soviet collapse. The political costs of continued involvement in Africa, Asia, and Latin America were disastrous at a time when people in Moscow and other cities were beginning to count their own part of each expense within a declining economy. The Afghanistan war became the symbol of these expenses, in lives as well as resources. The Soviet leaders who had brought about the intervention were, by the end of the 1980s, seen as fools or knaves, and the critique of the war and the way it had been fought undermined the faith many people had in the Soviet state. Together with the economic decline, the Chernobyl nuclear disaster, and the revolutions in Eastern Europe, the image of having fought unnecessary wars and supported unviable regimes destroyed the legitimacy of the government, creating an impression of unending mismanagement and failure. When the servants of the Kremlin had to decide where they stood during the coup attempt in August 1991, they themselves deserted the CPSU in droves just for these reasons.

Within the Soviet elites, the main cost of interventionism was its demolition of Marxist political theory. As had been proclaimed in the 1970s, the new Third World regimes were indeed seen as a mirror of socialism, but the longer even high CPSU officials looked at it, the less they liked the image they beheld. For many, Soviet allies in the Third World seemed to perform a mockery of the advanced socialist humanism that they viewed themselves as representing. But they also recognized this wayward performance as a reflection of parts of their own ideology and of some of their own practices. By the late 1980s – within the elites themselves – the mirror of socialism transmitted images of what was wrong with the Soviet Union. For some of them, socialism came to mean permanent underdevelopment, while capitalism promised a modernity that worked. Opting for that other version of modernity was a sacrifice for the Soviet elites, since the majority among them were still thinking within some form of a socialist framework. But when the coup attempt of August 1991 – and the possible return to Stalinism that it implied – forced their hand, they abandoned the party and abandoned socialism, thereby opening up for both a democratization of Russian society and for the extraordinary pillage of national and state resources of the 1990s.

While one Cold War superpower collapsed, the other went on to become the hyperpower of our times. As is becoming clear from the new Cold War history, it is unlikely that historians of the future will date the emergence of the United States as a hyperpower to the beginning of the 1990s; indeed, it is likely that many will see America as entering this phase at the beginning rather than the end of the last century. From this, it follows that the Cold War era never saw two equal superpowers – one was distinctly more "super" than the other, even though its power was never limitless. America just had more of everything: power, growth, ideas, modernity. The expansion of all of these aspects of the United States is one important part of the history of the Cold War, both domestically and internationally.

Karl Marx was right in foreseeing the United States becoming the main revolutionary power of the twentieth century, a power that would sweep long-established economic, political, and cultural patterns before it on its way to global supremacy. It transformed trade and financial markets, creating a new form of world economy. It defeated its enemies – Germany, Japan, the Soviet Union – while setting the terms for the democratic revolutions that reshaped their politics and societies. It inspired fundamental changes inside and among its European allies, helping to do away with privileges and social obedience and to create more open societies, while assisting in a process of transnational integration aimed at creating a European Union. It created a new form of audiovisual culture and the patterns of consumption this stimulated. And it created the Third World, by repeated interventions, by its need for raw materials, and – first and foremost – by its vision of development.

Surveying these massive processes of change, some historians have tended to confuse power with morality. Seeing the United States as – generally – a force for good in the world, they have concluded that an inherent morality is both the cause and the principle for America's international role. Such a near-sighted conclusion can only be explained in ideological terms – the identification with the vision of the future that Washington represents is so strong that the moral qualities of that vision outshine all its other aspects. In a manner strikingly similar to that of its Communist opponents, the aim thereby outweighs the character of the actions. Such an approach is not only intellectually faulty, but – as the Soviet case shows – dangerous in the extreme. That the United States – for a variety of reasons – is an immensely attractive society for many people around the world, does not excuse the violence with which it has attempted to influence the world, especially in Asia, Africa, and Latin America.

Seen from a Third World perspective, the results of America's interventions are truly dismal. Instead of being a force for good – which they were no doubt intended to be – these incursions have devastated many societies and left them more vulnerable to further disasters of their own making. So far, the combination of stable growth and stable democracies that Washington has ostensibly sought may be visible in two half-states (South Korea and Taiwan), but is absent in around thirty other countries in which the United States has intervened, directly or indirectly, since 1945. The human tragedies – for friend and foe – that this scorecard reflects are enormous. Moreover, for many countries these are ongoing tragedies, with enough landmines and other weapons in place to destroy lives well into a generation yet to be born.

One of the most frightening aspects of how the Cold War ended was that the negotiated surrender of Communism in Eastern Europe and the Soviet Union came to obscure the results of decades of disastrous interventions in the Third World. If Communism collapsed at least in part as a result of a successful US foreign policy – the thinking went – then some of this success should be reflected even in what had hitherto been commonly seen as low points in America's foreign engagements, such as the war in Vietnam. Reading history backwards, some claimed that through its anti-Communist interventions in the Third World, the United States had bought time, so that the capitalist transformation of areas such as Southeast Asia could take place from within. These changes, in turn, had paved the way for a true globalization of finance and markets in the 1990s. American sacrifice, in other words, had made it possible for all countries and individuals to aspire to take part in the post-Cold War boom. The idea was that through its ultimate triumph in the Cold War, the United States had released those forces of liberty that would – of their own accord – transform the world into liberal democracies and market economies.

This triumphalism was the main reason why the 1990s – in spite of the Gulf War, Somalia, and Kosovo – stand out as a relatively quiet period for US interventions. In addition, of course, there were no immediate threats to US global supremacy and, after the frenzy of the 1980s, there was a certain war-weariness in the population as a whole. With the economy steaming ahead and consumerism offering more products to a larger percentage of Americans than ever before, most people could not care less about Third World conflicts and suffering. As the CIA's Afghan specialist Milton Bearden put it: "Did we really give a shit about the long-term future of Nangarhar? Maybe not. As it turned out, guess what? We didn't."[13] The Clinton administration put the tough questions – such as the debt crisis, increasing world poverty, and security time bombs in Korea or Palestine – aside for others to deal with. With matters taking their natural course toward improvement in the Third World, places such as Nangarhar – one of the birthplaces of the Taliban – could afford to wait. They even faded from view in the US intelligence community. As one CIA officer put it in the summer of 2001: "Operations that include diarrhea as a way of life don't happen."[14]

In spite of the temporary reliance on the natural forces of history in the 1990s, the new and rampant interventionism we have seen after the Islamist attacks on America in September 2001 is not an aberration but a continuation – in a slightly more extreme form – of US policy during the Cold War. The main difference is, of course, that now there is no other global power to keep US intentions in check, just as the Soviet Union did at least in a few cases. But the ideology of interventionism is the same, with the same overall aims: only by changing markets and changing minds on a global scale can the United States really be secure. The new offensive – undertaken, to be sure, in the face of massive provocation, aims big and its slogan is more strongly put forward than ever before. As the State Department official spokesman Richard Boucher put it in a Thanksgiving address in London the year before the invasion of Iraq:

I declare myself an unabashed simplistic American. I believe in freedom as a right, a responsibility, a destiny, a force that cannot be vanquished. And, in my line of work, it is more than a faith: freedom is a foreign policy. The United States will defend freedom relentlessly . . . to me that is what it is all about – plain and simple. The United States stands for freedom, defends freedom, advances freedom, and enlarges the community of freedom because we think it is the right thing to do.[15]

The American-led invasion and occupation of Iraq offers a prime example of how freedom and security have been, and remain today, the driving forces of US foreign policy. As often happens when the most powerful country goes to war, the security aspects are diminished when the intervention gets under way and the opposing state folds. In the Iraq case, of course, the reduction of the security scare turned to farce when no huge arsenals of chemical, biological, or nuclear weapons – the pro-claimed reason for the timing of the attack – were found. What remains is the ideological quest for freedom, threatening to turn Iraq into a night-mare of unending conflict in the same way as happened so often to countries during the Cold War.

Can there be an end to American interventionism? I see it as unlikely, but not impossible. As this book has shown, the United States has been an interventionist power for most of its existence, and its emergence as global hyperpower has made this into a permanent state of affairs. But there is also another America, symbolized by the resistance to the war in Vietnam, the protests against intervention in Central America, and the opposition to the invasion and occupation of Iraq. This anti-interventionist fringe is strongest when it can demonstrate how wars abroad defeat improvements at home. In ideological terms, the only way of breaking the bond between what Jefferson described as interventionist "tastes" and democratic "theory" is probably – as it should be in all democratic politics – through appeals to what serves the country best. It is a debate that America needs now, because as global resistance to US interven-tionism increases, its democratic practices will come under increasing pressure at home. Without a genuine reorientation of its foreign policy, American democracy may end up suffering the same fate as Soviet socialism.

At the end of the Cold War about one out of four of the world's inhabitants lived in areas with improving standards of living. Today the lucky few number less than one out of six, and the difference between the numbers is increasing rapidly. In the long run it will be impossible for a dwindling privileged minority to impose its economic, political, and military fiat worldwide. Unless there is a reversal of the processes of impoverishment, the impoverished majority will begin to turn the tables on the United States and the pan-European world, through intervening in its affairs in the same way as it has – over centuries – intervened in theirs. In this context, the crime against the people in the Twin Towers of New York City was no bigger, or smaller, than those committed against the peoples of Luanda or Kabul during the Cold War. In light of the history of the recent past, the greatest shock of 11 September 2001 was certainly where it happened, not the murderous act itself.

Much of the future may therefore depend on how we revise our actions in order to reduce the potential for violent conflict. If there is one big lesson of the Cold War, it is that unilateral military intervention does not work to anyone's advantage, while open borders, cultural interaction, and fair economic exchange benefit all. This is not a pacifist argument – I believe firmly in the right to self-defense when attacked. But it is an argument that recognizes that in a world that is becoming increasingly diverse ideologically, just as communications tie us closer together, the only way of working against increased conflict is by stimulating inter-action while recognizing diversity, and, when needed, acting multilaterally to forestall disastrous events. The Cold War remains a dire example of what the world looks like when the opposite happens and regimes of global intervention take hold.

Notes

INTRODUCTION

1. Jasper Griffin, "It's All Greek!," *New York Review of Books*, 18 December 2003. The study of the ancient world may have more to offer Cold War historians than most of us think. When reviewing the role of local elites in the Cold War (see chapter 3), I am reminded of the people of Corcyra's message to the Athenians, offering one of the superpowers of the Greek world a fateful alliance in about 433 BCE: "Now there are many reasons why in the event of your compliance you will congratulate yourselves on this request having been made to you. First, because your assistance will be rendered to a power which, herself inoffensive, is a victim to the injustice of others. Secondly, because all that we most value is at stake in the present contest, and your welcome of us under these circumstances will be a proof of good will which will ever keep alive the gratitude you lay up in our hearts" (Thucydides, *The History of the Peloponnesian War*, trans. Richard Crawley [Oxford: Oxford University Press, 1960], ch. 2, § 33).
2. George Orwell, "You and the Atomic Bomb," *Tribune*, 19 October 1945.
3. See for instance the furious debate over *Tiermondisme* (Third-Worldism) in France in the late 1980s and early 1990s reflected in Claude Liauzu, *L'enjeu tiersmondiste: débats et combats* (The *Tiermondiste* Stakes: Debates and Battles) (Paris: Harmattan, 1987). For the historical background, see Denis Pelletier, *Economie et humanisme: de l'utopie communautaire au combat pour le tiers-monde: 1941–1966* (Economy and Humanism: From Communitarian Utopia to Struggle for the Third World) (Paris: Éditions du Cerf, 1996).
4. I am borrowing Immanuel Wallerstein's use of the term; see his "Cultures in Conflict? Who are We? Who are the Others?", Y. K. Pao Distinguished Chair Lecture, Center for Cultural Studies, Hong Kong University of Science and Technology, 20 September 2000.
5. Nirad Chaudhury, *Autobiography of an Unknown Indian* (London: Macmillan, 1951).

1 THE EMPIRE OF LIBERTY: AMERICAN IDEOLOGY AND FOREIGN INTERVENTIONS

1. William Jennings Bryan, "Imperialism," in *Under Other Flags: Travels, Lectures, Speeches* (Lincoln, NB: Woodruff-Collins Printing Co., 1904).

2. Jefferson quoted in Bradford Perkins, *The Cambridge History of American Foreign Relations, vol. I, The Creation of a Republican Empire, 1776–1865* (Cambridge: Cambridge University Press, 1993), p. 93.

3. Michael H. Hunt, *Ideology and US Foreign Policy* (New Haven, CT: Yale University Press, 1987).

4. Jefferson to John Adams, 28 October 1813, in Joyce Appleby and Terence Ball, eds., *Thomas Jefferson: Political Writings* (Cambridge: Cambridge University Press, 1999), p. 190.

5. Jefferson to the Marquis de Lafayette, 30 November 1813, *ibid.*, pp. 191–192.

6. The 1781 Articles of Confederation explicitly reserved a place for Canada in the new state.

7. The genocide against the Native American nations was, Frederick Hoxie argues convincingly, as much a result of US greed for land and resources as it was a consequence of the ideology that positioned them as enemies; see Frederick Hoxie et al., eds., *Native Americans and the Early Republic* (Charlottesville, VA: University of Virginia Press, 1999).

8. Matthew Frye Jacobson, *Barbarian Virtues: The United States Encounters Foreign Peoples at Home and Abroad, 1876–1917* (New York: Hill & Wang, 2000), p. 83.

9. Adams, 4 July 1865, cited in *The Cambridge History of American Foreign Relations* (Cambridge: Cambridge University Press, 1993), vol. III, pp. 149–150.

10. As Frye Jacobsen notes, Walker was eventually overthrown, not by Nicaraguan guerrillas, but by Cornelius Vanderbilt, whose shipping interests Walker had crossed (*Barbarian Virtues*, p. 39).

11. Arthur S. Link, *Woodrow Wilson: Revolution, War, and Peace* (Arlington Heights, IL: Harlan Davidson, 1979), p. 117.

12. Richard Wright, *Black Boy* (New York: Library of America, 1991 [1943/1944]).

13. Roosevelt, State of the Union Address 1938, *The Public Papers and Addresses of Franklin D. Roosevelt*, vol. VII (New York: Random House, n.d.).

14. Roosevelt, speech to the Foreign Policy Association, 21 October 1944, in *Vital Speeches*, 11 (1 November 1944), p. 38. For more on the perceptual links between the two world wars, see John Fousek, *To Lead the Free World: American Nationalism and the Cultural Roots of the Cold War* (Chapel Hill, NC: University of North Carolina Press, 2000), especially pp. 35–43.

15. Lars Schoultz, *Beneath the United States: A History of US Policy Toward Latin America* (Cambridge, MA: Harvard University Press, 1998), p. 386.

16. Eric Foner, *The Story of American Freedom* (New York: Norton, 1998), p. 134. In the 1950s Aguinaldo, who died in 1964, wrote a book in which he praised American freedom; Aguinaldo with Vicente Albano Pacis, *A Second Look at America* (New York: R. Speller, 1957). As late as 1952 the Philippines were still the largest recipient of US aid in the Third World.

17. US Army film, 1945, quoted in John W. Dower, *Embracing Defeat: Japan in the Wake of World War II* (New York: Norton, 2000), p. 215.

18. Paul G. Hoffman, *Peace Can Be Won* (New York: Doubleday, 1951), p. 130.

19. Robert E. Wood, *From Marshall Plan to Debt Crisis: Foreign Aid and Development Choices in the World Economy* (Berkeley, CA: University of California Press, 1986), p. 1.

20. *Major Speeches and Debates of Senator Joseph McCarthy Delivered in the United States Senate 1950–1951* (New York: Garden Press, 1975).
21. Marshall quoted in Joyce and Gabriel Kolko, *The Limits of Power: The World and United States Foreign Policy, 1945–1954* (New York: Harper & Row, 1972), p. 558.
22. *Official Proceedings of the Democratic National Convention Held in Kansas City, Mo., July 4, 5 and 6, 1900* (Chicago, IL: McLellan Printing Co., 1900), pp. 205–227.
23. "Statement of Students for a Democratic Society, National Convention Meeting in Port Huron, Michigan, June 11–15, 1962," on http://www.coursesa. matrix.msu.edu/~lhst306/documents/huron.html.
24. Jacobsen, *Barbarian Virtues*, p. 46.
25. Stanley L. Engerman and Robert E. Gallman, eds., *The Cambridge Economic History of the United States*, vol. II (Cambridge: Cambridge University Press, 2000), pp. 4–6; Robert E. Lipsey, "US Foreign Trade and the Balance of Payments, 1800–1913," *ibid.*, pp. 685–732. See also Irving B. Kravis, "Trade as a Handmaiden of Growth: Similarities between the Nineteenth and Twentieth Centuries," *Economic Journal*, 80 (1970): 850–872.
26. Lance E. Davis and Robert J. Cull, "International Capital Movements, Domestic Capital Markets, and American Economic Growth, 1820–1914," in Engerman and Gallman, eds., *Cambridge Economic History of the United States*, vol. II, pp. 733–812.
27. The importance of new foreign markets seems to have been mainly to provide higher "price elasticity" for US goods; when technology increases production, a slump in prices at home could be avoided through exporting the surplus; see Lipsey, "US Foreign Trade," pp. 700–732.
28. Bennett D. Baack and Edward John Ray, "Tariff Policy and Comparative Advantage in the Iron and Steel Industry, 1870–1929," *Explorations in Economic History*, 11 (1974): 103–121.
29. On new immigration laws and their connection to the Cold War, see Foner, *Story of American Freedom*, pp. 281–282.
30. Wood, *From Marshall Plan to Debt Crisis*, p. 124.
31. Dulles to C. P. Jackson, 24 August 1954, Jackson Papers, quoted from H. W. Brands, *The Specter of Neutralism: The United States and the Emergence of the Third World, 1947–1960* (New York: Columbia University Press, 1989), p. 108.
32. Wood, *From Marshall Plan to Debt Crisis*, p. 70.
33. Foner, *Story of American Freedom*, p. 271. See also Robert W. Haddow, *Pavilions of Plenty: Exhibiting American Culture Abroad in the 1950s* (Washington, DC: Smithsonian Institution Press, 1997) and Karal Ann Marling, *As Seen on TV: The Visual Culture of Everyday Life in the 1950s* (Cambridge, MA: Harvard University Press, 1996).
34. *Social Science Research Council Annual Report 1956–1957* (Washington, DC: SSRC, 1957), pp. 19–20.
35. Gabriel Almond, "Introduction," in Gabriel Almond and James S. Coleman, eds., *The Study of Developing Areas* (Princeton, NJ: Princeton University Press, 1960), pp. 3–4.

36. Max F. Millikan and W. W. Rostow, *A Proposal: Key to an Effective Foreign Policy* (New York: Harper & Row, 1957), pp. 2–8.

37. *Ibid.*, p. 8.

38. *Public Papers of the Presidents of the United States* (hereafter *PPP-US*), *John F. Kennedy*, vol. I (Washington, DC: US Printing Office, 1962), pp. 204–206, John F. Kennedy, special message to Congress on foreign aid, 22 March 1961.

39. Henry A. Kissinger, *The Necessity for Choice: Prospects of American Foreign Policy* (London: Chatto & Windus, 1960). Kissinger devotes a chapter to his views "On Political Evolution: The West, Communism, and the New Nations," in which he combines a modernization theory approach with considerable pessimism about America's ability to face up to the challenge of Third World transitions. "A Russian seeing the growth of the Communist empire over the past fifteen years would not naturally come to the conclusion that its system of political organization was basically wrong," he writes. "If the issue is simply the relative capacity to promote economic development, the outcome is foreordained [in favor of Communism]."

40. Quoted in Gerard T. Rice, *The Bold Experiment: JFK's Peace Corps* (Notre Dame, IN: University of Notre Dame Press, 1985), p. 15. See also Elizabeth Cobbs Hofman, "Decolonization, the Cold War, and the Foreign Policy of the Peace Corps," in Peter L. Hahn and Mary Ann Heiss, eds., *Empire and Revolution: The United States and the Third World since 1945* (Columbus, OH: Ohio State University Press, 2001), pp. 123–153.

41. Schlesinger to Kennedy, 10 March 1961, quoted in Michael E. Latham, *Modernization as Ideology: American Social Science and Nation-Building in the Kennedy Era* (Chapel Hill, NC: University of North Carolina Press, 2000), p. 81.

42. Memorandum of conversation between Kennedy and Mobutu, 31 May 1963, in *Foreign Relations of the United States* (hereafter *FRUS*), *1961–1963*, vol. XX, pp. 858–863.

43. Rostow to Kennedy, 11 November 1961, *FRUS*, *1961–1963*, vol. I, pp. 574–575.

44. Latham, *Modernization as Ideology*, p. 189.

45. Martin Luther King, Jr., speech at Riverside Church, New York City, 4 April 1967, in *I Have a Dream: Writings and Speeches that Changed the World* (San Francisco, CA: Harper, 1992), pp. 138–139.

46. Malcolm, speech at Palm Gardens, New York, 8 April 1964, in *Malcolm X Speaks* (New York: Pathfinder Press, 1965), p. 50.

2   THE EMPIRE OF JUSTICE: SOVIET IDEOLOGY AND FOREIGN INTERVENTIONS

1. Quoted in Andreas Kappeler, *Russland als Vielvölkerreich: Entstehung, Geschichte, Zerfall* (Russia as a Multiethnic Empire: Formation, History, Collapse) (Munich: C. H. Beck, 1992), p. 146.

2. Quoted *ibid.*, p. 163.

3. Quoted in Dominic Lieven, *Empire: The Russian Empire and its Rivals* (London: John Murray, 2000), p. 218.

4. *Ibid.*, p. 257.

5. Lenin, "The Heritage We Renounce," in *Collected Works*, 4th English edn. (Moscow: Progress, 1972), vol. II, pp. 493–534.

6. By far the most comprehensive examination of the causes of Russian revolution is Richard Pipes's *The Russian Revolution 1899–1919* (New York: Knopf, 1990). For a comparative view of the structural causes, see Theda Skocpol, *States and Social Revolutions: A Comparative Analysis of France, Russia and China* (Cambridge: Cambridge University Press, 1979).

7. Nikolai Berdiaev, "Materialism Destroys the Eternal Spirit," on http://www.cjd.org/paper/roots/rmateri.html.

8. S. N. Bulgakov, "Geroizm i podvizhnichestvo" (Heroism and Martyrdom), in *Vekhi: sbornik statei o russkoi intelligentsii* (Landmarks: A Collection of Articles about the Russian Intelligentsia) (1909; Moscow: Novosti, 1990), p. 33; see also Robert English's fascinating overview *Russia and the Idea of the West: Gorbachev, Intellectuals, and the End of the Cold War* (New York: Columbia University Press, 2000), p. 23.

9. Lenin, "The Attitude of the Workers Party to Religion," May 1909, in *Collected Works*, vol. XV, pp. 402–413. Interestingly, Lenin's article was written in part as a response to Anatoli Lunacharskii's *Marxism and Religion* (1907), in which the future church-burning Culture Commissar drew analogies between the struggle for the dictatorship of the proletariat and the struggle for a Kingdom of God – the three wise men, Owen, Bakunin, and Marx, bow down at the manger of the newly born proletariat.

10. Lenin, "The Right of Nations to Self-Determination," in *Collected Works*, vol. XX, pp. 393–454. This article was written between February and May 1914 and was serialized in the journal *Posveshcheniie* (see nos. 4–6, April–June 1914).

11. Lenin, "Report on Foreign Policy, Delivered at a Joint Meeting of the All-Russia Central Executive Committee and the Moscow Soviet," 14 May 1918, in *Collected Works*, vol. XXVII, pp. 365–381.

12. Lenin, "Manifesto to the Ukrainian People, with an Ultimatum to the Ukrainian Rada," 3 December 1917, in *Collected Works*, vol. XXVI, pp. 361–363.

13. Stalin, "The Immediate Tasks of Communism in Georgia and Transcaucasia: Report to a General Meeting of the Tiflis Organisation of the Communist Party of Georgia," 6 July 1921, in *Works* (Moscow: Foreign Languages Publishing House, 1953), vol. V, pp. 90–102, quote on pp. 95–96, originally published in *Pravda Gruzii*, 108 (13 July 1921).

14. Lenin, notes dictated 20 December 1922, in *Collected Works*, vol. XXXVI, pp. 593–611.

15. Reinhard Eisener, "The Emergence of the Ferghana *Basmacis*," on http://www.yeniturkiye.com.

16. Karl Marx, "The Future Results of the British Rule in India," *New York Daily Tribune*, 22 July 1853.

17. Lenin, *Imperialism: The Highest Stage of Capitalism: A Popular Outline* (1917; London: Pluto, 1996).

18. Lenin, "Address to the Second All-Russia Congress of Communist Organisations of the Peoples of the East," 22 November 1919, in *Polnoe*

sobranie sochinenii (Collected works) (5th edn; Moscow: Gos. izd-vo polit. lit-ry, 1960–70), vol. XXXIX, pp. 318–331.

19. Lenin, "Letter to the Propaganda and Action Council of the Peoples of the East," December 1921, in V. I. Lenin, *ibid.*, vol. XXXIXIV, p. 282.

20. Chernomordyuk to Mongolian People's Revolutionary Party leaders, n.d., quoted in Babaar, *Twentieth-Century Mongolia*, ed. C. Kaplonski, trans. D. Sühjargalmaa et al. (Cambridge: White Horse Press, 1999), p. 304. For an overview, see Irina Morozova, *The Comintern and Revolution in Mongolia* (Isle of Skye: White Horse Press, 2002).

21. See Kai Schmidt-Soltau, *Eine Welt zu gewinnen! Die antikoloniale Strategie-Debatte in der Kommunistischen Internationale zwischen 1917 und 1929 unter besonderer Berücksichtigung der Theorien von Manabendra Nath Roy* (A World to Gain! The Debate over Anti-Colonial Strategy in the Communist International between 1917 and 1929, with Particular Attention to the Theories of Manabendra Nath Roy) (Bonn: Pahl Rugenstein, 1994).

22. Sultan Galiev quoted in Ayse Azade Rorlich, "Mirsaid Sultan Galiev and National Communism," on http://www.yeniturkiye.com.

23. *Zhizn natsionalnostei* (Nationalities Life), 38 (5 October 1919).

24. Sultan Galiev was arrested in 1928 and shot in prison in 1941. For a good overview, see Rorlich, "Galiev and National Communism." See also Alexandre Bennigsen and Chantal Lemercier-Qelquejay, *Sultan Galiev, le père de la révolution tiers-mondiste* (Paris: Fayard, 1986) and *Les mouvements nationaux chez les Musulmans de Russie*, 2 vols. (Paris: Mouton, 1960, 1964); Alexandre Bennigsen and S. Enders Wimbush, *Muslim National Communism in the Soviet Union: A Revolutionary Strategy for the Colonial World* (Chicago, IL: University of Chicago Press, 1979), pp. 191–254; Hélène Carrère d'Encausse and Stuart R. Schram, *Marxism and Asia: An Introduction with Readings* (London: Allen Lane, 1969), pp. 178–180. Galiev's writings have recently been published in Tatarstan: see *Statei, vystupleniia, dokumenty* (Articles, Speeches, Documents) (Kazan: Tatarskoe knizhnoe, 1992) and *Izbrannie trudy* (Selected Works) (Kazan: Gazyr, 1998); see also B. F. Sultanbekov and D. R. Sharafutdinov, comps., *Neizvestnyi Sultan-Galiev: rassekrechennye dokumenty i materialy* (The Unknown Sultan Gailiev: Declassified Documents and Materials) (Kazan: Tatarskoe knizhnoe, 2002).

25. Ken Post, *Revolution's Other World: Communism and the Periphery, 1917–39* (Houndsmills: Macmillan, 1997), p. 79.

26. Yang Kuisong, *Zhong gong yu Mosike de guanxi, 1920–1960* (The Relations Between the Chinese Communists and Moscow, 1920–1969) (Taibei: Dongda, 1997). Key texts for understanding the Stalinist view of the world are *History of the Communist Party of the Soviet Union (Bolsheviks): A Short Course* (Moscow: Foreign Languages Publishing House, 1939) and Joseph Stalin, *Foundations of Leninism* (New York: International Publishers, 1932).

27. By far the best overview of this crime is Robert Conquest, *The Harvest of Sorrow: Soviet Collectivization and the Terror-Famine* (London: Pimlico, 1986, 2002), but see also Lynne Viola, *Peasant Rebels under Stalin: Collectivization and the Culture of Peasant Resistance* (Oxford: Oxford University Press, 1996), Anne

Applebaum, *GULAG: A History of the Soviet Camps* (London: Allen Lane, 2003), and for harrowing testimony, Viktor Danilov et al., eds.-in-chief, *Tragediia sovetskoi derevni: kollektivizatsiia i raskulachivanie: dokumenty i materialy, 1927–1939* (The Tragedy of the Russian Village: Collectivization and De-Kulakization, 1927–1939), three vols. to date (Moscow: ROSSPEN, 1999–).

28. Post, *Revolutions's other World*, p. 136.

29. The Labor-Defender (November 1928), quoted from *The Complete Published Works of W. E. B. Du Bois* (Millwood, NY: Kraus-Thomson Organization, 1982), vol. II (1910–1934), p. 302. Du Bois, an admirer of the Soviet Union, finally applied to join the US Communist Party in 1961 at the age of 91.

30. Georgi Dimitrov, diary entry for 7 November 1937, in Ivo Banac, ed., *The Diary of Georgi Dimitrov, 1933–1949* (New Haven, CT: Yale University Press, 2003), p. 65.

31. Georgi Dimitrov, diary entry for 7 September 1939, *ibid.*, p. 115.

32. The new CC organizations were first known as the Department of International Information, then (from 1946) the Department of Foreign Policy, and from 1958 the International Departments. See Iurii A. Poliakov, "Posle rospuska kominterna" (After the Dissolution of the Comintern), *Novaia i noveishaia istoriia*, 1 (2003): 106–116.

33. Georgi Dimitrov, diary entry for 25 November 1940, in Banac, ed., *Diary of Dimitrov*, p. 137.

34. Report to the Central Committee by the All-Russian Society for Cultural Relations with Turkey (1946), quoted in Artiom Ulunian, "Soviet Cold War Perceptions of Turkey and Greece, 1945–1958," *Cold War History*, 3.2 (January 2003): 40.

35. According to the Central Committee, "the justifiable nature of the proposals submitted by the Soviet Government is provided by centuries-long historical experience, which has clearly shown how important it is for the Black Sea Powers to guard the access to the Straits. The joint defense of the Straits by Russia and Turkey, as was the case during the Napoleonic Wars, corresponds fully to the interests of both states and would provide real security for their Black Sea possessions." K. V. Bazilevich, "On 'the Black Sea Straits': The History of the Question," minutes of a public lecture given in Moscow on 18 October 1946, quoted in Ulunian, "Soviet Cold War Perceptions of Turkey and Greece," 40.

36. Litvinov to Molotov, 22 June 1945, Arkhiv vneshnei politiki Rossiiskoi Federatsii (Foreign Policy Archives of the Russian Federation; hereafter AVPRF), f. 0431/1, op. 1, pa. 5, d. 33, pp. 8–19; see also Sergei Mazov, "SSSR i sudba byvshykh italianskikh koloniov (1945–1950 gg.)" (The USSR and the Fate of the Former Italian Colonies), in N. Komolov, ed., *Rossiia i Italiia* (Moscow: Nauka, 1998), pp. 211–241, and a slightly different version in *Cold War History*, 3.3 (April 2003); Apollon Davidson and Sergei Mazov, eds., *Rossiia i Afrika. Dokumenty i materialy. XVIII v. – 1960* (Russia and Africa. Documents and materials. The Eighteenth Century – 1960), vol. II, *1918–1960* (Moscow: IVI RAN, 1999).

37. Litvinov to Molotov, AVPRF, f. 0431/1, op. 1, pa. 5, d. 33, pp. 17–18.

38. AVPRF, f. 0431/1, op. 1, pa. 5, d. 33, p. 45. Much later, Molotov admitted that "it was a difficult argument" (Feliks Chuev, *Sto sorok besed s Molotovim*

[One Hundred and Forty Conversations with Molotov] [Moscow: TERRA, 1992], p. 103).

39. Stalin to Molotov, 20 November 1946, quoted in Vladimir Pechatnov *"The Allies are pressing on you to break your will ...," Foreign Policy Correspondence between Stalin, Molotov, and other Politburo Members, September 1945–December 1946*, Cold War International History Project (hereafter CWIHP), Working Paper 26 (1999), p. 22. Litvinov's original proposals saw no such barriers in confronting British imperialism: Eritrea and Italian Somalia could be of interest as "intermediate bases between the Black Sea and the Far East, as well as an instrument of influence on the neighbouring Arab countries and Abyssinia." Somalia's ports were "naval (and air force) bases, threatening four important sea routes, having a lot of significance for England: the one around South Africa, the Suez-Bombay, Suez-Colombo and Zanzibar-Bombay routes." Eritrea's strategic significance was defined as follows: "(1) the gate to Abyssinia; (2) a potential bridgehead for military actions against Abyssinia, Somalia, British Sudan, Saudi Arabia, Yemen and Aden; (3) controls the sea routes across the Red Sea and the Bab el Mandeb Strait" (Litvinov to Molotov, AVPRF, f. 0431/1, op. 1, pa. 5, d. 33, pp. 9–13, quoted from Mazov, "SSSR i sudba byvshykh italianskikh," 52).

40. For Khomeini see Hamid Algar, "Religious Forces in Twentieth-Century Iran," *The Cambridge History of Iran*, vol. VII, *From Nadir Shah to the Islamic Republic* (Cambridge: Cambridge University Press, 1991), p. 752. Khomeini wrote *Kashf al-Asrar* (The Unveiling of Secrets) in 1944, in which he argued that the prophets, while fully absorbed in the contemplation of God, had fought to bring about transformations in the social and political conditions of men. He also condemned rule by foreign powers and their agents, like the Shah.

41. Beria to Stalin, 16 August 1944, Arkhiv Prezidenta Rossiiskoi Federatsii (Archive of the President of the Russian Federation; hereafter APRF), f. 6, op. 6, pa. 37, d. 37, pp. 15–18.

42. VKP(b) CC, Politburo to Mir Bagirov, 6 July 1945, quoted from Fernande Beatrice Scheid, "Stalin, Bagirov and Soviet Policies in Iran, 1939–1946," Ph.D. dissertation, Yale University, 2000, pp. 259–60.

43. See Natalia I. Yegorova, *The "Iran Crisis" of 1945–46: A View from the Russian Archives*, CWIHP, Working Paper 15 (1996), p. 11. For Bagirov's aims, see Scheid, "Stalin, Bagirov," p. 253.

44. Tudeh CC to VKP(b) CC, (11?) September 1945, Rossiiskii gosudarstvennyi arkhiv sotsialno-politicheskoi istorii (Russian State Archive of Socio-Political History; hereafter RGASPI), f. 17, op. 128, d. 819, p. 182; see also report by representatives of Tudeh, 11 October 1945, RGASPI, f. 17, op. 128, d. 819. The Soviets received detailed reports from Ardasher Ovanessian, a member of the Tudeh Politburo, on the political reactions among Iranian Communists to Stalin's Iranian policies; see letters dated 21 September to 5 October 1945, RGASPI, f. 17, op. 128, d. 819, pp. 32–88.

45. In August 1945 officers close to the *Tudeh* rebelled and seemed ready to march on Teheran, but the uprising collapsed after the Soviets had made their displeasure clear to the Iranian Communists.

46. Bagirov to Atakishiev, 15 November 1945, quoted from Scheid, "Stalin, Bagirov," p. 285.

47. William Eagleton Jr., *The Kurdish Republic of 1946* (Oxford: Oxford University Press, 1963), pp. 43–62, 103; for Qazi Mohammad see pp. 34–35.

48. For the British view of Qavam, see Sir Clarmont Skrine, *World War in Iran* (London: Constable, 1962), pp. 231–237.

49. Soviet notes on Qavam in AVPRF, f. 94, op. 37e, pa. 362a, d. 1, pp. 10–13.

50. Record of conversation between Qavam and Molotov, 23 February, 1946, AVPRF, f. 94, op. 37e, pa. 362a, d. 1, p. 27.

51. The full records of the talks are in a special collection in the AVPRF: "Sovetsko-iranskie peregovori v Moskve i Tegerane v fevrale-aprele 1946g – kratkaia spravka," AVPRF, f. 094, op. 37e, pa. 362a, d. 1. For the Tudeh's reaction to the talks, see record of conversation with Ardasher Ovanessian, Tudeh Politburo member, 15 February 1946, RGASPI, f. 17, op. 128, d. 848, pp. 11–12.

52. Record of conversation between Qavam and Molotov, 25 February 1946, AVPRF, f. 094, op. 37e, pa. 362a, d. 1, p. 37.

53. *Ibid.*, pp. 40–42.

54. Record of conversation between Bagirov and Pishevari, 4–5 April 1946, quoted from Scheid, "Stalin, Bagirov," p. 335.

55. Stalin to Pishevari, 8 May 1946, quoted from Yegorova, *"Iran Crisis,"* pp. 23–24.

56. Intelligence summary for the Politburo, 23 June 1947, quoted from Scheid, "Stalin, Bagirov," p. 353.

57. Stalin to Mao, 20 April 1948, APRF, f. 39, op. 1, d. 31, p. 28.

58. Stalin's remarks to Kim Il Sung during conversations in Moscow, April 1950, quoted from *DPRK Report* (Moscow), no. 23 (March–April 2000).

59. RGASPI, f. 558, op.11, d. 313, pp. 13–14, quoted from Larisa Efimova, "Stalin and the Revival of the Communist Party of Indonesia," unpublished manuscript. As to Indonesian proposals for "the overthrow of the domination of the inner reactionaries who are serving the imperialists" and "their replacement with a democratic coalition government," Stalin exclaimed: "Wrong!" The same was Stalin's reaction to the call for "the union with the USSR, China and the states of people's democracy."

60. Khrushchev, "Speech to a Closed Session of the CPSU Twentieth Party Congress," 25 February 1956, in Thomas P. Whitney, ed., *Khrushchev Speaks!* (Ann Arbor, MI: University of Michigan Press, 1963), pp. 259–265.

61. *Sovetskoe vostokovedenie*, 1 (1956): 6–9.

62. When referring to these CC departments I will use the abbreviation MO for both, since in reality they functioned as one unit under Ponomarev's leadership.

63. See Odd Arne Westad, ed., *Brothers in Arms: The Rise and Fall of the Sino–Soviet Alliance, 1945–1963* (Stanford, CA: Stanford University Press, 1998).

64. Record of conversation between Khrushchev and Mao, 2 October 1959, APRF, f. 52, op. 1, d. 499, pp. 1–33.

65. United Nations, General Assembly, Official Records, Fifteenth Session, pp. 68–84.

66. Khrushchev speech, 6 January 1961, in Whitney, ed., *Khrushchev Speaks!*, pp. 52–61.

3 THE REVOLUTIONARIES: ANTICOLONIAL POLITICS AND TRANSFORMATIONS

1. The total colonial population at the outbreak of World War II was around 800 million (Mary Evelyn Townsend, *European Colonial Expansion Since 1871* [Chicago, IL: J. P. Lippincott, 1941], p. 19).

2. Good surveys of the colonization of Africa and Asia in the nineteenth century are Thomas R. Metcalf, *Ideologies of the Raj* (Cambridge: Cambridge University Press, 1994), John D. Hargreaves, *West Africa Partitioned* (Houndsmills: Macmillan, 1974, 1985), Ronald Oliver and G. N. Sanderson, eds., *The Cambridge History of Africa*, vol. VI, *From 1870 to 1905* (Cambridge: Cambridge University Press, 1985), and Nicholas Tarling's aptly titled *Imperialism in Southeast Asia: A Fleeting Passing Phase* (London: Routledge, 2001). For a superb general overview, see David B. Abernethy, *The Dynamics of Global Dominance: European Overseas Empires, 1415–1980* (New Haven, CT: Yale University Press, 2000), especially pp. 81–104.

3. Davis also supports the view that the famine conditions made colonial penetration easier in parts of the Third World; see Mike Davis, *Late Victorian Holocausts: El Niño and the Making of the Third World* (London: Verso, 2001), pp. 117–210 for more detail on this argument. The lack of sustained and organized resistance during the first period of colonization is, of course, not the same as a lack of opposition, which in some cases was very successful, such as the Chechen and Maori in the 1840s, the Zulu at Isandlwana (1879), and the Ethiopians at Aduwa (1896).

4. One of these universities is the London School of Economics and Political Science, where I teach. Founded in 1895 to further "education, economics, efficiency, equality, and empire," the LSE today provides plentiful opportunities to mull over the postcolonial situation.

5. Sutan Sjahrir quoted from Abernethy, *Dynamics of Global Dominance*, p. 386.

6. Nirad Chaudhury, *A Passage to England* (London: Macmillan, 1959), p. 19.

7. The British colonial historian Christopher Bayly believes the beginnings of the diffusion of technology to be the cause of the many anticolonial uprisings of the mid-nineteenth century – namely, the Xhosa and Maori wars, as well as major rebellions in China, India, Jamaica, and the Caucasus. (See C. A. Bayly in Robin Winks, ed., *The Oxford History of the British Empire*, vol. V, *Historiography* (Oxford: Oxford University Press, 1999), pp. 54–72.

8. James C. Scott, *Seeing Like a State: How Certain Schemes to Improve the Human Condition have Failed* (New Haven, CT: Yale University Press, 1998), p. 97.

9. M. N. Roy, "Open Letter to His Excellency Woodrow Wilson, President of the United States of America, 1917," in M. N. Roy, *Selected Works* (Oxford: Oxford University Press, 1987–), vol. I, p. 25.

10. Nehru, incomplete review of Bertrand Russell's *Roads to Freedom* (1919), quoted from S. Gopal, gen. ed., *Selected Works of Jawaharlal Nehru*, vol. I (New Delhi: Orient Longman, 1972), pp. 140–144.

11. Samaren Roy, *The Restless Brahmin: The Early Life of M. N. Roy* (Bombay: Allied Publishers, 1970).

12. His original name was Narendranath Bhattacharya.

13. At the founding congress of the Chinese Communist Party in July, at least three out of thirteen delegates were police agents. See vol. I of Chen Yongfa, *Zhongguo gongchan geming qishi nian* (Seventy Years of Chinese Communist Revolution) (Taibei: Lianjing, 1998).

14. Stuart R. Schram, *Mao's Road to Power; Revolutionary Writings, 1912–1949*, vol. I, *The Pre-Marxist Period, 1912–1920* (Armonk, NY: W. E. Sharpe, 1992), p. 318, "Manifesto on the Founding of the Xiang River Review (14 July 1919); original in *Mao Zedong Zaoqi Wengao* (Mao Zedong Youth Manuscripts) (Changsha: Hunan, 1995).

15. To show how fluid the colonial situation was at the beginning of the twentieth century, nine years earlier, on first arriving in France, Ho had sent a letter to the French president requesting admission to a training school for colonial administrators. "I would like to become useful to France in relation to my compatriots," Ho wrote, "and would like at the same time to help them profit from the benefits of instruction" (quoted from Sophie Quinn-Judge, *Ho Chi Minh: The Missing Years* [Berkeley, CA: University of California Press, 2002], p. 32).

16. *Ibid.*, p. 32.

17. *Indonesia Accuses!: Soekarno's Defence Oration in the Political Trial of 1930*, ed., trans., annotated, and introduced by Roger K. Paget (Oxford: Oxford University Press, 1975), p. 78.

18. Political Manifesto, 1 July 1927, quoted from *Sandino without Frontiers: Selected Writings of Augusto César Sandino on Internationalism, Pan-Americanism, and Social Questions*, ed., annotated, and introduced by Karl Bermann (Hampton, VA: Comoita Publishing, 1988), pp. 48–51.

19. The counterexample is, of course, Mahatma Gandhi, who in his *Experiments with Truth*, vol. I (Ahmedabad: Navajivan, 1927) claimed that "peace will not come out of a clash of arms but out of justice lived and done by unarmed nations in the face of odds."

20. Frantz Fanon, *The Wretched of the Earth*, preface by Jean-Paul Sartre (1961; New York: Grove Weidenfeld, 1991), p. 73.

21. Aimé Césaire, *Discourse on Colonialism* (New York: Monthly Review Press, 1972), pp. 21–23.

22. Kemal, "Speech on the Tenth Anniversary of the Founding of the Republic," 1 November 1932, on http://www.columbia.edu/cu/tsa/ata/onuncuyil.html.

23. See the excellent summary of the effects of colonialism in Abernethy, *Dynamics of Global Dominance*, pp. 363–386.

24. Ho, Declaration of Independence of the Democratic Republic of Viet-Nam, 2 September 1945, on http://www.mtholyoke.edu/acad/intrel/vietdec.htm.

25. Boucif Mekhaled, *Chroniques d'un massacre: 8 mai 1945, Sétif, Guelma, Kherrata* (Paris: Syros, 1995). More than a hundred French colonists were killed in the fighting that followed, while the estimates of Algerian dead vary from more than one thousand up to six or seven thousand. In March 1947 there was a similar anticolonial uprising against French rule in Madagascar,

with more than ten thousand dead. See Solofo Randrianja, *Société et luttes anticoloniales à Madagascar: de 1896 à 1946* (Paris: Karthala, 2001).

26. Abernethy, *Dynamics of Global Dominance*, p. 167.
27. Quoted from "Independence," program number 22 in the BBC series *The Story of Africa*, first broadcast in the United Kingdom on 18 January 2002.
28. The US-educated Nkrumah, born in 1909, had spent two years in British prison before steering the Gold Coast through a peaceful decolonization from Britain in 1957. The quote is from his aptly entitled early memoirs, *Ghana: The Autobiography of Kwame Nkrumah* (Edinburgh: T. Nelson, 1957), p. x.
29. Abernethy, *Dynamics of Global Dominance*, p. 164.
30. Nkrumah, *Autobiography*, p. x.
31. "Response to the speech of the leader of the Soviet delegation to the Indian Science Congress," 7 January 1947, *Selected Works of Jawaharlal Nehru*, second series, vol. I (New Delhi: Jawaharlal Nehru Memorial Fund, 1984), pp. 380–381.
32. Abernethy, *Dynamics of Global Dominance*, p. 334.
33. See also James Scott on the Tanzanian example. The land reform strategy was undoubtedly most successful in Taiwan, where the state compensated landlords in bonds that could be used to buy shares in industry and services.
34. See Tom Molony and Kenneth King, eds., *Nyerere: Student, Teacher, Humanist, Statesman* (Edinburgh: Edinburgh University Press, 2000).
35. Cabral, Eduardo Mondlane Memorial Lecture delivered at Syracuse University, New York, on 20 February 1970; quoted from Amílcar Cabral, *Unity and Struggle: Speeches and Writings* (London: Heinemann, 1980), p. 146.
36. Lamming's later work, especially his essay collection *The Pleasures of Exile* (London: Michael Joseph, 1960), examines Caribbean politics, race, and culture in an international context.
37. Quoted from Matthew Connelly, *A Diplomatic Revolution: Algeria's Fight for Independence and the Origins of the Post-Cold War Era* (Oxford: Oxford University Press, 2002), p. 47.
38. In his opening speech at Bandung, Sukarno cited two key precedents: the 1928 Brussels conference and the 1949 consultative meeting in New Delhi.
39. Richard Wright, *The Colour Curtain: A Report on the Bandung Conference*, foreword by Gunnar Myrdal (London: Dobson, 1956).
40. The prime minister's concern for the state of public facilities during the conference presumably also had something to do with his upbringing. He instructed his ambassador to Indonesia that "we cannot take the slightest risk of lack of adequate arrangements ... we cannot afford to have everything messed up because they [the Indonesians] are sensitive. The harm to Indonesia will be very great indeed if all the world sees that they cannot organise the conference or organise it very badly ... Above all, one fact should be remembered, and this is usually forgotten in Indonesia. This fact is an adequate provision of bathrooms and lavatories, etc. People can do without drawing rooms, but they cannot do without bath rooms and lavatories" (Nehru to B. F. H. B. Tyabji, 20 February 1955, quoted from *Selected Works* second series, vol. XXVIII, p. 99).
41. Sukarno speech, 18 April 1955, quoted from *Let a New Asia and a New Africa Be Born!* (Jakarta: Ministry of Foreign Affairs, 1955).

42. *Ibid.*
43. *Ibid.*
44. "A cry of defiance and not of fear, / A voice in the darkness, a knock at the door, / And a word that shall echo for evermore ..."
45. Speech in the closed session of the Asian–African Conference, Bandung, April 1955, quoted from Nehru, *Selected Works*, second series, vol. XXVIII, p. 100.
46. The term was first used by Lenin in an 18 April 1920 interview with the *New York Evening Journal*: "Our plans in Asia? The same as in Europe: peaceful coexistence with the peoples, with the workers and peasants of all nations."
47. Li Qi et al., comp., *Zhou Enlai nianpu* (Chronology), vol. II (Beijing: Zhongyang wenjian, 1997). See also Xiang Huayuan, *Zhou Enlai chu deng shijie wutai* (Zhou Enlai Begins to Ascend the World Stage) (Shenyang: Liaoning renmin, 1999).
48. Speech in the closed session of the Asian–African Conference, Bandung, 22 April 1955, quoted from Nehru, *Selected Works*, second series, vol. XXVIII, p. 108.
49. *Ibid.*, p. 100.
50. Quoted from *Bandung 1955* (Colombo: Government Press, n.d.), pp. 30–31.
51. Speech in the closed session of the Asian–African Conference, Bandung, April 1955, quoted from Nehru, *Selected Works*, second series, vol. XXVIII, p. 124.
52. Quoted from Connelly, *Diplomatic Revolution*, p. 96.
53. Mikhail Kapitsa, former Soviet Vice-Foreign Minister, author's interview, 8 September 1992.
54. For the preparation of this meeting, see record of conversation between Nehru and Kardelj, 5 July 1955, Arkhiv Srbije i Crne Gore (Archives of Serbia and Montenegro; hereafter ASCG), A CK SKJ IX, 42/V-13.
55. Oleg Troianovskii, former Soviet UN ambassador, author's interview, 14 September 1992.
56. Record of conversation between Nehru and Gamal Abdel Nasser, 1 May 1955, quoted from Nehru, *Selected Works*, second series, vol. XXVIII, p. 219.
57. See James D. LeSueur, *Uncivil War: Intellectuals and Identity Politics During the Decolonization of Algeria* (Philadelphia, PA: University of Pennsylvania Press, 2001).
58. Statement of Students for a Democratic Society, Port Huron, 15 June 1962, on http://coursesa.matrix.msu.edu/~hst306/documents/huron.html.
59. Piero Gleijeses, *Conflicting Missions: Havana, Washington, and Africa, 1959–1976* (Chapel Hill, NC: University of North Carolina Press, 2002), p. 39.
60. Today the NAM has 116 member states.
61. Declaration of the First Conference of Non-Aligned Heads of State, Belgrade, September 1961, on http://www.nam.gov.za/background/history.htm.
62. Cabral, "Speech given on the occasion of the day dedicated to Kwame Nkrumah, 13 May 1972," in *Unity and Struggle*, p. 116. Nkrumah died from cancer in a Bucharest hospital on 27 April 1972.
63. For the clearest statement of the reasons for his own turn towards Marxism, see Cabral, "The Weapon of Theory", speech delivered on behalf of the peoples and nationalist organizations of the Portuguese colonies to the First

Solidarity Conference of the Peoples of Africa, Asia, and Latin America (Havana, 3–12 January 1966) in the plenary session on 6 January, quoted from *Unity and Struggle*, pp. 119–137.

4 CREATING THE THIRD WORLD: THE UNITED STATES CONFRONTS REVOLUTION

1. See Angus Maddison, *The World Economy: A Millennial Perspective* (Paris: OECD Development Centre, 2001).
2. "NSC 68: United States Objectives and Programs for National Security," 14 April 1950, in *Foreign Relations of the United States* (hereafter *FRUS*), *1950*, vol. I, pp. 237–286.
3. NSC 51, US policy towards Southeast Asia, 1 July 1949, Declassified Documents Reference Service (hereafter DDRS), on http://www.ddrs.psmedia.com.
4. CIA report, "Consequences of Dutch 'Police Action' in Indonesia, 27 January 1949," DDRS.
5. Record of conversation between Acheson and Stikker and van Kleffens, 31 March 1949, in *FRUS, 1949*, vol. IV, pp. 258–261. See also Robert J. McMahon, *Colonialism and Cold War: The United States and the Struggle for Indonesian Independence, 1945–49* (Ithaca, NY: Cornell University Press, 1981), p. 293.
6. According to the reminiscences of the then coordinator of the State Department working group on Indonesia, Frederick Nolting, "Sukarno was regarded, in those days, rightly or wrongly, as a genuine nationalist – untainted by an education in Moscow, untainted by charges of being a Communist. This changed later on, but in those days he was regarded as a genuine, popular nationalist" (oral history interview with Frederick Nolting, Charlottesville, Virginia, June 1975, by Richard D. McKinzie, Harry S. Truman Presidential Library, Independence, MO (hereafter HSTL), p. 7). Nolting later served as US ambassador to Vietnam in 1961–63.
7. Van Oss to Acheson, 4 December 1951, Kuala Lumpur Consulate General, confidential file, 1950–52, Record Group (RG) 84, US National Archives, College Park, MD (hereafter NA-CP).
8. Lutkins to Baldwin, 25 January 1952, Kuala Lumpur Consulate General, confidential file, 1950–52, RG 84, NA-CP. See also Thor-Egil Eide, "Outside the Perimeter? An Inquiry into US–Malayan Relations, 1948–1957," hovedfag dissertation, University of Oslo, 1998.
9. Edward Lansdale, journal no. 17, 24 August 1947, Manila, Lansdale Papers, Hoover Institution Archives, Stanford, CA.
10. Bohannan, quoted in Michael McClintock, "Instruments of Statecraft: US Guerrilla Warfare, Counterinsurgency, and Counterterrorism, 1940–1990," on http://www.statecraft.org/chapter4.html. See also the official US Army history of the operation, Lawrence M. Greenberg, "The Hukbalahap Insurrection: A Case Study of a Successful Anti-Insurgency Operation in the Philippines, 1946–1955," on http://www.army.mil/cmh-pg/books/coldwar/huk/huk-fm.htm.

11. McCarthy speech, US Senate, 6 December 1950, quoted from *Major Speeches and Debates by Senator Joseph McCarthy Delivered in the US Senate 1950–1951* (New York: Garden Press, 1975), pp. 157–160.

12. Eisenhower notes, 29 April 1950, quoted from *The Papers of Dwight D. Eisenhower*, ed. Alfred D. Chandler (Baltimore, MD: Johns Hopkins University Press, 1981), vol. XI, p. 1092.

13. Quoted from Robert D. Schulzinger, *A Time for War: The United States and Vietnam, 1941–1975* (Oxford: Oxford University Press, 1997), p. 55.

14. *Ibid.*, p. 58.

15. Stephen Kinzer, *All the Shah's Men: An American Coup and the Roots of Middle East Terror* (Hoboken, NJ: John Wiley, 2003), p. 158.

16. Quoted *ibid.*, p. 107.

17. *Ibid.*, p. 70.

18. Quoted from James F. Goode, *The United States and Iran: In the Shadow of Mussadiq* (New York: St. Martin's Press, 1997), p. 82.

19. Record of a meeting of the National Security Council, 4 March 1953, in *FRUS, 1952–1954*, vol. X, p. 693.

20. See CIA, "Clandestine Service History: Overthrow of Premier Mossadeq of Iran, November 1952–August 1953," on http://www.nytimes.com/library/world/mideast/iran-cia-intro.pdf. This internal CIA postmortem on the coup, which was leaked to the *New York Times* in 2000, stresses the difficulties the CIA station had had with its local allies: "Specifically, it had been realized that not all the Persians involved in the plan would take the action required of them, [and] that even those who took it might not follow through exactly as required … That the initial military aspects went astray may be charged directly to the Persians, who at the very end refused to continue to accept the guidance which the station felt was so essential." It is to be assumed that this goes in particular for Shaban 'No Brains' Jafari, the Teheran gang leader who was charged with engineering the street riots.

21. Douglas Little, *American Orientalism: The United States and the Middle East Since 1945* (London: I. B. Tauris, 2003), p. 217.

22. Gamal Abdel Nasser, "The Philosophy of the Revolution" (1954), in Sylvia G. Haim, ed., *Arab Nationalism: An Anthology* (Berkeley, CA: University of California Press, 1962), pp. 230–231. Nasser's reference is to the Italian playwright Luigi Pirandello's *Sei personaggi in cerca d'autore* (1921).

23. Little, *American Orientalism*, p. 166.

24. Mark Kramer, "New Evidence on Soviet Decision-Making and the 1956 Polish and Hungarian Crises," *Cold War International History Project (CWIHP) Bulletin*, (8–9); Csaba Bekes, *The 1956 Hungarian Revolution and World Politics*, CWIHP, Working Paper 16 (Washington, DC: Woodrow Wilson Center, n.d.). See also M. J. Cohen, "Prologue to Suez: Anglo-American Planning for Military Intervention in a Middle East War, 1955–1956," *Journal of Strategic Studies*, 26.2 (June 2003): 152–183.

25. Quoted from Little, *American Orientalism*, p. 174.

26. *Ibid.*, p. 176.

27. "The Suez Canal Problem, 26 July–22 September 1956," US Department of State publication no. 6392 (Washington: GPO, 1956), pp. 345–351.

28. Little, *American Orientalism*, p. 178.
29. Rossiiskii gosudarstvennyi arkhiv sotsialno-politicheskoi istorii (hereafter RGASPI), f. 3, op. 12, d. 995, pp. 1–19.
30. Truman, letter to Edward Jacobson, 27 February 1948, on http://www.trumanlibrary.org/.
31. "Draft: The Position of the United States with Respect to Palestine, NSC," 17 February 1948, on http://www.trumanlibrary.org/. The Joint Chiefs of Staff were skeptical toward the partition plan because they felt it would create too much Arab resistance and also for fear of the introduction of Soviet UN troops into the region.
32. Isaac Alteras, *Eisenhower and Israel: US–Israeli Relations, 1953–1960* (Gainesville, FL: University of Florida Press, 1993); Abraham Ben-Zvi, *Decade of Transition: Eisenhower, Kennedy, and the Origins of the American–Israeli Alliance* (New York: Columbia University Press, 1998). The key argument in the latter volume is that US policies changed dramatically during Eisenhower's second term in office.
33. Quoted from Audrey R. Kahin and George McT. Kahin, *Subversion as Foreign Policy: The Secret Eisenhower and Dulles Debacle in Indonesia* (New York: New Press, 1995), p. 75.
34. *Ibid.*, p. 94.
35. *Ibid.*, p. 124.
36. US and ROC pilots flew bombing missions from Taiwan as late as July 1958.
37. NSC Memorandum of Discussion, 7 August 1958, in *FRUS, 1958–1960*, vol. XIV, p. 20.
38. Gerhard Th. Molin, *Die USA und der Kolonialismus: Amerika als Partner und Nachfolger der belgischen Macht in Afrika 1939–1965* (Berlin: Akademie Verlag, 1996), p. 153. Niemeyer was a German refugee who served on the State Department Policy Planning Staff (he later became known as the author of the widely used pamphlet *An Inquiry into Soviet Mentality* [New York: Praeger, 1956]).
39. See Jonathan E. Helmreich, *United States Relations with Belgium and the Congo, 1940–1960* (Newark, DE: University of Delaware Press, 1998), especially pp. 149–172, and also his *Gathering Rare Ores: The Diplomacy of Uranium Acquisition, 1943–1954* (Princeton, NJ: Princeton University Press, 1986).
40. Bonnet to Schuman, 18 July 1950, MAE, B-Amérique, Etats-Unis 1944–52, vol. 106 quoted in Matthew Connelly, *A Diplomatic Revolution: Algeria's Fight for Independence and the Origins of the Post-Cold War Era* (Oxford: Oxford University Press, 2002), p. 50.
41. For an excellent overview of desegregation in the US Army, see Morris J. MacGregor Jr., *Integration of the Armed Forces 1940–1965* (Washington, DC: Center of Military History, United States Army, 1985). Executive Order 9981, signed by Truman on 26 July 1948, integrated the armed forces in principle, but it took several years for the order to be carried out in full in all branches.
42. Conversation between Bunche and de Muelenaere, 16 November 1942, quoted in Molin, *USA und der Kolonialismus*, pp. 101–102.
43. Robert McGregor to State, 14 October 1949, quoted in Thomas Borstelmann, *Apartheid's Reluctant Uncle: the United States and Southern Africa in the Early Cold War* (Oxford: Oxford University Press, 1993), p. 129.

44. George McGhee, *Envoy to the Middle World: Adventures in Diplomacy* (New York: Harper & Row, 1983), pp. 143–144.

45. Record of conversation between Eisenhower and Herter, 24 March 1960, in *FRUS, 1958–1960*, vol. XIV, pp. 741–742.

46. Record of conversation between Eisenhower and Macmillan, 28 March 1960, *ibid.*, p. 746.

47. NIE 73–60, "The Outlook for South Africa," 19 July 1960, *ibid.*, p. 754.

48. Harriman to Rusk, 1 July 1964, in *FRUS, 1964–1968*, vol. XXIV, p. 742. For an overview of US support for FNLA, see "Angola (heading not declassified)," State Department Bureau of Intelligence and Research report, 6 March 1967, *ibid.*, pp. 770–771.

49. State to Lisbon Embassy, 8 February 1968, *ibid.*, p. 781.

50. "Special Message to Congress on Foreign Aid," 22 March 1961, *Public Papers of the Presidents of the United States* (hereafter *PPP-US*) *John F. Kennedy*, vol. 1, pp. 340–343.

51. Bowles to Kennedy, n.d., "Report on a Mission to Africa, October 157–November 9, 1962," DDRS.

52. Dulles quoted in Mary L. Dudziak, *Cold War Civil Rights: Race and the Image of American Democracy* (Princeton, NJ: Princeton University Press, 2002), p. 131.

53. Malcolm, speech in Palm Gardens, New York, 8 April 1964, in *Malcolm X Speaks* (New York: Pathfinder Press, 1965), p. 55.

54. Connelly, *Diplomatic Revolution*, p. 253.

55. Lumumba, "Speech on Independence Day," 30 June 1960, on http://members.lycos.nl/pol/toespraaklum.htm.

56. NSC meeting, 5 May 1960, quoted in "Editorial Note" in *FRUS, 1958–1960*, vol. XIV, p. 274. For the rather unconvincing view that conflicts among business groups determined US Congo policy, see David N. Gibbs, *The Political Economy of Third World Intervention: Mines, Money, and US Policy in the Congo Crisis* (Chicago, IL: University of Chicago Press, 1991), especially pp. 28–33, 193–208. The best overview of US involvement in the Congo is Lise A. Namikas, "Battleground Africa: The Cold War and the Congo Crisis, 1960–1965," Ph.D. dissertation, University of Southern California, 2002.

57. Record of conversation, NSC, 21 July 1960, DDRS.

58. Lumumba quoted in Cumming to Herter, 25 July 1960, in *FRUS, 1958–1960*, vol. XIV, p. 356. For the Soviet view of Katanga, see "Shaba: etnoregionalizm i natsionalnaia politika" (Shaba: Ethnoregionalism and National Policy), *Vostok*, 2 (1993): 47–56.

59. Quoted in Madeleine G. Kalb, *The Congo Cables: The Cold War in Africa from Eisenhower to Kennedy* (New York: Macmillan, 1982), p. 37.

60. Record of conversation between Herter and Lumumba, 27 July 1960, in *FRUS, 1958–1960*, vol. XIV, pp. 359–366.

61. NSC, 18 August 1960, *ibid.*, p. 424.

62. Joint Chiefs of Staff study, quoted at NSC meeting on 1 August 1960, *ibid.*, p. 373.

63. Dulles to CIA Station Officer, Kinshasa, 26 August 1960, quoted in *Alleged Assassination Plots Involving Foreign Leaders: An Interim Report of the Select*

Committee to Study Governmental Operations with Respect to Intelligence Activities, United States Senate; Together with Additional, Supplemental, and Separate Views (hereafter *Interim Report, US Senate*) (New York: Norton, 1976), pp. 15; see also excerpts from minutes of NSC Special Committee, 25 August 1960, *ibid.*, pp. 60–61.

64. Embassy, Leopoldville (Kinshasa) to State, 18 September 1960, in *FRUS, 1958–1960*, vol. XIV, p. 494.

65. *Interim Report, US Senate* and Kalb, *Congo Cables*, p. xi. For the British view of Lumumba, see Alan James, *Britain and the Congo Crisis* (Houndsmills: Macmillan, 1996), pp. 53–63.

66. *FRUS, 1958–1960*, vol. XIV, p. 486.

67. Carl Mydans and Shelley Smith Mydans, *The Violent Peace* (New York: Athenaeum, 1968), p. 313.

68. The Belgian Parliament's Commission of Inquiry report into Lumumba's death: Chambre des Représentants de Belgique, "Enquête Parlementaire visant à déterminer les circonstances exactes de l'assassinat de Patrice Lumumba et l'implication éventuelle des responsables politiques belges dans celui-ci." Report made on behalf of the Commission of Inquiry by Daniel Bacquelaine et al., doc no. 50 0312/006, 16 November 2001. See also Ludo De Witte, *The Assasination of Lumumba* (London: Verso, 2002).

69. *FRUS, 1961–1963*, vol. XX, pp. 858–863.

70. Leopoldville (Kinshasa) to State, 25 October 1963, quoted in Kalb, *Congo Cables*, p. 377.

71. Record of conversation, NSC meeting on the Congo, 11 August 1964, DDRS.

72. Record of telephone conversation between LBJ and Ball, 25 November 1964, DDRS.

73. Record of telephone conversation between LBJ and Rusk, 26 November 1964, 12 p.m., tape number 6486, Lyndon Baines Johnson Presidential Library, Austin, Texas (hereafter LBJL).

74. Record of telephone conversatio between LBJ and Walter Reuther (UAW President), 24 November 1964, 10 a.m., tape number 6474, LBJL.

75. Gleijeses, *Conflicting Missions*, p. 72. For a Soviet view, see Iurii Vinokurov, "Povstancheskoe dvizhenie 1963–1965 gg. v Kongo" (The Rebel Movement of 1963–65 in the Congo), *Narody Azii i Afriki*, 5 (1981): 102–109.

76. Ambassador Godley to State, 30 October 1965, DDRS.

77. Ahmed Ben Bella, quoted in Gleijeses, p. 65.

78. Malcolm, speech in Palm Gardens, New York, 8 April in 1964, in *Malcolm X Speaks*, p. 55.

79. Lars Schoultz, *Beneath the United States: A History of US Policy Toward Latin America* (Cambridge, MA: Harvard University Press, 1998), p. 115.

80. See Jürgen Buchenau, *In the Shadow of the Giant: The Making of Mexico's Central American Policy, 1876–1930* (Tuscaloosa, AL: University of Alabama Press, 1996).

81. Sandino's letter to the rulers of Latin America, 4 August 1928, on http://www.latinamericastudies.org/sandino/sandino8-4-28.htm.

82. CIA, "Soviet Objectives in Latin America," ORE 16/1, 1 November 1947, on http://www.foia.cia.gov.

83. CIA, Special Estimate, "Probable Developments in the World Situation through Mid-1953," 24 September 1951, on http://www.foia.cia.gov.

84. CIA, Information Report, "Personal Political Orientation of President Arbenz/ Possibility of a Left-Wing Coup," September 1952, on http://www.foia.cia.gov.

85. Arbenz quoted in Gleijeses, *Conflicting Missions*, p. 150. For an outline of Arbenz agrarian policy, see *ibid.*, pp. 149–170 and Douglas W. Trefzger, "Guatemala's 1952 Agrarian Reform Law: A Critical Reassessment," *International Social Science Review*, 77.1–2 (2002): 32–46.

86. CIA, Special Report on the Political Situation of Guatemala and its Relation to Hemispheric Security, 3 March 1953, and Memorandum for Director of Central Intelligence, "Indications of Soviet Involvement in ALFHEM shipment; Possibility of Further Shipments," 20 May 1954, both on http://www.foia.cia.gov.

87. Nick Cullather, *Secret History: The CIA's Classified Account of its Operations in Guatemala, 1952–1954* (Stanford, CA: Stanford University Press, 1999), p. 69.

88. *Ibid.*, pp. 62–63.

89. See Russ Olson, "You Can't Spit on a Foreign Policy," *SHAFR Newsletter* (September 2000).

90. "Che" Guevara, *Back on the Road: A Journey to Central America* (London: Vintage, 2002), p. 67.

91. Cullather, *Secret History*, p. 110.

92. Record of conversation between Alexis Johnson, McGeorge Bundy and others, 28 March 1964, subject: Brazil, DDRS.

93. Record of telephone conversation between LBJ, the Under Secretary of State George Ball, and Assistant Secretary of State Thomas Mann, 31 March 1964, 2:38 p.m. tape number 2718, LBJL.

94. Record of telephone conversation between LBJ and Mann, 3 April 1964, 12:06 p.m., tape number 2843, LBJL; record of telephone conversation between LBJ and McGeorge Bundy, 14 April 1964, 12:50 p.m., tape number 3025, LBJL. In a meeting with the President on 1 April, Secretary McNamara reported on the status of the task force: "It sailed this morning and would be in the vicinity of Santos by the 11th of April. The arms and ammunition are now being assembled for airlift in New Jersey and the airlift would take 16 hours from the time of decision. As to POL [petroleum, oil, lubricants], the earliest Navy tanker, diverted from the Aruba area, would be in place on the 10th or 11th of April. There is, however, a Norwegian tanker chartered by Esso in the South Atlantic loaded with the necessary motor and aviation gasoline. It is headed for Buenos Aires and should arrive there on the 5th or 6th of April" (record of conversation, 1 April 1964, in *FRUS, 1964–1968*, vol. XXXI. The task force was recalled on 3 April, when it was clear that the coup had succeeded.

95. Embassy, Rio de Janeiro to Secretary of State, 10 June 1964, DDRS. For US–Brazilian relations up to the coup, see Michael W. Weis, "The Twilight of Pan-Americanism: The Alliance for Progress, Neo-Colonialism, and Non-Alignment in Brazil, 1961–1964," *International History Review*, 23. 2 (2001): 322–344. On the Brazilian side, see *Visões do golpe: a memória militar sobre 1964* (Visions of a Coup: On Military Memories of 1964), introduced and

compiled by Maria Celina D'Araújo, Gláucio Ary Dillon Soares, and Celso Castro (Rio de Janeiro: Relume-Dumará, 1994).

96. CIA, "The Policies of the Castelo Branco Regime in Brazil: Achievements and Potential Conflicts," 31 December 1964, DDRS.

97. Dwight H. Perkins et al., *Economics of Development* (New York: Norton, 2001), p. 121.

98. Brasilia to Secretary of State, 25 September 1964, DDRS.

99. Montevideo to Secretary of State, 27 July 1965, DDRS.

100. CIA, Intelligence Information Cable, 26 April 1965, DDRS.

101. Record of telephone conversation between LBJ and Mansfield, 30 April 1965, 11:51 a.m., tape number 7410, LBJL. According to President Johnson, "Admiral Raborn [Director of Central Intelligence] said that Castro is taking over."

102. Record of telephone conversation between LBJ and Fortas and McNamara, 30 April 1965, 10:50 a.m., tape number 6504, LBJL.

103. Record of telephone conversation between LBJ and McGeorge Bundy, 1 May 1965, 2:21 p.m., tape number 7506, LBJL.

104. Record of telephone conversation between LBJ and Fortas, 16 May 1965, 12:30 p.m., tape number 6505, LBJL.

105. Clara Nieto, *Masters of War: Latin America and United States Aggression from the Cuban Revolution through the Clinton Years* (New York: Seven Stories Press, 2003), p. 101.

106. Embassy, Paris to Secretary of State, 4 May 1965, DDRS.

107. Some of Johnson's key advisers thought the President ought to have been more careful in blaming unrest in the Dominican Republic on Castro. At the height of the crisis Secretary of Defense McNamara told Johnson, "I think you've got a pretty tough job to prove that, Mr. President. As president. The rest of us can say things like that and we don't have to prove it … You don't know that Castro is trying to do anything. You'd have a hard time proving to any group that Castro has done more than train these people. *We*'ve trained a lot of people. He's trained a lot of people. I think this puts your own status and prestige too much on the line … [unclear] shown any evidence that I've seen that Castro has been directing this or has had any control over those people once they got back there" (record of telephone conversation between LBJ and McNamara, 30 April 1965, 5:05 p.m., tape number 6504, LBJL.

108. Komer to Bundy, 7 July 1965, DDRS.

109. See, for instance, Kevin H. O'Rourke and Jeffrey G. Williamson, *Globalization and History: The Evolution of a Nineteenth-Century Atlantic Economy* (Cambridge, MA: MIT Press, 1999).

110. Kunibert Raffer and H. W. Singer, *The Economic North–South Divide: Six Decades of Unequal Development* (Northampton, MA: Edward Elgar, 2001), p. 25. International trade is, of course, of different significance to different Third World countries; while the postwar average for Ethiopia is 13 percent, it is 48 percent for Nigeria.

111. While industrial production grew by 3.9 percent on average per year between 1963 and 1986, consumption of raw materials grew by only 1.5 percent (Perkins et al., *Economics of Development*, p. 635).

112. US Agency for International Development (USAID), "US Overseas Loans and Grants and Assistance from International Organizations: Obligations and Loan Authorizations, July 1, 1945–September 30, 2001," on http://www.dec.org/pdf_docs/PNACR900.pdf.

113. Special Message to Congress on Foreign Aid, 22 March 1961, *PPP-US, John F. Kennedy*, vol. 1, pp. 204–206.

114. Lizette Alvarez, "Lifting History's Curtain: Nixon Considered Seizing Oil Fields in '73," *International Herald Tribune*, 2 January 2004.

5   THE CUBAN AND VIETNAMESE CHALLENGES

1. "Nikita Khrushchev's speech to the December (1963) CC CPSU Plenum," 13 December 1963, Rossiiskii gosudarstvennyi arkhiv noveishei istorii (Russian State Archive of Contemporary History; hereafter RGANI), f. 2, op. 1, d. 679, pp. 126–127.

2. For the genesis of this concept from 1958 and for Mao's use of the term "intermediate zone," see Pang Xianzhi and Jin Chongji, chief eds., *Mao Zedong zhuan, 1949–1976* (Beijing: Zhongyang wenxian, 2003), vol. II, pp. 905–909.

3. Hoover to Jenkins (White House), FBI report on January 1964 visit to Indonesia by Canadian and Bulgarian Communists, 7 April 1964, Declassified Documents Reference Service (hereafter DDRS).

4. Record of conversation between Soviet and Chinese delegations, Moscow, 12 July 1963, Stiftung Archiv der Parteien und Massenorganisationen in Bundesarchiv, Berlin (hereafter SAPMO-BArch), DY-30, JIV 2/207 698.

5. Both quoted in Sergei Radchenko, "North Korea: The Soviet Union's Unreliable Ally," on http://www.radchenko.net/nkresearch.shtm.

6. Kim Il Sung, *The Present Situation and the Task of our Party (Report at the KWP Party Conference – 05.10.66)* (Pyongyang: Foreign Languages Publishing House, 1970), p. 6.

7. Soviet Embassy, Beijing to Foreign Minister, Moscow, "On the CC CCP's reaction to the CC CPSU letters dated 21 February and 30 March 1963," 17 May 1963, Arkhiv vneshnei politiki Rossiiskoi Federatsii (hereafter AVPRF), f. 0100, op. 56, pa. 506, d. 67, p. 94. I am grateful to Sergey Radchenko for drawing my attention to this document; see Sergey Radchenko, "The China Puzzle: Soviet Politics and the Conflict with Beijing, 1962–1969," Ph.D. thesis, London School of Economics, 2005.

8. Foreign Ministry, Far Eastern Department, "Report on the Splitting Activities of the CCP Leadership in Third Countries," 10 December 1963, AVPRF, F. 0100, op. 56, pa. 506, d. 67, p. 197.

9. *Ibid.*, p. 206.

10. *Ibid.*, p. 209.

11. *Ibid.*, p. 210.

12. "Kosygin's remarks at a private luncheon," 10 February 1967, National Archives of the United Kingdom, Public Record Office (hereafter PRO), PREM 13/1840, p. 65.

13. Telephone conversation between President Johnson and Former President Eisenhower, 25 June 1967, in *Foreign Relations of the United States* (hereafter *FRUS*), *1964–1968*, vol. XIV, on http://www.state.gov/r/pa/ho/frus/johnsonlb/xiv/.

14. *Pravda*, 2 September 1964, p. 2.

15. Andrei Aleksandrov-Agentov, *Ot Kollontai do Gorbacheva: vospominaniia diplomata sovetnika A. A. Gromyko, pomoshchnika L. I. Brezhneva, Iu. V. Andropova, K. U. Chernenko i M. S. Gorbacheva* (From Kollontai to Gorbachev: The Memoirs of a Diplomat and Adviser to A. A. Gromyko, and Aide to L. I. Brezhnev, Iu. V. Andropov, K. U. Chernenko, and M. S. Gorbachev) (Moscow: Mezhdunarodnye otnosheniia, 1994), p. 112.

16. "Castro speaks before Havana rally," 21 January 1959, Castro Speech Archive on http://lanic.utexas.edu.

17. Quoted in Leycester Coltman, *The Real Fidel Castro* (New Haven, CT: Yale University Press, 2003), p. 133.

18. *Ibid.*

19. Quoted *ibid.*, p. 185.

20. See http://www.pacifica.org/programs/slcuba.html.

21. Piero Gleijeses, *Conflicting Missions: Havana, Washington, and Africa, 1959–1976* (Chapel Hill, NC: University of North Carolina Press, 2002), p. 18.

22. Coltman, *Real Castro*, p. 175.

23. GDR Deputy Foreign Minister Winzer to Ulbricht, 28 October 1960, SAPMO-BArch, Büro Walter Ulbricht, DY 30/3465.

24. Aleksandr Fursenko and Timothy Naftali, *One Hell of a Gamble: Khruschshev, Castro, and Kennedy, 1958–1963* (New York: Norton, 1998), pp. 71, 160–165.

25. Record of conversation between Casto and Mikoyan, 3 November 1962, quoted in "Mikoyan's Mission to Havana: Cuban–Soviet Negotiations, November 1962," *Cold War International History Project (CWIHP) Bulletin* 5.

26. "Fidel Castro Speech at University," 13 March, Havana Domestic Radio and Television Services 0302, GMT, 14 March 1965, Castro Speech Archive on http://lanic.utexas.edu.

27. "Castro Speech on Playa Giron Anniversary," Havana Domestic Radio and Television Services in Spanish 0341, GMT, 20 April 1965, on-line *ibid.*

28. Enesto Guevara, *Guerrilla Warfare* (New York: Monthly Review Press, 1961), ch. 1. For a critical overview, see Matt D. Childs, "An Historical Critique of the Emergence and Evolution of Ernesto Che Guevara's *Foco* Theory," *Journal of Latin American Studies*, 27 (1995): 593–624.

29. Rostow to Johnson, 11 October 1967, in *FRUS, 1964–1968*, vol. XXXI.

30. Ernesto Guevara, *The African Dream: The Diaries of the Revolutionary War in the Congo* (London: Harvill Press, 2000).

31. *Ibid.*, pp. 224, 226.

32. Chin Peng, as told to Ian Ward and Norma Miraflor, *Alias Chin Peng: My Side of History* (Singapore: Media Masters, 2003), p. 354.

33. Record of conversation between Soviet ambassador Leonid Sokolov and Pham Van Dong, 3 May 1960, AVPRF, f. 079, op. 15, pa. 28, d. 6, pp. 101–104.

34. See Mari Olsen, "Changing Alliances: Moscow's Relations with Hanoi and the Role of China, 1949–1964," Ph.D. dissertation, University of Oslo, 2004.
35. Record of conversation between Zimyanin and Li Zhimin, 18 September 1957, AVPRF, f. 079, op. 12, pa. 17, d. 6, p. 69.
36. See Matthew Jones, *Conflict and Confrontation in Southeast Asia: Britain, the United States, Indonesia and the Creation of Malaysia* (Cambridge: Cambridge University Press, 2001).
37. Sukarno, as told to Cindy Williams, *Sukarno: An Autobiography* (Indianapolis, IN: Bobbs-Merrill, 1965).
38. Quoted in John Legge, *Sukarno: A Political Biography*, 3rd edn (Singapore: Archipelago Press, 2003), p. 396.
39. Record of conversation between Tito and Sukarno, Cairo, 5 October 1964, Arkhiv Srbije i Crne Gore (hereafter ASCG), A CK SKJ IX, 43/IV-30.
40. Hoover to Jenkins (White House), 7 April 1964, FBI report on January 1964 visit to Indonesia by Canadian and Bulgarian Communists, DDRS.
41. Soviet Embassy, Jakarta, to Foreign Minister, "Report on comments in the PKI newspaper Harian Rakjat on Soviet domestic and foreign policy," April 1965, RGANI, f. 5, op. 55, d. 144, pp. 4–14; see also embassy report on Aidid, n.d. (spring 1965), AVPRF, f. 091, op. 16, pa. 22, d. 20, pp. 2–8. The archives of the International Departments of the former Communist Party of the Soviet Union, now part of the Russian State Archive of Contemporary History, RGANI, in Moscow, is by far the most important source for the study of Soviet Third World policies in the late Cold War era. It consists of a very large collection of materials with differing provenances – among them embassy reports, documents created for the Politburo or the party Secretariat, intelligence summaries, and records of conversations with foreign leaders. A very large percentage of the files in RGANI are unfortunately still classified.
42. Soviet Embassy, Jakarta, to MO (n.d., early 1964), "On the position of the PKI leadership," RGANI, f. 5, op. 55, d. 116, p. 7. See also *ibid.*, pp. 10–14, on Soviet views of recent Chinese policy toward Southeast Asia.
43. Soviet ambassador to MO, 16 October 1965, "On the political situation in Indonesia in connection with the 30 September 1965 affair," RGANI, f. 5, op. 33, d. 218. I am grateful to Pål Johansen for alerting me to this key document. On Nasution's relations with the Soviets, see record of conversation between Soviet ambassador and General Nasution, 29 May 1964, RGANI, f. 5, op. 55, d. 116, pp. 18–22, and CIA intelligence information cable, "Sukarno's Actions and Plans to Balance the Power of Forces in Indonesia," 14 May 1965, DDRS.
44. US Embassy, Jakarta, to Department of State, 24 August 1964, in *FRUS, 1964–1968*, vol. XXVI.
45. Memorandum prepared in the Central Intelligence Agency, 9 November 1965, "Covert Assistance to the Indonesian Armed Forces Leaders," *ibid.*
46. For a discussion, see Theodore Friend, *Indonesian Destinies* (Cambridge, MA: Belknap, 2003).
47. Komer to Johnson, 12 March 1966, in *FRUS, 1964–1968*, vol. XXVI.
48. 557th Meeting of the National Security Council on 10 May 1966, in *FRUS, 1964–1968*, vol. IV.

49. Jose Maria Sison with Rainer Werning, *The Philippine Revolution: The Leader's View* (New York: Crane Russak, 1989), especially pp. 27–32.

50. Hans-Jürgen Krahl, speech in court, 1968, in Lutz Schulenburg, ed., *Das Leben ändern, die Welt verändern* (Hamburg: Nautilus, 1998), p. 391.

51. Günther Grass, *Denkzettel: Politische Reden und Aufsätze* (Darmstadt: Luchterhand, 1978), p. 85.

52. Memorandum from President Nixon to his Assistant (Haldeman), his Assistant for Domestic Affairs (Ehrlichman), and his Assistant for National Security Affairs (Kissinger), Washington, 2 March 1970, in *FRUS, 1969–1976*, vol. I, p. 204.

53. Memorandum from Marshall Wright of the National Security Council Staff to the President's Assistant for National Security Affairs (Kissinger), 10 January 1970, *ibid.*, p. 163. Showing the plight of policy advisers everywhere, Wright continued: "That being true, there is (or at least, I can find) no broad and positive conceptual base which can credibly be put forward to explain why we do what we do in Africa and the UN. The real base we cannot mention. The task then is to put the best possible face upon essentially negative roles, and to try to make them sound more positive and more integrated than they actually are."

54. Kissinger to Nixon, "Analysis of changes in international politics since World War II and their implications for our basic assumptions about US foreign policy," 20 October 1969, *ibid.*

55. Notes from Legislative Leadership Meeting, 17 February 1970, *ibid.*

56. On 25 July 1969, during a tour of Asia, President Nixon met with reporters in Guam; see *ibid.*

57. 12 October 1970, President Nixon and Henry Kissinger; see *ibid.*

58. For a useful but selective collection of documents on Soviet policy toward the Middle East from 1947 to 1967, see V. V. Naumkin, chief ed., *Blizhnevostochnyi konflikt: iz dokumentov Arkhiva vneshnei politiki Rossiiskoi Federatsii* (The Near East Conflict: From the Documents of the Foreign Policy Archive of the Russian Federation) (2 vols.; Moscow: Mezhdunarodnyi fond "Demokratiia," 2003).

59. Nasser quoted in Mohammad H. Heikal, *The Road to Ramadan* (New York: Ballantine, 1975), p. 80. For an overview of Egyptian criticism of the Soviets, see the records of conversations with the Yugoslav ambassador in Cairo in the autumn of 1967, ASCG, A CK SKJ IX, 43/IV-75.

60. Record of conversation, conference of the Communist and Workers' parties and chiefs of governments of the socialist countries on the situation in the Middle East, Budapest, 11–12 July 1967, CWIHP on http://www.wwics.si.edu.

61. See Fred Wehling, *Irresolute Princes: Kremlin Decision Making in Middle East Crises, 1967–1973* (London: Palgrave, 1997), p. 72.

62. Vinogradov quoted in Isabella Ginor, "'Under the Yellow Arab Helmet Gleamed Blue Russian Eyes': Operation *Kavkaz* and the War of Attrition, 1969–1970," *Cold War History*, 3.1 (2002): 127–156. See also Isabella Ginor, "The Russians were Coming: The Soviet Military Threat in the 1967 Six-Day War," *Middle East Review of International Affairs*, 4.4 (December 2000).

63. Karen N. Brutents, former first deputy head of the Central Committee's International Department, interview with author, Moscow, 5 October 1993 (hereafter "Brutents interview" and date). Ginor claims 50,000, citing an article by Vladimir Voronov in the Tel Aviv newspaper *Ekho*, 13 September 1999.

64. Urgent telegram from GDR ambassador Bierbach (Cairo) to Politburo, Berlin, 18 July 1972, SAPMO-BArch, DY30 J IV 2/2J/4211. For overviews, see Vladimir Safonov, ed., *Grif "sekretno" sniat: kniga ob uchastii sovetskikh voennosluzhashchikh v arabo-izrailskom konflikte* (Secret Classification Removed: A Book on the Participation of Soviet Military Servicemen in the Arab–Israeli Conflict) (Moscow: Sovet veteranov boevykh deistvii v Egipte, 1997); Vladimir A. Zolotarev et al., *Rossiya (SSSR) v lokal'nykh voynakh i vooruzhennykh konfliktakh vtoroy poloviny XX veka* (Russia [USSR] in Local Wars and Military Conflicts in the Second Half of the Twentieth Century) (Moscow: Ministerstvo oboroni Rossiiskoi Federatsii, 2000); and M. S. Meier et al., eds., *Togda v Egipte ...: kniga op pomoshchi SSSR Egiptu v voennom protivostoianii s Izrailem* (When in Egypt ...: A Book on the Soviet Support for Egypt in the Wars to Resist Israel) (Moscow: Institut stran Azii i Afriki pri MGU im. M. V. Lomonosova, 2001).

65. Grüneberg (Abteilung Internationale Vertretungen [hereafter AIV]) to Politburo, report on Arafat's visit to the GDR, 6–8 August 1974, SAPMO-BArch, DY30 J IV 2/2J/5412. On Iraq, see report on visit of First Secretary of the Iraq Communist Party, Aziz Mohamed, to the GDR, 27 October– 5 November 1973, SAPMO-BArch, DY30 J IV 2/2J/5007 and AIV report to Politburo on the situation in the Syrian Communist Party, 20 June 1974, SAPMO-BArch, DY30 J IV 2/2J/5337.

66. Kissinger to Secretary of State, 25 July 1972, "Follow-Up on the President's Talk with the Shah of Iran," DDRS.

67. William V. Broe (Chief, Western Hemisphere Division), "Memorandum for the Record: Genesis of Project FUBELT," 16 September 1970, held at State Department Freedom of Information Act Electronic Reading Room, see http://www.foia.state.gov/.

68. Handwritten notes, Richard Helms, "Meeting with President of Chile at 15.25 Sept. 15 '70, Present: John Mitchell and Henry Kissinger," on http://www.foia.state.gov/.

69. Memorandum, Kissinger to Nixon, "NSC Meeting, November 6 –Chile," 5 November 1970, Nixon Presidential Materials Project (hereafter NPMP) NSC IF, box H029. See also Tanya Harmer, "US-Chilean Relations and Nixon's Cold War in Latin America 1970–1973," Ph.D. thesis, London School of Economics, 2006.

70. Kissinger to Bunker, 15 January 1972, NPMP, NSC Series, box 872, for the President's Files – Lord–Vietnam Negotiations.

71. Celeste A. Wallander, "Third World Conflict in Soviet Military Thought," *World Politics*, 42.1 (October 1989): 31–37; Bruce D. Porter, *The USSR in Third World Conflicts: Soviet Arms and Diplomacy in Local Wars 1945–1980* (Cambridge: Cambridge University Press, 1984), pp. 36–59. See also Samuel P. Huntington, "Patterns of Intervention: Americans and Soviets in the Third World," *National Interest* (spring 1987): 39–47.

72. Other supporters of a more activist Third World policy in the early 1970s were the acting head of the Central Committee's Agitation and Propaganda Department, Aleksandr Iakovlev, and especially his deputy, Vadim Medvedev. Like Zagladin, Brutents, and Shakhnazarov, both Iakovlev and Medvedev ended up spearheading the Gorbachev reforms fifteen years later.

73. Karen N. Brutents, *Sovremennye natsionalno-osvoboditelnye revoliutsii. (Nekotorye voprosy teorii)* (Contemporary National Liberation Revolutions [Some Theoretical Questions]) (Moscow: Politizdat, 1974). Brutents' views here are in part based on a pamphlet he published in 1969, *Politika imperializma SShA v razvivaiushchikhsia stranakh* (US Imperialist Policy towards Developing Countries) (Moscow: Znanie).

74. Huntington, "Patterns of Intervention," p. 43; on Soviet interest groups, see Jan S. Adams, "Incremental Activism in Soviet Third World Policy: The Role of the International Department of the CPSU Central Committee," *Slavic Review*, 48.4 (winter 1989): 614–30, and for an insider's view of one of the institutions, former head of the KGB First Chief Directorate Leonid V. Shebarshin, *Ruka Moskvy: Zapiski nachalnika sovetskoi razvedki* (The Arm of Moscow: Reports by the Head of Soviet Intelligence) (Moscow: Tsentr-100, 1992) and his *Iz zhizni nachalnika razvedki* (From the Life of the Head of Intelligence) (Moscow: Mezhdunarodnye otnoshenii, 1994).

6 THE CRISIS OF DECOLONIZATION: SOUTHERN AFRICA

Some of the material in this chapter was previously used in my "Moscow and the Angolan Crisis, 1974–1976: A New Pattern of Intervention," *Cold War International History Project (CWIHP) Bulletin*, 8–9.

1. Verwoerd quoted in T. R. H. Davenport and Christopher Saunders, *South Africa: A Modern History* (5th edn; Houndsmills: Macmillan, 2000), p. 392.

2. Record of conversation between Rusk and Caetano, 19 November 1968, *Foreign Relations of the United States* (hereafter *FRUS*), *1964–1968*, vol. XII.

3. Neto, "Haste," written in prison in Lisbon in 1960, in *Sacred Hope: Poems by Agostinho Neto*, trans. Marga Holness (London: Journeyman, 1988), p. 129. For overviews of MPLA history from two very different perspectives, see Lúcio Lara, *Documentos e comentários para a história do MPLA* (Lisbon: Dom Quixote, 2000), and Mario Pinto de Andrade, in collaboration with José Eduardo Agualusa, *Origens do nacionalismo africano: continuidade e ruptura nos movimentos unitários emergentes da luta contra a dominaçao colonial portuguesa, 1911–1961* (The Origins of African Nationalism: Continuity and Change in the Unified Movements that Emerged from the Struggle against Portuguese Colonial Domination, 1911–1961) (Lisbon: Dom Quixote, 1997).

4. Interview at the Second Conference of the CONCP (Conferência das Organizações Nacionalistas das colonias Portuguesas), 3–8 October 1965. Document in author's possession; translated from French.

5. Interdepartmental Group for Africa (National Security Council), "Study in Response to National Security Memorandum 39: Southern Africa," 9 December 1969, Declassified Documents Reference Service (hereafter DDRS).

6. Notes on talk between Minister of Foreign Affairs and US Secretary of State, Dr. Kissinger, 5 October 1973, South African Department of Foreign Affairs Archives (hereafter SADFAA), 1/33/3, vol. 31.

7. Piero Gleijeses, *Conflicting Missions: Havana, Washington, and Africa, 1959–1976* (Chapel Hill, NC: University of North Carolina Press, 2002), p. 187.

8. Quoted *ibid.*, p. 189.

9. "We told him [Castro] openly that much of what they are doing is dangerous [and] that we do not concur with many things," Brezhnev had told visiting Polish Politburo member Zenon Kliszko on 24 June 1967 (record of conversation, CWIHP e-dossier no. 13, on http://wwics.si.edu).

10. GDR Ministerium fur Auswärtige Angelegenheiten report, "Einige Aspekte der politisch-ideologischen Entwicklung in Kuba," 21 April 1971, Stiftung Archiv der Parteien und Massenorganisationen in Bundesarchiv, Berlin (hereafter SAPMO-BArch), DY30 J IV 2/2J/3429; SKJ Presidium report on Cuban–Yugoslav relations, 23 May 1966, Arkhiv Srbijei Crne Gore (hereafter ASCG), A CK SKJ IX, 67–148.

11. Dohlus to Honecker, 3 July 1973, with enclosed record of conversation between Dohlus and Raul Castro, 22 June 1973, SAPMO-BArch, DY30 J IV 2/2J/4800.

12. Brutents interview, 17 December 1994; see also GDR Abteilung Internationale Vertretungen (hereafter AIV) report to SED Politburo on Southern Africa, 30 January 1975, SAPMO-BArch, DY30 J IV 2/2J/5652.

13. KGB to MO, 13 April 1970, Rossiiskii gosudarstvenni arkhiv noveishei istorii (hereafter RGANI), f. 5, op. 62, d. 535, pp. 7–9. This report, which is primarily an analysis of the preparations for the third summit conference of nonaligned nations in Lusaka, also notes that this conference will mean a step forward for Soviet diplomacy, that China's influence within the group is receeding, and that the United States is increasingly isolated in the Third World. See also KGB (Andropov) to MO, 6 May 1970, *ibid.*, pp. 32–35. On the KGB's influence on Brezhnev's thinking, see interview with Oleg Troianovskii, former Soviet UN ambassador, Moscow, 14 September 1992.

14. KGB to MO, 4 June 1970, RGANI, f. 5, op. 62, d. 536, pp. 73–76; KGB (Chebrikov) to MO, 26 November 1970, RGANI, f. 5, op. 62, d. 535, pp. 115–118. The latter report is based on an evaluation of European policies toward Portugal, originating with an analysis of materials from the British Conservative Party. The GRU, in a major report on US strategies in Africa, noted that the continent had become more important for the Americans both strategically and in terms of its natural resources. "Capitalist states," said the GRU, "[are] putting pressure on African countries to enter into base agreements and military assistance plans" (*ibid.*, pp. 71–90, 80).

15. Generalnii shtab voorushennikh sil SSSR (General Staff of the Armed Forces of the USSR), Glavnoie razvedivatelnoie upravleniie (Chief Intelligence Directorate of the General Staff; hereafter GRU) to MO, 15 September 1970, RGANI, f. 5, op. 62, d. 535, pp. 63–68; GRU to MO, "Po meropriiaiiam, napravlennim na oslablenie pozitsii KNR v Afrike" (On Measures (and) Directions to Weaken the Positions of the PRC in Africa), n.d., *ibid.*, pp. 96–101.

16. KGB (Andropov) to MO, 6 May 1970, *ibid.*, pp. 32–35, 35.

17. GRU report on China's military, economic, and political activities in Africa, 15 September 1970, and GRU report on measures to influence and weaken Chinese positions in Africa, 5 October 1970, *ibid.*, pp. 63–68, 96–101.

18. Report from an international conference of Communist and workers' parties, Moscow, 1969, Records of the ANC, London, Mayibuye Archives, University of the Western Cape, Belleville, South Africa (hereafter ANC papers, MA-UWC), box 21 (SACP; ANC: Dr. Y. Dadoo). See also GDR AIV, report on a visit by Yossuf Dadoo to the GDR, 26–30 November 1973 (dated 12 December 1973), SAPMO-BArch, DY30 J IV 2/2J/5069. For a Soviet view of the situation inside South Africa, see GRU to Politburo, "Voennoe-ekonomicheskie vozmoshnosti iushno-afrikanskoi respublikii" (The Republic of South Africa's military-economic potential), RGANI, f. 5, op. 62, d. 535, pp. 38–62.

19. Vladimir Shubin, *ANC: A View from Moscow* (Belleville, South Africa: Mayibuye Books, 1999), pp. 84–100, and Joe Slovo, "Thoughts on the Future of the Alliance," April 1969, ANC papers, MA-UWC, box 21 (SACP; ANC: Dr. Y. Dadoo). See also GRU(?) to MO, 29 September 1970, RGANI, f. 5, op. 62, d. 535, pp. 92–94 on Soviet attempts at relocating some of the ANC fighters in other African countries, for instance Algeria.

20. V. N. Bezukladnikov (councellor, Lusaka) to MO and attached letter from Neto to CPSU Central Committee concerning request for receiving MPLA members for military training, 24 June 1970, RGANI, f. 5, op. 62, d. 535, pp. 99–102; D. Z. Belokolos to MO, 14 July 1970, RGANI, f. 5, op. 62, d. 536, pp. 195–200.

21. Belokolos to MO, 25 July 1970, RGANI, f. 5, op. 62, d. 536, pp. 215–218; Embassy, Lusaka, to MO, Politpismo: "Perspektivy razvitiia borby naroda Angoly protiv portugalskikh kolonizatorov" (Perspectives on the Development of the Angolan People's Struggle against the Portuguese Colonizers), n.d. (October 1970), *ibid.*, pp. 219–228, 224. Soviet intelligence services still suspected that Neto kept the China option in reserve; see KGB to MO, 8 October 1970, *ibid.*, p. 212.

22. Soviet Embassy, Kinshasa, to MO, 16 January 1973, "K voprosu o primirenii mezhdu FNLA i MPLA" (On the question of reconciliation between the FNLA and the MPLA), RGANI, f. 5, op. 66, d. 843, pp. 4–9; Belokolos to MO, 10 October 1973, RGANI, f. 5, op. 66, d. 844, pp. 121–123.

23. Letter from Neto to Soviet Embassy, Zambia, 7 December 1972, with attached comments, RGANI, f. 5, op. 66, d. 844, pp. 2–5.

24. John Marcum, *The Angolan Revolution*, vol. II, *Exile Politics and Guerrilla Warfare, 1962–1976* (Cambridge, MA: MIT Press 1978), p. 199.

25. MPLA (Pedro Van Dunem) to CC CPSU, 11 December 1972, RGANI, f. 5, op. 66, d. 844, p. 22; Soviet Embassy, Kinshasa, to MO, 16 January 1973, "K voprosu o primirenii mezhdu FNLA i MPLA" (On the question of reconciliation between the FNLA and the MPLA), RGANI, f. 5, op. 66, d. 843, pp. 4–9; Soviet Embassy, Kinshasa, to MO, 12 April 1973, "K voprosu ob otnosheniiakh mezhdu MPLA i FNLA" (On the question of relations between the MPLA and the FNLA), RGANI, f. 5, op. 66, d. 843,

pp. 54–57; Neto to CC CPSU, 23 June 1973, RGANI, f. 5, op. 66, d. 844, p. 91; Belokolos to MO, 7 February 1974 (conversation with Daniel Chipenda), RGANI, f. 5, op. 67, d. 758, pp. 5–8.

26. Belokolos to MO, 25 October 1973, RGANI, f. 5, op. 66, d. 844, pp. 118–120; E. I. Afanasenko (ambassador, Brazzaville) to MO, 30 March 1974, Politpismo: "O poloshenii v 'Narodnom dvishenii za osvoboshdenie Angoli' (MPLA)" (On the situation in 'The People's Movement for the Liberaton of Angola' [MPLA]), RGANI, f. 5, op. 67, d. 758, pp. 37–45, 40. See also Ambassador Belokolos' conversation with Oliver Tambo, 5 July 1973, in which they discuss the future prospects of the MPLA, RGANI, f. 5, op. 66, d. 844, pp. 82–86.

27. AIV report to SED Politburo on Neto's stay in the GDR, 14–27 November 1971, SAPMO-BArch, DY30 J IV 2/2J/3880.

28. António de Spínola, *Portugal e o futuro: análise da conjuntura nacional* (Portugal and the Future: An Analysis of the National Prospect) (Lisbon: Arcádia, 1974).

29. For the attitudes and concerns of the coup plotters, see Manuel Bernardo, *Equívocos e realidades: Portugal, 1974–1975* (Equivocations and Realities: Portugal, 1974–1975) (2 vols.; Lisbon: Nova arrancada, 1999), and Jaime Nogueira Pinto, *O fim do estado nova e as origens do 25 de Abril* (The End of the New Order and the Origins of 25 April) (2nd edn; Lisbon: DIFEL, 1995).

30. For US aims with regard to Portugal before the April coup, see record of Secretary's Staff Meeting, 28 January 1974, Nixon Presidential Materials Project (hereafter NPMP). I am grateful to Mario del Pero for sharing with me this document and the one quoted below.

31. Record of conversation between Kissinger and Pedro Cortina Mauri, 9 October 1974, NPMP.

32. Iu. A. Iukalov (chargé d'affaires, Dar-es-Salam) to MO, 22 May 1974, RGANI, f. 5, op. 67, d. 758, pp. 70–71; E. I. Afanasenko to MO, 8 June 1974, *ibid.*, pp. 78–81.

33. Marcum, *Angolan Revolution*, vol. II, pp. 245–248.

34. *Ibid.*, pp. 249–250, George Wright, *US Policy Towards Angola: The Kissinger Years, 1974–1976* (Leeds: University of Leeds Press, 1990), pp. 18–23.

35. Afanasenko to MO, 10 October 1974, RGANI, f. 5, op. 67, d. 758, pp. 121–122. See also Marcum, *Angolan Revolution*, vol. II, pp. 251–253.

36. Marcum, *Angolan Revolution*, vol. II, p. 253; Michael Wolfers and Jane Bergerol, *Angola in the Front Line* (London: Zed Books, 1983), pp. 109–122 presents the MPLA view of events.

37. Afanasenko to MO, 4 December 1974, RGANI, f. 5, op. 68, d. 1962, pp. 11–12. Raymond Garthoff correctly concludes that the Soviet decision "preceded the American funding in January 1975, although it probably followed the military efforts of the FNLA in November" (*Détente and Confrontation: American-Soviet Relations from Nixon to Reagan* [rev. edn; Washington, DC: Brookings Institute, 1994], p. 507).

38. Soviet Embassy, Brazzaville, to MO, 25 December 1974, RGANI, f. 5, op. 68, d. 1941, pp. 10–21, 21, 17.

39. For the Soviet reaction to Alvor, see record of conversation between the Soviet ambassador to Tanzania, S. A. Slipchenko, and representatives of

the MO with Oliver Tambo (ANC), 21 March 1975, RGANI, f. 5, op. 68, d. 1982. See also Marcum, *Angolan Revolution*, vol. II, pp. 257–258; Garthoff, *Détente and Confrontation*, pp. 533–534.

40. B. Putilin (first secretary, Soviet Embassy, Brazzaville) to MO, n.d. (late January 1975), RGANI, f. 5, op. 68, d. 1941, pp. 10–21; Afanasenko to MO, 30 January 1975, RGANI, f. 5, op. 68, d. 1962, p. 26. Direct US support for Holden Roberto – with whom the CIA for several years had had "an intelligence gathering relationship" – was limited to "non-lethal equipment" up to July 1975 ("Talking points for secretary Kissinger. NSC meeting on Angola, Friday, June 27, 1975," National Security Archive [hereafter NSArch], Angola collection). Robert E. Gates, *From the Shadows: The Ultimate Insider's Story of Five Presidents and how they Won the Cold War* (New York: Simon & Schuster, 1996), pp. 65–69 has a useful account of CIA initiatives on Angola.

41. Slipchenko to MO, 6 February 1975, RGANI, f. 5, op. 68, d. 1982, pp. 48–54, 51; Slipchenko to MO, 24 August 1975, *ibid.*, pp. 238–246.

42. Soviet Embassy, Brazzaville, to MO, 14 April 1975, RGANI, f. 5, op. 68, d. 1941, pp. 50–53, 53. For relationships between the Angolan groups, see Franz-Wilhelm Heimer, *The Decolonization Conflict in Angola, 1974–76: An Essay in Political Sociology* (Geneva: Institut Universitaire de Hautes Etudes Internationales, 1979).

43. V. V. Aldoshin (chargé d'affaires, embassy, Dar-es-Salaam) to MO, 20 April 1975, RGANI, f. 5, op. 68, d. 1982, pp. 153–156; Institut Afriki Akademiia Nauk SSSR (Africa Institute, USSR Academy of Sciences) to MO, 19 June 1975, "Protsess dekolonizatsii v Angole i politika imperialisticheskikh derzhav" (The Decolonization Process in Angola and the Policies of the Imperialist Powers), RGANI, f. 5, op. 68, d. 1941, pp. 87–110; Soviet Embassy, Brazzaville, to MO, 14 April 1975, RGANI, f. 5, op. 68, d. 1941, pp. 50–53.

44. Interviews with Chinese Africa experts, Beijing, May 2004.

45. S. A. Slipchenko (Soviet ambassador, Dar-es-Salaam) to MO, 30 December 1974 (conversation with Oscar Oramas, Cuban Foreign Ministry; later ambassador to Luanda), RGANI, f. 5, op. 68, d. 1982, pp. 3–7; Afanasenko to MO, 10 January 1975 (conversation with Cuban ambassador A. Columbié Alvarez), RGANI, f. 5, op. 68, d. 1962, pp. 17–18. See also Jorge I. Dominguez, *To Make a World Safe for Revolution: Cuba's Foreign Policy* (Cambridge, MA: Harvard University Press, 1989), pp. 130–137; William M. LeoGrande, "Cuban–Soviet Relations and Cuban Policy in Africa," *Cuban Studies*, 10.1 (January 1980): 1–48.

46. AIV report on the situation in Southern Africa, 30 January 1975, SAPMO-BArch, DY30 J IV 2/2J/5652.

47. Nina D. Howland, "The United States and Angola, 1974–88: A Chronology," in *Department of State Bulletin*, 89.2143 (February 1989): 16–19; John Stockwell, *In Search of Enemies: A CIA Story* (London: André Deutsch, 1978), pp. 40–57. See also Assistant Secretary of State for African Affairs Nathaniel Davis to Under Secretary Joseph J. Sisco, 12 July 1975, and Sisco to Deputy to the National Security Adviser Brent Scowcroft, 15 July 1975, both in NSArch, Angola collection. The American covert military aid was in

addition to US civilian assistance and military and financial aid procured by the United States from US allies in the region, notably Zaire. (Hearing before the subcommittee on Africa of the Committee on International Relations, House of Representatives, 95th Congress, Second Session, 25 May 1978; see also Garthoff, *Détente and Confrontation*, pp. 560–570.

48. Stockwell, *In Search of Enemies*.
49. I am grateful to Ambassador David Tothill for discussing these aspects of South Africa's policy with me.
50. Botha to Secretary for Foreign Affairs, Pretoria, 8 January 1975, SADFAA, 1/33/3, vol. 30.
51. Embassy, Washington, to Pretoria, meeting with Colby and Walters, 25 March 1975, *ibid*.
52. Bureau for State Security to Secretary of Foreign Affairs, "When the Unthinkable Becomes the Inevitable," 16 September 1975, SADFAA, 1/33/3, vol. 31; E. M. Malone to Department of Foreign Affairs, 6 June 1975, SADFAA, 1/22/3, vol. 5; E. M. Malone to Department of Foreign Affairs, 23 April 1975, SADFAA, 1/22/3, vol. 5. See also Coetzee (BOSS) to Secretary of Foreign Affairs, 5 June 1975 on co-opting UNITA.
53. For the South African Department of Foreign Affairs reporting from June–July 1975, see SADFAA, 1/22/3, vols. 5 and 6. For good overviews by South African military historians with access to South African Defense Force archives, see Peter Stiff, *The Silent War: South African Recce Operations 1969–1994* (Cape Town: Galago, 1999), and Hilton Hamann, *The Days of the Generals: The Untold Story of South Africa's Apartheid-Era Military Generals* (Cape Town: Zebra Press, 2001).
54. From South African ambassador Beukes, Washington DC, to the Secretary of Foreign Affairs, Cape Town, "The Angola Question and Possible Developments in American/South African Relations as a result thereof," 9 February 1976, SADFAA, 1/33/3, vol. 32. Embassy traffic from Washington to Department of Foreign Affairs in Cape Town and Pretoria, "The Leadership Crisis in the USA and its Effect on Relations with South Africa," 26 February 1976, *ibid*. For the whole extent of US–RSA contacts, see "The United States of America: Further Developments of the Situation in 1974/75," n.d., SADFAA, 1/33/3, vol. 31.
55. Afanasenko to MO, 14 June 1975, RGANI, f. 5, op. 68, d. 1962, p. 137; Afanasenko to MO, RGANI, f. 5, op. 68, d. 1962, pp. 180–182. On Soviet difficulties with the PR Congo, see also AIV, "Zur internationalen Position der VR Kongo," n.d. (1974), SAPMO-BArch, DY-30/IV B 2/20/293.
56. Afanasenko to MO, 4 July 1975, RGANI, f. 5, op. 8, d. 1962, pp. 136–138; Slipchenko to MO, 10 February 1975, RGANI, f. 5, op. 68, d. 1982, pp. 44–47, 46.
57. Iu. K. Naumov (counsellor, Dar-es-Salaam) to MO, 2 August 1975, RGANI, f. 5, op. 68, d. 1982, pp. 226–227; record of conversation between Afanasenko and Congolese Prime Minister Henri Lopez, 17 June 1975, RGANI, f. 5, op. 68, d. 1962, pp. 113–114. On the Cuban role, see Putilin to MO, 14 April 1975, RGANI, f. 5, op. 68, d. 1941, pp. 50–53. See also Edward Gonzalez,

"Cuba, the Soviet Union, and Africa," in David E. Albright, *Communism in Africa* (Bloomington, IN: Indiana University Press, 1980).

58. M. A. Manasov (chargé d'affaires, embassy, Havana) to MO, 15 August 1975, RGANI, f. 5, op. 68, d. 1941, p. 122. This document is a record of the conversation between Manasov and Oscar Cienfuegos, an assistant to Fidel Castro who brought the Cuban leader's message to the Soviet embassy. No copy of the message itself could be found in the MO records. Georgi M. Kornienko, former Soviet first vice-foreign minister, interview with author (hereafter "Kornienko interview"), Moscow, 5 October 1993; Brutents interview, 3 October 1994; Brutents in Odd Arne Westad, ed., *Workshop on US–Soviet Relations and Soviet Foreign Policy Toward the Middle East and Africa in the 1970s* (oral history transcript, Lysebu, 1–3 October 1994; Oslo: Norwegian Nobel Institute, 1994) (hereafter "Lysebu I'), pp. 68–69.

59. Díaz Argüelles to R. Castro, 11 August 1975, quoted in Gleijeses, *Conflicting Missions*, p. 255. This and other key Cuban documents concerning its intervention in Angola are probably in the archives of the Centro de Información de la Defensa de las Fuerzas Armadas Revolucionarias in Havana, an archive that is still not open to scholars.

60. Afanasenko to MO, 17 August 1975, RGANI, f. 5, op. 68, d. 1962, pp. 196–203, 196. No record of Carreira's conversations in Moscow have been found.

61. Kornienko interview, 2 October 1994; Brutents interview, 4 June 1998.

62. Brutents interview, 4 June 1998.

63. Georgi Kornienko later recalled that the Soviet leadership tried to stop the Cubans: "I read a cable from our ambassador in Conakry which said, among many other things, that the Cuban ambassador had told him that the next day some planes with Cuban troops will land in Conakry for refueling on the way to Angola. I asked Gromyko, do you know anything? He called Andropov, he called Grechko. Nobody knew anything. All of them were against it and reported it immediately to the Politburo and suggested that we stop Castro. It took some hours to write the report, to get the decision, and to send the message to Castro. By this time the planes were in the air. You could rightly ask: How could it be – Soviet planes, stationed on Cuba, but it was Soviet planes and we had quite a few military people there … I checked. Well, technically, our people were involved, our planes were there for Cuban use, our advisers were involved, but they were completely convinced that a political decision had been taken [in Moscow]" (Kornienko interview, 5 October 1993). Gleijeses, supported by Cuban documents, claims that the aircraft were Cuban rather than Soviet (*Conflicting Missions*, p. 265) and stresses that the Cuban soldiers were primarily instructors rather than combat troops (p. 271). See also Gabriel García Márquez, "Operation Carlota: Cuba's Role in Angolan Victory," *Venceremos*, 4.5 (February 1977): 1–8; Arthur Jay Klinghoffer, *The Angolan War: A Study in Soviet Policy in the Third World* (Boulder, CO: Westview Press, 1980), pp. 109–120.

64. Soviet Embassy, Brazzaville, to MO, 15 September 1975, RGANI, f. 5, op. 68, d. 1941, pp. 118–121; Slipchenko to MO, 30 October 1975, RGANI, f. 5, op. 68, d. 1982, pp. 313–320. The military situation in Angola at the time

of the Cuban intervention is still under dispute. Piero Gleijeses, who has studied the Angolan war based on Cuban documents, believes that through the first half of October the MPLA was winning the war (Gleijeses, personal communication to author). The MPLA reports to Moscow (and presumably also to Havana) are much less optimistic (see Naumov to MO, 3 and 20 October 1975, RGANI, f. 5, op. 68, d. 1982, pp. 268–270, 280–281).

65. Kornienko interview, 4 October 1994; Slipchenko to MO, 30 October 1975, *ibid.*, pp. 313–320; Iu. K. Naumov to MO, 20 October 1975, *ibid.*, pp. 280–281. Kornienko, Brutents, and others discuss the rationale for the Soviet involvement in Lysebu I. See also Jiri Valenta, "Soviet Decision-Making on the Intervention in Angola," in David E. Albright, ed., *Communism in Africa* (Bloomington, IN: Indiana University Press, 1980). Several of the MO documents dealing with this issue are not yet declassified.

66. Soviet Embassy, Brazzaville, to MO, 15 September 1975, RGANI, f. 5, op. 68, d. 1941, p. 118 (the Brazzaville station also underlined that the FNLA as late as August 1975 was still receiving assistance from Romania and North Korea); Kornienko interview, 5 October 1993. See also Karen N. Brutents, *Tridtsat let na Staroi Ploshchadi* (Thirty Years at Staroia Ploshchad) (Moscow: Mezhdunarodnie otnosheniia, 1998), pp. 203–215.

67. Slipchenko to MO, 3 November 1975 (conversation with J. Nyerere), RGANI, f. 5, op. 68, d. 1962, pp. 305–307.

68. CPSU CC Secretariat card index, 192 meeting, 5 November 1975, RGANI; Afanasenko to MO, 4 November 1975, RGANI, f. 5, op. 68, d. 1962, pp. 230–231. Gleijeses points out that there was in fact no Cuban "artillery regiment" involved in the fighting at Qifangondo in late October, and it is likely that Ambassador Colombié exaggerated, misspoke, or was misquoted by the Soviet ambassador. There is no doubt, however, that Cuban soldiers participated in the fighting there.

69. Hamann, *Days of the Generals*, pp. 34–36.

70. G. A. Zverev (chargé d'affaires, Luanda) to MO, 1 March 1976, political report: entitled "Nekotorye voprosy voenno-politicheskoi i ekonomicheskoi obstnovki v Angole" (On Some Questions Concerning the Military-Political and Economic Situation in Angola), RGANI, f. 5, op. 9, d. 2513 (hereafter "Zverev report"), appendix. Having looked at the Cuban documents, Gleijeses finds no trace of Soviet support for the airlift before January 1976.

71. Zverev report.

72. *Ibid.*, appendix. See also head of the US and Canada Institute of the Soviet Academy of Sciences Georgi Arbatov's account of the discussions in Moscow on Angola, in *The System: An Insider's Life in Soviet Politics* (New York: Times Books, 1992), p. 194, where Brezhnev's chief foreign policy adviser Andrei Aleksandrov-Agentov is quoted as saying that the Soviets "could not avoid our internationalist duty" in Africa.

73. Zverev report, pp. 13–23; V. N. Rykov (ambassador, Algiers) to MO, 20 December 1975, RGANI, f. 5, op. 69, d. 2513, pp. 1–4; CPSU CC Secretariat card index, 197 meeting, 23 December 1975, RGANI. The archive of the Soviet General Staff is still not open for scholarly research. According to the East German archives, the South African Communists also offered to send

volunteers to fight in Angola, but Neto declined in order not to provoke the South African government further (record of conversation between Rudi Guttmann [deputy head AIV] and Dadoo, Berlin, 18 November 1975, SAPMO-BArch, DY30 J IV 2/2/J6091).

74. Donald Rothchild and Caroline Hartzell, "The Case of Angola: Four Power Intervention and Disengagement," in Ariel E. Levite, Bruce W. Jentleson, and Larry Berman, eds., *Foreign Military Intervention: The Dynamics of Protracted Conflict* (New York: Columbia University Press, 1992), pp. 163–208.

75. B. Putilin (first secretary, Luanda) to MO, 27 March 1976, report entitled "O poloshenii v MPLA" (On the Situation in the MPLA), RGANI, f. 5, op. 69, d. 2513, pp. 29–34; Klinghoffer, *Angolan War*, pp. 61–71.

76. Stockwell, *In Search of Enemies*, pp. 227–248; Fred Bridgland, *Jonas Savimbi: A Key to Africa* (London: Coronet Books, 1988), pp. 174–181.

77. Brutents in Lysebu I, pp. 76–77.

78. John H. Chettle, "Some Suggestions for a New Foreign Policy for South Africa," National Archives of South Africa (NASA), 144/1, Annex Jacket 1977. The South Africa-born Chettle was US director of the South Africa Foundation, one of the country's major business organizations.

79. Soviet Embassy, Luanda, to MO, 15 May 1976, report on discussions during meeting between Raul Castro and Jorge Risquet (Cuba) and I. F. Ponomarenko and A. I. Dubenko (USSR Ministry of Defense), RGANI, f. 5, op. 69, d. 2513 (hereafter "Castro discussions"), pp. 42–48; on Vietnam, Mikhail Kapitsa, former vice-foreign minister, author's interview, Moscow, 7 September 1992. See also Galia Golan, *The Soviet Union and National Liberation Movements in the Third World* (New York: Unwin Hyman, 1988); Mark Katz, *The Third World in Soviet Military Thought* (Baltimore, MD: Johns Hopkins University Press, 1982); Neil Matheson, *The "Rules of the Game" of superpower Military Intervention in the Third World, 1975–1980* (Washington, DC: University Press of America, 1982).

80. G. A. Zverev to MO, 1 March 1976, political report entitled "Nekotorye voprosy voenno-politicheskoi i ekonomicheskoi obstnovki v Angole" (On Some Questions Concerning the Military-Political and Economic Situation in Angola), RGANI, f. 5, op. 9, d. 2513, pp. 13–23, 15–16.

81. *Ibid.*, p. 23; Soviet Embassy, Luanda, to MO, 15 May 1976, report on discussions during a meeting between Raul Castro and Jorge Risquet (Cuba) and I. F. Ponomarenko and A. I. Dubenko (USSR Ministry of Defense), RGANI, f. 5, op. 69, d. 2513, pp. 42–48. For the history of the Cuban–Soviet relationship, see Dominguez, *World Safe for Revolution*, pp. 78–84.

82. G. A. Zverev to MO, 1 March 1976, political report entitled "Nekotorye voprosy voenno-politicheskoi i ekonomicheskoi obstnovki v Angole" (On Some Questions Concerning the Military-Political and Economic Situation in Angola), RGANI, f. 5, op. 9, d. 2513, pp. 13–14.

83. G. A. Zverev to MO, MemCon, Raúl Valdés Vivó (Head, General Department for International Relations, Cuban Communist Party) – Zverev, 28 May 1976, RGANI, f. 5, op. 69, d. 2513, pp. 53–54; Soviet Embassy, Luanda, to MO, 15 May 1976, report on discussions during a meeting between Raul Castro and Jorge Risquet (Cuba) and I. F. Ponomarenko and A. I. Dubenko (USSR

Ministry of Defense), RGANI, f. 5, op. 69, d. 2513, p. 45. On the size of the Cuban forces, see record of conversation between Honecker and Castro, 3 April 1977, SAPMO-BArch, DY-30/J IV 2/201/1292.

84. B. Putilin (first secretary, Luanda) to MO, 27 March 1976, report entitled "O poloshenii v MPLA" (On the Situation in the MPLA), RGANI, f. 5, op. 69, d. 2513, pp. 29–34.

85. *Ibid.*

86. Soviet Embassy, Luanda, to MO, 21 June 1976, report entitled "Ob informmatsionno-propagandistskoi rabote za II kvartal 1976 g." (On Information and Propaganda Work in the Second Quarter of 1976), *ibid.*, pp. 60–62. The embassy did, however, find it difficult to dispose of "several" sets of Lenin's collected works in French – not surprising, since more than 90 percent of all Angolans were illiterate and those who were able to read mostly did so in Portuguese.

87. Castro discussions; F. D. Kudashkin (counsellor, Luanda) to MO, 30 July 1976, *ibid.*, pp. 82–83. By the end of the year the Soviet authorities were hard pressed in their efforts to find the Marxist-Leninist avant-garde in Angola. See N. P. Tolubeev (Soviet ambassador, Havana) to MO, 10 December 1976, memorandum of conversation between Jorge Risquet and Tolubeev, *ibid.*, pp. 121–123.

88. On Fidel Castro see Marquez, "Operation Carlota," pp. 1–2; Castro discussions, p. 46; G. A. Zverev to MO, 28 May 1976, memorandum of conversation between Raúl Valdés Vivó and Zverev, *ibid.*, pp. 49–54.

89. Castro discussions, *ibid.*, pp. 43, 47.

90. Soviet Embassy, Luanda, to MO, 15 August 1976, *ibid.* These concerns persisted throughout 1976; see report on the visit of a SED delegation to Angola, 6–12 December 1976, SAPMO-BArch, DY-30/IV B 2/20/72.

91. Brutents interview, 5 October 1993. For a discussion, see Steven R. David, "Soviet Involvement in Third World Coups," *International Security*, 11 (summer 1986): 3–36.

92. Note headlined "1975," box 1, Dadoo Papers, MCH05, Mabuiye Centre, University of Western Cape, Belleville, South Africa (hereafter Mabuiye Centre).

93. "Notes: Some negative factors in the contemporary Southern African situation (1974)," box 3, Dadoo Papers, MCH05, Mabuiye Centre.

94. Fidel Castro, "Speech on the 23rd Anniversary of the Assault on Moncada Barracks," 26 July 1976, Castro Speech Database, http://www1.lanic.utexas.edu/la/cb/cuba/castro.html.

95. Wolfers and Bergerol, *Angola in the Front Line*, pp. 85–99 is a generally reliable account of the Alves coup, but see also the analysis of Alves political constituency in the second volume of Jean-Michel Mabeko-Tali, *Dissidencia e poder de estado – O MPLA perante si proprio (1962–1977)* (Dissidence and State Power: The MPLA Encounters Itself) (2 vols.; Luanda: Nzila, 2001). See also the official Angolan version, in "Report on a visit by a Party and State delegation from the GDR to Libya, Angola, Zambia, and Mozambique, February 1979," SAPMO-BArch, DY-30/J IV 2/201/1454. Alves may have used his close personal relations with some Soviet officers, and especially with two KGB agents in Luanda, to facilitate

his bid for power (Soviet officer stationed in Angola 1976–77, author's interview, Moscow, September 1998). For the later development of Soviet–Angolan relations, see Scott Christopher Monje, "Alliance Politics in Escalating Conflict: The Soviet Union and Cuba in Angola, 1974–1991," Ph.D. dissertation, Columbia University, 1995; and Mark Webber, "Soviet–Angolan Relations, 1975 to the Present," Ph.D. thesis, University of Birmingham, 1991.

96. Record of conversation, State Department, subject "Department Policy," 18 December 1975, reprinted in Mark Hertsgaard, "The Secret Life of Henry Kissinger: Minutes of a 1975 Meeting with Lawrence Eagleburger," *Nation*, 29 October 1990; on China's role, see also Steven F. Jackson, "China's Third World Foreign Policy: The Case of Angola and Mozambique, 1961–93," *China Quarterly*, 142 (1995): 388–422.

97. Minutes, National Security Council meeting, 7 April 1976, at Gerald Ford Presidential Library website, http://www.ford.utexas.edu/library/document/ nscmin/760407.pdf.

98. *Ibid.*

99. Henry Kissinger, *Years of Renewal* (New York: Simon & Schuster, 1999), p. 934.

100. Botha to Muller (Vorster), 15 May 1976, SADFAA, 1/33/3, vol. 33. See also Botha to Fourie (for Vorster), 7 June 1976, *ibid.* An updated BOSS intelligence profile of Kissinger is in the same file.

101. Embassy, Jakarta, to Secretary of State, 6 December 1975, quoted from William Burr and Michael L. Evans, eds., "East Timor Revisited: Ford, Kissinger, and the Indonesian Invasion, 1975–76," National Security Archive Electronic Briefing Book no. 62 (December 2001).

102. Reagan's radio broadcast, 31 March 1976, on http://www.reagan.com/ ronald/speeches/rrspeech07.shtml. Kissinger denies ever making the remarks Reagan attributes to him. For more on the debates that followed Angola, see Thomas J. Noer, "International Credibility and Political Survival: The Ford Administration's Intervention in Angola," *Presidential Studies Quarterly*, 23.4 (1993): 771–785.

103. Presidential campaign debate between Gerald R. Ford and Jimmy Carter, 6 October 1976, transcript on http://www.ford.utexas.edu/library/speeches/ 760854.htm.

104. Brzezinski, *Power and Principle: Memoirs of the National Security Adviser* (New York: Fanar, Straus, Giroux, 1983), pp. 149–150.

7 THE PROSPECTS OF SOCIALISM: ETHIOPIA AND THE HORN

I am grateful to Ilya Gaiduk for help in the Russian archives when I was preparing this chapter.

1. Anatolii Chernaiev, author's interview, Washington, 20 April 2002. For the PDRY regime, see Fred Halliday, *Revolution and Foreign Policy: The Case of South Yemen, 1967–1987* (new edn; Cambridge: Cambridge University Press, 2002).

2. There are several useful broader works on the Ethiopian revolution from very different perspectives; see Andargachew Tiruneh, *The Ethiopian Revolution 1974–1987: A Transformation from an Aristocratic to a Totalitarian Autocracy* (Cambridge: Cambridge University Press, 1993); Tefarra Haile-Selassie, *The Ethiopian Revolution 1974–1991: From a Monarchical Autocracy to a Military Oligarchy* (London: Kegan Paul, 1997); Edmond J. Keller, *Revolutionary Ethiopia: From Empire to People's Republic* (Bloomington, IN: Indiana University Press, 1988); Fred Halliday and Maxine Molyneux, *The Ethiopian Revolution* (London: New Left Books, 1981); and Edmond J. Keller and Donald Rothchild (eds.), *Afro-Marxist Regimes: Ideology and Public Policy* (Boulder, CO: Lynne Rienner, 1987).

3. Bruce D. Porter, *The USSR in Third World Conflicts: Soviet Arms and Diplomacy in Local Wars, 1945–1980* (Cambridge: Cambridge University Press, 1984), p. 200.

4. In 1983 and 1984 the total amount of nonmilitary aid was $542 million, which was more than 60 percent of the total aid given to sub-Saharan Africa; see Abraham S. Becker, "The Soviet Union and the Third World: The Economic Dimension," in Andrzej Korbonski and Francis Fukuyama, eds., *The Soviet Union and the Third World: The Last Three Decades* (Ithaca, NY: Cornell University Press, 1987), p. 78.

5. Tiruneh, *Ethiopian Revolution*, p. 13.

6. For a view of Haile Selassie in his later years, see Ryszard Kapuscinski, *The Emperor: Downfall of an Autocrat* (New York: Vintage Books, 1984).

7. Memorandum of conversation between Johnson and Haile Selassie, 14 February 1967, *Foreign Relations of the United States* (hereafter *FRUS*), *1964–1968*, vol. XXIV, p. 565.

8. Special National Intelligence Estimate 76.1–61, 24 January 1961, *FRUS*, *1961–1963*, vol. XXI, pp. 425–428.

9. For the relationship between the Ethiopian revolution, Christian missions, and Western Marxism, see Donald L. Donham's brilliant *Marxist Modern: An Ethnographic History of the Ethiopian Revolution* (Berkeley, CA: University of California Press, 1999), especially pp. 126–127.

10. Tiruneh, *Ethiopian Revolution*, pp. 17–34.

11. Haile-Selassie, *Ethiopian Revolution*, pp. 86–93.

12. Tiruneh, *Ethiopian Revolution*, pp. 60–81.

13. The Emperor was arrested on 12 September, by which time illness had made him unable to understand what was going on around him He was killed a year later. The monarchy was still formally in place under his son, until the prince wisely decided against returning from Europe, where he had been at the time of the coup. General Aman, who had been appointed head of the armed forces and, effectively, head of state by the Derg in June, was probably assassinated because of his attempts to negotiate with the Eritrean liberation movements (see Paul B. Henze, *Layers of Time: A History of Ethiopia* [New York: St. Martin's Press, 2000], pp. 285–287).

14. René Lefort, *Ethiopie: la révolution hérétique* (Paris: François Maspero, 1981) p. 63.

15. There is still no good biography of Mengistu, in English or in Amharic. This information is from Soviet advisers who worked with him in the late 1970s.

16. Tiruneh, *Ethiopian Revolution*, pp. 85–112.
17. Hoben, "Social Soundness of Agrarian Reform in Ethiopia," USAID report, 1976, pp. 92–93, quoted from Donham, *Marxist Modern*, p. 33.
18. Tiruneh, *Ethiopian Revolution*, pp. 131–151; see also Haile-Selassie, *Ethiopian Revolution*, pp. 207–209.
19. Haile-Selassie, *Ethiopian Revolution*, p. 172; the National Democratic Revolution Program of Ethiopia (NDRPE) was almost certainly drafted by the head of the All Ethiopia Socialist Movement (Meison), Haile Fida, who was a key adviser to the Derg until he fell out with Mengistu and was arrested. He was executed in 1979. His deputy, Negade Gobeze, another key Marxist intellectual, fled to Cuba.
20. Tiruneh, *Ethiopian Revolution*, pp. 182–184.
21. Henze, Layers of Time, p. 285.
22. Kissinger to Ford, 18 May 1975, Declassified Documents Reference Service (hereafter DDRS). See also Deputy Secretary of State Robert Ingersoll to Ford, 28 April 1975, DDRS. Ingersoll asked the President to extend special terms for military sales to Ethiopia. "It is desirable that the USA have maximum flexibility in dealing with this situation," Ingersoll noted.
23. Scowcroft to Kissinger, n.d. (probably early spring 1976), DDRS.
24. Transcript of NSC meeting, 11 May 1976, DDRS. On early Derg foreign relations, see Halliday, *Revolution and Foreign Policy*, pp. 213–267.
25. Henze to Brzezinski, 28 March 1977, DDRS.
26. Henze to Brzezinski, 22 April 1977, DDRS.
27. Brzezinski to Jimmy Carter, 3 June 1977, National Security Archive (hereafter NSArch), Carter–Brezhnev collection.
28. Record of conversation between Somalian Ambassador Addou and Carter and Brzezinski, 16 June 1977, NSArch, Carter–Brezhnev collection.
29. Henze to Brzezinski, 17 August 1977, DDRS. See also Secretary of State Cyrus Vance's conversation with Chinese Foreign Minister Huang Hua in Beijing, 23 August 1977, DDRS, in which the Secretary said that the "French, British, and Germans ... agreed that we would supply different kinds of equipment to the Somalis," and confirmed the US belief that the Somalians would reach their military aims. In a follow-up, Vance told Huang in September that the United States had given "Soviet friends" (presumably meaning the Ethiopians) photos of Soviet missiles around the Somalian port of Berbera (handwritten record of conversation, 28 September 1977, UN, box 41, Vertical File – China, Jimmy Carter Presidential Library [hereafter JCPL]).
30. Soviet Embassy, Addis Ababa, report to Foreign Minister Gromyko, March 1974, Rossiiskii gosudarstvennyi arkhiv noveishei istorii (hereafter RGANI), f. 5, op. 67, d. 796, pp. 40, 46.
31. *Ibid.*, p. 49.
32. Soviet Embassy, Addis Ababa, report to Foreign Minister Gromyko, 9 June 1974, *ibid.*, p. 223.
33. RGANI, f. 5, op. 67, d. 797, p. 292.
34. Record of conversation between Sinitsyn and Fereda, 21–22 September 1974, *ibid.* For Sinitsyn's own not very detailed account of his involvement in Ethiopian affairs, see Sergei Sinitsyn, *Missiia v Efiopii: Efiopiia, Afrikanskii*

Rog i politika SSSR glazami sovetskogo diplomata, 1956–1982 gg. (Mission to Ethiopia: Ethiopia and the Horn of Africa through the Eyes of a Soviet Diplomat, 1956–1982) (Moscow: XXI vek, 2001).

35. From Ratanov to MO, March 1975, RGANI, f. 5, op. 68, d. 1985, p. 121.
36. Record of conversation between Romashkin and Gedda, 1 November 1974, RGANI, f. 5, op. 67, d. 797, pp. 338–339; see also Soviet Embassy, Addis Ababa, "Statements of the PMAC Leadership on the Perspectives of Development of the Soviet–Ethiopian Relations and some Embassy's Considerations on Possible Actions of the Soviet Union in Political Sphere," 23 April 1976, RGANI, f. 5, op. 69, d. 2580, p. 37.
37. Soviet Embassy's Political Report for 1974, RGANI, f. 5, op. 67, d. 798, p. 67.
38. Record of conversation between Ratanov and Bante, 25 January 1975, RGANI, f. 5, op. 68, d. 1989, pp. 12–18.
39. Report on the Second Congress of the Congolese Workers' Party, p. 11, Archives of the Central Committee of the Italian Communist Party, Fondazione Istituto Gramsci, Rome (hereafter PCI Archives), 202, vol. IV, I° bimestre 1975.
40. Text of the Soviet ambassador's statement on behalf of the Soviet government (RGANI, f. 5, op. 68, d. 1989, pp. 53–54). The statement strongly stressed that the dispute between Ethiopia and Somalia should be resolved by means of negotiations.
41. Record of conversation between Ambassador Ratanov and Chairman of the PMAC Teferi Bante and other Ethiopian leaders, 11 March 1975, RGANI, f. 5, op. 68, d. 1989; pp. 81–83.
42. Keller, *Revolutionary Ethiopia*, pp. 196–201.
43. Kissinger to Ford, 18 May 1975, DDRS; James T. Lynn to Ford, 21 May 1975, DDRS; Kissinger to Ford, 24 June 1975, DDRS; Assistant Secretary for African Affairs, William Schaufele, quoted in Halliday, *Revolution and Foreign Policy*, p. 222. See also David A. Korn, *Ethiopia, the United States and the Soviet Union, 1974–1985* (London: Croom Helm, 1986), pp. 13, 21.
44. Ratanov to MO, March 1975, RGANI, f. 5, op. 68, d. 1985, p. 128.
45. Ratanov to MO, 20 and 24 March 1975, RGANI, f. 5, op. 68, d. 1989, p. 135.
46. Ratanov to MO, 9 April 1975, RGANI, f. 5, op. 68, d. 1989, pp. 123–126. On the coexistence of US and Soviet materiel in the Ethiopian Army, see also record of conversation between Ratanov and Head of the Political Committee of the PMAC Sisay Habte, 9 April 1975, *ibid.*, pp. 121–122.
47. *Ibid.*, pp. 167–173.
48. Record of conversation between Ratanov and Teferi Bante, 15 July 1975. RGANI, f. 5, op. 68, d. 1989, p. 204.
49. See, for example, the records of conversations between Ratanov and Teferi Bante, 15 July 1975, RGANI, f. 5, op. 68, d. 1989, pp. 201–205; between Ratanov and Minister of Defense Ayalew Mandefro, 6 August 1975, *ibid.*, pp. 228–230; between Soviet Embassy Counsellor S. Sinitsyn and Sisay Habte, 20 September 1975, *ibid.*, pp. 262–264.
50. Record of conversation between Sinitsyn and Member of the PMAC Lieutenant Silesi, 24 March 1975, RGANI, f. 5, op. 68, d. 1989, p. 138.

51. Ratanov to Foreign Minister Gromyko, 27 March 1976, RGANI, f. 5, op. 69, d. 2580, pp. 22–24.

52. Soviet Embassy, Addis Ababa, to Moscow, 23 April 1976, RGANI, f. 5, op. 69, d. 2580, p. 46.

53. "The Armed Forces of Ethiopia and its Role and Place in the Political Life of the Country," 31 January 1975, RGANI, f. 5, op. 68, d. 1985, p. 38.

54. Soviet Embassy, Addis Ababa, to Moscow, 21 June 1975, *ibid.*, p. 168.

55. See, for example, "Statements of the PMAC Leaders on the Perspectives of the Development of Soviet–Ethiopian Relations and the Embassy's Consideration on the Next Possible Steps of the Soviet Union in the Political Sphere," 23 April 1976, RGANI, f. 5, op. 69, d. 2580, pp. 34–54.

56. Memorandum of conversation between Soviet Ambassador A. Ratanov and Chairman of the PMAC Teferi Bante, 15 July 1975, RGANI, f. 5, op. 68, d. 1989, p. 204.

57. Soviet Embassy, Addis Ababa, to Foreign Ministry, Moscow, "Considerations and Proposals with Regard to Possible High Level Soviet–Ethiopian Negotiations," 16 June 1976, RGANI, f. 5, op. 69, d. 2580, pp. 60–95. See also "On the Reaction in Ethiopia to the Results of the High Level Soviet–Ethiopian Negotiations in Moscow," 11 September 1976, *ibid.*, pp. 143–156.

58. RGANI, f. 5, op. 69, d. 2580, p. 148.

59. Record of conversation between Ratanov and Mengistu Haile Mariam, 21 February 1975, RGANI, f. 5, op. 68, d. 1989, p. 57.

60. Keller, *Revolutionary Ethiopia*, p. 197.

61. "Annual Report of the USSR Embassy in Ethiopia for 1976," RGANI, f. 5, op. 73, d. 1634, pp. 1–11.

62. *Ibid.*

63. Soviet Embassy, Addis Ababa, to Foreign Ministry, Moscow, "On the Question of Perspectives for a Peace Settlement in Eritrea," 22 June 1975, RGANI, f. 5, op. 68, d. 1987, p. 33.

64. Korn, *Ethiopia*, p. 29.

65. Report concerning a trip to the Democratic Republic of Somalia by a delegation from the CC SED, 31 January–1 February 1977, RGANI, f. 5, op. 77, d. 1618, pp. 1–5.

66. Third Africa Department, Soviet Foreign Ministry, report on Somali–Ethiopian territorial disputes, 2 February 1977, RGANI, f. 5, op. 73, d. 1632, pp. 39–44.

67. Records of conversation between Ratanov and Mengistu, 4 and 19 February 1977, RGANI, f. 5, op. 73, d. 1636, pp. 31–32, 33–38.

68. Mengistu to Honecker, 9 March 1977, Stiftung Archiv der Parteien and Massenorganisationen in Bundesarchiv, Berlin (hereafter SAPMO-BArch), DY-30 2419.

69. Presumably MI-8Ts.

70. Records of conversation between Ratanov and Berhanu Bayih and Ratanov and Mengistu Haile Mariam, n.d., RGANI, f. 5, op. 73, d. 1636, pp. 46, 50, 55–57, 58.

71. Korn, *Ethiopia*, p. 29.

72. CPSU CC to SED CC, information concerning visit of Mengistu to Moscow, 13 May 1977, SAPMO-BArch, J IV 2/202/583; record of conversation between Kurt Seibt and Saddam Hussein, n.d., during Baath Party thirtieth anniversary, 6–13 April 1977, SAPMO-BArch, DY-30 IV B 2/20/87. Saddam underlined what he saw as a continued and strong US position in Ethiopia.

73. "On the PMAC's Measures to Achieve the Curtailment of the US Presence in Ethiopia," 26 May 1977, RGANI, f. 5, op. 73, d. 1633, p. 198. See also Diana L. Ohlbaum, "Identity and Interests in Soviet Foreign Policy: The Case of Ethiopia, 1974–1991," Ph.D. dissertation, Johns Hopkins University, 1998.

74. A good overview, mainly based on Ethiopian sources, is Gebru Tareke, "The Ethiopia–Somalia War of 1977 Revisited," *International Journal of African Historical Studies*, 33.3 (2000): 635–667.

75. Record of conversation between Ratanov and Mengistu Haile Mariam, 26 August 1977, RGANI, f. 5, op. 73, d. 1636, pp. 88–89. This record was circulated to members of the Soviet Politburo.

76. Record of conversation between the Soviet chargé d'affaires in Ethiopia S. Sinitsyn and Major Berhanu Bayeh, 18 March 1977, RGANI, f. 5, op. 73, d. 1638, pp. 93–97 (on the Cuban–Yemeni mediation effort in mid-March 1977).

77. Record of conversation between Honecker and Fidel Castro, 3 April 1977, SAPMO-BArch, DY-30 J IV 2/201/1292.

78. Archiv Prezidenta Rossiiskoi Federatsii (hereafter APRF), f. 3, op. 120, d. 37, pp. 44, 48.

79. Report from CPSU CC to SED CC on a visit to the Soviet Union by Somalian Vice President Samanta, late May–early June 1977, SAPMO-BArch, DY-30 J IV 2/202 584.

80. Records of conversation between Ratanov and Mengistu, 21 and 31 July 1977 and 1 August 1977, RGANI, f. 5, op. 73, d. 1636, pp. 110–112, 125–126.

81. Record of conversation between Ratanov and Cuban military official Arnaldo Ochoa, 17 July 1977, *ibid.*, pp. 141–146.

82. Mengistu speech on general mobilization, 21 August 1977, quoted from Haile-Selassie, *Revolutionary Ethiopia*, p. 214.

83. Report from CPSU CC to SED CC on the results of Podgorny's visit to Africa, late March 1977, n.d., SAPMO-BArch, J IV 2/202 58.

84. Korn, *Ethiopia*, p. 41.

85. For early discussion of the planning of a Soviet air operation, see record of conversation between Ratanov and Legesse Asfaw, 9 August 1977, RGANI, f. 5, op. 73, d. 1636, p. 106.

86. Keller, *Revolutionary Ethiopia*, p. 206.

87. CPSU CC to SED CC, "Information on the 30–31 October 1977 Closed Visit of Mengistu Haile Mariam to Moscow," 8 November 1977, SAPMO-BArch, J IV 2/202/583.

88. Record of conversation between Ratanov and an East German official, Addis Ababa, 6 December 1977, SAPO-BArch, DY-30 IV 2/2.035/126.

89. Record of conversation between Boris N. Ponomarev and Paul Markovski (SED), 10 February 1978, SAPMO-BArch, DY-30 IV 2/2.035/127.

90. Record of conversation between Eberhard Heinrich (SED) and Ratanov in Addis Ababa, 13 March 1978, SAPMO-BArch, DY-30 IV 2/2.035/127.

91. On Soviet direct involvement in the war, see Soviet Foreign Ministry Third Africa Department's background report on Soviet–Ethiopian relations, 3 April 1978, RGANI, f. 5, op. 75, d. 1175, pp. 24–32; on Libya's attempts to mediate, see "Memorandum on Soviet Reaction to Libyan Proposal on Somali–Ethiopian Conflict," 4 April 1978, SAPMO-BArch, DY-30 IV 2/2.035/127. The Russian literature on the Soviet military intervention is very weak, but see P. A. Golitsyn, "Tretia moia voina: o roli sovetskikh voennykh v Efiopii v otrazhenii somaliiskoi agressii" (My Third War: The Role of Soviet Soldiers in Ethiopia in Repelling the Somalian Aggression), *Voenno-istoricheskii zhurnal*, 3 (1994): 54–60. For the immediate US reaction, see SCC meeting, 26 January 1978, box 28, subject file-meetings, Brzezinski collection, JCPL.

92. For some of the opportunties and the challenges, see Soviet Foreign Ministry and CPSU CC International Department, "Background Report on the Somali-Ethiopian Conflict," 3 April 1978, RGANI, f. 5, op. 75, d. 1175, pp. 13–23.

93. For the party question and an interesting comparison with Afghanistan, see Eremias Abebe, "The Vanguard Party: Imperial Instrument of Soviet Third World Policy (1976–1986) (A Comparative Study of Soviet Party-to-Party Relations with Afghanistan and Ethiopia)," Ph.D. dissertation, University of Maryland, 1994.

94. The Soviets attempted to explore relations with the EPLF's traditional rival, the ELF, but, again, to no avail. See SED Abteilung Internationale Vertretungen (hereafter AIV), information concerning talks with Ahmed Nasser (ELF-RC) in the USSR Solidarity Committee, 7–8 June 1978, SAPMO-BArch, DY-30 IV 2/2.035/127.

95. Brutents interview, 5 October 1993.

96. Record of conversation between Friedel Trappen (SED) and Karen Brutents, 7 November 1977, SAPMO-BArch, DY-30 IV 2/2.035/126; the Palestinian go-between was Abu Nidal, the then head of the Fatah Revolutionary Council, a PLO splinter group based in Baghdad (record of conversation between Markovski [SED] and Ponomarev, Moscow, 10 February 1978, SAPMO-BArch, DY-30 IV 2/2.035/127).

97. SED AIV, "Report on Conversation with [Cuban Vice-President] Carlos Rafael Rodriguez," 13 February 1978, Havana, SAPMO-BArch, DY-30 IV 2/2.035/127.

98. Draft letter from Honecker to Brezhnev on Ethiopian–Eritrean Talks, 19 April 1978, SAPMO-BArch, DY-30 IV 2/2.035/12.

99. Bayerlacher (GDR ambassador, Addis Ababa) to GDR Foreign Ministry, 11 April 1978, SAPMO-BArch, DY-30 2419.

100. Record of conversation between Trappen (SED) and Ulianovskii (CPSU MO), 11 May 1978, SAPMO-BArch, DY-30 IV 2/2.035/127; see also record of conversation between Lamberz (SED) and Pepe (Cuban

Ambassador to Ethiopia), Addis Ababa, 3 March 1978, SAPMO-BArch, DY-30 IV 2/2.035/127. For an overview of East Germany's secret involvement in the Eritrean conflict, see SED AIV, "Information on the Development and Events of the Activities Undertaken by the SED during the 1970s in Support of a Peaceful Solution to the Eritrea Problem" (n.d., late 1979?), SAPMO-BArch, DY-30 2419.

101. GDR Embassy in Moscow, 19 June 1978, record of conversation between Grabowski (SED) and Sinitsyn (then head of the Third Africa Department of the Soviet Foreign Ministry), SAPMO-BArch, DY-30 IV 2/2.035/127.

102. Minutes of a meeting of the CPSU CC Politburo, 14 July 1978 (excerpt), APRF, f. 3, op. 120, d. 40, pp. 45, 10–12.

103. In their note to the Politburo before the 14 July meeting, Gromyko, Andropov, and Ponomarev said: "According to the communication from the Soviet Ambassador in Addis Ababa, and also according to the information from the Cuban friends, events are taking place that bear witness to manifestations of nationalistic moods among certain parts of the Ethiopian leadership following the victory over Somalia in the Ogaden, which already is beginning to exert a negative influence on Ethiopia's relations with several countries of the Socialist community. From the Ethiopian side, in particular, a certain dissatisfaction is being expressed regarding the progress of cooperation with these countries above all in the economic area, complaints connected with the development of trade-economic relations, not always grounded in fact, are being put forth. This type of mood in one way or another shows up in the approach of the Ethiopian leadership to a resolution of the Eritrean issue" (APRF, f. 3, op. 91, d. 272, pp. 140–143).

104. Brzezinski, *Power and Principle: Memoirs of the National Security Adviser* (New York: Fonar, Straus, Giroux, 1983), p. 189. For the administration's views of the consequences for the wider region, see State Department to US embassies Teheran et al., 13 December 1977, box 27, subject file – meetings, Brzezinski collection, JCPL.

105. Record of conversation between Carter and Gromyko, 27 May 1978, NSArch, Carter–Brezhnev collection. The Soviets undoubtedly intensified Carter's suspicion about their motives by lying about the degree of their involvement. Gromyko told the president that "the presence of a Soviet general in Enthiopia [was] a myth ... There was no Soviet Napoleon in Africa. Evidently the president was being fed completely fantastic information." In December 1977, as the airlift got under way, the foreign minister had told U.S. Ambassador Toon that the "Soviet arms supply to Ethiopia is insignificant (record of conversation between Gromyko and Toon, 12 December 1977, box 27, subject file – meetings, Brzezinski collection, JCPL).

106. Record of NSC Special Coordination Committee meeting, 2 March 1978, in Odd Arne Westad, ed., *The Fall of Détente: Soviet–American Relations during the Carter Years* (Oslo: Scandinavian University Press, 1997), p. 267.

107. Carter to Brzezinski, 17 May 1978, NSArch, Carter–Brezhnev collection. See also Henze to Brzezinski, 10 March 1978, "The Carter Administration and the Horn: What We Have Learned," box 28, subject file – meetings, Brzezinski collection, JCPL.

108. Ronald Reagan, speech on 25 March 1978, on http://www.reaganlegacy.
org/speeches/.

109. For Primakov's views, see his "Zakon neravnomernosti razvitiia i istoriches-
koi sudby osvobodivshikhsia stran" (The laws of uneven development and
the historical fate of newly independent countries), *Mirovaia ekonomika i
mezhdunarodnie otnosheniia*, 12 (1980): 27–39. For Bogomolov's institute,
see Oleg Bogomolov, "Some Considerations of the Foreign Policy Results
of the 1970s (Main Points)," 20 January 1980, published in *Moscow News*,
1989, no. 30. According to Robert English, the highly critical comments on
Soviet Third World policy in this report to the CPSU Central Committee
was authored by Viachislav Dashichev, head of the foreign policy section at
the Institute of the Economy of the World Socialist System (IEMSS)
(Robert English, *Russia and the Idea of the West: Gorbachev, Intellectuals, and
the End of the Cold War* [New York: Columbia University Press, 2000], p. 304).

110. Record of conversation between Mohammed Aziz and Paul Werner (SED
Politburo), 19 February 1979, with enclosed transcript of meeting between
Saddam Hussein and Iraqi Communist leaders, 24 January 1979, SAPMO-
BArch, DY-30 IV B 2/20/87. See also the SED International Department
(Winkelmann) report on Baath persecution of the ICP, 24 May 1978;
Honecker to al-Bakr, 20 May 1978; and al-Bakr's reply (n.d., but read by
Honecker on 11 June 1976), all *ibid*.

111. AIV report, "On Questions Concerning the Current Relationship between
the SED and the Iraqi Baath Party," 22 May 1980, SAPMO-BArch, DY-30
IV B 2/20/87.

112. "The 'Westernizers' [in Addis Ababa] are making use of the fact that certain
of the socialist countries are conducting themselves with restraint with
regard to the development of economic collaboration with Ethiopia.
These countries include Poland, Hungary, Bulgaria, and also Romania,
although this is for different reasons" (Soviet Embassy in Addis Ababa,
background report on "Ethiopia's Relations with Western Countries,"
14 August 1978, RGANI, f. 5, op. 75, d. 1173, pp. 155–161).

113. Dawit quoted in Jospeh Tubiana, comp., *La révolution Ethiopienne comme
phénomène de société: témoignages et documents* (Paris: Harmattan, 1990),
p. 235. See also Robert D. Kaplan, *Surrender or Starve: The Wars Behind
the Famine* (Boulder, CO: Westview Press, 1988). The consequences of the
Derg's policies are laid bare in Markos Ezra, *Ecological Degradation, Rural
Poverty, and Migration in Ethiopia: A Contextual Analysis* (New York:
Population Council Press, 2001). There is an excellent memorial website
to the victims of the Red Terror in Ethiopia at http://www.ethiopians.com/
qey_shibir.htm.

8   THE ISLAMIST DEFIANCE: IRAN AND
     AFGHANISTAN

Some of the material in this chapter was previously used in my "Concerning the
situation in 'A': New Russian Evidence on the Soviet Intervention in
Afghanistan," *Cold War International History Project (CWIHP) Bulletin*, 8–9;

"Prelude to Invasion: The Soviet Union and the Afghan Communists, 1978–1979," *International History Review*, 16.1 (1994): 49–69; and in "Nakanune vvoda sovetskikh voisk v Afganistan. 1978–1979" (On the Eve of Sending Soviet Troops to Afghanistan. 1978–1979), *Novaia i noveishaia istoriia*, 2 (1994): 19–35.

1. For an excellent overview see Kirsten E. Schulze, "The Rise of Political Islam, 1928–2000," in Antony Best et al., eds., *The Twentieth Century: An International History* (London: Routledge, 2003).

2. The key figures in the early Islamist awakening are Jamal al-Din al-Afghani (1839–97), Muhammad Abdu (1849–1905), and, especially, Mohammad Rashid Rida (1865–1935).

3. See Mark J. Gasiorowski, *US Foreign Policy and the Shah: Building a Client State in Iran* (Ithaca, NY: Cornell University Press, 1991) and Barry Rubin, *Paved with Good Intentions: The American Experience in Iran* (Oxford: Oxford University Press, 1980).

4. Memorandum from the Department of State Executive Secretary (Brubeck) to the President's Special Assistant for National Security Affairs (Bundy), 21 January 1963, in *Foreign Relations of the United States* (hereafter *FRUS*), *1962–1963*, Near East, p. 311.

5. For a critique see Ali M Ansari, "The Myth of the White Revolution: Mohammad Reza Shah, 'Modernization' and the Consolidation of Power," *Middle Eastern Studies*, 37.3 (2001): 1–24.

6. Mohammed Reza Pahlavi, speech at Harvard University, 13 June 1968, on http://www.sedona.net/pahlavi/harvard.html.

7. Department of State to US Embassy, Teheran, 16 July 1963, including Kennedy–Pahlavi message, *FRUS, 1961–1963*, vol. XVIII.

8. Polk to Rostow, 17 December 1963, *FRUS, 1961–1963*, vol. XVIII.

9. Baqer Moin, *Khomeini: Life of the Ayatollah* (London: I. B. Tauris, 1999), p. 104.

10. *Ibid.*, p. 155.

11. Khomeini speech in Qum, 27 October 1964, on http://www.irib.ir/worldservice/imam/speech/.

12. Henry Kissinger, *Years of Renewal* (New York: Simon & Schuster, 1999), p. 582.

13. Jonathan Randal, *Kurdistan: After Such Knowledge, What Forgiveness?* (London: Bloomsbury, 1998), p. 175.

14. Kissinger, *Years of Renewal*, pp. 592–596; Randal, *Kurdistan*, pp. 153–193.

15. Mohammed Reza Pahlavi, *Answer to History* (New York: Stein & Day, 1980), p. 156. See also Abbas Milani, *The Persian Sphinx: Amir Abbas Hoveyda and the Riddle of the Iranian Revolution* (Washington, DC: Mage, 2000). For a useful discussion of different views on the causes of the Iranian revolution, see Farhad Kazemi, "Models of Iranian Politics, the Road to the Islamic Revolution, and the Challenge of Civil Society," *World Politics*, 47.4 (July 1995): 555–580.

16. For economic causes of revolution, see Robert E. Looney, *Economic Origins of the Iranian Revolution* (New York: New York University Press, 1982). For the relationship between political "traditionalists" and the clergy, see Mohammad Gholi Majd, *Resistance to the Shah: Landowners and Ulama in Iran* (Gainesville,

FL: University Press of Florida, 2000). A very useful comparison of the role of the Islamic opposition within the countries of the region can be found in A. Banuazizi and M. Weiner, eds., *The State, Religion, and Ethnic Politics: Afghanistan, Iran, and Pakistan* (Syracuse, NY: Syracuse University Press, 1986).

17. Peter G. Bourne, *Jimmy Carter: A Comprehensive Biography from Plains to Postpresidency* (New York: Scribner, 1997), p. 453.
18. *Ibid.*, pp. 266, 453.
19. Talbot to Rusk, 6 June 1963, *FRUS, 1961–1963*, vol. XVIII, p. 570.
20. See Mohsen M. Milani, *The Making of Iran's Islamic Revolution: From Monarchy to Islamic Republic* (2nd edn; Boulder, CO: Westview Press, 1994).
21. See S. A. Arjomand, "Iran's Islamic Revolution in Comparative Perspective," *World Politics*, 38 (1986): 383–400.
22. Paul Vieille and Farhad Khosvokhavar, *Le discours populaire de la revolution Iranienne* (Paris: Contempéranité, 1990), vol. II, p. 354.
23. Moin, *Khomeini*, p. 276.
24. Khomeini, message to pilgrims, 12 September 1980, in Hamid Algar, ed. and trans., *Islam and Revolution: Speeches and Declarations*, of Imam Khomeini (Berkeley, CA: Mizan Press, 1981), p. 302.
25. Tulsiram, *History of Communist Movement in Iran* (Bhopal: Grafix, 1981), pp. 157–158. See also Dr. Zayar, "The Iranian Revolution: Past, Present and Future," on http://www.marxist.com/iran/index.html. For an overview of Soviet views, see Richard Herrmann, "The Role of Iran in Soviet Perceptions and Policy, 1946–1988," in Nikki R. Keddie and Mark J. Gasiorowski, eds., *Neither East Nor West: Iran, the Soviet Union, and the United States* (New Haven, CT: Yale University Press, 1990), pp. 63–69.
26. Record of conversation between Brezhnev und Honecker, 4 October 1979, Stiftung Archiv der Parteien und Massenorganisationen in Bundesarchiv, Berlin (hereafter SAPMO-BArch), DY30 JIV 2/201/1342.
27. The Islamists had some of their lists of Communists, as well as some of the "evidence" for Communist espionage, from British intelligence, who had helped one of Shebarshin's KGB deputies in Teheran, Major Vladimir Kuzichkin, defect to the West in June 1982. Both Shebarshin and deputy head of the MO, Ulianovskii, deny that Tudeh members were recruited as agents, but admit that the KGB were responsible for "technical communications" with the Communist leaders (see Alexei Vassiliev, *Russian Policy in the Middle East: From Messianism to Pragmatism* [Reading: Ithaca Press, 1993], p. 165). The best books in English on the destruction of the Iranian Left are Sepehr Zabih, *The Left in Contemporary Iran: Ideology, Organisation and the Soviet Connection* (London: Croom Helm, 1986) and Maziar Behrooz, *Rebels with a Cause: The Failure of the Left in Iran* (London: I. B. Tauris, 1999). For a view of Soviet–Iranian relations with an emphasis on the 1980s, see Haim Shemesh, *Soviet–Iraqi Relations, 1968–1988: In the Shadow of the Iraq–Iran Conflict* (Boulder, CO: Lynne Rienner, 1992).
28. Puzanov quoted in David Gai and Vladimir Snegirev, "Vtorzhenie: opyt zhurnalistskogo rassledovaniia" (Invasion: The Experience of Journalistic Investigation), *Znamia*, 3 (1991): 200.

29. For biographical information on Taraki, Amin, and Karmal, see Beverley Male, *Revolutionary Afghanistan: A Reappraisal* (New York: St. Martin's Press, 1982), pp. 20–51. On Karmal's background, see also the interview with him in *Trud*, 24 October 1991.

30. Hekmatyar himself escaped with Pakistani help; Gulbuddin Hekmatyar, author's interview, Peshawar, 12 March 1985.

31. Soviet Embassy, Kabul, report to Foreign Ministry, Moscow, 26 April 1978, quoted from Vasily Mitrokhin, *The KGB in Afghanistan*, ed. Odd Arne Westad and Christian Ostermann, CWIHP Working Paper 34 (Washington, DC: Woodrow Wilson Center, 2001), p. 23. The KGB agreed with the ambassador's assessment, saying in a telegram on the same day that "[t]he possibility cannot be excluded that Mossad [Israeli intelligence] is willfully provoking the military organization of this party to take action against the government in order to deal it a blow."

32. Puzanov had a high degree of seniority within the Soviet diplomatic establishment. He had had several ambassadorial postings before coming to Kabul, and he was a member of the CPSU Central Committee. See also General Valentin Varennikov's comments in "The Intervention in Afghanistan and the Fall of Détente. Transcript of an International Conference, Lysebu, September 1995," Norwegian Nobel Institute, 1995 (hereafter "Lysebu II"), p. 12. For the American reaction to the coup, see Harold H. Saunders to Cyrus R. Vance, "Briefing Memorandum: The Coup in Afghanistan," 27 April 1978, National Security Archives, comp., *Afghanistan: The Making of US Policy, 1973–1990. Guide and Index* (Alexandria, VA: Chadwyck-Healy, 1990) (hereafter NSArch, *Afghanistan*), microfiche. Saunders was the State Department's assistant secretary for Near Eastern and South Asian Affairs. For general Soviet policies, see Steven R. David, "Soviet Involvement in Third World Coups," *International Security*, 11.1 (summer 1986): 3–36.

33. Aleksandr M. Puzanov to MO, 5 May 1978, "Politpismo: o vnutripolitiches-kom poloshenii v DRA" (On the Domestic Political Situation in the DRA [Democratic Republic of Afghanistan]), Rossiiskii gosudarstvennyi arkhiv noveishei istorii (hereafter RGANI), f. 5, op. 75, d. 1179, pp. 2–6, 16. Most of Puzanov's reports went both to the Foreign Ministry and to the International Department of the party. A *politpismo* is a periodical political report which Soviet ambassadors were required to send to Moscow.

34. *Ibid.*, pp. 13–14, 16.

35. Simonenko, Gankovskov, and Smirnov to MO, 23 May 1978, RGANI f. 5, op. 75, d. 1181, p. 7.

36. Amin to CPSU CC, 23 May 1978, RGANI, f. 5, op. 75, d. 1182, pp. 1–8. Amin visited Moscow briefly in mid-May.

37. Puzanov to MO, 05, May 1978, "Politpismo: op. vnutripoliticheskom poloshenii v DRA" (On the Domestic Political Situation in the DRA), RGANI, f. 5, op. 75, d. 1179, pp. 7, 9–10.

38. Puzanov to MO, 17 May 1978, RGANI, f. 5, op. 75, d. 1181, pp. 1–3.

39. Puzanov to MO, 11 June 1978, *ibid.*, pp. 10–11, 13.

40. Puzanov to MO, 17 June 1978, *ibid.*, pp. 18–19; Puzanov to MO, 11 June 1978, *ibid.*, p. 13.

41. Puzanov to MO, 18 June 1978, *ibid.*, pp. 25–26, 27.
42. Puzanov to MO, 26 August 1978, *ibid.*, p. 77.
43. *Ibid.*, pp. 75–76.
44. *Ibid.*, pp. 76–77.
45. Gai and Snegirev, "Vtorzhenie," p. 201.
46. Puzanov to MO, 26 August 1978, RGANI, f. 5, op. 75, d. 1181, p. 77.
47. Ponomarev quoted in Gai and Snegirev, "Vtorzhenie," p. 201.
48. *Ibid.* For the KGB's suspicions of Amin, see also Aleksandr Morosov, "Kabulskii resident" *Novoe vremia*, 41 (1991): 29. Morosov was KGB deputy resident in Kabul from 1975 to 1979.
49. Gai and Snegirev "Vtorzhenie," p. 201; former Vice-Foreign Minister Mikhail Kapitsa, author's interview, 7 September 1992.
50. *Ibid.*
51. Puzanov to MO, 14 November 1978, RGANI, f. 5, op. 75, d. 1181, pp. 123–129.
52. Puzanov to MO, 17 December 1978, RGANI, f. 5, op. 76, d. 1044, p. 8; Puzanov to MO, 14 November 1978, f. 5, op. 76, d. 1181, p. 125.
53. On Iran, Puzanov to MO, 28 December 1978, RGANI, f. 5, op. 76, d. 1045, pp. 4–5 and Puzanov to MO, 15 January 1979, *ibid.*, p. 13. On technical advisers and assistance, Puzanov to MO, 17 December 1978, *ibid.*, pp. 1–3. On intelligence, Puzanov to MO, 28 December 1978, *ibid.*, p. 5.
54. Puzanov to MO, 30 December 1978, RGANI, f. 5, op. 76, d. 1044, pp. 6–7, 9.
55. Excerpt from the protocol of the 137th session of the Politburo of the CPSU CC on 7 January 1979, osobaia papka (special file; hereafter "OP"), RGANI, f. 89 – kollektsiia, perechen 14, dokument 24. The materials in this file were transferred from the Kremlin Presidential Archive to the RGANI in late 1992.
56. Arkhipov to MO, 28 February 28 1979, RGANI, f. 5, op. 76, d. 1044, pp. 20–23, 26–27.
57. Puzanov to MO, 1 July 1978, RGANI, f. 5, op. 75, d. 1181, p. 31; Puzanov to MO, 22 August 1978, *ibid.*, pp. 64–69; Puzanov to MO, 19 February 1979, RGANI, f. 5, op. 76, d. 1045, pp. 23–24.
58. Anthony Hyman, *Afghanistan under Soviet Domination, 1964–1991* (3rd edn; Houndsmills: Macmillan, 1992), pp. 100–101.
59. Fred Halliday and Zahir Tanin, "The Communist Regime in Afghanistan 1978–1992," *Europe–Asia Studies*, 50 (1998): 1357–1380.
60. Puzanov to MO, 19 March 1979, RGANI, f. 5, op. 76, d. 1044, pp. 36–38, 37.
61. *Kartoteka Sekretariata TsK KPSS* (card files of the Secretariat of the Central Committee of the CPSU; hereafter *KSTsK*), 151th session (20 March 1979), item 4, in RGANI; Puzanov to MO, 25 March 1979, RGANI, f. 5, op. 76, d. 1044, pp. 40–41.
62. Record of conversation between Kosygin, Gromyko, Ustinov, Ponomarev, and Taraki, 20 March 1979, OP, RGANI, f. 89 – kollektsiia, perechen 14, dokument 26.
63. Record of conversation between Brezhnev and Taraki, 20 March 1979, OP, RGANI, f. 89 – kollektsiia, perechen 14, dokument 25.

64. Puzanov to MO, 22 March 1979, RGANI, f. 5, op. 76, d. 1044, p. 29. Taraki used the new direct phone link with the Kremlin often during the Herat crisis. The record of another of his phone calls (to Prime Minister Aleksei Kosygin on 18 March) is published in *Moskovskie novosti*, 7 June 1992, p. 12. On the phone link to Moscow, see *KSTsK*, 150th session (13 March 1979), item 10, in RGANI.

65. Puzanov to MO, 10 April 1979, RGANI, f. 5, op. 76, d. 1044, pp. 43, 45–46.

66. Mark Urban, *War in Afghanistan* (2nd edn; Houndsmills: Macmillan, 1990), pp. 32–36.

67. Excerpt from the protocol of the 149th session of the CPSU CC Politburo on 12 April 1979. Political report, "O nashii dalneishei linii v sviazi s polozheniem v Afganistane" (On our future line in connection with the situation in Afghanistan), signed by Gromyko, Andropov, Ustinov, and Ponomarev, OP, RGANI, f. 89 – kollektsiia, perechen 14, dokument 27.

68. Safronchuk to MO, 2 July 1979, RGANI, f. 5, op. 76, d. 1046, pp. 38–40; Bruce J. Amstutz to Department of State, 25 June 1979, confidential cable 4888; Amstutz to State et al., 18 July 1979, confidential cable 5433, Amstutz to State, 19 July 1979, confidential cable 5463, all on microfiche in NSArch, *Afghanistan*. Safronchuk informed Amstutz, the US chargé d'affaires, about the Soviet plans for a "restructuring" of the Afghan government, probably in an attempt to defuse American criticism of Soviet military involvement in Afghanistan. See also V. Safronchuk, "Afganistan vremen Taraki" (Afghanistan in Taraki's Time), *Mezhdunarodnaia zhizn*, 12 (1990): 86–96.

69. Puzanov quoting Amin in Gai and Snegirev, "Vtorzhenie," p. 201.

70. Puzanov to MO, 21 July 1979, RGANI, f. 5, op. 76, d. 1045, p. 94; see also Ivanov and Osadchy to KGB Center, 16 June and 16 July, quoted in Mitrokhin, *KGB in Afghanistan*.

71. Gai and Snegirev, "Vtorzhenie," pp. 218, 223; Puzanov to MO, 21 July 1979, RGANI, f. 5, op. 76, d. 1045, pp. 95–97; Aleksandr Liakhovskii, *Tragediia i doblest afgana*, (Afghan Tragedy and Valor) (Mascow: Iskona, 1995) pp. 84–89.

72. Puzanov to MO, 6 August 1979, RGANI, f. 5, op. 76, d. 1044, pp. 81–84.

73. On the Epishev mission, see NSArch, *Afghanistan*, p. 77; see also Gorelov to Ogarkov, 14 March 1979, RGANI, f. 5, op. 76, d. 1045, p. 216; on the Pavlovskii mission, Pavlovskii to Ustinov, 20 and 25 August, *ibid.*, p. 217. Ustinov's report to the Politburo after Pavlovskii's return on 22 October is in Archiv Prezidenta Rossiiskoi Federatsii (hereafter APRF), f. 3, op. 82, d. 149, pp. 120–122. See also G. N. Sevostianov, "Dokumenty sovetskogo rukovodstva o polozhenii v Afganistane, 1979–1980" (Documents of the Soviet Leadership on the Situation in Afghanistan, 1979–1980), *Novaia i noveishaia istoriia*, 3 (1996): 91–99. For the military's viewpoints, see Artem Borovik, "Afganistan: podvodia itogi" (Afghanistan: The Conclusions), interview with General Valentin Varennikov, *Ogonyok*, 12 (1989): 6–8, 30–31.

74. Gai and Snegirev, "Vtorzhenie," pp. 204–208; former Vice-Foreign Minister Mikhail Kapitsa, author's interview, 7 September, 1992; see also Bhabani Sen Gupta, *Afghanistan: Politics, Economics, and Society* (London: Pinter, 1986), p. 82.

75. Gai and Snegirev, "Vtorzhenie," p. 205. The Soviet military attaché was Lieutenant General Lev Gorelov, the KGB resident was Lieutenant General Boris Ivanov.

76. *Ibid.*

77. Puzanov's diary, 19 September 1979, quoted by Mitrokhin, *KGB in Afghanistan.*

78. Morosov, "Kabulskii resident," pp. 28–31. General Leonid Shebarshin, who was KGB resident in Teheran at the time, claims that the KGB was not involved in the attempt to assassinate Amin (author's conversation, Oslo, 18 September 1995); see also Lysebu II, pp. 78–79. Mitrokhin's account of the episode, based on the KGB reports at the time, is also unclear on whether Soviet intelligence was directly involved.

79. Bogdanov to Kryuchkov, reporting meeting with Amin on 9 October 1979, quoted by Mitrokhin, *KGB in Afghanistan.*

80. Gai and Snegirev, "Vtorzhenie,", p. 210.

81. Puzanov to MO, 27 October 1979, RGANI, f. 5, op. 76, d. 1045, p. 112.

82. Conversation with Abdul Karim Misaq (Minister of Finance), Puzanov to MO, 5 November 1979, *ibid.*, pp. 125–126; conversation with Mohammad Siddiq Alemyar (Minister of Planning), Puzanov to MO, 10 November 1979, *ibid.*, pp. 134–136; conversation with Major Yaqub (Head of General Staff), Puzanov to MO, 13 November 1979, *ibid.*, pp. 140–143. Puzanov also met with Mahmoud Soma (Minister of Higher Education), Faqir Mohammad Faqir (Minister of Interior), and Shah Wali (Minister of Foreign Affairs).

83. Amstutz to Department of State, 30 September 1979, cable 7232, and Archer K. Blood to Department of State, 28 October 1979, cable 7726, both in NSArch, *Afghanistan*; in one conversation with Safronchuk, Amin particularly emphasized his contacts with the Americans; see Safronchuk to MO, 29 October 1979, RGANI, f. 5, op. 76, d. 1046, pp. 67–70.

84. Puzanov to MO, 19 November 1979, RGANI, f. 5, op. 76, d. 1045, pp. 144–146.

85. KGB (G. Tsinev) to MO, 10 October 1979, report entitled "Rukovodstvo Irana o vneshnei bezopasnosti strani" (The Iranian Leadership on the Country's Foreign Security), RGANI, f. 5, op. 76, d. 1355, pp. 18, 19–20.

86. Vasilii Safronchuk, "Afganistan vremen Amina" (Afghanistan in Amin's Time), *Mezhdunarodnaia zhizn*, 1 (1991): 124–142; V. P. Kapitanov to MO, n.d. (late fall 1979), RGANI, f. 5, op. 76, d. 1337, pp. 5–7. For the military situation, see Urban, *War in Afghanistan*, pp. 36–37.

87. Tabeev to MO, 6 December 1979, RGANI, f. 5, op. 76, d. 1045, pp. 152–153. See also Pavel Demchenko, "Kak eto nachinalos v Afganistane" (How it Began in Afghanistan), *Ekho planety*, 46 (1989): 26–32.

88. Record of CPSU Politburo meeting, 18 March 1979, in Odd Arne Westad, ed., *The Fall of Détente: Soviet–American Relations during the Carter Years* (Oslo: Scandinavian University Press, 1997), p. 302.

89. Author's conversation, Oslo, 18 September 1995.

90. *Ibid.* See also Lysebu II, pp. 75–94.

91. Mitrokhin, *KGB in Afghanistan*, pp. 85–86.

92. Lysebu II.

93. *Ibid.*, p. 177.
94. Karen N. Brutents, *Tridtsat let na Staroi Ploshchadi* (Thirty Years at Storoia Ploshchad) (Moscow: Mezhdunarodnie Otnosheniia, 1998), pp. 451–504.
95. Mirokhin, *KGB in Afghanistan*, p. 91. The KGB reported that after the murder of Amin, Kapustin became "quiet and withdrawn."
96. Lysebu II, p. 81.
97. *Ibid.*, pp. 90–91. This document, which probably was written on 2 December 1979, was hand-copied by Ambassador Dobrynin from sources in the APRF during his preparations for the Lysebu conference.
98. Lysebu II, pp. 83–86; author's interview with Varennikov, Oslo, 18 September 1995. The account of the final decision-making in Moscow that follows is based on the transcript of the September 1995 conference at Lysebu, supplemented by the author's conversations and interviews with the Russian participants at that conference and on later occasions. See also Diego Cordovez and Selig S. Harrison, *Out of Afghanistan: The Inside Story of the Soviet Withdrawal* (Oxford: Oxford University Press, 1995), pp. 44–49.
99. Document quoted by Ambassador Dobrynin at Lysebu, Lysebu II, pp. 91–92.
100. The KGB suffered considerable losses in the attack on Dar-ul-Aman. At least one hundred members were killed, something which according to Mitrokhin led Andropov to deviate from the KGB tradition of "hanging portraits in mourning frames of heroes killed whilst carrying out their noble international mission in the halls and corridors as this would attract unnecessary attention" (Mitrokhin, *KGB in Afghanistan*, p. 95).
101. Panjshiri played an unclear role in connection with the invasion. A valued KGB informant (under the codename "Richard"), he was implicated in the plotting against Amin, but seems to have had second thoughts and supported the party leadership at the time leading up to the Soviet intervention. After his release from prison in January 1980 he was reinstated in the PDPA Politburo.
102. See, for instance, Puzanov's political reports of 4 April 1979 and 27 June 1979 entitled "O nekotorikh momentakh vnutripoliticheskogo polozheniia v Demokraticheskoi Respublike Afganistan" (On some aspects of the domestic political situation in the Democratic Republic of Afghanistan), and "Ob osushchestvlenii v DRA zemelnoi reformi i ee vliianii na razvitie vnutripoliticheskoi obstanovki" (On the implementation of land reform in the DRA and its influence on the development of the domestic political situation), RGANI, f. 5, op. 76, d. 1042, pp. 1–15, 16–27.
103. Mitrokhin, *KGB in Afghanistan*, p. 105.
104. Male, *Revolutionary Afghanistan*, p. 28; Puzanov to MO, 19 February 1979, RGANI, f. 5, op. 76, d. 1045, pp. 23–24.
105. Hyman, *Afghanistan under Soviet Domination*, p. 106.
106. Puzanov to MO, 1 July 1978 and 18 July 1978, RGANI, f. 5, op. 75, d. 1181, pp. 29–33, 36–40. See also his political report of 27 June 1979, "Ob osushchestvlenii v DRA zemelnoi reformi i ee vliianii na razvitie vnutripoliticheskoi obstanovki" (On the implementation of land reform in the DRA and its influence on the development of the domestic political

situation), RGANI, f. 5, op. 76, d. 1042, pp. 16–27. For a good comparative discussion of Soviet interventions, see Bruce D. Porter, *The USSR in Third World Conflicts: Soviet Arms and Diplomacy in Local Wars, 1945–1980* (Cambridge: Cambridge University Press, 1984). Samuel P. Huntington has attempted a typology of Soviet and American interventions, which emphasizes Moscow's preparedness to offer military assistance; see for instance his "Patterns of Intervention: America and the Soviets in the Third World," *National Interest* (spring 1987): 39–47.

107. See Russian General Staff, *The Soviet–Afghan War: How a Superpower Fought and Lost*, trans. and ed. Lester W. Grau and Michael A. Gress (Lawrence, KN: University of Kansas Press, 2002).

108. Former Vice Foreign Minister Mikhail Kapitsa, author's interview, 8 September 1992.

109. On the KGB, see Morosov, "Kabulskii resident," *Novoe vremia* (1991), no. 38, pp. 36–39, no. 39, pp. 32–33, no. 40, pp. 36–37, no. 41, pp. 28–31; and also Boris Ponomarev, quoted in Gai and Snegirev, "Vtorzhenie," p. 226. On the military, see Ivan Pavlovskii, quoted in Gai and Snegirev, "Vtorzhenie,", p. 218.

110. The KGB, especially, saw the two threats merging: "The USA was hoping that, by giving financial and military aid to the [Afghan] rebels, it would please Khomeini and lead him to adopt a compromise to the question of the release of the hostages." KGB Center to KGB Station Beijing, 8 January 1980, in Mitrokhin, *KGB in Afghanistan*, typescript version, copy in author's possession.

111. Brezhnev made these remarks to Ambassador Dobrynin during a conversation in mid-January 1980 (Dobrynin, author's interview, Oslo, 22 September 1995; hereafter Dobrynin interview).

112. Brzezinski to Carter, 26 December 1979, NSArch, Carter–Brezhnev collection.

113. See Frank Reynolds' interview with Carter, a transcript of which appeared in the *New York Times*, 1 January 1980.

114. Record of NSC meeting, 2 January 1980, NSArch, Carter–Brezhnev collection.

115. Robert E. Gates, *From the Shadows: The Ultimate Insider's Story of Five Presidents and how they Won the Cold War* (New York: Simon & Schuster, 1996), p. 147.

116. The phrase is Brzezinski's; see Brzezinski to Carter, 26 December 1979, NSArch, Carter–Brezhnev Collection.

117. Turner's personal cover note to Brzezinski on CIA report on Soviet Third World policies, mid-April 1980, quoted in Gates, *From the Shadows*, p. 148.

118. *Ibid.*, p. 150.

119. Henry S. Bradsher, *Afghan Commmunism and Soviet Intervention* (Oxford: Oxford University Press, 1999), p. 105.

120. Prince Turki quoted in Steve Coll, *Ghost Wars: The Secret History of the CIA, Afghanistan, and Bin Laden, from the Soviet Invasion to September 11, 2001* (Harmondsworth: Penguin, 2004), p. 72. The prince, who became

the key funder for the Afghan Islamists at the beginning of the war, is aptly portrayed by Coll as "a champion of Saudi Arabia's austere Islam, a promoter of women's rights, a multimillionaire, a workaholic, a pious man, a sipper of banana daiquiris, an intriguer, an intellectual, a loyal prince, a sincere friend of Americans, [and] a generous funder of anti-American causes" (p. 73).

121. Mitrokhin, *KGB in Afghanistan*, p. 104. See also Vinogradov's own somewhat inaccurate account in "Audientsiin na rassvetie" (Audience at Dawn), *Mezhdunarodnaia zhizn* (1991).

122. Khomeini, message to pilgrims, in Algar, *Speeches and Declarations*.

9   THE 1980S: THE REAGAN OFFENSIVE

1. There is already a substantial literature on Reagan's Third World policies; by far the best overview is James M. Scott, *Deciding to Intervene: The Reagan Doctrine and American Foreign Policy* (Durham, NC: Duke University Press, 1996), but see also Peter W. Rodman, *More Precious than Peace: The Cold War and the Struggle for the Third World* (New York: Schribner's Sons, 1994), Robert A. Kagan, *A Twilight Struggle: American Power and Nicaragua, 1977–1990* (New York: Free Press, 1996), and Chester Crocker, *High Noon in Southern Africa: Making Peace in a Rough Neighborhood* (New York: Norton, 1992). The latter three were all written by State Department officials in the Reagan administration.

2. Gary Sick, author's conversation, 18 September 1995, Lysebu.

3. The concept of "totalitarianism" was first used, as a political goal, by the Italian Fascists in the 1920s. Its use in the 1960s drew on the supposed lessons of the defeat of Nazi Germany, Italy, and Japan, and was inspired by Hannah Arendt's *Origins of Totalitarianism*, first published in 1951.

4. There is, in Brzezinski's thinking, a curious contradiction between his apocalyptic vision of America's role and his Kissingerian emphasis on Soviet learning through US actions.

5. Radio address, 31 March 1976, on http://www.reaganlegacy.org/speeches/.

6. *Wall Street Journal*, 3 June 1980.

7. For an excellent contemporary overview, see Jagdish N. Bhagwati, ed., *The New International Economic Order: The North–South Debate* (Cambridge, MA: MIT Press, 1977)

8. Kofi Buenor Hadjor, *Penguin Dictionary of Third World Terms* (Harmondsworth: Penguin, 1993), p. 223.

9. For some interesting comparisons between state policies, see Peter B. Evans, *Embedded Autonomy: States and Industrial Transformation* (Princeton, NJ: Princeton University Press, 1995); see also, from the perspective of Western advisers, William Easterly, *The Elusive Quest for Growth: Economists' Adventures and Misadventures in the Tropics* (Cambridge, MA: MIT Press, 2001).

10. See Forrest D. Colburn, *The Vogue of Revolution in Poor Countries* (Princeton, NJ: Princeton University Press, 1994), especially pp. 97–105.

11. For an important discussion of the concepts of state and nation in the Third World during the Cold War, see Bertrand Badie, *L'état importé: essai sur*

l'occidentalisation de l'ordre politique (Paris: Fayard, 1992), especially pp. 169–200. See also Dawa Norbu, *Culture and the Politics of Third World Nationalism* (London: Routledge, 1992), and Nicola Weber and Andreas Biermayer, *Das Chamäleon Ideologie im Kontext einer "Neuen Ordnung" mit alten Strukturen* (Münster: Lit, 1993).

12. See, for instance, Martin Ravallion and Shaohua Chen, "Distribution and Poverty in Developing and Transition Economies: New Data on Spells during 1981–93," *World Bank Economic Review*, 11 (1997).

13. CIA, "The Soviet Economy in 1978–79 and Prospects for 1980: A Research Paper," June 1980, on http://www.foia.cia.gov. Recent Russian figures confirm the downward trend in growth in the 1970s and also point to 1979 as a particularly difficult year; see V. A. Vinogradov, chief ed., *Ekonomicheskaia istoriia Rossii XIX–XX vv: sovremennyi vzgliad* (The Economic History of Russia in the Nineteenth and Twentieth Centuries: A Contemporary View) (Moscow: Rosspen, 2000).

14. Andropov himself began using a similar term in 1983 – *perekhitrit*; literally "overreached" – on Soviet foreign engagements (interview with former Soviet Vice-Foreign Minister Mikhail Kapitsa, Moscow, 8 September 1992).

15. Record of CPSU CC Politburo meeting 31 May 1983 *Cold War International History Project (CWIHP) Bulletin*, 4.

16. See Beth Fischer, *The Reagan Reversal: Foreign Policy and the End of the Cold War* (Columbia, MO: University of Missouri Press, 1997) and James M. Scott, *Deciding to Intervene: The Reagan Doctrine and American Foreign Policy* (Durham, NC: Duke University Press, 1996), especially pp. 14–39.

17. Elie Krakowski at CWIHP Afghanistan conference, Washington, DC, April 2002.

18. Author's interview with Richard Pipes, Oslo, May 1993.

19. V. Vorotnikov to CC CPSU, 15 December 198, RGANI, f. 5, op. 84, d. 584, pp. 1–27; record of conversation between Rodriguez and Haig, 23 November 1981, National Security Archive (hereafter NSArch). Rodriguez' response to Haig's charges on Central America was that "The Soviet Union in no way wants to be entangled in anything which is seen to be a revolutionary process in which it does not desire to participate."

20. Interview with Walter Cronkite of CBS News, 3 March 1981.

21. For an overview of the history of the Sandinistas, see Matilde Zimmermann, *Sandinista: Carlos Fonseca and the Nicaraguan Revolution* (Durham, NC: Duke University Press, 2000), and Dennis Gilbert, *Sandinistas: The Party and the Revolution* (Oxford: Basil Blackwell, 1988).

22. For a good overview, see Thomas W. Walker, ed., *Nicaragua in Revolution* (New York: Praeger, 1982).

23. Kagan, *Twilight Struggle*, p. 91.

24. See, for instance, the memoirs of Tomás Borge, one of the key Sandinista leaders, *The Patient Impatience: From Boyhood to Guerrilla. A Personal Narrative of Nicaragua's Struggle for Liberation* (Willimantic, CT: Curbstone Press, 1992).

25. Kagan, *Twilight Struggle*, p. 197.

26. See Ortega's own testimony in *60 preguntas a un sandinista: entrevista a Daniel Ortega Saavedra* (Sixty Questions to a Sandinista: Interview with Daniel Ortega Saavedra) (Managua: Radio la Primerísima, 1994).

27. Kagan, *Twilight Struggle*, p. 192.

28. Much of the US support for the E1 Salvadorean government had been prepared by the Carter administration; see "Presidential Determination on Nicaraguan Support for Salvadorean Guerrillas," 1 October 1981, box 33, subject file – meetings, Brzezinski collection, Jimmy Carter Presidential Library, and Bob Woodward, *Veil: The Secret Wars of the CIA, 1981–1987* (New York: Simon & Schuster, 1987). The first part of the record of this conversation was submitted by the Nicaraguan government to the International Court of Justice (ICJ) in 1986; see ICJ, Military and Paramilitary Activities in and against Nicaragua (Nicaragua v. United States of America), Merits, Judgment 27 June 1986; see also William M. LeoGrande, *Our Own Backyard: The United States in Central America, 1977–1992* (Chapel Hill, NC: University of North Carolina Press, 1998), p. 120.

29. Soviet Ambassador to Cuba Vorotnikov, memorandum of conversation with Raul Castro, 1 September 1979, *CWIHP Bulletin*, 8–9; GDR report on a visit to Nicaragua, June 1981, Stiftung Archiv der Parteien und Massenorganisationen in Bundesarchiv, Berlin (herafter SAPMO-BArch), J IV 2/20/149.

30. Record of conversation between Abteilung Internationale Vertretungen (hereafter AIV) and Carlos Nuñez Téllez, 20 July 1981, SAPMO-BArch, J IV 2/20/149.

31. Interview with Daniel Ortega for CNN Cold War television series, on-line at http://www.cnn.com/SPECIALS/cold.war/episodes/18/interviews/ortega/.

32. For an overview of Nicaraguan–Eastern Bloc interaction in 1981–84, see record of conversation, between Honecker and Daniel Ortega, Berlin, 20 June 1984, SAPMO-BArch, DY-30 JIV 2/201/1586; see also Danuta Paszyn, *The Soviet Attitude to Political and Social Change in Central America, 1979–1990: Case-Studies on Nicaragua, El Salvador and Guatemala* (Houndsmills: Macmillan, 2000), pp. 39–55.

33. Interview with Walter Cronkite of CBS News, 3 March 1981.

34. Remarks to an Outreach Working Group on United States Policy in Central America, 18 July 1984, on http://www.reagan.utexas.edu/resource/speeches/1984/71884d.htm.

35. Originally in published in *Commentary* (January 1981), reprinted as "US Security and Latin America" in Jeane J. Kirkpatrick, *Dictatorships and Double Standards: Rationalism and Reason in Politics* (New York: Simon & Schuster, 1982), p. 89.

36. High-ranking Reagan administration official, author's interview, Washington, DC, August 1999.

37. Fred C. Iklé, "US Policy for Central America: Can We Succeed?" Iklé was Undersecretary of Defense for Policy in the Reagan administration.

38. Elizabeth Wood, *Insurgent Collective Action and Civil War in El Salvador* (Cambridge: Cambridge University Press, 2003), p. 201.

39. *Ibid.*, pp. 117–118.

40. Question-and-answer session with high school students on domestic and foreign policy issues, 25 March 1983, *Public Papers of the Presidents of the United States* (hereafter *PPP-US*), *Ronald Wilson Reagan*, on http://www.reagan.utexas.edu/resource/speeches/1983/32583c.htm.

41. Tomás Borge, 1 May 1982 speech in Managua, reprinted in *Intercontinental Press*, 31 May 1982.

42. For the effects of the El Salvadorean civil war, see Margaret L. Popkin, *Peace without Justice: Obstacles to Building the Rule of Law in El Salvador* (University Park, PA: Pennsylvania State University Press, 2000), and Manuel Montobbio, *La metamorfosis de pulgarcito: transición política y proceso de paz en El Salvador* (Tom Thumb's Transformation: Political Transition and Peace Process in El Salvador) (Barcelona: Icaria, 1999).

43. This, one may assume, was easier said than done. As Henry S. Bradsher points out, Karmal's new cabinet included, as first deputy premier, Sarwari, who had been publicly accused of personally torturing the second deputy premier, Keshtmand, while the latter spent time in prison in 1978. See Henry S. Bradsher, *Afghan Communism and Soviet Intervention* (Oxford: Oxford University Press, 1999), p. 121.

44. See Gilles Dorronsoro, *La révolution afghane: des communistes aux tâlebân* (Paris: Karthala, 2000), especially pp. 109–154. Dorronsoro's book is by far the best available introduction to Afghan politics in the 1980s.

45. According to General Mohammed Youssaf, the deputy head of Pakistani military intelligence, by early 1984 "Zia's patience snapped, and he issued a directive at 2.00 a.m. that the Parties were to form a Seven-Party Alliance and issue a joint announcement to that effect within 72 hours. He did not say what he would do if they declined. The leaders were well aware that without Pakistan's, and that meant Zia's, backing, everything was finished." Mohammed Youssaf with Mark Adkin, *Afghanistan: The Bear Trap. The Defeat of a Superpower* (Havertown, PA: Casemate Publishers, 2001), p. 35. General Youssaf's book provides an excellent overview of Pakistani intelligence's involvement with the Afghan resistance.

46. Russian General Staff, *The Soviet–Afghan War: How a Superpower Fought and Lost*, trans. and ed. Lester W. Gran and Michael A. Gress (Lawrence, KS: University of Kansas Press, 2002).

47. *Ibid.*, p. 19.

48. Dorronsoro, *Revolution afghane*, pp. 193–227; Fred Halliday and Zahir Tanin, "The Communist Regime in Afghanistan 1978–1992," *Europe–Asia Studies*, 50 (1998): 1357–1380.

49. Dobrynin interview; see also "The Intervention in Afghanistan and the Fall of Détente. Transcript of an International Conference, Lysebu, September 1995," Norwegian Nobel Institute, 1995 (hereafter Lysebu II).

50. For Zia's aims, see his 3 June 1980 speech to the nation, published as "Islamic Order, Our Goal" (Islamabad: Directorate of Films and Publications, Ministry of Information and Broadcasting, Govt. of Pakistan, [1980]).

51. Information from author's interviews in Pakistan in 1986 and 1991. Unfortunately none of the informants can be listed by name.

52. Information from oral testimony by Elie Krakowski, Milton Bearden, and Nicholas Veliotes at the conference "Towards an International History of the War in Afghanistan, 1979–89," organized by the Cold War International History Project in Washington, DC, 29–30 April 2002.

53. Secretary of State to US Embassy, Islamabad, for Undersecretary Eagleburger and Ambassador Spiers, n.d. (November 1982), NSArch, Afghanistan collection.

54. Veliotes to Secretary of State, 29 November 1982, NSArch, Afghanistan collection.

55. Shultz to Reagan, 29 November 1982, NSArch, Afghanistan collection.

56. Record of conversation between Shultz and Zia, 6 December 1982 NSArch, Afghanistan collection.

57. Tsongas and Ritter had proposed a resolution on providing more effective material aid to the Mujahedin already in 1982, but it was not passed until 1984 because of the administration's attempts at linking support for the Afghans to support for "freedom fighters" elsewhere (i.e., Nicaragua – a policy that a majority in Congress opposed) and doubts in Congress about where to find the money for the Afghan venture.

58. US Embassy, Islamabad, to Secretary of State, June 1983, NSArch, Afghanistan collection.

59. Elie D. Krakowski, author's conversation, 29 April 2002.

60. Jay Winik, *On the Brink: The Dramatic Behind-the-Scenes Saga of the Reagan Era and the Men and Women who Won the Cold War* (New York: Simon & Schuster, 1996), p. 447. See also McFarlane to Shultz, "US–Soviet Relations: A Framework for the Future," where the National Security Adviser argues that it is in the Third World that the Soviet Union will find it most difficult to find grounds for accommodation with the United States, for reasons of doctrine (24 February 1984, NSArch, Afghanistan collection).

61. Joseph E. Persico, *Casey: From the OSS to the CIA* (New York: Viking, 1990), p. 226.

62. These new initiatives are summed up in Reagan's National Security Decision Directive (NSDD) 166, "US Policy, Programs, and Strategy in Afghanistan," 27 March 1985. This NSDD is still not declassified.

63. The CIA's then station chief in Islamabad, Milton Bearden, estimated a total of 2 to 3,000 foreign Muslims fighting in Afghanistan in 1986 (conversation with author, Washington, DC, 19 April 2002). It is still very difficult to determine the full extent of this network. In addition to the training camps in Pakistan, there was one such camp in Egypt and probably one in one of the Gulf states, both operated locally but with CIA assistance. The Chinese trained some Afghans and possibly also foreigners in a camp in southwestern China. The Thatcher government – true to style – "privatized" its Afghan military assistance, using public money to pay for mercenaries to train ISI specialists (information gathered in Peshawar by author in 1985 and 1986; conversations with Charles Coogan and Milton Bearden, Washington, DC, April 2002). Unfortunately, one of the main sources of information, John K. Cooley's *Unholy Wars: Afghanistan, America, and International Terrorism* (2nd edn; London: Pluto Press, 2000), is unreliable; some of the information

Cooley uses obviously originates in Soviet disinformation from the 1980s (interview with "Vasiliy Mitrokhin," London, October 2001; see also Mitrokhin's *The KGB in Afghanistan*, ed. Christian Ostermann and O. A. Westad, [Washington, DC: Cold War International History Project, 2002]).

64. According to General Youssaf, Congressman Wilson went to Afghanistan with the ISI several times in the mid-1980s, where "he enjoyed himself, being photographed on a white pony dressed as a Mujahideen, with a bandolier of bullets across his chest. He was most excited when he came under spasmodic shellfire ... Because we had several Stingers with us we tried to tempt a helicopter to come within range, as the Mujahideen wanted to show off their skill, and Wilson was equally enthusiastic to see one brought down. Unfortunately, they kept well away" (Youssaf, *Bear Trap*, pp. 54–55).

65. Woodward, *Veil*; high-ranking Reagan administration official, author's interview, Washington, August 1999.

66. The Bank of Credit and Commerce International (BCCI), which collapsed in 1991, for a time held some of the accounts of the Saudi royal family as well as the accounts of the bin Laden family – one of the bin Laden brothers served on its board. See the penultimate draft of "The BCCI Affair: A Report to the Committee on Foreign Relations, United States Senate, by Senator John Kerry and Senator Hank Brown, December 1992," on http://fas.org/irp/congress/1992_rpt/bcci/.

67. The Mujahedin had British-made "Blowpipe" ground-to-air missiles and some light-weight Soviet-designed SA-7 missiles since late 1983, but, although effective at first, these weapons were far too easy to avoid for both helicopters and fighter-bombers.

68. According to one of his assistants, Shultz had been looking for a way to put more pressure on the Soviets since 1983, when he was deeply moved by the plight of Afghan refugees after a visit to one of the camps in Pakistan (Nicholas Veliotis, interview, Washington, DC, April 2002).

69. Youssaf, *Bear Trap*, p. 73. See also Steve Coll, *Ghost Wars: The Secret History of the CIA, Afghanistan, and Bin Laden, from the Soviet Invasion to September 11, 2001* (Harmondsworth: Penguin, 2004).

70. The head of the ISI Afghan Bureau, General Youssaf, sees Hekmatyar as "a staunch believer in an Islamic government for Afghanistan, an excellent administrator and, as far as I could discover, scrupulously honest. Despite his comparative wealth, he lives a frugal life. He is also ruthless, arrogant, inflexible, a stern disciplinarian, and he does not get on with Americans" (Youssaf, *Bear Trap*, p. 36).

71. Sayaaf's group got a curious afterlife when one of the foreign fighters who had joined it in the 1980s, Ustadz Abdurajack Janjalani, returned home to the Philippines in 1989, there turning from soft-spoken Islamic preacher to talk-show host, to head of the Islamic insurgent group known as the Abu Sayaaf.

72. Hekmatyar's group singled out moderate religious leaders and the Afghan intelligentsia in exile for intimidation or assassination. Their murder of the main independent Afghan writer on the war, Sayed Bahauddin Majrooh, in Peshawar on 11 February 1988 stands out as particularly gruesome. Hekmatyar's view of the United States from author's interview, 12 March

1985. The CIA, meanwhile, continued to defend the group. "Gulbuddin is not as bad as you fear," a CIA officer told his French counterpart (quoted from Coll, *Ghost Wars*, p. 151).

73. Russian General Staff, *Soviet-Afghan War*, especially chs. 7 (Combat Support) and 9 (Morale).

74. Ronald Reagan, "The Agenda is Victory," 26 February 1982, on http://www.thereaganlegacy.com.

75. Kirkpatrick, "Dictatorships and Double Standards," *Commentary* (November 1979).

76. Ronald Reagan speech entitled "America's Purpose," 25 March 1978, online at http://www.reaganlegacy.org/speeches/. US allies were still, of course, exempted: "President Mobutu continues to hold to his courageous, difficult programs of economic reform, compliance with IMF requirements, and a liberal human rights policy," National Security Adviser McFarlane reported to President Reagan, 27 February 1984, box 42, African Affairs, NSC Executive Secretariat, Ronald Reagan Presidential Library, Simi Valley, CA.

77. IMF director Jacques de Larosière de Champfeu, quoted in Wood, *Insurgent Collective Action*, p. 300. Interestingly, both of the crusading free-market directors of the IMF in the 1980s, de Larosière and his successor from 1987, Michel Camdessus, were converts from the distinctly nonmonetarist tradition of the French Ecole Nationale d'Administration, from which they both had graduated.

78. Wood, *Insurgent Collective Action*, p. 267.

79. Philip Armstrong, Andrew Glyn, and John Harrison, *Capitalism Since 1945* (Cambridge, MA: Blackwell, 1991), p. 293.

80. See also Ibrahima Ly's magnificent novel *Toiles d'araignées* (Paris: Harmattan, 1985). Eric Toussant, *La bourse ou la vie: la finance contre les peuples* (Paris: Editions Syllepse, 1998), p. 157.

81. South African Truth and Reconciliation Commission, "The Case of Samora Machel," on http://www.contrast.org/truth/html/summary.html.

10   THE GORBACHEV WITHDRAWAL AND THE END OF THE COLD WAR

1. For the development of Gorbachev's views, see Anatolii Cherniaev's various memoirs, especially *My Six Years with Gorbachev*, trans. and ed. Robert D. English and Elizabeth Tucker (University Park, PA: Pennsylvania State University Press, 2000), and also the memoirs of another key Gorbachev aide, Aleksandr N. Iakovlev.

2. Record of conversation between Gorbachev and Raul Castro, 5 April 1985, Gorbachev Foundation Archives. Gorbachev's meeting with Pakistani leader Zia ul-Haq, who came to Moscow for Chernenko's funeral, was, according to one of Zia's close aides, filled with Soviet accusations and threats.

3. Record of conversation between Reagan and Gorbachev, 19 November 1985, 2nd Plenary Meeting, National Security Archive (hereafter NSArch).

4. Excerpt from Cherniaev's diary, 17 October 1985, in Chernyaev, *Six Years with Gorbachev*, p. 42.

5. CIA, Directorate of Intelligence. "The Costs of Soviet Involvement in Afghanistan: An Intelligence Assessment," February 1987, pp. iv, 2, on http://www.foia.cia.gov.

6. See Mohammed Youssaf with Mark Adkin, *Afghanistan: The Bear Trap. The Defeat of a Superpower* (Havetown, PA: Casemate Publishers, 2001), ch. 12, and Steve Coll, *Ghost Wars: The Secret History of the CIA, Afghanistan, and Bin Laden, from the Soviet Invasion to September 11, 2001* (Harmondsworth: Penguin, 2004), pp. 161–162 Also Georgii Kornienko, former Soviet first vice-foreign minister, interview with author, 5 October 1993.

7. Record of conversation between Dubinin and Armacost, 1 December 1986, Declassified Documents Reference Service (hereafter DDRS). US personnel did at least occasionally interrogate Soviets who were held prisoner by the Mujahedin (former CIA official, author's interview, Washington, DC, November 1999).

8. *Mirovaia ekonomika i mezhdunarodnye otnosheniia*, 5 (1985), but see also Leonid Abalkin's article in the same issue, "Leninskoia teoriia imperializma v svete sovremennykh realnosti" (The Leninist Theory of Imperialism in Light of Contemporary Realities.)

9. Record of conversation between Reagan and Gorbachev, 19 November 1985, NSArch.

10. Record of conversation, 19 November 1985, 2nd Plenary Meeting, NSArch.

11. Anatolii Cherniaev, author's interview, Washington, DC, 20 April 2002; record of conversation between Honecker and Castro, Moscow, 3 March 1986, Stiftung Archiv der Parteien und Massenorganisationen in Bundesarchiv, Berlin (hereafter SAPMO-BArch), DY30 2462. Castro also said that "no one can predict that the Reagan administration will not intervene militarily in Nicaragua or El Salvador."

12. On the origins of the Soviet–PCI conflict, see record of conversation between Enrico Berlinguer and Kirilenko and Zagladin, Bologna, 24 March 1975, Archives of the Central Commitee of the Italian Communist Party (hereafter PCI Archives), 204, vol. III, 2° bimestre 1975; for the extent of PCI criticism of the Soviet domestic record in the 1970s, see *Unità*, 6 December 1976, and for Soviet responses to PCI criticism of its Third World policy, SUCP CC to PCI CC (Berlinguer), (received) 7 March 1977, PCI Archives, 297, 1496–97.

13. NSDD 194, "Meeting with Soviet Leaders in Geneva: Themes and Perceptions," 25 October 1985, NSArch.

14. Record of conversation, special session of the North Atlantic Council, 21 November 1985, NSArch.

15. Cherniaev, *Six Years with Gordachev*, p. 52.

16. Cherniaev notes, Politburo meeting, 15 April 1986, NSArch.

17. Cherniaev notes, NSArch. These notes are probably from the Politburo meeting on either 23 or 26 February 1987. Cherniaev's book has a slightly different version, (*Six Years with Gorbachev*, p. 106).

18. Cherniaev notes from 13 November 1986 Politburo meeting, NSArch.

19. Cherniaev notes, Politburo meetings, 23 and 26 February 1987, NSArch.

20. Cherniaev notes, Politburo meeting, 12 December 1986, NSArch.

21. Cherniaev, *Six Years with Gorbachev*, p. 100. See also Cherniaev's notes from the Politburo meeting of 2 April 1987, when Gorbachev discussed Thatcher's visit, Archive of the Gorbachev Foundation, Moscow.
22. The death of DCI William Casey in May 1987 also strengthened this perception.
23. The new General Secretary was known as Najib up to October 1987 when he – in a telling sign of the times – reverted to using the postfix "ullah" (of God). The Soviets had encouraged the name change, although they, when referring to him in private, kept the name of God out of it.
24. Khadimat-e atal'at-e dowlati (KhAD) translates as State Information Service.
25. Record of conversation between Reagan and Gorbachev, Washington, DC, 9 December 1987, and record of conversation between Reagan and Gorbachev at working luncheon, 10 December 1987, both at NSArch.
26. According to General Mohammed Youssaf, Zia was willing to agree to a power-sharing arrangement in Kabul after the Geneva accords were reached, but only as a tactical measure.
27. Cherniaev, *Six Years with Gorbachev*, p. 208.
28. Rachik M. Avakov, "Novoe mishlenie i problema izucheniia razvivaiush-chikhsia stran" (The New Thinking and Problem of Studying the Developing Countries), *Mirovaia ekonomika i mezhdunarodnye otnosheniia*, 11 (1987): 48–62.
29. *Ibid.*
30. For the KGB and the Afghan case in particular, see Vladimir Kriuchkov, *Lichnoe delo* (Private File) (Moscow: Olimp, 1996), especially vol. I.
31. See Shakhnazarov's notes on the Yemen in *Tsena svobody: Reformatsiia Gorbacheva glazami ego pomoshchnika* (The Price of Freedom: Gorbachev's Reformation through the Eyes of his Assistant) (Moscow: Rossika Zevs, 1993), pp. 386–387.
32. Cherniaev, *Six Years with Gorbachev*, p. 144.
33. Record of conversation between Günther Kleber (SED Politburo) and Castro, Havanna, 26 March 1987, SAPMO-BArch, DY30 2462.
34. Cherniaev, *Six Years with Gorbachev*, pp. 204–205.
35. Interview with Elena Erofeieva, *Izvestia*, 10 July 1989. Resolution of the Supreme Soviet of the USSR, 13 June 1990.
36. Dmitri Volskii, *Izvestia*, 22 December 1988.
37. *Pravda*, 3 November 1987.
38. Andrei I. Kolosovskii, "Regionalye konflikti i globalnaia bezupasnost" (Regional Conflicts and Global Security), *Mirovaia ekonomika i mezhdunar-odnye otnosheniia*, 6 (1988): 32–41.
39. Andrey Kozyrev, "Confidence and the Balance of Interests," *International Affairs*, 11 (Moscow, 1988): 3–12.
40. All quotes are taken from records of conversations between Reagan and Gorbachev, 29 May and 1 June 1988, NSArch.
41. "Dear President Savimbi," Reagan had written in 1987, "I know that you are very busy these days on the field of battle . . . I wish to take this opportunity to extend my best wishes once again to you and to the proud forces of UNITA as

you struggle to bring freedom to Angola. My thoughts will be with you in the trying weeks and months ahead" (Reagan to Savimbi, 10 August 1987, box 91630, Herman Cohen files, White House staff files, Ronald Reagan Presidential Library). For the development of US–Angolan and Soviet–Angolan relations, see José Patrício, *Angola-EUA: os caminhos do bom-senso* (Lisbon: Publicações Dom Quixote, 1998), and Michael McFaul, "The Demise of the World Revolutionary Process: Soviet–Angolan Relations under Gorbachev," *Journal of Southern African Studies*, 16.1 (1990): 165–189; for the peace process, see Chester A. Crocker, *High Noon in Southern Africa: Making Peace in a Rough Neighborhood* (New York: Norton, 1992); Anthony G. Pazzanita, "The Conflict Resolution Process in Angola," *Journal of Modern African Studies*, 29.1 (1991): 83–114; and, from a Soviet perspective, M. V. Maiorov, "Mezhdunarodnoe posrednichestvo: iz opyta otechestvennoi diplomatii" (International Mediation: The Experience of Patriotic Diplomacy), *Novaia i noveishaia istoriia*, 6 (2000): 17–34.

42. Human Rights Watch Arms Project, "Still Killing: Landmines in Southern Africa," on http://hrw.org/reports/1997/lmsa/.

43. Thabo Mbeki, speech given at a seminar in Ottawa, Canada, 19–22 February 1978, available on-line at http://www.anc.org.za/ancdocs/history/mbeki/pre-1994/. Compare this with Mbeki's statements in his speech to South African newspaper editors, 26 November 1990. See also Sean Jacobs and Richard Calland, eds., *Thabo Mbeki's World: The Politics and Ideology of the South African President* (London: Zed Books, 2003).

44. Nelson Mandela, speech in Matanzas, Cuba, 26 July 1991, on http://www1.lanic.utexas.edu/la/cb/cuba/castro.

45. Chernaiev, *Six Years with Gorbachev*, p. 204.

46. Castro to Honecker, 3 October 1989, SAPMO-BArch, DY30 2462.

47. Castro, speech given during a ceremony honoring Cuban internationalists fallen in Angola, El Cacahual Mausoleum, Havana, 7 December 1989, available on-line at http://www.lanic.utexas.edu.

48. Robert A. Kagan, *A Twilight Struggle for the Third World* (New York: Free Press, 1996), p. 644.

49. Member of the Land Defense Committee, Las Marías, El Salvador to Elizabeth Wood in 1992, quoted in her *Insurgent Collective Action and Civil War in El Salvador* (Cambridge: Cambridge University Press, 2003).

CONCLUSION: REVOLUTIONS, INTERVENTIONS, AND GREAT POWER COLLAPSE

1. Joseph Conrad, *Heart of Darkness* (1902; Harmondsworth: Penguin, 1994).

2. James C. Scott, *Seeing Like a State* (New Haven, CT: Yale University Press, 1998), p. 377, quoting David Harvey, *The Condition of Post-Modernity: An Enquiry into the Origins of Social Change* (Oxford: Basil Blackwell, 1989), p. 35.

3. For attempt at understanding the destruction wrought by antigovernment forces, see Thandika Mkandawire, "The Terrible Toll of Post-Colonial

'Rebel Movements' in Africa: Towards an Explanation of the Violence against the Peasantry," *Journal of Modern African Studies*, 40.2 (2002): 181–215.

4. Speech delivered 26 February 1965, quoted from John Gerassi, ed., *Venceremos! The Speeches and Writings of Ernesto Che Guevara* (New York: Macmillan, 1968), pp. 378–385.

5. A. M. Baryalai, ed., *Democratic Republic of Afghanistan Annual: 1979* (Kabul: Kabul Times Publishing Agency, 1979), pp. 62–70.

6. UNDP, Human Development Report 1990, on http://hdr.undp.org/reports/global/1990/en/pdf/hdr_1990_ch2.pdf.

7. Speech delivered 17 September 1979, quoted from Emine Engin, ed., *The Revolution in Afghanistan* (n.p. (Istanbul?): İşçinin Sesi, 1982). The reference is to Lenin's "Two Tactics of Social-Democracy in the Democratic Revolution," in *Collected Works*, (4th English edn; Moscow: Progress, 1972), vol. IX, pp. 15–140.

8. Memorandum from Kenneth Young to Walt Rostow, 17 February 1961, NSF, Box 325, John K. Kennedy Presidential Library, quoted from David Milne, "America's Mission Civilisatrice: The Strategic Hamlet Program for South Vietnam," unpublished paper.

9. Bertrand Badie, *La fin des territoires: essai sur le désordre international et sur l'utilité sociale du respect*, (Paris: Fayard, 1995) p. 214.

10. Richard Wright, *The Color Curtain: A Report on the Bandung Conference*, forward Gunnar Myrdal (London: Dobson, 1956).

11. Boris Piliatskin, *Izvestia*, 10 December 1993. See also Moscow Protestant Chaplaincy's Task Force on Racial Attacks, "Report on Anti-African Racism in Moscow," on http://www.moscowprotestantchaplaincy.org. Daniel Williams, "From Russia with Hate: Africans Face Racism," *Washington Post*, 12 January 1998; and, for a view of how racism influences Russia's wars in the Caucasus, Roman L. Meredith, "Making Caucasians Black: Moscow since the Fall of Communism and the Racialization of non-Russians," *Journal of Communist Studies and Transition Politics*, 18.2 (2000): 1–27.

12. Russian economist Stanislav Menshikov in *Voprosy ekonomiki*, 7 (July 1999).

13. Bearden quoted in Steve Coll, *Ghost Wars: The Secret History of the CIA, Afghanistan, and Bin Laden, from the Soviet Invasion to September 11, 2001* (Harmondsworth: Penguin, 2004), P. 173.

14. Quoted by Ruel Marc Gerecht in the *Atlantic* (July–August 2001).

15. Quoted from the *Independent* (London), 29 November 2002.

Index